Microeconomics for Today

SECOND EDITION

Microeconomics for Today

Irvin B. Tucker

University of North Carolina at Charlotte

South-Western College Publishing
Thomson Learning

Australia • Canada • Denmark • Japan • Mexico • New Zealand • Philippines
Puerto Rico • Singapore • South Africa • Spain • United Kingdom • United States

Microeconomics for Today, 2nd edition ISBN: 0-324-00623-3

Vice President / Team Director: Jack W. Calhoun
Acquisitions Editor: Keri L. Witman
Senior Developmental Editor: Susanna C. Smart
Marketing Manager: Lisa L. Lysne
Production Editor: Peggy K. Buskey
Manufacturing Coordinator: Georgina Calderon
Promotions Project Manager: Jon Schneider
Internal Design: Carolyn Deacy Design / San Francisco
Cover Design: Tin Box Studio / Cincinnati
Cover Photography: Guildhaus Photography / Cincinnati
Photo Editor: Cary Benbow
Photo Researcher: Fred Middendorf
Production House: Lachina Publishing Services, Inc.
Printer: R.R. Donnelley & Sons Company, Willard Manufacturing Division

Printed in the United States of America
    3 4 02 01

For more information contact South-Western College Publishing, 5101 Madison Road, Cincinnati, Ohio, 45227. Or you can visit our Internet site at http://www.swcollege.com

For permission to use material from this text or product contact us by
• **telephone: 1-800-730-2214**
• **fax: 1-800-730-2215**
• **web: http://www.thomsonrights.com**

Library of Congress Cataloging-in-Publication Data
Tucker, Irvin B.
    Microeconomics for today / Irvin B. Tucker. — 2nd ed.
        p.   cm.
    Includes bibliographical references and index.
    ISBN 0-324-00623-3
    1. Microeconomics. 2. United States—Economic conditions—1981–
  I. Title.
  HB172.T789   1999
  338.5—dc21   99-30239

This book is printed on acid-free paper.

To Sharon Adams-Poore

For her faith in my work

Text with a Mission

As with the first edition, the purpose of *Microeconomics for Today*, 2nd Edition, is to teach in an engaging style the basic operations of the U.S. economy to students who will take a two-term economics course. Rather than taking an encyclopedic approach to economic concepts, *Microeconomics for Today* focuses on the most important tool in economics supply and demand analysis and applies it to clearly explain real-world economic issues.

In a nutshell, every effort has been made to make *Microeconomics for Today* the most "student friendly" text on the market. This text was written to simplify the often confusing array of economic analyses that forces students to simply memorize in order to pass the course. Instead, *Microeconomics for Today* presents a straight-forward and unbiased approach that effectively teaches the application of basic economic principles. After reading this text, the student should be able to say "that economics stuff in the news finally makes sense."

How It Fits Together

The text presents the core principles of microeconomics and inter-national economics. The first 14 chapters introduce the logic of economic analysis and develop the core of microeconomic analysis. Here students learn the role of demand and supply in determining prices in competitive versus monopolistic markets. This part of the book explores such issues as minimum wage laws, rent control, and pollution. The text concludes with three chapters devoted entirely to international issues. For example, students will learn how the supply of and demand for currencies determine exchange rates and what the complications of a strong or a weak dollar are.

New to the Second Edition

While the basic layout remains the same, the following are key improvements in the second edition:

- New "Online Exercises" at the end of each chapter. These exercises also appear on the *Economics for Today* Web Site at **http://tucker.swcollege.com** with links directly to each address.

- New "Internet Margin Notes" throughout the text provide Internet addresses of sites relevant to the topics being discussed, and encourage students to visit the sites for more information.

- New "International Economics" features highlight global situations that serve as examples of the chapter topics.

- New visual "Summary" at the end of each chapter includes graphs and causation chains to refresh students' memories of the chapter topics.

Instructor's Manual

The Instructor's Manual, prepared by Douglas Copeland of Johnson County Community College, provides valuable course assistance to instructors. It includes chapter outlines, instructional objectives, critical thinking/group discussion questions, hints for effective teaching, answers to the Analyze the Issue questions, and summary quizzes with answers. It also features a list of transparency masters for figures and tables from the text, and the solutions to the Homework Sets.

ISBN: 0-324-00780-9

Test Bank

As with the study guide, the test bank was prepared by the author to conform to the text. In addition, it has been reviewed for accuracy and greatly expanded to include nearly 6,000 multiple-choice and true-false questions. Most questions have been thoroughly tested in the classroom by the author and classified by topic and degree of difficulty.

Microeconomics Version ISBN: 0-324-00783-3

Macroeconomics Version ISBN: 0-324-00782-5

Thomson Learning Testing Tools™

The Thomson Learning Testing Tools™ computerized testing program contains all of the questions in the printed test bank. Thomson Learning Testing Tools™ is an easy-to-use test creation software compatible with Microsoft Windows. Instructors can add or edit questions, instructions, and answers, and select questions by previewing them on the screen, select them randomly, or select them by number. Instructors can also create and administer quizzes online, whether over the Internet, a local area network (LAN), or a wide area network (WAN).

Microeconomics Version ISBN: 0-324-00793-0

Macroeconomics Version ISBN: 0-324-00794-9

ITP Call-In Testing

Adopters may take advantage of the ITP Call-In Testing Service. Contact your sales representative or call 1-800-423-0563, or fax 1-606-647-5020, for details.

Color Transparency Acetates

A set of full-color transparency acetates for key figures and tables from the text is available to use in classroom presentation.

ISBN: 0-324-00788-4

Transparency Masters

A set of transparency masters is available for figures in the text that have not been prepared in color acetates.

ISBN: 0-324-00787-6

CNN Economics Video

The CNN Economics video provides a variety of video clips of current events. Thought-provoking real-world current events come to life in your classroom through this exclusive CNN Principles of Economics Update video.

ISBN: 0-538-86839-2

PowerPoint Presentation Package

Developed by Ken Long of New River Community College, this state-of-the-art multimedia presentation software provides instructors with visual support in the classroom. This new package includes vivid and easy-to-read animated graphs, highlights of important concepts, student tutorials with thought-provoking questions, and links to the text Web Site's Online exercises. Instructors can edit the PowerPoint presentations or create their own exciting in-class presentations that include text, graphics, and animation. The PowerPoint package is available on the text Web Site at **http://tucker.swcollege.com**.

Online Course Creation and Delivery Systems

South-Western College Publishing now makes taking your course online as easy as typing. Adopters of *Economics for Today*, 2nd edition, can use Thomson World Class Learning™ to create an online course, or to create a Web Site for a traditional course. Visit the South-Western Economics Resource Center at **http://economics.swcollege.com** or contact your ITP/South-Western sales representative to learn more about these exciting tools.

Tucker *Economics for Today* Web Site

Go to **http://tucker.swcollege.com** to visit the text Web Site. This one-stop
site provides updates to the text, economic debates online, online exercises, a
PowerPoint Presentation Package, a PowerPoint Tutorial, links to economics web
sites, economic news summaries, a forum to talk to the author, and much more.
A link to *Survey of Economics*, 2nd Edition, the one-semester principles text by
Irvin Tucker, is also provided.

ACKNOWLEDGMENTS

A deep debt of gratitude is owed to the reviewers for their expert assistance. Each comment and suggestion was carefully evaluated and served to improve the final product. To each of the following reviewers of both the first and this second edition, I give my sincerest thanks.

Jack E. Adams
University of Arkansas–Little Rock

John W. Alderson, III
East Arkansas Community College

James Q. Aylsworth
Lakeland Community College

Klaus G. Becker
Texas Tech University

Randall W. Bennett
Gonazaga University

John P. Blair
Wright State University

Tantatape Brahmasrene
Purdue University North Central

William Dougherty
Carroll County Community College

James W. Eden
Portland Community College

Ronald Elkins
Central Washington University

John L. Ewing-Smith
Burlington County College

Chris Fawson
Utah State University

Arthur A. Fleisher, III
Metropolitan State College of Denver

Arthur Friedberg
Mohawk Valley Community College

J. P. Gilbert
Mira Costa College

Sanford D. Gordon
University of South Florida

Gary Greene
Manatee Community College

Gail A. Hawks
Miami Dade Community College

R. Jack Inch
Oakland Community College

Barbara H. John
University of Dayton

Randall G. Kesselring
Arkansas State University

Harry T. Kolendrianos
Danville Community College

Margaret Landman
Bridgewater State College

Stephen E. Lile
Western Kentucky University

Thomas Maloy
Muskegon Community College

Robert A. Margo
Vanderbilt University

Melanie Marks
Longwood College

James C. McBrearty
University of Arizona

Diana L. McCoy
Truckee Meadows Community College

Donald P. McDowell
Florida Community College

Margaret Moore
Franklin University

Kevin J. Murphy
Oakland University

Peter K. Olson
Indiana University

Patrick B. O'Neill
University of North Dakota

Jan Palmer
Ohio University

Michael L. Palmer
Maple Woods Community College

Kathy Parkison
Indiana University–Kokomo

Donald W. Pearson
Eastern Michigan University

Martin Perline
Wichita State University

Maurice Pfannestiel
Wichita State University

L. Wayne Plumly, Jr.
Valdosta State University

Renee Prim
Central Piedmont Community College

J. Patrick Raines
University of Richmond

Steve Robinson
University of North Carolina at Wilmington

Kurt A. Schwabe
Ohio University

Alden W. Smith
Anne Arundel Community College

Rebecca Summary
Southeast Missouri State University

Richard Trieff
Des Moines Area Community College

Roy van Til
University of Maine-Farmington

Harold Warren
East Tennessee State University

Robert G. Welch
Midwestern State University

Herbert D. Werner
University of Missouri

Michael D. White
St. Cloud State University

Gwen Williams
Alvernia College

Virginia S. York
Gulf Coast Community College

Paul Young
Dodge City Community College

Special Thanks

I especially wish to offer my deepest appreciation to Peter Schwarz, my colleague at UNC Charlotte, who provided inspiration and ideas throughout the development of both *Survey of Economics* and *Microeconomics for Today*, and who authored the environmental economics chapter. Many of the ideas in the You're the Economist sections are the result of brainstorming sessions with Professor Schwarz. Special thanks also go to Douglas Copeland of Johnson County Community College, who, besides writing the Instructor's Manual, provided invaluable suggestions for improvement, as well as the Internet margin notes and many of the Internet exercises. A sincere thanks also goes to Ken Long, New River Community College, for his outstanding work in creating the new PowerPoint Presentation Package. I also would like to thank Dave Hart for the suggestion to create a visual summary. Special acknowledgments also go to the reviewers of the test bank and study guide.

My appreciation goes to Jack Calhoun, Team Director, and Keri Witman, Acquisitions Editor for South-Western College Publishing Company. My thanks also to Susanna Smart, Developmental Editor, and Peggy Buskey, Production Editor, who put all the pieces of the puzzle together and brought their creative talent to this text. Sherry Goldbecker was superb in her copyediting of the manuscript. I am also grateful to Kurt Gerdenich, Media Technology Editor, for developing the text's Web Site and to Lisa Lysne for her skillful marketing. Finally, I give my sincere thanks for a job well done to the entire team at South-Western College Publishing Company.

STUDENT LEARNING GUIDE

How to Study Economics

EXHIBIT A-6

Changes in Price, Quantity, and Income in Two Dimensions

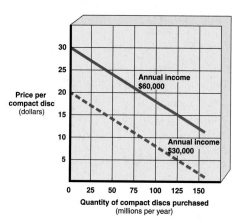

Economists use a multicurve graph to represent a three-variable relationship in a two-dimensional graph. A decrease in the price per compact disc causes a movement downward along each curve. As the annual income of consumers rises, there is a shift rightward in the position of the demand curve.

To some students, studying economics is a little frightening because many chapters are full of graphs. An often-repeated mistake is for students to prepare for tests by trying to memorize the lines of graphs. When their graded tests are returned, the students using this strategy will probably exclaim, "What happened?" The answer to this query is that the student should have learned the economic concepts first, and then the graphs would be understood as illustrations of these underlying concepts. Stated simply, superficial cramming for economics quizzes does not work.

For students with an anxiety over using graphs, there is a brief review of graphical analysis in the appendix to Chapter 1. In addition, the Graphing Primer and the Study Guide contain step-by-step features on how to interpret graphs.

a curve. Here's how to tell the difference. A change in one of the variables shown on either of the coordinate axes of the graph causes *movement along* a curve. On the other hand, a change in a variable not shown on one of the coordinate axes of the graph causes a *shift in* a curve's position on the graph.

> **Conclusion** *A shift in a curve occurs only when the ceteris paribus assumption is relaxed and a third variable not on either axis of the graph is allowed to change.*

A Helpful Study Hint Using Graphs

Don't be the student who tries to memorize the graphs and then wonders why he or she failed economics. Instead of memorizing graphs, you should use graphs as a valuable aid to learning the economic concepts these graphs

Motivational Pedagogical Features

Microeconomics for Today strives to push out the boundaries of traditional pedagogy with the following features:

Chapter Previews

Each chapter begins with a preview designed to pique the student's interest and reinforce how the chapter fits into the overall scheme of the book. Each preview appeals to one's "Sherlock Holmes" impulses by posing several economics puzzles that can be solved by understanding the material presented in the chapter.

Margin Definitions

Key concepts introduced in the chapter are highlighted in bold and then defined in the text and again in the margins. This feature avoids forcing the student to search through the text in order to locate and comprehend the key concepts. The body of the text and the margin definitions therefore serve as a quick reference.

Model
A simplified description of reality used to understand and predict the relationship between variables.

Internet Margin Notes

This edition contains Internet addresses in the margins that direct students to sites relevant to the topics being discussed. The addresses sometimes send students to sites that will give them additional information about a topic, and sometimes send them to sites that will simply be relevant and interesting. In either case, students will become familiar with using the Internet for economics topics, and will be more prepared for the Internet exercises an instructor may wish to assign.

 *Visit Haggle Online, an internet auction site at* http://www.haggle.com. *What type of products are being auctioned? Look at the history of the bidding process for a few products. From this information, what can you conclude about the demand for each product?*

Conclusion Statements

Throughout the chapters highlighted conclusion statements of key concepts appear at the ends of sections and tie together the material just learned. Students will be able to see quickly if they have understood the main points of the section. These statements are summarized at the end of each chapter as well, and provide a useful study aid.

sidy amount is payable at any price along the demand curve, the demand curve shifts rightward until the efficient equilibrium price and quantity are reached.

Conclusion *When externalities are present, market failure gives incorrect price and quantity signals, and as a result, resources are misallocated. External costs cause the market to overallocate resources, and external benefits cause the market to underallocate resources.*

Public Goods

National defense is an example of a **public good**, a good that the govern-

*that, once
properties:
ely consume
here is no way
do not pay*

You're the Economist

Each chapter includes boxed inserts that provide the acid test of "relevance." This feature gives the student an opportunity to encounter timely real-world extensions of the explanations of economic theory. For example, students read about how Fred Smith wrote an economics term paper explaining his plan to create Federal Express—and find out how well he did! So that the student wastes no time figuring out which economic concepts apply to the article, applicable concepts are listed after each feature's title. Also, many of these boxed features include information from newspaper articles that may span a period of years. This method is used to demonstrate that economics concepts apply to everyday life and remain relevant over time.

International Economics

Today's economic environment is a global one. *Microeconomics for Today* carefully integrates international topics throughout the text and presents the material using a highly readable and accessible approach designed for students with no training in international economics. To highlight international economics, all sections of the text that present international economics are identified by a special global icon in the text margin and in "International Economics" boxes. In addition, the final three chapters of the book are devoted entirely to international economics.

Analyze the Issue

losses forces Congress to perform a difficult balancing act by offering voters the reassurance that a minimum-wage increase is not too large, but just large enough to help the working poor.

Some politicians claim that raising the minimum wage is a way to help the working poor without cost to taxpayers. Others believe the cost is hidden in inflation and lost employment opportunities for marginal workers, such as teenagers, the elderly, and minorities.

Another problem with raising the minimum wage to aid the working poor is that studies show that the minimum wage is a blunt weapon to redistribute wealth. Only a small percentage of minimum-wage earners are full-time workers whose family income falls below the poverty line. This means nonpoor workers receive most

this issue in Chapter 4 as an application of supply and demand analysis.

ANALYZE THE ISSUE

1. Identify two positive and two normative statements given concerning raising the minimum wage. List other minimum-wage arguments not discussed in the You're the Economist, and classify them as either positive or normative economics.

2. Give a positive and a normative argument why a business leader would oppose raising the minimum wage. Give a positive and a normative argument why a

This feature follows each "You're the Economist" and "International Economics" article. *Microeconomics for Today* leaves nothing to chance by merely including newspaper articles and expecting the student to understand the applications. Instead, "Analyze the Issue" asks specific questions that require students to test their knowledge of how the featured material is relevant to the applicable chapter concept, promoting economic analysis skills and active learning. To allow for these questions to be used in classroom discussions or homework assignments, answers are provided in the Instructor's Manual rather than in the text.

Checkpoint

Who said learning economics can't be fun? Watch for these features that add a unique approach to generating interest and stimulating critical thinking. These questions spark students to check their progress by presenting challenging economics puzzles in a game-like style. Students enjoy thinking through and answering the questions, and then checking the answers at the end of the chapter. A student who answers correctly earns the satisfaction of knowing he or she has mastered the concepts.

Illustrations

Clarity in graphical presentations is essential for any successful economics textbook. Each exhibit has been carefully analyzed to ensure that the key concepts being represented stand out clearly. Brief descriptions are included with the graphs to provide guidance for the student as he or she studies the graph. When actual data are used, the web site reference is provided so that students can easily locate the data source. Color is an important feature of the graphs. For example, throughout the text Demand lines are in blue, and Supply lines are in red.

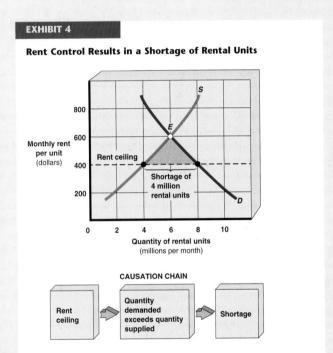

EXHIBIT 4

Rent Control Results in a Shortage of Rental Units

CAUSATION CHAIN

If no rent controls exist, the equilibrium rent for a hypothetical apartment is $600 per month at point E. However, the government imposes a rent ceiling of $400 per month, and a shortage of 4 million rental units occurs. Because rent cannot rise by law, one outcome is that consumers must

Causation Chains

This will be one of your favorite features! The highly successful "Causation Chains" have proven to be invaluable to students as a learning tool and are included under many graphs throughout the text. This pedagogical device helps students visualize complex economic relationships in terms of simple box diagrams that illustrate how one change causes another change, and drives understanding of cause-and-effect analysis.

Visual Summaries

Each chapter ends with a brief point-by-point "Summary" of the key concepts. In this edition, many of these summarized points include miniaturized versions of the important graphs and causation chains that illustrate numerous key concepts. These are intended to serve as visual reminders for students as they finish the chapters, and are also useful in reviewing and studying for quizzes and exams.

SUMMARY

■ **Three fundamental economic questions** facing any economy are *What, How,* and *For Whom* to produce goods. The What question asks exactly which goods are to be produced and in what quantities. The How question requires society to decide the resource mix used to produce goods. The For Whom problem concerns the division of output among society's citizens.

■ **Opportunity cost** is the best alternative foregone for a chosen option. This means no decision can be made without cost.

■ **Marginal analysis** examines the impact of changes from a current situation and is a technique used extensively in economics. The basic approach is to compare the additional benefits of a change with the additional costs of the change.

fully employed. (2) The resource base is not allowed to vary during the time period. (3) *Technology*, which is the body of knowledge applied to the production of goods, remains constant. **Inefficient** production occurs at any point inside the production possibilities curve. All points along the curve are **efficient** points because each point represents a maximum output possibility.

Production possibilities curve

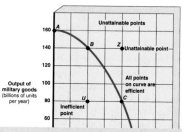

Summaries of Conclusion Statements

Each chapter also includes a summary of the key conclusion statements introduced throughout the chapter. This approach ensures understanding and aids in review by presenting important conclusions in a clear and concise format.

SUMMARY OF CONCLUSION STATEMENTS

■ Under the law of demand, any decrease in price along the vertical axis will cause an increase in quantity demanded, measured along the horizontal axis.

■ Changes in nonprice determinants can produce only a shift in the demand curve and not a movement along the demand curve, which is caused by a change in price.

■ Under the law of supply, any increase in price along the vertical axis will cause an increase in quantity supplied, measured along the horizontal axis.

■ Changes in nonprice determinants can produce only a shift in the supply curve and not a movement along the supply curve.

■ Graphically, the intersection of the supply curve and

Study Questions and Problems

The end-of-chapter questions and problems offer a variety of levels ranging from straightforward recall to deeply thought-provoking applications. The answers to odd-numbered questions and problems are in the back of the text. This feature gives students immediate feedback without requiring the instructor to check their work.

STUDY QUESTIONS AND PROBLEMS

1. Market researchers have studied the market for milk, and their estimates for the supply of and the demand for milk per month are as follows:

Price per gallon (millions of gallons)	Quantity demanded (millions of gallons)	Quantity supplied (millions of gallons)
$2.50	100	500
2.00	200	400
1.50	300	300
1.00	400	200
0.50	500	100

b. Suppose the government enacts a milk support price of $2.00 per gallon. Indicate this action on your graph, and explain the effect on the milk market. Why would the government establish such a support price?

c. Now assume the government decides to set a price ceiling of $1.00 per gallon. Show and explain how this legal price affects your graph of the milk market. What objective could the government be trying to achieve by establishing such a price ceiling?

2. Use a graph to show the impact on the price of Japanese cars sold in the United States if the United States enacts import quotas on Japanese cars. Now draw another graph to show the effect of the change in the price of Japanese cars on the price of American-made

Online Exercises

These exercises are designed to spark student excitement about exploring the Internet to access economic data and information, and then answer questions related to the content of the chapter. All Internet exercises are repeated on the *Economics for Today* Web Site with direct links to the addresses so that students will not have the tedious and error-prone task of entering long web site addresses. See http://tucker.swcollege.com.

Answers to Checkpoints

Answers to each Checkpoint are found at the end of every chapter so students can check their answers easily. The student who answers correctly earns the satisfaction of knowing he or she has mastered the concepts.

 CHECKPOINT ANSWERS

Can Gasoline Become an Exception to the Law of Demand?

As the price of oil began to rise, the expectation of still higher prices caused buyers to buy more now, and, therefore, demand increased. As shown in Exhibit 13, suppose the price per gallon of gasoline was initially at P_1 and the quantity demanded was Q_1 on demand curve D_1 (point A). Then the Iraqi invasion caused the demand curve to shift rightward to D_2. Along the new demand curve, D_2, consumers increased their quantity demanded to Q_2 at the higher price of P_2 per gallon of gasoline (point B).

The expectation of rising gasoline prices in the future caused "an increase in demand," rather than "an increase in quantity demanded," in response to a higher price. If you said there are no exceptions to the law of demand, YOU ARE CORRECT.

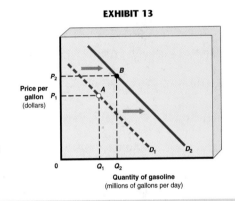

EXHIBIT 13

Practice Quizzes

A great help before in-class quizzes! Many instructors in principles courses test students using multiple-choice questions. For this reason, the final section of each chapter provides the type of multiple-choice questions given in the instructor's Test Bank. The answers to all of these questions are given in the back of the text.

PRACTICE QUIZ

For a visual explanation of the correct answers, visit the tutorial at http://tucker.swcollege.com.

1. Suppose prices for new homes have risen, yet sales of new homes have also risen. We can conclude that
   a. the demand for new homes has risen.
   b. the law of demand has been violated.
   c. new firms have entered the construction industry.
   d. construction firms must be facing higher costs.

5. An increase in the wage paid to grape pickers will cause the
   a. demand curve for grapes to shift to the right, resulting in higher prices for grapes.
   b. demand curve for grapes to shift to the left, resulting in lower prices for grapes.
   c. supply curve for grapes to shift to the left, resulting in lower prices for grapes.
   d. supply curve for grapes to shift to the left, result-

In addition, students may utilize the PowerPoint tutorial found at http://tucker.swcollege.com to obtain a visual explanation of each correct answer. Here you can actually see the graphs shift and arrows point to key changes in prices, output, and other key variables.

STUDENT LEARNING GUIDE

A Supplements Package Designed for Success

To learn more about these supplements, visit the *Economics for Today* Web Site, http://tucker.swcollege.com. You can order any of these items online, through your college bookstore, or by calling the ITP Customer Service Center at 1-800-347-7707.

Study Guide

The Study Guide is recommended for each student using the text. It is perhaps the best way to prepare for quizzes. To ensure that the Study Guide material fits the text, it was written by the text author. In addition, it was reviewed for accuracy. The Study Guide contains features such as the chapter in a nutshell, key concept review, fill-in-the-blank questions, step-by-step interpretation of the graph boxes, multiple-choice questions, true-false questions, and crossword puzzles.

Comprehensive Version ISBN: 0-324-00784-1

Microeconomics Version ISBN: 0-324-00786-8

Macroeconomics Version ISBN: 0-324-00785-X

South-Western Economics Tutorial Software

This tutorial program allows students to interact electronically through a series of modules covering major macro and micro topics. The software guides students through a series of interactive graphical exercises covering key concepts in the text. Students create, modify, and interact with key graphs and they are able to record their progress through each chapter. It is available on the *Economics for Today* Web Site at http://tucker.swcollege.com.

Online Quizzes

Test your understanding of each chapter's concepts with these interactive quizzes. Each quiz contains fifteen multiple-choice questions, like those found on a typical exam. Questions include detailed feedback for each answer, so you'll know instantly why you have answered correctly or incorrectly. In addition, you may email yourself and/or your instructor the results of the quiz, with a listing of correct and incorrect answers. Finally, check your results against those of other students—previous scores to quizzes are displayed online. Find the quizzes at **http://tucker.swcollege.com**.

PowerPoint Tutorial

This PowerPoint tutorial is perfect for test preparation. Ken Long of New River Community College has developed practice quiz questions and answers for each chapter that are available at the Tucker *Economics for Today* Web Site **http://tucker.swcollege.com**. First, the question appears on the screen and then correct answers are explained. Many answers include animated graphs that shift with a click of the mouse, and help students master the graphing process.

Graphing Primer

Graphs in economics are one of the more difficult challenges to students. The Graphing Primer provides students with the practice they need to master the process of creating, interpreting, and understanding graphs.

ISBN: 0-538-85360-3

International Economics Issues Reader

This reader, prepared by Peter Schwarz of UNC Charlotte, contains a collection of articles on global economics topics. Each article is selected to critically examine economics principles that affect people's daily lives in a global economy.

ISBN: 0-314-20913-1

Homework Sets

These sets of exercises, prepared by William V. Weber of Eastern Illinois University and Amy Myers of Parkland College, review economic concepts presented in the text. They can be given as homework assignments or used by students to practice for exams. Answers are available in the Instructor's Manual.

Microeconomics Version ISBN: 0-324-00791-4

Macroeconomics Version ISBN: 0-324-00790-6

Economics Alive!: Principles and Applications CD-ROMs

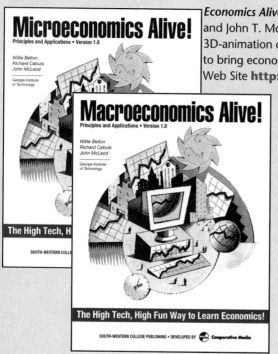

Economics Alive!: Principles and Applications by Richard J. Cebula, Willie J. Belton, and John T. McLeod Jr. These interactive CD-ROMs with captivating 3D-animation combine mulitimedia lessons, graphing tools, and simulations to bring economic concepts to life. To learn more visit the *Economics Alive!* Web Site **http://econalive.swcollege.com**.

Microeconomics Alive! CD-ROM ISBN 0-538-84650-X

Macroeconomics Alive! CD-ROM ISBN: 0-538-86850-3

Tucker *Economics for Today* Web Site

Go to **http://tucker.swcollege.com** to visit the text Web Site. This one-stop site provides updates to the text, economic debates online, online exercises, a PowerPoint Presentation Package, a PowerPoint Tutorial, links to economics web sites, economic news summaries, a forum to talk to the author, and much more. A link to *Survey of Economics*, 2nd Edition, the one-semester principles text by Irvin Tucker, is also provided.

Brief Contents

Contents

CHAPTER 2

Production Possibilities and Opportunity Cost   33

CHAPTER 3

Market Demand and Supply   53

PART III   MARKET STRUCTURES   181

CHAPTER 8   Perfect Competition   181

CHAPTER 11   ## Labor Markets   258

PART IV   **MICROECONOMIC POLICY ISSUES   281**

CHAPTER 14

Environmental Economics   332

About the Author

IRVIN B. TUCKER has over twenty years of experience teaching introductory economics at the University of North Carolina at Charlotte and the University of South Carolina. He earned his B.S. in economics at N.C. State University and his M.A. and Ph.D. in economics from the University of South Carolina.

Dr. Tucker is former Director of the Center for Economic Education at the University of North Carolina at Charlotte and long-time member of the National Council on Economic Education. He is recognized for his ability to relate basic principles to economic issues and public policy. His work has received national recognition by being awarded the Meritorious Leavy Award for Excellence in Private Enterprise Education, the Federation of Independent Business Award for Postsecondary Educator of the Year in Entrepreneurship and Economic Education, and the Freedom Foundation's George Washington Medal for Excellence in Economic Education. In addition, he has published numerous professional journal articles on a wide range of topics including studies of industrial organization, entrepreneurship, and sports economics. Dr. Tucker is also the author of the highly successful second edition of *Survey of Economics*, a text for one-semester economics courses, published by South-Western College Publishing.

Introducing the Economic Way of Thinking

Welcome to an exciting and useful subject economists call "the economic way of thinking." As you learn this reasoning technique, it will become infectious. You will discover that the world is full of economic problems requiring more powerful tools than just common sense. As you master the methods explained in this book, you will appreciate economics as a valuable reasoning approach to solving economic puzzles. Stated differently, the economic way of thinking is important because it provides a logical framework within which to organize thoughts and understand an economic issue or event. Just to give a sneak preview, you will study the perils of government price-fixing for gasoline and health care. You will also find out why colleges and universities charge different tuitions to students for the same education. You will investigate why to worry or not to worry whether the federal government balances its budget. You will learn that the island of Yap uses large stones with holes in the center as money. In the final chapter, you will study why some countries grow rich, while others remain poor and less developed. And the list of fascinating and relevant topics explained continues throughout each chapter. As you read these pages, your efforts will be rewarded by an understanding of just how economic theories and policies affect our daily lives—past, present, and future.

Chapter 1 acquaints you with the foundation of the economic way of thinking. The first building blocks joined are the concepts of scarcity and choice. The next building blocks are the steps in the model-building process that economists use to study the choices people make. Then we look at some pitfalls of economic reasoning and explain why economists might disagree with one another.

In this chapter, you will learn to solve these economics puzzles:

■ Can you prove there is no person worth a trillion dollars?

■ Why would you purchase more Coca-Cola when the price increases?

■ How can we explain the relationship between the Super Bowl winner and changes in the stock market?

The Problem of Scarcity

Scarcity
The condition in which human wants are forever greater than the available supply of time, goods, and resources.

Our world is a finite place where people, both individually and collectively, face the problem of **scarcity**. Scarcity is the condition in which human wants are forever greater than the available supply of time, goods, and resources. Because of scarcity, it is impossible to satisfy every desire. Pause for a moment to list some of your unsatisfied wants. Perhaps you would like a big home, thick steaks, designer clothes, clean air, better health care, shelter for the homeless, more leisure time, and so on. Unfortunately, nature does not offer the Garden of Eden, where every desire is fulfilled. Instead, there are always limits on the economy's ability to satisfy unlimited wants. Alas, scarcity is pervasive, so "You can't have it all."

You may think your scarcity problem would disappear if you were rich, but wealth does not solve the problem. No matter how affluent an individual is, the wish list continues to grow. We are familiar with the "rich and famous" who never seem to have enough. Although they live well, they still desire finer homes, faster planes, and larger yachts. In short, the condition of scarcity means all individuals, whether rich or poor, are dissatisfied with their material well-being and would like more. What is true for individuals also applies to society. States are debating whether to use lotteries to raise funds to improve the quality of their schools. The federal government's desire to spend for the poor, education, highways, police, and national defense exceeds the tax revenue it receives to pay for these programs. So not even Uncle Sam escapes the problem of scarcity.

Of course, scarcity is a fact of life throughout the world. In much of South America, Africa, and Asia, the problem of scarcity is often life threatening. On the other hand, in North America, Western Europe, and some parts of Asia, there has been substantial economic growth and development. Although life is much less grueling in the more advanced countries, the problem of scarcity exists because individuals and countries never have as much of all the goods and services as they would like to have.

Scarce Resources and Production

Resources
The basic categories of inputs used to produce goods and services. Resources are also called factors of production. Economists divide resources into three categories: land, labor, and capital.

Because of the economic problem of scarcity, no society has enough **resources** to produce all the goods and services necessary to satisfy all human wants. Resources are the basic categories of inputs used to produce goods and services. Resources are also called *factors of production*. Economists divide resources into three categories: *land, labor,* and *capital.* See Exhibit 1.

EXHIBIT 1

Three Categories of Resources

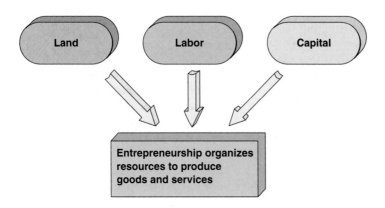

Resources are the basic categories of inputs organized by entrepreneurship (a special type of labor) to produce goods and services. Economists divide resources into the three categories of land, labor, and capital.

Land

Land is a shorthand expression for any natural resource provided by nature. Land includes those resources that are gifts of nature available for use in the production process. Farming, building factories, and constructing oil refineries would be impossible without land. Land includes anything natural above or below the ground, such as forests, gold, diamonds, oil, wildlife, and fish. Other examples are rivers, lakes, sea, air, the sun, and the moon. Two broad categories of natural resources are *renewable resources* and *nonrenewable resources*. Renewable resources are basic inputs that nature will automatically replace without interference from man. Examples include lakes, crops, and clean air. Nonrenewable resources are basic inputs that nature will not automatically replace. There is only so much coal, oil, and natural gas in the world. When these fossil fuels disappear, we must use substitutes.

Land
A shorthand expression for any natural resource provided by nature.

Labor

Labor is the mental and physical human capacity of workers to produce goods and services. The services of farmers, assembly-line workers, lawyers, professional football players, and economists are all *labor*. Both the number of people available for work and the skills or quality of workers measure the labor resource. One reason nations differ in their ability to produce is that human characteristics, such as the education, experience, health, and motivation of workers, differ among nations.

Labor
The mental and physical capacity of workers to produce goods and services.

Entrepreneurship
The creative ability of individuals to seek profits by combining resources to produce innovative products.

Entrepreneurship is a special type of labor. Entrepreneurship is the creative ability of individuals to seek profits by combining resources to produce innovative products. The *entrepreneur* is a motivated person who seeks profits by undertaking such risky activities as starting new businesses, creating new products, or inventing new ways of accomplishing tasks. Entrepreneurship is a scarce human resource because relatively few are willing or able to innovate and make decisions involving greater than normal chances for failure.

Entrepreneurs are the agents of change who bring material progress to society. The birth of the Levi Strauss Company is a classic entrepreneurial success story. In 1850, at the age of 24, Levi Strauss sailed from New York to join the California Gold Rush. His idea was not to dig for gold, but to sell cloth. When he arrived in San Francisco, he had sold most of his cloth to those on the ship. The only cloth left was a roll of canvas for tents and covered wagons. On the dock, he met a miner who wanted a pair of pants that would last while digging for gold. Presto! Strauss knew a good thing when he saw it, so he hired workers, built factories, and became the largest pants maker in the world. As a reward for bearing business risks, organizing production, and introducing a product, the Levi Strauss Company earned profits, and Strauss became rich and famous.

Capital

Capital
The physical plants, machinery, and equipment used to produce other goods. Capital goods are man-made goods that do not directly satisfy human wants.

Capital is the physical plants, machinery, and equipment used to produce other goods. Capital goods are man-made goods that do not directly satisfy human wants. *Capital* before the Industrial Revolution meant a tool, such as a hoe, an axe, or a bow and arrow. In those days, these items served as capital to build a house or to provide food for the dinner table. Today, capital also consists of factories, office buildings, warehouses, robots, trucks, and distribution facilities. College buildings, the printing presses used to produce this textbook, and pencils are also examples of capital.

The term *capital* as it is used in the study of economics can be confusing. Economists know that capital in everyday conversations means money or the money value of paper assets, such as stocks, bonds, or a deed to a house. This is actually financial capital. In the study of economics, capital does not refer to money assets. Instead, capital in economics means a factor of production, such as a factory or machinery. Stated simply, you must pay special attention to this point: "Money is not capital and is therefore not a resource."

Conclusion *Financial capital by itself is not productive; instead, it is only a paper claim on economic capital.*

Economics: The Study of Scarcity and Choice

Economics
The study of how society chooses to allocate its scarce resources to the production of goods and services in order to satisfy unlimited wants.

The perpetual problem of scarcity forcing people to make choices is the basis for the definition of **economics**. Economics is the study of how society chooses to allocate its scarce resources to the production of goods and services in order to satisfy unlimited wants. You may be surprised by this definition of economics. People often think economics means studying supply and demand, the stock market, money, and banking. In fact, there are many ways one could define *economics*, but economists accept the definition given here because it includes the link between *scarcity* and *choices*.

Society makes two kinds of choices: economywide or macro choices and individual or micro choices. The prefixes *macro* and *micro* come from the Greek words meaning "large" and "small," respectively. Reflecting the macro and micro perspectives, economics consists of two main branches: *macroeconomics* and *microeconomics*.

Macroeconomics

The old saying "Looking at the forest rather than the trees" fits **macroeconomics**. Macroeconomics is the branch of economics that studies decision-making for the economy as a whole. Macroeconomics applies an overview perspective to an economy by examining economywide variables, such as inflation, unemployment, growth of the economy, the money supply, and the national incomes of developing countries. Macroeconomic decision-making considers such "big picture" policies as the effect of balancing the federal budget on unemployment and the effect of changing the money supply on prices.

Microeconomics

Examining individual trees, leaves, and pieces of bark, rather than surveying the forest, illustrates **microeconomics**. Microeconomics is the branch of economics that studies decision-making by a single individual, household, firm, industry, or level of government. Microeconomics applies a microscope to specific parts of an economy, as one would examine cells in the body. The focus is on small economic units, such as economic decisions of particular groups of consumers and businesses. An example would be to use microeconomic analysis to study economic units involved in the market for ostrich eggs. Will suppliers decide to supply more, less, or the same amount of ostrich eggs to the market in response to price changes? Will individual consumers of these eggs decide to buy more, less, or the same amount at a new price?

We have described macroeconomics and microeconomics as two separate branches, but they are related. Because the overall economy is the sum or aggregation of its parts, micro changes impact on the macro economy, and macro changes produce micro changes.

The Methodology of Economics

Economists use the same *scientific method* used by other disciplines, such as criminology, biology, chemistry, and physics. The scientific method is a step-by-step procedure for solving problems by developing a theory, gathering data, and testing whether the data are consistent with the theory. Exhibit 2 summarizes the model-building process.

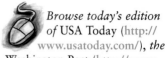

Browse today's edition of USA Today (http://www.usatoday.com/), *the* Washington Post (http://www.washingtonpost.com/), *the* International Herald Tribune (http://www.iht.com/), *or the* Sydney Morning Herald (http://www.smh.com.au/). *Can you find a headline story involving economics?*

Macroeconomics
The branch of economics that studies decision-making for the economy as a whole.

Microeconomics
The branch of economics that studies decision-making by a single individual, household, firm, industry, or level of government.

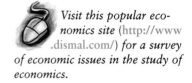

Visit this popular economics site (http://www.dismal.com/) for a survey of economic issues in the study of economics.

The Steps in the Model-Building Process

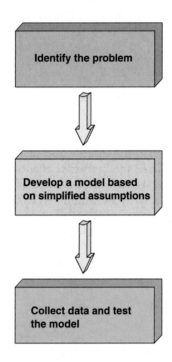

The first step in developing a model is to identify the problem. The second step is to select the critical variables necessary to formulate a model that explains the problem under study. Eliminating other variables that complicate the analysis requires simplifying assumptions. In the third step, the researcher collects data and tests the model. If the evidence supports the model, the model is accepted. If not, the model is rejected.

Problem Identification

The first step in applying the scientific method is to define the problem. Suppose an economist wishes to investigate the microeconomic problem of why U.S. motorists cut back on gasoline consumption in a given year from, for example, 100 billion gallons per month in September to 80 billion gallons per month in December.

Model Development

The second step in our hypothetical example toward finding an explanation is for the economist to build a **model**. A model is a simplified description of reality used to understand and predict the relationship between variables. A model and a *theory* are interchangeable. A model emphasizes only those variables that are most important to explaining an event. As

Model

A simplified description of reality used to understand and predict the relationship between variables.

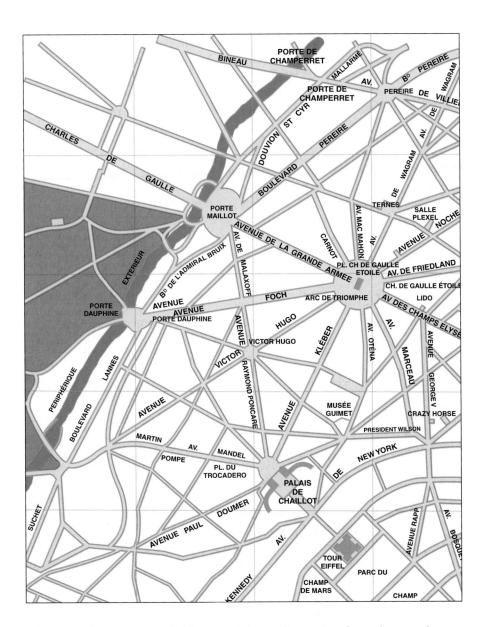

The map of Paris is a model because it is an abstraction from the actual beauty of the city. A key assumption is that one can rationally interpret this model.

Albert Einstein said, "Theories should be as simple as possible, but not more so." The purpose of a model is to construct an abstraction from real-world complexities and make events understandable. A map of Paris, for example, is far from a precise duplication of a real trip to this beautiful city. But a map of the city does help a visitor understand the best way to see the sights by leaving out the clutter of details.

A model requires simplified assumptions in order to be useful. Someone must decide, for example, whether a map will include only symbols for the major highways or the details of hiking trails through mountains. In our gasoline consumption example, several variables might be related to the quantity of gasoline consumed, including consumer incomes, the price of goods other than gasoline, the price of gasoline, the fuel economy of cars, and weather conditions. Because a theory focuses only on the main or critical variables, the economist must be a Sherlock Holmes and use a keen sense of observation to form a model. Using his or her expertise, the economist must select the relevant variables that are related to gasoline consumption and reject variables that have only slight or no relationship to gasoline consumption. In this simple case, the economist removes the cloud of complexity by formulating the theory that increases in the price of gasoline *cause* the quantity of gasoline consumed to decrease during the time period.

Theory Testing

To find materials and data resources used by economists on the Internet, visit http://www.helsinki.fi/WebEc/ WebEc.html.

An economic model can be stated as a verbal argument, numerical table, graph, or mathematical equation. You will soon discover that a major part of this book is devoted to building and using economic models. The purpose of an economic model is to *forecast* or *predict* the results of various changes in variables. An economic theory can be expressed in the form "If *A*, then *B*, other things held constant." An economic model is useful only if it yields accurate predictions. When the evidence is consistent with a theory that *A* causes outcome *B*, there is confidence in the theory's validity. When the evidence is inconsistent with the theory that *A* causes outcome *B*, the researcher rejects this theory.

In the third step, the economist gathers data to test the theory that if the price of gasoline rises, then gasoline purchases fall—all other relevant factors held constant. Suppose the investigation reveals that there was a sharp rise in the price of gasoline between September and December of the given year. The data are therefore consistent with the theory that the quantity of gasoline consumed per month falls when its price rises, assuming no other relevant factors change. Thus, the theory is valid if, for example, consumer incomes or population does not change at the same time gasoline prices rise.

Hazards of the Economic Way of Thinking

Models help us understand and predict the impact of changes in economic variables. A model is an important tool in the economist's toolkit, but it must be handled with care. The economic way of thinking seeks to avoid reasoning mistakes. Two of the most common pitfalls to clear thinking are (1) failing to understand the *ceteris paribus assumption* and (2) confusing *association* and *causation*.

CHECKPOINT   Can You Prove There Is No Trillion-Dollar Person?

Suppose a theory says no U.S. citizen is worth $1 trillion. You decide to test this theory and send researchers to all corners of the nation to check financial records to see whether someone qualifies by owning assets valued at $1 trillion or more. The researchers return after years of checking, and they report not a single person worth at least $1 trillion. Do you conclude that the evidence proves the theory?

The Ceteris Paribus Assumption

As you work through a model, try to think of a host of relevant variables assumed to be "standing still," or "held constant." **Ceteris paribus** is a Latin phrase that means that while certain variables change, "all other things remain unchanged." As in the gasoline example discussed earlier, a key simplifying assumption of the model is that changes in consumer incomes and certain other variables do not occur and complicate the analysis. The ceteris paribus assumption holds everything else constant and therefore allows us to concentrate on the study of the relationship between two key variables: changes in the price of gasoline and the quantity of gasoline purchased per month.

> **Ceteris paribus**
> *A Latin phrase that means that while certain variables change, "all other things remain unchanged."*

Now suppose an economist wishes to explain the model for the price and quantity purchased of Coca-Cola. Assume the theory is "If the price increases, then the quantity of Coca-Cola purchased decreases, ceteris paribus." A pitfall in reasoning occurs if you observe that the price of Coca-Cola increased one summer and some people actually bought more and not less. Based on this real-world observation, you declare the theory is incorrect. Think again! The economist responds that the model is valid based on the assumption of ceteris paribus and that your observation gives us no reason to reject the model. The reason the model appeared flawed is that another factor, a sharp rise in the temperature, *caused* people to buy more Coca-Cola in spite of its higher price. If the temperature and all other factors are held constant as the price of Coca-Cola rises, then people will indeed buy less Coca-Cola, as the model predicts.

> **Conclusion** *A theory cannot be tested legitimately unless its ceteris paribus assumption is satisfied.*

Association Versus Causation

Another of the most common errors in reasoning is confusing *association* (or correlation) and *causation* between variables. Stated differently, you err when you read more into a relationship between variables than is actually

Should Minnesota State Join a Big-Time Athletic Conference?

Minnesota State (a mythical university) stood by while Penn State, Florida State, the University of Miami, and the University of South Carolina joined big-time athletic conferences. Minnesota State officials are pondering whether to remain independent or to pursue membership in a conference noted for high-quality football and basketball programs. An editorial in the newspaper advocates joining and cites a study showing that universities belonging to major athletic conferences have higher graduation rates than nonmembers. Because educating its students is the number-one goal of Minnesota State, will this evidence influence Minnesota State officials to join a big-time conference?

The Council of Economic Advisors (http://www .whitehouse.gov/WH/ EOP/CEA/html/CEA.html) *and the Bank of America* (http:// www.bankamerica.com/econ_ indicator/econ_indicator.html) *are just two examples of organizations that hire economists to predict how the economy will behave and also provide the latest data on economic performance.*

there. A model is valid only when a cause-and-effect relationship is stable over time, rather than being an association that occurs by chance and eventually disappears. Suppose a witch doctor performs a voodoo dance during three different months and stock market prices skyrocket during each of these months. The voodoo dance is *associated* with the increase in stock prices, but this does not mean the voodoo dance *caused* the event. Even though there is a statistical relationship between two variables in a number of observations, eventually the voodoo dance will be performed, and stock prices will fall or remain unchanged. The reason is that there is no true economic relationship between voodoo dances and stock market prices.

Further investigation may reveal that stock prices actually responded to changes in interest rates during the months voodoo dances were performed. Changes in interest rates affect borrowing and, in turn, profits and stock market prices. On the other hand, there is no real economic relationship between voodoo dances and stock market prices, and, therefore, the voodoo model is not valid.

Conclusion *The fact that one event follows another does not necessarily mean that the first event caused the second event.*

Throughout this book, you will study economic models or theories that include variables linked by stable cause-and-effect relationships. For example, the theory that a change in the price of a good *causes* a change in the quantity purchased is a valid microeconomic model. The theory that a change in the money supply *causes* a change in interest rates is an example of a valid macroeconomic model. The following You're the Economist gives some amusing examples of the "association means causation" reasoning pitfall.

Mops and Brooms, the Boston Snow Index, the Super Bowl, and Other Economic Indicators

Applicable Concept: association versus causation

Although the Commerce Department, The Wharton School, the Federal Reserve Board, and other organizations publish economic forecasts and data on key economic indicators, they are not without armchair competition. For example, the chief executive of Standex International Corporation, Daniel E. Hogan, reports that his company can predict economic downturns and recoveries from sales reports of its National Metal Industries subsidiary in Springfield, Massachusetts. National makes metal parts for about 300 U.S. manufacturers of mops and brooms. A drop in National's sales always precedes a proportional fall in consumer spending. The company's sales always pick up slightly before consumer spending does.[1]

The Boston Snow Index (BSI) is the brainchild of one of the vice presidents of a New York securities firm. It predicts that next year will see a rising economy if there is snow on the ground in Boston on Christmas Day. The BSI has predicted correctly about 73 percent of the time over the past 30 years. However, its creator, Mr. David L. Upshaw, does not take it too seriously and views it as a spoof of other forecasters' methods.

Greeting card sales are another tried and true indicator, according to a vice president of American Greetings. Before a recession sets in, there is an increase in the sale of higher-priced greeting cards. It seems that people substitute the cards for gifts, and since there is no gift, the card must be fancier.

Then there are some other less well-known indicators. For example, one economist says that the surliness of waiters is a countercyclical indicator. If they are nice, expect that bad times are coming, but if they are rude, expect an upturn. Waiters, on the other hand, counter that a fall in the average tip usually precedes a downturn in the economy. A Super Bowl win by an NFC team has been associated with the stock market the following December being up from the year before. A win by an old AFL team has been associated with a dip in the stock market.

Finally, Anthony Chan, chief economist for Bank One Investment Advisers, studied marriage trends over a 34-year period. He discovered that when the number of marriages increases, the economy rises significantly and a slowdown in marriages is followed by a decline in the economy. Chan explains there is usually about a one-year lag between a change in the marriage rate and the economy.[2]

ANALYZE THE ISSUE

Which of the above indicators are examples of causation? Explain.

---

[1]"Economic Indicators, Turtles, Butterflies, Monks, and Waiters," *Wall Street Journal*, August 27, 1979, pp. 1, 16.
[2]Sandra Block, "Worried? Look at Wedding Bell Indicator," *Charlotte Observer*, April 15, 1995, p. 8A.

Why Do Economists Disagree?

Why might one economist say a clean environment is most important and another economist say economic growth should be our goal? If economists share the economic way of thinking and carefully avoid reasoning pitfalls, then why do they disagree? Why are economists known for giving advice by saying, "On the one hand, if you do this, then *A* results, and, on the other hand, doing this causes result *B*"? In fact, President Harry Truman once jokingly exclaimed, "Find me an economist with one hand." George Bernard Shaw offered another famous line in the same vein: "If you took all the economists in the world and laid them end to end, they would never reach a conclusion." These famous quotes imply that economists should agree, but ignore the fact that physicists, doctors, business executives, lawyers, and all professionals often disagree.

It may appear that economists disagree more than other professions partly because it is more interesting to report disagreements than agreements. Actually, economists agree on a wide range of issues. Many economists, for example, agree on free trade among nations, the elimination of farm subsidies and rent ceilings, government deficit spending to recover from recession, and many other issues. When disagreements do exist, the reason can often be explained by the difference between *positive economics* and *normative economics*.

Positive Economics

Positive economics
An analysis limited to statements that are verifiable.

Positive economics deals with facts and therefore addresses "what is" or "verifiable" questions. Positive economics is an analysis limited to statements that are verifiable. Positive statements can be proven either true or false. Often a positive statement is expressed "If *A*, then *B*." For example, if the national unemployment rate rises to 7 percent, then teenage unemployment exceeds 80 percent. This is a positive "if-then" prediction, which may or may not be correct. The accuracy of the statement is not the criterion for being a positive statement. The key consideration for a positive statement is whether the statement is *testable* and not whether it is true or false. Suppose the data show that if the nation's overall unemployment rate is close to 7 percent, the unemployment rate for teenagers never reaches 80 percent. Based on these facts, we would conclude that this positive statement is false. (In 1993, the overall unemployment rate was 6.8 percent, and the rate for teenagers was 19 percent.)

Now we can explain one reason why economists' forecasts can diverge. The statement "If event *A* occurs, then event *B* follows" can be thought of as a *conditional* positive statement. For example, two economists may agree that if the federal government cuts spending by 10 percent this year, prices will fall about 2 percent next year. However, their predictions about the fall in prices may differ because one economist assumes Congress will not cut spending, while the other economist assumes Congress will cut spending by 10 percent.

Conclusion *Forecasts of economists can differ because, using the same methodology, economists can agree that event* A *causes event* B, *but disagree over the assumption that event* A *will occur.*

Normative Economics

Instead of using objective statements, an argument can be phrased subjectively. **Normative economics** attempts to determine "what should be." Normative economics is an analysis based on value judgment. Normative statements express an individual or collective opinion on a subject and cannot be proven by facts to be true or false. Certain words or phrases tell us clearly that we have entered the realm of normative economics. These include the words *good, bad, need, should,* and *ought to.*

The point here is that people wearing different-colored glasses see the same facts differently. Each of us has individual subjective preferences that we apply to a particular subject. An animal rights activist says that no one *should* purchase a fur coat. Or one senator argues, "We *ought to* see that every teenager who wants a job has one." Another senator counters by saying, "Maintaining the purchasing power of the dollar is *more important* than teenage unemployment."

Normative economics
An analysis based on value judgment.

Conclusion *When opinions or points of view are not based on facts, they are scientifically untestable.*

When considering a debate, make sure to separate the arguments into their positive and normative components. This distinction allows you to determine if you are choosing a course of action related to factual evidence or to opinion. The material presented in this textbook, like most of economics, takes pains to stay within the boundaries of positive economic analysis. In our everyday lives, however, politicians, business executives, relatives, and friends use mostly normative statements to discuss economic issues. Economists also might associate themselves with a political position and use normative arguments for or against some economic policy. When using value judgments, an economist's normative judgment might have no greater validity than those of others. Biases or preconceptions can cloud an economist's thinking about deficit spending or whether to increase taxes on gasoline. Like beginning economics students, economists are human.

For more on the minimum wage go to: http://www.911dispatch.com/super_book/FSLA_guide.html.

Does Raising the Minimum Wage Help the Working Poor?

Applicable Concepts: positive and normative analyses

In 1938, Congress enacted the federal Fair Labor Standards Act, commonly known as the "minimum-wage law." Today, a minimum-wage worker who works full-time still earns a deplorably low annual income. One approach to help the working poor earn a living wage might be to raise the minimum wage.

The dilemma for Congress is that a higher minimum wage for the employed is enacted at the expense of jobs for unskilled workers. Opponents forecast that the increased labor cost from a high minimum-wage hike jeopardizes hundreds of thousands of unskilled jobs. For example, employers may opt to purchase more capital and less expensive labor. The fear of such sizeable job losses forces Congress to perform a difficult balancing act by offering voters the reassurance that a minimum-wage increase is not too large, but just large enough to help the working poor.

Some politicians claim that raising the minimum wage is a way to help the working poor without cost to taxpayers. Others believe the cost is hidden in inflation and lost employment opportunities for marginal workers, such as teenagers, the elderly, and minorities.

Another problem with raising the minimum wage to aid the working poor is that studies show that the minimum wage is a blunt weapon to redistribute wealth. Only a small percentage of minimum-wage earners are full-time workers whose family income falls below the poverty line. This means nonpoor workers receive most increases in the minimum wage. For example, many minimum-wage workers are students living at home or workers whose spouse earns a much higher income. To help only the working poor, some economists argue that the government should target only those who need it, rather than using the "shotgun" approach of raising the minimum wage.

Supporters are not convinced by the case against raising the minimum wage. They say it is outrageous that a worker can work full-time and still be in poverty. Moreover, this side of the debate believes that opponents exaggerate the dangers to the economy from a higher mini-

mum wage. Economist Lester Thurow of Massachusetts Institute of Technology, for example, argues that a high minimum wage will force employers to upgrade the skills and productivity of workers. Increasing the minimum wage may therefore be a win-win proposition, rather than a win-lose proposition. Professor Thurow is supported by the research of David Card and Alan B. Krueger. These economists studied data including the 1992 increase in New Jersey's minimum wage, the 1988 rise in California's minimum wage, and the 1990–1991 increases in the federal minimum wage. In each case, their evidence shows that modest increases in the minimum wage have resulted in little or no loss of jobs.[1] Note that we will return to this issue in Chapter 4 as an application of supply and demand analysis.

ANALYZE THE ISSUE

1. Identify two positive and two normative statements given concerning raising the minimum wage. List other minimum-wage arguments not discussed in the You're the Economist, and classify them as either positive or normative economics.

2. Give a positive and a normative argument why a business leader would oppose raising the minimum wage. Give a positive and a normative argument why a labor leader would favor raising the minimum wage.

3. Explain your position on this issue. Identify positive and normative reasons for your decision. Are there alternative ways to aid the working poor?

---

[1]David Card and Alan B. Krueger, *Myth and Measurement: The New Economics of the Minimum Wage* (Princeton, N.J.: Princeton University Press, 1995).

KEY CONCEPTS

Scarcity
Resources
Land
Labor

Entrepreneurship
Capital
Economics

Macroeconomics
Microeconomics
Model

Ceteris paribus
Positive economics
Normative economics

SUMMARY

■ **Scarcity** is the fundamental economic problem that human wants exceed the availability of time, goods, and resources. Individuals and society therefore can never have everything they desire.

■ **Resources** are factors of production classified as land, labor, and capital. Entrepreneurship is a special type of labor. An entrepreneur combines resources to produce innovative products.

■ **Economics** is the study of how individuals and society choose to allocate scarce resources in order to satisfy unlimited wants. Faced with unlimited wants and scarce resources, we must make choices among alternatives.

■ **Macroeconomics** applies an economywide perspective that focuses on such issues as inflation, unemployment, and the growth rate of the economy.

■ **Microeconomics** examines individual decision-making units within an economy. Microeconomics studies such topics as a consumer's response to changes in the price of coffee and the reasons for changes in the market price of personal computers.

■ **Models** are simplified descriptions of reality used to understand and predict economic events. An economic model can be stated verbally or in a table, graph, or equation. If the evidence is not consistent with the model, the model is rejected.

■ **Ceteris paribus** holds "all other factors unchanged" that might affect a particular relationship. If this assumption is violated, a model cannot be tested. Another reasoning pitfall is to think that *association* means *causation*.

■ Use of **positive** versus **normative economic analysis** is a major reason for disagreement among economists. **Positive economics** uses testable statements. Often a positive argument is expressed as an "*if-then*" statement. **Normative economics** is based on value judgments or opinions and uses words such as *good, bad, ought to*, and *ought not to.*

SUMMARY OF CONCLUSION STATEMENTS

■ Financial capital by itself is not productive; instead, it is only a paper claim on economic capital.

■ A theory cannot be tested legitimately unless its ceteris paribus assumption is satisfied.

■ The fact that one event follows another does not necessarily mean that the first event caused the second event.

■ Forecasts of economists can differ because, using the same methodology, economists can agree that event *A* causes *B*, but disagree over the assumption that event *A* will occur.

■ When opinions or points of view are not based on facts, they are scientifically untestable.

STUDY QUESTIONS AND PROBLEMS

1. Explain why both nations with high living standards and nations with low living standards face the problem of scarcity. If you won $1 million in a lottery, would you escape the scarcity problem?

2. Why isn't money considered capital in economics?

3. Computer software programs are an example of
   a. capital.
   b. labor.
   c. a natural resource.
   d. none of the above.

4. Explain the difference between macroeconomics and microeconomics. Give examples of the areas of concern to each branch of economics.

5. Which of the following are microeconomic issues? Which are macroeconomic issues?
   a. How will an increase in the price of Coca-Cola affect the quantity of Pepsi-Cola sold?
   b. What will cause the rate of inflation in the nation to fall?
   c. How does a quota on textile imports affect the textile industry?
   d. Does a large federal budget deficit reduce the rate of unemployment in the economy?

6. A model is defined as a
   a. value judgment of the relationship between variables.
   b. presentation of all relevant aspects of real-world events.
   c. simplified description of reality used to understand the way variables are related.
   d. data set adjusted for irrational actions of people.

7. Explain the importance of an economic model being an abstraction from the real world.

8. Explain the importance of the ceteris paribus assumption for an economic model.

9. Having won the Cold War, Congress cuts spending for the military, and then unemployment rises in the U.S. defense industry. Is there causation in this situation, or are we observing an association between events?

10. Which of the following is an example of a proposition from positive economics?
    a. If George Bush had been re-elected president, taxpayers would have been treated more fairly than they are under Bill Clinton.
    b. The average rate of inflation was higher during Bush's presidency than during Clinton's presidency.
    c. In economic terms, Bush was a better president than Clinton.
    d. Clinton's policies are more just toward poor people than Bush's.

11. "The government should collect higher taxes from the rich and use the additional revenues to provide greater benefits to the poor." This statement is an illustration of a
    a. testable statement.
    b. basic principle of economics.
    c. statement of positive economics.
    d. statement of normative economics.

12. Analyze the positive versus normative arguments in the following case. Which statements of positive economics are used to support requiring airbags? What normative reasoning is used?

Should the Government Require Airbags?

Airbag advocates say airbags will save lives and the government should require them in all cars. Airbags are estimated to add up to $600 to the cost of a car, compared to about $100 for a set of regular seat belts. Opponents argue that, because airbags are electronic devices, they are subject to failures and have produced injury or death. For example, air bags have killed both adults and children whose heads are within the inflation zone at the time of deployment. Opponents therefore believe the government should leave the decision of whether to spend an extra $600 or so for an airbag to the consumer. The role of the government should be limited to providing information on the risks of having or not having an airbag.

ONLINE EXERCISES

Exercise 1

Does the Internet raise or lower the cost of making friends? As you consider this question, visit a virtual meeting place: the American Intercultural Student Exchange (http://www.sibling.org). Or you may wish to participate in a live chat with other people on the Internet—if so, visit Yahoo! (http://chat.yahoo.com). Explain how scarcity relates to the Internet.

Exercise 2

Visit World Factbook (http://www.odci.gov/cia /publications/factbook/index.html), and follow these steps:

1. Select Countries and then United States.
2. Note the land area and population size in the United States.
3. Compute the land area per person by dividing the land area of the United States by its population size.
4. Select Japan. Repeat steps 2 and 3 for Japan.

5. How does the scarcity of land influence land-use choices? Would you find as many golf courses in Japan as in the United States? Explain.

Exercise 3

Visit Job Openings for Economists (http://www.eco .utexas.edu/joe/) and select the most recent issue. Browse the Academic, Foreign, or Nonacademic job openings for economists. Study the job descriptions and earnings for economists.

Exercise 4

Visit the White House home page—http://www .whitehouse.gov/. Look under The Briefing Room. Click on Summaries of today's press releases. Choose a topic you think pertains to economics. Does the subject matter pertain to macroeconomics or microeconomics? Is the analysis primarily normative or positive?

CHECKPOINT ANSWERS

Can You Prove There Is No Trillion-Dollar Person?

How can researchers ever be certain they have seen all the rich people in the United States? There is always the possibility that there is a person who qualifies somewhere. Had the researchers found one, you could have rejected the theory. Because they did not, you can only fail to reject the theory. If you said that the evidence can support, but never prove the theory, YOU ARE CORRECT.

Should Minnesota State Join a Big-Time Athletic Conference?

Suppose universities that belong to big-time athletic conferences do indeed have higher graduation rates than nonmembers. This is not the only possible explanation for the statistical correlation (or association) between the graduation rate and membership in a big-time athletic conference. A more plausible explanation is that improving academic variables, such as tuition, quality of faculty, and student/faculty ratios, and not athletic conference membership, improves the graduation rate. If you said correlation does not mean causation, and therefore Minnesota State officials will not necessarily accept the graduation rate evidence, YOU ARE CORRECT.

PRACTICE QUIZ

For a visual explanation of the correct answers, visit the tutorial at http://tucker.swcollege.com.

1. Scarcity exists
   a. when people consume beyond their needs.
   b. only in rich nations.
   c. in all countries of the world.
   d. only in poor nations.

2. Which of the following would eliminate scarcity as an economic problem?
   a. Moderation of people's competitive instincts.
   b. Discovery of sufficiently large new energy reserves.
   c. Resumption of steady productivity growth.
   d. None of the above because scarcity cannot be eliminated.

3. Which of the following is *not* a resource?
   a. Land
   b. Labor
   c. Money
   d. Capital

4. Economics is the study of
   a. how to make money.
   b. how to operate a business.
   c. people making choices because of the problem of scarcity.
   d. the government decision-making process.

5. Microeconomics approaches the study of economics from the viewpoint of
   a. individual or specific markets.
   b. the operation of the Federal Reserve.
   c. economywide effects.
   d. the national economy.

6. A review of the performance of the U.S. economy during the 1990s is primarily the concern of
   a. macroeconomics.
   b. microeconomics.
   c. both macroeconomics and microeconomics.
   d. neither macroeconomics nor microeconomics.

7. An economic theory claims that a rise in gasoline prices will cause gasoline purchases to fall, ceteris paribus. The phrase "ceteris paribus" means that
   a. other relevant factors like consumer incomes must be held constant.
   b. the gasoline prices must first be adjusted for inflation.
   c. the theory is widely accepted, but cannot be accurately tested.
   d. consumers' need for gasoline remains the same regardless of price.

8. An economist notices that sunspot activity is high just prior to recessions and concludes that sunspots cause recessions. The economist has
   a. confused association and causation.
   b. misunderstood the ceteris paribus assumption.
   c. used normative economics to answer a positive question.
   d. built an untestable model.

9. Which of the following is a statement of positive economics?
   a. The income tax system collects a lower percentage of the incomes of the poor.
   b. A reduction in tax rates of the rich makes the tax system more fair.
   c. Tax rates ought to be raised to finance health care.
   d. All of the above are primarily statements of positive economics.

10. Which of the following is a statement of positive economics?
    a. An unemployment rate greater than 8 percent is good because prices will fall.
    b. An unemployment rate of 7 percent is a serious problem.
    c. If the overall unemployment rate is 7 percent, black unemployment rates will average 15 percent.
    d. Unemployment is a more severe problem than inflation.

11. Which of the following is a statement of normative economics?
    a. The minimum wage is good because it raises wages for the working poor.
    b. The minimum wage is supported by unions.
    c. The minimum wage reduces jobs for less skilled workers.
    d. The minimum wage encourages firms to substitute capital for labor.

12. Select the normative statement that completes the following sentence: If the minimum wage is raised rapidly, then
    a. inflation increases.
    b. workers will gain their rightful share of total income.
    c. profits will fall.
    d. unemployment will rise.

Applying Graphs to Economics

Economists are famous for their use of graphs. The reason is "A picture is worth a thousand words." Graphs are used throughout this text to present economics models. By drawing a line, you can use a two-dimensional illustration to analyze the effects of a change in one variable on another. You could describe the same information using other model forms, such as verbal statements, tables, or equations. But the graph provides the simplest way to present and understand the relationship between economic variables.

Don't be worried that graphs will "throw you for a loop." Relax! This appendix explains all the basic graphical language you will need. The following illustrates the simplest use of graphs for economic analysis.

A Direct Relationship

Basic economic analysis typically concerns the relationship between two variables, both having positive values. Hence, we can confine our graphs to the upper right-hand (northeast) quadrant of the coordinate number system. In Exhibit A-1, notice that the scales on the horizontal axis (x-axis) and the vertical axis (y-axis) do not necessarily measure the same numerical values.

The horizontal axis in Exhibit A-1 measures annual income, and the vertical axis shows the amount spent per year for a personal computer (PC). In

EXHIBIT A-1

A Direct Relationship Between Variables

Expenditure for a Personal Computer at Different Annual Incomes

Point	Personal computer expenditure (thousands of dollars per year)	Annual income (thousands of dollars)
A	$1	$10
B	2	20
C	3	30
D	4	40

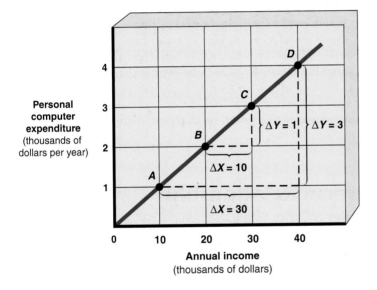

The line with a positive slope shows that the expenditure per year for a personal computer has a direct relationship to annual income, ceteris paribus. As annual income increases along the horizontal axis, the amount spent on a personal computer also increases, as measured by the vertical axis. Along the line, each 10-unit increase in annual income results in a 1-unit increase in expenditure for a personal computer. Because the slope is constant along a straight line, we can measure the same slope between any two points. Between points B and C or between points A and D, *the slope is* $\Delta Y/\Delta X = +3/+30 = +1/+10 = 1/10$.

the absence of any established traditions, we could decide to measure income on the vertical axis and purchases on the horizontal axis. The intersection of the horizontal and the vertical axes is the *origin* and the point where both income and expenditure are zero. In Exhibit A-1, each point is a coordinate that matches the dollar value of income and the corresponding expenditure for a PC. For example, point *A* on the graph shows that people with an annual income of $10,000 spent $1,000 per year for a PC. Other incomes are associated with different expenditure levels. For example, at $30,000 per year (point *C*), $3,000 will be the annual amount spent for a PC.

The straight line in Exhibit A-1 allows us to determine the direction of change in PC expenditure as annual income changes. This relationship is *positive* because PC expenditure, measured along the vertical axis, and annual income, measured along the horizontal axis, move in the same direction. PC expenditure increases as annual income increases. As income declines, so does the amount spent on a personal computer. Thus, the straight line representing the relationship between income and PC expenditure is a **direct relationship**. A direct relationship is a positive association between two variables. When one variable increases, the other variable increases, and when one variable decreases, the other variable decreases. In short, both variables change in the *same* direction.

Finally, this is an important point to remember. A two-variable graph, like any model, isolates the relationship between two variables and holds all other variables constant under the ceteris paribus assumption. In Exhibit A-1, for example, such factors as the prices of PCs and education are held constant by assumption. In Chapter 3, you will learn that allowing variables not shown in the graph to change can shift the position of the curve.

Direct relationship

A positive association between two variables. When one variable increases, the other variable increases, and when one variable decreases, the other variable decreases.

An Inverse Relationship

Now consider the relationship between the price of compact discs and the quantity consumers will buy per year, shown in Exhibit A-2. These data indicate a *negative* relationship between the price and quantity variables. When the price is low, consumers purchase a greater quantity of compact discs than when the price is high.

In Exhibit A-2, there is an **inverse relationship** between the price per compact disc and the quantity consumers buy. An inverse relationship is a negative association between two variables. When one variable increases, the other variable decreases, and when one variable decreases, the other variable increases. Stated simply, both variables move in *opposite* directions.

The line drawn in Exhibit A-2 is an inverse relationship. By long-established tradition, economists put price on the vertical axis and quantity on the horizontal axis. In Chapter 3, we will study in more detail the relationship between price and quantity called the *law of demand*.

In addition to the slope, you must interpret the *intercept* at point *A* in the figure. The intercept in this case means that at a price of $25 no consumer is willing to buy a single compact disc.

Inverse relationship

A negative association between two variables. When one variable increases, the other variable decreases, and when one variable decreases, the other variable increases.

EXHIBIT A-2

An Inverse Relationship Between Variables

Quantity of Compact Discs Consumers Purchase at Different Prices

Point	Price per compact disc	Quantity of compact discs purchased (millions per year)
A	$25	0
B	20	25
C	15	50
D	10	75
E	5	100

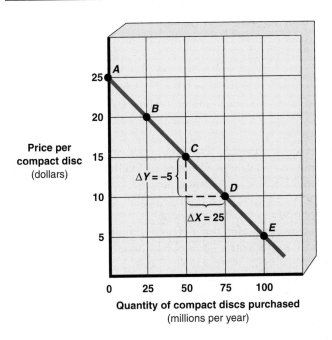

The line with a negative slope shows an inverse relationship between the price per compact disc and the quantity of compact discs consumers purchase, ceteris paribus. As the price of a compact disc rises, the quantity of compact discs purchased falls. A lower price for compact discs is associated with more compact discs purchased by consumers. Along the line, with each $5 decrease in the price of compact discs, consumers increase the quantity purchased by 25 units. The slope = $\Delta Y / \Delta X = -5/+25 = -1/5$.

The Slope of a Straight Line

Plotting numbers gives a clear visual expression of the relationship between two variables, but it is also important to know how much one variable changes as another variable changes. To find out, we calculate the **slope**. The slope is the ratio of the change in the variable on the vertical axis (the rise or fall) to the change in the variable on the horizontal axis (the run). Algebraically, if Y is on the vertical axis and X on the horizontal axis, the slope is expressed as follows (the delta symbol, Δ, means "change in"):

$$\text{Slope} = \frac{\text{rise}}{\text{run}} = \frac{\text{change in vertical axis}}{\text{change in horizontal axis}} = \frac{\Delta Y}{\Delta X}$$

Consider the slope between points B and C in Exhibit A-1. The change in expenditure for a PC, Y, is equal to $+1$ (from \$2,000 up to \$3,000 per year), and the change in annual income, X, is equal to $+10$ (from \$20,000 up to \$30,000 per year). The slope is therefore $+1/+10$. The sign is positive because computer expenditure is directly or positively related to annual income. The steeper the line, the greater the slope because the ratio of ΔY to ΔX rises. Conversely, the flatter the line, the smaller the slope. Exhibit A-1 also illustrates that the slope of a straight line is constant. That is, the slope between any two points along the line, such as between points A and D, is equal to $+3/+30 = 1/10$.

What does the slope of 1/10 mean? It means that a \$1,000 increase (decrease) in PC expenditure each year occurs for each \$10,000 increase (decrease) in annual income. The line plotted in Exhibit A-1 has a *positive slope*, and we describe the line as "upward sloping."

On the other hand, the line in Exhibit A-2 has a *negative slope*. The change in Y between points C and D is equal to -5 (from \$15 down to \$10), and the change in X is equal to 25 (from 50 million up to 75 million compact discs purchased per year). The slope is therefore $-5/+25 = -1/5$, and this line is described as "downward sloping."

What does this slope of $-1/5$ mean? It means that raising (lowering) the price per compact disc by \$1 decreases (increases) the quantity of compact discs purchased by 5 million per year.

Suppose we calculate the slope between any two points—say, points B and C in Exhibit A-3. In this case, there is no change in Y (expenditure for toothpaste) as X (annual income) increases. Consumers spend \$20 per year on toothpaste regardless of annual income. It follows that $\Delta Y = 0$ for any ΔX, so that the slope is equal to 0. The two variables along a flat line (horizontal or vertical) have an **independent relationship**. An independent relationship is a zero association between two variables. When one variable changes, the other variable remains unchanged.

The Slope of a Curve

The slope of a curve changes from one point to another. Suppose the relationship between the expenditure for a PC per year and annual income is not a straight line, but an upward-sloping curve, as drawn in Exhibit A-4.

Slope
The ratio of change in the variable on the vertical axis (the rise or fall) to change in the variable on the horizontal axis (the run).

Independent relationship
A zero relationship between two variables. When one variable changes, the other variable remains unchanged.

EXHIBIT A-3

An Independent Relationship Between Variables

Expenditure for Toothpaste at Different Annual Incomes

Point	Toothpaste expenditure (dollars per year)	Annual income (thousands of dollars)
A	$20	$10
B	20	20
C	20	30
D	20	40

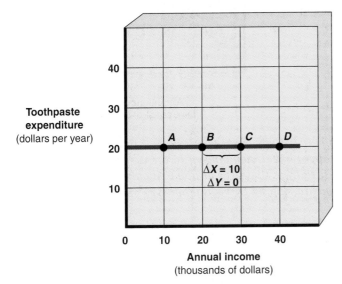

The flat line with a zero slope shows that the expenditure per year for toothpaste is unrelated to annual income. As annual income increases along the horizontal axis, the amount spent each year for toothpaste remains unchanged at 20 units. If annual income increases 10 units, the corresponding change in expenditure is zero. The slope $= \Delta Y/\Delta X = 0/+10 = 0$.

This means the slope of the curve is *positive* as we move along the curve. To calculate the slope of a given point on the curve requires two steps. For example, at point *A*, the first step is to draw a tangent line that just touches the curve at this point without crossing it. The second step is to determine the slope of the tangent line. In Exhibit A-4, the slope of the tangent line, and therefore the slope of the curve at point *A*, is $+2/+30 = +1/+15 = 1/15$. What does this slope of 1/15 mean? It means that at point *A* there will be a $1,000 increase (decrease) in PC expenditure each year for each $15,000 increase (decrease) in annual income.

EXHIBIT A-4

The Slope of an Upward-Sloping Curve

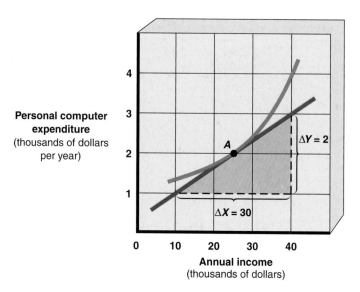

The slope of a curve at any given point, such as point A, is equal to the slope of the straight line drawn tangent to the curve at that point. The tangent line just touches the curve at point A without crossing it. The slope of the upward-sloping curve at point A is +2/+30 = +1/+15 = 1/15.

Now consider that the relationship between the price per compact disc and the quantity demanded by consumers per year is the downward-sloping curve shown in Exhibit A-5. In this case, the slope of the curve is *negative* as we move along the curve. To calculate the slope at point *A*, draw a line tangent to the curve at point *A*. Thus, the slope of the curve at point *A* is −10/+50 = −1/+5 = −1/5.

A Three-Variable Relationship in One Graph

The two-variable relationships drawn so far conform to a two-dimensional flat piece of paper. For example, the vertical axis measures the price per compact disc variable, and the horizontal axis measures the quantity of compact discs purchased variable. All other factors, such as consumer income, that may affect the relationship between the price and quantity variables are held constant by the ceteris paribus assumption. But reality is frequently not so accommodating. Often a model must take into account

The Slope of a Downward-Sloping Curve

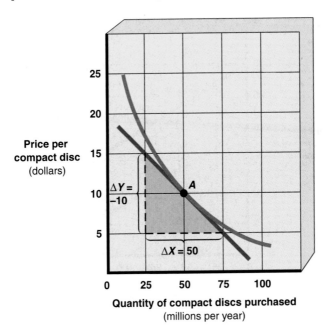

Price per compact disc (dollars)

$\Delta Y = -10$

A

$\Delta X = 50$

Quantity of compact discs purchased (millions per year)

In this exhibit, the negative slope changes as one moves from point to point along the curve. The slope at any given point, such as point A, can be determined by the slope of the straight line tangent to that point. The slope of the downward-sloping curve at point A is $-10/+50 = -1/+5 = -1/5$.

the impact of changes in a third variable (consumer income) drawn on a two-dimensional piece of graph paper.

The favorite method of economists to depict a three-variable relationship is shown in Exhibit A-6. As explained earlier, the cause-and-effect relationship between price and quantity of compact discs determines the downward-sloping curve. A change in the price per compact disc causes a movement downward along either of the two separate curves. As the price falls, consumers increase the quantity of compact discs demanded. The location of each curve on the graph, however, depends on the annual income of consumers. As the annual income variable increases from $30,000 to $60,000 and as consumers can afford to pay more, the price–quantity demanded curve shifts rightward. Conversely, as the annual income variable decreases and as consumers can afford to pay less, the price–quantity demanded curve shifts leftward.

This is an extremely important concept you must understand: Throughout this book, you must distinguish between *movements along* and *shifts in*

Changes in Price, Quantity, and Income in Two Dimensions

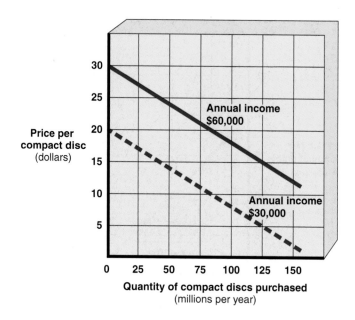

Economists use a multicurve graph to represent a three-variable relation-ship in a two-dimensional graph. A decrease in the price per compact disc causes a movement downward along each curve. As the annual income of consumers rises, there is a shift rightward in the position of the demand curve.

a curve. Here's how to tell the difference. A change in one of the variables shown on either of the coordinate axes of the graph causes *movement along* a curve. On the other hand, a change in a variable not shown on one of the coordinate axes of the graph causes a *shift in* a curve's position on the graph.

Conclusion *A shift in a curve occurs only when the ceteris paribus assumption is relaxed and a third variable not on either axis of the graph is allowed to change.*

A Helpful Study Hint Using Graphs

Don't be the student who tries to memorize the graphs and then wonders why he or she failed economics. Instead of memorizing graphs, you should use graphs as a valuable aid to learning the economic concepts these graphs illustrate. After studying a chapter, go back to the graphs one by one. Cover up the brief description accompanying each graph, and describe to yourself or other students what the graph means. Next, uncover the description, and check your interpretation. If you still fail to understand the graph, read the text again, and correct the problem before proceeding to the next chapter.

KEY CONCEPTS

Direct relationship   Slope
Inverse relationship   Independent relationship

SUMMARY

■ **Graphs** provide a means to clearly show economic relationships in two-dimensional space. Economic analysis is often concerned with two variables confined to the upper right-hand (northeast) quadrant of the coordinate number system.

★ A **direct relationship** is one in which two variables change in the *same* direction.

Direct relationship

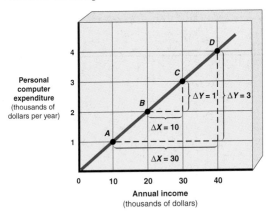

★ An **inverse relationship** is one in which two variables change in *opposite* directions.

Inverse relationship

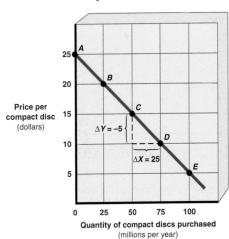

★ An **independent relationship** is one in which two variables are unrelated.

Independent relationship

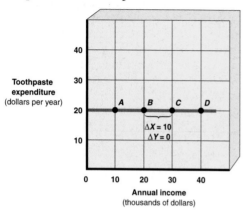

★ **Slope** is the ratio of the vertical change (the rise or fall) to the horizontal change (the run). The slope of an *upward-sloping* line is *positive*, and the slope of a *downward-sloping* line is *negative*.

Positive slope of an upward-sloping curve

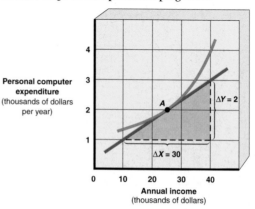

Negative slope of a downward-sloping curve

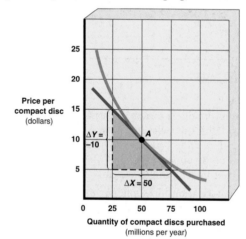

SUMMARY OF CONCLUSION STATEMENTS

■ A shift in a curve occurs only when the ceteris paribus assumption is relaxed and a third variable not on either axis of the graph is allowed to change.

STUDY QUESTIONS AND PROBLEMS

1. Draw a graph without specific data for the expected relationship between the following variables:
   a. The probability of living and age
   b. Annual income and years of education
   c. Inches of snow and sales of bathing suits
   d. The number of football games won and the athletic budget

   In each case, state whether the expected relationship is *direct* or *inverse*. Explain an additional factor that would be included in the ceteris paribus assumption because it might change and influence your theory.

2. Assume a research firm collects survey sales data that reveal the relationship between the possible selling prices of hamburgers and the quantity of hamburgers consumers would purchase per year at alternative prices. The report states that if the price of a hamburger is $4.00, 20,000 will be bought. However, at a price of $3.00, 40,000 hamburgers will be bought. At $2.00, 60,000 hamburgers will be bought, and at $1.00, 80,000 hamburgers will be purchased.

   Based on these data, describe the relevant relationship between the price of a hamburger and the quantity consumers are willing to purchase, using
   a. a verbal statement.
   b. a numerical table.
   c. a graph.
   Which model do you prefer and why?

PRACTICE QUIZ

For a visual explanation of the correct answers, visit the tutorial at http://tucker.swcollege.com.

1. Straight line *CD* in Exhibit A-7 shows that
   a. increasing the values of *X* will increase the value of *Y*.
   b. decreasing the values of *X* will decrease the value of *Y*.
   c. there is a direct relationship between *X* and *Y*.
   d. all of the above are true.

2. In Exhibit A-7, the slope of straight line *CD* is
   a. 3.
   b. 1.
   c. −1.
   d. 1/2.

3. In Exhibit A-7, the slope of straight line *CD* is
   a. positive.
   b. zero.
   c. negative.
   d. variable.

4. Straight line *AB* in Exhibit A-8 shows that
   a. increasing the value of *X* reduces the value of *Y*.
   b. decreasing the value of *X* increases the value of *Y*.
   c. there is an inverse relationship between *X* and *Y*.
   d. all of the above are true.

5. As shown in Exhibit A-8, the slope of straight line *AB*
   a. decreases with increases in *X*.
   b. increases with increases in *X*.
   c. increases with decreases in *X*.
   d. remains constant with changes in *X*.

EXHIBIT A-7   Straight Line

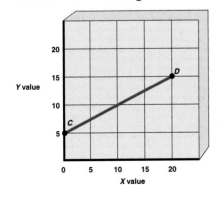

EXHIBIT A-8   Straight Line

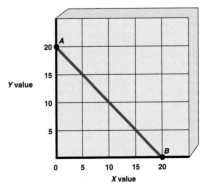

6. In Exhibit A-8, the slope for straight line *AB* is
   a. 3.
   b. 1.
   c. −1.
   d. −5.

7. A shift in a curve represents a change in
   a. the variable on the horizontal axis.
   b. the variable on the vertical axis.
   c. a third variable that is not on either axis.
   d. any variable that is relevant to the relationship being graphed.

8. A change in a third variable not on either axis of a graph is illustrated with a
   a. horizontal or vertical line.
   b. movement along a curve.
   c. shift of a curve.
   d. point of intersection.

CHAPTER TWO

Production Possibilities and Opportunity Cost

This chapter continues building on the foundation laid in the preceding chapter. Having learned that *scarcity* forces *choices*, here you will study the choices people make in more detail. This chapter begins by examining the three basic choices: *What, How,* and *For Whom* to produce. Next, you will learn that the process of answering these basic questions introduces two other key building blocks in the economic way of thinking—*opportunity cost* and *marginal analysis.* Once you understand these important concepts stated in words, it will be easier to interpret our first formal economic model, the *production possibilities curve.* This model illustrates how economists use graphs as a powerful tool to supplement words and develop an understanding of basic economic principles. You will discover that

the production possibilities model teaches many of the most important concepts in economics, including scarcity, the law of increasing opportunity costs, efficiency, investment, and economic growth. For example, the chapter concludes by using the production possibilities curve to explain why underdeveloped countries do not achieve economic growth and thereby improve their standard of living. As you read the chapter, watch for the relevance of the sailboat on this page.

In this chapter, you will learn to solve these economics puzzles:

■ Why do so few rock stars or movie stars go to college?

■ Why would you spend an extra hour reading this text, rather than going to a movie or sleeping?

■ Why are investment and economic growth so important?

The Three Fundamental Economic Questions

Whether rich or poor, every nation must answer these same three fundamental economic questions: (1) *What* products will be produced? (2) *How* will they be produced? (3) *For Whom* will they be produced? The chapter on comparative economic systems introduces various types of economic systems and describes how each deals with these three economic choices.

What to Produce?

Should society devote its limited resources to producing more military goods and fewer consumer goods and services? Should society produce more CDs and fewer computer software programs? Should more small cars and fewer large cars be produced, or should more buses be produced instead of cars? The problem of scarcity imposes a restriction on the ability to produce everything we want during a given period, so the choice to produce "more" of a good requires producing "less" of another good.

How to Produce?

After deciding which products to make, the second question for society to decide is how to mix technology and scarce resources in order to produce these goods. For instance, a towel can be sewn primarily by hand (labor), partially by hand and partially by machine (labor and capital), or primarily by machine (capital). In short, the How question asks whether a production technique will be more or less capital-intensive.

Education plays an important role in answering the How question. Education improves the ability of workers to perform their work. Because the quality and quantity of education vary among nations, this is one reason economies differ in their capacities to apply resources and technology to answer the How question. For example, the United States is striving to catch up with Japan in the use of robotics. Answering the question "How to improve our robotics?" requires engineers and employees with the proper training in the installation and operation of robots.

For Whom to Produce?

Once the What and How questions are resolved, the third question is For Whom. Among all those desiring the produced goods, who actually receives them? Who is fed well? Who drives a Mercedes? Who receives organ transplants? Should economics professors earn a salary of $1 million a year and others pay higher taxes to support economists? The For Whom question means that society must have a method to decide who will be "rich and famous" and who will be "poor and unknown."

Opportunity Cost

Because of scarcity, the three basic questions cannot be answered without sacrifice or cost. But what does the term *cost* really mean? The common response would be to say that the purchase price is the cost. A movie ticket *costs* $5.00, or a shirt *costs* $50.00. Applying the economic way of think-ing, however, *cost* is a relative concept. A well-known phrase in economics is, "There is no such thing as a free lunch." This expression captures the links among the concepts of scarcity, choice, and cost. Because of scarcity, people must make choices, and each choice incurs a cost (sacrifice). Once one option is chosen, another option is given up. The money you spend on a movie ticket cannot also buy a videotape. A business may purchase a new textile machine to manufacture towels, but this same money cannot be used to buy a new recreation facility for employees.

The videotape and the recreation facility examples illustrate that the true cost of these decisions is the **opportunity cost** of a choice, not the pur-chase price. Opportunity cost is the best alternative sacrificed for a chosen alternative. This principle states that some most highly valued opportunity must be foregone in all economic decisions. The actual good or use of time given up for the chosen good or the use of time measures the opportunity cost. We may leave off the word "opportunity" before the word "cost," but the concept remains just the same.

Examples are endless, but let's consider a few. Suppose your economics professor decides to become a rock star in the Rolling in Dough band. Now all his or her working hours are devoted to creating hit music, and the opportunity cost is the educational services no longer provided. Now a personal example: The opportunity cost of dating a famous model or movie star (name your favorite) might be the loss of your current girl-friend or boyfriend. Opportunity cost also applies to national economic decisions. Suppose the federal government decides to spend tax revenues on a space station. The opportunity cost depends on the next best program *not* funded. Assume roads and bridges are the highest valued projects not built as a result of the decision to purchase the space station. Then roads and bridges are the opportunity cost of the decision to devote resources to the space station and not the money actually spent to buy the space station.

To illustrate the relationship between time and opportunity cost, ask yourself what you would be doing if you were not reading this book. Your answer might be studying another subject, watching television, or sleeping. If sleeping is your choice, the opportunity cost of studying this text is the sleep you sacrifice. Rock stars or movie stars, on the other hand, must for-feit a large amount of income to attend college. Now you know why you see so few of these stars in class.

Marginal Analysis

At the heart of many important decision-making techniques used through-out this text is **marginal analysis**. Marginal analysis examines the effects of additions to or subtractions from a current situation. This is a very valu-able tool in the economic-way-of-thinking toolkit because it considers the effects of change. For example, you must decide how to use your scarce time. Should you devote an extra hour to reading this book, going to a movie, watching television, talking on the phone, or sleeping? There are many ways to spend your time. Which option do you choose? The answer

Opportunity cost
The best alternative sacrificed for a chosen alternative.

🖱 *What is the opportunity cost of attending college? To learn more about the costs and benefits of attending col-lege, visit the U.S. Department of Education at* http://www.ed.gov/.

Marginal analysis
An examination of the effects of additions to or subtractions from a current situation.

depends on marginal analysis. If you decide the benefit of a higher grade in economics exceeds the opportunity cost of, say, sleep, then you allocate the extra hour to studying economics. Excellent choice!

Similarly, producers use marginal analysis. For example, a farmer plants corn without fertilizer at a cost of $50 per acre. The farmer asks if he or she should add fertilizer. Using marginal analysis, the farmer estimates that the corn revenue yield will be about $75 per acre without fertilizer and about $100 per acre using fertilizer. If the cost of fertilizer is $20 per acre, marginal analysis tells the farmer to fertilize. The additional fertilizer will increase profit by $5 per acre because fertilizing adds $25 to the value of each acre at a cost of $20 per acre.

Marginal analysis is an important concept when government considers changes in various programs. For example, as demonstrated in the next section, it is useful to know that an increase in the production of military goods will result in an opportunity cost of fewer consumer goods produced.

The Production Possibilities Curve

Production possibilities curve

A curve that shows the maximum combinations of two outputs that an economy can produce, given its available resources and technology.

The economic problem of scarcity means that society's capacity to produce combinations of goods is constrained by its limited resources. This condition can be represented in a model called the **production possibilities curve**. The production possibilities curve shows the maximum combinations of two outputs that an economy can produce, given its available resources and technology. Three basic assumptions underlie the production possibilities curve model:

1. *Fixed Resources.* The quantities and qualities of all resource inputs remain unchanged during the time period. But the "rules of the game" do allow an economy to shift any resource from the production of one output to the production of another output. For example, an economy might shift workers from producing consumer goods to producing capital goods. Although the number of workers remains unchanged, this transfer of labor will produce fewer consumer goods and more capital goods.

2. *Fully Employed Resources.* The economy operates with all its factors of production fully employed and producing the greatest output possible without waste or mismanagement.

Technology

The body of knowledge applied to how goods are produced.

3. *Technology Unchanged.* Holding existing **technology** fixed creates limits, or constraints, on the amounts and types of goods any economy can produce. Technology is the body of knowledge applied to how goods are produced.

Exhibit 1 shows a hypothetical economy that has the capacity to manufacture any combination of military goods ("guns") and consumer goods ("butter") per year along its production possibilities curve (*PPC*), including points *A*, *B*, *C*, and *D*. For example, if this economy uses all its resources to make military goods, it can produce a *maximum* of 160 billion units of

EXHIBIT 1

The Production Possibilities Curve for Military Goods and Consumer Goods

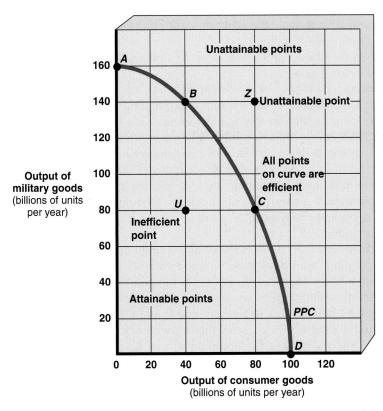

Output of military goods (billions of units per year)

Output of consumer goods (billions of units per year)

The Production Possibilities for Military Goods and Consumer Goods per Year

Output (billions of units per year)	Production possibilities			
	A	**B**	**C**	**D**
Military goods	160	140	80	0
Consumer goods	0	40	80	100

All points along the production possibilities curve (PPC) are maximum possible combinations of military goods and consumer goods. One possibility, point A, would be to produce 160 billion units of military goods and zero units of consumer goods each year. At the other extreme, point D, an economy uses all its resources to produce 100 billion units of consumer goods and zero units of military goods each year. Points B and C are obtained by using some resources to produce each of the two outputs. If the economy fails to utilize its resources fully, the result is the inefficient point U. Point Z lies beyond the economy's present production capabilities and is unattainable.

military goods and zero units of consumer goods (combination *A*). Another possibility is for the economy to use all its resources to produce a *maximum* of 100 billion units of consumer goods and zero units of military goods (point *D*). Between the extremes of points *A* and *D* lie other production possibilities for combinations of military and consumer goods. If combination B is chosen, the economy will produce 140 billion units of military goods and 40 billion units of consumer goods. Another possibility (point *C*) is to produce 80 billion units of military goods and 80 billion units of consumer goods.

Visit a few pacifist organizations, such as the Center for Economic Conversion at http://www.conversion .org/ *and the American Peace Network at* http://www.apn.org/. *What arguments do these organizations make for decreasing the size of the military? Do these arguments take into account the concept of opportunity cost?*

What happens if the economy does not use all its resources to their capacity? For example, some workers may not find work, or plants and equipment may be idle for any number of reasons. The result is that our hypothetical economy fails to reach any of the combinations along PPC. In Exhibit 1, point *U* illustrates an *inefficient* output level for any economy operating without all its resources fully employed. At point *U*, our model economy is producing 80 billion units of military goods and 40 billion units of consumer goods per year. Such an economy is underproducing because it could satisfy more of society's wants if it were producing at some point along *PPC*.

Even if an economy fully employs all its resources, it is impossible to produce certain output quantities. Any point outside the production possibilities curve is *unattainable* because it is beyond the economy's present production capabilities. Point *Z*, for example, represents an unattainable output of 140 billion units of military goods and 80 billion units of consumer goods. Society would prefer this combination to any combination along, or inside, *PPC*, but the economy cannot reach this point with its existing resources and technology.

Conclusion *Scarcity limits an economy to points on or below its production possibilities curve.*

Because all the points along the curve are *maximum* output levels with the given resources and technology, they are all called *efficient* points. A movement between any two efficient points on the curve means that *more* of one product is produced only by producing *less* of the other product. In Exhibit 1, moving from point *A* to point *B* produces 40 billion additional units of consumer goods per year, but only at a cost of sacrificing 20 billion units of military goods. Thus, a movement between any two efficient points graphically illustrates "There is no such thing as a free lunch."

Conclusion *The production possibilities curve consists of all efficient output combinations where an economy can produce more of one good only by producing less of the other good.*

The Law of Increasing Opportunity Costs

Why is the production possibilities curve shaped the way it is? Exhibit 2 will help us answer this question. It presents a production possibilities curve for a hypothetical economy that must choose between producing

EXHIBIT 2

The Law of Increasing Opportunity Costs

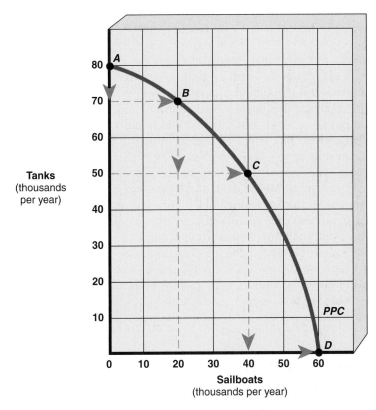

Production Possibilities for Tanks and Sailboats per Year

Output (thousands per year)	Production possibilities			
	A	**B**	**C**	**D**
Tanks	80	70	50	0
Sailboats	0	20	40	60

A hypothetical economy produces equal increments of 20,000 sailboats per year as we move from point A through point D on the production possibilities curve (PPC). If the hypothetical economy moves from point A to point B, the opportunity cost of 20,000 sailboats is a reduction in tank output of 10,000 per year. This opportunity cost rises to 20,000 tanks by selecting point C, instead of point B. Finally, production at point D, rather than point C, results in an opportunity cost of 50,000 tanks per year. The opportunity cost rises because workers are not equally suited to making tanks and sailboats.

tanks and producing sailboats. Consider expanding the production of sail-boats in 20,000-unit increments. Moving from point *A* to point *B*, the *opportunity cost* is 10,000 tanks; between point *B* and point *C*, the *opportunity cost* is 20,000 tanks; and the *opportunity cost* of producing at point *D*, rather than point *C*, is 50,000 tanks.

Law of increasing opportunity costs

The principle that the opportunity cost increases as the production of one output expands.

Exhibit 2 illustrates the **law of increasing opportunity costs**. The law of increasing opportunity costs states that the opportunity cost increases as production of one output expands. Holding the stock of resources and technology constant (ceteris paribus), the law of increasing opportunity costs causes the production possibilities curve to display a *bowed-out* shape.

Why must our hypothetical economy sacrifice larger and larger amounts of tank output in order to produce each additional 20,000 sailboats? The reason is that all workers are not equally suited to producing one good, compared to another good. To expand the output of sailboats, workers must be used who are less suited to producing sailboats than producing tanks. Suppose our hypothetical economy produces no sailboats (point *A*) and decides to expand its production of sailboats. At first, the least skilled tank workers are transferred to making sailboats, and 10,000 tanks are sacrificed. As the economy moves from point *B* to point *C*, more highly skilled tankmakers become sailboat makers, and the opportunity cost rises to 20,000 tanks. Finally, the economy can decide to move from point *C* to point *D*, and the opportunity cost increases even more to 50,000 tanks. Now the remaining tank workers, who are superb tank makers, but poor sailboat makers, must adapt to the techniques of sailboat production.

Shifting the Production Possibilities Curve

Economic growth

The ability of an economy to produce greater levels of output, represented by an outward shift of its production possibilities curve.

The economy's production capacity is not permanently fixed. If either the resource base increases or technology advances, the economy experiences **economic growth,** and the production possibilities curve shifts outward. Economic growth is the ability of an economy to produce greater levels of output, represented by an outward shift of its production possibilities curve. Exhibit 3 illustrates the importance of an outward shift. (Note the causation chain, which is often used in this text to focus on a model's cause-and-effect relationship.) At point *A* on production possibilities curve PPC_1, a hypothetical full-employment economy produces 40,000 computers and 200 million pizzas per year. If the curve shifts outward to new curve PPC_2, the economy can expand its full-employment output options. One option is to produce at point *B* and increase computer output to 70,000 per year. Another possibility is to increase pizza output to 400 million per year. Yet another choice is to produce more of both at some point between points *B* and *C*.

Changes in Resources

One way to accelerate economic growth is to gain additional resources. Any increase in resources—for example, more natural resources, a "baby boom," or more factories—will shift the production possibilities curve outward.

An Outward Shift of the Production Possibilities Curve for Computers and Pizzas

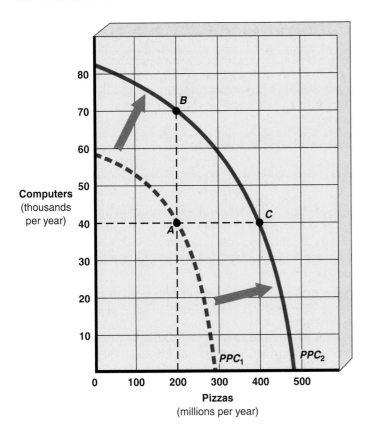

CAUSATION CHAIN

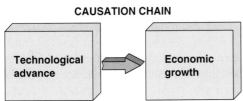

| Technological advance | → | Economic growth |

The economy begins with the capacity to produce combinations along production possibilities curve PPC₁. Growth in the resource base or technological advance shifts the production possibilities curve outward from PPC₁ to PPC₂. Points along PPC₂ represent new production possibilities previously impossible. This outward shift permits the economy to produce greater quantities of output. Instead of producing combination A, the economy can produce, for example, more computers at point B, or it can produce more pizzas at point C. If the economy produces at a point between B and C, more of both pizzas and computers can be produced, compared to point A.

CHECKPOINT

What Does the Peace Dividend Really Mean?

The easing of Cold War tensions gave the Clinton administration and Congress the opportunity to reverse the military buildup of the 1980s. The "peace dividend" is the well-known phrase used to describe this situation. Does the peace dividend represent a possible shift of the production possibilities curve or a movement along it?

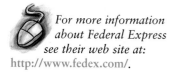

The Agricultural Research Service (ARS) in the U.S. Department of Agriculture (http://www.ars.usda.gov/) *is the main agricultural research agency of the federal government. What types of research does the ARS conduct, and how might this research push out the production possibilities curve for the subjects of this research?*

For more information about Federal Express see their web site at: http://www.fedex.com/.

In Exhibit 3, assume curve PPC_1 represents Japan's production possibilities for clothing and food in a given year. Suddenly, Japan discovers within its borders new sources of labor and other resources. Such new resources will result in Japan having an expanded capacity to produce any combination along an expanded curve, such as curve PPC_2.

Reductions in resources will cause the production possibilities curve to shift inward. Assume curve PPC_2 describes Japan's economy before World War II and the destruction of its factors of production in the war caused Japan's curve to shift leftward to curve PPC_1. Over the years, Japan trained its workforce, built new factories and equipment, and used new technology to shift its curve outward and surpass its original production capacity at curve PPC_2.

Technological Change

Another way to achieve economic growth is through research and development of new technologies. The knowledge of how to transform stone into a wheel vastly improved the prehistoric standard of living. Technological change also makes it possible to shift the production possibilities curve outward by producing more from the same resources base. One source of technological change is *invention*. The light bulb, the transistor, the computer chip, and the satellite are all examples of technological advances resulting from the use of science and engineering knowledge.

Technological change is also the result of the innovations of entrepreneurship introduced in the previous chapter. Innovation involves creating and developing new products or productive processes. Seeking profits, entrepreneurs create new, better, or less expensive products. This requires organizing an improved mix of resources, which expands the production possibilities curve.

One entrepreneur, Henry Ford, changed auto industry technology by pioneering the use of the assembly line for making cars. Another entrepreneur, Edwin Land, invented the Polaroid Land camera, which changed instant camera technology. Another entrepreneur, Chester Carlson, a law

Federal Express Wasn't an Overnight Success

Applicable Concept: entrepreneurship

Frederick W. Smith's story is a variation on the classic entrepreneur's saga: Poor boy from humble origins never goes to college but with hard work and a good idea, makes a fortune. Fred Smith came from a wealthy family—his father built Greyhound's bus system in the South. Young Fred went to Yale University, founded Federal Express Corp., worked like crazy and made a lot of money.

Moral: When you guarantee to "absolutely, positively" beat the pants off the U.S. Postal Service, rich parents and a Yale degree aren't that much of a handicap.

In a college economics class term paper in the 1960s, Smith spelled out his idea for a nationwide overnight parcel delivery system. He got a "C" grade. Perhaps the professor thought the idea was too far out. Certainly lots of others did.

In 1969, after a tour as a Marine pilot in Vietnam, the 24-year old Smith began selling corporate jets in Little Rock, Ark. He also started shopping his parcel delivery plan. Most of the financiers he approached were skeptical. But in two years, and with $4 million of his family's money as a sweetener, he persuaded a handful of venture capitalists to put up $80 million. It was the largest venture capital package ever assembled.

Two years later, in 1973, Federal Express kicked off its delivery service. A fleet of 14 French built Falcon jets connected a network of 25 cities. On the first night, 16 packages showed up.

Smith's entrepreneurial plan rested on a single concept—reliability. People, he said, would pay a fancy price if they truly believed their packages would arrive at their destination the following morning. To make it work, Smith incorporated two American industrial innovations, time and motion study and computers.

In a sort of nocturnal, airborne assembly line, Federal Express planes converge nightly on Memphis, Tenn., chosen for its central U.S. location and because its airport has little bad weather to cause landing delays.

The operation is carefully timed. Between 11 P.M. and 1 A.M., planes from around the U.S. fly in and out of Memphis. Items are unloaded, sorted, then rerouted on other airplanes to destination airports, where vans battle rush-hour traffic to make deliveries before noon. Computers track each item, giving nervous customers updates on their shipments.

It was two years before Smith looked like a genius. The company posted a $27 million loss, turned the corner in 1976, and then took off, helped by a 1981 decision to add letters to its basic package delivery service. Smith's basic strategy hasn't changed in 16 years, but the scale of the operation has exploded. Now, one million items is an average night for Federal Express. The company flies 255 planes, painted a distinctive purple, orange and white. There are 24,000 computerized delivery vans and a 57,000 person work force.

The Postal Service [USPS] may be miffed with Smith, but the Smithsonian Institution has rendered its ultimate accolade. It snapped up an early Federal Express jet for its collection, displaying it for a time in the Air and Space Museum in Washington, D.C., not far from the Wright Brothers' first airplane.[1]

Like many private businesses, the federal government often needs to send urgent, overnight mail. So whom does it turn to for delivery of 8 million express letters and packages each year? Federal Express. Why not the U.S. Postal Service? Because the USPS is forbidden by law from lowering its prices to bid for competitive contracts. No wonder, then, that the government recently signed a five-year, $300 million contract with FedEx, which can deliver its overnight mail $3 cheaper per letter than its own 221-year-old Postal Service.[2]

ANALYZE THE ISSUE

Draw a production possibilities curve for an economy producing only pizzas and computers. Explain how Fred Smith and other entrepreneurs affect the curve.

[1]Eugene Carlson, "Federal Express Wasn't an Overnight Success," June 6, 1989, p. B2. Reprinted by permission of the *Wall Street Journal*, © 1989 Dow Jones & Company, Inc. All Rights Reserved Worldwide.
[2]Douglas Stanglin, "Don't Return to Sender," *U.S. News and World Report*, October 7, 1996, p. 49.

student, worked on his own to develop photocopying because the problem of copying documents frustrated him. After years of disappointment, a small firm named Xerox Corporation accepted Carlson's invention and transformed a good idea into a revolutionary product. These, and a myriad of other business success stories, illustrate that entrepreneurs are important because they transform their new ideas into production and practical use.

Present Investment and Future Production Possibilities Curve

When the decision for an economy involves choosing between capital and consumer goods, the output combination for the present period can determine future production capacity.

Exhibit 4 compares two countries producing different combinations of capital and consumer goods. Part (a) shows the production possibilities curve for the low-investment economy of Alpha. This economy was producing combination A in 1990, which is an output of C_a of consumer goods and an output of K_a of capital goods per year (depreciation). Let's assume K_a is just enough capital output to replace the capital being worn out each year. As a result, Alpha fails to accumulate the net gain of factories and equipment required to expand its production possibilities curve outward in future years.[1] Why wouldn't Alpha simply move up along its production curve by shifting more resources to capital goods production? The problem is that sacrificing consumer goods for capital formation causes the standard of living to fall.

Comparing Alpha to Beta illustrates the importance of being able to do more than just replace worn-out capital. Beta operated in 1990 at point A in part (b), which is an output of C_b of consumer goods and K_b of capital goods. Assuming K_b is more than enough to replenish worn-out capital, Beta is a high-investment economy, adding to its capital stock and creating extra production capacity. This process of accumulating capital (*capital formation*) is **investment**. Investment is the accumulation of capital, such as factories, machines, and inventories, that is used to produce goods and services. Newly manufactured factories, machines, and inventories in the present provide an economy with the capacity to expand its production options in the future. For example, the outward shift of its curve allows Beta to produce C_c consumer goods at point B in the year 2010. This means Beta will be able to improve its standard of living by producing

Investment

The accumulation of capital, such as factories, machines, and inventories, that is used to produce goods and services.

----

[1]Recall from the Appendix in Chapter 1 that a third variable can affect the variables measured on the vertical and the horizontal axes. In this case, the third variable is the quantity of capital worn out per year.

EXHIBIT 4

Alpha's and Beta's Present and Future Production Possibilities Curves

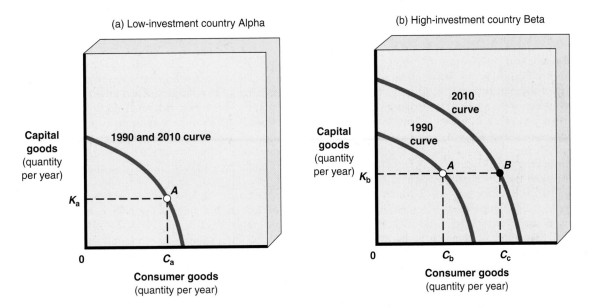

In part (a), each year Alpha produces only enough capital (K_a) to replace existing capital being worn out. Without greater capital and assuming other resources remain fixed, Alpha is unable to shift its production possibilities curve outward. In part (b), each year Beta produces K_b capital, which is more than the amount required to replenish its depreciated capital. In the year 2010, this expanded capital provides Beta with the extra production capacity to shift its production possibilities curve to the right. If Beta chooses point B on its curve, it has the production capacity to increase the amount of consumer goods from C_b to C_c without producing fewer capital goods.

$C_c - C_b$ extra consumer goods, while Alpha's standard of living remains unchanged because the production of consumer goods remains unchanged.

> **Conclusion** *A nation can accelerate economic growth by increasing its production of capital goods in excess of the capital being worn out in the production process.*

INTERNATIONAL ECONOMICS

When Japan Tumbles, Where Is It on the Curve?
Applicable Concept: production possibilities curve

In spite of recent economic woes, Japan is known for quality products produced by dedicated workers who seek ways to avoid wasting resources—and management listens to them. Although this practice is changing, workers in large industrial companies are given lifetime employment, and this job security diminishes worker resistance to technological change. Japan uses twice as many robots as industry in the United States and Western Europe combined.

One key to Japanese production is a bit of management genius called "just in time delivery." The goal is to produce products at precisely the right time with a minimum inventory on hand. This inventory-on-demand system allows the industrial giants to focus on assembling the final product, while smaller firms make and stock parts. For example, Mazda's workers have a small bin of headlights beside the assembly line so that parts can be quickly picked up and installed. A production manager constantly checks the supply of headlights and other parts to make sure there is no surplus of materials. As soon as more headlights are needed to fill the assembly-line bin, Mazda orders its headlights from an outside small subcontractor

located in Tokyo. The headlights arrive in a matter of hours. Mazda's only concern is installing the headlights quickly and not having to invest in large inventories of headlights and other auto parts.

Many subcontractors supplying parts to the industrial giants have businesses located in their homes. Mom, Pop, and children operate a small factory on the first floor of their apartment on the kitchen table and living room floor. Small children are cared for upstairs by a female member of the family who works downstairs when the children take naps. Women and children usually deliver orders, allowing men to continue producing parts at home.

Scarcity of housing is an acute problem in Japan. In fact, the average poor American has a third more living space than the average Japanese. In Tokyo, for example, few public parks are built because of the opportunity cost in terms of factories or apartment buildings. The typical Japanese family of four in Tokyo lives in an apartment with a tiny kitchen, two small rooms, and no yard. The living room by day serves as the bedroom by night. Each morning family members simply roll up their mattress beds into a

closet. In addition to limited space, many houses lack central heating, so the Japanese must warm themselves with small electric heaters. Moreover, most areas of Japan do not have sewers, so people must use septic tanks. These reasons explain why couples save so much in Japan; it is the only way they can hope to afford better housing. (The last chapter of this book explains in more detail how saving allows a country to invest and thereby create economic growth and development by shifting its production possibilities curve outward.)

ANALYZE THE ISSUE

Construct a production possibilities curve that represents Japan's goal of producing both cars and housing. Assume the Japanese economy is in a downturn, and indicate with an X the point on your graph at which the Japanese are operating. (*Hint:* Compare an inefficient point to an efficient point.) Give examples to explain the location you have chosen for point X. Also, based on examples in the above article, explain how the Japanese move their production possibilities curve outward.

KEY CONCEPTS

What, How, and
   For Whom questions
Opportunity cost

Marginal analysis
Production possibilities
   curve

Technology
Law of increasing
   opportunity costs

Economic growth
Investment

SUMMARY

- **Three fundamental economic questions** facing any
  economy are *What*, *How*, and *For Whom* to produce
  goods. The What question asks exactly which goods
  are to be produced and in what quantities. The How
  question requires society to decide the resource mix
  used to produce goods. The For Whom problem concerns the division of output among society's citizens.

- **Opportunity cost** is the best alternative foregone for a
  chosen option. This means no decision can be made
  without cost.

- **Marginal analysis** examines the impact of changes
  from a current situation and is a technique used
  extensively in economics. The basic approach is to
  compare the additional benefits of a change with the
  additional costs of the change.

- ★ A **production possibilities curve** illustrates an economy's capacity to produce goods, subject to the con-
  straint of scarcity. The production possibilities curve
  is a graph of the maximum possible combinations of
  two outputs that can be produced in a given period of
  time, subject to three conditions: (1) All resources are

fully employed. (2) The resource base is not allowed
to vary during the time period. (3) *Technology*, which
is the body of knowledge applied to the production of
goods, remains constant. **Inefficient** production occurs
at any point inside the production possibilities curve.
All points along the curve are **efficient** points because
each point represents a maximum output possibility.

Production possibilities curve

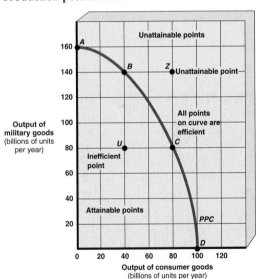

■ The **law of increasing opportunity costs** states that the opportunity cost increases as the production of an output expands. The explanation for the law of increasing opportunity costs is that the suitability of resources declines sharply as greater amounts are transferred from producing one output to producing another output.

■ **Investment** means that an economy is producing and accumulating capital. Investment consists of factories, machines, and inventories (capital) produced in the present that are used to shift the production possibilities curve outward in the future.

★ **Economic growth** is represented by the production possibilities curve shifting outward as the result of an increase in resources or an advance in technology.

Economic growth

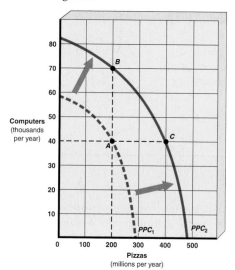

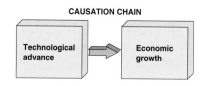

CAUSATION CHAIN

SUMMARY OF CONCLUSION STATEMENTS

■ Scarcity limits an economy to points on or below its production possibilities curve.

■ The production possibilities curve consists of all efficient output combinations where an economy can produce more of one good only by producing less of the other good.

■ A nation can accelerate economic growth by increasing its production of capital goods in excess of the capital being worn out in the production process.

STUDY QUESTIONS AND PROBLEMS

1. Explain why scarcity forces individuals and society to incur opportunity costs. Give specific examples.

2. Suppose a retailer promotes his or her store by advertising a drawing for a "free car." Is this car *free* because the winner pays *zero* for it?

3. Explain verbally the statement "There is no such thing as a free lunch" in relation to scarce resources.

4. Which of the following decisions has the greatest opportunity cost? Why?
   a. A decision to use an undeveloped lot in Tokyo's financial district for an apartment building
   b. A decision to use a square mile in the desert for a gas station

5. Attending college is expensive, is time-consuming, and requires effort. Why do people decide to attend college?

6. The following is a set of hypothetical production possibilities for a nation.

Combination	Automobiles (thousands)	Beef (thousands of tons)
A	0	10
B	2	9
C	4	7
D	6	4
E	8	0

a. Plot these production possibilities data. What is the opportunity cost of the first 2,000 automobiles produced? Between which points is the opportunity cost per thousand automobiles highest? Between which points is the opportunity cost per thousand tons of beef highest?

b. Label a point *F* inside the curve. Why is this an inefficient point? Label a point *G* outside the curve. Why is this point an unattainable point? Why are points *A* through *E* all efficient points?

c. Does this production possibilities curve reflect the law of increasing opportunity costs? Explain.

d. What assumptions could be changed to shift the production possibilities curve?

7. The following table shows the production possibilities for pies and flowerboxes. Fill in the opportunity cost (pies foregone) of producing the first through the fifth flowerbox.

Combination	Pies	Flowerboxes	Opportunity cost
A	30	0	
B	26	1	____
C	21	2	____
D	15	3	____
E	8	4	____
F	0	5	____

8. Why does a production possibilities curve have a bowed-out shape?

9. Interpret the phrases "There is no such thing as a free lunch" and "A free lunch is possible" in terms of the production possibilities curve.

10. Suppose, unfortunately, both your mathematics and your economics professors have decided to give tests two days from now and you realize that you can spend only a total of 12 hours studying for both exams. After some thought, you conclude that dividing your study time equally between each subject will give you an expected grade of C in each course. For each increase of 3 hours study time for one of the subjects, your letter grade will increase for that subject, and your letter grade will fall for the other subject.

a. Construct a table for the production possibilities and corresponding number of hours of study in this case.

b. Plot these production possibilities data in a graph.

c. Does this production possibilities curve reflect the law of increasing opportunity costs? Explain.

11. Draw a production possibilities curve for a hypothetical economy producing capital goods and consumer goods. Suppose a major technological breakthrough occurs in the capital goods industry and the new technology is widely adopted only in this industry. Draw the new production possibilities curve. Now assume that a technological advance occurs in producing consumer goods, but not in producing capital goods. Draw the new production possibilities curve.

12. The choice between investing in capital goods and producing consumer goods now affects the ability of an economy to produce in the future. Explain.

ONLINE EXERCISES

Exercise 1

Visit GPO Gate, Catalog for Economic Report of the President (http://www.gpo.ucop.edu/catalog/erp97 _appen_b.html). Select Table B-33, and follow these steps:

1. Note the increase in the civilian labor force and the decrease in the unemployment rate between 1992 and 1996.

2. Draw a graph to illustrate the effect of an increase in the civilian labor force and a decrease in the unemployment rate on the production possibilities curve.

Exercise 2

Visit Map States (http://www.census.gov/datamap/www /index.html), and follow these steps:

1. On the map of the United States, select the state in which you live.

2. Select State Profile, and then choose State Government Finances.

3. Note the government expenditure categories for Education and Correction.

4. Select the Back button, and select State Abstract. Note the state population for the most recent year given, and divide each of the categories listed above (Education and Correction) by the population size.

5. In your opinion, what is the opportunity cost of money spent on correction?

Exercise 3

Visit Department of Economics Links (http://www .csuchico.edu/econ/links/econlinks.html), and browse Resources for Economists on the Internet. Do not select the Index of Jokes about Economics or Economists.

Exercise 4

How might the officials of the People's Republic of China answer the three fundamental economic questions? For one perspective, visit the China Council for the Promotion of International Trade (CCPIT): http://www.ccpit .org/.

CHECKPOINT ANSWERS

What Does the Peace Dividend Really Mean?

The "peace dividend" suggests resources are allocated away from military production and used for greater nonmilitary production. If you said that this phrase represents a movement along the production possibilities curve, YOU ARE CORRECT.

PRACTICE QUIZ

For a visual explanation of the correct answers, visit the tutorial at http://tucker.swcollege.com.

1. Which of the following decisions must be made by all economies?
   a. How much to produce? When to produce? How much does it cost?
   b. What is the price? Who will produce it? Who will consume it?
   c. What to produce? How to produce it? For whom to produce?
   d. None of the above.

2. A student who has one evening in which to prepare for two exams on the following day has the following two alternatives:

Possibility	Score in economics	Score in accounting
A	95	80
B	80	90

   The opportunity cost of receiving a 90, rather than an 80, on the accounting exam is represented by how many points on the economics exam?
   a. 15 points
   b. 80 points
   c. 90 points
   d. 10 points

3. Opportunity cost is the
   a. purchase price of a good or service.
   b. value of leisure time plus out-of-pocket costs.
   c. best option given up as a result of choosing an alternative.
   d. undesirable sacrifice required to purchase a good.

4. On a production possibilities curve, the opportunity cost of good X in terms of good Y is represented by
   a. the distance to the curve from the vertical axis.
   b. the distance to the curve from the horizontal axis.
   c. the movement along the curve.
   d. all of the above.

5. A farmer is deciding whether or not to add fertilizer to his or her crops. If the farmer adds 1 pound of fertilizer per acre, the value of the resulting crops rises from $80 to $100 per acre. According to marginal analysis, the farmer should add fertilizer if it costs less than
   a. $12.50 per pound.
   b. $20 per pound.
   c. $80 per pound.
   d. $100 per pound.

6. On a production possibilities curve, the opportunity cost of good X in terms of good Y is a production possibilities curve; a change from economic inefficiency to economic efficiency is obtained by
   a. movement along the curve.
   b. movement from a point outside the curve to a point on the curve.
   c. movement from a point inside the curve to a point on the curve.
   d. a change in the slope of the curve.

7. Any point inside the production possibilities curve is a (an)
   a. efficient point.
   b. nonfeasible point.
   c. inefficient point.
   d. maximum output combination.

8. Using a production possibilities curve, unemployment is represented by a point located
   a. near the middle of the curve.
   b. at the top corner of the curve.
   c. at the bottom corner of the curve.
   d. outside the curve.
   e. inside the curve.

9. Along a production possibilities curve, an increase in the production of one good can be accomplished only by
   a. decreasing the production of another good.
   b. increasing the production of another good.
   c. holding constant the production of another good.
   d. producing at a point on the corner of the curve.

10. Education and training that improve the skill of the labor force are represented on the production possibilities curve by a (an)
    a. movement along the curve.
    b. inward shift of the curve.
    c. outward shift of the curve.
    d. movement toward the curve from an exterior point.

11. A nation can accelerate its economic growth by
    a. reducing the number of immigrants allowed into the country.
    b. adding to its stock of capital.
    c. printing more money.
    d. imposing tariffs and quotas on imported goods.

CHAPTER THREE

Market Demand and Supply

A cornerstone of the U.S. economy is the use of markets to answer the basic economic questions discussed in the previous chapter. Consider baseball cards, compact discs, physical fitness, gasoline, soft drinks, alligators, tennis shoes, and cocaine. In a *market economy*, each is bought and sold by individuals coming together as buyers and sellers in markets. Of course, cocaine is a product sold in an illegal market, but it is a market that determines the price and the quantity exchanged. This chapter is extremely important because it introduces basic supply and demand analysis. This technique will prove to be valuable because it is applicable to a multitude of real-world choices of buyers and sellers facing the problem of scarcity. For example, one of the You're the Economist sections asks you to consider the highly controversial

issue of international trade in human organs.

Demand represents the choice-making behavior of consumers, while supply represents the choices of producers. The chapter begins by looking closely at demand and then supply. Finally, it combines these forces to see how prices and quantities are determined in the marketplace. Market supply and demand analysis is the basic tool of microeconomic analysis.

In this chapter, you will learn to solve these economics puzzles:

■ What is the difference between a "change in quantity demanded" and a "change in demand"?

■ Can Congress repeal the law of supply in order to control oil prices?

■ Does the price system eliminate scarcity?

The Law of Demand

Economics might be referred to as "graphs and laughs" because economists are so fond of using graphs to illustrate demand, supply, and many other economic concepts. Unfortunately, some students taking economics courses say they miss the laughs.

Exhibit 1 reveals an important "law" in economics called the **law of demand**. The law of demand states there is an inverse relationship between the price of a good and the quantity buyers are willing to purchase in a defined time period, ceteris paribus. The law of demand makes good sense. At a "sale," consumers buy more when the price of merchandise is cut.

In Exhibit 1, the *demand curve* is formed by the line connecting the possible price and quantity purchasing responses of an individual consumer. The demand curve therefore allows you to find the quantity demanded by a buyer at any possible selling price by moving along the curve. For example, Bob is a sophomore at Marketplace College. Bob loves listening to music on his stereo while studying. Bob's demand curve shows that at a price of $15 per compact disc his quantity demanded is 6 compact discs purchased annually (point *B*). At the lower price of $10, Bob's quantity demanded increases to 10 compact discs per year (point *C*). Following this procedure, other price and quantity possibilities for Bob are read along the demand curve.

Note that until we know the actual price, we do not know how many compact discs Bob will actually purchase annually. The demand curve is simply a summary of Bob's buying intentions. Once we know the market price, a quick look at the demand curve tells us how many compact discs Bob will buy.

Market Demand

To make the transition from an *individual* demand curve to a *market* demand curve, we total, or sum, the individual demand schedules. Suppose the owner of Rap City, a small chain of retail music stores serving a few states, tries to decide what to charge for compact discs and hires a consumer research firm. For simplicity, we assume Fred and Mary are the only two buyers in Rap City's market, and they are sent a questionnaire that asks how many compact discs each would be willing to purchase at several possible prices. Exhibit 2 reports their price–quantity demanded responses in tabular and graphical form.

The market demand curve, D_{total}, in Exhibit 2 is derived by summing *horizontally* the two individual demand curves, D_1 and D_2, for each possible price. At a price of $20, for example, we sum Fred's 2 compact discs demanded per year and Mary's 1 compact disc demanded per year to find that the total quantity demanded at $20 is 3 compact discs per year. Repeating the same process for other prices generates the market demand curve, D_{total}. For example, at a price of $5, the total quantity demanded is 12 compact discs.

Law of demand
The principle that there is an inverse relationship between the price of a good and the quantity buyers are willing to purchase in a defined time period, ceteris paribus.

Visit Haggle Online, an internet auction site at http://www.haggle.com. *What types of products are being auctioned? Look at the history of the bidding process for a few products. From this information, what can you conclude about the demand for each product?*

EXHIBIT 1

An Individual Buyer's Demand Curve for Compact Discs

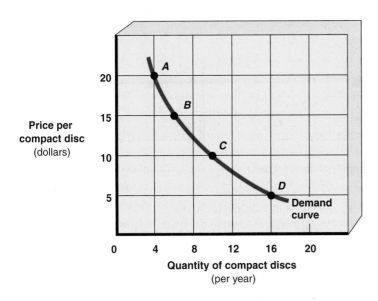

Individual Buyer's Demand Schedule for Compact Discs

Point	Price per compact disc	Quantity demanded (per year)
A	$20	4
B	15	6
C	10	10
D	5	16

Bob's demand curve shows how many compact discs he is willing to purchase at different possible prices. As the price of compact discs declines, the quantity demanded increases, and Bob purchases more compact discs. The inverse relationship between price and quantity demanded conforms to the law of demand.

The Distinction Between Changes in Quantity Demanded and Changes in Demand

Price is not the only variable that determines how much of a good or service consumers will buy. Recall from Chapter 1 that the price and quantity variables in our model are subject to the ceteris paribus assumption.

EXHIBIT 2

The Market Demand Curve for Compact Discs

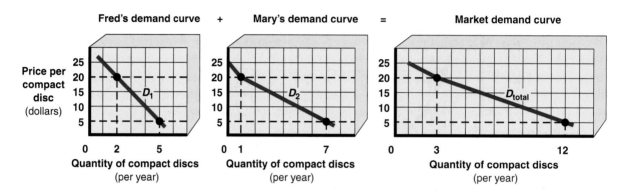

Fred's demand curve + Mary's demand curve = Market demand curve

Market Demand Schedule for Compact Discs

Price per compact disc	Quantity demanded (per year)		
	Fred +	Mary =	Total demand
$25	1	0	1
20	2	1	3
15	3	3	6
10	4	5	9
5	5	7	12

Individual demand curves differ for consumers Fred and Mary. Assuming these are the only two buyers in the market, the market demand curve, D_{total}, is derived by summing horizontally the individual demand curves, D_1 and D_2.

If we relax this ceteris paribus assumption and allow other variables held constant to change, a variety of factors can influence the position of the demand curve. Because these factors are not the price of the good itself, these variables are called *nonprice determinants*. The major nonprice determinants include (1) the number of buyers; (2) tastes and preferences; (3) income; (4) expectations of future changes in prices, income, and availability of goods; and (5) prices of related goods.

Change in quantity demanded

A movement between points along a stationary demand curve, ceteris paribus.

Before discussing these nonprice determinants of demand, we must pause to explain an important and possibly confusing distinction in terminology. We have been referring to a **change in quantity demanded**, which results solely from a change in the price. A change in quantity demanded is a movement between points along a stationary demand curve, ceteris

EXHIBIT 3

Movement Along a Demand Curve Versus a Shift in Demand

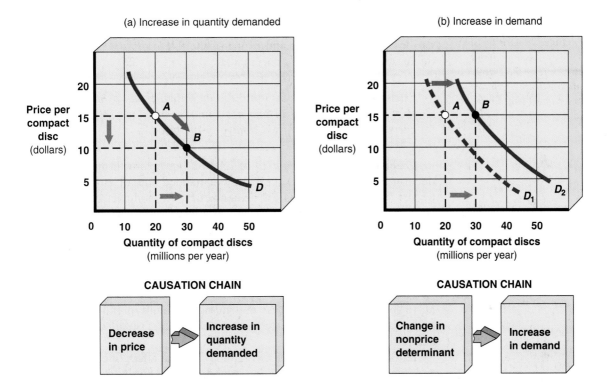

(a) Increase in quantity demanded

(b) Increase in demand

CAUSATION CHAIN

CAUSATION CHAIN

Part (a) shows the demand curve, D, for compact discs per year. If the price is $15 at point A, the quantity demanded by consumers will be 20 million discs. If the price decreases to $10 at point B, the quantity demanded will increase from 20 million to 30 million compact discs.

Part (b) illustrates an increase in demand. A change in some nonprice determinant can cause an increase in demand from D_1 to D_2. At a price of $15 on D_1 (point A), 20 million compact discs would be the quantity demanded per year. At this price on D_2 (point B), the quantity demanded increases to 30 million.

paribus. In Exhibit 3(a), at the price of $15, the quantity demanded is 20 million compact discs per year. This is shown as point *A* on the demand curve, *D*. At the lower price of, say, $10, a larger quantity demanded of 30 million compact discs per year occurs, shown as point *B*. Verbally, we describe the impact of the price decrease as an increase in the quantity demanded of 10 million compact discs per year. We show this relationship on the demand curve as a movement down along the curve from point *A* to point *B*.

Conclusion *Under the law of demand, any decrease in price along the vertical axis will cause an increase in quantity demanded, measured along the horizontal axis.*

Change in demand

An increase or decrease in the quantity demanded at each possible price. An increase in demand is a rightward shift in the entire demand curve. A decrease in demand is a leftward shift in the entire demand curve.

A **change in demand** is an increase (rightward shift) or a decrease (leftward shift) in the quantity demanded at each possible price. If ceteris paribus no longer applies and if one of the five nonprice factors changes, the location of the demand curve shifts.

Conclusion *Changes in nonprice determinants can produce only a shift in the demand curve and not a movement along the demand curve, which is caused by a change in the price.*

Comparing parts (a) and (b) of Exhibit 3 is helpful in making the distinction between a change in quantity demanded and a change in demand. In part (b), suppose the market demand curve for compact discs is initially at D_1 and there is a shift to the right (an increase in demand) from D_1 to D_2. This means that at *all* possible prices consumers wish to purchase a larger quantity than before the shift occurred. At $15 per compact disc, for example, 30 million CDs (point *B*) would be consumed each year, rather than 20 million CDs (point *A*).

Now suppose a change in some nonprice factor causes demand curve D_1 to shift leftward (a decrease in demand). The interpretation in this case is that at *all* possible prices consumers will buy a smaller quantity than before the shift occurred.

Exhibit 4 summarizes the terminology for the effect of changes in price and nonprice determinants on the demand curve.

Nonprice Determinants of Demand

Distinguishing between a change in quantity demanded and a change in demand requires some patience and practice. The following discussion of specific changes in nonprice factors will clarify how each nonprice variable affects demand.

Number of Buyers

Why does Sunkist (http://www.sunkist .com/), a major producer of oranges, provide free orange recipes? To increase the demand for oranges, of course.

Look back at Exhibit 2, and imagine the impact of adding individual demand curves to the individual demand curves of Fred and Mary. At all possible prices, there is extra quantity demanded by the new customers, and the market demand curve for compact discs shifts rightward (an increase in demand). Population growth therefore tends to increase the number of buyers, which shifts the market demand curve for a good or service rightward. Conversely, a population decline shifts most market demand curves leftward (a decrease in demand).

EXHIBIT 4   Terminology for Changes in Price and Nonprice Determinants of Demand

Change	Effect	Terminology
Price increases	Upward movement along the demand curve	Decrease in quantity demanded
Price decreases	Downward movement along the demand curve	Increase in quantity demanded
Nonprice determinant	Leftward or rightward shift in the demand curve	Decrease or increase in demand

The number of buyers can be specified to include both foreign and domestic buyers. Suppose the market demand curve D_1 in Exhibit 3(b) is for compact discs purchased in the United States by customers at home and abroad. Also assume Japan restricts the import of compact discs into Japan. What would be the effect of Japan removing this trade restriction? The answer is that the demand curve shifts rightward from D_1 to D_2 when Japanese consumers add their individual demand curves to the U.S. market demand for compact discs.

Tastes and Preferences

Fads, fashions, advertising, and new products can influence consumer preferences to buy a particular good or service. Beanie Babies became the rage in the 1990s, and the demand curve for these products shifted to the right. When people tire of this product, the demand curve will shift leftward. The physical fitness trend in the 1980s and 1990s increased the demand for health clubs and exercise equipment. On the other hand, have you noticed how many stores sell hula hoops?

*Advertising is designed to increase demand. The Clio Awards (*http://www.clioawards.com/index.html*) highlight the best advertising campaigns in print, radio, and television.*

Income

Most students are all too familiar with how changes in income affect demand. There are two possible categories for the relationship between changes in income and changes in demand: (1) **normal goods** and (2) **inferior goods**.

A normal good is any good for which there is a direct relationship between changes in income and its demand curve. For many goods and services, an increase in income causes buyers to purchase more at any possible price. As buyers receive higher incomes, the demand shifts rightward for such *normal goods* as cars, steaks, vintage wine, cleaning services, and compact discs. A decline in income has the opposite effect, and demand shifts leftward.

An inferior good is any good for which there is an inverse relationship between changes in income and its demand curve. A rise in income can

Normal good
Any good for which there is a direct relationship between changes in income and its demand curve.

Inferior good
Any good for which there is an inverse relationship between changes in income and its demand curve.

result in reduced purchases of a good or service at any possible price. This might happen with such *inferior goods* as generic brands, Spam, and bus service. Instead of buying these inferior goods, higher incomes allow consumers to buy brand names, steaks, or a car. Conversely, a fall in income causes the demand curve for inferior goods to shift rightward.

Expectations of Buyers

What is the effect on demand in the present when consumers anticipate future changes in prices, incomes, or availability? What happened in 1990 when Iraq invaded Kuwait? Expectations that there would be a shortage of gasoline induced consumers to say "fill-er-up" at every opportunity, and demand increased. Suppose students learn the price of the textbooks for several courses they plan to take next semester will double soon. Their likely response is to buy now, which causes an increase in the demand curve for these textbooks. Another example is a change in the weather, which can indirectly cause expectations to shift demand for some products. Suppose a hailstorm destroys a substantial portion of the peach crop. Consumers reason that the reduction in available supply will soon drive up prices, and they dash to stock up before it is too late. This change in expectations causes the demand curve for peaches to increase.

Prices of Related Goods

Possibly the most confusing nonprice factor is the influence of other prices on the demand for a particular good or service. The term *nonprice* seems to forbid any shift in demand resulting from a change in the price of *any* product. This confusion exists when one fails to distinguish between changes in quantity demanded and changes in demand. Remember that ceteris paribus holds all prices of other goods constant. Therefore, movement along a demand curve occurs solely in response to changes in the price of a product, that is, its "own" price. When we draw the demand curve for Coca-Cola, for example, we assume the prices of Pepsi-Cola and other colas remain unchanged. What happens if we relax the ceteris paribus assumption and the price of Pepsi rises? Many Pepsi buyers switch to Coca-Cola, and the demand curve for Coca-Cola shifts rightward (an increase in demand). Coca-Cola and Pepsi-Cola are one type of related goods called **substitute goods**. A substitute good competes with another good for consumer purchases. As a result, there is a direct relationship between a price change for one good and the demand for its "competitor" good. Other examples of substitutes include margarine and butter, domestic cars and foreign cars, and audio cassettes and compact discs.

Compact discs and compact disc players illustrate a second type of related goods called **complementary goods**. A complementary good is jointly consumed with another good. As a result, there is an inverse relationship between a price change for one good and the demand for its "go-together" good. Although buying a compact disc and buying a compact disc player can be separate decisions, these two purchases are related.

Substitute good
A good that competes with another good for consumer purchases. As a result, there is a direct relationship between a price change for one good and the demand for its "competitor" good.

Complementary good
A good that is jointly consumed with another good. As a result, there is an inverse relationship between a price change for one good and the demand for its "go together" good.

CHECKPOINT Can Gasoline Become an Exception to the Law of Demand?

The Iraqi invasion of Kuwait in 1990 was followed by sharply climbing gasoline prices. Consumers feared future oil shortages if war cut off oil supplies, and they rushed to fill up their gas tanks. In this case, as the price of gas increased, consumers bought more, not less. Is this an exception to the law of demand?

The more disc players consumers buy, the greater is the demand for compact discs. What happens if the price of compact disc players falls sharply from, say, $250 to $50? The market demand curve for compact discs shifts rightward (an increase in demand) because new owners of players add their individual demand curves to those of persons already owning players and buying compact discs. Conversely, a sharp rise in the price of tuition decreases the demand for textbooks.

Exhibit 5 summarizes the relationship between changes in the nonprice determinants of demand and the demand curve, accompanied by examples for each type of nonprice factor change.

The Law of Supply

In everyday conversations, the term *supply* refers to a specific quantity. A "limited supply" of golf clubs at a sporting goods store means there are only so many for sale and that's all. This interpretation of supply is *not* the economist's definition. To economists, supply is the relationship between ranges of possible prices and quantities supplied, which is stated as the **law of supply**. The law of supply states there is a direct relationship between the price of a good and the quantity sellers are willing to offer for sale in a defined time period, ceteris paribus. Interpreting the individual *supply curve* for Rap City, shown in Exhibit 6, is basically the same as interpreting Bob's demand curve shown in Exhibit 1. Each point on the curve represents a quantity supplied (measured along the horizontal axis) at a particular price (measured along the vertical axis). For example, at a price of $10 per disc (point *C*), the quantity supplied by the seller, Rap City, is 35,000 compact discs per year. At the higher price of $15, the quantity supplied increases to 45,000 compact discs per year (point *B*).

Why are sellers willing to sell more at a higher price? Suppose Farmer Brown is trying to decide whether to devote more of his land, fertilizer, labor, and barn space to the production of soybeans. Recall from Chapter 2 the

Law of supply
The principle that there is a direct relationship between the price of a good and the quantity sellers are willing to offer for sale in a defined time period, ceteris paribus.

EXHIBIT 5   Summary of the Impact of Changes in Nonprice Determinants of Demand on the Demand Curve

Nonprice Determinant of Demand	Relationship with the Demand Curve	Examples
1. Number of buyers	Direct	■ The Japanese remove import restrictions on American compact discs, and Japanese consumers increase the demand for American CDs. ■ A decline in the birthrate reduces the demand for baby clothes.
2. Tastes and preferences	Direct	■ For no apparent reason, consumers want Beanie Babies, and demand increases, but after awhile, the fad dies, and demand declines.
3. Income (a) Normal goods	Direct	■ There is an increase in consumers' income, and the demand for steaks increases. ■ A decline in income decreases the demand for air travel.
(b) Inferior goods	Inverse	■ There is an increase in consumers' income, and the demand for hamburger decreases. ■ A decline in income increases the demand for bus service.
4. Expectations of buyers	Direct	■ Consumers expect that gasoline will be in short supply next month and that prices will rise sharply. Consequently, consumers fill the tanks in their cars this month, and there is an increase in demand for gasoline. Months later consumers expect the price of gasoline to fall soon, and the demand for gasoline decreases.
5. Prices of related goods (a) Substitute goods	Direct	■ A reduction in the price of tea decreases the demand for coffee. ■ An increase in the price of bus fares causes higher demand for airline transportation.
(b) Complementary goods	Inverse	■ A decline in the price of compact disc players increases the demand for compact discs. ■ A higher price for peanut butter decreases the demand for jelly.

production possibilities curve and the concept of increasing opportunity cost developed in that chapter's Exhibit 2. If Farmer Brown devotes few of his resources to producing soybeans, the opportunity cost of, say, producing milk is small. But increasing soybean production means a higher opportunity cost, measured by the quantity of milk not produced. The logical question is, What would induce Farmer Brown to produce more soybeans for sale and overcome the higher opportunity cost of producing less milk? You guessed it! There must be the *incentive* of a higher price for soybeans.

EXHIBIT 6

An Individual Seller's Supply Curve for Compact Discs

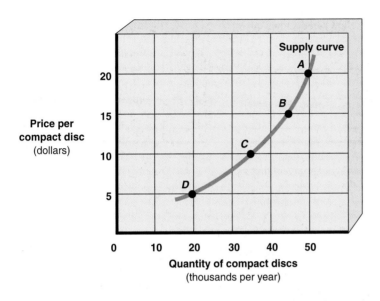

An Individual Seller's Supply Schedule for Compact Discs

Point	Price per compact disc	Quantity supplied (thousands per year)
A	$20	50
B	15	45
C	10	35
D	5	20

The supply curve for an individual seller, such as Rap City, shows the quantity of compact discs offered for sale at different possible prices. As the price of compact discs rises, a retail store has an incentive to increase the quantity of compact discs supplied per year. The direct relationship between price and quantity supplied conforms to the law of supply.

Conclusion *Only at a higher price will it be profitable for sellers to incur the higher opportunity cost associated with producing and supplying a larger quantity.*

Market Supply

To construct a *market* supply curve, we follow the same procedure used to derive a market demand curve. That is, we *horizontally* sum all the quantities supplied at various prices that might prevail in the market.

EXHIBIT 7

The Market Supply Curve for Compact Discs

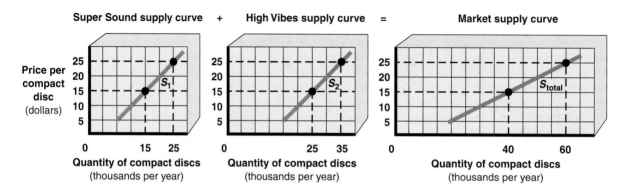

The Market Supply Schedule for Compact Discs

Price per compact disc	Quantity supplied (thousands per year)		
	Super Sound +	High Vibes =	Total supply
$25	25	35	60
20	20	30	50
15	15	25	40
10	10	20	30
5	5	15	20

Super Sound and High Vibes are two individual businesses selling compact discs. If these are the only two firms in the compact disc market, the market supply curve, S$_{total}$, can be derived by summing horizontally the individual supply curves, S$_1$ and S$_2$.

Let's assume Super Sound Company and High Vibes Company are the only two firms selling compact discs in a given market. You can see in Exhibit 7 that the market supply curve S_{total} slopes upward to the right. At a price of $25, Super Sound would supply 25,000 compact discs per year, and High Vibes would supply 35,000 compact discs per year. Thus, summing the two individual supply curves, S_1 and S_2, *horizontally*, the total of 60,000 compact discs is plotted at this price on the market supply curve, S_{total}. Similar calculations at other prices along the price axis generate a market supply curve, telling us the total amount of compact discs these businesses offer for sale at different selling prices.

The rising oil prices of the early 1990s in response to the Iraqi invasion of Kuwait were nothing new. The country experienced two oil shocks during the 1970s in the aftermath of Middle East tensions. Congress said no to high oil prices by passing a law prohibiting prices above a legal limit. Supporters of such price controls said this was a way to ensure adequate supply without allowing oil producers excess profits. Did price controls increase, decrease, or have no effect on U.S. oil production during the 1970s?

The Distinction Between Changes in Quantity Supplied and Changes in Supply

Similar to demand theory, the price of a product is not the only factor that influences how much sellers offer for sale. Once we relax the ceteris paribus assumption, there are six principal *nonprice determinants* that can shift the supply curve's position: (1) the number of sellers, (2) technology, (3) resource prices, (4) taxes and subsidies, (5) expectations, and (6) prices of other goods. We will discuss these nonprice determinants in more detail momentarily, but first we must distinguish between a **change in quantity supplied** and a **change in supply**.

A change in quantity supplied is a movement between points along a stationary supply curve, ceteris paribus. In Exhibit 8(a), at the price of $10, the quantity supplied is 30 million compact discs per year (point *A*). At the higher price of $15, sellers offer a larger "quantity supplied" of 40 million compact discs per year (point *B*). Economists describe the effect of the rise in price as an increase in the quantity supplied of 10 million compact discs per year.

Conclusion *Under the law of supply, any increase in price along the vertical axis will cause an increase in the quantity supplied, measured along the horizontal axis.*

A change in supply is an increase (rightward shift) or a decrease (leftward shift) in the quantity supplied at each possible price. If ceteris paribus no longer applies and if one of the six nonprice factors changes, the impact is to alter the supply curve's location.

Conclusion *Changes in nonprice determinants can produce only a shift in the supply curve and not a movement along the supply curve.*

Change in quantity supplied
A movement between points along a stationary supply curve, ceteris paribus.

Change in supply
An increase or decrease in the quantity supplied at each possible price. An increase in supply is a rightward shift in the entire supply curve. A decrease in supply is a leftward shift in the entire supply curve.

EXHIBIT 8

Movement Along a Supply Curve Versus a Shift in Supply

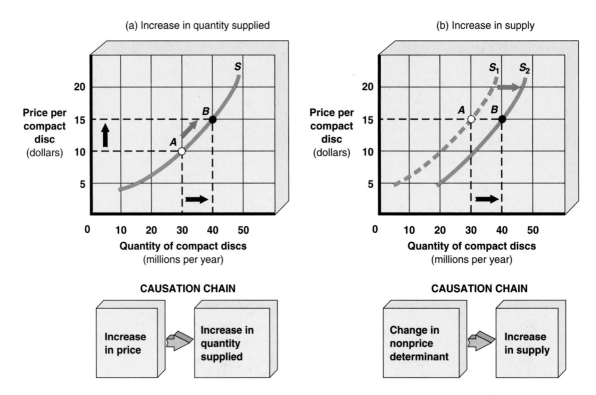

Part (a) presents the market supply curve, S, for compact discs per year. If the price is $10 at point A, the quantity supplied by firms will be 30 million discs. If the price increases to $15 at point B, the quantity supplied will increase from 30 million to 40 million compact discs.

Part (b) illustrates an increase in supply. A change in some nonprice determinant can cause an increase in supply from S_1 to S_2. At a price of $15 on S_1 (point A), 30 million compact discs would be the quantity supplied per year. At this price on S_2 (point B), the quantity supplied increases to 40 million.

In Exhibit 8(b), the rightward shift (an increase in supply) from S_1 to S_2 means that at all possible prices sellers offer a greater quantity for sale. At $15 per compact disc, for instance, sellers provide 40 million for sale annually (point B), rather than 30 million (point A).

Another case is that some nonprice factor changes and causes a leftward shift (a decrease in supply) from supply curve S_1. As a result, a smaller quantity will be offered for sale at any price.

EXHIBIT 9 Terminology for Changes in Price and Nonprice Determinants of Supply

Change	Effect	Terminology
Price increases	Upward movement along the supply curve	Increase in quantity supplied
Price decreases	Downward movement along the supply curve	Decrease in quantity supplied
Nonprice determinant	Leftward or rightward shift in the supply curve	Decrease or increase in supply

Exhibit 9 summarizes the terminology for the effect of changes in price and nonprice determinants on the supply curve.

Nonprice Determinants of Supply

Now we turn to how each of the six basic nonprice factors affects supply.

Number of Sellers

What happens when a severe drought destroys wheat or a frost ruins the orange crop? The damaging effect of the weather may force orange growers out of business, and supply decreases. When the government eases restrictions on hunting alligators, the number of alligator hunters increases, and the supply curve for alligator meat and skins increases. Internationally, the United States may decide to lower trade barriers on textile imports, and this action increases supply by allowing new foreign firms to add their individual supply curves to the U.S. market supply curve for textiles. Conversely, higher U.S. trade barriers on textile imports shift the U.S. market supply curve for textiles leftward.

Technology

Never have we experienced such an explosion of new production techniques. Throughout the world, new and more efficient technology is making it possible to manufacture more products at any possible selling price. For example, new, more powerful PCs reduce production costs and increase the supply of all sorts of goods and services. In the compact disc industry, robots have been developed that allow you to select a compact disc, listen to it, and then just put your money or charge card in the slot if you wish to buy it. Installing these robots makes it possible to offer more discs for sale per year at a lower cost per disc, and the entire supply curve shifts to the right.

Resource Prices

Natural resources, labor, capital, and entrepreneurship are all required to produce products, and the prices of these resources affect supply. Suppose many firms are competing for computer programmers to design their software and the salaries of these highly skilled workers increase. This increase in the price of labor adds to the cost of production. As a result, the supply of computer software decreases because sellers must charge more than before for any quantity supplied. Any reduction in production cost caused by a decline in the price of resources will have an opposite effect and increase supply.

Taxes and Subsidies

Certain taxes, such as sales taxes, have the same effect on supply as an increase in the price of a resource. The impact of a sales tax would be similar to that of a rise in the salaries of computer programmers. An increase in the sales tax imposes an additional production cost on, for example, compact discs, and the supply curve shifts leftward. Conversely, a payment from the government for each compact disc produced (an unlikely subsidy) would have the same effect as lower prices for resources or a technological advance. That is, the supply curve for compact discs shifts rightward.

Expectations of Producers

Expectations affect both current demand and current supply. For example, the 1990 Iraqi invasion of Kuwait caused oil producers to believe that oil prices would rise dramatically. Their initial response was to hold back a portion of the oil in their storage tanks and make greater profits later when oil prices rose. One approach used by the major oil companies was to place limits on the amount of gasoline delivered to independent distributors. This response by the oil industry shifted the supply curve to the left. Now suppose farmers anticipate the price of wheat will soon fall sharply. Their reaction is to sell their inventories stored in silos today before the downturn in price occurs tomorrow. Such a response shifts the supply curve for wheat to the right.

Prices of Other Goods the Firm Could Produce

Businesses are always considering shifting resources from producing one good to producing another good. A rise in the price of one product relative to the prices of other products signals to suppliers that switching production to the product with the higher relative price yields higher profit. If the price of tomatoes rises while the price of corn remains the same, many farmers will divert more of their land to tomatoes and less to corn. The result is an increase in the supply of tomatoes and a decrease in the supply of corn. This happens because the opportunity cost of growing corn, measured in foregone tomato profits, increases.

PC Prices Fall Below $400

Applicable Concept: nonprice determinants of demand and supply

Radio was in existence for 38 years before 50 million people tuned in. Television took 13 years to reach that benchmark. Sixteen years after the first PC kit came out, 50 million people were using one. Once it was opened to the public, the Internet crossed that line in four years.[1]

An Associated Press article reported:

Personal computers, which tumbled below the $1,000-price barrier just 18 months ago, now are breaking through the $400-price-mark—putting them within reach of the average U.S. family.

The plunge in PC prices reflects declining wholesale prices for computer parts, such as microprocessors, memory chips, and hard drives.

"We've seen a massive transformation in the PC business," said Andrew Peck, an analyst with Cowen & Co., based in Boston.

But PC makers also are responding to a profound shift in U.S. buying habits: Today's consumers care more about bargains than the latest technology for running fancy software, like PC games with 3-D imagery.

Micro Center, a Columbus, Ohio–based chain of 13 computer stores, early this month began selling a $399 computer under the Power Spec label. On Thursday, Precision Tec LLC, a maker based in Costa Mesa, Calif., introduced its Gazelle machine for the same price, for sale over the Internet through Egghead.com and other Web-site companies. . . .

Many of the new buyers are expected to be from families making less than $30,000 a year, expanding the pool of traditional buyers, who usually come from families making $50,000 or more.

The lower-income buyers "just don't need as much computing power," Sargent said. "They are only willing to pay a certain amount of money for it."

But for many new computer users and second-time buyers, those lower prices don't necessarily sacrifice computer performance.

Today's computers costing below $1,000 are equal to or greater in power than PCs costing $1,500 and more just a few years ago—working well for word processing, spread-sheet applications, and Internet access, the most popular computer uses.[2]

ANALYZE THE ISSUE

Identify changes in quantity demanded, changes in demand, changes in quantity supplied, or changes in supply described in the article. If there is a change in demand or supply, also identify the nonprice determinant causing the change.

---

[1] *The Emerging Digital Economy*, (U.S. Department of Commerce, 1998), Chap. 1, p. 1 (http://www/ecommerce.gov /chapter1.htm).
[2] David E. Kalish, "PC Prices Fall Below $400, Luring Bargain-Hunters," Associated Press/*Charlotte Observer*, August 25, 1998, p. 3D.

EXHIBIT 10   Summary of the Impact of Changes in Nonprice Determinants of Supply on the Supply Curve

Nonprice Determinant of Supply	Relationship with the Supply Curve	Examples
1. Number of sellers	Direct	■ The United States lowers trade restrictions on foreign textiles, and the supply of textiles in the United States increases. ■ A severe drought destroys oranges, and the supply of oranges decreases.
2. Technology	Direct	■ The development of new methods of producing automobiles reduces production costs, and there is an increase in the supply of automobiles. ■ Technology is destroyed in war, and production costs increase; the result is a decrease in the supply of good X.
3. Resource prices	Inverse	■ A decline in the price of computer chips increases the supply of computers. ■ An increase in the cost of farm equipment decreases the supply of soybeans.
4. Taxes and subsidies	Inverse and Direct	■ An increase in the per-pack tax on cigarettes reduces the supply of cigarettes. ■ A government payment to dairy farmers on the basis of the number of gallons produced increases the supply of milk.
5. Expectations	Inverse	■ Oil companies anticipate a substantial rise in future oil prices, and this expectation causes these companies to decrease their current supply of oil. ■ Farmers expect the future price of wheat to decline, so they increase the present supply of wheat.
6. Prices of other goods and services	Inverse	■ A rise in the price of brand-name drugs causes drug companies to decrease the supply of generic drugs. ■ A decline in the price of tomatoes causes farmers to increase the supply of cucumbers.

Exhibit 10 summarizes the relationship between changes in the non-price determinants of supply and the supply curve, accompanied by examples for each type of nonprice factor change.

A Market Supply and Demand Analysis

Market

Any arrangement in which buyers and sellers interact to determine the price and quantity of goods and services exchanged.

A drum roll please! Buyer and seller actors are on center stage to perform a balancing act in a **market**. A market is any arrangement in which buyers and sellers interact to determine the price and quantity of goods and services exchanged. Let's consider the retail market for tennis shoes. Exhibit 11 displays hypothetical market demand and supply data for this product. Notice in column 1 of the table that price serves as a common variable for both supply and demand relationships. Columns 2 and 3 list the quantity demanded and the quantity supplied for pairs of tennis shoes per year.

EXHIBIT 11   Demand, Supply, and Equilibrium for Tennis Shoes (Pairs per Year)

(1) Price per Pair	(2) Quantity Demanded	(3) Quantity Supplied	(4) Difference (3) – (2)	(5) Market Condition	(6) Pressure on Price
$105	25,000	75,000	+50,000	Surplus	Downward
90	30,000	70,000	+40,000	Surplus	Downward
75	40,000	60,000	+20,000	Surplus	Downward
60	50,000	50,000	0	Equilibrium	Stationary
45	60,000	35,000	−25,000	Shortage	Upward
30	80,000	20,000	−60,000	Shortage	Upward
15	100,000	5,000	−95,000	Shortage	Upward

The important question for market supply and demand analysis is: Which selling price and quantity will prevail in the market? Let's start by asking what will happen if retail stores supply 75,000 pairs of tennis shoes and charge $105 a pair. At this relatively high price for tennis shoes, consumers are willing and able to purchase only 25,000 pairs. As a result, 50,000 pairs of tennis shoes remain as unsold inventory on the shelves of sellers (column 4), and the market condition is a **surplus** (column 5). A surplus is a market condition existing at any price where the quantity supplied is greater than the quantity demanded.

How will retailers react to a surplus? Competition forces sellers to bid down their selling price in order to attract more sales (column 6). If they cut the selling price to $90, there will still be a surplus of 40,000 pairs of tennis shoes, and pressure on sellers to cut their selling price will continue. If the price falls to $75, there will still be an unwanted surplus of 20,000 pairs of tennis shoes remaining as inventory, and pressure will persist to charge a lower price.

Now let's assume sellers slash the price of tennis shoes to $15 per pair. This price is very attractive to consumers, and the quantity demanded is 100,000 pairs of tennis shoes each year. However, sellers are willing and able to provide only 5,000 pairs at this price. The good news is that some consumers buy these 5,000 pairs of tennis shoes at $15. The bad news is that potential buyers are willing to purchase 95,000 more pairs at that price, but cannot because the shoes are not on the shelves for sale. This out-of-stock condition signals the existence of a **shortage**. A shortage is a market condition existing at any price where the quantity supplied is less than the quantity demanded.

In the case of a shortage, unsatisfied consumers compete to obtain the product by bidding to pay a higher price. Because sellers are seeking the higher profits that higher prices make possible, they gladly respond by setting a higher price of, say, $30 and increasing the quantity supplied to 20,000 pairs annually. At the price of $30, the shortage persists because the quantity demanded still exceeds the quantity supplied. Thus, a price of $30 will also be temporary because the unfulfilled quantity demanded

Surplus
A market condition existing at any price where the quantity supplied is greater than the quantity demanded.

Shortage
A market condition existing at any price where the quantity supplied is less than the quantity demanded.

CHECKPOINT

Can the Price System Eliminate Scarcity?

You visit Cuba and observe that at "official" prices there is a constant shortage of consumer goods in government stores. People explain that in Cuba scarcity is caused by the low prices combined with the low production quotas set by the government. Many Cuban citizens say that the condition of scarcity will be eliminated if the government will allow markets to respond to supply and demand. Will the price system eliminate scarcity?

Equilibrium

A market condition that occurs at any price for which the quantity demanded and the quantity supplied are equal.

provides an incentive for sellers to further raise their selling price and offer more tennis shoes for sale. Suppose the price of tennis shoes rises to $45 a pair. At this price, the shortage falls to 25,000 pairs, and the market still gives the message to sellers to move upward along their market supply curve and sell for a higher price.

Equilibrium Price and Quantity

Assuming sellers are free to sell their product at any price, trial and error will make all possible price-quantity combinations unstable except at **equilibrium**. Equilibrium occurs at any price for which the quantity demanded and the quantity supplied are equal. Economists also refer to *equilibrium* as *market-clearing*.

In Exhibit 11, $60 is the *equilibrium* price, and 50,000 pairs of tennis shoes is the *equilibrium* quantity per year. Equilibrium means that the forces of supply and demand are in balance and there is no reason for price or quantity to change, ceteris paribus. In short, all prices and quantities except a unique equilibrium price and quantity are temporary. Once the price of tennis shoes is $60, this price will not change unless a nonprice factor changes demand or supply.

English economist Alfred Marshall compared supply and demand to a pair of scissor blades. He wrote, "We might as reasonably dispute whether it is the upper or the under blade of a pair of scissors that cuts a piece of paper, as whether value is governed by utility (demand) or cost of production (supply)."[1] Joining market supply and market demand in Exhibit 12 allows us to see clearly the "two blades," that is, the demand curve, *D*, and the supply curve, *S*. We can measure the amount of any surplus or shortage by the horizontal distance between the demand and the supply curves.

---

[1]Alfred Marshall, *Principles of Economics*, 8th ed. (New York: Macmillan, 1982), p. 348.

EXHIBIT 12

The Supply and Demand for Tennis Shoes

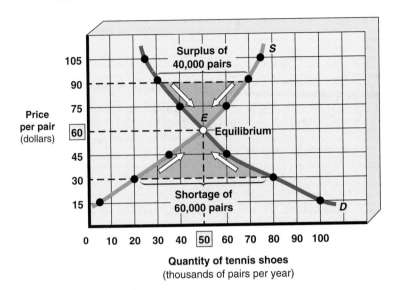

CAUSATION CHAINS

| Quantity supplied exceeds quantity demanded | ⇨ | Surplus | ⇨ | Price decreases to equilibrium price |

| Quantity demanded exceeds quantity supplied | ⇨ | Shortage | ⇨ | Price increases to equilibrium price |

The supply and demand curves represent a market for tennis shoes. The intersection of the demand curve, D, and the supply curve, S, at point E indicates the equilibrium price of $60 and the equilibrium quantity of 50,000 pairs bought and sold per year. At any price above $60, a surplus prevails, and pressure exists to push the price downward. At $90, for example, the excess quantity supplied of 40,000 pairs remains unsold. At any price below $60, a shortage condition provides pressure to push price upward. At $30, for example, the excess quantity demanded of 60,000 pairs encourages consumers to bid up the price.

INTERNATIONAL ECONOMICS

The Market Approach to Organ Shortages
Applicable Concept: price system

The Chinese government has been charged with selling organs from political and criminal prisoners it puts to death. Witnesses report that immediately after prisoners are shot to death, surgeons stand by in nearby vans to remove the organs. In the Chinese culture, there are few voluntary organ donations because people believe it desecrates the body.

Economist James R. Rinehart wrote the following in a journal article on this subject.

If you were in charge of a kidney transplant program with more potential recipients than donors, how would you allocate the organs under your control? Life and death decisions cannot be avoided. Some individuals are not going to get kidneys regardless of how the organs are distributed because there simply are not enough to go around. Persons who run such programs are influenced in a variety of ways. It would be difficult not to favor friends, relatives, influential people, and those who are championed by the press. Dr. John la Puma, at the Center for Clinical Medical Ethics, University of Chicago, suggested recently that we use a lottery system for selecting transplant patients. He feels that the present rationing system is unfair.

The selection process frequently takes the form of having the patient wait at home until a suitable donor is found. What this means is that, at any given point in time, many potential recipients are just waiting for an organ to be made available. In essence, the organs are rationed to those who are able to survive the wait.

In many situations, patients are simply screened out because they are not considered to be suitable candidates for a transplant. For instance, patients with heart disease and overt psychosis often are excluded. Others with end-stage liver disorders are denied new organs on the grounds that the habits that produced the disease may remain to jeopardize recovery. . . .

Under the present arrangements, owners receive no monetary compensation; therefore, suppliers are willing to supply fewer organs than potential recipients want. Compensating a supplier monetarily would encourage more people to offer their organs for sale. It also would be an excellent incentive for us to take better care of our organs. After all, who would want an enlarged liver or a weak heart . . . ?[1]

The following quote from a newspaper article illustrates the controversy.

Mickey Mantle's temporary deliverance from death, thanks to a liver transplant, illustrated how the organ-donations system is heavily weighted against poor potential recipients who cannot pass what University of Pennsylvania medical ethicist Arthur Caplan calls the "wallet biopsy." . . . Thus, affluent patients like Mickey Mantle may get evaluated and listed simultaneously in different regions to increase their odds of finding a donor. The New Yorker found his organ donor in Texas' Region 4. Such a system is not only highly unfair, but it leads to other kinds of abuses.[2]

But altruism isn't working. About 50,000 people are waiting for organ transplants, and about 4,000 die each year waiting.[3]

ANALYZE THE ISSUE

1. Should foreigners have the right to buy U.S. organs and U.S. citizens have the right to buy foreign organs?
2. What are some arguments against using the price system to allocate organs?

---

[1] Reprinted with permission from the *Journal of Health Care Marketing*, published by the American Marketing Association, "The Market Approach to Organ Shortages," James R. Rinehart, March 1988 / v. 8 no. 1 and pp. 72–75.
[2] Carl Senna, "The Wallet Biopsy," *Providence Journal*, June 13, 1995, p. B-7.
[3] *USA Today*, April 17, 1998, p. 1A.

At any price *above* equilibrium—say, $90—there is an *excess quantity supplied* (surplus) of 40,000 pairs of tennis shoes. For any price *below* equilibrium—$30, for example—the horizontal distance between the curves tells us there is an *excess quantity demanded* (shortage) of 60,000 pairs. When the price per pair is $60, the market supply curve and the market demand curve intersect at point *E*, and the quantity demanded equals the quantity supplied at 50,000 pairs per year.

Conclusion *Graphically, the intersection of the supply curve and the demand curve is the market equilibrium price-quantity point. When all other nonprice factors are held constant, this is the only stable coordinate on the graph.*

Our analysis leads to an important conclusion. The predictable or stable outcome in the tennis shoes example is that the price will eventually come to rest at $60 per pair. All other factors held constant, the price may be above or below $60, but the forces of surplus or shortage guarantee that any price other than the equilibrium price is temporary. This is in theory how the **price system** operates. The price system is a mechanism that uses the forces of supply and demand to create an equilibrium through rising and falling prices. Stated simply, price plays a rationing role. At the equilibrium price of $60, only those consumers willing to pay $60 per pair get tennis shoes, and there is no sale for buyers willing to pay less.

For statistics pertaining to organ shortages see http://www.mayo.edu /news/Mayo_ROCHESTER /transplant/donorstats.html.

Price system

A mechanism that uses the forces of supply and demand to create an equilibrium through rising and falling prices.

KEY CONCEPTS

Law of demand	Inferior good	Change in quantity supplied	Surplus
Change in quantity demanded	Substitute good	Change in supply	Shortage
Change in demand	Complementary good	Market	Equilibrium
Normal good	Law of supply		Price system

SUMMARY

■ The **law of demand** states there is an inverse relationship between the price and the quantity demanded, ceteris paribus. A market demand curve is the horizontal summation of individual demand curves.

★ A **change in quantity demanded** is a movement along a stationary demand curve caused by a change in price. When any of the nonprice determinants of demand changes, the demand curve responds by shifting. An *increase in demand* (rightward shift) or a *decrease in demand* (leftward shift) is caused by a change in one of the nonprice determinants.

Change in quantity demanded

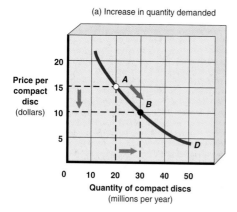

(a) Increase in quantity demanded

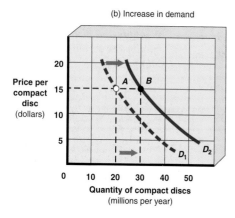

(b) Increase in demand

★ A **change in quantity supplied** is a movement along a stationary supply curve caused by a change in price. When any of the nonprice determinants of supply changes, the supply curve responds by shifting. An *increase in supply* (rightward shift) or a *decrease in supply* (leftward shift) is caused by a change in one of the nonprice determinants.

Change in quantity supplied

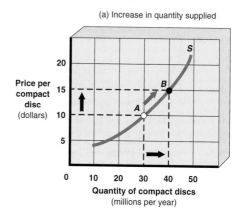

(a) Increase in quantity supplied

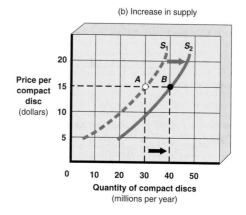

(b) Increase in supply

- ■ **Nonprice determinants of demand** are
  a. the number of buyers,
  b. tastes and preferences,
  c. income (normal and inferior goods),
  d. expectations of future price and income changes, and
  e. prices of related goods (substitutes and complements).

- ■ The **law of supply** states there is a direct relationship between the price and the quantity supplied, ceteris paribus. The market supply curve is the horizontal summation of individual supply curves.

- ■ **Nonprice determinants of supply** are
  a. the number of sellers,
  b. technology,
  c. resource prices,
  d. taxes and subsidies,
  e. expectations of future price changes, and
  f. prices of other goods.

■ A **surplus or shortage** exists at any price where the quantity demanded and the quantity supplied are not equal. When the price of a good is greater than the equilibrium price, there is an excess quantity supplied called a *surplus*. When the price is less than the equilibrium price, there is an excess quantity demanded called a *shortage*.

★ **Equilibrium** is the unique price and quantity established at the intersection of the supply and the demand curves. Only at equilibrium does quantity demanded equal quantity supplied.

Equilibrium

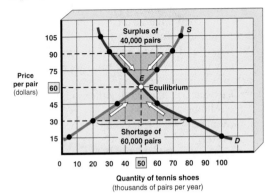

■ The **price system** is the supply and demand mechanism that establishes equilibrium through the ability of prices to rise and fall.

SUMMARY OF CONCLUSION STATEMENTS

■ Under the law of demand, any decrease in price along the vertical axis will cause an increase in quantity demanded, measured along the horizontal axis.

■ Changes in nonprice determinants can produce only a shift in the demand curve and not a movement along the demand curve, which is caused by a change in price.

■ Only at a higher price will it be profitable for sellers to incur the higher opportunity cost associated with producing and supplying a larger quantity.

■ Under the law of supply, any increase in price along the vertical axis will cause an increase in quantity supplied, measured along the horizontal axis.

■ Changes in nonprice determinants can produce only a shift in the supply curve and not a movement along the supply curve.

■ Graphically, the intersection of the supply curve and the demand curve is the market equilibrium price-quantity point. When all other nonprice factors are held constant, this is the only stable coordinate on the graph.

STUDY QUESTIONS AND PROBLEMS

1. Some people will pay a higher price for brand-name goods. For example, some people buy Rolls Royces and Rolex watches to impress others. Does knowingly paying higher prices for certain items just to be a "snob" violate the law of demand?

2. Draw graphs to illustrate the difference between a decrease in quantity demanded and a decrease in

demand for Mickey Mantle baseball cards. Give a possible reason for change in each graph.

3. Suppose oil prices rise sharply for years as a result of a war in the Persian Gulf. What happens and why to the
   a. demand for cars?
   b. demand for home insulation?
   c. demand for coal?
   d. demand for tires?

4. Draw graphs to illustrate the difference between a decrease in the quantity supplied and a decrease in supply for condominiums. Give a possible reason for change in each graph.

5. Use supply and demand analysis to explain why the quantity of word processing software exchanged increases from one year to the next.

6. Predict what will happen to either supply or demand in the following situations:

   a. Several new companies enter the home computer industry.

   b. Consumers suddenly decide large cars are unfashionable.

   c. The U.S. surgeon general issues a report that tomatoes prevent colds.

   d. Frost threatens to damage the coffee crop, and consumers expect the price to rise sharply in the future.

   e. The price of tea falls. What is the effect on the coffee market?

   f. The price of sugar rises. What is the effect on the coffee market?

   g. Tobacco lobbyists convince Congress to remove the tax paid by sellers on each carton of cigarettes sold.

   h. A new type of robot is invented that will pick peaches.

   i. Nintendo anticipates that the future price of its games will fall much lower than the current price.

7. Explain and illustrate graphically the effect of the following situations:

   a. Population growth surges rapidly.

   b. The prices of resources used in the production of good X increase.

   c. The government is paying a $1.00-per-unit subsidy for each unit of good produced.

   d. The income of consumers of normal good X increases.

   e. The income of consumers of inferior good Y decreases.

   f. Farmers are deciding what crop to plant and learn that the price of corn has fallen relative to the price of cotton.

8. Explain why the market price is not the same as the equilibrium price.

9. If a new breakthrough in manufacturing technology reduces the cost of producing compact disc players by half, what would happen to the

   a. supply of compact disc players?

   b. demand for compact disc players?

   c. equilibrium price and quantity of compact disc players?

   d. demand for compact discs?

10. The U.S. Postal Service now faces increased competition from firms providing overnight delivery of packages and letters. Additional competition has emerged because messages can be sent over computers and fax machines. What will be the effect of this competition on the market demand for mail delivered by the post office?

11. There is a shortage of college basketball and football tickets for some games, and a surplus occurs for other games. Why do shortages and surpluses exist for different games?

12. Explain the statement "People respond to incentives and disincentives" in relation to the demand curve and supply curve for good X.

ONLINE EXERCISES

Exercise 1

Visit Business Cycle Indicators Home Page (http://www.globalexposure.com/). Select Income/Consumer, and follow these steps:

1. Under Personal Income, select Personal income, and review the changes for recent years.

2. Draw a graph to illustrate the effect of a change in personal income on the demand curve for Spam.

3. Select the Back button and, under Indexes of Consumer attitudes, choose Consumer expectations, The Conference Board.

4. Draw a graph to illustrate the effect of changes in consumer expectations in recent years on the demand curve for automobiles.

Exercise 2

At the same site, select Wages/Labor, and follow these steps:

1. Under Productivity, select Index of output per hour, all persons, business sector, and review the trend for recent years.
2. Would the productivity change affect the demand or the supply curve? Show its effect by drawing the appropriate demand or supply curve.

Exercise 3

If water is inexpensive and readily available, why does the demand for bottled water, which can cost more than $2 for a 12-ounce bottle, remain strong? Why are consumers willing to pay such a steep price for bottled water? For references, visit the Evian water website at http://www.evian.com/.

Exercise 4

Go to http://price.bus.okstate.edu/archive/Econ3113 _963/Shows/Chapter2/chap_02.htm to view a slide show on supply, demand, and market equilibrium.

 CHECKPOINT ANSWERS

Can Gasoline Become an Exception to the Law of Demand?

As the price of oil began to rise, the expectation of still higher prices caused buyers to buy more now, and, therefore, demand increased. As shown in Exhibit 13, suppose the price per gallon of gasoline was initially at P_1 and the quantity demanded was Q_1 on demand curve D_1 (point A). Then the Iraqi invasion caused the demand curve to shift rightward to D_2. Along the new demand curve, D_2, consumers increased their quantity demanded to Q_2 at the higher price of P_2 per gallon of gasoline (point B).

The expectation of rising gasoline prices in the future caused "an increase in demand," rather than "an increase in quantity demanded," in response to a higher price. If you said there are no exceptions to the law of demand, YOU ARE CORRECT.

EXHIBIT 13

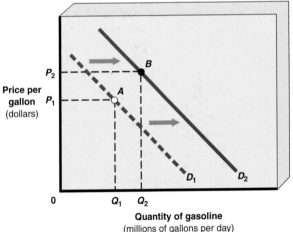

Price per gallon (dollars)

Quantity of gasoline (millions of gallons per day)

Can the Law of Supply Be Repealed?

There is not a single quantity of oil—say, 3 million barrels—for sale in the world on a given day. The supply curve for oil is not vertical. As the law of supply states, higher oil prices will cause greater quantities of oil to be offered for sale. At lower prices, oil producers have less incentive to drill deeper for oil that is more expensive to discover.

The government cannot repeal the law of supply. Price controls discourage producers from oil exploration and production, which causes a reduction in the quantity supplied. If you said U.S. oil production decreased in the 1970s when the government put a lid on oil prices, YOU ARE CORRECT.

Can the Price System Eliminate Scarcity?

Recall from Chapter 1 that scarcity is the condition in which human wants are forever greater than the resources available to satisfy those wants. Using markets free from government interference will not solve the scarcity problem. Scarcity exists at any price for a good or service. This means scarcity occurs at any disequilibrium price where a shortage or surplus exists and scarcity remains at any equilibrium price where no shortage or surplus exists.

Although the price system can eliminate shortages (or surpluses), if you said it cannot eliminate scarcity, YOU ARE CORRECT.

PRACTICE QUIZ

For a visual explanation of the correct answers, visit the tutorial at http://tucker.swcollege.com.

1. If the demand curve for good X is downward-sloping, this means that an increase in the price will result in
   a. an increase in the demand for good X.
   b. a decrease in the demand for good X.
   c. no change in the quantity demanded for good X.
   d. a larger quantity demanded for good X.
   e. a smaller quantity demanded for good X.

2. The law of demand states that the quantity demanded of a good changes, other things being equal, when
   a. the price of the good changes.
   b. consumer income changes.
   c. the prices of other goods change.
   d. a change occurs in the quantities of other goods purchased.

3. Which of the following is the result of a decrease in the price of tea, other things being equal?
   a. A leftward shift in the demand curve for tea
   b. A downward movement along the demand curve for tea
   c. A rightward shift in the demand curve for tea
   d. An upward movement along the demand curve for tea

4. Which of the following will cause a movement along the demand curve for good X?
   a. A change in the price of a close substitute
   b. A change in the price of good X
   c. A change in consumer tastes and preferences for good X
   d. A change in consumer income

5. Assuming beef and pork are substitutes, a decrease in the price of pork will cause the demand curve for beef to
   a. shift to the left as consumers switch from beef to pork.
   b. shift to the right as consumers switch from beef to pork.
   c. remain unchanged, since beef and pork are sold in separate markets.
   d. do none of the above.

6. Assuming coffee and tea are substitutes, a decrease in the price of coffee, other things being equal, results in a (an)
   a. downward movement along the demand curve for tea.
   b. leftward shift in the demand curve for tea.
   c. upward movement along the demand curve for tea.
   d. rightward shift in the demand curve for tea.

7. Assuming steak and potatoes are complements, a decrease in the price of steak will
   a. decrease the demand for steak.
   b. increase the demand for steak.
   c. increase the demand for potatoes.
   d. decrease the demand for potatoes.

8. Assuming steak is a normal good, a decrease in consumer income, other things being equal, will
   a. cause a downward movement along the demand curve for steak.
   b. shift the demand curve for steak to the left.
   c. cause an upward movement along the demand curve for steak.
   d. shift the demand curve for steak to the right.

9. An increase in consumer income, other things being equal, will
   a. shift the supply curve for a normal good to the right.
   b. cause an upward movement along the demand curve for an inferior good.
   c. shift the demand curve for an inferior good to the left.
   d. cause a downward movement along the supply curve for a normal good.

10. Yesterday seller *A* supplied 400 units of a good *X* at $10 per unit. Today seller *A* supplies the same quantity of units at $5 per unit. Based on this evidence, seller *A* has experienced a (an)
    a. decrease in supply.
    b. increase in supply.
    c. increase in quantity supplied.
    d. decrease in quantity supplied.
    e. increase in demand.

11. An improvement in technology causes a (an)
    a. leftward shift of the supply curve.
    b. upward movement along the supply curve.
    c. firm to supply a larger quantity at any given price.
    d. downward movement along the supply curve.

12. Suppose autoworkers receive a substantial wage increase. Other things being equal, the price of autos will rise because of a (an)
    a. increase in the demand for autos.
    b. rightward shift of the supply curve for autos.
    c. leftward shift of the supply curve for autos.
    d. reduction in the demand for autos.

13. Assuming both soybeans and tobacco can be grown on the same land, an increase in the price of tobacco, other things being equal, causes a (an)
    a. upward movement along the supply curve for soybeans.
    b. downward movement along the supply curve for soybeans.
    c. rightward shift in the supply curve for soybeans.
    d. leftward shift in the supply curve for soybeans.

14. If Q_d = quantity demanded and Q_s = quantity supplied at a given price, a shortage in the market results when
    a. Q_s is greater than Q_d.
    b. Q_s equals Q_d.
    c. Q_d is less than or equal to Q_s.
    d. Q_d is greater than Q_s.

15. Assume the equilibrium price for a good is $10. If the market price is $5, a
    a. shortage will cause the price to remain at $5.
    b. surplus will cause the price to remain at $5.
    c. shortage will cause the price to rise toward $10.
    d. surplus will cause the price to rise toward $10.

EXHIBIT 14 Supply and Demand Curves

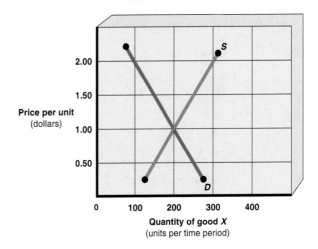

16. In the market shown in Exhibit 14, the equilibrium price and quantity of good *X* are
    a. $0.50, 200.
    b. $1.50, 300.
    c. $2.00, 100.
    d. $1.00, 200.

17. In Exhibit 14, at a price of $2.00, the market for
    good X will experience a
    a. shortage of 150 units.
    b. surplus of 100 units.
    c. shortage of 100 units.
    d. surplus of 200 units.

18. In Exhibit 14, if the price of good X moves from
    $1.00 to $2.00, the new market condition will put
    a. upward pressure on price.
    b. no pressure on price to change.
    c. downward pressure on price.
    d. no pressure on quantity to change.

CHAPTER FOUR

Markets in Action

Once you understand how buyers and sellers respond to changes in equilibrium prices, you are progressing well in your quest to understand the economic way of thinking. This chapter begins by showing that changes in supply and demand influence the equilibrium price and quantity of goods and services exchanged around you every day. For example, you will study the impact of changes in supply and demand curves on the markets for Caribbean cruises, new homes, and AIDS vaccinations. Then you will see why the laws of supply and demand cannot be repealed. Using market supply and demand analysis, you will learn that government policies to control markets have predictable consequences. For example, you will understand

what happens when the government limits the maximum rent landlords can charge and who benefits and who loses from the federal minimum wage law.

In this chapter, you will also study situations in which the market mechanism fails. Have you visited Los Angeles and lamented over the smog that blankets the beautiful surroundings? Or have you ever wanted to use a stream for swimming or fishing, but could not because of industrial waste? These are obvious cases in which market-

system magic failed and the government must consider cures to reach socially desirable results.

In this chapter, you will learn to solve these economics puzzles:

■ How does the spotted owl affect the price of homes?

■ Why might government warehouses overflow with cheese and milk?

■ What do ticket scalping and rent controls have in common?

Changes in Market Equilibrium

Using market supply and demand analysis is like putting on glasses if you are nearsighted. Suddenly, the fuzzy world around you comes into clear focus. In the following examples, you will open your eyes and see that economic theory has something important to say about so many things in the real world.

Changes in Demand

The Caribbean cruise market shown in Exhibit 1(a) assumes market supply, S, is constant and market demand increases from D_1 to D_2. Why has the demand curve shifted rightward in the figure? We will assume the popularity of cruises to these vacation islands has suddenly risen sharply due to extensive advertising (changes in tastes and preferences). Given supply curve S and demand curve D_1, the initial equilibrium price is $600 per cruise, and the initial equilibrium quantity is 8,000 cruises per year, shown as point E_1. After the impact of advertising, the new equilibrium point, E_2, becomes 12,000 cruises per year at a price of $900 each. Thus, the increase in demand causes both the equilibrium price and the equilibrium quantity to increase.

It is important to understand the force that caused the equilibrium to shift from E_1 to E_2. When demand initially increased from D_1 to D_2, there was a temporary shortage of 8,000 cruises at $600 per cruise. Firms in the cruise business responded to excess demand by hiring more people, offering more cruises to the Caribbean, and raising the price. Cruise lines will therefore move upward along the supply curve (increasing quantity supplied, but not changing supply). During some period of trial and error, Caribbean cruise sellers will increase their price and quantity supplied until a shortage no longer exists at point E_2. Therefore, the increase in demand causes both the equilibrium price and the equilibrium quantity to increase.

What will happen to the demand for gas-guzzler automobiles (for example, SUVs) if the price of gasoline triples? Because gasoline and automobiles are complements, a rise in the price of gasoline decreases the demand for such automobiles from D_1 to D_2 in Exhibit 1(b). At the initial equilibrium price of $30,000 per gas guzzler ($E_1$), the quantity supplied now exceeds the quantity demanded by 20,000 automobiles per month. This unwanted inventory forces automakers to reduce the price and quantity supplied. As a result of this movement downward on the supply curve, market equilibrium changes from E_1 to E_2. The equilibrium price falls from $30,000 to $20,000, and the equilibrium quantity falls from 30,000 to 20,000 gas guzzlers per month.

Changes in Supply

Now reverse the analysis by assuming demand remains constant, and allow some nonprice determinant to shift the supply curve. In Exhibit 2(a), begin at point E_1 in the video rental industry with an equilibrium price of $3.00 per rental and 40 million video rentals per month. Then word spreads to

EXHIBIT 1

The Effects of Shifts in Demand on Market Equilibrium

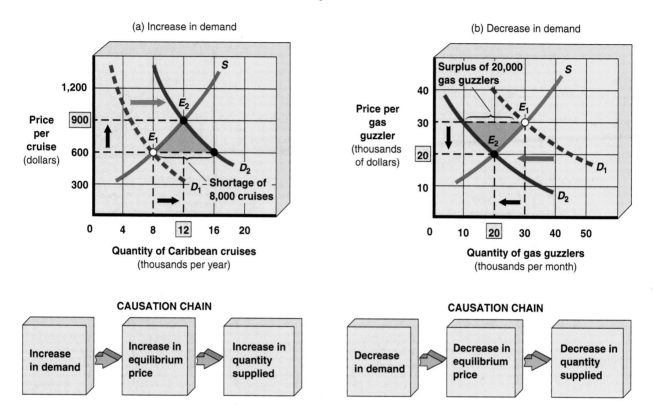

In part (a), there is an increase in the demand for Caribbean cruises because of extensive advertising, and the demand curve shifts rightward from D_1 to D_2. This shift in demand causes a temporary shortage of 8,000 cruises per year at the initial equilibrium of E_1. This disequilibrium condition encourages firms in the cruise business to move upward along the supply curve to a new equilibrium at E_2.

Part (b) illustrates a decrease in the demand for gas-guzzler automobiles caused by a sharp rise in the price of gasoline (a complement). This leftward shift in demand from D_1 to D_2 results in a temporary surplus of 20,000 gas guzzlers per month at the initial equilibrium of E_1. This disequilibrium condition forces automobile sellers of these cars to move downward along the supply curve to equilibrium E_2.

entrepreneurs that the video business is a hot prospect for earning profits. New firms enter the video rental market, and the market supply curve shifts from S_1 to S_2. This creates a temporary surplus of 40 million video rentals at point E_1. Video rental firms respond to having so many unrented videos on their shelves by reducing the rental price and the number available for rent. As the price falls, buyers move down along their demand curve

EXHIBIT 2

The Effects of Shifts in Supply on Market Equilibrium

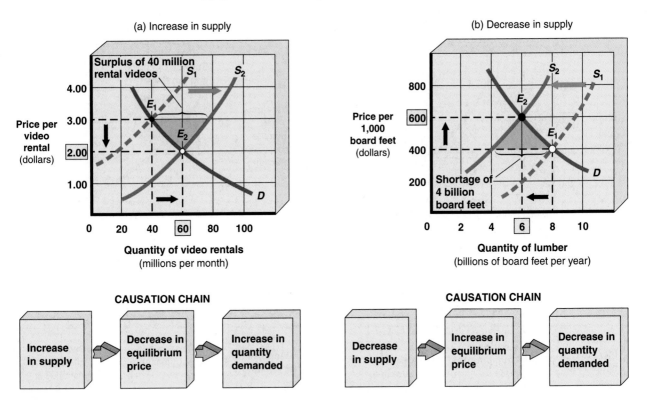

(a) Increase in supply

(b) Decrease in supply

CAUSATION CHAIN

Increase in supply → Decrease in equilibrium price → Increase in quantity demanded

CAUSATION CHAIN

Decrease in supply → Increase in equilibrium price → Decrease in quantity demanded

In part (a), begin at equilibrium E_1 in the video rental industry, and assume an increase in the number of video rental firms shifts the supply rightward from S_1 to S_2. This shift in supply causes a temporary surplus of 40 million video rentals per month. This disequilibrium condition causes a movement downward along the demand curve to a new equilibrium at E_2. At E_2, the equilibrium rental price declines, and the equilibrium quantity rises.

In part (b), steps to protect the environment cause the supply curve for lumber to shift leftward from S_1 to S_2. This shift in supply results in a temporary shortage of 4 billion board feet per year. Customer bidding for the available lumber raises the price. As a result, the market moves upward along the demand curve to a new equilibrium at E_2, and the quantity demanded falls.

and rent more videos per month. When the rental price falls to $2.00, the market is in equilibrium again at point E_2, instead of E_1, and consumers rent 60 million videos per month.

Exhibit 2(b) illustrates the market for lumber. Suppose this market is at equilibrium E_1, the going price is $400 per thousand board feet, and 8 bil-

EXHIBIT 3   Effect of Shifts in Demand and Supply on Market Equilibrium

Change	Effect on equilibrium price	Effect on equilibrium quantity
Demand increases	Increases	Increases
Demand decreases	Decreases	Decreases
Supply increases	Decreases	Increases
Supply decreases	Increases	Decreases

lion board-feet are bought and sold per year. Now suppose a new Endangered Species Act is passed and the federal government sets aside huge forest resources to protect the spotted owl and other wildlife. This means the market supply curve shifts leftward from S_1 to S_2 and a temporary shortage of 4 billion board feet of lumber exists at point E_1. Suppliers respond by hiking their price from $400 to $600 per thousand board feet, and a new equilibrium is established at E_2, where the quantity is 6 billion board feet. This higher cost of lumber, in turn, raises the price of a new 1,800-square-foot home by $4,000, compared to the price of an identical home the previous year. One proposed solution to higher lumber prices is to reduce sales of logs to foreign countries. Why might this be a good idea?

Exhibit 3 gives a concise summary of the impact of changes in demand and supply on market equilibrium.

Can the Laws of Supply and Demand Be Repealed?

In some markets, the objective of Congress and the state legislatures is to prevent prices from rising to the equilibrium price. In other markets, the government's goal is to maintain a price higher than the equilibrium price. Market supply and demand analysis is a valuable tool to understand what happens when the government fixes prices. There are two types of price controls: *price ceilings* and *price floors*.

Price Ceilings

What happens if the government prevents the price system from setting a market price "too high" by mandating a price ceiling? A **price ceiling** is a legally established maximum price a seller can charge. Rent controls are an example of the imposition of a price ceiling in the market for rental units. New York City, Washington, D.C., Los Angeles, San Francisco, and Boston are among the many U.S. cities that have adopted rent controls. The rationale for rent control is to provide an "essential service" that would be

Price ceiling
A legally established maximum price a seller can charge.

CHECKPOINT

Why the Higher Price for Lower Cholesterol?

A few years ago a number-one best-selling book proclaimed the virtues of oat bran in reducing cholesterol. More and more consumers added oat bran cereal and muffins to their diets. At the same time, producers switched over to oat bran production from other agricultural crops. Within a two-month period, the price of a pound of oat bran shot up from $0.99 to $2.59. During this two-month period, which increased more—demand, supply, or neither?

unaffordable to many people at the equilibrium rental price. Let's see why most economists believe that rent controls are counterproductive.

Exhibit 4 is a supply and demand diagram for the quantity of rental units demanded and supplied per month in a hypothetical city. We begin the analysis assuming no rent controls exist and the equilibrium is at point *E*, with a monthly rent of $600 per month and 6 million units occupied. Next, assume the city council imposes a rent control (ceiling price) that by law forbids any landlord to rent a unit for more than $400 per month. What does market supply and demand theory predict will happen? At the low rent ceiling of $400, the quantity demanded of rental units will be 8 million, while the quantity supplied will be only 4 million. Consequently, the price ceiling creates a persistent market shortage of 4 million rental units because the rental price cannot rise without suppliers being subjected to legal penalty.

It should be noted that a rent ceiling at or above $600 per month would have no effect. If a rent control is set at the equilibrium rent of $600, the quantities of rental units demanded and rental units supplied are equal regardless of the price control. If the rent ceiling is set above the equilibrium rent, the quantity of rental units supplied exceeds the quantity of rental units demanded, and this surplus will cause the market to adjust to the equilibrium rent of $600.

What might be the impact of rent controls on consumers? First, consumers must spend more time on waiting lists and searching for housing, as a substitute for paying higher prices. This means consumers incur an *opportunity cost* added to the $400 rent set by government. Second, an illegal market, or *black market*, can arise because of the excess quantity demanded. Because the price of rental units is artificially low, a profit motive exists that encourages tenants to risk breaking the law in order to sublet the unit to the highest bidder over $400 per month.

From the seller's perspective, rent control encourages two undesirable effects. First, a mandated low rent means landlords may cut maintenance expenses, and housing deterioration will reduce the stock of rental units in

See http://millennianet .com/glondon/honolulu .html *for the impact of rent controls on the city and county of Honolulu.*

EXHIBIT 4

Rent Control Results in a Shortage of Rental Units

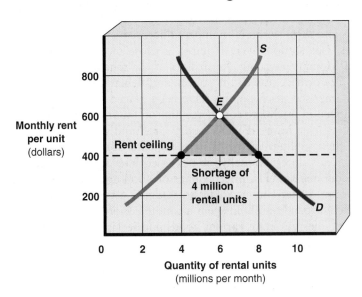

CAUSATION CHAIN

Rent ceiling ⇨ Quantity demanded exceeds quantity supplied ⇨ Shortage

If no rent controls exist, the equilibrium rent for a hypothetical apartment is $600 per month at point E. However, the government imposes a rent ceiling of $400 per month, and a shortage of 4 million rental units occurs. Because rent cannot rise by law, one outcome is that consumers must search for available units instead of paying a higher rent. Other outcomes include a black market, bribes, discrimination, and other illegal methods to deal with a shortage of 4 million rental units per month.

the long run. Second, landlords may use discriminatory practices to replace the price system. Once owners realize there is an excess demand for rentals at the controlled price, they may resort to preferences based on pet ownership, family size, race, and so on in order to determine how to allocate scarce rental space.

The government placed price ceilings on most nonfarm prices during World War II and to a lesser extent during the Korean War. In 1971, President Nixon "froze" virtually all wages, prices, and rents for 90 days in an attempt to control inflation. As a result of an oil embargo in late 1973, the government imposed a price ceiling of 55 cents per gallon of gasoline. To deal with the shortage, nonprice rationing schemes were introduced in 1974. Some states used a first-come, first-served system, while other states allowed consumers with even-numbered license plates to buy gas on even-numbered days and those with odd-numbered license plates to buy on odd-numbered days. Gas stations were required to close on Friday night and not open until Monday morning. Regardless of the scheme, long waiting lines for gasoline formed, just as the supply and demand model predicts. Finally, legally imposed price ceilings have been placed on such items as natural gas shipped in interstate commerce and on interest rates for loans. Maximum interest rate laws are called *usury laws*, and state governments have adopted these ceilings in the past to regulate home mortgage and other types of loans. Internationally, as discussed later in the chapter on comparative economic systems, price ceilings on food and rent were common in the former Soviet Union. Soviet sociologists estimated that members of the typical urban household spent a combined total of 40 hours per week standing in lines to obtain various goods and services.

Price Floors

Price floor

A legally established minimum price a seller can be paid.

The other side of the price-control coin is that the government sets a *price floor* because it fears that the price system might establish a price viewed as "too low." A **price floor** is a legally established minimum price a seller can be paid. We now turn to two examples of price floors. The first is the minimum wage, and the second is agricultural price supports.

Case 1: The Minimum Wage Law In the first chapter, the second You're the Economist involved *normative* and *positive* reasoning applied to the issue of the minimum wage. Now you are prepared to apply market supply and demand analysis (positive reasoning) to this debate. Begin by noting that the demand for unskilled labor is the downward-sloping curve shown in Exhibit 5. The wage rate on the vertical axis is the price of unskilled labor, and the amount of unskilled labor employers are willing to hire varies inversely with the wage rate. At a higher wage rate, businesses will hire fewer workers. At a lower wage rate, they will employ a larger quantity of workers.

On the supply side, the wage rate determines the number of unskilled workers willing and able to work per year. At higher wages, workers will give up leisure or schooling to work, and lower wages will result in fewer workers available for hire. The upward-sloping curve in Exhibit 5 is the supply of labor.

Assuming the freedom to bargain, the price system will establish an equilibrium wage rate of W_e and an equilibrium quantity of labor employed of Q_e. But suppose the government enacts a minimum wage, W_m, which is a price floor above the equilibrium wage, W_e. The intent of the legislation is to make lower-paid workers better off, but consider the undesirable con-

EXHIBIT 5

A Minimum Wage Results in a Surplus of Labor

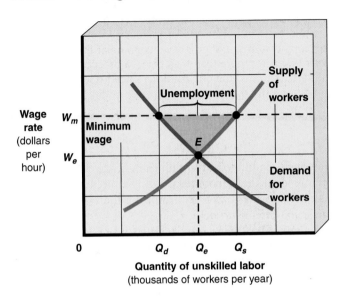

When the federal or state government sets a wage-rate floor above the
equilibrium wage, a surplus of unskilled labor develops. The supply curve
is the number of workers being offered jobs per year at possible wage
rates. The demand curve is the number of workers employers are willing
and able to hire at various wage rates. Equilibrium wage, W_e, will be the
result if the price system is allowed to operate without government interference. At the minimum wage of W_m, there is a surplus of unemployed
workers, $Q_s - Q_d$.

---

sequences. One result of an artificially high minimum wage is that the
number of workers willing to offer their labor increases upward along the
supply curve to Q_s and the number of workers firms are willing to hire
decreases to Q_d on the demand curve. The predicted outcome is a labor
surplus of unskilled workers, $Q_s - Q_d$, who are unemployed. Moreover,
employers are encouraged to substitute machines and skilled labor for the

CHECKPOINT

Is There Price Fixing at the Ticket Window?

At sold-out concerts, sports contests, and other events, some of those with tickets try to resell their tickets for more than they paid—a practice known as scalping. For scalping to occur, must the original ticket price be set by a price floor, at the equilibrium price, or by a price ceiling?

unskilled labor previously employed at equilibrium wage W_e. The minimum wage is therefore considered counterproductive because employers lay off the lowest-skilled workers, who are ironically the type of workers minimum wage legislation intends to help.

Supporters of the minimum wage are quick to point out that those employed (Q_d) are better off. Even though the minimum wage causes a reduction in employment, some economists argue that a more equal or fair income distribution is worth the loss of some jobs. Moreover, the shape of the labor demand curve may be much more vertical than shown in Exhibit 5. If this is the case, the unemployment effect of a rise in the minimum wage would be small. In addition, they claim opponents ignore the possibility that unskilled workers lack bargaining power versus employers.

Finally, a minimum wage set at or below the equilibrium wage rate is ineffective. If the minimum wage rate is set at the equilibrium wage rate of W_e, the quantities of labor demanded and labor supplied are equal regardless of the minimum wage. If the minimum wage rate is set below the equilibrium wage rate, the forces of supply of and demand for labor establish the equilibrium wage regardless of the minimum wage rate.

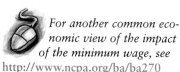

For another common economic view of the impact of the minimum wage, see http://www.ncpa.org/ba/ba270 .html.

Case 2: Agricultural Price Supports A farm price support is a well-known price floor, which results in government purchases of surplus food and in higher food prices. Agricultural price support programs began in the 1930s as a means of raising the income of farmers, who were suffering from low market prices during the Great Depression. Under these programs, the government guarantees a minimum price above the equilibrium price and agrees to purchase any quantity the farmer is unable to sell at the legal price.

A few of the crops that have received price supports are corn, peanuts, soybeans, wheat, cotton, rice, tobacco, and dairy products. As predicted by market supply and demand analysis, a price support above the equilibrium price causes surpluses. Government warehouses therefore often overflow with such perishable products as butter, cheese, and dry milk purchased with taxpayers' money. The following You're the Economist on the dairy industry provides one of the best-known examples of U.S. government interference with agricultural market prices.

Rigging the Market for Milk

Applicable Concept: price supports

Each year the question in the milk industry is: What does the federal government plan to do about its dairy price support program, which has helped boost farmers' income since 1949? Under the price support program, the federal government agrees to buy storable milk products, such as cheese, butter, and dry milk. If the farmers cannot sell all their products to consumers at a price exceeding the support price level, the federal government will purchase any unsold grade A milk production. Although state-run dairy commissions set their own minimum prices on milk, state price supports closely follow federal levels and are kept within 3 percent of levels in bordering states in order to reduce interstate milk price competition.

Members of Congress who advocate changes in the price support programs worry that milk surpluses are costing taxpayers too much. Each year the federal government pays billions to dairy farmers for milk products held in storage at a huge cost. Moreover, the problem is getting worse because the federal government encourages dairy producers to use ultramodern farming techniques to increase the production per cow. Another concern is that the government pays the biggest price support checks to the largest farmers, while the number of dairy farmers continues to decline.

Congress is constantly seeking a solution to the milk price-support-program problem. The following are some of the ideas that have been considered:

1. Freeze the current price support level. This prospect dismays farmers, who are subject to increasing expenses for feed, electricity, and other resources.
2. Eliminate the price support gradually in yearly increments over the next five years. This would subject the milk market to the price fluctuations of the free market, and farmers would suffer some bad years from low milk prices.

3. The Agriculture Department can charge dairy farmers a tax of 50 cents for every 100 pounds of milk they produce. The farmers oppose this approach because it would discourage production and run small farmers out of business.
4. The federal government can implement a "whole herd buyout" program. The problem is that using taxpayers' money to get farmers out of the dairy business pushes up milk product prices and rewards drop-out dairy farmers who own a lot of cows. Another problem with this idea is what to do with the cows after the government has purchased them.

Finally, opponents of the dairy price support program argue that the market for milk is inherently a competitive industry and that consumers and taxpayers are better served without government price supports for milk.

ANALYZE THE ISSUE

1. Which proposal do you think best serves the interest of the small dairy farmers and why?
2. Which proposal do you think best serves the interest of the consumer and why?
3. Which proposal do you think best serves the interest of a member of Congress and why?
4. Draw a supply and demand graph to illustrate the problem described in the case study, and prescribe your own solution.

Market Failure

In this chapter and the previous chapter, you gained an understanding of how markets operate. Through the price system, society coordinates economic activity, but markets are not always "Prince Charmings." It is now time to step back with a critical eye and consider markets that become "ugly frogs," producing socially unacceptable results. **Market failure** means the price system creates a problem for society or fails to achieve society's goals. In this section, you will study four important cases of market failure: lack of competition, externalities, public goods, and income inequality.

Market failure

A situation in which the price system creates a problem for society or fails to achieve society's goals.

Lack of Competition

There must be competition among both producers and consumers for markets to function properly. In *Wealth of Nations*, Adam Smith stated, "People of the same trade seldom meet together, even for merriment and diversion, but the conversation ends in a conspiracy against the public, or in some diversion to raise prices."[1] This famous quote clearly underscores the fact that in the real world businesses will seek ways to replace consumer sovereignty with "big business sovereignty." What happens when a few firms rig the market and they become the market's boss? By restricting supply through artificial limits on the output of a good, firms could enjoy higher prices and profits. As a result, firms may waste resources and retard technology and innovation.

Exhibit 6 illustrates how IBM, Apple, Gateway, and other suppliers of personal computers could benefit from rigging the market. Without collusive action, the competitive price for personal computers is $1,500, the quantity of 200,000 per month is sold, and efficient equilibrium prevails at point E_1. It is in the best interest of sellers, however, to take steps that would make personal computers artificially scarce and raise the price. Graphically, the sellers wish to shift the competitive supply curve, S_1, leftward to the restricted supply curve, S_2. This could happen for a number of reasons, including these: an agreement among sellers to restrict supply (collusion) and government action. For example, the sellers could lobby the government to pass a law allowing an association of PC suppliers to set production quotas. The proponents might argue this action raises prices and, in turn, profits. Higher profits mean the industry can invest in new capital and become more competitive in world markets.

Opponents of artificially restricted supply argue that whether the producers benefit or not, the lack of competition means the economy loses. The result of restricting supply is that the efficient equilibrium point, E_1, changes to the inefficient equilibrium point, E_2. At point E_2, the higher price of $2,000 is charged, and the lower equilibrium quantity means that

[1]Adam Smith, *An Inquiry into the Nature and Causes of the Wealth of Nations* (1776; reprint, New York: Random House, The Modern Library, 1937), p. 128.

EXHIBIT 6

Rigging the PC Market

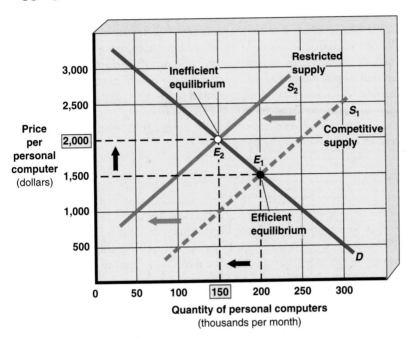

At efficient equilibrium point E_1, sellers compete. As a result, the price per PC charged is $1,500, and the quantity of PCs exchanged is 200,000. Suppose suppliers use collusion, government intervention, or other means to restrict the supply of this product. The decrease in supply from S_1 to S_2 establishes inefficient equilibrium E_2. At E_2, firms charge the higher price of $2,000, and the equilibrium quantity of PCs falls to 150,000. Thus, the outcome of restricted supply is that the market fails because firms use too few resources to produce PCs at an artificially higher price.

firms devote too few resources to producing PCs and charge an artificially high price. Note that under antitrust laws in the United States, the Justice Department is responsible for prosecuting firms that collude to restrict supply in order to force higher prices.

Externalities

There must be competition among both producers and consumers for markets to function properly. However, even if markets are competitive, some markets may still fail because they suffer from the presence of side effects economists call **externalities**. An externality is a cost or benefit imposed on

Externality
A cost or benefit imposed on people other than the consumers and producers of a good or service.

people other than the consumers and producers of a good or service. Externalities are also called *spillover effects* or *neighborhood effects*. People other than consumers and producers who are affected by these side effects of market exchanges are called *third parties*. Externalities may be either negative or positive; that is, they may be detrimental or beneficial. Suppose you are trying to study and your roommate is listening to Metallica at full blast on the stereo. The action of your roommate is imposing an unwanted *external cost* or *negative externality* on you and other third parties who are trying to study or sleep. Externalities can also result in an *external benefit* or *positive externality* to nonparticipating parties. When a community proudly displays its neat lawns, gorgeous flowers, and freshly painted homes, visitors are third parties who did none of the work, but who enjoy the benefit of the pleasant scenery.

For some new ideas in pollution regulation, see the World Bank's Internet site at http://www.worldbank .org/nipr/newappr.htm.

A Graphical Analysis of Pollution Exhibit 7 provides a graphical analysis of two markets that fail to include externalities in their market prices unless the government takes corrective action. Exhibit 7(a) shows a market for steel in which steel firms burn high-sulfur coal and pollute the environment. Demand curve D and supply curve S_1 establish the inefficient equilibrium E_1 in the steel market. Not included in S_1 are the *external costs* to the public because the steel firms are not paying for the damage from smoke emissions. If steel firms discharge smoke and ash into the atmosphere, foul air reduces property values, raises health care costs, and, in general, erodes the quality of life. Because supply curve S_1 does not include these external costs, they are also not included in the price of steel, P_1. In short, the absence of the cost of pollution in the price of steel means the firms produce more steel and pollution than is socially desirable.

S_2 is the supply curve that would exist if the external costs of respiratory illness, dirty homes, and other undesirable side effects are included. Once S_2 includes the charges for environmental damage, the equilibrium price rises to P_2, and the equilibrium quantity becomes Q_2. At the efficient equilibrium point, E_2, the steel market achieves allocative efficiency. At E_2, steel firms are paying the full cost and using fewer resources to produce the lower quantity of steel at Q_2.

> **Conclusion** *When the supply curve fails to include external costs, the equilibrium price is artificially low and the equilibrium quantity artificially high.*

Regulation and pollution taxes are two ways society can correct the market failure of pollution:

1. *Regulation.* Legislation can set standards that force firms to clean up their emissions as a condition of remaining in business. This means a firm must buy, install, and maintain pollution-control equipment. When the extra cost of the pollution equipment is added to the production cost per ton of steel, the initial supply curve, S_1, shifts leftward to supply curve S_2. This means regulation has forced the mar-

EXHIBIT 7

Externalities in the Steel and AIDS Vaccination Markets

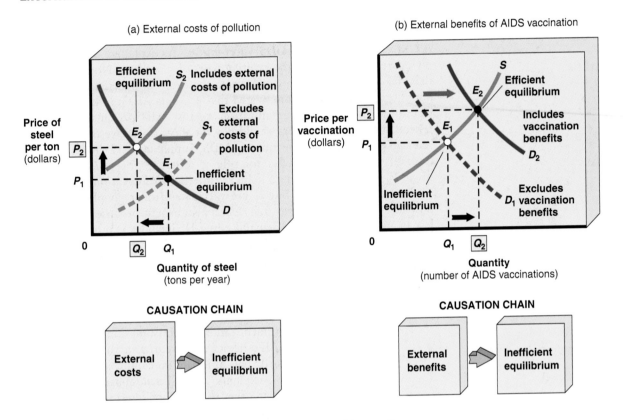

(a) External costs of pollution

(b) External benefits of AIDS vaccination

CAUSATION CHAIN

External costs ➡ Inefficient equilibrium

CAUSATION CHAIN

External benefits ➡ Inefficient equilibrium

In part (a), resources are overallocated at inefficient equilibrium E_1 because steel firms do not include the cost per ton of pollution. Supply curve S_2 includes the external costs of pollution. If firms are required to purchase equipment to remove the pollution or to pay a tax on pollution, the economy achieves the efficient equilibrium of E_2.

Part (b) demonstrates that external benefits cause an underallocation of resources. At equilibrium point E_2, the efficient output is obtained if people are required to purchase AIDS shots or if the government pays a subsidy equal to the external benefit per shot.

ket equilibrium to change from E_1 to E_2. At point E_2, the firm uses fewer resources to produce Q_2 compared to Q_1 output of steel per year, and, therefore, the firm operates efficiently.

2. *Pollution Taxes.* Another approach would be for the government to levy a tax per ton equal to the external cost imposed on society when the firm dumps pollution into the air. This action inhibits production by imposing an additional production cost per ton from the

pollution taxes and shifts the supply curve leftward from S_1 to S_2. The objective is again to change the equilibrium from E_1 to E_2 and eliminate the overuse of resources devoted to steel production and its pollution. The tax revenue could be used to compensate those damaged by the pollution.

A Graphical Analysis of AIDS Vaccinations   As explained above, the supply curve can understate the *external costs* of a product. Now you will see that the demand curve can understate the external benefits of a product. Suppose a vaccination is discovered that prevents AIDS. Exhibit 7(b) illustrates the market for immunization against AIDS. Demand curve D_1 reflects the price consumers would pay for shots to receive the benefit of a reduced probability of infection by AIDS. Supply curve S shows the quantities of shots suppliers offer for sale at different prices. At equilibrium point E_1, the market fails to achieve an efficient allocation of resources. The reason is that when buyers are vaccinated, other people who do not purchase AIDS shots (called *free riders*) also benefit because this disease is less likely to spread. Once demand curve D_2 includes external benefits to nonconsumers of AIDS vaccinations, the efficient equilibrium of E_2 is established. At Q_2, sellers devote greater resources to AIDS vaccinations, and the underallocation of resources is eliminated.

How can society prevent the market failure of AIDS vaccinations? Two approaches follow:

1. *Regulation.* The government can boost consumption by requiring all citizens to purchase AIDS shots each year, and this will shift the demand curve rightward. This approach to capturing external benefits in market demand explains why all school-age children must take polio, smallpox, and other shots before entering school.

2. *Special Subsidies.* Another possible solution would be for the government to pay consumers for each AIDS vaccination. This would mean the government pays each citizen a dollar payment equal to the amount of external benefits per shot purchased. Since the subsidy amount is payable at any price along the demand curve, the demand curve shifts rightward until the efficient equilibrium price and quantity are reached.

Conclusion *When externalities are present, market failure gives incorrect price and quantity signals, and as a result, resources are misallocated. External costs cause the market to overallocate resources, and external benefits cause the market to underallocate resources.*

Public good

A good or service that, once produced, has two properties: (1) Users collectively consume benefits, and (2) there is no way to bar people who do not pay (free riders) from consuming the good or service.

Public Goods

National defense is an example of a **public good**, a good that the government must provide, rather than the price system, because of its special characteristics. A public good is a good or service that, once produced, has

Should There Be a War on Drugs?

The U.S. government fights the use of drugs, such as marijuana and cocaine, in a variety of ways, including spraying crops with poisonous chemicals; imposing jail sentences for dealers and users; and confiscating drug-transporting cars, boats, and planes. What is the market failure that motivates the government to interfere with the market for drugs: lack of competition, externalities, public goods, or income inequality?

two properties: (1) Users collectively consume benefits, and (2) there is no way to bar people who do not pay (free riders) from consuming the good or service.

To see why the marketplace fails, imagine that Patriot Missiles, Inc., offers to sell missile defense systems to people who want private protection against attacks from incoming missiles. First, once the system is operational, everyone in the defense area benefits from increased safety. Second, the *nonexclusive* nature of a public good means it is impossible or very costly for any owner of a Patriot missile defense system to prevent nonowners, the free riders, from reaping the benefits of its protection.

Given the two properties of a public good, why would any private individual purchase a Patriot missile defense system? Why not take a free ride and wait until someone else buys a missile system? Each person therefore wants a Patriot system, but each person does not want to bear the cost of the system when everyone shares in the benefits. As a result, the market fails to provide Patriot missile defense systems, and everyone hopes no missile attacks occur before someone finally decides to purchase one. Government can solve this public goods problem by producing Patriot missiles and taxing the public to pay. Unlike a private citizen, the government can use force to collect payments and prevent the free-rider problem. Other examples of public goods include the judicial system, the national emergency warning system, air traffic control, prisons, and traffic lights.

Conclusion *If public goods are available only in the marketplace, people wait for someone else to pay, and the result is an underproduction or zero production of public goods.*

Income Inequality

In the cases of insufficient competition, externalities, and public goods, the marketplace allocates too few or too many resources to producing output. Although very controversial, the market may also result in a very unequal

Can Vouchers Fix Our Schools?

Applicable Concept: public goods

Years ago economists Milton Friedman and Rose Friedman proposed the voucher plan:

> One way to achieve a major improvement [in education], to bring learning back into the classroom, especially for the most disadvantaged, is to give all parents greater control over their children's schooling. . . . One simple and effective way to assure parents greater freedom to choose, while at the same time retaining present sources of finance, is a voucher plan. Suppose your child attends a public elementary or secondary school. On the average, countrywide, it costs the taxpayer—you and me—about $6,000 [updated] per year for every child enrolled. If you withdraw your child from a public school and send him to a private school, you save taxpayers about $6,000 per year—but you get no part of that saving except as it is passed on to all taxpayers, in which case it would amount to at most a few cents off your tax bill. You have to pay private tuition in addition to taxes—a strong incentive to keep your child in a public school.
>
> Suppose, however, the government said to you: "If you relieve us of the expense of schooling your child, you will be given a voucher, a piece of paper redeemable for a designated sum of money, if and only if, it is used to pay the cost of schooling your child at an approved school." The sum of money might be $6,000, or it might be a lesser sum, say $5,000 or $4,000, in order to divide the saving between you and the other taxpayers. But whether the full amount or the lesser amount, it would remove at least a part of the financial penalty that now limits the freedom of parents to choose.
>
> The voucher plan embodies exactly the same principle as the GI bill that provides for educational benefits to military veterans. The veteran gets a voucher good only for educational expenses and he or she is completely free to choose the school at which it is used, provided that it satisfies certain standards.
>
> Parents could, and should, be permitted to use the vouchers not only at private schools but also at other public schools—and not only at schools in their own

distribution of income. Under the impersonal price system, Tom Cruise earns a huge income for acting in movies, while homeless people roam the streets penniless. The controversy is therefore over how equal the distribution of income should be and how much government intervention is required to achieve this goal. Some people wish to remove most inequality of income. Others argue for the government to provide a "safety net" minimum income level for all citizens. Still others see high income as an incentive and a "fair" reward for productive resources.

district, city, or state, but at any school that is willing to accept their child. That would both give every parent a greater opportunity to choose and at the same time require public schools to finance themselves by charging tuition (wholly, if the voucher corresponded to the full cost; at least partly, if it did not). The public schools would then have to compete both with one another and with private schools.

This plan would relieve no one of the burden of taxation to pay for schooling. It would simply give parents a wider choice as to the form in which their children get the schooling that the community has obligated itself to provide. The plan would also not affect the present standards imposed on private schools in order for attendance at them to satisfy the compulsory attendance laws.[1]

In 1990, Milwaukee began an experiment with school vouchers. The program gave selected children from low-income families federal vouchers to allow them to attend private schools. There has been a continuing heated debate among parents, politicians, and educators over the results. In 1998, Wisconsin's highest court ruled in a 4–2 decision that Milwaukee can use public money for vouchers for students who attend religious schools without violating the constitutional separation of church and state.

Some experts predict more states will launch similar voucher programs.[2]

ANALYZE THE ISSUE

1. In recent years, school choice has been a hotly debated issue. Explain whether or not education is a public good. If education is not a public good, why should the government provide it?
2. The article presents a very one-sided view of the benefits of a voucher system. Other economists disagree about the potential effectiveness of vouchers. Do you support a voucher system for education? Explain your reasoning.

[1]Excerpts from FREE TO CHOOSE: A PERSONAL STATEMENT, pp. 160–161, copyright © 1980 by Milton Friedman and Rose D. Friedman, reprinted by permission of Harcourt Brace & Company.
[2]Mary Beth Marklein, "Voucher Use in Religious Schools Ruled Constitutional in Wisconsin," *USA Today*, June 11, 1998, p. 1A.

To create a more equal distribution of income, the government uses various programs to transfer money from people with high incomes to those with low incomes. For example, unemployment compensation and food stamps are such programs. The federal minimum wage is another type of government attempt to raise the earnings of low-income workers.

KEY CONCEPTS

Price ceiling   Market failure   Public good
Price floor   Externality

SUMMARY

★ **Price ceilings** and **price floors** are maximum and minimum prices enacted by law, rather than allowing the forces of supply and demand to determine prices. A *price ceiling* is a maximum price mandated by government, and a *price floor,* or *support price* for agricultural products, is a minimum legal price. If a price ceiling is set below the equilibrium price, a shortage will persist. If a price floor is set above the equilibrium price, a surplus will persist.

Price ceiling

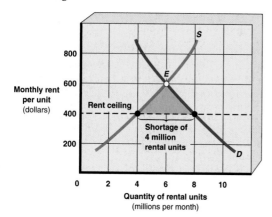

Price floor

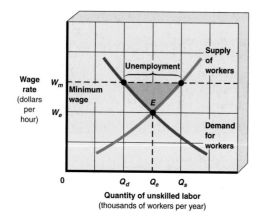

■ **Market failure** means the market mechanism does not achieve desirable results. Sources of market failure include lack of competition, externalities, public goods, and income inequality. Although controversial, government intervention is a possible way to correct market failure.

★ An **externality** is a cost or benefit of a good imposed on people who are not buyers or sellers of that good. Pollution is an example of an *external cost,* which means too many resources are used to produce the product responsible for the pollution. Two basic approaches to solve this market failure are regulation and pollution taxes. Vaccinations provide *external benefits,* which means sellers devote too few resources to produce this product. Two basic solutions to this type of market failure are laws to require consumption and special subsidies.

Externalities

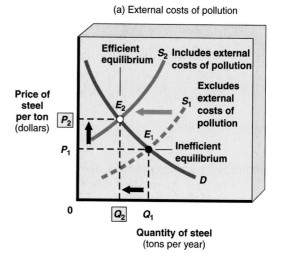

(a) External costs of pollution

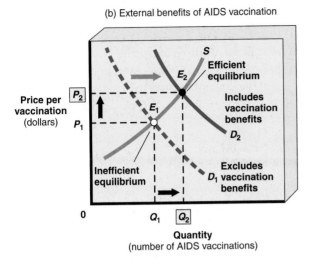

(b) External benefits of AIDS vaccination

- **Public goods** are goods that are consumed by everyone regardless of whether they pay or not. National defense, air traffic control, and other public goods can benefit many individuals simultaneously and are provided by the government.

SUMMARY OF CONCLUSION STATEMENTS

- When the supply curve fails to include external costs, the equilibrium price is artificially low and the equilibrium quantity artificially high.

- When externalities are present, market failure gives incorrect price and quantity signals, and as a result, resources are misallocated. External costs cause the market to overallocate resources, and external benefits cause the market to underallocate resources.

- If public goods are available only in the marketplace, people wait for someone else to pay, and the result is an underproduction or zero production of public goods.

STUDY QUESTIONS AND PROBLEMS

1. Market researchers have studied the market for milk, and their estimates for the supply of and the demand for milk per month are as follows:

Price per gallon (millions of gallons)	Quantity demanded (millions of gallons)	Quantity supplied (millions of gallons)
$2.50	100	500
2.00	200	400
1.50	300	300
1.00	400	200
0.50	500	100

a. Using the above data, graph the demand for milk and the supply of milk. Identify the equilibrium point as E, and use dotted lines to connect E to the equilibrium price on the price axis and the equilibrium quantity on the quantity axis.

b. Suppose the government enacts a milk support price of $2.00 per gallon. Indicate this action on your graph, and explain the effect on the milk market. Why would the government establish such a support price?

c. Now assume the government decides to set a price ceiling of $1.00 per gallon. Show and explain how this legal price affects your graph of the milk market. What objective could the government be trying to achieve by establishing such a price ceiling?

2. Use a graph to show the impact on the price of Japanese cars sold in the United States if the United States enacts import quotas on Japanese cars. Now draw another graph to show the effect of the change in the price of Japanese cars on the price of American-made cars in the United States. Explain the market outcome in each graph and the link between the two graphs.

3. Using market supply and demand analysis, explain why labor union leaders are strong advocates of raising the minimum wage above the equilibrium wage.

4. What are the advantages and disadvantages of the price system?

5. Suppose a market is in equilibrium and both the demand and the supply curves increase. What happens to the equilibrium price if demand increases more than supply?

6. Consider this statement: "The government is inherently inefficient." Do you agree or disagree? Explain.

7. Suppose coal-burning firms are emitting excessive pollution into the air. Suggest two ways the government can deal with this market failure.

8. Explain the impact of external costs and external benefits on resource allocation.

9. Why are public goods not produced in sufficient quantities by private markets?

10. Which of the following are public goods?
    a. Air bags
    b. Pencils
    c. Cycle helmets
    d. Smoking
    e. Contact lenses

ONLINE EXERCISES

Exercise 1

Visit GPO Gate, Catalog for Economic Report of the President (http://www.gpo.ucop.edu/catalog/erp98 _appen_b.html). Select Table B-60, and follow these steps:

1. Select the Entertainment series and Food and Beverage series for the last 10 years.

2. Plot both series on one graph.

3. Explain each of the series in terms of how demand and supply affected the price trend for each of the series over the last two years.

Exercise 2

Visit the Bureau of Labor Statistics' Most Requested Series (http://stats.bls.gov/top20.html). Under Prices & Living Conditions, select Average Price Data. Choose Milk, All Types, Per Gallon. Follow these steps:

1. Select All Years, and observe changes in the average price per one-half gallon of milk for January of each year.

2. Choose the Back button, and choose Red Delicious Apples. Select All Years, and observe changes in the average price for January of each year.

3. Using supply and demand analysis, explain the observed differences in the price changes between milk and Red Delicious apples.

Exercise 3

Browse Dairy Policy Issues (http://www.cnie.org/nle /ag-29.html), and select "Background and Analysis." What economic concepts are at play in this case?

Exercise 4

One solution often suggested for lessening the parking problems at colleges and universities is to promote alternative forms of transportation. For example, some people propose the increased use of bicycles to alleviate automobile parking problems during peak hours. Review Bicycle Parking at the Workplace at http://www.bts.gov /NTL/DOCS/mapc.html, a study conducted by the Metropolitan Area Planning Council. What suggestions does this study offer? Does the study advance a viable argument? Why?

Exercise 5

Many areas of the country experience water shortages, especially in the hot, dry summer months. Municipalities in these areas have requested or required conservation plans. For a general overview of these plans, review "How to Conserve Water and Use It Effectively" at http://www.epa.gov/OW/you/chap3.html, an Environmental Protection Agency report. What economic strategies might a municipality employ to prevent water shortages and promote the conservation of water?

CHECKPOINT ANSWERS

Why the Higher Price for Lower Cholesterol?

As shown in Exhibit 8, an increase in demand leads to higher prices, while an increase in supply leads to lower prices. Because the overall direction of price in the oat bran market was up, the demand increase must have been larger than the supply increase.

If you said demand increased by more than supply because consumers reacted more quickly than producers, YOU ARE CORRECT.

EXHIBIT 8

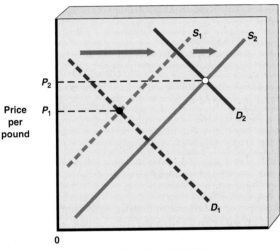

Is There Price Fixing at the Ticket Window?

Scalpers are evidence of a shortage whereby buyers are unable to find tickets at the official price. As shown in Exhibit 9, scalpers (often illegally) sell tickets above the official price in order to profit from the shortage. Shortages result when prices are restricted below equilibrium,

just as is the case when there is a price ceiling. If you said scalping occurs when there is a price ceiling because scalpers charge more than the official maximum price, YOU ARE CORRECT.

EXHIBIT 9

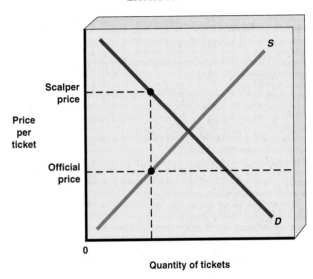

Should There Be a War on Drugs?

Drug use affects not only the person using the drugs, but other members of society as well. Higher crime rates are largely attributable to increased drug usage. Even the spread of AIDS often begins with users injecting drugs with nonsterile needles. When one person's actions affect others not involved in the decision to buy or sell, the market fails to operate efficiently. If you said the market failure motivating government intervention in the drug market is externalities because drug users impose costs on nonusers, YOU ARE CORRECT.

PRACTICE QUIZ

For a visual explanation of the correct answers, visit the tutorial at http://tucker.swcollege.com.

1. Suppose prices for new homes have risen, yet sales of new homes have also risen. We can conclude that
   a. the demand for new homes has risen.
   b. the law of demand has been violated.
   c. new firms have entered the construction industry.
   d. construction firms must be facing higher costs.

2. Which of the following statements is true of a market?
   a. An increase in demand, with no change in supply, will increase the equilibrium price and quantity.
   b. An increase in supply, with no change in demand, will decrease the equilibrium price and the equilibrium quantity.
   c. A decrease in supply, with no change in demand, will decrease the equilibrium price and increase the equilibrium quantity.
   d. All of the above are true.

3. Consider the market for chicken. An increase in the price of beef will
   a. decrease the demand for chicken, creating a lower price and a smaller amount of chicken purchased in the market.
   b. decrease the supply of chicken, creating a higher price and a smaller amount of chicken purchased in the market.
   c. increase the demand for chicken, creating a higher price and a greater amount of chicken purchased in the market.
   d. increase the supply of chicken, creating a lower price and a greater amount of chicken purchased in the market.

4. An increase in consumer income increases the demand for oranges. As a result of the adjustment to a new equilibrium, there is a (an)
   a. leftward shift of the supply curve.
   b. downward movement along the supply curve.
   c. rightward shift of the supply curve.
   d. upward movement along the supply curve.

5. An increase in the wage paid to grape pickers will cause the
   a. demand curve for grapes to shift to the right, resulting in higher prices for grapes.
   b. demand curve for grapes to shift to the left, resulting in lower prices for grapes.
   c. supply curve for grapes to shift to the left, resulting in lower prices for grapes.
   d. supply curve for grapes to shift to the left, resulting in higher prices for grapes.

6. If the federal government wants to raise the price of cheese, it will
   a. take cheese from government storage and sell it.
   b. encourage farmers to research ways to produce more cheese.
   c. subsidize purchases of farm equipment.
   d. encourage farmers to produce less cheese.

7. Which of the following is *least* likely to result from rent controls set below the equilibrium price for rental housing?
   a. Shortages and black markets will result.
   b. The existing rental housing will deteriorate.
   c. The supply of rental housing will increase rapidly.
   d. People will demand more apartments than are available.

8. Suppose the equilibrium price set by supply and demand is lower than the price ceiling set by the government. The result will be
   a. a shortage.
   b. that quantity demanded is equal to quantity supplied.
   c. a surplus.
   d. a black market.

9. A good that provides external benefits to society has
   a. too few resources devoted to its production.
   b. too many resources devoted to its production.
   c. the optimal resources devoted to its production.
   d. not provided profits to producers of the good.

10. Pollution from cars is an example of
    a. a harmful opportunity cost.
    b. a negative externality.
    c. a production dislocation.
    d. none of the above.
11. Which of the following is the *best* example of a public good?
    a. Pencils
    b. Education
    c. Defense
    d. Trucks
12. A public good may be defined as any good or service that
    a. allows users to collectively consume benefits.
    b. must be distributed equally to all citizens in equal shares.
    c. is never produced by government.
    d. is described by answers a and c above.

Applying Supply and Demand Analysis to Health Care

One out of every seven dollars spent in the United States is spent for health care services. This is a greater percentage than in any other industrialized country.[1] The topic of health care arouses deep emotions and generates intense media coverage. How can we understand many of the important health-care issues? One approach is to listen to the normative statements made by politicians and other concerned citizens. Another approach is to use supply and demand theory to analyze the issue. Here the objective is to again bring textbook theory to life and use it to provide you with a deeper understanding of health service markets.

The Impact of Health Insurance

There is a downward-sloping demand curve for health care services just as there is for other goods and services. Following the same law of demand that applies to cars, clothing, entertainment, and so on, movements along the demand curve for health care occur because consumers respond to changes in the price of health care. As shown in Exhibit A-1, we assume that health care, including doctor visits, medicine, hospital bills, and other medical services, can be measured in units of health care. Without health insurance, consumers buy Q_1 units of health-care services per year at a

---

[1] *Statistical Abstract of the United States, 1997,* http://www.CENSUS.gov/prod/www/abs /cc97stab.html, Table 1341.

EXHIBIT A-1

The Impact of Insurance on the Health-Care Market

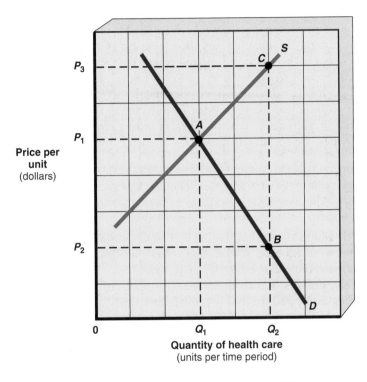

Without health insurance, the market is in equilibrium at point A, with a price of P_1 and a quantity demanded of Q_1. Total spending is $0P_1AQ_1$. With copayment health insurance, consumers pay the lower price of P_2, and the quantity demanded increases to Q_2. Total health care costs rise to $0P_3CQ_2$, with $0P_2BQ_2$ paid by consumers and P_2P_3CB paid by insurers. As a result, the quantity supplied increases from point A to point C, where it equals the quantity demanded of Q_2.

price of P_1 per unit. Assuming supply curve S represents the quantity supplied, the market is in equilibrium at point A. At this point, the total cost of health care can be computed by the price of health care (P_1) times the quantity demanded (Q_1) or represented geometrically by the rectangle $0P_1$ AQ_1.

Analysis of the demand curve for health care is complicated by the way health care is financed. About 80 percent of all health care is paid for by *third parties*, including private insurance companies and government programs, such as Medicare and Medicaid. The price of health-care services therefore depends on the *copayment rate*, which is the percentage of the cost of services consumers pay out-of-pocket. In order to understand the impact, it is therefore more realistic to assume consumers are insured and extend the analysis represented in Exhibit A-1. Because patients pay only 20 percent of the bill, the quantity of health care demanded in the figure increases to Q_2 at a lower price of P_2. At point B on the demand curve, insured consumers pay an amount equal to rectangle $0P_2BQ_2$, and insurers pay an amount represented by rectangle P_2P_3CB. Health-care providers respond by increasing the quantity supplied from point A to point C on supply curve S, where the quantity supplied equals the quantity demanded of Q_2. The reason that there is no shortage in the health-care market is that the combined payments from the insured consumers and insurers equal the total payment required for the movement upward along the supply curve. Stated in terms of rectangles, the total health care payment of $0P_3CQ_2$ equals $0P_2BQ_2$ paid by consumers plus P_2P_3CB paid by insurers.

Conclusion *Compared to a health-care market without insurance, the quantity demanded, the quantity supplied, and the total cost of health care are increased by copayment health care insurance.*

Finally, it should be noted that Exhibit A-1 represents an overall or general model of the health-care market. Individual health-care markets are subject to *market failure*. For example, there would be a lack of competition if hospitals, doctors, health maintenance organizations (HMOs), or drug companies conspired to fix prices. Externalities provide another source of market failure, as illustrated for vaccinations in Exhibit 7(b) of Chapter 4. We are also concerned that health care be distributed in a fair or just way. This concern explains why the government Medicare and Medicaid programs help the elderly and poor afford health care.

Shifts in the Demand for Health Care

While changes in the price of health care cause movements along the demand curve, other factors can cause the demand curve to shift. The following are some of the nonprice determinants that can change the demand for health care.

Number of Buyers

As the population increases, the demand for health care increases. In addition to the number of people, the distribution of older people in the population is important. As more people move into the 65-and-older age group, the demand for health care services becomes greater because older people have more frequent and prolonged spells of illness. An increase in substance abuse, involving alcohol, tobacco, and drugs, also increases the demand for health care. For example, if the percentage of babies born into poor, drug-prone families increases, the demand for health care will shift rightward.

Tastes and Preferences

Changes in consumer attitudes toward health care can also change demand. For example, television, movies, magazines, and advertising might be responsible for changes in people's preferences for cosmetic surgery. Moreover, medical science has improved so much that we believe there must be a cure for most ailments. This means that consumers are willing to buy larger quantities of medical services at each possible price.

In addition to the media, doctors influence consumer preferences by prescribing treatment. It is often argued that some doctors guard against malpractice suits or boost their incomes by ordering more tests or office visits than are really needed. Some estimates suggest that fraud and abuse account for about 10 percent of total health-care spending. These studies reveal that as many as one-third of some procedures are inappropriate.[2]

Income

Health care is a normal good. Rising inflation-adjusted incomes of consumers in the United States cause the demand curve for health-care services to shift to the right. On the other hand, if real median family income remains unchanged, there is no influence on the demand curve.

Prices of Substitutes

The prices of goods and services that may be substituted for medical services can change and, in turn, influence the demand for medical services. For example, treatment of a back problem by a chiropractor is an alternative for many of the conditions treated by orthopedic doctors. If the price of orthopedic therapy rises, then some people will switch to treatment by a chiropractor. As a result, the demand curve for chiropractic therapy shifts rightward.

Shifts in the Supply of Health Care

Changes in the following nonprice factors change the supply of health care.

Number of Sellers

Sellers of health care include hospitals, nursing homes, physicians in private practice, HMOs, drug suppliers, chiropractors, psychologists, and a host of other suppliers. To ensure the quality and safety of health care, virtually every facet of the industry is regulated and licensed by the government or controlled by the American Medical Association (AMA). The AMA limits the number of persons practicing medicine primarily through medical school accreditation and licensing requirements. The federal Food and Drug Administration (FDA) delays the introduction of new drugs.

---

[2] *Economic Report of the President, 1994*, Chart 4-5, p. 144.

Tighter restrictions on the number of sellers shift the health-care supply curve leftward, and reduced restrictions shift the supply curve rightward.

Resource Prices

An increase in the costs of resources underlying the supply of health care shifts the supply curve leftward. By far the single most important factor behind increasing health-care spending has been technological change. New diagnostic, surgical, and therapeutic equipment is used extensively in the health-care industry, and the result is higher costs. Wages, salaries, and other costs, such as the costs of malpractice suits, also influence the supply curve. If hospitals, for example, are paying higher prices for inputs used to produce health care, the supply curve shifts to the left because the same quantities may be supplied only at higher prices.

Health-Care Reform Proposals

In October 1993, the Clinton administration submitted a 1,336-page proposal for health-care reform to Congress. After a much-publicized and heated debate, Congress rejected this complex and controversial proposal. The cornerstone of President Clinton's plan was universal health care. First, all employers would be required to provide their employees with health insurance. Second, those persons who were unemployed or not in the labor force would obtain health care through regional health alliances established in each state. In addition, the plan considered taxing destructive personal behavior that increases health-care costs, such as cigarette smoking and alcohol abuse.

The critics of the Clinton plan argued that the quantity of health care cannot be extended to meet the demands of everyone without enormous additional costs. The result would be price controls and the rationing of health care (recall Exhibit 4 of Chapter 4). In short, critics viewed the Clinton proposal as creating a system of new bureaucracies and employer mandates that would produce an unwarranted increase in the government's role in the health-care industry.

In 1996, Congress passed a bill cosponsored by former Republican Senator Nancy Kassebaum from Kansas and Democratic Senator Edward Kennedy from Massachusetts that bars insurance companies from denying coverage because of pre-existing medical conditions of the employee or members of the employee's family. This bill allows workers changing jobs to retain their coverage. The Kassebaum-Kennedy bill does not set rates the insurance companies can charge for being forced to accept higher risks, and critics predict that the average premium will increase dramatically.

CHAPTER FIVE

Price Elasticity of Demand and Supply

Suppose you are the manager of the Steel Porcupines rock group. You are considering raising your ticket price, and you wonder how the fans will react. You have studied economics and know the law of demand. When the price of a ticket rises, the quantity demanded goes down, ceteris paribus. So you really need to know how many tickets fans will purchase if the band boosts the ticket price. If the ticket price for a Steel Porcupines concert is $25, 20,000 tickets will be sold. On the other hand, at $30 per ticket, 10,000 tickets will be sold. Thus, a $5 increase per ticket cuts in half the number of tickets sold.

Which ticket price should you choose? Is it better to charge a higher ticket price and sell fewer tickets or to charge a lower ticket price and sell more tickets? The answer depends on changes in *total revenue* or sales as we move upward along points on Steel Porcupines' demand curve. At $30 per ticket, sales will be $300,000. If you charge $25, the group will take in $500,000 for a concert. Okay, you say, what happens at $20 per ticket?

This chapter teaches you to calculate the percentage change in the quantity demanded when the price changes by a given percentage. Then you will see how this relates to total revenue. This knowledge of the sensitivity of demand is vital for pricing and targeting markets for goods and services. Next, you will see how changes in consumer income and the prices of related goods affect percentage changes in the quantity demanded. The chapter concludes by relating the concept of price elasticity to supply and the impact of taxation.

In this chapter, you will learn to solve these economics puzzles:

■ Can total revenue from a Steel Porcupines concert remain unchanged regardless of changes in the ticket price?

■ How sensitive is the quantity of cigarettes demanded to changes in the price of cigarettes?

■ What happens to the sales of Mercedes, BMWs, and Jaguars in the United States if Congress prevents sales of luxury Japanese cars in this country?

Price Elasticity of Demand

In Chapter 3, you studied the demand curve. The focus was on the law of demand. That is, there is an inverse relationship between the price and the quantity demanded of a good or service. This chapter stresses measuring the *relative size* of changes in the price and the quantity demanded. Now we ask, By *what percentage* does the quantity demanded rise when the price falls by, say, 10 percent?

The Price Elasticity of Demand Midpoints Formula

Price elasticity of demand
The ratio of the percentage change in the quantity demanded of a product to a percentage change in its price.

Economists use a **price elasticity of demand** formula to measure the degree of consumer responsiveness, or sensitivity, to a change in price. Price elasticity of demand is the ratio of the percentage change in the quantity demanded of a product to a percentage change in its price. Suppose a university's enrollment drops by 20 percent because tuition rises by 10 percent. Therefore, the price elasticity of demand is 2 (−20 percent/+10 percent). The number 2 means that the quantity demanded (enrollment) changes 2 percent for each 1 percent change in price (tuition). Note there should be a minus sign in front of the 2. This is because price and quantity under the law of demand move in *opposite* directions. However, economists drop the minus sign because we know from the law of demand that quantity demanded and price are inversely related.

The number 2 is an *elasticity coefficient*, which economists use to measure the degree of elasticity. The elasticity formula is

$$E_d = \frac{\text{percentage change in quantity demanded}}{\text{percentage change in price}}$$

where E_d is the elasticity of demand coefficient. Here you must take care. *There is a problem using this formula.* Let's return to our rock group example from the Chapter Preview. Suppose Steel Porcupines raises its ticket price from \$25 to \$30 and the number of seats sold falls from 20,000 to 10,000. We can compute the elasticity coefficient as

$$E_d = \frac{\%\Delta Q}{\%\Delta P} = \frac{\dfrac{10{,}000 - 20{,}000}{20{,}000}}{\dfrac{30 - 25}{25}} = \frac{50\%}{20\%} = 2.5$$

Now consider the elasticity coefficient computed between these same points on Steel Porcupines' demand curve when the price is lowered. Starting at $30 per ticket and lowering the ticket price to $25 cause the number of seats sold to rise from 10,000 to 20,000. In this case, the rock group computes a much different elasticity coefficient, as follows:

$$E_d = \frac{\%\Delta Q}{\%\Delta P} = \frac{\dfrac{20{,}000 - 10{,}000}{10{,}000}}{\dfrac{25 - 30}{30}} = \frac{100\%}{17\%} = 5.9$$

There is a reason for the disparity in the elasticity coefficients between the same two points on a demand curve (2.5 if price is raised, 5.9 if price is cut). The natural approach is to select the initial point as the base and then compute a percentage change. But price elasticity of demand involves changes between two possible initial base points (P_1, Q_1 or P_2, Q_2). Economists solve this problem of different base points by using the *midpoints* as the base points of changes in prices and quantities demanded. The *midpoints formula* for price elasticity of demand is

$$E_d = \frac{\text{change in quantity}}{\text{sum of quantities}/2} \div \frac{\text{change in price}}{\text{sum of prices}/2}$$

which can be expressed as

$$E_d = \frac{\%\Delta Q}{\%\Delta P} = \frac{\dfrac{Q_2 - Q_1}{(Q_1 + Q_2)/2}}{\dfrac{P_2 - P_1}{(P_1 + P_2)/2}}$$

where Q_1 represents the first quantity demanded, Q_2 represents the second quantity demanded, and P_1 and P_2 are the first and second prices. Expressed this way, we divide the change in quantity demanded by the *average* quantity demanded. Then this value is divided by the change in the price divided by the *average* price.[1]

It does not matter if Q_1 or P_1 is the first number in each term. This is because we are finding averages. Also note that you can drop the 2 as a divisor of both the ($Q_1 + Q_2$) and the ($P_1 + P_2$) terms. The reason is that the 2s in the numerator and the denominator cancel out. Now we can use the midpoints formula to calculate the price elasticity of demand of 3.7 regardless of whether Steel Porcupines raises the ticket price from $25 to $30 or lowers it from $30 to $25.

---

[1]The midpoints formula is also commonly called the *arc elasticity formula*.

$$E_d = \frac{\dfrac{Q_2 - Q_1}{Q_1 + Q_2}}{\dfrac{P_2 - P_1}{P_1 + P_2}} = \frac{\dfrac{10{,}000 - 20{,}000}{20{,}000 + 10{,}000}}{\dfrac{30 - 25}{25 + 30}} = \frac{33\%}{9\%} = 3.7$$

and

$$E_d = \frac{\dfrac{Q_2 - Q_1}{Q_1 + Q_2}}{\dfrac{P_2 - P_1}{P_1 + P_2}} = \frac{\dfrac{20{,}000 - 10{,}000}{10{,}000 + 20{,}000}}{\dfrac{25 - 30}{30 + 25}} = \frac{33\%}{9\%} = 3.7$$

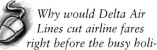 *Why would Delta Air Lines cut airline fares right before the busy holiday season? Delta is betting that the demand for airline tickets is price elastic. Specifically, Delta believes that if prices are lower, the quantity of tickets demanded will more than offset the decline in price. To discover more about Delta Air Lines and its airfare strategies, visit Delta Air Lines SkyLinks (http://www.delta-air .com/).*

Elastic demand

A condition in which the percentage change in quantity demanded is greater than the percentage change in price.

Total revenue

The total number of dollars a firm earns from the sale of a good or service, which is equal to its price multiplied by the quantity demanded.

The Total Revenue Test of Price Elasticity of Demand

As reflected in the midpoints formula, the *responsiveness* of the quantity demanded to a change in price determines the value of the elasticity coefficient. Three possibilities are (1) the numerator is greater than the denominator, (2) the numerator is less than the denominator, and (3) the numerator equals the denominator. Exhibit 1 presents three cases that the Steel Porcupines rock band may confront.

Elastic Demand ($E_d > 1$) Suppose Steel Porcupines' demand curve is as depicted in Exhibit 1(a). Using the above midpoints formula, which drops the 2 as a divisor, if the group decreases its ticket price from \$30 to \$20, the quantity demanded increases from 10,000 to 30,000. Using the midpoints formula, this means that a 20 percent reduction in ticket price brings a 50 percent increase in quantity demanded. Thus, $E_d = 2.5$, and demand is **elastic**. Elastic demand is a condition in which the percentage change in quantity demanded is greater than the percentage change in price. Demand is elastic when the elasticity coefficient is greater than 1. Because the percentage change in quantity is greater than the percentage change in price, the drop in price causes **total revenue** to rise. Total revenue is the total number of dollars a firm earns from the sale of a good or service, which is equal to its price multiplied by the quantity demanded. Perhaps the simplest way to tell whether demand is elastic, unitary elastic, or inelastic is to observe the response of total revenue as the price of a product changes. For example, in Exhibit 1(a), the total revenue at \$30 is \$300,000. The total revenue at \$20 is \$600,000. Compare the shaded rectangles under the demand curve, representing total revenue at each price. The dark area is an amount of total revenue unaffected by the price change. Note that the lighter shaded area gained at \$20 per ticket (\$400,000) is greater than the lighter shaded area lost at \$30 per ticket (\$100,000). This net gain of \$300,000 causes the total revenue to increase by this amount when Steel Porcupines lowers the ticket price from \$30 to \$20.

EXHIBIT 1

The Impact of a Decrease in Price on Total Revenue

(a) Elastic demand ($E_d > 1$)

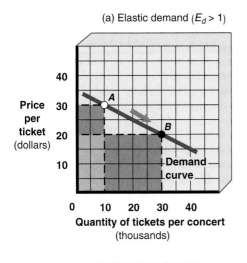

(b) Inelastic demand ($E_d < 1$)

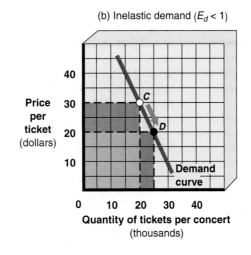

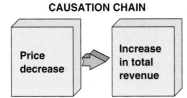

CAUSATION CHAIN

Price decrease → Increase in total revenue

CAUSATION CHAIN

Price decrease → Decrease in total revenue

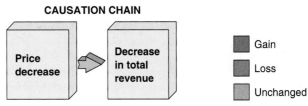

■ Gain
■ Loss
■ Unchanged

(c) Unitary elastic demand ($E_d = 1$)

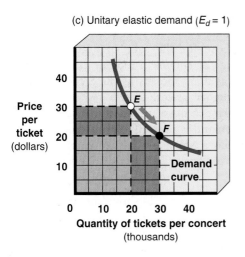

CAUSATION CHAIN

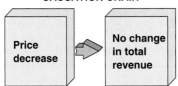

Price decrease → No change in total revenue

These three different demand curve graphs show the relationship between a decrease in concert ticket price and an increase in total revenue.

In part (a), the demand curve is elastic between points A and B. The percentage change in quantity demanded is greater than the percentage change in price, $E_d > 1$. As the ticket price falls from $30 to $20, total revenue increases from $300,000 to $600,000.

Part (b) shows a case in which the demand curve is inelastic between points C and D. The percentage change in quantity demanded is less than the percentage change in price, $E_d < 1$. As the ticket price decreases over the same range, total revenue falls from $600,000 to $500,000.

Part (c) shows a unitary elastic demand curve. The percentage change in quantity demanded equals the percentage change in price between points E and F, $E_d = 1$. As the concert ticket price decreases, total revenue remains unchanged at $600,000.

Inelastic demand

A condition in which the percentage change in quantity demanded is less than the percentage change in price.

Inelastic Demand ($E_d < 1$) The demand curve in Exhibit 1(b) is inelastic. The quantity demanded is less responsive to a change in price. Here a fall in Steel Porcupines' ticket price from $30 to $20 causes the quantity demanded to increase by just 5,000 tickets (20,000 to 25,000 tickets). Using the midpoints formula, a 20 percent fall in the ticket price causes an 11 percent rise in the quantity demanded. This means $E_d = .55$ and demand is **inelastic**. Inelastic demand is a condition in which the percentage change in quantity demanded is less than the percentage change in price. Demand is inelastic when the elasticity coefficient is less than 1. When demand is inelastic, the drop in price causes total revenue to fall from $600,000 to $500,000. Note the net change in the shaded rectangles.

Unitary Elastic Demand ($E_d = 1$) An interesting case exists when demand curves are neither elastic nor inelastic. Exhibit 1(c) is a demand curve in which the change in quantity demanded responds in exact proportion to the change in price. This situation occurs when the total amount of money spent on a good or service does not vary with changes in price. If Steel Porcupines drops the ticket price from $30 to $20, the quantity demanded rises from 20,000 to 30,000. Therefore, using the midpoints formula, a 20 percent decrease in price brings about a 20 percent increase in quantity demanded. If this is the case, demand is **unitary elastic** ($E_d = 1$), and the total revenue remains unchanged at $600,000. Unitary elastic demand is a condition in which the percentage change in quantity demanded is equal to the percentage change in price. Because the percentage change in price equals the percentage change in quantity, total revenue does not change regardless of price.

Unitary elastic demand

A condition in which the percentage change in quantity demanded is equal to the percentage change in price.

Perfectly Elastic Demand ($E_d = \infty$) Two extreme cases are shown in Exhibit 2. These represent the limits between which the three demand curves explained above fall. Suppose for the sake of argument that a demand curve is perfectly horizontal, as shown in Exhibit 2(a). At a price of $20, buyers are willing to buy as many tickets as the Steel Porcupines are willing to offer for sale. At higher prices, buyers buy nothing. For example, this means that at $20.01 per ticket or higher buyers will buy zero tickets. If so, $E_d = \infty$, and demand is **perfectly elastic**. Perfectly elastic demand is a condition in which a small percentage change in price brings about an infinite percentage change in quantity demanded.

Perfectly elastic demand

A condition in which a small percentage change in price brings about an infinite percentage change in quantity demanded.

Perfectly Inelastic Demand ($E_d = 0$) Exhibit 2(b) shows the other extreme case, in which a demand curve is perfectly vertical. No matter how high or low the Steel Porcupines' ticket price is, the quantity demanded is 20,000 tickets. Such a demand curve is **perfectly inelastic**, and $E_d = 0$. Perfectly inelastic demand is a condition in which the quantity demanded does not change as the price changes.

Exhibit 3 summarizes the ranges for price elasticity of demand.

Perfectly inelastic demand

A condition in which the quantity demanded does not change as the price changes.

EXHIBIT 2

Perfectly Elastic and Perfectly Inelastic Demand

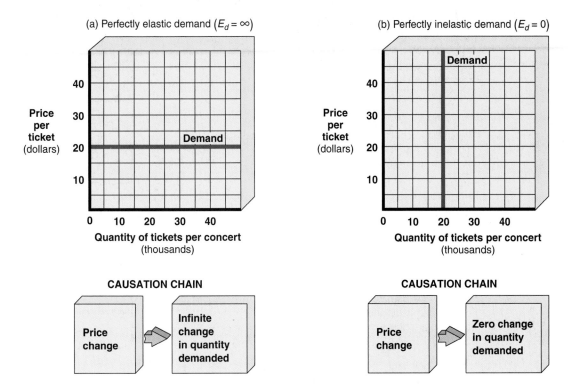

Here two extreme demand curves for Steel Porcupines concert tickets are represented. Part (a) shows a demand curve that is a horizontal line. Such a demand curve is perfectly elastic. At $20 per ticket, Steel Porcupines can sell as many concert tickets as they wish. At any price above $20, the quantity demanded falls from an infinite number to zero.

Part (b) shows a demand curve that is a vertical line. This demand curve is perfectly inelastic. No matter what the ticket price, the quantity demanded remains unchanged at 20,000 tickets.

Price Elasticity of Demand Variations Along a Demand Curve

The price elasticity of demand for a downward-sloping straight-line demand curve varies as we move along the curve. Look at Exhibit 4, which shows a linear demand curve in part (a) and the corresponding total revenue curve in part (b). Begin at $40 on the demand curve, and move down

EXHIBIT 3   Price Elasticity of Demand Terminology

Elasticity Coefficient	Definition	Demand	Graph
$E_d > 1$	Percentage change in quantity demanded is greater than the percentage change in price	Elastic	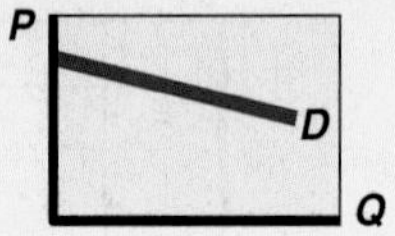
$E_d < 1$	Percentage change in quantity demanded is less than the percentage change in price	Inelastic	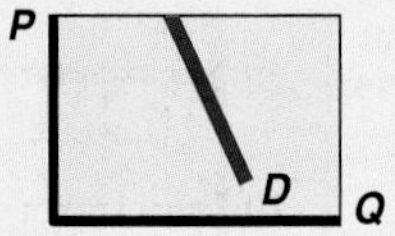
$E_d = 1$	Percentage change in quantity demanded is equal to the percentage change in price	Unitary elastic	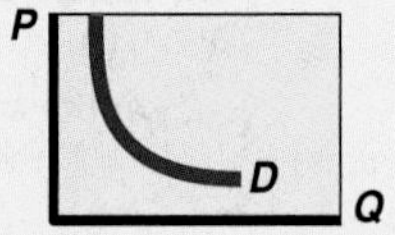
$E_d = \infty$	Percentage change in quantity demanded is infinite in relation to the percentage change in price	Perfectly elastic	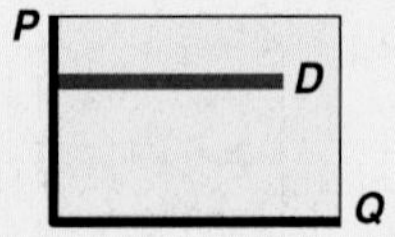
$E_d = 0$	Quantity demanded does not change as the price changes	Perfectly inelastic	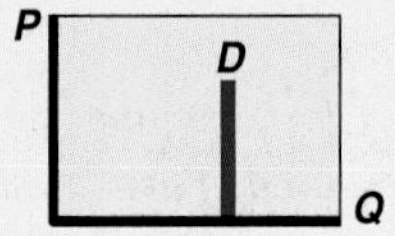

to $35, to $30, to $25, and so on. The table in Exhibit 4 lists variations in the total revenue and the elasticity coefficient (E_d) at different ticket prices. As we move down the upper segment of the demand curve, price elasticity of demand falls, and total revenue rises. For example, measured over the price range of $35 to $30, the price elasticity of demand is 4.13, and, therefore, this segment of demand is elastic ($E_d > 1$). Between these two prices, total revenue increases from $175 to $300. At $20, price elasticity is unitary elastic ($E_d = 1$), and total revenue is maximized at $400. As we move down the lower segment of the demand curve, price elasticity of demand falls below a value of 1.0, and total revenue falls. Over the price range of $15 to $10, for example, the price elasticity of demand is 0.45, and, therefore, this segment of demand is inelastic ($E_d < 1$). Between these two prices, total revenue decreases from $375 to $300.

EXHIBIT 4

The Variation in Elasticity and Total Revenue Along a Hypothetical Demand Curve

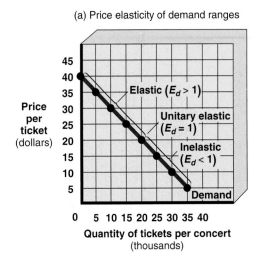

(a) Price elasticity of demand ranges

Calculation of Total Revenue and Elasticity Along a Hypothetical Demand Curve

Price	Quantity	Total revenue (thousands of dollars)	Elasticity coefficient (E_d)	Demand
$40	0	$0		
			15.00	Elastic
35	5	175		
			4.33	Elastic
30	10	300		
			2.20	Elastic
25	15	375		
			1.29	Elastic
20	20	400	1.00	Unitary elastic
			0.78	Inelastic
15	25	375		
			0.45	Inelastic
10	30	300		
			0.23	Inelastic
5	35	175		

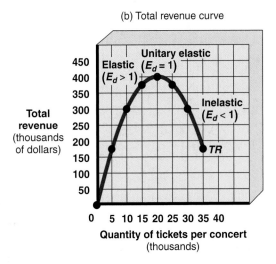

(b) Total revenue curve

Part (a) shows a straight-line demand curve and its three elasticity ranges. In the $40–$20 price range, demand is elastic. As price decreases in this range, total revenue increases. At $20, demand is unitary elastic, and total revenue is at its maximum. In the $20–$5 price range, demand is inelastic. As price decreases in this range, total revenue decreases. The total revenue (TR) curve is plotted in part (b) in order to trace its relationship to price elasticity.

CHECKPOINT   Will Fliers Flock to Low Summer Fares?

USAirways is concerned over low sales and announces special cuts in its fares this summer. The New York to Los Angeles fare, for example, is reduced from $500 to $420. Does USAirways think demand is elastic, unitary elastic, or inelastic?

Conclusion *The price elasticity of demand applies only to a specific range of prices.*

It is no coincidence that the demand curve in Exhibit 4(a) has elastic, unitary elastic, and inelastic segments. In fact, *any downward-sloping straight-line demand curve has ranges of all three of these types of price elasticity of demand.* As we move downward, first, there is an elastic range; second, a unitary elastic range; and, third, an inelastic range. Why? Recall that price elasticity of demand is a ratio of percentage changes. At the upper end of the demand curve, quantities demanded are lower, and prices are higher. A change of 1 unit in quantity demanded is a large percentage change. On the other hand, a $1 price change is a relatively small percentage change. At the lower end of the curve, the situation reverses. A 1-unit change in quantity demanded is a small percentage change. A $1 price change is a relatively larger percentage change. Now pause and refer back to parts (a) and (b) of Exhibit 1. If we examine changes in price along the entire length of these demand curves, they would have elastic, unitary elastic, and inelastic segments.

Exhibit 5 summarizes the relationships among elasticity, price change, and total revenue.

EXHIBIT 5   Relationships Among Elasticity, Price Change, and Total Revenue

Price Elasticity of Demand	Elasticity Coefficient	Price	Total Revenue
Elastic	$E_d > 1$	↑	↓
Elastic	$E_d > 1$	↓	↑
Unitary elastic	$E_d = 1$	↑↓	No change
Inelastic	$E_d < 1$	↑	↑
Inelastic	$E_d < 1$	↓	↓

Determinants of Price Elasticity of Demand

Economists estimate price elasticity of demand for various goods and services. Exhibit 6 presents some of these estimates, and the elasticity coefficients vary a great deal. For example, the demand for automobiles and for chinaware is elastic. On the other hand, the demand for jewelry and watches and for theater and opera tickets is inelastic. The demand for tires and tubes is approximately unitary elastic. What makes the price elasticities of demand for these products different? The following factors cause these differences.

Availability of Substitutes

By far the most important cause of price elasticity of demand is the availability of substitutes. Demand is more elastic for a good or service with close substitutes. If the price of cars rises, consumers can switch to buses, trains, bicycles, and walking. The more public transportation is available, the more responsive quantity demanded is to a change in the price of cars. When consumers have limited alternatives, the demand for a good or service is more price inelastic. If the price of tobacco rises, people addicted to it have few substitutes. Not smoking is not very appealing to most users.

Coke and Pepsi are close substitutes, and the demand for each is relatively elastic. What strategies do Coca-Cola (http://www.cocacola.com/home.html) and Pepsi-Cola (http://www.pepsiworld.com/index2.html) use to make the demand for their products less elastic?

EXHIBIT 6   Estimated Price Elasticities of Demand

Item	Elasticity Coefficient	
	Short Run	**Long Run**
Automobiles	1.87	2.24
Chinaware	1.54	2.55
Movies	0.87	3.67
Tires and tubes	0.86	1.19
Commuter rail fares	0.62	1.59
Jewelry and watches	0.41	0.67
Medical care	0.31	0.92
Housing	0.30	1.88
Gasoline	0.20	0.70
Theater and opera tickets	0.18	0.31
Foreign travel	0.14	1.77
Air travel	0.10	2.40

Sources: Robert Archibald and Robert Gillingham, "An Analysis of the Short-Run Consumer Demand for Gasoline Using Household Survey Data," *Review of Economics and Statistics* 62 (November 1980): 622–628; Hendrik S. Houthakker and Lester D. Taylor, *Consumer Demand in the United States: Analyses and Projections* (Cambridge: Harvard University Press, 1970): 56–149; Richard Voith, "The Long-Run Elasticity of Demand for Commuter Rail Transportation," *Journal of Urban Economics* 30 (November 1991): 360–372.

INTERNATIONAL ECONOMICS

Cigarette Smoking Around the World
Applicable Concept: price elasticity of demand

Worldwide, only 12 percent of women smoke, compared with 47 percent of men. In the United States, smoking rates for men and women are roughly equal at about 25 percent. . . . Although fledgling antismoking activists are beginning to make their presence felt overseas, U.S. tobacco manufacturers are likely to prosper abroad for a long time. And no one really expects Big Tobacco to surrender one of its last bastions of growth without a huge fight.[1]

The following are some thumbnail reports on the status of smoking in some countries around the world:

- *Germany.* Smoking is restricted in restaurants and banned at railway stations and on public transportation.
- *Sweden.* Smoking is banned in some public places, and no-smoking sections are required in restaurants. Smoking ads are not permitted on billboards or posters.
- *Spain.* Segregated smoking areas are designated in public buildings, and smoking is prohibited on public transportation.

- *Canada.* Smoking is prohibited in all public areas and on all flights of Canadian airlines. All cigarette advertising is banned, and high sales taxes are imposed at both the federal and the provincial levels. Cigarette taxes are used to help pay for the national health-care program.
- *Japan.* Smoking has become a vice of the Japanese. Smoking fits the frantic lifestyle of the Japanese, and most Japanese men smoke. Smoking ads are prohibited on billboards.

- *Great Britain.* The British government imposes an extra tax on high-tar and high-nicotine cigarettes.
- *USA.* Since 1964, health warnings have been mandated on tobacco advertising, including billboards and printed advertising. In 1971, television advertising was prohibited. Most states have banned smoking in state buildings, and the federal government has restricted smoking in federal offices and military facilities. In 1998, the Senate engaged in heated debate and finally set aside broad legislation to curb smoking by teenagers. This bill would have raised the price of cigarettes by $1.10 a pack over five years, and the tobacco industry would have paid $369 billion over the next 25 years. Opponents argued that this price increase was a massive tax on low-income Americans that would generate huge revenues to finance additional government programs and spending. Proponents countered that the bill was not about taxes. Instead, the bill was an attack on the death march of 418,000 Americans a year who die early from tobacco-related

Conclusion *The price elasticity coefficient of demand is directly related to the availability of good substitutes for a product.*

Price elasticity also depends on the market used to measure demand. For example, studies show the price elasticity of Chevrolets is greater than that of automobiles in general. Chevrolets compete with other cars sold by Ford, GM, Chrysler, Toyota, and other automakers and with buses and trains—all of which are their substitutes. But using the broad class of cars eliminates these specific types of cars as competitors. Instead, substitutes diseases. Finally, the Senate was so divided on the issue that it was impossible, at least for that year, to pass a tobacco bill.

The following research provides an analysis of the price elasticity of demand for cigarettes in the United States:

In a 1994 issue of *The American Economic Review*, Gary Becker, Michael Grossman, and Kevin Murphy tested a model to determine the short-run and long-run effects of a change in the price of cigarettes on cigarette consumption. The results of this research indicate that the demand for cigarettes is inelastic and that the responsiveness to price change varies over time. Based on this study, a 10-percent permanent increase in the price per pack of cigarettes reduced current consumption 4 percent in the short run and 7.5 percent in the long run. Thus, the long-run price elasticity of demand is almost twice as large as the short-run price elasticity.[2]

The price elasticity of demand for cigarettes also appears to vary by education. In a 1991 study published in the *Journal of Political Economy*, Frank Chaloupka found that less-educated adults are more responsive to price changes than better-educated adults. Individuals with less than a high school education were estimated to have a long-run price elasticity of demand of −0.60. However, more educated individuals were found to be unresponsive to changes in price. This finding supports the theory that less-educated people are more present-oriented, or "myopic," than more-educated people. Thus, less-educated individuals tend to be more influenced by current changes in the price of a pack of cigarettes.[3]

A 1991 study published in the *Journal of Health Economics* finds the price elasticity of demand for cigarettes has changed over time. Researchers Jeffrey Wasserman, Willard Manning, Joseph Newhouse, and John Winkler estimated that in the 1970s consumption of cigarettes was almost unresponsive to changes in price. However, between 1980 and 1988, the demand for cigarettes became more responsive to changes in price.[4]

ANALYZE THE ISSUE

According to the above, what factors influence the price elasticity of demand for cigarettes? What other factors not mentioned in the article might also influence the price elasticity of demand for cigarettes?

[1]Susan Headden, "The Marlboro Man Lives! Restrained at Home, Tobacco Firms Step Up Their Marketing Overseas," *U.S. News & World Report*, September 21, 1998, 58–59.

[2]Gary S. Becker, Michael Grossman, and Kevin M. Murphy, "An Empirical Analysis of Cigarette Addiction," *American Economic Review* 84, no. 3 (June 1994): 396–418.

[3]Frank Chaloupka, "Rational Addictive Behavior and Cigarette Smoking," *Journal of Political Economy* 99, no. 4 (August 1991): 722–742.

[4]Jeffrey Wasserman, Willard Manning, Joseph Newhouse, and John Winkler, "The Effect of Excise Taxes and Regulations on Cigarette Smoking," *Journal of Health Economics* 10, no. 1 (May 1991): 43–65.

for automobiles include buses and trains, which are also substitutes for Chevrolets. In short, there are more close substitutes for Chevrolets than there are for all cars.

Share of Budget Spent on the Product

When the price of salt changes, consumers pay little attention. Why should they notice? The price of salt or matches can double, and this purchase will remain a small percentage of one's budget. If, however, college tuition, the price of dinners at restaurants, or housing prices double, people will look for alternatives. These goods and services account for a large part of people's budgets.

Conclusion *The price elasticity coefficient of demand is directly related to the percentage of one's budget spent for a good or service.*

Adjustment to a Price Change over Time

Exhibit 6 separates the elasticity coefficients into short-run and long-run categories. As time passes, buyers can respond fully to a change in the price of a product by finding more substitutes. Consider the demand for gasoline. In the short run, people find it hard to cut back the amount they buy when the price rises sharply. They are accustomed to driving back and forth to work alone in their cars. The typical short-run response is to cut luxury travel and reduce speed on trips. If high prices persist over time, car buyers will find ways to cut back. They can buy cars with better fuel economy (more miles per gallon), form car pools, and ride buses or commuter trains. This explains why the short-run elasticity coefficient of gasoline in the exhibit is more inelastic at 0.2 than the long-run elasticity coefficient of 0.7.

Conclusion *In general, the price elasticity coefficient of demand is higher the longer a price change persists.*

Other Elasticity Measures

The elasticity concept has other applications beyond calculating the price elasticity of demand. Broadly defined, it is a technique for measuring the response of one variable to changes in some other variable.

Income Elasticity of Demand

Income elasticity of demand
The ratio of the percentage change in the quantity demanded of a good or service to a given percentage change in income.

Recall from Chapter 3 that an increase in income can increase the demand curve for a normal good or service and decrease the demand curve for an inferior good or service. To measure exactly how consumption responds to changes in income, economists calculate the **income elasticity of demand.** Income elasticity of demand is the ratio of the percentage change in the quantity demanded of a good or service to a given percentage change in income. We use a midpoint formula similar to the one we used for calculating price elasticity of demand:

$$E_Y = \frac{\text{percentage change in quantity demanded}}{\text{percentage change in income}}$$

CHECKPOINT   Can Trade Sanctions Affect Elasticity
of Demand for Cars?

Assume Congress prevents Lexus, Acura, Infiniti, Mazda 929, and other luxury
Japanese cars from being sold in the United States. How would this affect the
price elasticity of demand for Mercedes, BMWs, and Jaguars in the United
States?

$$E_Y = \frac{\%\Delta Q}{\%\Delta Y} = \frac{\dfrac{Q_2 - Q_1}{Q_1 + Q_2}}{\dfrac{Y_2 - Y_1}{Y_1 + Y_2}}$$

where E_Y is the income elasticity of demand coefficient, Q_1 and Q_2 represent quantities demanded before and after the income change, and Y_1 and Y_2 represent income before and after the income change. (Note that economists often use Y to represent income.)

For a *normal* good or service, the income elasticity of demand is *positive*, $E_Y > 0$. Recall that for this type of good demand and income move in the same direction. Thus, the variables change in the numerator and denominator in the same direction. For an *inferior* good or service, the reverse is true, and the income elasticity of demand is *negative*, $E_Y < 0$.

Why is the income elasticity coefficient important? Returning to our rock group example, the Steel Porcupines need to know the impact of a recession on ticket sales. During a downturn when consumers' income falls, if a rock concert is a *normal good*, the quantity of ticket sales falls. Conversely, if a rock concert is an *inferior good*, the quantity of ticket sales rises. To illustrate, suppose consumers' income increases from $1,000 to $1,250 per month. As a result, the quantity of tickets demanded increases from 10,000 to 15,000. Based on these data, is a rock concert a normal or an inferior good? We compute as follows:

$$E_Y = \frac{\dfrac{Q_2 - Q_1}{Q_1 + Q_2}}{\dfrac{Y_2 - Y_1}{Y_1 + Y_2}} = \frac{\dfrac{15,000 - 10,000}{10,000 + 15,000}}{\dfrac{1,250 - 1,000}{1,250 + 1,000}} = \frac{.20}{.11} = 1.8$$

The computed income elasticity of demand coefficient of 1.8 summarizes the relationship between changes in rock concert ticket purchases and changes in income. First, E_Y is a positive number, and, therefore, a rock concert is a normal good because people buy more when their income rises.

Rothstein-Tauber, Inc., is one of a number of consulting firms that estimate price elasticities. You can access its Internet site at http://www.rtimarketresearch.com/rt03008.htm.

Cross-elasticity of demand
The ratio of the percentage change in the quantity demanded of a good or service to a given percentage change in the price of another good or service.

Second, ticket purchases are very responsive to changes in income. When income rises by 11 percent, ticket sales increase by more (20 percent).

Exhibit 7 lists estimated income elasticity of demand for selected products.

Cross-Elasticity of Demand

In Chapter 3, we learned that a change in the price of one good—say, *Y*—can cause the consumption of another good—say, *X*—to change (see prices of related goods in Exhibit 5 in Chapter 3. In Exhibit 1(b) in Chapter 4, for example, a sharp rise in the price of gasoline (a complement) caused the number of gas guzzlers purchased to decline. This responsiveness of the quantity demanded to changes in the price of some other good is estimated by the **cross-elasticity of demand**. Cross-elasticity of demand is the ratio of the percentage change in the quantity demanded of a good or service to a given percentage change in the price of another good or service. Again, we use the midpoint formula as follows to compute the cross-elasticity coefficient of demand:

$$E_c = \frac{\text{percentage change in quantity demanded of one good}}{\text{percentage change in price of another good}}$$

$$E_c = \frac{\%\Delta Q_X}{\%\Delta P_Y} = \frac{\dfrac{Q_{X_2} - Q_{X_1}}{Q_{X_1} + Q_{X_2}}}{\dfrac{P_{Y_2} - P_{Y_1}}{P_{Y_1} + P_{Y_2}}}$$

where E_c is the cross-elasticity coefficient, Q_1 and Q_2 represent quantities before and after the price of another good or service changes, and P_1 and P_2 represent the price of another good or service before and after the price change.

The cross-elasticity coefficient reveals whether a good or service is a *substitute* or a *complement*. For example, Coke increases its price 10 percent, which causes consumers to buy 5 percent more Pepsi. The cross-elasticity of demand for Pepsi is a *positive* .50 (+5 percent/+10 percent). Since $E_c >$ 0, Coke and Pepsi are *substitutes* because the numerator and denominator variables change in the same direction. The larger the positive coefficient, the greater the substitutability between the two goods.

Now suppose there is a 50 percent increase in the price of motor oil and the quantity demanded of gasoline decreases by 10 percent. The cross-elasticity of demand for gasoline is a *negative* .20 (−10 percent/+50 percent). Since $E_c <$ 0, these two goods are complements. The larger the negative coefficient, the greater the complementary relationship between the two goods. The variables in the numerator and denominator change in the opposite direction.

EXHIBIT 7   Estimated Income Elasticities of Demand

Item	Elasticity Coefficient	
	Short Run	**Long Run**
Potatoes	N.A.	−0.81
Furniture	2.60	0.53
Dental services	0.38	1.00
Automobiles	5.50	1.07
Physician services	0.28	1.15
Clothing	0.95	1.17
Shoes	0.90	1.50
Gasoline and oil	0.55	1.36
Jewelry and watches	1.00	1.60
Toilet articles	0.25	3.74

Sources: Hendrik S. Houthakker and Lester D. Taylor, *Consumer Demand in the United States: Analyses and Projections* (Cambridge: Harvard University Press, 1970); Dale M. Helen, "The Structure of Food Demand: Interrelatedness and Duality," *American Journal of Agricultural Economics* 64, no. 2 (May 1982): 213–221.

Price Elasticity of Supply

The **price elasticity of supply** closely follows the price elasticity of demand concept. Price elasticity of supply is the ratio of the percentage change in the quantity supplied of a product to the percentage change in its price. This elasticity coefficient is calculated using the following formula:

$$E_s = \frac{\text{percentage change in quantity supplied}}{\text{percentage change in price}}$$

where E_s is the price elasticity of supply coefficient. Since price and quantity supplied change in the same direction, the elasticity coefficient is a positive value. Economists use terminology corresponding to that for the elasticity of demand. Supply is *elastic* when $E_s > 1$, *unit elastic* when $E_s = 1$, *inelastic* when $E_s < 1$, *perfectly elastic* when $E_s = \infty$, and *perfectly inelastic* when $E_s = 0$. Exhibit 8 shows three of these cases.

In Chapter 8, we will explain why the time period of analysis is a primary determinant of the shape of the supply curve. It will be shown that price elasticity of supply is greater in the long run than in the short run. Thus, the long-run supply curve will be flatter.

Exhibit 9 gives a summary of the three elasticity concepts presented in this section.

Price elasticity of supply

The ratio of the percentage change in the quantity supplied of a product to the percentage change in its price.

EXHIBIT 8

Price Elasticity of Supply

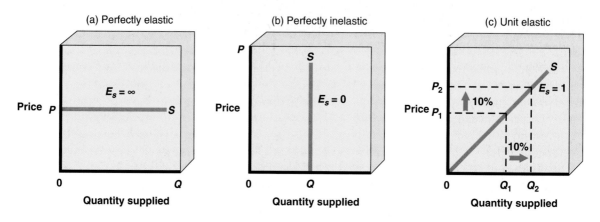

This figure shows three supply curves. As shown in part (a), a small change in price changes the quantity supplied by an infinite amount: $E_s = \infty$. Part (b) shows the quantity supplied is unaffected by a change in price: $E_s = 0$, and supply is perfectly inelastic. In part (c), the percentage change in quantity supplied is equal to the percentage change in price: $E_s = 1$.

Price Elasticity and the Impact of Taxation

Who pays a tax levied on sellers of goods such as gasoline, cigarettes, and alcoholic beverages? One way to answer this question is to say that if the government places a tax on, say, gasoline, the gasoline companies pay the tax. They collect the tax when they sell gas and write the checks to the government for the tax. But this is not the whole story. Instead of looking simply at who writes the checks, economists use the elasticity concept to analyze who "really" pays a tax. **Tax incidence** is the share of a tax ultimately paid by consumers and sellers. In this section, we show that even though taxes are collected from sellers, buyers do not escape a share of the tax burden. The tax incidence depends on the price elasticities of demand and supply. Let's look at two examples.

Tax incidence

The share of a tax ultimately paid by consumers and sellers.

Suppose the federal government decides to raise the gasoline tax $.50 per gallon. Exhibit 10 shows the impact of the tax. At E_1, the equilibrium price before the tax is $1 per gallon, and the equilibrium quantity is 30 million gallons per day. The effect of the tax is to shift the supply curve upward from S_1 to S_2. From the sellers' viewpoint, the cost of each gallon of gasoline increases $.50 per gallon. The effect is exactly the same as if the price of crude oil or any resource used to produce gasoline increased.

Sellers would like consumers to pay the entire amount of the tax. This would occur if consumers would pay $1.50 per gallon for the same 30 mil-

EXHIBIT 9   Summary of Other Elasticity Concepts

Type	Definition	Elasticity Coefficient Possibilities	Terminology
Income elasticity of demand	Percentage change in quantity demanded / Percentage change in income	$E_Y > 0$	Normal good
		$E_Y < 0$	Inferior good
		$E_Y > 1$	Income elastic
		$E_Y < 1$	Income inelastic
		$E_Y = 1$	Income unitary elastic
Cross-elasticity of demand	Percentage change in quantity demanded of one good / Percentage change in price of another good	$E_c < 0$	Complements
		$E_c > 0$	Substitutes
Price elasticity of supply	Percentage change in quantity supplied / Percentage change in price	$E_s > 1$	Elastic
		$E_s = 1$	Unit elastic
		$E_s < 1$	Inelastic
		$E_s = \infty$	Perfectly elastic
		$E_s = 0$	Perfectly inelastic

lion gallons per day they purchased before the tax. But the leftward shift in supply establishes a new equilibrium at E_2. The new equilibrium price is $1.25 per gallon, and the equilibrium quantity falls to 25 million gallons per day. At E_2, the entire shaded area represents the tax revenue. The government collects $12.5 million per day, which equals the $.50 per gallon tax times the 25 million gallons sold each day. The vertical line between points E_2 and T represents the $.50 tax per gallon. Since consumers now pay $1.25 instead of $1.00 per gallon, they pay one-half of the tax. The sellers pay the remaining half of the tax. Now the sellers send $.50 to Uncle Sam and keep $.75 compared to the $1.00 per gallon they kept before the tax.

Conclusion *If the demand curve slopes downward and the supply curve slopes upward, sellers cannot raise the price by the full amount of the tax.*

Part (b) of Exhibit 10 is a special case in which the market price increases by the full amount of the tax per gallon. Here the demand for gasoline is perfectly inelastic. In this case, the decrease in supply caused by the tax does not result in buyers responding by decreasing the quantity demanded. The quantity demanded is 30 million gallons per day before and after the

EXHIBIT 10

The Tax Incidence of a Tax on Gasoline

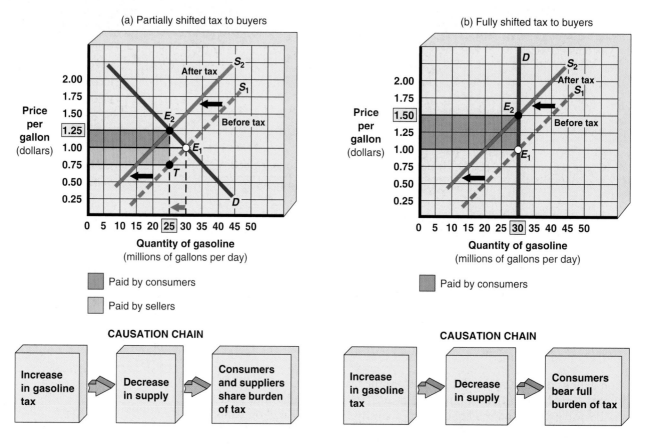

Paid by consumers
Paid by sellers

Paid by consumers

CAUSATION CHAIN

Increase in gasoline tax ⇒ Decrease in supply ⇒ Consumers and suppliers share burden of tax

CAUSATION CHAIN

Increase in gasoline tax ⇒ Decrease in supply ⇒ Consumers bear full burden of tax

In parts (a) and (b), S_1 is the supply curve before the imposition of a tax of $.50 per gallon on gasoline. The demand curve is not affected by this tax collected from the sellers. The initial equilibrium is E_1. Before the tax, the price is $1 per gallon, and 30 million gallons are bought and sold.

In part (a), the equilibrium price rises to $1.25 per gallon at E_2 as a result of the tax. After the tax is paid, sellers are paid only $.75 per gallon (point T) instead of $1.00, as they were before the tax. Thus, buyers pay $.25 of the tax per gallon, and sellers bear the remaining $.25. The shaded area is their total tax collected.

As shown in part (b), a tax collected from sellers can be fully shifted to buyers in the unlikely case that demand is perfectly inelastic. Since the quantity of gasoline purchased is unresponsive to a change in price, sellers receive $1 per gallon before and after they pay the tax.

CHECKPOINT   Can Honda Compete with Itself?

When Honda introduced the Acura to compete with European luxury cars, there was a danger that the new line would take sales away from the Accord. To make Acura more competitive with other luxury cars, suppose Honda cuts the price of Acura, while the price of Accord remains unchanged. If Honda's fear has come true, will it find a negative cross-elasticity of demand, a negative income elasticity of demand, or a positive cross-elasticity of demand?

tax. The price, however, increases by exactly the amount of tax per unit from $1 to $1.50 per gallon. After paying the tax, sellers receive a net price of $1 per gallon. The total tax revenue collected by the government is the shaded area. Each day $15 million is collected, which equals the $.50 per gallon tax multiplied by 30 million gallons sold each day.

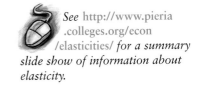

See http://www.pieria .colleges.org/econ /elasticities/ *for a summary slide show of information about elasticity.*

Conclusion *In the case where demand is perfectly inelastic, sellers can raise the price by the full amount of a tax.*
                              price change.

KEY CONCEPTS

Price elasticity of demand	Inelastic demand	Perfectly inelastic demand	Cross-elasticity of demand
Elastic demand	Unitary elastic demand	Income elasticity	Price elasticity of supply
Total revenue	Perfectly elastic demand	of demand	Tax incidence

SUMMARY

■ **Price elasticity of demand** is a measure of the responsiveness of the quantity demanded to a change in price. Specifically, price elasticity of demand is the ratio of the percentage change in quantity demanded to the percentage change in price.

$$E_d = \frac{\%\Delta Q}{\%\Delta P} = \frac{\dfrac{Q_2 - Q_1}{(Q_1 + Q_2)/2}}{\dfrac{P_2 - P_1}{(P_1 + P_2)/2}}$$

★ **Elastic demand** is a change of more than 1 percent in quantity demanded in response to a 1 percent change in price. Demand is elastic when the elasticity coefficient is greater than 1 and *total revenue* (price times quantity) varies inversely with the direction of the

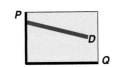

★ **Inelastic demand** is a change of less than 1 percent in quantity demanded in response to a 1 percent change in price. Demand is inelastic when the elasticity coefficient is less than 1 and total revenue varies directly with the direction of the price change.

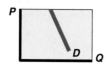

★ **Unitary elastic demand** is a 1 percent change in quantity demanded in response to a 1 percent change in price. Demand is unitary elastic when the elasticity coefficient equals 1 and total revenue remains constant as the price changes.

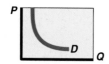

★ **Perfectly elastic demand** is a decline in quantity demanded to zero for even the slightest rise or fall in price. This is an extreme case in which the demand curve is horizontal and the elasticity coefficient equals infinity.

★ **Perfectly inelastic demand** is no change in quantity demanded in response to price changes. This is an extreme case in which the demand curve is vertical and the elasticity coefficient equals zero.

■ **Determinants of price elasticity of demand** include (a) the availability of substitutes, (b) the percentage of budget spent on the product, and (c) the length of time allowed for adjustment. Each of these factors is directly related to the elasticity coefficient.

■ **Income elasticity of demand** is the percentage change in quantity demanded divided by the percentage change in income. For a *normal* good or service, income elasticity of demand is positive. For an *inferior* good or service, income elasticity of demand is negative.

■ **Cross-elasticity of demand** is the percentage change in the quantity demanded of one product caused by a change in the price of another product. When the cross-elasticity of demand is negative, the two products are complements.

■ **Price elasticity of supply** is a measure of the responsiveness of the quantity demanded to a change in price. Price elasticity of supply is the ratio of the percentage change in quantity supplied to the percentage change in price.

★ **Tax incidence** is the share of a tax ultimately paid by buyers and sellers. Facing a downward-sloping demand curve and an upward-sloping supply curve, sellers cannot raise the price by the full amount of the tax. If the demand curve is vertical, sellers will raise the price by the full amount of a tax.

Tax incidence

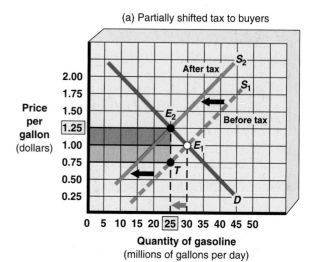

Quantity of gasoline
(millions of gallons per day)

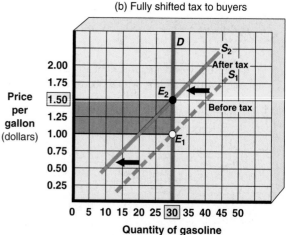

Quantity of gasoline
(millions of gallons per day)

SUMMARY OF CONCLUSION STATEMENTS

- The price elasticity of demand applies only to a specific range of prices.
- The price elasticity coefficient of demand is directly related to the availability of good substitutes for a product.
- The price elasticity coefficient of demand is directly related to the percentage of one's budget spent for a good or service.

- In general, the price elasticity coefficient of demand is higher the longer a price change persists.
- If the demand curve slopes downward and the supply curve slopes upward, sellers cannot raise the price by the full amount of the tax.
- In the case where demand is perfectly inelastic, sellers can raise the price by the full amount of a tax.

STUDY QUESTIONS AND PROBLEMS

1. If the price of a good or service increases and the total revenue received by the seller declines, is the demand for this good over this segment of the demand curve elastic or inelastic? Explain.

2. Suppose the price elasticity of demand for farm products is inelastic. If the federal government wants to follow a policy of increasing income for farmers, what type of programs will the government enact?

3. Suppose the price elasticity of demand for used cars is estimated to be 3. What does this mean? What will be the effect on the quantity demanded for used cars if the price rises by 10 percent?

4. Consider the following demand schedule:

Price	Quantity demanded	Elasticity coefficient
$25	20	_____
20	40	_____
15	60	_____
10	80	_____
5	100	_____

What is the price elasticity of demand between
a. $P = \$25$ and $P = \$20$?
b. $P = \$20$ and $P = \$15$?
c. $P = \$15$ and $P = \$10$?
d. $P = \$10$ and $P = \$5$?

5. Suppose a university raises its tuition from $3,000 to $3,500. As a result, student enrollment falls from 5,000 to 4,500. Calculate the price elasticity of demand. Is demand elastic, unitary elastic, or inelastic?

6. Will each of the following changes in price cause total revenue to increase, decrease, or remain unchanged?
a. Price falls, and demand is elastic.
b. Price rises, and demand is elastic.
c. Price falls, and demand is unitary elastic.
d. Price rises, and demand is unitary elastic.
e. Price falls, and demand is inelastic.
f. Price rises, and demand is inelastic.

7. Suppose the movie theater raises the price of popcorn 10 percent, but customers do not buy any less of it. What does this tell you about the price elasticity of demand, and what will happen to total revenue as a result of the price increase?

8. Charles loves Mello Yello and will spend $10 per week on the product no matter what the price. What is his price elasticity of demand for Mello Yello?

9. Which of the following goods has the higher price elasticity of demand?
a. Oranges or Sunkist oranges
b. Car or salt
c. Foreign travel in the short run or foreign travel in the long run

10. Energizer's "Can't stop the Energizer Bunny" ad campaign for batteries has been very successful. Explain the relationship between this slogan and the firm's price elasticity of demand and total revenue.

11. Suppose the income elasticity of demand for furniture is 3 and the income elasticity of demand for physician services is 0.3. Compare the impact on furniture and physician services of a recession that reduces consumer income by 10 percent.

12. How might you determine whether compact discs and cassettes are in competition with each other?

13. Assume that the cross-elasticity of demand for car tires with respect to the price of cars is −2. What does this tell you about the relationship between car tires and cars when the price of cars rises by 10 percent?

14. Consider the following supply schedule:

Price	Quantity supplied	Elasticity coefficient
$10	50	_____
8	40	_____
6	30	_____
4	20	_____
2	10	_____
0	0	_____

What is the price elasticity of supply between
a. $P = \$10$ and $P = \$8$?
b. $P = \$8$ and $P = \$6$?
c. $P = \$6$ and $P = \$4$?
d. $P = \$4$ and $P = \$2$?
e. $P = \$2$ and $P = 0$?

15. Why would consumers prefer that the government tax products with elastic, rather than inelastic, demand?

16. Opponents of increasing the tax on gasoline argue that the big oil companies just pass the tax along to the consumers. Do you agree or disagree? Explain your answer.

ONLINE EXERCISES

Exercise 1

Visit a few of the major antitobacco groups: the American Lung Association (http://www.lungusa.org/), the tobacco Control Resource Center (http://www.tobacco.neu.edu), and Smoke-Free Kids, an initiative by the U.S. Department of Health and Human Services (http://www.smokefree.gov/). What are these groups doing to increase the elasticity of demand for cigarettes?

Exercise 2

Does the federal government take economic concepts (such as elasticity) into consideration when it formulates energy and environmental policies? Visit the Environmental Protection Agency (EPA), and review its materials on the economy and the environment (http://www.epa.gov/oppe/eaed/eedhmpg.htm). Also visit the Department of Energy, Energy Information Administration (http://www.eia.doe.gov/).

Exercise 3

Cindy Crawford is not the only personality to advertise products. One well-known person who is in numerous print ads and television commercials is Michael Jordan. There is even a Michael Jordan cologne. Visit the Michael Jordan web site (http://www.michael-jordan-cologne.com/), and see what company manufactures the Michael Jordan cologne. Why did the company want a cologne named after Jordan?

Exercise 4

The Kelley Blue Book Official Guide is a major source of new and used car prices (http://www.kbb.com/). Find the new car prices for two popular cars: Honda Accord and Ford Taurus. Are the two cars closely priced? Do you think physically similar goods are closer substitutes when they are more closely priced than when they are less closely priced? Or do you think the issue of closeness in price is irrelevant to the degree of substitution? Explain your answer. Do you think the cross-price elasticity of demand between Accord and Taurus is positive or negative? Explain your answer.

CHECKPOINT ANSWERS

Will Fliers Flock to Low Summer Fares?

USAirways must believe the quantity of airline tickets demanded during the summer is quite responsive to a price cut. In order for total revenue to rise with a price cut, the quantity demanded must increase by a larger percentage than the percentage decrease in the price. For this to occur, the price elasticity of demand must exceed 1. If you said USAirways believes demand is elastic, **YOU ARE CORRECT.**

Can Trade Sanctions Affect Elasticity of Demand for Cars?

Because U.S. consumers are denied the availability of substitutes (Japanese luxury cars), the quantity demanded of Mercedes, BMWs, and Jaguars sold in the United States would be less responsive to changes in the price for these cars. If you said the price elasticity of demand for Mercedes, BMWs, and Jaguars would become less elastic, **YOU ARE CORRECT.**

Can Honda Compete with Itself?

Seeing the effect of cutting the Acura's price on sales of Accords calls for cross-elasticity. Once the price of Acura is cut, Honda would calculate the change in the quantity of Accords demanded. If Acura's decrease in price causes people to buy fewer Accords, Honda is indeed competing with itself. If you said a positive cross-elasticity of demand indicates the two goods are substitutes, **YOU ARE CORRECT.**

PRACTICE QUIZ

For a visual explanation of the correct answers, visit the tutorial at http://tucker.swcollege.com.

1. If an increase in bus fares in Charlotte, North Carolina, reduces total revenue of the public transit system, this is evidence that demand is
   a. price elastic.
   b. price inelastic.
   c. unitary elastic.
   d. perfectly elastic.

2. Which of the following is the result of an increase in total revenue?
   a. Price increases when demand is elastic.
   b. Price decreases when demand is elastic.
   c. Price increases when demand is unitary elastic.
   d. Price decreases when demand is inelastic.

3. You are on a committee that is considering ways to raise money for your city's symphony program. You would recommend increasing the price of symphony tickets only if you thought the demand curve for these tickets was
   a. inelastic.
   b. elastic.
   c. unitary elastic.
   d. perfectly elastic.

4. The price elasticity of demand for a horizontal demand curve is
   a. perfectly elastic.
   b. perfectly inelastic.
   c. unitary elastic.
   d. inelastic.
   e. elastic.

5. Suppose the quantity of steak purchased by the Jones family is 110 pounds per year when the price is $2.10 per pound and 90 pounds per year when the price is $3.90 per pound. The price elasticity of demand coefficient for this family is
   a. 0.33.
   b. 0.50.
   c. 1.00.
   d. 2.00.

6. If a 5 percent reduction in the price of a good produces a 3 percent increase in the quantity demanded, the price elasticity of demand over this range of the demand curve is
   a. elastic.
   b. perfectly elastic.
   c. unitary elastic.
   d. inelastic.
   e. perfectly inelastic.

7. A manufacturer of Beanie Babies hires an economist to study the price elasticity of demand for this product. The economist estimates that the price elasticity of demand coefficient for a range of prices close to the selling price is greater than 1. The relationship between changes in price and quantity demanded for this segment of the demand curve is
   a. elastic.
   b. inelastic.
   c. perfectly elastic.
   d. perfectly inelastic.
   e. unitary elastic.

8. A downward-sloping demand curve will have a
   a. higher price elasticity of demand coefficient along the top of the demand curve.
   b. lower price elasticity coefficient along the top of the demand curve.
   c. constant price elasticity of demand coefficient throughout the length of the demand curve.
   d. positive slope.

9. The price elasticity of demand coefficient for a good will be less
   a. if there are few or no substitutes available.
   b. if a small portion of the budget will be spent on it.
   c. in the short run than in the long run.
   d. if all of the above are true.

10. The income elasticity of demand for shoes is estimated to be 1.50. We can conclude that shoes
    a. have a relatively steep demand curve.
    b. have a relatively flat demand curve.
    c. are a normal good.
    d. are an inferior good.

11. To determine whether two goods are substitutes or complements, an economist would estimate the
    a. price elasticity of demand.
    b. income elasticity of demand.
    c. cross-elasticity of demand.
    d. price elasticity of supply.

12. If the government wanted to raise tax revenue and shift most of the tax burden to the sellers, it would impose a tax on a good with a
    a. steep (inelastic) demand curve and a steep (inelastic) supply curve.
    b. steep (inelastic) demand curve and a flat (elastic) supply curve.
    c. flat (elastic) demand curve and a steep (inelastic) supply curve.
    d. flat (elastic) demand curve and a flat (elastic) supply curve.

CHAPTER SIX

Consumer Choice Theory

This chapter expands our understanding of demand by investigating more deeply *why* people buy goods and services. In Chapter 3, the law of demand rested on a foundation of common sense and everyday observation. When the price of a Big Mac falls, people *do* buy more, and a price rise causes people to buy less. But there is more to the story.

The focus of this chapter is the logic of consumer choice. Why does a consumer buy one bundle of goods, rather than another? Suppose someone asked why you bought a milkshake and french fries, rather than a Coke and a hot dog. You would probably answer that given the money you had to spend, the Coke and hot dog would have given you less satisfaction. In this chapter, you will transform this simple explanation into consumer choice theory and then connect this theory to the law of demand. The chapter ends with another way to explain the demand curve, which involves effects related to income and the prices of other goods.

In this chapter, you will learn to solve these economics puzzles:

■ Under what conditions might you be willing to pay $10,000 for a gallon of water and 1 cent for a one-carat diamond?

■ When ordering Big Macs, milkshakes, pizza, and other goods, how can you obtain the highest possible satisfaction?

■ Do white rats obey the law of demand?

From Utility to the Law of Demand

The basis of the law of demand is self-interested behavior. Consumers spend their limited budget to satisfy some want, such as listening to a compact disc or driving a new car. The motivation to consume goods and services is to gain **utility**. Utility is the satisfaction, or pleasure, that people receive from consuming a good or service. Utility is want-satisfying power "in the eye of the beholder." Just as wants differ among people, utility received from consumption varies from person to person. Fred's utility from consuming a BMW is probably going to differ from Maria's utility. In spite of the subjective nature of utility, this section develops in steps the derivation of a demand curve based on the utility concept.

Total Utility and Marginal Utility

Actual measurement of utility is impossible. This is because only you know the satisfaction from consuming four Big Macs in one day. But suppose we could gauge your **total utility** of consuming four Big Macs in a day. Total utility is the amount of satisfaction received from all the units of a good or service consumed. That is, the utility of the first unit consumed added to that of the second unit, and so on. What units can be used to measure total utility? Economists use a mythical unit called a *util*, which allows us to quantify our thinking about consumer behavior.

No one has invented a "utility meter," but assume we could hook such a meter to your brain. Like taking your temperature, we could read the **marginal utility** each time you eat a Big Mac. Marginal utility is the change in total utility from one additional unit of a good or service. Instead of the total pleasure from eating *X* number of Big Macs, the question is how much *extra* satisfaction the first, second, or third Big Mac gives you. For example, Exhibit 1(a) shows your marginal utility data for eating four Big Macs in a day. You munch down the first Big Mac. Ah, the util meter hits an 8. You grab another Big Mac and eat it a little more slowly. The util meter hits 4 this time. You're starting to feel full, but you eat a third Big Mac. This one gets a 2. Even though you are pretty full, there is room for one more. You eat the fourth Big Mac very slowly, and it gives you less satisfaction than any of the previous burgers. Your utility meter reads 1. This trend conforms to the **law of diminishing marginal utility**. The law of diminishing marginal utility is the principle that the extra satisfaction of a good or service declines as people consume more in a given period. Economists have found that this is a universal principle of human consumption behavior. Exhibit 1(a) is a marginal utility (*MU*) graph. Consistent with the law of diminishing marginal utility, the *MU* curve slopes downward as you consume more Big Macs. This reflects a steady decline in the utility of each additional Big Mac consumed. If you continued to eat Big Macs, a quantity of Big Macs is eventually reached at which the marginal utility is zero. Here you say to yourself, "If I eat another bite, I'll be sick." Then if you did eat another bite after all, marginal utility would be negative. A rational person never consumes goods when the marginal utility is negative (disutility) unless he or she is paid enough to do so. In our example, we assume you are rational and will not eat a Big Mac that gives you a

Utility
The satisfaction, or pleasure, that people receive from consuming a good or service.

Total utility
The amount of satisfaction received from all the units of a good or service consumed.

Marginal utility
The change in total utility from one additional unit of a good or service.

Law of diminishing marginal utility
The principle that the extra satisfaction of a good or service declines as people consume more in a given period.

Universal Studios in Florida claims that guests who visit for one day will want "just one more day—or two more days, or even a year's worth of fun." But the law of diminishing marginal utility states that by year's end guests would probably no longer find it enjoyable. See http://www.usf.com.

EXHIBIT 1

Diminishing Marginal Utility and Total Utility Curves for Consuming Big Macs

(a) Marginal utility

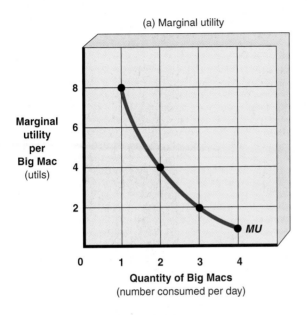

(b) Total utility

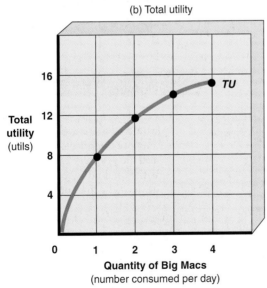

Part (a) shows that, as more Big Macs are consumed per day, the utility from each additional Big Mac declines. The utils are only imaginary because utility cannot be measured. When the marginal utility of each Big Mac consumed is summed, we obtain the total utility curve shown in part (b).

Why Is Water Less Expensive Than Diamonds?

Applicable Concepts: total utility and marginal utility

Adam Smith posed a paradox in *The Wealth of Nations*. Water is essential to life and therefore should be of great value. On the other hand, diamonds are unessential to life, and people should value them less than water. Even though water provides more utility, it is cheaper than diamonds. Smith's puzzle came to be known as the diamond-water paradox. Now you can use marginal utility analysis to explain something that baffled the father of economics.

Early economists failed to find the key to the diamond-water puzzle because they did not distinguish between marginal and total utility. Marginal utility theory was not developed until the late nineteenth century. Water is life-giving and does indeed yield much higher total utility than diamonds. However, marginal utility, and not total utility, determines the price. Water is plentiful in most of the world, so its marginal utility is low. This follows the law of diminishing marginal utility.

Jewelry-quality diamonds, on the other hand, are scarce. Because we have relatively few diamonds, the quantity of diamonds consumed is not large. As a result, the marginal utility of diamonds and the price buyers are willing to pay for them are quite high. Thus, scarcity raises marginal utility and price regardless of the size of total utility.[1]

Exhibit 2 presents a graphical analysis that you can use to unravel the alleged paradox. Part (a) shows the marginal utility per carat you receive from each diamond consumed, and part (b) represents marginal utility per gallon of water consumed. The vertical line, *S*, in each graph is the supply of water or diamonds available per year. Since water is much more plentiful than diamonds, the supply curve for water intersects the marginal utility curve at MU_w, which is close to zero. Conversely, the supply curve for diamonds intersects the marginal utility curve at a much higher marginal utility, MU_d. Because of the relative marginal utilities of water and diamonds, you are willing to pay much more for one more carat of a diamond than for one more gallon of water.

1. Can you imagine a situation in which water would be more expensive than diamonds?
2. Suppose the price per gallon of water is 1 cent and the price per carat of a diamond is $10,000. Is the total utility of diamonds 10,000 times as great as the total utility received from water?

---

[1]In our time, jewelry-quality diamonds are scarce because De-Beers, a South African company, controls and restricts the world-wide distribution of diamonds. Actually, the world supply of rough diamonds is quite large.

EXHIBIT 2

The Diamond-Water Paradox

(a) Marginal utility of diamonds

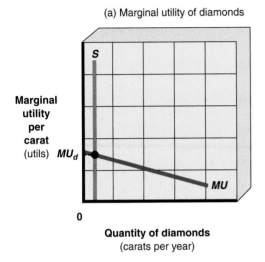

(b) Marginal utility of water

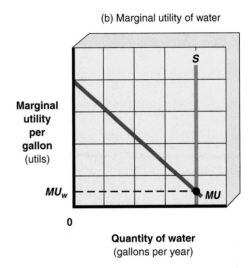

negative marginal utility and a stomachache. Also keep in mind that the *MU* curve for a good is different for different circumstances and individuals. Your *MU* curve would be much higher if you had not eaten in days. On the other hand, a vegetarian would receive no positive marginal utility from consuming a Big Mac.

Exhibit 1(b) shows how the shape of the total utility (*TU*) curve varies with marginal utility as you consume more Big Macs each day. The total utility of Big Macs increases steadily because each hamburger provides *additional* satisfaction to the sum of all the Big Macs already consumed. However, the total utility curve becomes flatter as the marginal utility diminishes. This is because the positive pleasure per Big Mac declines, and, in turn, each Big Mac adds less to total utility as you consume more.

Consumer Equilibrium

We will now make our example of consumer choice more realistic. Let's examine how Bob Moore, a sophomore at Seaview College, might behave, given a limited budget and the choice between two goods. Suppose Bob goes to McDonald's for lunch with $8 in his pocket to spend for Big Macs and milkshakes. The price of a Big Mac is $2, and the price of a milkshake is also $2. How can Bob enjoy the maximum total utility with his limited money?

Recall from Chapter 2 the concept of *marginal analysis*. This is the method Bob uses to decide how many Big Macs and milkshakes to order.

EXHIBIT 3   Marginal Utility for Big Macs and Milkshakes (Utils per Day)

Quantity	Big Macs MU	Big Macs MU/P	Milkshakes MU	Milkshakes MU/P
1	8	4	6	3
2	4	2	4	2
3	2	1	1	1/2
4	1	1/2	0	0

Note: The price per Big Mac and per milkshake is $2.

Exhibit 3 shows Bob's marginal utility for each Big Mac and milkshake consumed. The *marginal utility per dollar (MU/P)* is the ratio of the marginal utility of each good to its price. In making purchases, the key consideration is how additional satisfaction relates to price. Using marginal decision-making before giving an order, Bob compares the marginal utility of one Big Mac to the marginal utility of one milkshake. Being a rational consumer, Bob sees that spending his first $2 on a Big Mac gives more "bang for the buck." The first Big Mac gives him 4 utils per dollar, but the same $2 spent on a milkshake gives him 3 utils per dollar. Next, Bob ponders how to spend his next $2. The best buy now is a milkshake because it gives 3 utils per dollar compared to 2 utils per dollar for a second Big Mac.

Spending Bob's last $4 is a toss-up. Both the second Big Mac and the second milkshake give the same 2 utils per dollar. So Bob can spend $2 for a second Big Mac and his last $2 for a second milkshake. Or he can spend $2 for a second milkshake and his last $2 for a second Big Mac. The order does not matter. Now that Bob has spent all his income, the marginal utility per dollar of the last Big Mac is equal to the marginal utility per dollar of the last milkshake.

> **Conclusion** *If the marginal utility per last dollar spent on each good is equal and the entire budget is spent, total utility is maximized.*

To convince yourself that two Big Macs and two milkshakes do indeed maximize total utility, consider any other combination Bob could buy with $8. All others yield lower total utility. Suppose Bob were to buy three Big Macs and one milkshake. The third Big Mac adds 2 utils, but giving up the second milkshake subtracts 4 utils. As a result, total utility falls by 2 utils. Or can Bob maximize utility if he were to eat only one Big Mac and drink three milkshakes? The extra utility of the third milkshake is 1 util, but this is less than the 4 utils he would lose by saying no to the second Big Mac. In this case, total utility would fall by 3 utils.

The above example demonstrates the utility-maximizing concept of **consumer equilibrium**. Consumer equilibrium is a condition in which total utility cannot increase by spending more of a given budget on one good

Consumer equilibrium
A condition in which total utility cannot increase by spending more of a given budget on one good and spending less on another good.

and spending less on another good. Suppose Bob knows not only the exact marginal utility of consuming Big Macs and milkshakes, but also the marginal utility of french fries, pizza, and other goods. To obtain the highest possible satisfaction, Bob allocates a budget so the last dollar spent on good *A*, the last on good *B*, and so on yield equal *MU/P* ratios. Consumer equilibrium can be restated algebraically as

$$\frac{MU \text{ of good } A}{\text{price of good } A} = \frac{MU \text{ of good } B}{\text{price of good } B} = \frac{MU \text{ of good } Z}{\text{price of good } Z}$$

The letters *A, B, . . . Z* indicate all the goods and services purchased by the consumer with a given budget.

From Consumer Equilibrium to the Law of Demand

Understanding the law of diminishing marginal utility and consumer equilibrium provides you with a new set of tools to explore the law of demand. Let's begin with a straightforward link between the law of diminishing marginal utility and the demand curve. Declining marginal utility from consuming more Big Macs and milkshakes means each extra quantity consumed is less important or valuable to the consumer. Therefore, as the quantity consumed increases and the marginal utility falls, Bob is willing to pay less per Big Mac and milkshake. Thus, Bob's individual demand curve conforms to the law of demand and is downward-sloping.

A more complete explanation of the law of demand combines diminishing marginal utility and consumer equilibrium. Suppose Bob reaches consumer equilibrium as follows:

$$\frac{MU \text{ of Big Mac}}{\text{price of Big Mac}} = \frac{MU \text{ of milkshake}}{\text{price of milkshake}}$$

$$\frac{4 \text{ utils}}{\$2} = \frac{4 \text{ utils}}{\$2}$$

Now suppose the price of a Big Mac falls to $1 and upsets the above equality. This changes the formula to the following:

$$\frac{MU \text{ of Big Mac}}{\text{price of Big Mac}} > \frac{MU \text{ of milkshake}}{\text{price of milkshake}}$$

$$\frac{4 \text{ utils}}{\$1} > \frac{4 \text{ utils}}{\$2}$$

Now Bob gains more utility per dollar by buying a Big Mac, rather than a milkshake. To restore maximum total utility, he spends more on Big Macs. The marginal utility of a Big Mac must fall as he buys more. At the same time, the marginal utility of a milkshake must rise as Bob buys fewer. A fall in the price of Big Macs therefore causes Bob to buy more Big Macs. Voila! The law of demand.

A number of commercial firms conduct research on consumer choices and preferences. Visit USADATA at http://www.usadata.com.

When Dining Out, Do You Eat Smart?

Welcome to José's Hacienda! The menu lists beside each dish the total utility from each item. If you have $10 to spend, which meal will you order to achieve consumer equilibrium?

José's Hacienda Menu

Tacos—$3 each	Flan*—$2 each	Coke—$1 each
1 taco (99 utils)	1 flan (40 utils)	1 Coke (25 utils)
2 tacos (162 utils)	2 flans (48 utils)	2 Cokes (30 utils)
3 tacos (174 utils)	3 flans (50 utils)	3 Cokes (32 utils)

*Mexican dessert.

Income and Substitution Effects and the Law of Demand

Since utility is not measurable, it is desirable to have an alternative explanation of demand. Economists offer the following two complementary explanations for the law of demand, which do not rely on utility.

Income Effect

One reason people buy more of a good when the price falls is the effect of a price change on real income. The *nominal* or *money* amount of your paycheck is simply the number of dollars you earn. On the other hand, price changes alter your *real* income. A rise in prices decreases purchasing power, and a fall in prices increases purchasing power, ceteris paribus.

Suppose your weekly nominal income is $100 and you decide to stock up on Pepsi-Cola (a normal good). If the price per quart is $1, you can afford to buy 100 quarts this week. If the price is instead $.50 per quart and the prices of other goods remain constant, you are richer because of the rise in purchasing power. As a result, you can buy 200 quarts of Pepsi-Cola without giving up any other goods or less than 200 quarts and more of other goods. As predicted by the law of demand, the lower price for Pepsi-Cola causes real income to rise and, in turn, causes the quantity demanded to rise. This relationship between changes in real income and your ability to buy goods and services is the **income effect**. The income effect is the change in quantity demanded of a good or service caused by a change in real income (purchasing power).

Income effect

The change in quantity demanded of a good or service caused by a change in real income (purchasing power).

CHECKPOINT   Does the Substitution Effect Apply to Buying a Car?

Brad Moore wants to buy a new car, and the annual gasoline expense is a major consideration. His present car gets 25 miles per gallon (mpg), and he is looking at a new car that gets 40 mpg. Brad now drives about 12,000 miles per year and pays $1.25 per gallon of gasoline. Brad therefore calculates an annual gasoline consumption of 480 gallons for his 25-mpg car (12,000 miles/25 mpg), compared to 300 gallons consumed per year for the 40-mpg car (12,000 miles/ 40 mpg). Since driving the higher mileage car would use 180 gallons less per year, Brad estimates the new car will save him $225 in gasoline expense per year (180 gallons × $1.25 per gallon). Suppose Brad buys the 40-mpg car. Do you predict Brad will have an annual gasoline savings equal to $225, less than $225, or more than $225?

Substitution Effect

There is another reason why the change in a good's price causes a change in the quantity demanded. This reason has to do with changing *relative prices*, that is, the price of one good compared to that of another. If the price of Pepsi falls and the price of Coke remains unchanged, Pepsi becomes a better buy. As a result, many consumers will switch from Coke and other beverages and buy Pepsi. Just as the law of demand predicts, this is an increase in quantity demanded. With the price of Pepsi lower than before, the **substitution effect** causes people to substitute Pepsi for the now relatively more expensive Coke. The substitution effect is the change in quantity demanded of a good or service caused by the change in its price relative to substitutes.

Above we discussed the income and the substitution effects separately, but they are complementary explanations for the downward-sloping demand curve.

> **Conclusion** *When the price of a normal good falls, the income effect and the substitution effect combine to cause the quantity demanded to increase.*

Some students express relief that this conclusion has no reference to the untidy word *utility*.

Substitution effect
The change in quantity demanded of a good or service caused by the change in its price relative to substitutes.

Testing the Law of Demand with White Rats

Applicable Concept: substitution effect

Economists often envy the controlled laboratory experiments of biologists and other scientists. In the real world, the economist is unable to observe consumer behavior without prices of other goods, expectations, and other factors changing. So it is no wonder that the idea of studying the behavior of white rats to study the law of demand is intriguing. The question is whether the consumer choice of a white rat supports the downward-sloping demand curve.

Standard laboratory rats were placed in experimental cages with two levers. If a rat pressed one lever, one liquid—say, nonalcoholic Collins mix—was the reward. Depressing the second lever rewarded the rat with another liquid—say, root beer. It seems rats are fond of these two beverages. Each rat was given a limited "income" of lever presses per day. After, say, 300 presses, a light above the lever went out, signaling the daily budget was gone. The next day the light was turned on, and the rat was given a new income of lever presses. The "price" of each good corresponded to the number of lever pushes required to obtain one milliliter of liquid. For example, if the number of pushes per milliliter for Collins mix released doubled, this equaled a 50 percent increase in the price of Collins mix.

The crucial test was to measure the substitution effect resulting from a change in price. As explained in the text, a change in price sets in motion both an income effect and a substitution effect. In the experiment, the price of Collins mix was lowered by decreasing the pushes per milliliter. At the same time, the price of root beer was raised by increasing the pushes per milliliter. To eliminate the income effect, the number of lever presses was raised to compensate for loss of purchasing power. For example, if a rat purchased 4 milliliters of Collins mix per day and 11 milliliters of root beer before the price change, it would be given enough extra pushes after the price change to still purchase these quantities.

In one experiment, a male albino rat was given 300 pushes per day for two weeks, and both liquids were priced at 20 pushes per milliliter. The rat soon settled into a consistent consumption pattern of 4 milliliters of Collins mix and 11 milliliters of root beer per day. Then the experimenters made changes in prices and income. The price (pushes per milliliter) of Collins mix was cut in half, and the price of root beer was doubled. At the same time, the total income of pushes was increased just enough to allow the rat to afford its initial consumption pattern. Stated differently, the income effect was eliminated in order to focus on the substitution effect.

After two weeks of decisions under the new conditions, the rat changed its consumption pattern to 17 milliliters of Collins mix and 8 milliliters of root beer per day.

ANALYZE THE ISSUE

Based on the behavior of the rat described above, what do you conclude about the substitution effect and the slope of the demand curve?

Source: Adapted by permission from John H. Kagel, Raymond C. Battalio, Howard Rachlin, and Leonard Green, "Demand Curves for Animal Consumers," *Quarterly Journal of Economics* 96 (February 1981): 1–16.

KEY CONCEPTS

Utility
Total utility
Marginal utility

Law of diminishing
   marginal utility
Consumer equilibrium

Income effect
Substitution effect

SUMMARY

■ **Utility** is the satisfaction or pleasure derived from consumption of a good or service. Actual measurement of utility is impossible, but economists assume it can be measured by a fictitious unit called the *util*.

★ **Total utility** is the total level of satisfaction derived from all units of a good or service consumed. *Marginal utility* is the change in total utility from a one-unit change in the quantity of a good or service consumed.

Total utility

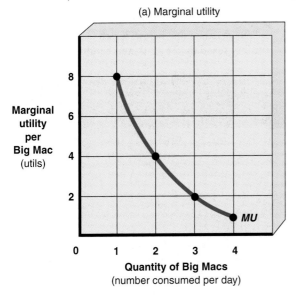

(a) Marginal utility

Marginal utility per Big Mac (utils)

MU

Quantity of Big Macs (number consumed per day)

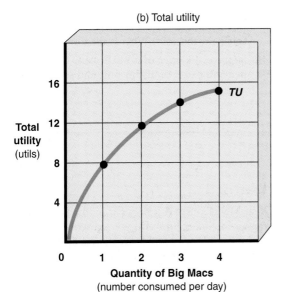

(b) Total utility

Total utility (utils)

TU

Quantity of Big Macs (number consumed per day)

■ The **law of diminishing marginal utility** states that the marginal utility of a good or service eventually declines as consumption increases.

■ **Consumer equilibrium** is the condition of reaching the maximum level of satisfaction, given a budget, when the marginal utility per dollar spent on each good purchased is equal. Consumer equilibrium and the law of diminishing marginal utility can be used to derive a downward-sloping demand curve. When the price of a good falls, consumer equilibrium no longer holds because the marginal utility per dollar for the good rises. To restore equilibrium, the consumer must increase consumption. As the quantity demanded increases, the marginal utility falls until equilibrium is again achieved. Thus, the price falls and the quantity demanded rises, as predicted by the law of demand.

$$\frac{MU \text{ of good } A}{\text{price of good } A} = \frac{MU \text{ of good } B}{\text{price of good } B} = \frac{MU \text{ of good } Z}{\text{price of good } Z}$$

■ The **income effect** and the **substitution effect** are complementary explanations for the law of demand. When the price changes, these effects work in combination to change the quantity demanded in the opposite directions. As the price falls, real purchasing power increases, causing an increase in the consumer's willingness and ability to purchase a good or service. This is the *income effect*. Also, as the price falls, the consumer substitutes the cheaper good for other goods that are now relatively more expensive. This is the *substitution effect*.

SUMMARY OF CONCLUSION STATEMENTS

- If the marginal utility per last dollar spent on each good is equal and the entire budget is spent, total utility is maximized.

- When the price of a normal good falls, the income effect and the substitution effect combine to cause the quantity demanded to increase.

STUDY QUESTIONS AND PROBLEMS

1. Does a dollar given to a rich person raise the rich person's total utility more than a dollar given to a poor person raises the poor person's total utility?

2. Do you agree with the following statement? "If you like tacos, you should consume as many as you can."

3. This week you have gone to two parties. Assume the total utility you gained from these parties is 100 utils. Then you go to a third party, and your total utility rises to 110 utils. What is the marginal utility of the third party attended per week? Given the law of diminishing marginal utility, what will happen to total utility and marginal utility when you go to a fourth party this week?

4. Suppose your marginal utility for meals at the campus cafeteria this week has fallen to zero. Explain what has happened to your total utility curve derived from consuming these meals. Now explain what will happen to total utility if you eat more meals at the cafeteria this week.

5. Suppose you consume 3 pounds of beef and 5 pounds of pork per month. The price of beef is $1.50 per pound, and pork is $2 per pound. Assuming you have studied economics and achieved consumer equilibrium, what is the ratio of the marginal utility of beef to the marginal utility of pork?

6. Suppose the marginal utility of a Coke is 15 utils and its price is $1. The marginal utility of a pizza is 20 utils, and its price is $2. If you buy one unit of each

good, will you achieve consumer equilibrium? If not, how can greater total utility be obtained?

7. Explain the relationship between the law of diminishing marginal utility and the law of demand.

8. Consider the table below, which lists James's marginal utility schedule for steak and hamburger meals:

Steak meals per month	Marginal utility of steak meals	Price per steak meal	Hamburger meals per month	Marginal utility of hamburger meals	Price per hamburger meal
1	20	$10	1	15	$5
2	15	10	2	8	5
3	12	10	3	6	5
4	10	10	4	4	5
5	8	10	5	2	5

Given a budget of $55, how many steak and hamburger meals will James buy per month to maximize his total utility? What is the total utility realized?

9. Using the marginal utility schedule in question 8, begin in consumer equilibrium, and assume the price per hamburger meal falls from $5 to $2, all other factors held constant. What is the total utility realized?

10. Suppose the price of a BMW falls. Explain the law of demand based on the income and substitution effects.

ONLINE EXERCISES

Exercise 1

Visit the *Journal of Applied Behavioral Analysis* (http://www.envmed.rochester.edu/wwwrap/behavior/jaba/jabahome.htm). Browse this journal for studies of animal behavior that reflects economic concepts.

Exercise 2

Visit MediaSource (http://www.usadata.com/ms/magazine/index.htm). Do you subscribe to any of these magazines? In terms of consumer equilibrium analysis, how would a subscriber allocate a given budget among different magazines?

Exercise 3

How many different kinds and flavors of yogurt are there? Take a look at what Dannon (http://www.dannon .com/fyog_us.html) has. Why so many flavors?

Exercise 4

Visit the Diamond Information Center at http://www .adiamondisforever.com/. What statement does this site make about the marginal utility of diamonds?

 CHECKPOINT ANSWERS

When Dining Out, Do You Eat Smart?

Start with 1 taco (99 marginal utils/$3, or 33 marginal utils/$1). Then order a Coke (25 marginal utils/$1). Next order another taco (63 marginal utils/$3, or 21 marginal utils/$1). Now treat yourself to a flan (40 marginal utils/ $2, or 20 marginal utils/$1). Finish it all with a second Coke (5 marginal utils/$1). You have now spent your entire $10 budget. If you said you would order 2 Cokes, 2 tacos, and 1 flan following the principle of consumer equilibrium, although not a very nutritious choice, **YOU ARE CORRECT.**

Does the Substitution Effect Apply to Buying a Car?

Buying a higher-mpg car will reduce the cost per mile of driving relative to substitutes, such as riding a bus, train, or airplane. As the cost of driving falls, the substitution effect predicts Brad will drive more in the 40-mpg car than the 12,000 miles he now drives per year in the 25-mpg car. The extra cost of gasoline for driving over 12,000 miles per year in the 40-mpg must be subtracted from the $225 savings that was based on the assumption that Brad's miles driven per year would remain unchanged when he bought the 40-mpg car. If you said Brad will save less than $225, **YOU ARE CORRECT.**

PRACTICE QUIZ

For a visual explanation of the correct answers, visit the tutorial at http://tucker.swcollege.com.

1. As an individual consumes more of a given good, the marginal utility of that good to the consumer
   a. rises at an increasing rate.
   b. rises at a decreasing rate.
   c. falls.
   d. rises.

2. The amount of added utility that a consumer gains from the consumption of one more unit of a good is called
   a. incremental utility.
   b. total utility.
   c. diminishing utility.
   d. marginal utility.

3. A certain consumer buys only food and compact discs. If the quantity of food bought increases, while that of compact discs remains the same, the marginal utility of food will
   a. fall relative to the marginal utility of compact discs.
   b. rise relative to the marginal utility of compact discs.
   c. rise, but not as fast as the marginal utility of compact discs rises.
   d. fall, but not as fast as the marginal utility of compact discs falls.

4. Rational consumers will continue to consume two goods until the
   a. marginal utility per dollar's worth of the two goods is the same for the last dollar spent on each good.
   b. marginal utility is the same for each good for the last dollar spent on each good.
   c. prices of the two goods are equal for the last dollar spent on each good.
   d. prices of the two goods are unequal.

5. Assume a person's consumption of just the right amounts of pork and chicken is in equilibrium. We can conclude that the
   a. marginal utility of pork must equal the marginal utility of chicken.
   b. price of pork must equal the price of chicken.
   c. ratio of marginal cost to price must be the same in both the pork and the chicken markets.
   d. ratio of marginal utility to price must be the same for pork and chicken.

6. Assume an individual consumes only milk and dough-nuts and he/she has arranged consumption so that the last glass of milk yields 12 utils and the last doughnut 6 utils. If the price of milk is $1 per glass and the price of a doughnut is $.50, we can conclude that the
   a. consumer should consume less milk and more doughnuts.
   b. price of milk is too high relative to doughnuts.
   c. consumer should consume more milk and fewer doughnuts.
   d. consumer is in equilibrium.

7. Suppose an individual consumes pizza and cola. To reach consumer equilibrium, the individual must con-sume pizza and cola so that the
   a. price paid for the two goods is the same.
   b. marginal utility of the two goods is equal.
   c. ratio of marginal utility to price is the same for both goods.
   d. ratio of the marginal utility of cola to the marginal utility of pizza is 1.

8. A state of consumer equilibrium for goods consumed prevails when the
   a. marginal utility of all goods is the same for the last dollar spent for each good.
   b. marginal utility per dollar's worth of two goods is the same for the last dollar spent for each good.
   c. price of two goods is the same for the last dollar spent for each good.
   d. marginal cost per dollar spent on two goods is the same for the last dollar spent for each good.

9. The change in quantity demanded resulting from a change in purchasing power is known as the
   a. income effect.
   b. substitution effect.
   c. law of demand.
   d. consumer equilibrium effect.

EXHIBIT 4 Total Utility for Multiplex Tickets, Video Rentals, and Popcorn

Total Utility from Multiplex Tickets	Total Utility from Video Rentals	Total Utility from Popcorn
1 movie (30 utils)	1 video (14 utils)	1 bag (8 utils)
2 movies (54 utils)	2 videos (24 utils)	2 bags (13 utils)
3 movies (72 utils)	3 videos (30 utils)	3 bags (15 utils)
4 movies (84 utils)	4 videos (32 utils)	4 bags (16 utils)

10. In Exhibit 4, assume Multiplex tickets cost $6 each, video rentals cost $2 each, and bags of popcorn cost $1 each. What is the marginal utility of renting a third video?
    a. 6 utils
    b. 8 utils
    c. 10 utils
    d. 30 utils

11. In Exhibit 4, assume Multiplex tickets cost $6 each, video rentals cost $2 each, and bags of popcorn cost $1 each. Suppose the consumer has $12 per week to spend on Multiplex tickets, video rentals, and pop-corn. What combination of goods will give the con-sumer the most utility?
    a. 1 movie, 3 videos, and no popcorn
    b. 1 movie, 2 videos, and 2 bags of popcorn
    c. 1 movie, 1 video, and 4 bags of popcorn
    d. 2 movies, no videos, and no bags of popcorn

CHAPTER SEVEN

Production Costs

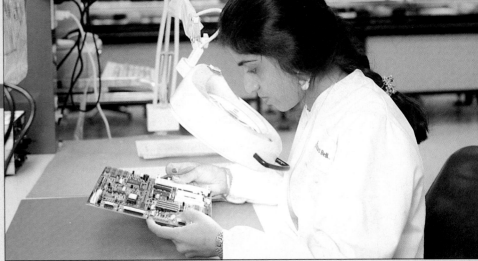

Suppose you dream of owning your own company. That's right! You want to be an entrepreneur. You crave the excitement of starting your own firm and making it successful. Instead of working for someone else, you want to be your own boss. You are under no illusions; it is going to take hard work and sacrifice.

You are an electrical engineer who is an expert at designing electronic components for bank teller machines and similar applications. So you quit your job and invest your nest egg in starting Computech (a mythical company). You lease factory space, hire employees, and purchase raw materials, and soon your company's products begin rolling off the assembly line. And production cost considerations influence each decision you make in this new business venture.

The purpose of this chapter is to study production and its relationship to various types of costs. Whether your company is new and small or an international giant, understanding costs is essential for success. In this chapter and the next chapter, you will follow Computech and learn the basic principles of production and the way various types of costs vary with output.

In this chapter, you will learn to solve these economics puzzles:

■ Why would an accountant say a firm is making a profit and an economist say it is losing money?

■ What is the difference between the short run and the long run?

■ Why are multi-screen movie theaters replacing single-screen theaters?

Costs and Profit

A basic assumption in economics is that the motivation for business decisions is profit maximization. Economists realize that managers of firms may sometimes pursue other goals, such as contributing to the United Way or building an empire for the purpose of ego satisfaction. But the profit maximization goal has proven to be the best theory to explain why managers of firms choose a particular level of output or price. To understand profit as a driving force for business firms, we must distinguish between the way economists measure costs and the way accountants measure costs.

Explicit and Implicit Costs

Explicit costs

Payments to nonowners of a firm for their resources.

Implicit costs

The opportunity costs of using resources owned by the firm.

Economists define the total opportunity cost of a business as the sum of **explicit costs** and **implicit costs**. Explicit costs are payments to nonowners of a firm for their resources. In our Computech example, explicit costs include the wages paid to labor, the rental charges for a plant, the cost of electricity, the cost of materials, and the cost of medical insurance. These resources are owned outside the firm and must be purchased with an actual payment to these "outsiders."

Implicit costs are the opportunity costs of using resources owned by the firm. These are opportunity costs of resources owned by the firm itself, and, therefore, the firm makes no actual payment to outsiders. When you started Computech, you gave up the opportunity to earn a salary as an electrical engineer for someone else's firm. When you invested your nest egg in your own enterprise, you gave up earning interest. You also used a building you own to warehouse Computech products. Although you made no payment to anyone, you gave up the opportunity to earn rental payments.

Economic and Accounting Profit

In everyday use, the word *profit* is defined as follows:

$$\text{Profit} = \text{total revenue} - \text{total cost}$$

Economists call this concept *accounting profit*. This popular formula is expressed in economics as

$$\text{Accounting profit} = \text{total revenue} - \text{total explicit cost}$$

Economic profit

Total revenue minus explicit and implicit costs.

Because economic decisions include implicit as well as explicit costs, economists use the concept **economic profit** instead of accounting profit. Economic profit is total revenue minus explicit and implicit costs. Economic profit can be positive, zero, or negative (an economic loss). Expressed as an equation:

$$\text{Economic profit} = \text{total revenue} - \text{total opportunity costs}$$

EXHIBIT 1   Computech's Accounting Versus Economic Profit

Item	Accounting Profit	Economic Profit
Total revenue	$500,000	$500,000
Less explicit costs:		
Wages and salaries	400,000	400,000
Materials	50,000	50,000
Interest paid	10,000	10,000
Other payments	10,000	10,000
Less implicit costs:		
Forgone salary	0	50,000
Forgone rent	0	10,000
Forgone interest	0	5,000
Equals profit	$30,000	−$ 35,000

or

Economic profit = total revenue − (explicit costs + implicit costs)

Exhibit 1 illustrates the importance of the difference between accounting profit and economic profit. Computech must know how well it is doing, so you hire an accounting firm to prepare a financial report. The exhibit shows that Computech earned total revenue of $500,000 in its first year of operation. Explicit costs for wages, materials, interest, and other payments totaled $470,000. Based on standard accounting procedures, this left an accounting profit of $30,000.

If the analysis ends with accounting profit, Computech is profitable. But accounting practice overstates profit. Because implicit costs are too subjective and therefore difficult to measure, accounting profit ignores implicit costs. A few examples will illustrate the importance of implicit costs. Your $50,000-a-year salary as a manager was forgone in order to spend all your time as owner of Computech. Also forgone were $10,000 in rental income and $5,000 in interest that you would have earned during the year by renting your building and putting your savings in the bank. Subtracting both explicit and implicit costs from total revenue, Computech had an economic loss of $35,000. The firm is failing to cover the opportunity costs of using its resources in the electronics industry. Thus, the firm's resources would earn a higher return if used for other alternatives.

How would you interpret a zero economic profit? It's not as bad as it sounds. Economists call this condition **normal profit**. Normal profit is the

Normal profit
The minimum profit necessary to keep a firm in operation. A firm that earns normal profit earns total revenue equal to its total opportunity cost.

Publishers Experiment with Lower Prices

Applicable Concepts: accounting profit and economic profit

Bantam Books this week is shipping to bookstores almost 100,000 copies of "Creature," a 329-page horror novel by John Saul. A hardcover novel of that length would normally carry a retail price of $18.95. But to entice Mr. Saul's large paperback audience to buy his book in hard cover, Bantam has priced it at $12.95. . . .

Indeed, book pricing is anything but an exact science. Determining the suggested retail price of a book is a matter of combining a mathematical formula with instinct.

"You have a basic formula—how much it costs you to make the book, the author's royalties and how much you'll spend to promote it," said Roger Donald, publisher of Little, Brown adult trade books. "But the formula is rarely right because you don't know how many copies it will sell. Yet you have to put a price, so you do it on the basis of your best guess."

The average novel or nonfiction book costs $1.50 to $2 a copy to manufacture, although the manufacturing cost of a heavily illustrated book like an art book can reach $10 a copy. The suggested retail price must also include the cost of composition, typesetting and jacket design as well as fixed costs like office space and editorial salaries. Advertising and promotion usually get 5 percent to 7 percent.

In addition, bookstores and wholesalers receive an average discount off the suggested retail price of 45 to 47 percent, meaning they pay the publishers a little more than $10 for a book they can sell for almost $20. Author royalties, also based on the cover price, range from 10 to 15 percent. Moreover, because books can be returned for full credit, the cover price must reflect a return rate currently averaging almost 40 percent for hardcover books.

When all those costs are subtracted, a publisher is lucky to make $1 on a book with a cover price of $19.95. In fact, publishers say they rarely make money on first printings, whether of 5,000 copies or 500,000. Their profit comes from subsequent printings, and from selling reprint rights for a paperback edition, a transaction in which the hardcover publisher splits the income with the author.

ANALYZE THE ISSUE

1. Suppose Bantam Books' accounting profit for the novel *Creature* is $1 per copy. Give an example of how an economist's calculation of profit would be different.
2. The above excerpt states that royalties paid to authors range from 10 to 15 percent of the cover price. Why don't the authors publish their own books? To simplify the analysis, assume that both the author-publisher company and Bantam Books can publish a book for the same explicit costs for typesetting, paper, warehousing, promotion, and so on.

Source: Edwin McDowell, "Publishers Experiment with Lower Prices," *New York Times*, May 8, 1989, p. D10. Copyright 1989 by The New York Times Company. Reprinted by permission.

minimum profit necessary to keep a firm in operation. Zero economic profit signifies there is just enough total revenue to pay the owners for all explicit and implicit costs. Stated differently, there is no benefit from reallocating resources to another use. For example, assume an owner earns zero economic profit, including an implicit (forfeited) cost of $50,000 per year that could be earned working for someone else. This means he or she earned as much as would have been earned in the next best employment opportunity.

CHECKPOINT

Should the Professor Go or Stay?

Professor Martin is considering leaving the university and opening a consulting business. For her services as a consultant, she would be paid $75,000 a year. To open this business, Professor Martin must convert a house from which she collects rent of $10,000 per year into an office and hire a secretary at a salary of $15,000 per year. Also, she must withdraw $10,000 from savings for miscellaneous expenses and forego earning 10 percent interest per year. The university pays Professor Martin $50,000 a year. Based only on economic decision-making, do you predict the professor will leave the university to start a new business?

Conclusion *Since business decision-making is based on economic profit, rather than accounting profit, the word* profit *in this text always means economic profit.*

Short-Run Production Costs

Having presented the basic definitions of total cost, the next step is to study cost theory. In this section, we explore the relationship between output and cost in the short run. In the next section, the time horizon shifts to the long run.

Short Run Versus Long Run

Suppose I asked you, "What is the difference between the short run and the long run?" Your answer might be that the short run is less than a year and the long run is over a year. Good guess, but wrong! Economists do not partition production decisions based on any specific number of days, months, or years. Instead, the distinction depends on the ability to vary the quantity of inputs or resources used in production. There are two types of inputs—**fixed inputs** and **variable inputs**. A fixed input is any resource for which the quantity cannot change during the period of time under consideration. For example, the physical size of a firm's plant and the production capacity of heavy machines cannot change easily within a short period of time. They must remain as fixed amounts while managers decide to vary output. In addition to fixed inputs, the firm uses *variable inputs* in the production process. A variable input is any resource for which the quantity can change during the period of time under consideration. For example, managers can hire fewer or more workers during a given year. They can also change the amount of materials and electricity used in production.

Now we can link the concepts of fixed and variable inputs to the **short run** and the **long run**. The short run is a period of time so short that there

Fixed input
Any resource for which the quantity cannot change during the period of time under consideration.

Variable input
Any resource for which the quantity can change during the period of time under consideration.

Short run
A period of time so short that there is at least one fixed input.

Long run
A period of time so long that all inputs are variable.

is at least one fixed input. For example, the short run is a period of time during which a firm can increase output by hiring more workers (variable input), while the size of the firm's plant (fixed input) remains unchanged. The firm's plant is the most difficult input to change quickly. The long run is a period of time so long that all inputs are variable. In the long run, the firm can build new factories or purchase new machinery. New firms can enter the industry, and existing firms may leave the industry.

The Production Function

Production function
The relationship between the maximum amounts of output a firm can produce and various quantities of inputs.

Having defined inputs, we can now describe the transforming of these inputs into outputs, using a concept called a **production function**. A production function is the relationship between the maximum amounts of output a firm can produce and various quantities of inputs. An assumption of the production function model we are about to develop is that the level of technology is fixed. Technological advances would mean more output is possible from a given quantity of inputs.

Exhibit 2(a) presents a short-run production function for Eaglecrest Vineyard. The variable input is the number of workers employed per day, and each worker is presumed to have equal job skills. The acreage, amount of fertilizer, and all other inputs are assumed to be fixed, and, therefore, our production model is operating in the short run. Employing zero workers produces no bushels of grapes. A single worker can produce 10 bushels per day, but a lot of time is wasted when one worker picks, loads containers, and transports the grapes to the winery. Adding the second worker raises output to 22 bushels per day because the workers divide the tasks and specialize. Adding four more workers raises total product to 50 bushels per day.

Marginal Product

Marginal product
The change in total output produced by adding one unit of a variable input, with all other inputs used being held constant.

The relationship between changes in total output and changes in labor is called the **marginal product**. Marginal product is the change in total output produced by adding one unit of a variable input, with all other inputs used being held constant. When Eaglecrest increases labor from zero to one worker, output rises from zero to 10 bushels produced per day. This increase is the result of the addition of one more worker. Therefore, the marginal product so far is 10 bushels per worker. Similar marginal product calculations generate the marginal product curve shown in Exhibit 2(b). Note that marginal product is plotted at the midpoints shown in the table because the change in total output occurs between each additional unit of labor used.

The Law of Diminishing Returns

Law of diminishing returns
The principle that beyond some point the marginal product decreases as additional units of a variable factor are added to a fixed factor.

A long-established economic law called the **law of diminishing returns** determines the shape of the marginal product curve. The law of diminishing returns states that beyond some point the marginal product decreases as additional units of a variable factor are added to a fixed factor. Because the law of diminishing returns assumes fixed inputs, this principle is a short-run, rather than a long-run, concept.

EXHIBIT 2

A Production Function and the Law of Diminishing Returns

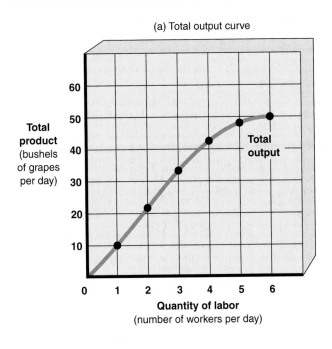

(a) Total output curve

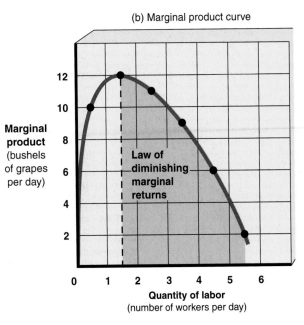

(b) Marginal product curve

Short-Run Production Function of Eaglecrest Vineyard

(1) Labor input (number of workers per day)	(2) Total output (bushels of grapes per day)	(3) Marginal product (bushels of grapes per day) [Δ(2)/Δ(1)]
0	0	
		10
1	10	
		12
2	22	
		11
3	33	
		9
4	42	
		6
5	48	
		2
6	50	

Part (a) shows how the total output of bushels of grapes per day increases as the number of workers increases while all other inputs remain constant. This figure is a short-run production function, which relates outputs to a one-variable input while all other inputs are fixed.

Part (b) illustrates the law of diminishing returns. The first worker adds 10 bushels of grapes per day, and marginal product is 10 bushels per day. Adding a second worker adds another 12 bushels of grapes per day to total output. This is the range of increasing marginal returns. After 2 workers, diminishing marginal returns set in, and marginal product declines continuously.

This law applies to production of both agricultural and nonagricultural products. Returning to Exhibit 2, we can identify and explain the law of diminishing returns in our Eaglecrest example. Initially, the total output curve rises quite rapidly as this firm hires the first two workers. The marginal product curve reflects the change in the total output curve because marginal product is the slope of the total output curve. As shown in Exhibit 2(b), the range from zero to two workers hired is called *increasing marginal returns*. In this range of output, the last worker adds more to total output than the previous worker.

Diminishing returns begin after the second worker is hired and the marginal product reaches its peak. Beyond two workers, diminishing returns occur, and the marginal product declines. The short-run assumption guarantees this condition. Eventually, the amount of land per worker falls as more workers are added to fixed quantities of land and other inputs used to produce wine. Similar reasoning applies to the Computech example introduced in the Chapter Preview. Assume Computech operates with a fixed plant size and a fixed number of machines and all other inputs except the number of workers are fixed. Those in the first group of workers hired divide the most important tasks among themselves, specialize, and achieve increasing returns. Then diminishing returns begin and continue as Computech employs each additional worker. The reason is that as more workers are added, they must share fixed inputs, such as machinery. Some workers are underemployed because they are standing around waiting for a machine to become available. Also, as more workers are hired, there are fewer important tasks to perform. As a result, marginal product declines. In the extreme case, marginal product would be negative. At some number of workers, they start stepping on each other's toes when they must work with limited floor space, machines, and other fixed inputs. No profit-seeking firm would ever hire workers with zero or negative marginal product. Chapter 11 explains the labor market in more detail and shows how Computech decides exactly how many workers to hire.

Short-Run Cost Formulas

In order to make production decisions in either the short run or the long run, a business must determine the costs associated with producing various levels of output. Using Computech, you will study the relationship between two "families" of short-run costs and output: first, the total cost curves and, next, the average cost curves.

Total Cost Curves

Total Fixed Cost   As production expands in the short run, costs are divided into two basic categories—**total fixed cost** and **total variable cost.** Total fixed cost consists of costs that do not vary as output varies and that must be paid even if output is zero. These are payments that the firm must make in the short run regardless of the level of output. Even if a firm, such as Computech, produces nothing, it still must pay rent, interest on loans, property taxes, and fire insurance. Fixed costs are therefore beyond man-

Total fixed cost
Costs that do not vary as output varies and that must be paid even if output is zero. These are payments that the firm must make in the short run, regardless of the level of output.

Total variable cost
Costs that are zero when output is zero and vary as output varies.

agement's control in the short run. The total fixed cost (*TFC*) for Computech is $100, as shown in column 2 of Exhibit 3.

Total Variable Cost   As the firm expands from zero output, total variable cost is added to total fixed cost. Total variable cost consists of costs that are zero when output is zero and vary as output varies. These costs relate to the costs of variable inputs. Examples include wages for hourly workers, electricity, fuel, and raw materials. As a firm uses more input to produce output, its variable costs will increase. Management can control variable costs in the short run by changing the level of output. Exhibit 3 lists the total variable cost (*TVC*) for Computech in column 3.

Total Cost   Given total fixed cost and total variable cost, the firm can calculate **total cost**. Total cost is the sum of total fixed cost and total variable cost at each level of output. As a formula:

$$TC \; = \; TFC \; + \; TVC$$

Total cost
The sum of total fixed cost and total variable cost at each level of output.

Total cost (*TC*) for Computech is shown in column 4 of Exhibit 3. Exhibit 4(a) uses data in Exhibit 3 to construct graphically the relationships among total cost, total fixed cost, and total variable cost. Note that the *TVC* curve varies with the level of output and the *TFC* curve does not. The *TC* curve is simply the *TVC* curve plus the vertical distance between the *TC* and *TVC* curves, which represents *TFC*.

Average Cost Curves

In addition to total cost, the *per-unit cost*, or *average cost*, interests firms. Average cost, like product price, is stated on a per-unit basis. The last three columns in Exhibit 3 are *average fixed cost* (*AFC*), *average variable cost* (*AVC*), and *average total cost* (*ATC*). These average, or per-unit, curves are also shown in Exhibit 4(b). These three concepts are defined as follows:

Average Fixed Cost   As output increases, **average fixed cost** (*AFC*) falls continuously. Average fixed cost is total fixed cost divided by the quantity of output produced. Written as a formula:

$$AFC = \frac{TFC}{Q}$$

Average fixed cost
Total fixed cost divided by the quantity of output produced.

As shown in Exhibit 4(b), the *AFC* curve approaches the horizontal axis as output expands. This is because larger output numbers divide into *TFC* and cause *AFC* to become smaller and smaller.

Average Variable Cost   The **average variable cost** (*AVC*) in our example forms a U-shaped curve. Average variable cost is total variable cost divided by the quantity of output produced. Written as a formula:

$$AVC = \frac{TVC}{Q}$$

Average variable cost
Total variable cost divided by the quantity of output produced.

EXHIBIT 3　Short-Run Cost Schedule for Computech

(1) Total Product (Q)	(2) Total Fixed Cost (TFC)	(3) Total Variable Cost (TVC)	(4) Total Cost (TC)	(5) Marginal Cost (MC)	(6) Average Fixed Cost (AFC)	(7) Average Variable Cost (AVC)	(8) Average Total Cost (ATC)
0	$100	$ 0	$100		—	—	—
				$ 50			
1	100	50	150		$100	$50	$150
				34			
2	100	84	184		50	42	92
				24			
3	100	108	208		33	36	69
				19			
4	100	127	227		25	32	57
				23			
5	100	150	250		20	30	50
				30			
6	100	180	280		17	30	47
				38			
7	100	218	318		14	31	45
				48			
8	100	266	366		13	33	46
				59			
9	100	325	425		11	36	47
				75			
10	100	400	500		10	40	50
				95			
11	100	495	595		9	45	54
				117			
12	100	612	712		8	51	59

The *AVC* curve is also drawn in Exhibit 4(b). At first, the *AVC* curve falls, and then after an output of 6 units per hour, the *AVC* curve rises. Thus, the *AVC* curve is U-shaped. The explanation for the shape of the *AVC* curve is given in the next section.

Average total cost
Total cost divided by the quantity of output produced.

Average Total Cost　Average total cost (*ATC*) is sometimes referred to as *per-unit cost*. The average total cost is total cost divided by the quantity of output produced. Written as a formula:

$$ATC = AFC + AVC = \frac{TC}{Q}$$

EXHIBIT 4

Short-Run Cost Curves

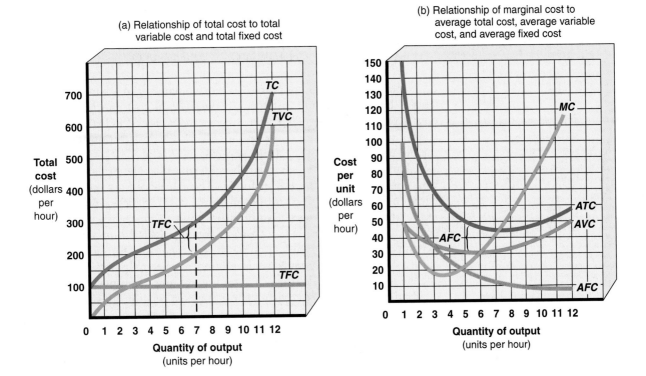

(a) Relationship of total cost to total variable cost and total fixed cost

(b) Relationship of marginal cost to average total cost, average variable cost, and average fixed cost

The curves in this exhibit are derived by plotting data from Exhibit 3. Part (a) shows that the total cost (TC) at each level of output is the sum of total variable cost (TVC) and total fixed cost (TFC). Because the TFC curve does not vary with output, the shape of the TC curve is determined by the shape of the TVC curve. The vertical distance between the TC and the TVC curves is TFC.

In part (b), the marginal cost (MC) curve at first decreases, then reaches a minimum, and then increases as output increases. The MC curve intersects both the average variable cost (AVC) curve and the average total cost (ATC) curve at the minimum point on each of these cost curves. The average fixed cost (AFC) curve declines continuously as output expands. AFC is also the difference at any quantity of output between the ATC and the AVC curves.

Like the *AVC* curve, the *ATC* curve is U-shaped, as shown in Exhibit 4(b). At first, the *ATC* curve falls because its component parts—*AVC* and *AFC*—are falling. As output continues to rise, the *AVC* curve begins to rise, while the *AFC* curve falls continuously. Beyond the output of 7 units per hour, the rise in the *AVC* curve is greater than the fall in the *AFC* curve, which causes the *ATC* curve to rise in a U-shaped pattern.

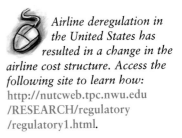

Airline deregulation in the United States has resulted in a change in the airline cost structure. Access the following site to learn how: http://nutcweb.tpc.nwu.edu /RESEARCH/regulatory /regulatory1.html.

Marginal cost

The change in total cost when one additional unit of output is produced.

Marginal Cost   Marginal analysis asks how much it costs to produce an *additional* unit of output. Column 5 in Exhibit 3 is **marginal cost.** Marginal cost is the change in total cost when one additional unit of output is produced. Stated differently, marginal cost is the ratio of the change in total cost to a one-unit change in output. Written as a formula:

$$MC = \frac{\text{change in } TC}{\text{change in } Q} = \frac{\text{change in } TVC}{\text{change in } Q}$$

Note that marginal cost can also be calculated from changes in *TVC*. This is because the only difference between total cost and total variable cost is total fixed cost. Thus, the changes in *TC* and *TVC* with each unit change in output are the same amount. To check this relationship, look at the per-unit changes in *TC*, *TVC*, and *MC* in Exhibit 3.

Changing output by one unit at a time simplifies the marginal cost calculations in our Computech example. The marginal cost data are listed between output levels to show that marginal cost is the change in total cost as the output level changes. Exhibit 4(b) shows this marginal cost schedule graphically. In the short run, a firm's marginal cost falls initially as output expands, eventually reaches a minimum, and then rises, forming a J-shaped curve. Note that marginal cost is plotted at the midpoints because the change in cost occurs between each additional unit of output.

Exhibit 5 summarizes a firm's short-run cost relationships.

Marginal Cost Relationships

Part (b) of Exhibit 4 presents two important relationships that require explanation. First, we will explain the rule that links the marginal cost curve to the average cost curves. Second, we will return to the marginal product curve in Exhibit 2(b) and explain its connection to the marginal cost curve.

The Marginal-Average Rule

Marginal-average rule

The rule that states when marginal cost is below average cost, average cost falls. When marginal cost is above average cost, average cost rises. When marginal cost equals average cost, average cost is at its minimum point.

Observe that the *MC* curve in Exhibit 4(b) intersects both the *AVC* curve and the *ATC* curve at their minimum points. This is not accidental. It is a result of a relationship called the **marginal-average rule.** The marginal-average rule states that when marginal cost is below average cost, average cost falls. When marginal cost is above average cost, average cost rises. When marginal cost equals average cost, average cost is at its minimum point. The marginal-average rule applies to grades, weights, and any average figure.

Perhaps the best way to understand this rule is to apply it to a noneconomic example. Suppose there are 20 students in your classroom and each student has a grade point average (GPA) of 4.0. The average GPA of the class is therefore 4.0. Now let another student who has a GPA of 2.0 join the class. The new average GPA of 21 students in the class falls to 3.9. The average GPA was pulled down because the *marginal* GPA of the additional student was less than the *average* GPA of the other students. On the other

EXHIBIT 5   Short-Run Cost Formulas

Cost Concept	Formula	Graph
Total cost (*TC*)	$TC = TFC + TVC$	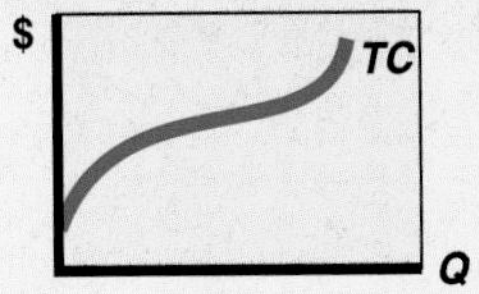
Marginal cost (*MC*)	$\dfrac{\text{change in } TC}{\text{change in } Q} = \dfrac{\text{change in } TVC}{\text{change in } Q}$	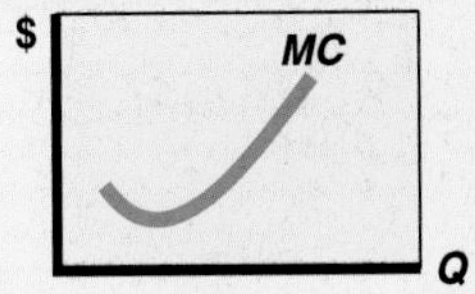
Average fixed cost (*AFC*)	$AFC = \dfrac{TFC}{Q}$	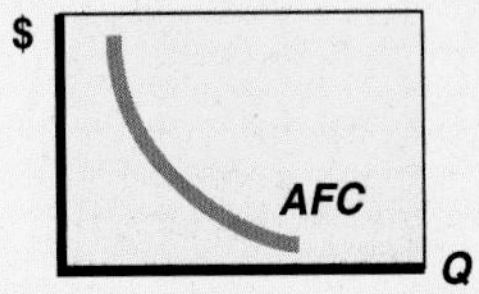
Average variable cost (*AVC*)	$AVC = \dfrac{TVC}{Q}$	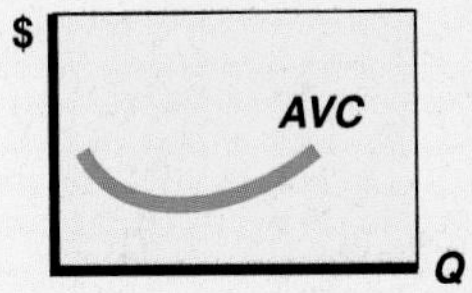
Average total cost (*ATC*)	$ATC = \dfrac{TC}{Q}$	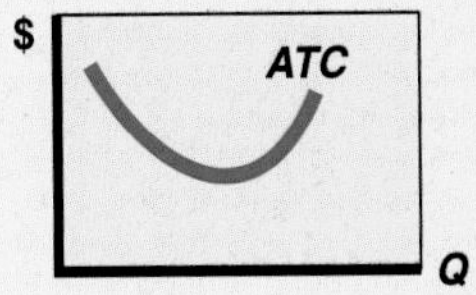

hand, let's start with 20 students with a 2.0 GPA and add a student who has a 4.0 GPA. In this case, the new average GPA of 21 students rises from 2.0 to 2.1. Thus, the *marginal* GPA of the last student was greater than the *average* GPA of all students in class before the addition of new students.

Now consider the *MC* curve in part (b) of Exhibit 4. In the range of output from 0 to 6 units per hour, the *MC* curve is below the *AVC* curve, and *AVC* is falling. Beyond 6 units per hour, the *MC* curve is above *AVC*,

Did Michael Jordan Beat the Marginal-Average Rule?

Michael Jordan, formerly of the Chicago Bulls, is one of the finest players in the history of basketball. Suppose he has an average of 33 points per game over the first 10 games of the season and then scores 20, 25, 40, 50, and 20 points in the next five games. Did Michael Jordan beat the marginal-average rule?

and *AVC* is rising. Hence, the relationship between *AVC* and *MC* conforms to the marginal-average rule. It follows that the *MC* curve intersects the *AVC* at its lowest point. This analysis also applies to the relationship between the *MC* and *ATC* curves. Initially, the *MC* curve is less than the *ATC* curve is at its minimum. Beginning with 8 units of output, the *MC* curve exceeds the *ATC* curve, causing the ATC curve to rise.

Marginal Cost's Mirror Image

Since the *MC* curve determines the U-shape of the *AVC* and *ATC* curves, we must explain the J-shape of the *MC* curve. Exhibit 6 illustrates that the shape of the *MC* curve is the mirror reflection of the shape of the marginal product (*MP*) curve. Comparing parts (a) and (b) of Exhibit 6 gives this conclusion: *The marginal cost declines as the marginal product of a variable input rises if the wage rate is constant. Beginning at the point of diminishing returns, the marginal cost rises as the marginal product of a variable input declines.* As explained earlier in this chapter, the law of diminishing returns is the declining portion of the *MP* curve that corresponds to the rising portion of the *MC* curve.

To understand why this relationship exists, we return to the case of Eaglecrest Vineyard presented earlier in Exhibit 2. Now we again assume that labor is the only variable input and add the new important assumption that the wage rate is constant at $100 per day. When Eaglecrest moves from zero labor to hire one worker, its total output rises from zero to 10 bushels of grapes per day. As explained earlier, the marginal product is also 10 bushels, and the marginal cost is $100/10 = $10 ($\Delta TC/\Delta Q = \Delta TC/MP$). When Eaglecrest hires the second worker, total output rises by 12 bushels per day. Hiring this worker increases the firm's total cost by $100, while the marginal product rises to 12 bushels. The marginal cost of the second worker therefore falls to a minimum at $100/12 = $8.33. At this point, it is noteworthy that the minimum point on the *MC* curve corresponds to the maximum point on the *MP* curve. The third worker hired yields only 11 additional bushels of grapes per day, so marginal cost rises to $9.09. Thus, diminishing returns begin with the third worker, and the marginal cost continues to rise as more workers are hired.

EXHIBIT 6

The Inverse Relationship Between Marginal Product and Marginal Cost

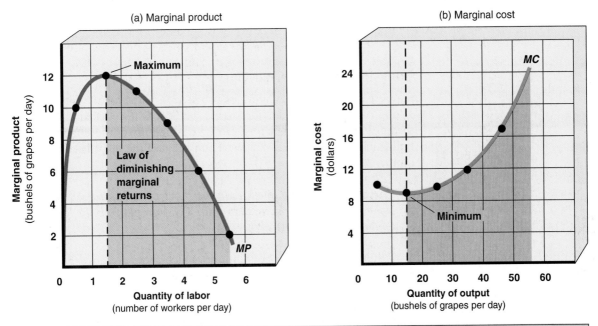

(1) Labor input (number of workers per day)	(2) Total output (bushels of grapes per day)	(3) Marginal product (bushels of grapes per day) [Δ(2)/Δ(1)]	(4) Total cost per day [$100x(1)]	(5) Marginal cost [Δ(4)/(3)]
0	0		$ 0	
		10		$10.00
1	10		100	
		12		8.33
2	22		200	
		11		9.09
3	33		300	
		9		11.11
4	42		400	
		6		16.66
5	48		500	
		2		50.00
6	50		600	

Part (a) represents the marginal product of labor (MP) curve. At first, each additional worker hired adds more to output than does the previously hired worker, and the MP curve rises until a maximum is reached at two workers hired. At three workers, the law of diminishing returns sets in, and each additional worker hired adds less output than previously hired workers.

Part (b) shows the marginal cost (MC) curve is a U-shaped curve that is inversely related to the MP curve. Assuming the wage rate remains constant, as the MP curve rises, the MC curve falls. When the MP curve reaches a maximum at 2 workers, the MC curve is at a minimum. As diminishing returns set in and the MP curve falls, the MC curve rises.

Long-Run Production Costs

As explained earlier in this chapter, the long run is a time period long enough to change the quantity of all fixed inputs. A firm can, for example, build a larger or smaller factory or vary the capacity of its machinery. In this section, we will discuss how varying factory size, and *all* other inputs, in the long run affects the relationship between production and costs.

Long-Run Average Cost Curves

Suppose Computech is making its production plans for the future. Taking a long-run view of production means the firm is not locked into a small-, medium-, or large-sized factory. However, once any of those factory sizes is built, the firm operates in the short run because the plant becomes a fixed input.

> **Conclusion** *A firm operates in the short run when there is insufficient time to alter some fixed input. The firm plans in the long run when all inputs are variable.*

Exhibit 7 illustrates a condition in which there are only three possible factory sizes Computech might select. Short-run cost curves representing these three possible plant sizes are labeled $SRATC_s$, $SRATC_m$, and $SRATC_l$. SR is the abbreviation for short run, and ATC stands for average total cost. The subscripts s, m, and l represent small, medium, and large plant size, respectively. In the previous sections, there was no need to use SR for short run because we were discussing only short-run cost curves and not long-run cost curves.

Suppose Computech estimates that it will be producing an output level of 6 units per hour for the foreseeable future. Which plant size should the company choose? It will build the plant size represented by $SRATC_s$ because this affords a lower cost of $30 per unit (point A) than the factory size represented by $SRATC_m$, which is $40 per unit (point B).

What if production is expected to be 12 units per hour? In this case, the firm will choose the plant size represented by $SRATC_l$. This plant size gives a cost of $30 per unit (point C), rather than a cost of $40 per unit (point D).

> **Conclusion** *The plant size selected by a firm in the long run depends on the expected level of production.*

Using the three short-run average cost curves shown in Exhibit 7, we can construct the firm's **long-run average cost curve** (*LRAC* curve). The long-run average cost curve traces the lowest cost per unit at which a firm can produce any level of output after the firm can build any desired plant size. The *LRAC* curve is often called the firm's planning curve. In Exhibit 8, the heavily shaded curve represents the *LRAC* curve.

Long-run average cost curve

The curve that traces the lowest cost per unit at which a firm can produce any level of output when the firm can build any desired plant size.

EXHIBIT 7

The Relationship Between Three Factory Sizes and the Long-Run Average Cost Curve

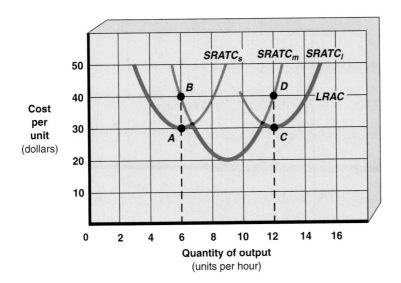

Each of the three short-run ATC curves in the exhibit corresponds to a different size. Assuming these are the only three plant-size choices, a firm can choose any one of these plant sizes in the long run. For example, a young firm may operate a small plant represented by U-shaped short-run average total cost curve SRATC$_s$. As a firm matures and demand for its product expands, it can decide to build a larger factory, corresponding to either SRATC$_m$ or SRATC$_l$. The long-run average cost (LRAC) curve is the heavily shaded scalloped curve joining the short-run curves below their intersections.

Exhibit 8 shows there are actually an infinite number of possible plant sizes from which managers can choose in the long run. As the intersection points of the short-run average total cost curves move closer and closer together, the lumps in the *LRAC* curve shown in Exhibit 8 disappear. With a great variety of plant sizes, the corresponding short-run ATC curves trace a smooth *LRAC* curve. When the *LRAC* curve falls, the tangency points are to the left of the minimum points on the short-run *ATC* curves. As the *LRAC* curve rises, the tangency points are to the right of the minimum points on the short-run *ATC* curves.

EXHIBIT 8

The Long-Run Average Cost Curve When the Number of Factory Sizes Is Unlimited

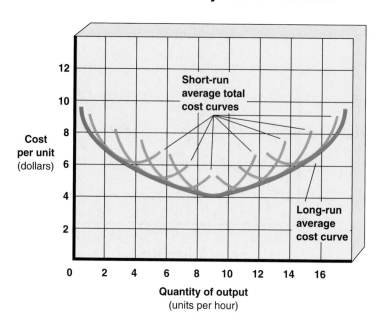

There are an infinite number of possible short-run ATC *curves that correspond to different plant sizes. The long-run average cost* (LRAC) *curve is the green curve tangent to each of the possible red short-run* ATC *curves.*

Different Scales of Production

Exhibit 8 depicted long-run average cost as a U-shaped curve. In this section, we will discuss the reasons why *LRAC* first falls and then rises when output expands in the long run. In addition, we will learn that the *LRAC* curve can have a variety of shapes. Note that the law of diminishing returns is not an explanation here because in the long run there are no fixed inputs.

For simplicity, Exhibit 9 excludes possible short-run *ATC* curves that touch points along the *LRAC* curve. Typically, a young firm starts small and builds larger plants as it matures. As the scale of operation expands, the *LRAC* curve can follow three different patterns. Over the lowest range of output from zero to Q_1, the firm experiences **economies of scale**. Economies of scale exist when the long-run average cost curve declines as the firm increases output.

There are several reasons for economies of scale. First, a larger firm can increase the *division of labor* and *use of specialization*. Adam Smith noted in *Wealth of Nations*, published in 1776, that the output of a pin factory is greater when one worker draws the wire, a second straightens it, a third

Economies of scale
A situation in which the long-run average cost curve declines as the firm increases output.

EXHIBIT 9

A Long-Run Average Cost Curve with Constant Returns to Scale

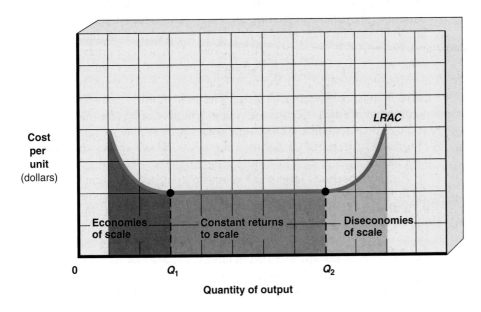

The long-run average cost (LRAC) curve illustrates a firm that experiences economies of scale until output level Q_1 is reached. Between output levels Q_1 and Q_2, the LRAC curve is flat, and there are constant returns to scale. Beyond output level Q_2, the firm experiences diseconomies of scale, and the LRAC curve rises.

cuts it, a fourth grinds the point, and a fifth makes the head of the pin. As a firm initially expands, having more workers allows managers to break a job into small tasks. Then each worker—including managers—can specialize by mastering narrowly defined tasks, rather than trying to be a jack-of-all-trades.[1] The classic example is Henry Ford's assembly line, which greatly reduced the cost of producing automobiles. Today, McDonald's trains workers at "Hamburger University"; then some workers prepare food, some specialize in taking orders, and a few workers specialize in the drive-in window operation.

Second, economies of scale result from greater *efficiency of capital*. Suppose machine A costs $1,000 and produces 1,000 units per day. Machine B costs $4,000, but it is technologically more efficient and has a capacity of 8,000 units per day. The low-output firm will find it too costly to purchase machine B, so it uses machine A, and its average cost is $1. The large-scale

Find information on economies of scale in rail-based transit systems at http://nutcweb.tpc.nwu.edu/RESEARCH/carrier/carrier.html.

McDonald's, with thousands of restaurants around the world, standardizes menus and operating procedures to take advantage of economies of scale. See their site at http://www.mcdonalds.com.

---

[1]Adam Smith, *An Inquiry into the Nature and Causes of the Wealth of Nations* (1776; reprint, New York: Random House, 1937): 4–6.

firm can afford to purchase machine *B* and produce more efficiently at a per-unit cost of only $.50.

The *LRAC* curve may not turn upward and form the U-shaped cost curve in Exhibit 8. Between some levels of output, such as Q_1 and Q_2 in Exhibit 9, the *LRAC* curve no longer declines. In this range of output, the firm increases its plant size, but the *LRAC* curve remains flat. Economists call this scale of operation **constant returns to scale**. Constant returns to scale exist when the long-run average cost curve does not change as the firm increases output. Economists believe this is the shape of the *LRAC* curve in most real-world industries. The scale of operation is important for competitive reasons. Consider a young firm producing less than output Q_1 and competing against a more established firm producing in the constant-returns-to-scale range of output. The *LRAC* curve shows that the older firm has an average cost advantage.

As a firm becomes large and expands output beyond some level, such as Q_2 in Exhibit 9, it encounters **diseconomies of scale**. Diseconomies of scale exist when the long-run average cost curve rises as the firm increases output. A large-scale firm becomes harder to manage. As the firm grows, the chain of command lengthens, and communication becomes more complex. Everyone must use forms to communicate instead of direct conversation. Firms become too bureaucratic, and operations bog down in red tape. Layer upon layer of management are paid big salaries to shuffle papers that have little or nothing to do with producing output. Consequently, it is no surprise that a firm can become too big and these management problems can cause the average cost of production to rise.

Steven Jobs, founder of Apple Computer Company, stated:

> *When you are growing [too big], you start adding middle management like crazy. . . . People in the middle have no understanding of the business, and because of that, they screw up communications. To them, it's just a job. The corporation ends up with mediocre people that form a layer of concrete.*[2]

Constant returns to scale
A situation in which the long-run average cost curve does not change as the firm increases output.

Diseconomies of scale
A situation in which the long-run average cost curve rises as the firm increases output.

---

[2]Deborah Wise and Catherine Harris, "Apple's New Crusade," *Business Week*, November 26, 1984, p. 156.

Invasion of the Monster Movie Theaters

Applicable Concept: economies and diseconomies of scale

A few decades ago most movie theaters had a single screen and offered just one film and few concession stand choices. Now theaters are bigger and better than ever. Megaplexes, defined as cinemas with 16 or more screens, offer several movies at the same time, espresso coffee, gourmet popcorn, Haagen Daz ice cream, and sometimes valet parking. These megaplexes, with stadium seating providing easier viewing, have become the industry standard.

The following article illustrates the competitive advantage of economies of scale:

The marquee at Water Tower Cinema [Gastonia, N.C.] was bare on Wednesday—a first in the theater's more than 10-year history. The four-screen theater that in its heyday sold out its weekend movies, shut down Tuesday, leaving Gaston County again without a discount movie house. Village Twin, a 99-cent theater formerly located on U.S. 29–74, closed in the summer of 1986 because of declining attendance.

An analyst who follows the movie theater industry for First Union Capital Markets in Charlotte said the owners of second-run theaters—especially small ones—face several challenges. "In the age of megaplexes, a four-screen theater stands out on the negative side. In general we're moving to a lot more screens and a lot less theaters," Bishop Cheen said. "If you only have four screens, you only have four reasons for a patron to leave home and spend money."[1]

Kurt Hall, executive vice president of United Artists Entertainment Co., stated his concern for diseconomies of scale:

When building new theaters, United Artists is limiting its screens per site to about 15, half as many as AMC [American Multi-Cinema, Inc.]. United Artists fears

that a larger megaplex won't pull in enough volume and could suffer a fate similar to Tandy Corp.'s Incredible Universe, the "big-box" electronics chain that closed this year. "Over 16 screens, the economics start to fall apart."[2]

1. Explain why the long-run average cost curve for movie theaters falls (economies of scale) as movie theaters add screens.
2. Explain why the long-run average cost curve for movie theaters rises (diseconomies of scale) beyond some number of screens.

[1]Audrey Y. Williams, "Cut-Rate Movie Theater Has Closed," *Charlotte Observer*, October 9, 1997, p. 1A.
[2]Kevin Helliker, "Monster Movie Theaters Invade the Cinema Landscape," *Wall Street Journal*, May 13, 1997, p. B1.

KEY CONCEPTS

Explicit costs
Implicit costs
Economic profit
Normal profit
Fixed input
Variable input
Short run

Long run
Production function
Marginal product
Law of diminishing
    returns
Total fixed cost

Total variable cost
Total cost
Average fixed cost
Average variable cost
Average total cost
Marginal cost

Marginal-average rule
Long-run average cost
    curve
Economies of scale
Constant returns to scale
Diseconomies of scale

SUMMARY

■ **Economic profit** is equal to total revenue minus both **explicit** and **implicit costs.** Implicit costs are the opportunity costs of forgone returns to resources owned by the firm. Economic profit is important for decision-making purposes because it includes implicit costs and accounting profit does not. Accounting profit equals total revenue minus explicit costs.

■ The **short run** is a time period during which a firm has at least one fixed input, such as its factory size. The **long run** for a firm is defined as a period during which all inputs are variable.

■ A **production function** is the relationship between output and inputs. Holding all other factors of production constant, the production function shows the total output as the amount of one input, such as labor, varies.

■ **Marginal product** is the change in total output caused by a one-unit change in a variable input, such as the number of workers hired. The **law of diminishing returns** states that after some level of output in the short run, each unit of the variable input yields smaller and smaller marginal product. This range of declining marginal product is the region of diminishing returns.

★ **Total fixed cost** consists of costs that cannot vary with the level of output, such as rent for office space. Total fixed cost is the cost of inputs that do not change as the firm changes output in the short run. **Total variable cost** consists of costs that vary with the level of output, such as wages. Total variable cost is the cost

of variable inputs used in production. **Total cost** is the sum of total fixed cost and total variable cost.

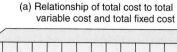

Total cost

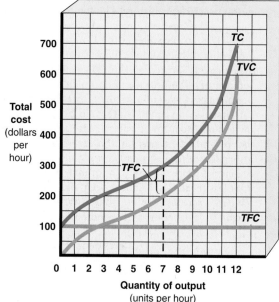

(a) Relationship of total cost to total variable cost and total fixed cost

★ **Marginal cost** is the change in total cost associated with one additional unit of output. **Average fixed cost** is the total fixed cost divided by total output. **Average** variable cost is the total variable cost divided by total output. **Average total cost** is the total cost, or the sum of average fixed cost and average variable cost, divided by output.

Average total cost

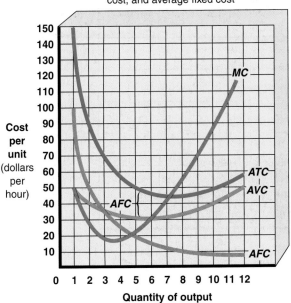

(b) Relationship of marginal cost to average total cost, average variable cost, and average fixed cost

- The **marginal-average rule** explains the relationship between marginal cost and average cost. When the marginal cost is less than the average cost, the average cost falls. When the marginal cost is greater than the average cost, the average cost rises. Following this rule, the marginal cost curve intersects the average variable cost curve and the average total cost curve at their minimum points.

★ **Marginal cost** and **marginal product** are mirror images of each other. Assuming a constant wage rate, marginal cost equals the wage rate divided by the marginal product. Increasing returns cause marginal cost to fall, and diminishing returns cause marginal

cost to rise. This explains the U-shaped marginal cost curve.

Marginal product

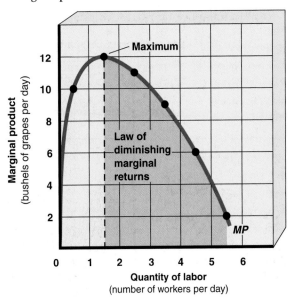

Marginal cost

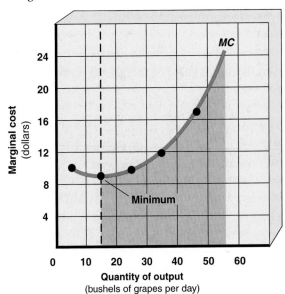

★ The **long-run average cost curve** is a curve drawn tangent to all possible short-run average total cost curves. When the long-run average cost curve decreases as output increases, the firm experiences **economies of scale**. If the long-run average cost curve remains unchanged as output increases, the firm experiences **constant returns to scale**. If the long-run average cost curve increases as output curve increases, the firm experiences **diseconomies of scale**.

Long-run average cost curve

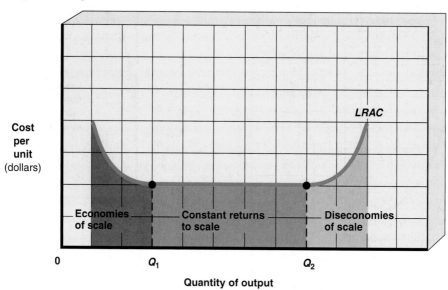

SUMMARY OF CONCLUSION STATEMENTS

■ Since business decision-making is based on economic profit, rather than accounting profit, the word *profit* in this text always means economic profit.

■ The marginal cost declines as the marginal product of a variable input rises if the wage rate is constant. Beginning at the point of diminishing returns, the marginal cost rises as the marginal product of a variable input declines.

■ A firm operates in the short run when there is insufficient time to alter some fixed input. The firm plans in the long run when all inputs are variable.

■ The plant size selected by a firm in the long run depends on the expected level of production.

STUDY QUESTIONS AND PROBLEMS

1. Indicate whether each of the following is an explicit cost or an implicit cost.
   a. A manager's salary
   b. Payments to IBM for computers
   c. A salary forgone by the owner of a firm by operating his or her own company
   d. Interest forgone on a loan an owner makes to his or her own company
   e. Medical insurance payments a company makes for its employees
   f. Income forgone while going to college

2. Suppose you own a video tape rental store. List some of the fixed inputs and variable inputs you would use in operating the store.

3. a. Construct the marginal product schedule for the following production function:

Labor	Total output	Marginal product
0	0	
1	8	_____
2	18	_____
3	30	_____
4	43	_____
5	55	_____
6	65	_____
7	73	_____
8	79	_____
9	82	_____
10	80	_____

b. Graph the total output and marginal product curves, and identify increasing and diminishing marginal returns.

4. Consider this statement: "Total output starts falling when diminishing returns occur." Do you agree or disagree? Explain.

5. What effect might a decrease in the demand for video tape recorders have on the short-run average total cost curve for this product?

6. a. Construct the following cost schedule for a firm operating in the short run:

b. Graph the average variable cost, average total cost, and marginal cost curves.

7. Explain why the average total cost curve and the average variable cost curve move closer together as output expands.

8. Ace Manufacturing produces 1,000 hammers per day. The total fixed cost for the plant is $5,000 per day, and the total variable cost is $15,000 per day. Calculate the average fixed cost, average variable cost, average total cost, and total cost at the current output level.

9. An owner of a firm estimates that the average total cost is $6.71 and the marginal cost is $6.71 at the current level of output. Explain the relationship between these marginal cost and average total cost figures.

10. What short-run effect might a decline in the demand for electronic components for bank teller machines have on Computech's average total cost curve?

11. For mathematically minded students, what is the algebraic relationship between the equation for output and the equation for marginal product in Exhibit 2? Explain the circumstances under which the long-run supply curve for an industry is a horizontal line. Next, explain the circumstances under which the long-run supply curve for an industry is an upward-sloping line.

Total Product (Q)	Total Fixed Cost (TFC)	Total Variable Cost (TVC)	Total Cost (TC)	Marginal Cost (MC)	Average Fixed Cost (AFC)	Average Variable Cost (AVC)	Average Total Cost (ATC)
0	$ 50	$ ___	$ 50	$ ___	$ ___	$ ___	___
1	___	___	$ 70	___	___	___	___
2	___	___	$ 85	___	___	___	___
3	___	___	$ 95	___	___	___	___
4	___	___	$100	___	___	___	___
5	___	___	$110	___	___	___	___
6	___	___	$130	___	___	___	___
7	___	___	$165	___	___	___	___
8	___	___	$215	___	___	___	___
9	___	___	$275	___	___	___	___

ONLINE EXERCISES

Exercise 1

Visit Business Cycle Indicators Home Page (http://www .globalexposure.com/). Select Wages/Labor, and follow these steps:

1. Under Wages and Compensation, choose Percent change from previous quarter, AR.

2. Under Productivity, choose Percent change over 1-quarter span, AR.

3. Explain how these two graphs are related to each other.

Exercise 2

Visit MovieLink (http://www.movielink.com/). Explain how movie theaters reflect both economies and diseconomies of scale.

Exercise 3

To view an original *Fortune* magazine article discussing "increasing returns," visit http://www.pathfinder.com /fortune/magazine/1996/960429/economy.html. Is this article confusing "increasing returns" with "economies of scale"?

Exercise 4

The Air Transport Association of America has produced an online Airline Handbook that provides information on airline economics and the structure of airline costs. Access this site at http://www.air-transport.org/handbk /chaptr04.htm. Summarize the major components of airline costs.

CHECKPOINT ANSWERS

Should the Professor Go or Stay?

In the consulting business, the accounting profit is $60,000. An accountant would calculate profit as the annual revenue of $75,000 less the explicit cost of $15,000 per year for the secretary's salary. However, the accountant would neglect implicit costs. Professor Martin's business venture would have implicit costs of $10,000 in forgone rent, $50,000 in forgone earnings, and $1,000 in forgone annual interest on the $10,000 she took out of savings. Her economic profit is −$1,000, calculated as the accounting profit of $60,000 less the total implicit costs of $61,000. If you said the professor will pass up the potential accounting profit and stay with the university to avoid an economic loss, **YOU ARE CORRECT.**

Did Michael Jordan Beat the Marginal-Average Rule?

Since Jordan's marginal points in games 11 and 12 were below his average points per game, Jordan reduced his average points per game from 33 to 31. Games 13 and 14

lifted his average from 31 to 33 points per game because his marginal points in both of these games exceeded his average points per game. Finally, the 20 points in game 15 again reduced his average back to 32 points per game. Thus, when Jordan's marginal points scored in a game were below his season's average points per game, his average fell. When Jordan's marginal points scored in a game were above his season's average points per game, his average rose. If you said even Michael Jordan cannot beat the marginal-average rule, **YOU ARE CORRECT.**

Game	Marginal Points	Average Points
10		33 over 10 games
11	20	32 = (33 × 10 + 20)/11 games
12	25	31 = (32 × 11 + 25)/12 games
13	40	32 = (31 × 12 + 40)/13 games
14	50	33 = (32 × 13 + 50)/14 games
15	20	32 = (33 × 14 + 20)/15 games

PRACTICE QUIZ

For a visual explanation of the correct answers, visit the tutorial at http://tucker.swcollege.com.

1. Explicit costs are payments to
   a. hourly employees.
   b. insurance companies.
   c. utility companies.
   d. all of the above.

2. Implicit costs are the opportunity costs of using the resources of
   a. outsiders.
   b. owners.
   c. banks.
   d. retained earnings.

3. Which of the following equalities is true?
   a. Economic profit = total revenue − accounting profit
   b. Economic profit = total revenue − explicit costs − accounting profit
   c. Economic profit = total revenue − implicit costs − explicit costs
   d. Economic profit = opportunity cost + accounting cost

4. Fixed inputs are factors of production that
   a. are determined by a firm's plant size.
   b. can be increased or decreased quickly as output changes.
   c. cannot be increased or decreased as output changes.
   d. are none of the above.

5. An example of a variable input is
   a. raw materials.
   b. energy.
   c. hourly labor.
   d. all of the above.

6. Suppose a car wash has 2 washing stations and 5 workers and is able to wash 100 cars per day. When it adds a third station, but no more workers, it is able to wash 150 cars per day. The marginal product of the third washing station is
   a. 100 cars per day.
   b. 150 cars per day.
   c. 5 cars per day.
   d. 50 cars per day.

7. If the units of variable input in a production process are 1, 2, 3, 4, and 5 and the corresponding total outputs are 10, 22, 33, 42, and 48, respectively, the marginal product of the fourth unit is
   a. 2.
   b. 6.
   c. 9.
   d. 42.

8. The total fixed cost curve is
   a. upward-sloping.
   b. downward-sloping.
   c. upward-sloping and then downward-sloping.
   d. unchanged with the level of output.

9. Assuming the marginal cost curve is a smooth U-shaped curve, the corresponding total cost curve has a (an)
   a. linear shape.
   b. S-shape.
   c. U-shape.
   d. reverse-S-shape.

10. If both the marginal cost and the average variable cost curves are U-shaped, at the point of minimum average variable cost, the marginal cost must be
    a. greater than the average variable cost.
    b. less than the average variable cost.
    c. equal to the average variable cost.
    d. at its minimum.

11. Which of the following is *true* at the point where diminishing returns set in?
    a. Both marginal product and marginal cost are at a maximum.
    b. Both marginal product and marginal cost are at a minimum.
    c. Marginal product is at a maximum and marginal cost at a minimum.
    d. Marginal product is at a minimum and marginal cost at a maximum.

EXHIBIT 10   Total Cost Curve

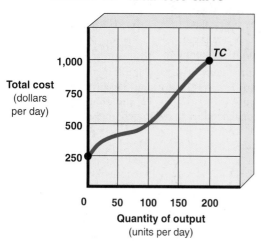

12. As shown in Exhibit 10, total fixed cost for the firm is
    a. zero.
    b. $250.
    c. $500.
    d. $750.
    e. $1,000.

13. As shown in Exhibit 10, the total cost of producing 100 units of output per day is
    a. zero.
    b. $250.
    c. $500.
    d. $750.
    e. $1,000.

14. In Exhibit 10, if the total cost of producing 99 units of output per day is $475, the marginal cost of producing the 100th unit of output per day is approximately
    a. zero.
    b. $25.
    c. $475.
    d. $500.

15. Each potential short-run average total cost curve is tangent to the long-run average cost curve at
    a. the level of output that minimizes short-run average total cost.
    b. the minimum point of the average total cost curve.
    c. the minimum point of the long-run average cost curve.
    d. a single point on the short-run average total cost curve.

16. Suppose a typical firm is producing X units of output per day. Using any other plant size, the long-run average cost would increase. The firm is operating at a point at which
    a. its long-run average cost curve is at a minimum.
    b. its short-run average total cost curve is at a minimum.
    c. both a and b are true.
    d. neither a nor b is true.

17. The downward-sloping segment of the long-run average cost curve corresponds to
    a. diseconomies of scale.
    b. both economies and diseconomies of scale.
    c. the decrease in average variable costs.
    d. economies of scale.

18. Long-run diseconomies of scale exist when the
    a. short-run average total cost curve falls.
    b. long-run marginal cost curve rises.
    c. long-run average total cost curve falls.
    d. short-run average variable cost curve rises.
    e. long-run average cost curve rises.

19. Long-run constant returns to scale exist when the
    a. short-run average total cost curve is constant.
    b. long-run average cost curve rises.
    c. long-run average cost curve is flat.
    d. long-run average cost curve falls.

CHAPTER EIGHT

Perfect Competition

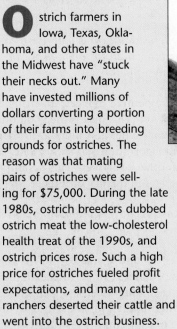

Ostrich farmers in Iowa, Texas, Oklahoma, and other states in the Midwest have "stuck their necks out." Many have invested millions of dollars converting a portion of their farms into breeding grounds for ostriches. The reason was that mating pairs of ostriches were selling for $75,000. During the late 1980s, ostrich breeders dubbed ostrich meat the low-cholesterol health treat of the 1990s, and ostrich prices rose. Such a high price for ostriches fueled profit expectations, and many cattle ranchers deserted their cattle and went into the ostrich business.

Adam Smith concluded that competitive forces are like an "invisible hand" that leads people who simply pursue their own interests to serve the interests of society. In a competitive market, when the profit potential in the ostrich business looks good, firms start raising ostriches. However, if more and more ostrich farmers flock to this market and the ostrich population explodes, prices and profits will tumble.

This chapter combines the demand, cost of production, and marginal analysis concepts from previous chapters to explain how competitive markets determine prices, output, and profits. Here firms are small, like an ostrich ranch or an alligator farm, rather than huge, like Sears, Exxon, or IBM.

Other types of markets in which large and powerful firms operate are discussed in the subsequent two chapters.

In this chapter, you will learn to solve these economics puzzles:

■ Why is the demand curve horizontal for a firm in a perfectly competitive market?

■ Why would a firm stay in business while losing money?

■ In the long run, can alligator farms earn an economic profit?

Perfect Competition

Firms sell goods and services under different market conditions, which economists call **market structures**. A market structure describes the key traits of a market, including the number of firms, the similarity of the products they sell, and the ease of entry into and exit from the market. Examination of the business sector of our economy reveals firms operating in different market structures. In this chapter, and the two chapters that follow, we will study four market structures. The first is **perfect competition**, to which this entire chapter is devoted. Perfect, or pure, competition is a market structure characterized by (1) a large number of small firms, (2) a homogeneous product, and (3) very easy entry into or exit from the market. Let's discuss each of these characteristics.

Characteristics of Perfect Competition

Large Number of Small Firms   How many sellers is a large number? And how small is a small firm? Certainly, one, two, or three firms in a market would not be a large number. In fact, the exact number cannot be stated. This condition is fulfilled when each firm in a market has no significant share of total output and therefore no ability to affect the product's price. Each firm acts independently, rather than coordinating decisions collectively. For example, there are thousands of independent egg farmers in the United States. If any single egg farmer raises the price, the going market price for eggs is unaffected.

> **Conclusion**   *The large-number-of-sellers condition is met when each firm is so small relative to the total market that no single firm can influence the market price.*

Homogeneous Product   In a perfectly competitive market, all firms produce a standardized or a homogeneous product. This means the good or service of each firm is identical. Farmer Brown's wheat is identical to Farmer Jones's wheat. Buyers may believe the transportation services of one independent trucker are about the same as another's services. This assumption rules out rivalry among firms in advertising and quality difference.

> **Conclusion**   *If a product is homogeneous, buyers are indifferent as to which seller's product they buy.*

Very Easy Entry and Exit   Very easy entry into a market means that a new firm faces no barriers to entry. These barriers can be financial, technical, or government-imposed barriers, including licenses, permits, and patents. Anyone who wants to try his or her hand at raising ostriches needs only a plot of land and feed. The flip side of easy entry is restraints on ceasing operation. An example of an exit restriction is a law restricting a firm's right to close its plants.

Market structure

A classification system for the key traits of a market, including the number of firms, the similarity of the products they sell, and the ease of entry into and exit from the market.

Perfect competition

A market structure characterized by (1) a large number of small firms, (2) a homogeneous product, and (3) very easy entry into or exit from the market. Perfect competition is also referred to as pure competition.

Conclusion *Perfect competition requires that resources be completely mobile to freely enter or exit a market.*

No real-world market exactly fits the three assumptions of perfect competition. The perfectly competitive market structure is a theoretical or ideal model, but some actual markets do approximate the model fairly closely. Examples include farm products markets, the stock market, and the foreign exchange market.

The Perfectly Competitive Firm as a Price Taker

For model-building purposes, suppose a firm operates in a market that conforms to all three of the above requirements for perfect competition. This would mean the perfectly competitive firm is a **price taker**. A price taker is a seller that has no control over the price of the product it sells. From the individual firm's perspective, market supply and demand conditions over which the firm has no influence determine the price of its products. Look again at the characteristics of a perfectly competitive firm: a small firm that is one among many firms, sells a homogeneous product, and is exposed to competition from new firms entering the market. These conditions make it impossible for the perfectly competitive firm to have the market power to affect the market price. Instead, the firm must adjust to or "take" the market price.

Exhibit 1 is a graphical presentation of the relationship between the market supply and demand for electronic components and the demand curve facing a firm in a perfectly competitive market. Here we will assume that the electronic components industry is perfectly competitive, keeping in mind that the real-world market does not exactly fit the model. Exhibit 1(a) shows market supply and demand curves for the quantity of output per hour. The theoretical framework for this model was explained in Chapter 4. The equilibrium price is $70 per unit, and the equilibrium quantity is 60,000 units per hour.

Because the perfectly competitive firm "takes" the equilibrium price, the individual firm's demand curve in Exhibit 1(b) is *perfectly elastic* (horizontal) at the $70 market equilibrium price. (Note the difference between the firm's units per hour and the industry's thousands of units per hour.) Recall from Chapter 5 that when a firm facing a perfectly elastic demand curve tries to raise its price one penny higher than $70, no buyer will purchase its product [see Exhibit 2(a) in Chapter 5]. The reason is that there are many other firms selling the same product at $70 per unit. Hence, the perfectly competitive firm will not set the price above the prevailing market price and risk selling zero output. Nor will the firm set the price below the market price because the firm can sell all it wants to at the going price, and, therefore, a lower price would reduce the firm's revenue.

Price taker
A seller that has no control over the price of the product it sells.

Auctions are often considered to be quite competitive markets. Auctions over the Internet are now quite common. For example, visit eBay's Auction Web to witness a Dutch auction (http://www.ebay.com /aw/). *To see a live Internet auction, visit ON-SALE Interactive Marketplace, a live Internet auction house offering computers and electronics* (http://www.onsale .com/). *For more about how auctions work, visit the Auction Marketing Institute (AMI), a nonprofit professional educational organization* (http://www.auctionweb.com /ami/).

The Market Price and Demand for the Perfectly Competitive Firm

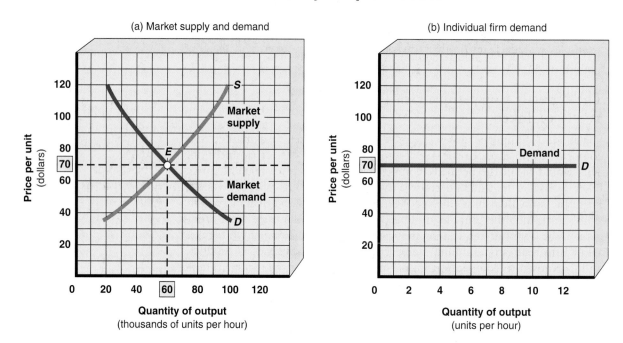

(a) Market supply and demand

(b) Individual firm demand

Price per unit (dollars)

Quantity of output (thousands of units per hour)

Quantity of output (units per hour)

In part (a), the market equilibrium price is $70 per unit. The perfectly competitive firm in part (b) is a price taker because it is so small relative to the market. At $70, the individual firm faces a horizontal demand curve, D. This means that the firm's demand curve is perfectly elastic. If the firm raises its price even one penny, it will sell zero output.

Short-Run Profit Maximization for a Perfectly Competitive Firm

Since the perfectly competitive firm has no control over price, what does the firm control? The firm makes only one decision—what quantity of output to produce that maximizes profit. In this section, we develop two profit maximization methods that determine the output level for a competitive firm. We begin by examining the total revenue–total cost approach for finding the profit-maximizing level of output. Next, we use marginal analysis to show another method for determining the profit-maximizing level of output. The framework for our analysis is the short run with some fixed input, such as factory size.

EXHIBIT 2 Short-Run Profit Maximization Schedule for Computech as a Perfectly Competitive Firm

(1) Output (units per hour)	(2) Total Revenue	(3) Total Cost	(4) Profit [(2) − (3)]	(5) Marginal Cost [Δ(3)/Δ(1)]	(6) Marginal Revenue [Δ(2)/Δ(1)]
0	$ 0	$100	−$100		
				$ 50	
1	70	150	−80		$70
				34	
2	140	184	−44		70
				24	
3	210	208	2		70
				19	
4	280	227	53		70
				23	
5	350	250	100		70
				30	
6	420	280	140		70
				38	
7	490	318	172		70
				48	
8	560	366	194		70
				59	
9	630	425	205		70
				75	
10	700	500	200		70
				95	
11	770	595	175		70
				117	
12	840	712	128		70

The Total Revenue–Total Cost Method

Exhibit 2 provides hypothetical data on output, total revenue, total cost, and profit for our typical electronic components producer—Computech. Using Computech as our example allows us to extend the data and analysis presented in previous chapters. The total cost figures in column 3 are taken from Exhibit 3 in Chapter 7. Total fixed cost at zero output is $100.

Total revenue is reported in column 2 of Exhibit 2 and is computed as the product price times the quantity. In this case, we assume the market equilibrium price is $70 per unit, as determined in Exhibit 1. Because Computech is a price taker, the total revenue from selling 1 unit is $70, from selling 2 units is $140, and so on. Subtracting total cost in column 3 from total revenue in column 2 gives the total profit or loss (column 4) that the firm earns at each level of output. From zero to 2 units, the firm earns losses, and then a *break-even point* (zero economic profit) occurs at about 3 units per hour. If the firm produces 9 units per hour, it earns the maximum profit of $205 per hour. As output expands, between 9 and 12 units of output, the firm's profit diminishes. Exhibit 3 illustrates graphically that the maximum profit occurs where the vertical distance between the total revenue and the total cost curves is at a maximum.

EXHIBIT 3

Short-Run Profit Maximization Using the Total Revenue–Total Cost Method

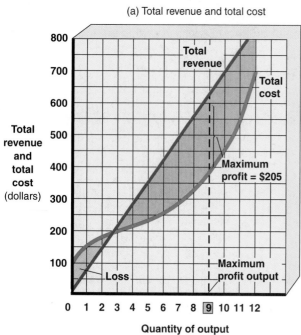

(a) Total revenue and total cost

This exhibit shows the profit-maximizing level of output chosen by a perfectly competitive firm, Computech. Part (a) shows the relationships among total revenue, total cost, and output, given a market price of $70 per unit. The maximum profit is earned by producing 9 units per hour. At this level of output, the vertical distance between the total revenue and the total cost curves is the greatest.

Profit maximization is also shown in part (b) of the figure. The maximum profit of $205 per hour corresponds to the profit-maximizing output of 9 units per hour, represented in part (a).

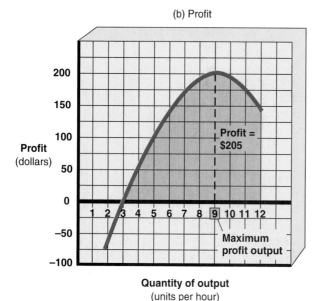

(b) Profit

The Marginal Revenue Equals Marginal Cost Method

A second approach uses *marginal analysis* to determine the profit-maximizing level of output by comparing marginal revenue (marginal benefit) and marginal cost. Column 5 of Exhibit 2 gives marginal cost data calculated in column 5 of Exhibit 3 in Chapter 7. Recall that marginal cost is the change in total cost as the output level changes one unit. As in Exhibit 3 in Chapter 7, these marginal cost data are listed between the quantity of output line entries.

Now we introduce **marginal revenue** (*MR*), a concept similar to marginal cost. Marginal revenue is the change in total revenue from the sale of one additional unit of output. Stated another way, marginal revenue is the ratio of the change in total revenue to a one-unit change in output. Mathematically,

$$MR = \frac{\text{change in total revenue}}{\text{one-unit change in output}}$$

As shown in Exhibit 1(b), the perfectly competitive firm faces a perfectly elastic demand curve. Because the competitive firm is a price taker, the sale of each additional unit adds to total revenue an amount equal to the price (average revenue, *TR/Q*). In our example, Computech adds $70 to its total revenue each time it sells one unit. Therefore, $70 is the marginal revenue for each additional unit of output in column 6 of Exhibit 2.

Conclusion *In perfect competition, the firm's marginal revenue equals the price that the firm views as a horizontal demand curve.*

Columns 2 and 3 in Exhibit 2 show that both total revenue and total cost rise as the level of output increases. Now compare marginal cost and marginal revenue in columns 5 and 6. As explained, marginal revenue remains equal to the price, but marginal cost follows the J-shaped pattern introduced in Exhibit 3 in Chapter 7. At first, marginal cost is below marginal revenue, and this means that producing each additional unit adds less to total cost than to total revenue. Economic profit therefore increases as output expands from zero until the output level reaches 9 units per hour. Over this output range, Computech moves from a $100 loss to a $205 profit per hour. Beyond an output level of 9 units per hour, marginal cost exceeds marginal revenue, and profit falls. This is because each additional unit of output raises total cost by more than it raises total revenue. In this case, profit falls from $205 to only $128 per hour if output increases from 9 to 12 units per hour.

Our example leads to this question: How does the firm use its marginal revenue and marginal cost curves to determine the profit-maximizing level of output? The answer is that the firm follows a guideline called the *MR* = *MC rule: The firm maximizes profit or minimizes losses by producing the output where marginal revenue equals marginal cost.* Exhibit 4 relates the marginal revenue curve equals marginal cost curve condition to profit maximization. In Exhibit 4(a), the perfectly elastic demand is drawn at the industry-determined price of $70. The average total cost curve is traced from data given earlier in column 8 of Exhibit 3 in Chapter 7. Note that Exhibit 4(a) is a reproduction of Exhibit 4(b) in Chapter 7, except for the omission of the *AFC* curve.

Marginal revenue
The change in total revenue from the sale of one additonal unit of output.

EXHIBIT 4

Short-Run Profit Maximization Using the Marginal Revenue Equals Marginal Cost Method

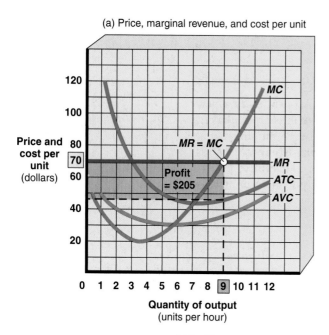

(a) Price, marginal revenue, and cost per unit

In addition to comparing total revenue and total cost, the profit-maximizing level of output can be found by comparing marginal revenue and marginal cost. As shown in part (a), profit is at a maximum where marginal revenue equals marginal cost at $70 per unit. The intersection of the marginal revenue and the marginal cost curves establishes the profit-maximizing output at 9 units per hour.

A profit curve is depicted separately in part (b) in order to show that the maximum profit occurs when the firm produces at the level of output corresponding to the marginal revenue equals marginal cost point.

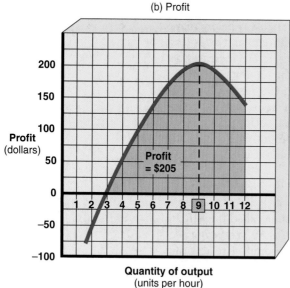

(b) Profit

Using marginal analysis, we can relate the $MR = MC$ rule to the same profit curve given in Exhibit 3(b). Between 8 and 9 units of output, the MC curve is below the MR curve ($59 < $70), and the profit curve rises to its peak. Beyond 9 units of output, the MC curve is above the MR curve, and the profit curve falls. For example, between 9 and 10 units of output, marginal cost is $75, and marginal revenue is $70. Therefore, if the firm produces at 9 units of output rather than, say, 8 or 10 units of output, the MR curve equals the MC curve, and profit is maximized.

You can also calculate profit directly from Exhibit 4(a). At the profit-maximizing level of output of 9 units, the vertical distance between the demand curve and the ATC curve is the *average profit per unit.* Multiplying the average profit per unit times the quantity of output gives the profit [($70 − $47.22) × 9 = $205.22].[1] The shaded rectangle also represents the maximum profit of $205 per hour. Note that we have arrived at the same profit-maximization amount ($205) derived by comparing the total revenue and the total cost curves.

Short-Run Loss Minimization for a Perfectly Competitive Firm

Because the perfectly competitive firm must take the price determined by market supply and demand forces, market conditions can change the prevailing price. When the market price drops, the firm can do nothing but adjust its output to make the best of the situation. Here only the marginal approach is used to predict output decisions of firms. Our model therefore assumes that business managers make their output decisions by comparing the *marginal* effect on profit of a *marginal* change in output.

A Perfectly Competitive Firm Facing a Short-Run Loss

Suppose a decrease in the market demand for electronic components causes the market price to fall to $35. As a result, the firm's horizontal demand curve shifts downward to the new position shown in Exhibit 5(a). In this case, there is no level of output at which the firm earns a profit because any price along the demand curve is below the *ATC* curve.

Since Computech cannot make a profit, what output level should it choose? The logic of the *MR* = *MC* rule given in the profit-maximization case applies here as well. At a price of $35, *MR* = *MC* at 6 units per hour. Comparing parts (a) and (b) of Exhibit 5 shows that the firm's loss will be minimum at this level of output. The minimum loss of $70 per hour is equal to the shaded area, which is the *average loss per unit* times the quantity of output [($35 − $46.66) × 6 = −$70].

Note that although the price is not high enough to pay the average total cost, the price is high enough to pay the average variable cost. Each unit sold also contributes to paying a portion of the average fixed cost, which is the vertical distance between the *ATC* and the *AVC* curves. This analysis leads us to extend the *MR* = *MC* rule: *The firm maximizes profit or minimizes loss by producing the output where marginal revenue equals marginal cost.*

---

[1]In Exhibit 3 in Chapter 7, the average total cost figure at 9 units of output was rounded to $47. It also should be noted that there is often no level of output for which marginal revenue exactly equals marginal cost when dealing with whole units of output.

EXHIBIT 5

Short-Run Loss Minimization

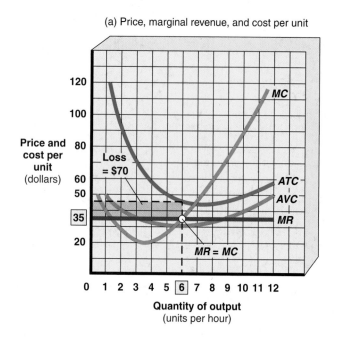

(a) Price, marginal revenue, and cost per unit

Price and cost per unit (dollars)

Quantity of output (units per hour)

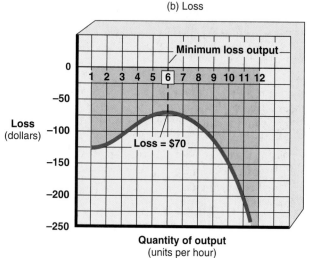

(b) Loss

Loss (dollars)

Quantity of output (units per hour)

If the market price is less than the average total cost, the firm will produce a level of output that keeps its loss to a minimum. In part (a), the given price is $35 per unit, and marginal revenue equals marginal cost at an output of 6 units per hour.

Part (b) shows that the firm's loss will be greater at any output other than where the marginal revenue and the marginal cost curves intersect. Because the price is above the average variable cost, each unit of output sold pays for the average variable cost and a portion of the average fixed cost.

A Perfectly Competitive Firm Shutting Down

What happens if the market price drops below the *AVC* curve, as shown in Exhibit 6? For example, if the price is $25 per unit, should Computech produce some level of output? The answer is no. The best course of action is for the firm to shut down. *If the price is below the minimum point on the AVC curve, each unit produced would not cover the variable cost per unit, and, therefore, operating would increase losses.* The firm would be better off shutting down and producing zero output. While shut down, the firm might keep its factory, pay fixed costs, and hope for higher prices soon. If the firm does not believe market conditions will improve, it will avoid fixed costs by going out of business.

EXHIBIT 6

The Short-Run Shutdown Point

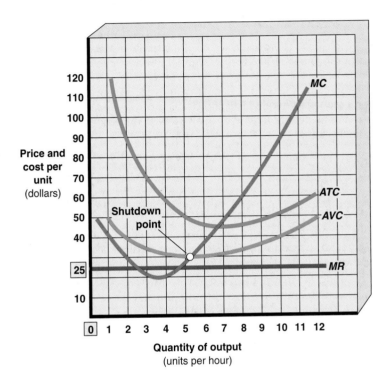

CAUSATION CHAIN

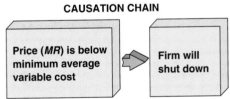

| Price (*MR*) is below minimum average variable cost | → | Firm will shut down |

If the price falls below the minimum point on the average variable cost curve, the firm shuts down. The reason is because operating losses are now greater than the total fixed cost. In this exhibit, the price is $25 per unit and is below the average variable cost curve at any level of output.

Short-Run Supply Curves Under Perfect Competition

The preceding examples provide a framework for a more complete explanation of the supply curve than was given earlier in Chapter 3. We now develop the short-run supply curve for an individual firm and then derive it for an industry.

Should Motels Offer Rooms at the Beach for Only $20 a Night?

Myrtle Beach, South Carolina, is lined with virtually identical motels. Summer-time rates run about $100 a night. During the winter, one can find rooms for as little as $20 a night. Assume the average fixed cost of a room per night, including insurance, taxes, and depreciation, is $50. The average guest-related cost for a room each night, including cleaning service and linens, is $15. Would these motels be better off renting rooms for $20 in the off-season or shutting down until summer?

The Perfectly Competitive Firm's Short-Run Supply Curve

Exhibit 7 reproduces the cost curves from our Computech example. Also represented in the exhibit are three different possible demand curves the firm might face—MR_1, MR_2, and MR_3. As the marginal revenue curve moves upward along the marginal cost curve, the $MR = MC$ point changes.

Suppose demand for electronic components begins at the market price close to $30. Point *A* therefore corresponds to a price equal to MR_1, which equals *MC* at the lowest point on the *AVC* curve. At any lower price, the firm cuts its loss by shutting down. At a price of about $30, however, the firm produces 5.5 units per hour. Point *A* is therefore the lowest point on the individual firm's short-run supply curve.

If the price rises to $45, represented in the exhibit by MR_2, the firm breaks even and earns a normal profit at point *B* with an output of 7 units per hour. As the marginal revenue curve increases, the firm's supply curve is traced by moving upward along its *MC* curve. At a price of $90, point *C* is reached. Now MR_3 intersects the *MC* curve at an output of 10 units per hour, and the firm earns an economic profit. If the price rises higher than $90, the firm will continue to increase the quantity supplied and increase its maximum profit.

We can now define a **perfectly competitive firm's short-run supply curve**. The perfectly competitive firm's short-run supply curve is its marginal cost curve above the minimum point on its average variable cost curve.

Perfectly competitive firm's short-run supply curve
The firm's marginal cost curve above the minimum point on its average variable cost curve.

The Perfectly Competitive Industry's Short-Run Supply Curve

Understanding that the firm's short-run supply curve is the segment of its *MC* curve above its *AVC* curve sets the stage for derivation of the **perfectly competitive industry's short-run supply curve**. The perfectly competitive industry's short-run supply curve is the horizontal summation of all firms' marginal cost curves in the industry above the minimum point of each firm's average variable cost curve.

In Exhibit 7 in Chapter 3, we drew a market supply curve. Now we will reconstruct this market, or industry, supply curve using more precision.

Perfectly competitive industry's short-run supply curve
The supply curve derived from the horizontal summation of all firms' marginal cost curves in the industry above the minimum point of each firm's average variable cost curve.

EXHIBIT 7

The Firm's Short-Run Supply Curve

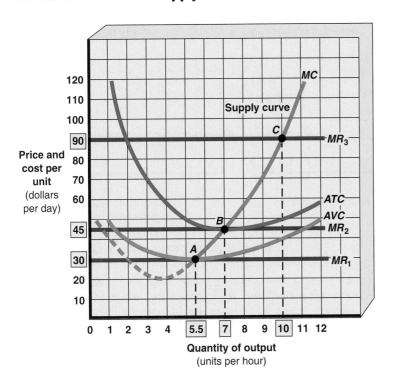

The exhibit shows how the short-run supply curve for Computech is derived. When the price is $30, the firm will produce 5.5 units per hour at point A. If the price rises to $45, the firm will move upward along its marginal cost curve to point B and produce 7 units per hour. At $90, the firm continues to set price equal to marginal cost, and it produces 10 units per hour. Thus, the firm's short-run supply curve is the marginal cost curve above its average variable cost curve.

Although in perfect competition there are many firms, we suppose for simplicity that the industry has only two firms, Computech and Western Computer Co. Exhibit 8 illustrates the *MC* curves for these two firms. Each firm's *MC* curve is drawn for prices above the minimum point on the *AVC* curve. At a price of $40, the quantity supplied by Computech would be 7 units, and the quantity supplied by Western Computer Co. would be 11 units. Now we horizontally add these two quantities and obtain one point on the industry supply curve corresponding to a price of $40 and 18 units. Following this procedure for all prices, we generate the short-run industry supply curve.

EXHIBIT 8

Deriving the Industry Short-Run Supply Curve

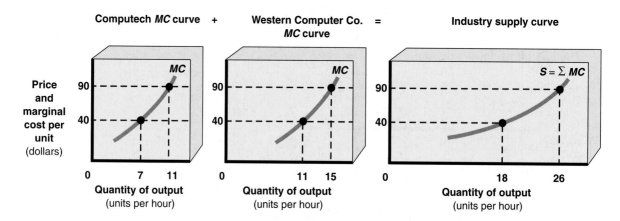

Computech *MC* curve   +   Western Computer Co.   =   Industry supply curve
                                          MC curve

Price and marginal cost per unit (dollars)

Quantity of output (units per hour)

Assuming input prices remain constant as output expands, the short-run supply curve for an industry is derived by the horizontal summation of quantities supplied at each price for all firms in the industry. In this exhibit, we assume there are only two firms in an industry. At $40, Computech supplies 7 units of output, and Western Computer Co. supplies 11 units. The quantity supplied by the industry is therefore 18 units. Other points forming the industry short-run supply curve are obtained similarly.

Note that the industry supply curve derived above is based on the assumption that input prices remain unchanged as output expands. In the next section, we will learn how changes in input prices affect derivation of the supply curve.

Short-Run Equilibrium for a Perfectly Competitive Firm

Exhibit 9 illustrates a condition of short-run equilibrium under perfect competition. Exhibit 9(a) represents the equilibrium price and cost situation for one of the many firms in an industry. As shown in the figure, the firm earns an economic profit in the short run by producing 9 units. Exhibit 9(b) depicts short-run equilibrium for the industry. As explained earlier, the industry supply curve is the aggregate of each firm's *MC* curve above the minimum point on the *AVC* curve. Including industry demand establishes the equilibrium price of $60 that all firms in the industry must take. The industry's equilibrium quantity supplied is 60,000 units. This state of short-run equilibrium will remain until some factor changes and causes a new equilibrium condition in the industry.

EXHIBIT 9

Short-Run Perfectly Competitive Equilibrium

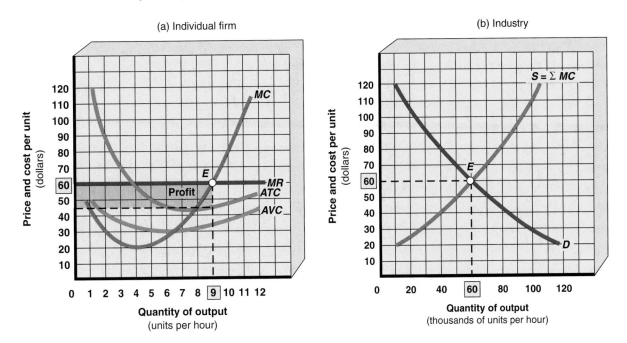

(a) Individual firm

(b) Industry

Short-run equilibrium occurs at point E. *The intersection of the industry supply and demand curves shown in part (b) determines the price of $60 facing the firm shown in part (a). Given this equilibrium price, the firm represented in part (a) establishes its profit-maximizing output at 9 units per hour and earns an economic profit shown by the shaded area. Note in part (b) that the short-run industry supply curve is the horizontal summation of the marginal cost curves of all individual firms above their minimum average variable cost points.*

Long-Run Supply Curves Under Perfect Competition

Recall from Chapter 7 that *all* inputs are variable in the long run. Existing firms in an industry can react to profit opportunities by building larger or smaller plants, buying and selling land and equipment, or varying other inputs that are fixed in the short run. Profits also attract new firms to an industry, while losses cause some existing firms to leave the industry. As you will now see, the free entry and exit characteristic of perfect competition is a crucial determinant of the shape of the long-run supply curve.

CHECKPOINT

Are You in Business for the Long Run?

You are considering building a Rent Your Own Storage Center. You are trying to decide whether to build 50 storage units at a total economic cost of $200,000, 100 storage units at a total economic cost of $300,000, or 200 storage units at a total economic cost of $700,000. If you wish to survive in the long run, which size will you choose?

Long-Run Equilibrium for a Perfectly Competitive Firm

Remember from Chapter 7 that in the long run a firm can change its plant size or any input used to produce a product. This means that an established firm can decide to *leave* an industry if it earns below normal profits (negative economic profits) and that new firms may enter an industry in which earnings of established firms exceed normal profits (positive economic profits). This process of entry and exit of firms is the key to long-run equilibrium. If there are economic profits, new firms enter the industry and shift the short-run supply curve to the right. This increase in short-run supply causes the price to fall until economic profits reach zero in the long run. On the other hand, if there are economic losses in an industry, existing firms leave, causing the short-run supply curve to shift to the left, and the price rises. This adjustment continues until economic losses are eliminated and economic profits equal zero in the long run.

Exhibit 10 shows a typical firm in long-run equilibrium. Supply and demand for the market as a whole set the equilibrium price. Thus, in the long run, the firm faces an equilibrium price of $60. Following the $MR = MC$ rule, the firm produces an equilibrium output of 6 units per hour. At this output level, the firm earns a normal profit (zero economic profit) because marginal revenue (price) equals the minimum point on both the short-run average total cost curve and the long-run average cost ($LRAC$) curve. Given the U-shaped $LRAC$ curve, the firm is producing with the optimal factory size.

These conditions for long-run perfectly competitive equilibrium can also be expressed as an equality:

$$P = MR = SRMC = SRATC = LRAC$$

As long as none of the variables in the above formula changes, there is no reason for a perfectly competitive firm to change its output level, factory size, or any aspect of its operation. Everything is just right! Because the typical firm is in a state of equilibrium, the industry is also at rest. Under

EXHIBIT 10

Long-Run Perfectly Competitive Equilibrium

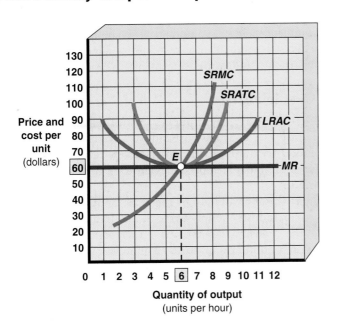

Quantity of output
(units per hour)

CAUSATION CHAIN

Entry and exit of firms → Zero long-run economic profit → Long-run equilibrium

Long-run equilibrium occurs at point E. *In the long run, the firm earns a normal profit. The firm operates where the price equals the minimum point on its long-run average cost curve. At this point, the short-run marginal cost curve intersects both the short-run average total cost curve and the long-run average cost curve at their minimum points.*

long-run equilibrium conditions, there are neither positive economic profits to attract new firms to enter the industry nor negative economic profits to force existing firms to leave. In long-run equilibrium, the adjustment process of firms moving into or out of the industry is complete, and the firms charge the lowest possible price to consumers. Next, we will discuss how the firm and industry adjust when market demand changes.

Perfectly competitive industry's long-run supply curve
The curve that shows the quantities supplied by the industry at different equilibrium prices after firms complete their entry and exit.

Constant-cost industry
An industry in which the expansion of industry output by the entry of new firms has no effect on the firm's cost curves.

Three Types of Long-Run Supply Curves

There are three possibilities for a **perfectly competitive industry's long-run supply curve**. The perfectly competitive industry's long-run supply curve shows the quantities supplied by the industry at different equilibrium prices after firms complete their entry and exit. The shape of each of these long-run supply curves depends on the response of input prices as new firms enter the industry. The following sections discuss each of these three cases.

Constant-Cost Industry

In a **constant-cost industry**, input prices remain constant as new firms enter or exit the industry. A constant-cost industry is an industry in which the expansion of industry output by the entry of new firms has no effect on the firm's cost curves. Exhibit 11 reproduces the long-run equilibrium situation from Exhibit 10.

Begin in part (b) of Exhibit 11 at the initial industry equilibrium point, E_1, with short-run industry supply curve S_1 and industry demand curve D_1. Now assume the industry demand curve increases from D_1 to D_2. As a result, the industry equilibrium moves temporarily to E_2. Correspondingly, the equilibrium price rises from \$60 to \$80, and industry output increases from 50,000 to 70,000 units.

The short-run result for the typical firm in the industry happens this way. As shown in part (a) of Exhibit 11, the firm takes the increase in price and adjusts its output from 6 to 7 units per hour. At the higher price and output, the firm changes from earning a normal profit to making an economic profit because the new price is above the *SRATC* curve. All the other firms in the industry make the same adjustment by moving upward along their *SRMC* curves.

In perfect competition, new firms are free to enter the industry in response to a profit opportunity, and they will do so. The addition of new firms shifts the short-run supply curve rightward from S_1 to S_2. Firms will continue to enter the industry until profit is eliminated. This occurs at equilibrium point E_3, where short-run industry demand curve D_2 intersects short-run supply curve S_2. Thus, the entry of new firms has restored the initial equilibrium price of \$60. The firm responds by moving downward along its *SRMC* curve until it once again produces 6 units and earns a normal profit.

As shown in the exhibit, the path of these changes in industry short-run equilibrium points traces a horizontal line, which is the industry's long-run supply curve.

Conclusion *The long-run supply curve in a perfectly competitive constant-cost industry is perfectly elastic.*

Now we reconsider Exhibit 11 and ask what happens when the demand curve shifts leftward from D_2 to D_1. Beginning in part (b) at point E_3, the decrease in demand causes the price to fall temporarily below \$60. As a result, firms earn short-run losses, and some firms leave the industry. The

EXHIBIT 11

Long-Run Supply in a Constant-Cost Industry

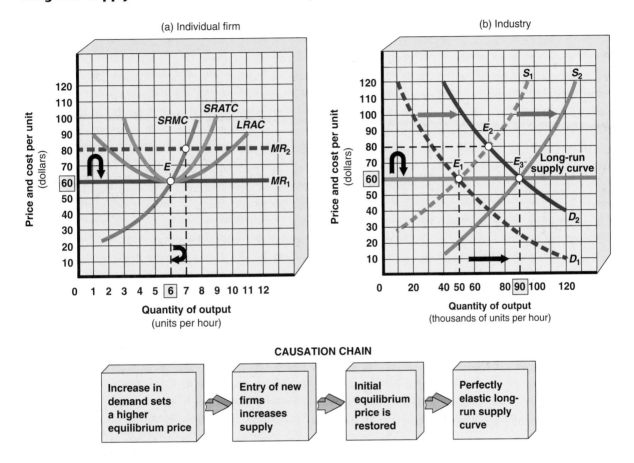

(a) Individual firm

(b) Industry

CAUSATION CHAIN

| Increase in demand sets a higher equilibrium price | Entry of new firms increases supply | Initial equilibrium price is restored | Perfectly elastic long-run supply curve |

Part (b) shows an industry in equilibrium at point E₁, producing 50,000 units per hour and selling units at $60 per unit. In part (a), the firm is in equilibrium, producing 6 units per hour and earning a normal profit. Then industry demand increases from D₁ to D₂, and the equilibrium price rises to $80. Industry output rises temporarily to 70,000 units per hour, and the individual firm increases output to 7 units per hour. Firms are now earning an economic profit, which attracts new firms into the industry. In the long run, the entry of these firms causes the short-run supply curve to shift rightward from S₁ to S₂, the price is re-established at $60, and a new industry equilibrium point, E₃, is established. At E₃, industry output rises to 90,000 units per hour, and the firm's output returns to 6 units per hour. Now the typical firm earns a normal profit, and new firms stop entering the industry. Connecting point E₁ to point E₃ generates the long-run supply curve.

exodus of firms shifts the short-run supply curve leftward from S_2 to S_1, establishing a new equilibrium at point E_1. This decrease in supply restores the equilibrium price to the initial price of $60 per unit. Once equilibrium is re-established at E_1, there is a smaller number of firms, each earning a normal profit.

Decreasing-Cost Industry

Decreasing-cost industry
An industry in which the expansion of industry output by the entry of new firms decreases the firm's cost curves.

Input prices fall as new firms enter a **decreasing-cost industry**, and output expands. A decreasing-cost industry is an industry in which the expansion of industry output by the entry of new firms decreases the firm's cost curves. For example, as production of electronic components expands, the price of computer chips may be lower. The reason is that greater sales volume allows the suppliers to achieve *economies of scale* and lower their input prices to firms in the electronic component industry. Exhibit 12 illustrates the adjustment process of an increase in demand based on the assumption that our example is a decreasing-cost industry.

> **Conclusion** *The long-run supply curve in a perfectly competitive decreasing-cost industry is downward-sloping.*

Increasing-Cost Industry

Increasing-cost industry
An industry in which the expansion of industry output by the entry of new firms increases the firm's cost curves.

Firms in increasing-cost industries, such as housing construction, in the long run encounter increased costs as output expands. To learn more about the economics of housing construction, visit the National Association of Home Builders (NAHB) (http://www.nahb.com/).

In an **increasing-cost industry**, input prices rise as new firms enter the industry, and output expands. As this type of industry uses more labor, and machines, the demand for greater quantities of these inputs drives up input prices. An increasing-cost industry is an industry in which the expansion of industry output by the entry of new firms increases the firm's cost curves. Suppose the electronic component disc business uses a significant proportion of all electrical engineers in the country. If this is the case, electrical engineering salaries will rise as firms hire more electrical engineers to expand industry output. In practice, most industries are increasing-cost industries, and, therefore, the long-run supply curve is upward-sloping.

Exhibit 13 shows what happens in an increasing-cost industry when an increase in demand causes output to expand. In part (b), the industry is initially in equilibrium at point E_1. As in the previous case, the demand curve shifts rightward from D_1 to D_2, establishing a new short-run equilibrium at E_2. This movement upward along short-run industry supply curve S_1 raises the price in the short run from $60 to $80, resulting in profit for the typical firm. Once again, new firms enter the industry, and the short-run supply curve shifts rightward from S_1 to S_2. Part (a) of Exhibit 13 shows that the response of the firm's ATC to the industry's expansion differs from that in the constant-cost industry case. In an increasing-cost industry, the firm's ATC curve shifts upward from ATC_1 to ATC_2, corresponding to the new short-run equilibrium at point E_3. At this final equilibrium point, the price is higher at $70 than the initial price of $60. Normal profits are re-established because profits are squeezed from both the price fall and the rise in the ATC curve.

EXHIBIT 12

Long-Run Supply in a Decreasing-Cost Industry

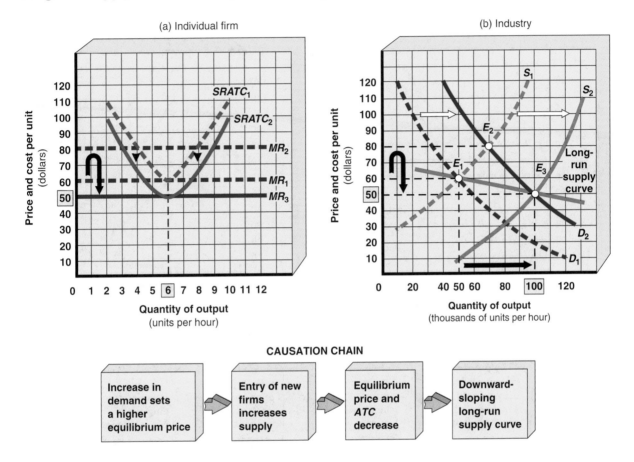

(a) Individual firm

(b) Industry

CAUSATION CHAIN

| Increase in demand sets a higher equilibrium price | ⇒ | Entry of new firms increases supply | ⇒ | Equilibrium price and *ATC* decrease | ⇒ | Downward-sloping long-run supply curve |

The long-run supply curve for a decreasing-cost industry is downward-sloping. The increase in industry demand shown in part (b) causes the price to rise to $80 in the short run. Temporarily, the typical firm illustrated in part (a) earns an economic profit. Higher profits attract new firms, and supply increases. As the industry expands, the average total cost curve for the firm shifts lower, and the firm re-establishes long-run equilibrium at the lower price of $50.

The long-run industry supply curve is drawn by connecting the two long-run equilibrium points of E_1 and E_3. Equilibrium point E_2 is not a long-run equilibrium point because it is not established after the entry of new firms has restored normal profits.

Conclusion *The long-run supply curve in a perfectly competitive increasing-cost industry is upward-sloping.*

EXHIBIT 13

Long-Run Supply in an Increasing-Cost Industry

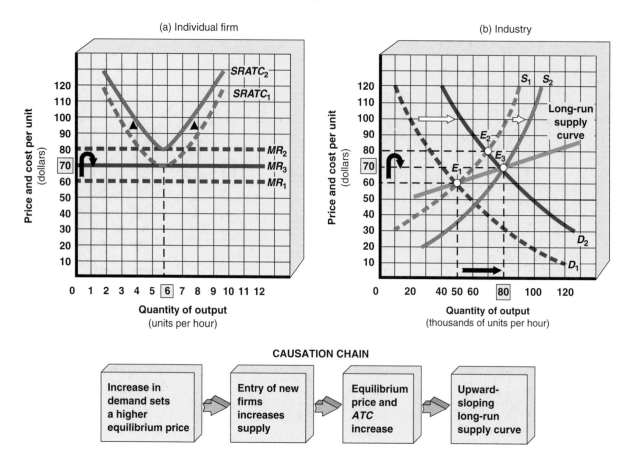

(a) Individual firm

(b) Industry

CAUSATION CHAIN

Increase in demand sets a higher equilibrium price ⇨ Entry of new firms increases supply ⇨ Equilibrium price and *ATC* increase ⇨ Upward-sloping long-run supply curve

This pair of graphs derives the long-run supply curve based on the assumption that input prices rise as industry output expands. Part (b) shows that an increase in demand from D_1 to D_2 causes the price to increase in the short run from $60 to $80. The typical firm represented in part (a) earns an economic profit, and new firms enter the industry, causing an increase in industry supply from S_1 to S_2. As output expands, input prices rise and push up the firm's short-run average total cost curve from $SRATC_1$ to $SRATC_2$. As a result, a new long-run equilibrium price is established at $70, which is above the initial equilibrium price. The long-run supply curve for an increasing-cost industry is upward-sloping.

Finally, given the three models presented above, you may ask which is the best choice. The answer is that all three versions are possible for any given industry. Only direct observation of the industry can tell which type of industry it is.

Gators: Snapping Up Profits

Applicable Concepts: short-run and long-run competitive equilibrium

A 1986 article describes the short-run gator market:

Attention, farmers! Tired of milking cows and slopping hogs? Fed up with slumping poultry prices? Have we got the animal for you—but keep a gun handy when you enter its pen.

Since its prehistoric heyday, the alligator has led a reclusive existence in the Florida wetlands, struggling to avoid extinction. Then came conservation, and wandering alligators are now such pests in Florida neighborhoods that residents must often call the police. Shrewd entrepreneurs saw big profits in the reptile surplus; with a hide suitable for leather goods and a meat that gives any menu an exotic flair, the gator could make an ideal farm animal. Today [1986] gator farming ranks as one of Florida's fastest-growing businesses. "Look, beef and poultry farmers are in trouble," says gator grower John Hudson, feeding a pitchfork full of rotten chicken wings to a six-foot specimen. "But the gator-meat industry is a coming thing."

The animal, in fact, spawned several hot industries. The lizard "look" has come back into vogue: fashion mavens sport gator-skin purses, shoes, and belts. Chic doesn't come cheap; in New York gator cowboy boots sell for $1,800, and attache cases retail for $4,000. These days you can order gator meat at trendy restaurants all along the East Coast. Dominique's in Washington, D.C., sells out its sauteed tail at $12 a plate. Even the Red Lobster seafood chain sees a future for the reptile. "Why not gator?" asked Red Lobster spokesman Dick Monroe. "Today's two-income households are looking for more variety. And tourists think it's neat to eat an animal that can eat them."

To meet the demand, Florida now has 26 licensed alligator farms, double the number of four years ago, when they functioned almost entirely as tourist attractions. Last year Florida farmers raised 37,000 gators; in 1986 that figure will increase by 50 percent. Revenues have soared as well. Frank Godwin, owner of Gatorland in Orlando, nets an estimated $270,000 from the 1,000 animals he harvests annually. Improved technology may boost profits even higher. Lawler Wells, owner of Hilltop Farms in Avon Park, raises his 7,000 gators in darkened hothouses that accelerate their growth. . . .

Understandably, gators are not yet a major cash crop. Most gator farms still earn big revenues from tourists. But Frank Godwin, who sells gator accessories, canned gator chowder, and "gator bites" (deep-fried appetizers), sees the possibilities. "Imagine gator bites selling like Chicken McNuggets," he says. Other alligator experts doubt that gator meat will ever rival the hamburger in appeal. Says one Florida game warden: "I like it, but to

most folks it's like eating a lizard."[1]

A few years later, an article in the *Washington Post* continues the gator tale: "During the late 1980s, gator ranching was booming, and the industry was being compared to a living gold mine. People rushed into the industry. Some farmers became temporarily rich."[2]

In 1995, an interview with a gator hunter provides evidence on long-run equilibrium: "Armed with a pistol barrel attached to the end of an 8-foot wooden pole, alligator hunter Bill Chaplin fires his "bank-stick" and dispatches a six-footer with a single round of .44 magnum ammunition. What's in it for him? Financially, very little. At $3.50 a pound for the meat and $45 a foot for the hide, an alligator is worth perhaps $100 a foot. After paying for skinning and processing, neither hunter nor landowner gets rich."[3] [Alligators have been off the endangered species list since 1988.]

ANALYZE THE ISSUE

1. Draw short-run firm and industry competitive equilibriums for a perfectly competitive gator-farming industry before the number of alligator farms in Florida doubled. For simplicity, assume the gator farm is earning zero economic profit. Now show the short-run effect of an increase in demand for alligators.

2. Assuming gator farming is perfectly competitive, explain the long-run competitive equilibrium condition for the typical gator farmer and the industry as a whole.

[1] Ron Moreau and Penelope Wang, "Gators: Snapping Up Profits," p. 68. From *Newsweek*, December 8, 1986, © 1986 Newsweek, Inc. All rights reserved. Reprinted by permission.
[2] William Booth, "Bag a Gator and Save the Species," *Washington Post*, August 25, 1993, p. A1.
[3] J. Taylor Buckley, "S. Carolina Lets Hunters Go for Gators Again," *USA Today*, September 21, 1995, News Section, p. A1.

KEY CONCEPTS

Market structure
Perfect competition
Price taker
Marginal revenue

Perfectly competitive
  firm's short-run
  supply curve
Perfectly competitive
  industry's short-run
  supply curve

Perfect competitive
  industry's long-run
  supply curve
Constant-cost industry
Decreasing-cost industry
Increasing-cost industry

SUMMARY

■ **Market structure** consists of three market characteristics: (1) the number of sellers, (2) the nature of the product, and (3) the ease of entry into or exit from the market.

■ **Perfect competition** is a market structure in which an individual firm cannot affect the price of the product it produces. Each firm in the industry is very small relative to the market as a whole, all the firms sell a homogeneous product, and firms are free to enter and exit the industry.

■ A **price-taker** firm in perfect competition faces a perfectly elastic demand curve. It can sell all it wishes at the market-determined price, but it will sell nothing above the given market price. This is because so many competitive firms are willing to sell at the going market price.

★ The **total revenue–total cost method** is one way the firm determines the level of output that maximizes profit. Profit reaches a maximum when the vertical difference between the total revenue and the total cost curves is at a maximum.

Total revenue–total cost method

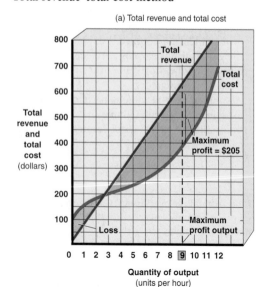

(a) Total revenue and total cost

★ The **marginal revenue equals marginal cost method** is a second approach to finding where a firm maximizes profits. **Marginal revenue** is the change in total revenue from a one-unit change in output. Marginal revenue for a perfectly competitive firm equals the market price. The $MR = MC$ *rule* states that the firm maximizes profit or minimizes loss by producing the output where marginal revenue equals marginal cost. If the price (average revenue) is below the minimum point on the average variable cost curve, the $MR = MC$ rule does not apply, and the firm shuts down to minimize its losses.

Marginal revenue

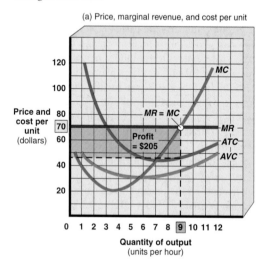

(a) Price, marginal revenue, and cost per unit

★ The **perfectly competitive firm's short-run supply curve** is a curve showing the relationship between the price of a product and the quantity supplied in the short run. The individual firm always produces along its marginal cost curve above its intersection with the average variable cost curve. The **perfectly competitive industry's short-run supply curve** is the horizontal summation of the short-run supply curves of all firms in the industry.

Short-run supply curve

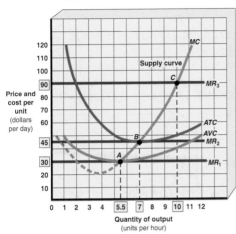

Long-run perfectly competitive equilibrium

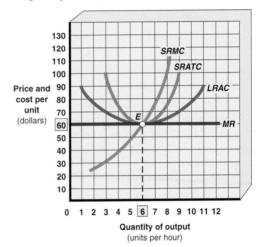

★ **Long-run perfectly competitive equilibrium** occurs when the firm earns a normal profit by producing where price equals minimum long-run average cost equals minimum short-run average total cost equals short-run marginal cost.

■ A **constant-cost industry** is an industry whose total output can be expanded without an increase in the firm's average total cost. Because input prices remain constant, the long-run supply curve in a constant-cost industry is perfectly elastic.

■ A **decreasing-cost industry** is an industry in which lower input prices result in a downward-sloping long-run supply curve. As industry output expands, the firm's average total cost curve shifts downward, and the long-run equilibrium market price falls.

■ An **increasing-cost industry** is an industry in which input prices rise as industry output increases. As a result, the firm's average total cost curve rises, and the long-run supply curve for an increasing-cost industry is upward-sloping.

SUMMARY OF CONCLUSION STATEMENTS

■ The large-number-of-sellers condition is met when each firm is so small relative to the total market that no single firm can influence the market price.

■ If a product is homogeneous, buyers are indifferent as to which seller's product they buy.

■ Perfect competition requires that resources be completely mobile to freely enter or exit a market.

■ In perfect competition, the firm's marginal revenue equals the price that the firm views as a horizontal demand curve.

■ In perfect competition, the firm maximizes profit or minimizes losses by producing the output where marginal revenue equals marginal cost.

■ In perfect competition, if the price is below the minimum point on the *AVC* curve, each unit produced would not cover the variable cost per unit. Therefore, the firm shuts down.

■ The long-run supply curve in a perfectly competitive constant-cost industry is perfectly elastic.

■ The long-run supply curve in a perfectly competitive decreasing-cost industry is downward-sloping.

■ The long-run supply curve in a perfectly competitive increasing-cost industry is upward-sloping.

STUDY QUESTIONS AND PROBLEMS

1. Explain why a perfectly competitive firm would or would not advertise.

2. Does a Kansas wheat farmer fit the perfectly competitive market structure? Explain.

3. Suppose the market equilibrium price of wheat is $2.00 per bushel in a perfectly competitive industry. Draw the industry supply and demand curves and the demand curve for a single wheat farmer. Explain why the wheat farmer is a price taker.

4. Assuming the market equilibrium price for wheat is $5 per bushel, draw the total revenue and the marginal revenue curves for the typical wheat farmer in the same graph. Explain how marginal revenue and price are related to the total revenue curve.

5. Consider the following cost data for a perfectly competitive firm in the short run:

Output (Q)	Total Fixed Cost (TFC)	Total Variable Cost (TVC)	Total Cost (TC)	Total Revenue (TR)	Profit
1	$100	$120	$___	$___	$___
2	100	200	___	___	___
3	100	290	___	___	___
4	100	430	___	___	___
5	100	590	___	___	___

If the market price is $150, how many units of output will the firm produce in order to maximize profit in the short run? Specify the amount of economic profit or loss. At what level of output does the firm break even?

6. Consider this statement: "A firm should increase output when it makes a profit." Do you agree or disagree? Explain.

7. Consider this statement: "When marginal revenue equals marginal cost, total cost equals total revenue, and the firm makes zero profit." Do you agree or disagree? Explain.

8. Consider Exhibit 14, which shows the graph of a perfectly competitive firm in the short run.
   a. If the firm's demand curve is MR_3, state whether the firm earns an economic profit or loss.
   b. Which demand curve(s) indicates the firm incurs a loss?

c. Which demand curve(s) indicates the firm would shut down?

d. Identify the firm's short-run supply curve.

EXHIBIT 14   Perfectly Competitive Firm

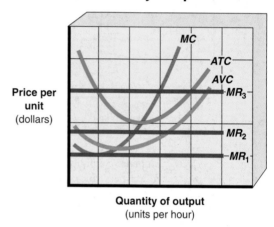

Quantity of output
(units per hour)

9. Consider this statement: "The perfectly competitive firm will sell all the quantity of output consumers will buy at the prevailing market price." Do you agree or disagree? Explain your answer.

10. Suppose a perfectly competitive firm's demand curve is below its average total cost curve. Explain the conditions under which a firm continues to produce in the short run.

11. Suppose the industry equilibrium price of residential housing construction is $100 per square foot and the minimum average variable cost for a residential construction contractor is $110 per square foot. What would you advise the owner of this firm to do? Explain.

12. Suppose independent truckers operate in a perfectly competitive industry. If these firms are earning positive economic profits, what happens in the long run to the following: the price of trucking services, the industry quantity of output, the profits of trucking firms? Given these conditions, is the independent trucking industry a constant-cost, an increasing-cost, or a decreasing-cost industry?

ONLINE EXERCISES

Exercise 1

Visit GPO Gate, Catalog for Economic Report of the President (http://www.gpo.ucop.edu/catalog/erp99 _appen_b.html). Select Table B-60, consumer price indexes for major expenditure classes, and follow these steps:

1. Note the Apparel and energy prices for the last 20 years.

2. Why does the price of energy fluctuate more than the price of apparel?

Exercise 2

Visit USA Today Market Scoreboard (http://www .usatoday.com). Click on Stocks, and follow these steps:

1. Under Markets, study the Dow Jones Industrial Average fluctuation in the chart.

2. Apply the characteristics of a perfectly competitive market structure to the stock market. Why do stock prices fluctuate so much?

CHECKPOINT ANSWERS

Should Motels Offer Rooms at the Beach for Only $20 a Night?

As long as price exceeds average variable cost, the motel is better off operating than shutting down. Since $20 is more than enough to cover the guest-related variable costs, the firm will operate. The $5 remaining after covering variable costs can be put toward the $50 of fixed costs. Were the firm to shut down, it could make no contribution to these overhead costs. If you said the Myrtle Beach motels should operate during the winter because they can get a price that exceeds their average variable cost, **YOU ARE CORRECT.**

Are You in Business for the Long Run?

In the long run, surviving firms will operate at the minimum of the long-run average cost curve. The average cost of 50 storage units is $4,000 ($200,000/50), the average cost of 100 storage units is $3,000 ($300,000/ 100), and the average cost of 200 storage units is $3,500 ($700,000/200). Of the three storage-unit quantities given, the one with the lowest average cost is closest to the minimum point on the *LRAC* curve. If you chose 100 storage units, **YOU ARE CORRECT.**

PRACTICE QUIZ

For a visual explanation of the correct answers, visit the tutorial at http://tucker.swcollege.com.

1. A perfectly competitive market is *not* characterized by
   a. many small firms.
   b. a great variety of different products.
   c. free entry into and exit from the market.
   d. any of the above.

2. Which of the following is a characteristic of perfect competition?
   a. Entry barriers
   b. Homogeneous products
   c. Expenditures on advertising
   d. Quality of service

3. Which of the following are the same at all levels of output under perfect competition?
   a. Marginal cost and marginal revenue
   b. Price and marginal revenue
   c. Price and marginal cost
   d. All of the above

4. If a perfectly competitive firm sells 100 units of output at a market price of $100 per unit, its marginal revenue per unit is
   a. $1.
   b. $100.
   c. more than $1, but less than $100.
   d. less than $100.

5. Short-run profit maximization for a perfectly competitive firm occurs where the firm's marginal cost equals
   a. average total cost.
   b. average variable cost.
   c. marginal revenue.
   d. all of the above.

6. A perfectly competitive firm sells its output for $100 per unit, and the minimum average variable cost is $150 per unit. The firm should
   a. increase output.
   b. decrease output, but not shut down.
   c. maintain its current rate of output.
   d. shut down.

7. A perfectly competitive firm's supply curve follows the upward-sloping segment of its marginal cost curve above the
   a. average total cost curve.
   b. average variable cost curve.
   c. average fixed cost curve.
   d. average price curve.

EXHIBIT 15
Marginal Revenue and Cost per Unit Curves

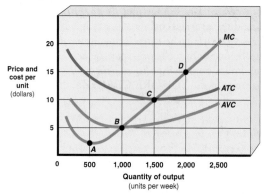

8. Assume the price of the firm's product in Exhibit 15 is $15 per unit. The firm will produce
   a. 500 units per week.
   b. 1,000 units per week.
   c. 1,500 units per week.
   d. 2,000 units per week.
   e. 2,500 units per week.

9. The lowest price in Exhibit 15 at which the firm earns zero economic profit in the short run is
   a. $5 per unit.
   b. $10 per unit.
   c. $20 per unit.
   d. $30 per unit.

10. Assume the price of the firm's product in Exhibit 15 is $6 per unit. The firm should
   a. continue to operate because it is earning an economic profit.
   b. stay in operation for the time being even though it is earning an economic loss.

   c. shut down temporarily.
   d. shut down permanently.

11. Assume the price of the firm's product in Exhibit 15 is $10 per unit. The maximum profit the firm earns is
   a. zero.
   b. $5,000 per week.
   c. $1,500 per week.
   d. $10,500 per week.

12. In Exhibit 15, the firm's total revenue at a price of $10 per unit pays for
   a. a portion of total variable costs.
   b. a portion of total fixed costs.
   c. none of the total fixed costs.
   d. all of the total fixed costs and total variable costs.

13. As shown in Exhibit 15, the short-run supply curve for this firm corresponds to which segment of its marginal cost curve?
   a. *A* to *D* and all points above
   b. *B* to *D* and all points above
   c. *C* to *D* and all points above
   d. *B* to *C* only

14. In long-run equilibrium, the perfectly competitive firm's price is equal to which of the following?
   a. Short-run marginal cost
   b. Minimum short-run average total cost
   c. Marginal revenue
   d. All of the above

15. In a constant-cost industry, input prices remain constant as
   a. the supply of inputs fluctuates.
   b. firms encounter diseconomies of scale.
   c. workers become more experienced.
   d. firms enter and exit the industry.

16. Suppose that, in the long run, the price of feature films rises as the movie production industry expands. We can conclude that movie production is a (an)
   a. increasing-cost industry.
   b. constant-cost industry.
   c. decreasing-cost industry.
   d. marginal-cost industry.

17. Which of the following is *true* of a perfectly competitive market?
   a. If economic profits are earned, then the price will fall over time.
   b. In long-run equilibrium, $P = MR = SRMC = SRATC = LRAC$.
   c. A constant-cost industry exists when the entry of new firms has no effect on their cost curves.
   d. All of the above are true.

CHAPTER NINE

Monopoly

Playing the popular board game of Monopoly teaches some of the characteristics of monopoly theory presented in this chapter. In the game version, players win by gaining as much economic power as possible. They strive to own railroads, utilities, Boardwalk, Park Place, and other valuable real estate. Then each player tries to bankrupt opponents by owning hotels that charge high prices. A player who rolls the dice and lands on another player's property has no choice—he or she must pay the price or lose the game.

In the last chapter, we studied perfect competition, which may be viewed as the paragon of economic virtue. Why? Under perfect competition, there are many sellers, each lacking any power to influence price. Perfect competition and monopoly are polar extremes. The word *monopoly* is derived from two Greek words meaning "single seller." A monopoly has the market power to set its price and not worry about competitors. Perhaps your college or university has only one bookstore where you can buy textbooks. If so, students are likely to pay higher prices for textbooks than would be the case if many sellers competed in the campus textbook market.

This chapter explains why firms do not or cannot enter a particular market and compete with a monopolist. Then we explore some of the interesting actual monopolies around the world. We study how a monopolist determines what price to charge and how much to produce. The chapter ends with a discussion of the pros and cons of monopoly. Most of the analytical tools required here have been introduced in previous chapters.

In this chapter, you will learn to solve these economics puzzles:

■ Why doesn't the monopolist gouge consumers by charging the highest possible price?

■ How can price discrimination be fair?

■ Are medallion cabs in New York City monopolists?

The Monopoly Market Structure

The model at the opposite extreme from perfect competition is monopoly. Under **monopoly**, the consumer has a simple choice—either buy the monopolist's product or do without it. Monopoly is a market structure characterized by (1) a single seller, (2) a unique product, and (3) impossible entry into the market. Unlike perfect competition, there are no close substitutes for the monopolist's product. Monopoly, like perfect competition, corresponds only approximately to real-world industries, but serves as a useful benchmark model. Following are brief descriptions of each monopoly characteristic.

Monopoly
A market structure characterized by (1) a single seller, (2) a unique product, and (3) impossible entry into the market.

Single Seller

In perfect competition, many firms make up the industry. In contrast, a monopoly means that a single firm *is* the industry. One firm provides the total supply of a product in a given market. Local monopolies are more common real-world approximations of the model than national or world market monopolies. For example, the campus bookstore, local telephone service, cable television company, and electric power company may be local monopolies. The only gas station in Nowhere County, Utah, and a hot dog stand at a football game are also examples of monopolies. Nationally, the U.S. Postal Service monopolizes first-class mail.

Congress has granted the U.S. Postal Service the exclusive right to deliver first-class mail. Check the USPS site at http://www.usps.com.

Unique Product

A unique product means there are *no close substitutes* for the monopolist's product. Thus, the monopolist faces little or no competition. In reality, however, there are few, if any, products that have no close substitutes. For example, students can buy used textbooks from sources other than the campus bookstore. Natural gas and oil furnaces are good substitutes for electric heat. Similarly, the fax machine and E-mail are substitutes for mail service, and a satellite dish can replace your local cable television service.

Impossible Entry

In perfect competition, there are no constraints to prevent new firms from entering an industry. In the case of monopoly, there are extremely high barriers that make it very difficult or impossible for new firms to enter an industry. Following are the three major barriers that prevent new sellers from entering a market and competing with a monopolist.

Ownership of a Vital Resource   Sole control of the entire supply of a strategic input is one way a monopolist can prevent a newcomer from entering an industry. A famous historical example is Alcoa's monopoly in the U.S. aluminum market from the late nineteenth century until the end of World War II. The source of Alcoa's monopoly was its control of bauxite ore, which is necessary to produce aluminum. It is very difficult for a new professional sports league to compete with the National Football League (NFL) and the National Basketball Association (NBA). Why? NFL and NBA teams have contracts with the best players and leases for the best stadiums and arenas.

Legal Barriers   The oldest and most effective barriers protecting a firm from potential competitors are the result of government franchises and licenses. The government permits a single firm to provide a certain product and excludes competing firms by law. For example, electric power, water and sewer service, natural gas, and cable television operate under monopoly franchises established by state and local government. In many states, the state government runs monopoly liquor stores and lotteries. The U.S. Postal Service also has a government franchise to deliver first-class mail.

Government-granted licenses restrict entry into some industries and occupations. For example, the Federal Communications Commission (FCC) must license radio and television stations. In most states, physicians, lawyers, dentists, nurses, teachers, real estate agents, barbers, taxicabs, liquor stores, funeral homes, and other professions and businesses are required to have a license.

Patents and copyrights are another form of government barrier to entry. The government grants patents to inventors, thereby legally prohibiting other firms from selling the patented product for 17 years. Copyrights give creators of literature, art, music, and movies exclusive rights to sell or license their works. The purpose behind granting patents and copyrights is to encourage innovation and new products by guaranteeing for a limited period exclusive rights to profit from new ideas.

Economies of Scale   Why might competition among firms be unsustainable, so that one firm becomes a monopolist? Recall the concept of *economies of scale* from the chapter on production costs. As a result of large-scale production, the long-run average cost of production falls. This means a monopoly can emerge in time *naturally* because of the relationship between average cost and the scale of an operation. As a firm becomes larger, its cost per unit of output is lower than a smaller competitor. In the long run, this "survival of the fittest" cost advantage forces the smaller firms to leave the industry. Because new firms cannot hope to produce and sell output equal or close to that of the monopolist, thereby achieving the low costs of the monopolist, they will not enter the industry. Thus, a monopoly can arise over time and remain dominant in an industry even though the monopolist does not own an essential resource or obtain legal barriers.

For over 60 years, DeBeers Consolidated Mines has struggled to maintain a worldwide monopoly on the diamond trade, owning most of the diamond mines in the world. See its site at http://www.edata.co.za/debeers.

For patents granted, patents pending, the process of patent issuance, or a search for patents, visit the following sites: http://www.uspto.gov, http://patents.uspto.gov, *and* http://www.patentspending.com. *Also see the National Association of Patent Practitioners (NAPP) for matters relating to patent laws, practice, and technological advances at* http://www.napp.org.

Natural monopoly
An industry in which the long-run average cost of production declines throughout the entire market. As a result, a single firm can supply the entire market demand at a lower cost than two or more smaller firms.

Economists call the situation in which one seller emerges in an industry because of economies of scale a **natural monopoly**. A natural monopoly is an industry in which the long-run average cost of production declines throughout the entire market. As a result, a single firm can supply the entire market demand at a lower cost than two or more smaller firms. Public utilities, such as the electric, natural gas, water, and local telephone companies, are examples of natural monopolies. The government grants an exclusive franchise to these industries in a geographic area so consumers benefit from the cost savings that occur when one firm in an industry with significant economies of scale sells a large output. The government then regulates these monopolies to prevent exploitation.

Exhibit 1 depicts the *LRAC* curve for a natural monopoly. A single firm can produce 100 units at an average cost of $15 and a total cost of $1,500. Another option is for two firms to each produce 50 units, and the total cost rises to $2,500. With five firms producing 20 units each, the total cost rises to $3,500. In the chapter on antitrust and regulation, regulation of a natural monopoly will be explored in greater detail.

Conclusion   *A single firm will produce output at a lower per-unit cost than two or more firms in the industry.*

Price and Output Decisions for a Monopolist

A major difference between perfect competition and monopoly is the shape of the demand curve, not the shapes of the cost curves. As explained in the previous chapter, a perfectly competitive firm is a *price taker*. In contrast, the next sections explain that a monopolist is a **price maker**. A price maker is a firm that faces a downward-sloping demand curve. This means a monopolist has the ability to select the product's price. In short, a monopolist can set the price with its corresponding level of output, rather than being a helpless pawn at the mercy of the going industry price. To understand the monopolist, we again apply the marginal approach to our hypothetical electronics company—Computech.

Price maker
A firm that faces a downward-sloping demand curve and therefore it can choose among price and output combinations along the demand curve.

Marginal Revenue, Total Revenue, and Price Elasticity of Demand

Suppose engineers for Computech discover an inexpensive miracle electronic device called "SAV-U-GAS," which anyone can easily attach to his or her car's engine. Once installed, the device raises gasoline mileage to over 100 miles per gallon. The government grants Computech a patent, and the company becomes a monopolist selling these gas-saver gizmos. Because of this barrier to entry, Computech is the only seller in the industry. Although other firms try to compete with this invention, they create poor substitutes. This means the downward-sloping demand curve for the industry and for the monopolist are identical.

EXHIBIT 1

Minimizing Costs in a Natural Monopoly

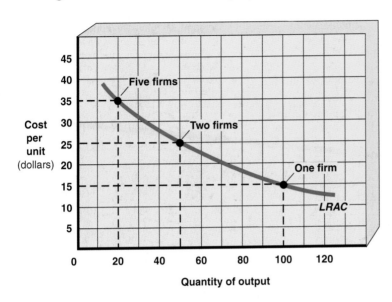

In a natural monopoly, a single firm can produce at a lower cost than two or more firms in an industry. This condition occurs because the LRAC curve for any firm decreases over the relevant range. For example, one firm can produce 100 units at an average cost of $15 and a total cost of $1,500. Two firms in the industry can produce 100 units of output (50 units each) for a total cost of $2,500, and five firms can produce the same output for a total cost of $3,500.

Exhibit 2(a) illustrates the demand and the marginal revenue curves for a monopolist such as Computech. As the monopolist lowers its price to increase the quantity demanded, changes in both price and quantity affect the firm's total revenue (price times quantity), as shown graphically in Exhibit 2(b). If Computech charges $150, consumers purchase zero units, and, therefore, total revenue is zero. To sell 1 unit, Computech must lower the price to $138, and total revenue rises from zero to $138. Because the marginal revenue is the increase in total revenue that results from a 1-unit change in output, the *MR* curve at the first unit of output is $138 ($138 − 0). Thus, the price and the marginal revenue from selling 1 unit are equal at $138. To sell 2 units, the monopolist must lower the price to $125, and total revenue rises to $250. The marginal revenue of the second unit is $112 ($250 − $138). Now the marginal revenue from selling the second unit is $13 less than the price received.

EXHIBIT 2

Demand, Marginal Revenue, and Total Revenue

(a) Demand and marginal revenue curves

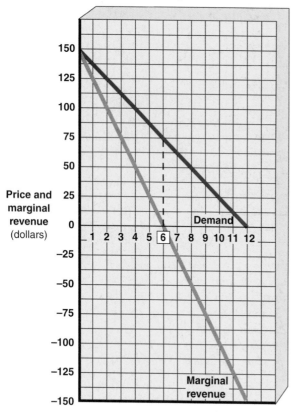

Price and marginal revenue (dollars)

Demand

Marginal revenue

Quantity of output
(units per hour)

Demand, Marginal Revenue, and Total Revenue for Computech as a Monopolist

Output per hour	Price	Total revenue	Marginal revenue
0	$150	$0	
			$138
1	138	138	
			112
2	125	250	
			89
3	113	339	
			61
4	100	400	
			40
5	88	440	
			10
6	75	450	
			0
7	63	441	−9
			−41
8	50	400	
			−58
9	38	342	
			−92
10	25	250	
			−107
11	13	143	
			−143
12	0	0	

(b) Total revenue curve

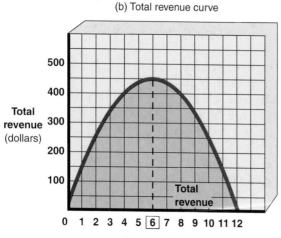

Total revenue (dollars)

Total revenue

Quantity of output
(units per hour)

Part (a) shows the relationship between the demand and the marginal revenue curves. The MR curve is below the demand curve. Between zero and 6 units of output, MR > 0; at 6 units of output, MR = 0; beyond 6 units of output, MR < 0.

The relationship between demand and total revenue is shown in part (b). When the price is $150, total revenue is zero. When the price is set at zero, total revenue is also zero. In between these two extreme prices, the price of $75 maximizes total revenue. This price corresponds to 6 units of output, which is where the MR curve intersects the quantity axis, halfway between the origin and the intercept of the demand curve.

INTERNATIONAL ECONOMICS

Monopolies Around the World
Applicable Concept: monopoly

This section briefly gives some interesting examples of monopolies in other countries. Let's begin with a historical example. Monarchs in the sixteenth through eighteenth centuries granted monopoly rights for a variety of businesses. For example, Queen Elizabeth I in 1600 chartered the British East India Company, and it was given a monopoly over England's trade with India. This company was even given the right to coin money and to make peace or war with non-Christian powers. As a result of its monopoly, the company made substantial profits from the trade in Indian cotton goods, silks, and spices. In the late 1700s, the growing power of the company and huge personal fortunes of its officers provoked more and more government control. Finally, its trade monopoly, great power, and patronage ended in 1858, when the company was abolished.

"Diamonds are forever," and perhaps so is the diamond monopoly. DeBeers, a South African corporation, is pretty close to a world monopoly. Through its Central Selling Organization (CSO) headquartered in London, DeBeers controls 80 percent of all the diamonds sold in the world. DeBeers controls the price of jewelry-quality diamonds by requiring suppliers in Russia, Australia, Zaire, Botswana, Namibia, and other countries to sell their rough diamonds through DeBeers's CSO. Why do the suppliers of rough diamonds allow DeBeers to set the price and quantity of diamonds sold throughout the world? The answer is that the CSO can put any uncooperative seller out of business. All the CSO has to do is to reach into its huge stockpile of diamonds and flood the market with the type of diamonds being sold by an independent seller. As a result, the price of diamonds plummets in the competitor's market, and it ceases to sell diamonds.

Genuine caviar, the salty black delicacy, is naturally scarce because it comes from the eggs of sturgeon harvested by fisheries from the Caspian Sea near the mouth of the Volga River. After the Bolshevik revolution in 1917, a caviar monopoly was established under the control of the Soviet Ministry of Fisheries and the Paris-based Petrosian Company. The Petrosian brothers limited exports of caviar and pushed up prices to as much as $1,000 a pound for some varieties. As a result of this worldwide monopoly, both the Soviet government and the Petrosian Company earned handsome profits. It is interesting to note that the vast majority of the tons of caviar harvested each year were consumed at government banquets or sold at bargain prices to top Communist party officials.

Then came the fall of the Soviet Union, and it was impossible for the Ministry of Fisheries to control all exports of caviar. Various former Soviet republics claimed jurisdiction and negotiated independent export contracts. Caviar export prices dropped sharply. But caviar lovers should not be too overjoyed. Today, the supply of caviar is dwindling because of overfishing and pollution of the Volga.

As shown in Exhibit 2(a), as a monopolist lowers its price, price is greater than marginal revenue after the first unit of output. Like all marginal measurements, marginal revenue is plotted midway between the quantities.

Conclusion *The demand and the marginal revenue curves of the monopolist are downward-sloping, in contrast to the horizontal demand and corresponding marginal revenue curves facing the perfectly competitive firm (compare Exhibit 2(a) with Exhibit 1(b) of the previous chapter).*

Starting from zero output, as the price falls, total revenue rises until it reaches a maximum at 6 units and then falls, which traces the "revenue hill" drawn in part (b). The explanation was presented earlier, in Chapter 5. Recall that a straight-line demand curve has an elastic ($E_d > 1$) upper half, a unit elastic ($E_d = 1$) midpoint, and an inelastic ($E_d < 1$) lower half (see Exhibit 4 in Chapter 5). Recall from Chapter 5 that when $E_d > 1$, total revenue rises as the price drops, and total revenue reaches a maximum where $E_d = 1$. When $E_d < 1$, total revenue falls as the price falls.

As shown in Exhibit 2(b), total revenue for a monopolist is related to marginal revenue. When the *MR* curve is above the quantity axis (elastic demand), total revenue is increasing. At the intersection of the *MR* curve and the quantity axis (unit elastic demand), total revenue is at its maximum. When the *MR* curve is below the quantity axis, total revenue is decreasing (inelastic demand). The monopolist will never operate on the inelastic range of its demand curve that corresponds to a negative marginal revenue. The reason is that cutting output and raising price in this inelastic range increase total revenue. In our example, Computech would not charge a price lower than $75 or produce an output greater than 6 units per hour. Now we turn to the question of what price the monopolist will charge to maximize profit.

In Exhibit 2(a), observe that the *MR* curve cuts the quantity axis at 6 units, half of 12 units. Following an easy rule helps locate the point along the quantity axis where marginal revenue equals zero: *The marginal revenue curve for a straight-line demand curve intersects the quantity axis halfway between the origin and the quantity axis intercept of the demand curve.*

Monopoly in the Short Run

Exhibit 3 reproduces the demand and the marginal revenue curves from Exhibit 2 and adds cost curves. Exhibit 3(a) illustrates a situation in which Computech can earn monopoly economic profit in the short run. As with the perfectly competitive firm, a monopolist maximizes profit by producing the quantity of output where *MR* = *MC* and charging the corresponding price on its demand curve. In this case, 4 units is the quantity at which *MR* = *MC*. As represented by point *A* on the demand curve, the price at 4 units is $100.

Point *B* represents the *ATC* of $75 at 4 units. Because price is greater than the *ATC* at the *MR* = *MC* output, the monopolist earns a profit of $25 per unit. At the hourly output of 4 units, total profit is $100 per hour, as shown by the shaded area.

Observe that a monopolist charges neither the highest possible price nor the revenue-maximizing price. In Exhibit 3(a), $100 is not the highest possible price. Because Computech is a *price maker*, it could have set a price above $100 and sold less output than 4 units. However, the monopolist does not charge the highest possible price in order to maximize profit. Any price above $100 does not correspond to the intersection of the *MR* and *MC* curves. Now note that 4 units is below the output level where

Profit Maximization and Loss Minimization for a Monopolist

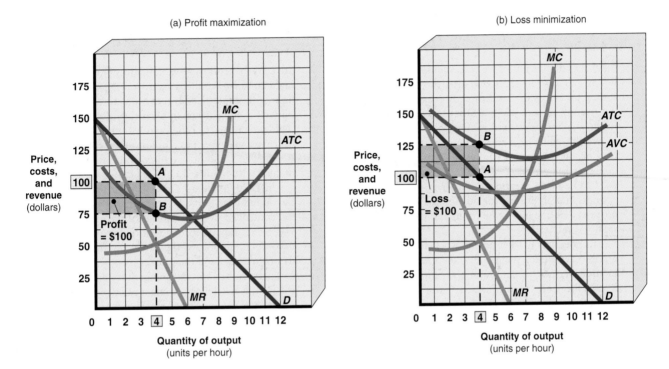

(a) Profit maximization

(b) Loss minimization

Part (a) illustrates a monopolist electronics firm—Computech—maximizing profit by producing 4 units of output, which corresponds to the intersection of the marginal revenue and the marginal cost curves. The price the monopolist charges is $100, which is point A on the demand curve. Because $100 is above the ATC of $75 at 4 units, the monopolist earns a short-run profit of $100 per hour, represented by the shaded area.

In part (b), Computech is a monopolist minimizing short-run losses by producing 4 units of output. Here the demand curve lies below the ATC curve at all points. At a price of $100, the shaded area shows that total revenue is less than total cost and the loss is $100 per hour. If the demand curve shifts leftward, preventing the firm from charging a price that covers the AVC, the monopolist loses less money by shutting down.

MR intersects the quantity axis and total revenue reaches its peak. Since $MR = 0$ and $E_d = 1$ when total revenue is maximum at 6 units of output, $MC = 0$ must also hold to maximize revenue and profit at the same time. A monopolist producing with zero marginal cost is an unlikely case. Hence, the price charged to maximize profit is higher on the demand curve than the price that maximizes total revenue.

The Standard Oil Company Monopoly

Applicable Concept: monopoly

Oil was discovered in western Pennsylvania by Colonel Edwin L. Drake in 1859, and after the Civil War, oil wells sprang up across the landscape. Because the supply of oil was plentiful, there was cutthroat competition, and the result was low prices and profits. John D. Rockefeller had grown up selling eggs and was at this time a young Cleveland produce wholesaler in his early twenties. He was doing well in produce, but realized that greater profits were to be made in refining oil, where there was less competition than in drilling for oil. So, in 1869, Rockefeller borrowed all the money he could and began with two small oil refineries.

To boost his market power, Rockefeller's Standard Oil of Ohio negotiated secret agreements with the railroads. In addition to information on his competitors' shipments, Rockefeller negotiated contracts with the railroads that paid rebates on oil shipments of not only Standard Oil, but also its competitors. Soon Standard Oil was able to buy 21 of its 26 refining competitors in the Cleveland

area. As its profits grew, Standard Oil expanded its refining empire by acquiring its own oil fields, railroads, pipelines, and ships. The objective was to control oil from the oil well to the consumer. Over time, Rockefeller came to own a major part of the petroleum industry. Rivals found railroads and pipelines closed to their oil shipments. Rivals who could not be forced out of business were merged with Standard Oil.

In 1870, Standard Oil controlled only 10 percent of the oil industry in the United States. By 1880, Standard Oil controlled over 90 percent of the industry, and its oil was being shipped throughout the world. The more Standard Oil monopolized the petroleum industry, the higher its profits rose, and the greater its power to eliminate competition became. As competitors dropped out of the industry, Rockefeller became a price maker. He raised prices, and profits soared for Standard Oil. Finally, in 1911, Standard Oil was broken up under the Sherman Antitrust Act of 1890.

Conclusion *The monopolist always maximizes profit by producing at a price on the elastic segment of its demand curve.*

The fact that a firm has a monopoly does not guarantee profits. A monopolist has no protection against changes in demand conditions. If the demand curve is lower than the *ATC* curve, as shown in Exhibit 3(b), total cost exceeds total revenue at any price charged. Because the *MR* = *MC* price of $100 (point *A*) is greater than the *AVC*, but not the *ATC*, the best Computech can do is to minimize its loss. This means the monopolist, like the perfectly competitive firm, produces in the short run where *MR* = *MC* as long as the price exceeds *AVC*. At a price of $100 (point *A*), the *ATC* is $125 (point *B*), and Computech takes a loss of $100 per hour, as represented by the shaded area ($25 × 4 units).

What if *MR* = *MC* at a price below the *AVC* for a monopolist? As under perfect competition, the monopolist will shut down. To operate would only add further to losses.

Monopoly in the Long Run

In perfect competition, economic profits are impossible in the long run. The entry of new firms into the industry drives the product's price down until profits reach zero. Extremely high barriers to entry, however, protect a monopolist.

> **Conclusion** *If the positions of a monopolist's demand and cost curves give it a profit and nothing disturbs these curves, the monopolist will earn profit in the long run.*

In the long run, the monopolist has great flexibility. The monopolist can alter its plant size to lower cost just as a perfectly competitive firm does. But firms such as Computech will not remain in business in the long run when losses persist—regardless of their monopoly status. Facing long-run losses, the monopolist will transfer its resources to a more profitable industry.

In reality, no monopolist can depend on barriers to protect it fully from competition in the long run. One threat is that entrepreneurs will find innovative ways to compete with a monopoly. For example, Computech must fear that firms will use their ingenuity to develop a better and cheaper gasoline-saving device, using new electronic discoveries. To dampen the enthusiasm of potential rivals, one alternative is to sacrifice short-run profits to earn greater profits in the long run. Returning to part (a) of Exhibit 2, the monopolist might wish to charge a price below $100 and produce an output greater than 4 units per hour.

Price Discrimination

Our discussion so far has assumed the monopolist charges each customer the same price. What if Computech decides to sell identical SAV-U-GAS units for, say, $50 to truckers and $100 to everyone else? Under certain conditions, a monopolist may practice **price discrimination** to maximize profit. Price discrimination occurs when a seller charges different prices for the same product not justified by cost differences.

Price discrimination
The practice of a seller charging different prices for the same product not justified by cost differences.

Conditions for Price Discrimination

All monopolists cannot engage in price discrimination. The following three conditions must exist before a seller can price discriminate:

1. The seller must be a price maker and therefore face a downward-sloping demand curve. This means monopoly is not the only market structure in which this practice may appear.
2. The seller must be able to segment the market by distinguishing between consumers willing to pay different prices. Momentarily, this separation of buyers will be shown to be based on different price elasticities of demand.
3. It must be impossible or too costly for customers to engage in **arbitrage**. Arbitrage is the practice of earning a profit by buying a good at a low price and reselling the good at a higher price. For example, suppose your campus bookstore tried to boost profits by selling textbooks at a 50 percent discount to seniors. It would not take

Arbitrage
The practice of earning a profit by buying a good at a low price and reselling the good at a higher price.

seniors long to cut the bookstore profits by buying textbooks at the low price, selling these texts under the list price to all the students who are not seniors, and pocketing the difference. In so doing, even without knowing the word *arbitrage*, the seniors would destroy the bookstore's price discrimination scheme.

Although not monopolies, college and university tuition policies meet the conditions for price discrimination. First, a lower tuition will increase the quantity of openings demanded. Second, an applicant's high school grades and SAT score allow the admissions office to classify "consumers" with different price elasticities of demand. Students with lower grades and SAT scores have fewer substitutes, and their demand curve is less elastic than that of students with higher grades and SAT scores. If the tuition price rises at University *X*, few students with lower grades will be lost because they have few offers of admission from other universities. On the other hand, the loss of students with higher grades and SAT scores is greater because they have more admissions opportunities. Third, the nature of the product prevents arbitrage. A student cannot buy University *X* admission at one tuition price and sell it to another student for a higher price.

Exhibit 4 illustrates how University *X* price discriminates. For simplicity, assume the marginal cost of providing education to students is constant and therefore represented by a horizontal *MC* curve. To maximize profit, University *X* follows the $MR = MC$ rule in each market. Given the different price elasticities of demand, the price at which $MR = MC$ differs for average and superior students. As a result, University *X* sets a higher tuition, T_1, in the average-student market, where demand is less responsive to the higher price. In the superior-student market, where demand is more responsive, these students receive scholarships, and their tuition is lower at T_2.

Is Price Discrimination Unfair?

Examples of price discrimination abound. Movie theaters offer lower prices for children than for adults. Electric utilities, which are monopolies, charge industrial users of electricity lower rates than residential users. Hotels and restaurants often give discounts to senior citizens. Airlines offer lower fares to groups of vacationers.

The typical reaction to price discrimination is that it is unfair. From the viewpoint of buyers who pay the higher prices, it is. But look at the other side of price discrimination. First, the seller is pleased because price discrimination increases profits. Second, many buyers benefit from price discrimination by not being excluded from purchasing the product. In Exhibit 4, price discrimination makes it possible for superior students who could not afford to pay a higher tuition to attend University *X*. It allows retired persons to enjoy hotels and restaurants they could not otherwise afford and more children to attend movies.

EXHIBIT 4

Price Discrimination

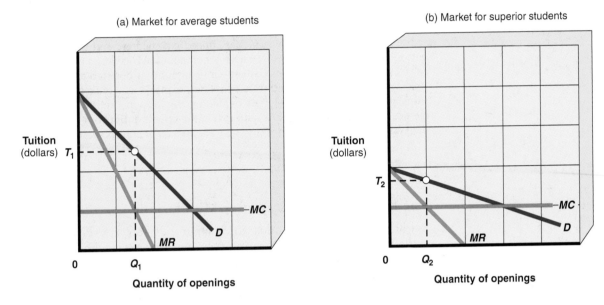

(a) Market for average students

(b) Market for superior students

To maximize profit, University X separates students applying for admission into two markets. The demand curve for admission of average students in part (a) is less elastic than the demand curve for admission of superior students in part (b). Profit maximization occurs when MR = MC in each market. Therefore, University X sets a tuition of T_1 for average students and gives scholarships to superior students, which lowers their tuition to T_2. Using price discrimination, University X earns a greater profit than it would by charging a single price to all students.

Comparing Monopoly and Perfect Competition

Now that the basics of the two extremes of perfect competition and monopoly have been presented, we can compare and evaluate these market structures. This is an important assessment because the contrast between the disadvantages of monopoly and the advantages of perfect competition is the basis for many government policies, such as antitrust laws. To keep the analysis simple, we assume the monopolist charges a single price, rather than engaging in price discrimination.

CHECKPOINT

Why Don't Adults Pay More for Popcorn at the Movies?

At the movies, adults pay a higher ticket price than children, and each group gets a different-colored ticket. However, when adults and children go to the concession stand, both groups pay the same amount for popcorn and other snacks. Which of the following statements best explains why price discrimination stops at the ticket window? (1) The demand curve for popcorn is perfectly elastic. (2) The theater has no way to divide the buyers of popcorn based on different price elasticities of demand. (3) The theater cannot prevent resale.

The Monopolist as a Resource Misallocator

Recall the discussion of market efficiency from Chapter 4. This condition exists when a firm charging the equilibrium price uses neither too many nor too few resources to produce a product, so there is no *market failure*. Now you can state this definition of market efficiency in terms of price and marginal cost, as follows: *A perfectly competitive firm that produces the quantity of output at which* P = MC *achieves an efficient allocation of resources*. This means production reaches the level of output where the price of the last unit produced matches the cost of producing it.

Exhibit 5(a) shows that a perfectly competitive firm produces the quantity of output at which $P = MC$. The price, P_c (marginal benefit), of the last unit produced equals the marginal cost of the resources used to produce it. In contrast, the monopolist shown in Exhibit 5(b) charges a price, P_m, greater than marginal cost, $P > MC$. Therefore, consumers are short-changed because the marginal benefit of the last unit produced exceeds the marginal cost of producing it. Consumers want the monopolist to use more resources and produce additional units, but the monopolist restricts output to maximize profit.

> **Conclusion** *A monopolist is characterized by inefficiency because resources are underallocated to the production of its product.*

Perfect Competition Means More Output for Less

Exhibit 6 presents a comparison of perfect competition and monopoly in the same graph. Suppose the industry begins as perfectly competitive. The market demand curve, D (equal to MR), and the market supply curve, S, establish a perfectly competitive price, P_c, and an output, Q_c. Recall from Exhibit 8 in the previous chapter that the competitive industry's supply curve, S, is the horizontal sum of the marginal cost curves of all the firms in the industry.

EXHIBIT 5

Comparing a Perfectly Competitive Firm and a Monopolist

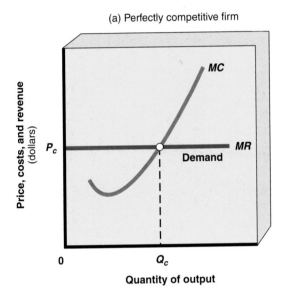

(a) Perfectly competitive firm

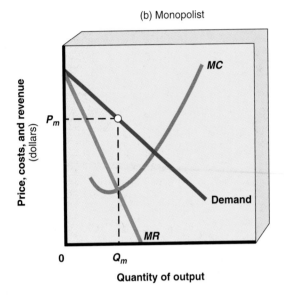

(b) Monopolist

The perfectly competitive firm in part (a) sets P = MC *and produces* Q_c
*output. Therefore, at the last unit of output, the marginal benefit is equal
to the marginal cost of resources used to produce it. This condition means
perfect competition achieves efficiency.*

Part (b) shows that the monopolist produces output Q_m *where* P >
MC. *By so doing, consumers are shortchanged because the marginal benefit of the last unit produced exceeds the marginal cost of producing it.
Under monopoly, inefficiency occurs because the monopolist underallo-
cates resources to the production of its product. As a result,* Q_m *is less
that* Q_c.

Now let's suppose the market structure changes when one firm buys
out all the competing firms and the industry becomes a monopoly. Assume
further that the demand and the cost curves are unaffected by this dramatic
change. In a monopoly, the industry demand curve *is* the monopolist's
demand curve. Because the single firm is a price maker, the *MR* curve lies
below the demand curve. The industry supply curve now becomes the marginal cost curve for the monopolist. To maximize profit, the monopolist
sets *MR* = *MC* by restricting the output to Q_m and raising the price to P_m.

Conclusion *Monopoly harms consumers on two fronts. The monopolist charges a higher price and produces a lower output than would
result under a perfectly competitive market structure.*

EXHIBIT 6

The Impact of Monopolizing an Industry

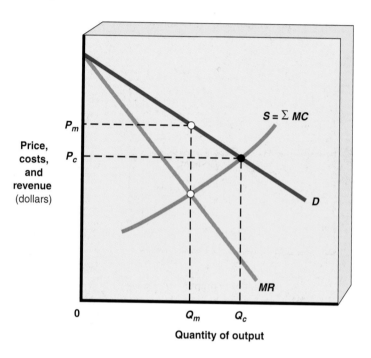

Price, costs, and revenue (dollars)

Assume an industry is perfectly competitive, with market demand curve D *and market supply curve* S. *The market supply curve is the horizontal summation of all the individual firms' marginal cost curves above their minimum average variable costs. The intersection of market supply and market demand establishes the equilibrium price of* P_c *and the equilibrium quantity of* Q_c. *Now assume the industry suddenly changes to a monopoly. The monopolist produces the* MR = MC *output of* Q_m, *which is less than* Q_c. *By restricting output to* Q_m, *the monopolist is able to charge the higher price of* P_m.

The Case Against and for Monopoly

So far, a strong case has been made against monopoly and in favor of perfect competition. Now it is time to pause and summarize the economist's case against monopoly, as follows:

- A monopolist "gouges" consumers by charging a higher price than would be the case under perfect competition.

- Because a monopolist restricts output in order to maximize profit, too few resources are used to produce the product. Stated differently, the monopolist misallocates resources by charging a price greater than marginal cost. In perfectly competitive industries, price is set equal to marginal cost, and the result is an optimal allocation of resources.

New York Taxicabs: Where Have All the Fare Flags Gone?

Applicable Concepts: perfect competition versus monopoly

In the 1920s, New York taxicabs were competitive. There was no limit on the number of taxis, and hack licenses were only $10. Cabbies could choose among three different flags to attach to their cars. A red flag cab would charge a surcharge for extra passengers. A white flag signaled no surcharge for extra passengers. A green flag meant the cabbie was offering a discount fare. Price wars often erupted, and the vast majority of cabbies would fly the green flags and charge bargain fares. One strategy was to fly the red flag (high rate) during rush hour and the green flag to offer discounts at off-peak times. Also, taxi companies offered a variety of cabs— old, new, big, and small.

As years passed, the system changed, and currently the Taxi and Limousine Commission sets rates and imposes regulations. One law passed creates a monopoly by requiring any cabs accepting street hails to be painted yellow and possess a medallion. The cost of that little plastic medallion on the yellow taxicabs' hood is about $300,000, and a 1937 law limits the numbers of medallions. On the other hand, it is illegal for cabs without medallions to cruise the streets and pick up passengers who hail them, although the law is often ignored. Nonmedallion cabs are authorized to respond only to customers who have ordered cabs in advance by phone or other means. There's no limit on the number of these cabs or what the drivers may charge.

A *New York Times* article describes results of this dual system:

> While today's 12,187 yellow cabs concentrate on Manhattan below 125th Street, there's a much larger fleet of radio-dispatched cars that handles business in upper Manhattan and the other boroughs. "The outer boroughs generally get better service because there's competition out there," Edward Rogoff [professor of management at Baruch College] says. "By and large, the nonmedallion cars are better vehicles with more experienced drivers who carry more insurance than the yellow cabs."[1]

In a personal interview with the author, Professor Rogoff stated, "I would estimate that, in general, nonmedallion vehicles charge about 25 percent less than medallion cabs."[2] However, established nonmedallion vehicle owners also want the city to make it tougher for new companies to enter the nonmedallion market. "What we want is a little monopoly help from the government," said Robert Mackle, an official of Skyline CreditRide, a cooperative of owner-drivers of black cars.[3]

ANALYZE THE ISSUE

Use a graph to compare the price and output of medallion yellow cab rides in New York City before and after the 1920s.

---

[1]John Tierney, "You'll Wonder Where the Yellow Went," *New York Times*, July 12, 1998, sec. 6, p. 18.
[2]Personal interview, 1998.
[3] Winston Williams, "Owners Bewail Flood of Cabs in New York," *New York Times*, April 10, 1989, p. B1.

- Long-run economic profit for a monopolist exceeds the zero economic profit in the long run for a perfectly competitive firm.

- To the extent that the monopolist is a rich John D. Rockefeller, for example, and consumers of oil are poor, monopoly alters the distribution of income in favor of the monopolist.

Not all economists agree that monopoly is bad. The late Joseph Schumpeter and John Kenneth Galbraith have praised monopoly power. They have argued that the rate of technological change is likely to be greater under monopoly than perfect competition. Their view is that monopoly profits afford giant monopolies the financial strength to invest in the well-equipped laboratories and skilled labor necessary to create technological change.

The counterargument is that monopolists are slow to innovate. Freedom from direct competition means the monopolist is not motivated and therefore tends to stick to the "conventional wisdom." As Nobel laureate Sir John Hicks put it, "The best of all monopoly profit is a quiet life." In short, monopoly offers the opportunity to relax a bit and not worry about the "rat race" of technological change.

What does research on this issue suggest? Not surprisingly, many attempts have been made to verify or refute the effect of market structure on technological change. Unfortunately, the results to date have been inconclusive. For all we know, a mix of large and small firms in an industry may be the optimal mix to create technological change.

KEY CONCEPTS

Monopoly	Price maker	Arbitrage
Natural monopoly	Price discrimination	

SUMMARY

- **Monopoly** is a single seller facing the entire industry demand curve because it is the industry. The monopolist sells a unique product, and extremely high barriers to entry protect it from competition.

- **Barriers to entry** that prevent new firms from entering an industry are (1) ownership of an essential resource, (2) legal barriers, and (3) economies of scale. Govern-

ment franchises, licenses, patents, and copyrights are the most obvious legal barriers to entry.

- ★ A **natural monopoly** arises because of the existence of economies of scale in which the *LRAC* curve falls as production increases. Without government restrictions, economies of scale allow a single firm to produce at a lower cost than any firm producing a smaller output. Thus, smaller firms leave the industry, new firms fear competing with the monopolist, and the result is that a monopoly emerges *naturally*.

Natural monopoly

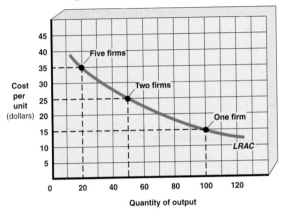

- A **price-maker** firm faces a downward-sloping demand curve. It therefore searches its demand curve to find the price-output combination that maximizes its profit and minimizes its loss.

- The **marginal revenue** and the demand curves are downward-sloping for a monopolist. The marginal revenue curve for a monopolist is below the demand curve, and the total revenue curve reaches its maximum where marginal revenue equals zero.

- **Price elasticity of demand** corresponds to sections of the marginal revenue curve. When *MR* is positive, price elasticity of demand is elastic, $E_d > 1$. When MR is equal to zero, price elasticity of demand is unit elastic, $E_d = 1$. When *MR* is negative, price elasticity of demand is inelastic, $E_d < 1$.

★ The **short-run-profit-maximizing monopolist**, like the perfectly competitive firm, locates the profit-maximizing price by producing the output where

the *MR* and the *MC* curves intersect. If this price is less than the *AVC* curve, the monopolist shuts down to minimize losses.

Short-run-profit-maximizing monopolist

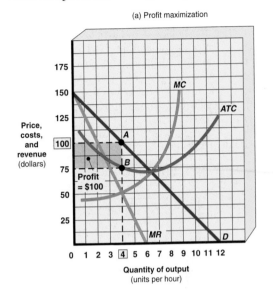

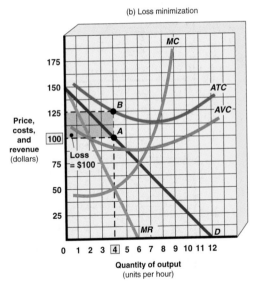

- The **long-run-profit-maximizing monopolist** earns a profit because of barriers to entry. If demand and cost conditions prevent the monopolist from earning a profit, it will leave the industry.

★ **Price discrimination** allows the monopolist to increase profits by charging buyers different prices, rather than a single price. Three conditions are necessary for price discrimination: (1) The demand curve must be downward-sloping, (2) buyers in different markets must have different price elasticities of demand, and (3) buyers must be prevented from reselling the product at a higher price than the purchase price.

★ **Monopoly disadvantages** are these: (1) A monopolist charges a higher price and produces less output than a perfectly competitive firm, (2) resource allocation is inefficient because the monopolist produces less than if competition existed, (3) monopoly produces higher long-run profits than if competition existed, and (4) monopoly transfers income from consumers to producers to a greater degree than under perfect competition.

Price discrimination

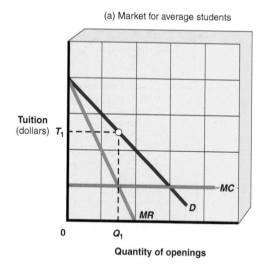

(a) Market for average students

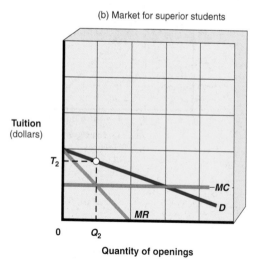

(b) Market for superior students

Monopoly disadvantages

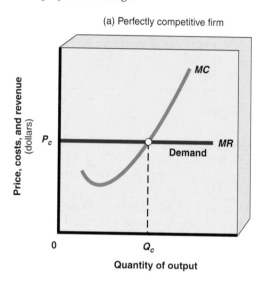

(a) Perfectly competitive firm

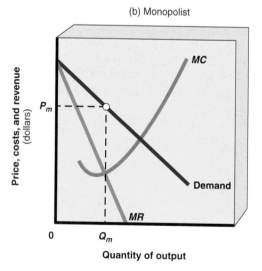

(b) Monopolist

SUMMARY OF CONCLUSION STATEMENTS

- A single firm will produce output at a lower per-unit cost than two or more firms in the industry.

- The demand and the marginal revenue curves of the monopolist are downward-sloping, in contrast to the horizontal demand and corresponding marginal revenue curves facing the perfectly competitive firm.

- The monopolist always maximizes profit by producing at a price on the elastic segment of its demand curve.

- If the positions of a monopolist's demand and cost curves give it a profit and nothing disturbs these curves, the monopolist will earn profit in the long run.

- A monopolist is characterized by inefficiency because resources are underallocated to the production of its product.

- Monopoly harms consumers on two fronts. The monopolist charges a higher price and produces a lower output than would result under a perfectly competitive market structure.

STUDY QUESTIONS AND PROBLEMS

1. Using the three characteristics of monopoly, explain why each of the following is a monopolist:
   a. Local telephone company.
   b. San Francisco 49ers football team.
   c. U.S. Postal Service.

2. Why is the demand curve facing a monopolist downward-sloping and the demand curve facing a perfectly competitive firm horizontal?

3. Suppose an investigator reveals that the prices charged for drugs at a hospital are higher than the prices charged for the same products at drugstores in the area served by the hospital. What may the explanation for this situation be?

4. Explain why you agree or disagree with the following statements:
   a. "All monopolies are created by the government."
   b. "The monopolist charges the highest possible price."
   c. "The monopolist never takes a loss."

5. Suppose the average cost of producing a kilowatt hour of electricity is lower for one firm than for another firm serving the same market. Without the government granting a franchise to one of these competing power companies, explain why a single seller is likely to emerge in the long run.

6. Use the following demand schedule for a monopolist to calculate total revenue and marginal revenue. For each price, indicate whether demand is elastic, unit elastic, or inelastic. Using the data from the demand schedule, graph the demand curve, the marginal revenue curve, and the total revenue curve. Identify the elastic, unit elastic, and inelastic segments along the demand curve.

Price	Quantity Demanded	Total Revenue	Marginal Revenue	Price Elasticity of Demand
$5.00	0	$ ___	$ ___	___
4.50	1	___	___	___
4.00	2	___	___	___
3.50	3	___	___	___
3.00	4	___	___	___
2.50	5	___	___	___
2.00	6	___	___	___
1.50	7	___	___	___
1.00	8	___	___	___
.50	9	___	___	___
0	10	___	___	___

7. Make the unrealistic assumption that production is costless for the monopolist in question 6. Given the data from the above demand schedule, what price will the monopolist charge, and how much output should the firm produce? How much profit will the firm earn? What will be the effect on the price and output of the monopolist when marginal cost is above zero?

8. Explain why a monopolist would never produce in the inelastic range of the demand curve.

9. In each of the following cases, state whether the monopolist would increase or decrease output:
   a. Marginal revenue exceeds marginal cost at the output produced.
   b. Marginal cost exceeds marginal revenue at the output produced.

10. Suppose the demand and the cost curves for a monopolist are as shown in Exhibit 7. Explain what price the monopolist should charge and how much output it should produce.

EXHIBIT 7   A Monopolist in the Short Run

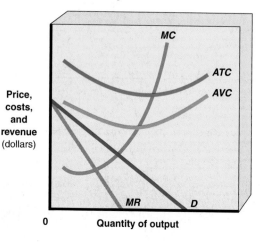

11. Which of the following are price discrimination?
    a. A department store has a 25-percent-off-the-price sale.
    b. A publisher sells economics textbooks at a lower price in North Carolina than in New York.
    c. The Japanese sell cars at higher prices in the United States than in Japan.
    d. The phone company charges higher long-distance rates during the day.

12. Suppose the candy bar industry approximates a perfectly competitive industry. Suppose also that a single firm buys all the assets of the candy bar firms and establishes a monopoly. Contrast these two market structures with respect to price, output, and allocation of resources. Draw a graph of the market demand and market supply for candy bars before and after the takeover.

ONLINE EXERCISES

Exercise 1

Visit Engagement Diamond FAQ (http://www.wam.umd.edu/~sek/wedding/mlynek.html), and select 3: From a Mine to Your Finger. This section gives some insight into how DeBeers has maintained a worldwide monopoly in diamonds.

Exercise 2

Visit your university's Internet site. If you are not sure of the address, visit http://www.universities.com/. Does your university specify admission standards at its site? Is anything said about scholarships? Does your university practice price discrimination?

Exercise 3

Consider the definition of a monopolist. Can the U.S. Postal Service (http://www.usps.com) be considered a monopoly in first-class postage? Why or why not? Federal Express Corporation (http://www.fedex.com) and United Parcel Service of America, Inc. (http://www.ups.com) also deliver letters and packages. What has happened to the price elasticity of demand for first-class letters?

Exercise 4

Why can't two baseball teams succeed in a city like Kansas City (http://www.majorleaguebaseball.com/al/kc/), while both the New York Yankees (http://www.yankees.com) and the New York Mets (http://www.majorleaguebaseball.com/nl/ny/) can succeed in New York City?

CHECKPOINT ANSWERS

Why Don't Adults Pay More for Popcorn at the Movies?

First, there are no other sellers in the lobby, so the theater is a price maker for popcorn, and the demand curve slopes downward. Second, the theater could easily set up different lines for adults and children and charge different

prices for popcorn. Third, is there a practical way to prevent resale? Does the theater want to try to stop children who resell popcorn to their parents, friends, and other adults? If you said theaters do not practice price discrimination at the concession counter because resale cannot be prevented, **YOU ARE CORRECT.**

PRACTICE QUIZ

For a visual explanation of the correct answers, visit the tutorial at http://tucker.swcollege.com.

1. A monopolist always faces a demand curve that is
   a. perfectly inelastic.
   b. perfectly elastic.
   c. unit elastic.
   d. the same as the market demand curve.

2. A monopolist sets the
   a. price at which marginal revenue equals zero.
   b. price that maximizes total revenue.
   c. highest possible price on its demand curve.
   d. price at which marginal revenue equals marginal cost.

3. A monopolist sets
   a. the highest possible price.
   b. a price corresponding to minimum average total cost.
   c. a price equal to marginal revenue.
   d. a price determined by the point on the demand curve corresponding to the level of output at which marginal revenue equals marginal cost.
   e. none of the above.

4. Which of the following is true for the monopolist?
   a. Economic profit is possible in the long run.
   b. Marginal revenue is less than the price charged.
   c. Profit-maximizing or loss-minimizing occurs when marginal revenue equals marginal cost.
   d. All of the above are true.

EXHIBIT 8
Profit Maximizing for a Monopolist

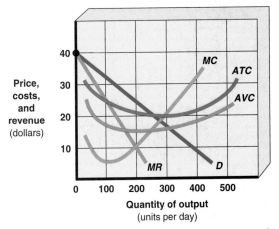

5. As shown in Exhibit 8, the profit-maximizing or loss-minimizing output for this monopolist is
   a. 100 units per day.
   b. 200 units per day.
   c. 300 units per day.
   d. 400 units per day.

6. As shown in Exhibit 8, this monopolist
   a. should shut down in the short run.
   b. should shut down in the long run.
   c. earns zero economic profit.
   d. earns positive economic profit.

7. To maximize profit or minimize loss, the monopolist in Exhibit 8 should set its price at
   a. $30.00 per unit.
   b. $25.00 per unit.
   c. $20.00 per unit.
   d. $10.00 per unit.
   e. $40.00 per unit.

8. If the monopolist in Exhibit 8 operates at the profit-maximizing output, it will earn total revenue to pay about what portion of its total fixed cost?
   a. None
   b. One-half
   c. Two-thirds
   d. All total fixed costs

9. For a monopolist to practice effective price discrimination, one necessary condition is
   a. identical demand curves among groups of buyers.
   b. differences in the price elasticity of demand among groups of buyers.
   c. a homogeneous product.
   d. none of the above.

10. What is the act of buying a commodity in one market at a lower price and selling it in another market at a higher price?
    a. Buying short
    b. Discounting
    c. Tariffing
    d. Arbitrage

11. Under both perfect competition and monopoly, a firm
    a. is a price taker.
    b. is a price maker.
    c. will shut down in the short run if price falls short of average total cost.
    d. always earns a pure economic profit.
    e. sets marginal cost equal to marginal revenue.

CHAPTER TEN

Monopolistic Competition and Oligopoly

uppose your favorite restaurant is Ivan's Oyster Bar. Ivan's does not fit either of the two extreme models studied in the previous two chapters. Instead, Ivan's characteristics are a blend of monopoly and perfect competition. For starters, similar to a monopolist, Ivan's demand curve is downward-sloping. This means Ivan's is a *price maker* because it can charge a higher price for seafood and lose some customers, but many loyal customers will keep coming. The reason is that Ivan's makes its product different from the competition by advertising, first-rate service, a great salad bar, and other factors. In short, like a monopolist, Ivan's has a degree of *market power*. But like a perfectly competitive firm, Ivan's is not the only place to buy a seafood dinner in town. It must share the market with many other restaurants within an hour's drive.

The small Ivan's Oyster Bars and the gigantic General Motors of the world represent most of the firms with which you deal. These firms compete in two market structures that fall in a category economists call **imperfect competition**. One model of imperfect competition is *monopolistic competition,* and the other model is *oligopoly.* Ivan's operates in the former, and General Motors belongs to the latter.

Unlike a monopolist, an imperfect competitor shares the market with competing firms. But like monopolies, they restrict output to maximize profit. The theories of perfect competition and monopoly learned in the previous two chapters will help you understand the impact of these market structures on price and output decisions.

Imperfect competition

A market structure between the extremes of perfect competition and monopoly. Monopolistic competition and oligopoly belong to the imperfect competition category.

In this chapter, you will learn to solve these economics puzzles:

- Why will Ivan's Oyster Bar make zero economic profit in the long run?

- Why do OPEC and other cartels tend to break down?

- Are Cheerios, Rice Krispies, and other brands sold by firms in the breakfast cereal industry produced under monopolistic competition or oligopoly?

- How does the NCAA Final Four basketball tournament use imperfect competition?

The Monopolistic Competition Market Structure

Monopolistic competition

A market structure characterized by (1) many small sellers, (2) a differentiated product, and (3) easy market entry and exit.

Economists define **monopolistic competition** as follows: Monopolistic competition is a market structure characterized by (1) many small sellers, (2) a differentiated product, and (3) easy market entry and exit. Monopolistic competition fits numerous real-world industries. Following is a brief explanation of each characteristic.

Many Small Sellers

Under monopolistic competition, as under perfect competition, the exact number of firms cannot be stated. Ivan's Oyster Bar, described in the Chapter Preview, is an example of a monopolistic competitor. Ivan assumes that his restaurant can set prices slightly higher or improve service *independently* without fear that competitors will react by changing their prices or giving better service. Thus, if any single seafood restaurant raises its price, the going market price for seafood dinners increases by a very small amount.

> **Conclusion** *The many-sellers condition is met when each firm is so small relative to the total market that each firm's pricing decisions have a negligible effect on the market price.*

Differentiated Product

Product differentiation

The process of creating real or apparent differences between goods and services.

The key feature of monopolistic competition is **product differentiation**. Product differentiation is the process of creating real or apparent differences between goods and services. A differentiated product means there are close, but not perfect, substitutes for the firm's product. While the products of each firm are highly similar, the consumer views them as somewhat different or distinct. There may be 25 seafood restaurants in a given city, but they are not all the same. They differ in location, atmosphere, quality of food, quality of service, and so on.

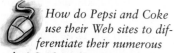 *How do Pepsi and Coke use their Web sites to differentiate their numerous colas? See http://www.pepsi.com and http://www.cocacola.com.*

Product differentiation can be real or imagined. It does not matter which is correct so long as consumers believe such differences exist. For example, many customers think Ivan's has the best seafood in town even though other restaurants actually offer a similar product. The importance of this consumer viewpoint is that they will be willing to pay a slightly higher price for Ivan's seafood. This gives Ivan the incentive to appear on local TV cooking shows and to buy ads showing him personally catching the fish he serves.

Conclusion *When a product is differentiated, buyers are not indifferent as to which seller's product they buy.*

The example of Ivan's restaurant makes it clear that under monopolistic competition rivalry centers not only on price competition, but also on **nonprice competition**. Nonprice competition is the situation in which a firm competes using advertising, packaging, product development, better quality, and better service, rather than lower prices. Nonprice competition means there is an important distinction among monopolistic competition, perfect competition, and monopoly. Under perfect competition, there is no nonprice competition because the product is identical for all firms. Likewise, the monopolist has little incentive to engage in nonprice competition because it sells a unique product.

Nonprice competition
The situation in which a firm competes using advertising, packaging, product development, better quality, and better service, rather than lower prices.

Easy Entry and Exit

Unlike a monopoly, firms in a monopolistically competitive market confront low barriers to entry. But entry into a monopolistically competitive market is not quite as easy as entry into a perfectly competitive market. Because monopolistically competitive firms sell differentiated products, it is somewhat difficult for new firms to become established. Many persons who want to enter the seafood restaurant business can get a loan, lease a building, and start serving seafood without too much trouble. However, new seafood restaurants may at first have difficulty attracting consumers because of Ivan's established reputation as the best seafood restaurant in town.

Monopolistic competition is by far the most common market structure in the United States. Examples include retail firms, such as grocery stores, hair salons, gas stations, video rental stores, diet centers, and restaurants.

The Monopolistically Competitive Firm as a Price Maker

Given the characteristics of monopolistic competition, you might think the monopolistic competitor is a *price taker*, but it is not. The primary reason is that its product is differentiated. This gives the monopolistically competitive firm, like the monopolist, limited control over its price. When the price is raised, brand loyalty means some customers will remain steadfast. As for a monopolist, the demand curve and the corresponding marginal revenue curve for a monopolistically competitive firm are downward-sloping. But the existence of close substitutes causes the demand curve for the monopolistically competitive firm to be more elastic than the demand curve for a monopolist. When Ivan's raises its price 10 percent, the quantity of seafood dinners demanded declines, say, 30 percent. Instead, if Ivan's has a monopoly, no close substitutes exist, and consumers are less sensitive to price changes. As a monopolist, the same 10 percent price hike might lose Ivan's only 15 percent of its quantity of seafood dinners demanded.

> **Conclusion** *The demand curve for a monopolistically competitive firm is less elastic (steeper) than for a perfectly competitive firm and more elastic (flatter) than for a monopolist.*

Advertising Pros and Cons

Before presenting the complete graphical models for monopolistic competition, let's pause to examine further the topic of advertising. As explained at the beginning of this chapter, a distinguishing feature of a monopolistically competitive firm is that it engages in nonprice competition by using expensive ads to differentiate its product. Instead of lowering the price, the goal is to convince customers that one firm's product is really different from its rivals' products. Monopolistically competitive firms are frequently running ads that feature reduced prices, a higher quality of service, or new products to win customers. Ads proclaim that products make you smarter, better looking, or nicer to be around. Graphically, the firm hopes advertising will make the demand curve less elastic and shift it rightward by changing consumers' tastes in favor of its product. Profit rises when advertising increases the firm's revenue more than the increase in the cost of the advertising.

Exhibit 1 illustrates the effect of advertising on the long-run average cost (*LRAC*) curve for Yummy Frozen Yogurt. Yummy competes with It Can't Be Yogurt and five other stores in the northeastern part of town. Without advertising, the $LRAC_1$ curve represents Yummy's average cost. At the given price charged, the quantity demanded is 6,000 frozen yogurt dishes per month, and the average cost is $2 per dish (point *A*).

To increase profits in the short run, Yummy decides to advertise. Yummy knows, however, that in the long run new entrants and rising costs will shrink all yogurt stores' economic profits to zero. Then Yummy has to come up with some new product to boost sales. But for now, suppose Yummy's advertising campaign is successful and demand increases; then two short-run effects occur. One is an upward shift in the average cost curve at any level of output from $LRAC_1$ to $LRAC_2$. The vertical distance between these two curves measures the additional average fixed cost of advertising. Another effect is that the quantity demanded increases to 12,000 frozen yogurt dishes per month. Now the average cost is $1.50 at point *B* on $LRAC_2$.

So far, our story illustrates a social benefit of advertising. Look again at Exhibit 1. The increased volume of sales caused by advertising leads to *economies of scale,* explained in Chapter 7. Without advertising, Yummy operated with a lower output and a higher average cost. With advertising, the benefit to consumers from the reduction in average total cost from *A* to *B* outweighs the boost in cost per unit from advertising.

On the other hand, suppose Yummy's advertising campaign is not successful and demand remains unchanged. In this case, the quantity demanded remains at the original 6,000 frozen yogurt dishes per month, but the aver-

The Effect of Advertising on Average Cost

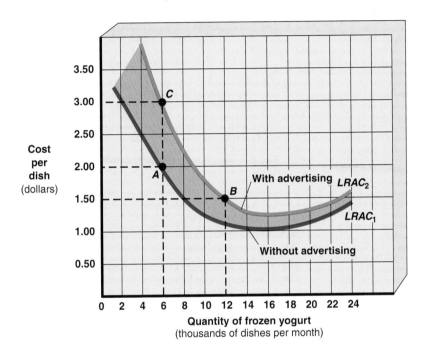

When Yummy Frozen Yogurt increases its advertising costs to sell more yogurt, the firm's average cost curve shifts upward from $LRAC_1$ to $LRAC_2$. If advertising increases the quantity demanded from 6,000 to 12,000 dishes per month, average total cost falls from $2.00 (point A) to $1.50 (point B). However, if the extra cost of advertising fails to increase the quantity demanded, average total cost rises from $2.00 (point A) to $3.00 (point C).

age total cost rises to $3.00 (point C). Critics of advertising argue this is the typical case and not the reduction from *A* to *B*. Instead of economies of scale, advertising is self-canceling. Yummy, It Can't Be Yogurt, and other firms spend large outlays on advertising just to keep their present market share. And in the process, the cost, and therefore the price, of yogurt is higher. Moreover, the higher cost of advertising does not improve the yogurt at all. The only purpose is to persuade or mislead consumers into buying something they do not need. From society's viewpoint, the resources used in advertising could be used for schools, software, or other useful products.

Proponents of advertising counter the argument that advertising is valueless. This side of the debate sees ads as information. Advertising informs consumers of sales, the availability of products, and the advantages of

The Advertising Game

Applicable Concepts: advertising, barriers to entry

You are probably familiar with newspaper ads, radio or television commercials, or even Yellow Pages ads that promise legal services at very reasonable rates. Lawyers were not always free to advertise. It was not until 1977 that the Supreme Court freed lawyers from the disciplinary actions of local bar authorities designed to prohibit lawyers from publicizing themselves. This case involved two young Phoenix lawyers, John Bates and Van O'Steen, who simply advertised their legal services, which was a violation of the Arizona Bar's rules. The bar's position was that the "hustle of the marketplace" would "tarnish the dignified public image of the profession." The high court rejected this argument and ruled that lawyers have a constitutional right to advertise their services.

In a 1983 study, the Federal Trade Commission (FTC) surveyed 3,200 lawyers in 17 states. The FTC concluded that fees for wills, bankruptcies, uncontested divorces, and uncomplicated accident cases were 5 to 13 percent lower in cities with the least restrictions on advertising.[1] However, lawyers are still split over the role of advertising. For example, the North Carolina State Bar approved in 1996 a 30-day delay on direct-mail solicitation of clients after an accident or arrest.

Another study compared prices of eyeglasses in states that had restrictions on advertising to prices in states that did not. It found that in states without advertising the retail prices of eyeglasses were 25 to 40 percent higher.[2]

Critics of advertising claim that it serves as a barrier to entry against new firms. Brand loyalty allows firms to raise their prices without losing many customers. Researchers conducted an experiment in which 150 subjects from Detroit were given two plates of turkey meat. One plate displayed an advertised brand name, and the other plate had an unknown brand. The advertised brand-name meat was preferred by 56 percent of the subjects; 34 percent preferred the unknown brand, and only 10 percent thought the two samples tasted alike. In fact, the slices of turkey meat in both samples came from the same turkey.[3]

In 1967, one study investigated the link between advertising expenditures and profits in 40 industries. The authors of the study reached the following conclusion:

It is evident that advertising is a highly profitable activity. Industries with high advertising outlays earn, on the average, a profit rate which exceeds that of other industries by nearly four percentage points.

This differential represents a 50 percent increase in profit rates. It is likely, moreover, that much of this profit rate differential is accounted for by the entry barriers created by advertising expenditures and by the resulting achievement of market power.[4]

Other economists claim that advertising is not a barrier to entry. In fact, a study by Yale Brozen found that advertising allows new entrants to penetrate markets dominated by long-established firms. Advertising gives new competitors a chance to introduce their products and win customers from their entrenched rivals.[5] A study by Woodrow Eckard is consistent with this theory. He found that market shares and profits of leading cigarette producers increased after the 1971 federal government ban on cigarette advertising. Also, new cigarette brand entry virtually stopped for four years after the ban.[6]

ANALYZE THE ISSUE

Advertising is tasteless, offensive, and a waste of resources; therefore, all advertising should be banned. Give three arguments against this idea.

[1]Ruth Marcus, "Practicing Law in the Advertising Age," *Washington Post,* June 30, 1987, p. A6.
[2]Lee Benham, "The Effect of Advertising on the Price of Eyeglasses," *Journal of Law and Economics* 15, no. 2 (1972): 337–352.
[3]James C. Makens, "Effect of Brand Preferences upon Consumers' Perceived Taste of Turkey Meat," *Journal of Applied Psychology* 49 (November 4, 1965): 261–263.
[4]William Comanor and Thomas Wilson, "Advertising, Market Structure, and Performance," *Review of Economics and Statistics* 49 (November 1967): 437. Further evidence of this view is presented in William Comanor and Thomas Wilson, *Advertising and Market Power* (Cambridge: Harvard University Press, 1974).
[5]Yale Brozen, "Entry Barriers: Advertising and Product Differentiation," in *Industrial Concentration: The New Learning,* ed. Harvey J. Goldschmid, H. Michael Mann, and J. Fred Weston (Boston: Little, Brown, 1974): 115–137.
[6]Woodrow Eckard, "Competition and the Cigarette TV Advertising Ban," *Economic Inquiry* 29, no. 1 (January 1991): 119–133.

products. So while the product costs a little more, this information saves consumers money and time. Ads also increase price competition among sellers. When Yummy offers discount coupons, other yogurt stores see these ads and respond with lower prices. Finally, consumers are rational and cannot be fooled by advertising. If a product is undesirable, customers will not buy it.

Does monopolistic competition lead to lower prices, greater output, and better-informed consumers? Or does this market structure simply raise prices and annoy customers with useless and often misleading information? This fascinating debate is perhaps best analyzed on a case-by-case basis. And the debate goes on. In the next section, you will learn that advertising to differentiate a product is also a key characteristic of oligopoly.

Price and Output Decisions for a Monopolistically Competitive Firm

Now we are prepared to develop the short-run and long-run graphical models for monopolistic competition. In the short run, you will see that monopolistic competition resembles monopoly. In the long run, however, entry by new firms leads to a more competitive market structure. This section presents a graphical analysis that shows why a monopolistically competitive firm is part perfectly competitive and part monopolistic.

Monopolistic Competition in the Short Run

Exhibit 2 shows the short-run equilibrium position for Ivan's Oyster Bar—a typical firm under monopolistic competition. As explained earlier, the demand curve slopes downward because customers believe, rightly or wrongly, that Ivan's product is a little better than its competitors' products. Customers like Ivan's family atmosphere, location, and quality of service. These nonprice factors differentiate Ivan's product and allow this restaurant to raise the price of sauteed alligator, shrimp, and oysters at least slightly without losing many sales.

Like the monopolist, the monopolistically competitive firm maximizes short-run profit by following the $MR = MC$ rule. In this case, the marginal cost and the marginal revenue curves intersect at an output of 600 seafood meals per week. The price per meal of $18 is the point on the demand curve corresponding to this level of output. Because the price exceeds the ATC of $15 per meal, Ivan's earns a short-run weekly economic profit of $1,800. As under monopoly, if the price equals the ATC curve, the firm earns a short-run normal profit. If the price is below the ATC curve, the firm suffers a short-run loss, and if the price is below the AVC curve, the firm shuts down.

Monopolistic Competition in the Long Run

The monopolistically competitive firm, unlike a monopolist, will not earn an economic profit in the long run. Rather, like a perfect competitor, the monopolistically competitive firm earns only a normal profit (that is, zero

EXHIBIT 2

A Monopolistically Competitive Firm in the Short Run

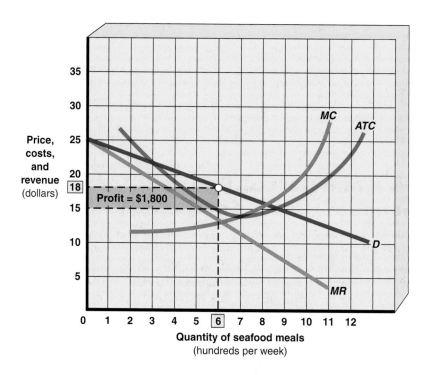

Ivan's Oyster Bar is a monopolistically competitive firm that maximizes short-run profit by producing the output where marginal revenue equals marginal cost. At an output of 600 seafood dinners per week, the price of $18 per dinner is dictated by its demand curve. Given the firm's costs, output, and prices, Ivan's will earn a weekly short-run profit of $1,800.

While small video rental stores were forced to close due to cable television and satellite technologies, Blockbuster Video has been able to increase its market share. See http://blockbuster.com.

economic profit) in the long run. The reason is that short-run profits and easy entry attract new firms into the industry. When Ivan's Oyster Bar earns a short-run profit, as shown in Exhibit 2, two things happen. First, Ivan's demand curve shifts downward as each seafood restaurant's market share is taken away by new firms seeking profit. Second, Ivan's, as well as other seafood restaurants, tries to recapture market share by advertising, improving the restaurant decor, and utilizing other forms of nonprice competition. As a result, long-run average costs increase, and the firm's *LRAC* curve shifts upward.

The combination of the leftward shift in the firms' demand curves and the upward shift in their *LRAC* curves continues in the long run until the firms earn zero or normal economic profit. The result is the long-run equilibrium condition shown in Exhibit 3. At a price of $17 per meal, the demand curve is tangent to the *LRAC* curve at the *MR* = *MC* output of

EXHIBIT 3

A Monopolistically Competitive Firm in the Long Run

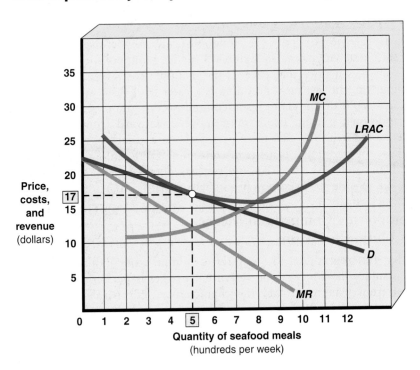

In the long run, the entry of new seafood restaurants decreases the demand for Ivan's seafood. In addition, Ivan's shifts the average cost curve upward by increasing advertising and other expenses in order to compete against new entrants. In the long run, the firm earns zero economic profit at a price of $17 per seafood meal and produces an MR = MC output of 500 meals per week.

500 meals per week. Once long-run equilibrium is achieved in a monopolistically competitive industry, there is no incentive for new firms to enter or leave.

Comparing Monopolistic Competition and Perfect Competition

Some economists argue that the long-run equilibrium condition for a monopolistically competitive firm, as shown in Exhibit 3, results in poor economic performance. Other economists contend that the benefits of a monopolistically competitive industry outweigh the costs. In this section, we again use the standard of perfect competition to understand both sides of this debate.

The Monopolistic Competitor as a Resource Misallocator

As in the case of monopoly, the monopolistically competitive firm fails the efficiency test. As shown in Exhibit 3, under monopolistic competition, Ivan's charges a price that exceeds the marginal cost. Thus, the value to consumers of the last meal produced is greater than the cost of producing it. Ivan's could devote more resources and produce more seafood. To sell this additional output, Ivan's must move downward along its demand curve by reducing the $17 price per meal. As a result, customers would purchase the additional benefits of consuming more seafood meals. However, Ivan's uses less resources and restricts output to 500 seafood meals per week in order to maximize profits where $MR = MC$.

Monopolistic Competition Means Less Output for More

Exhibit 4(a) reproduces the long-run condition from Exhibit 3. Exhibit 4(b) assumes that the seafood restaurant market is perfectly competitive. Recall from Chapter 8 that the characteristics for perfect competition include the condition that customers perceive seafood meals as *homogeneous* and that as a result no firms engage in advertising. Because we now assume for the sake of argument that Ivan's product is identical to all other seafood restaurants, Ivan's becomes a *price taker*. In this case, the industry's long-run supply and demand curves set an equilibrium price of $16 per meal. Consequently, Ivan's faces a horizontal demand curve with the price equal to marginal revenue. Also recall from Chapter 8 that long-run equilibrium for a perfectly competitive firm is established by the entry of new firms until the minimum point of $16 per meal on the firm's *LRAC* curve equals the price (*MR*).

A comparison of parts (a) and (b) of Exhibit 4 reveals two important points. First, both the monopolistic competitor and the perfect competitor earn zero economic profit in the long run. Second, the long-run equilibrium output of the monopolistically competitive firm is to the left of the minimum point on the *LRAC* curve. Like a monopolist, the monopolistically competitive firm therefore charges a higher price and produces less output than a perfectly competitive firm.

In our example, Ivan's would charge $1 less per meal and produce 300 more seafood meals per week in a perfectly competitive market. The extra 300 meals not produced are *excess capacity,* which represents underutilized resources. The criticism of monopolistic competition, then, is that there are too many firms producing too little output at inflated prices and wasting society's resources in the process. For example, on many nights, there are not enough customers for all the restaurants in town. Servers, cooks, tables, and other resources are therefore underutilized. With fewer firms, each would produce a greater output at a lower price and with a lower average cost.

EXHIBIT 4

A Comparison of Monopolistic Competition and Perfect Competition in the Long Run

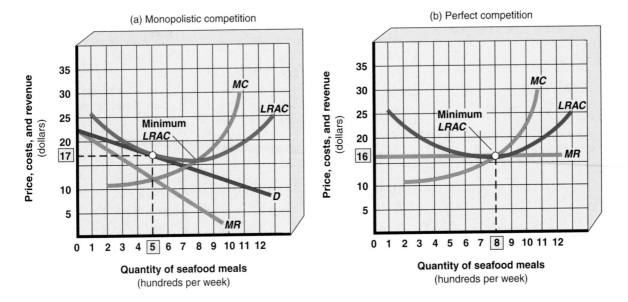

In part (a), Ivan's Oyster Bar is a monopolistically competitive firm that sets its price at $17 per seafood meal and produces 500 meals per week. As a monopolistic competitor, Ivan's earns zero economic profit in the long run and does not produce at the lowest point on its LRAC curve.

Under conditions of perfect competition in part (b), Ivan's becomes a price taker, rather than a price maker. Here the firm faces a flat demand curve at a price of $16 per seafood meal. The output is 800 meals per week, which corresponds to the lowest point on the LRAC curve. Therefore, the price is lower, and the excess capacity of 300 meals per week is utilized when Ivan's operates as a perfectly competitive firm, rather than as a monopolistically competitive firm.

On this issue, opinions vary concerning whether some of the benefits can be greater than the cost of monopolistic competition. Having many seafood restaurants offers consumers more choice and variety of output. Having Ivan's Oyster Bar and many similar competitors gives consumers extra quality and service options. If you do not like Ivan's sauteed alligator, you may be able to find another restaurant that serves this dish. Also, having many restaurants in a market saves consumers valuable time. Chances are better that you will not shed crocodile tears because your travel time required to enjoy an alligator meal is lower.

Strong frequent flier programs help major airlines dominate in the market and keep small airlines from expanding their market share. Check on the frequent flier program offered by Delta at http://www.delta-air.com/index.html or United at http://www.ual.com.

Oligopoly
A market structure characterized by (1) few sellers, (2) either a homogeneous or a differentiated product, and (3) difficult market entry.

Mutual interdependence
A condition in which an action by one firm may cause a reaction on the part of other firms.

The Oligopoly Market Structure

Now we turn to oligopoly, an imperfectly competitive market structure in which a few large firms dominate the market. Many manufacturing industries, such as steel, aluminum, automobiles, aircraft, drugs, and tobacco, are best described as oligopolistic. This is the "big business" market structure, in which firms aggressively compete by bombarding us with advertising on television and filling our mailboxes with junk mail.

Economists define an **oligopoly** as follows: Oligopoly is a market structure characterized by (1) few sellers, (2) either a homogeneous or a differentiated product, and (3) difficult market entry. Like monopolistic competition, oligopoly conforms to real-world industries. Let's examine each characteristic.

Few Sellers

Oligopoly is competition "among the few." Here we cover the range between monopolistic competition and monopoly. We use the "Big Three" or "Big Four" to mean that three or four firms dominate an industry. But what does "a few" firms really mean? Does this mean at least 2, but less than 10? As with other market structures, the answer is not that a specific number of firms must dominate an industry before it is an oligopoly. Basically, an oligopoly is a consequence of **mutual interdependence**. Mutual interdependence is a condition in which an action by one firm may cause a reaction on the part of other firms. Stated another way, a market structure with a few powerful firms makes it easier for oligopolists to collude. The large number of firms under perfect competition or monopolistic competition and the lack of firms in monopoly rule out mutual interdependence and collusion in these market structures.

When General Motors (GM) considers a price hike or a style change, it must predict how Ford and Chrysler will change their prices and styling in response. Therefore, the decisions under oligopoly are more complex than under perfect competition, monopoly, and monopolistic competition.

Conclusion *The few-sellers condition is met when these few firms are so large relative to the total market that they can affect the market price.*

Homogeneous or Differentiated Product

Under oligopoly, firms can produce either a homogeneous or a differentiated product. The steel produced by USX is identical to the steel from Republic Steel. The oil sold by Saudi Arabia is identical to the oil from Iran. Similarly, zinc, copper, and aluminum are standardized products. But cars produced by the "Big Three" are differentiated products. Tires, detergents, and breakfast cereals are also differentiated products sold in oligopolies.

Conclusion *Buyers in an oligopoly may or may not be indifferent as to which seller's product they buy.*

Difficult Entry

Similar to the monopoly, formidable barriers to entry in an oligopoly protect firms from new entrants. These barriers include exclusive financial requirements, control over an essential resource, patent rights, and other legal barriers. But the most significant barrier to entry in an oligopoly is *economies of scale*. For example, larger automakers achieve lower average total costs than those incurred by smaller automakers. Consequently, the U.S. auto industry has moved over time from more than 60 firms to only 3 major firms.

Price and Output Decisions for an Oligopolist

Mutual interdependence among firms in an oligopoly makes this market structure more difficult to analyze than perfect competition, monopoly, or monopolistic competition. The price-output decision of an oligopolist is not simply a matter of charging the price where $MR = MC$. Making price and output decisions in an oligopoly is like playing a game of chess. One player's move depends on the anticipated reactions of the opposing player. One player thinks, "If I move my rook here, my opponent might move her knight there." Likewise, there are many different possible reactions that one firm in an oligopoly can make to the price, nonprice, and output changes of another firm. Consequently, there are different oligopoly models because no single model can cover all cases. The following is a discussion of four well-known oligopoly models: (1) nonprice competition, (2) the kinked demand curve, (3) price leadership, and (4) the cartel.

Nonprice Competition

When we observe major oligopolies, they often compete using advertising and product differentiation. Instead of "slugging it out" with price cuts, oligopolies can try to capture business away from their rivals by better advertising campaigns and improved products. This model of behavior explains why advertising expenditures often are large in the cigarette, soft drink, athletic shoe, and automobile industries. It also explains why the research and development (R and D) function is so important to oligopolies. For example, much engineering effort is aimed largely at developing new products and improving existing products.

Why might oligopolies compete through nonprice competition, rather than price competition? The answer is that each oligopolist perceives that its rival will easily and quickly match any firm's price reduction. On the other hand, it is much more difficult to combat a clever and/or important product improvement.

Kinked demand curve

A demand curve facing an oligopolist that assumes rivals will match a price decrease, but ignore a price increase.

The Kinked Demand Curve

Unlike other market structures, different assumptions define different models for any given oligopolistic industry. Over time, the "rules of the game" change, and a new model becomes the best predictor of the behavior of oligopolists. We begin with the **kinked demand curve**. The strange shape of this curve explains why prices in an oligopolistic market selling cars would change far less often than prices in a perfectly competitive market selling wheat.

The kinked demand curve is a demand curve facing an oligopolist that assumes rivals will match a price decrease, but ignore a price increase. Without collusion, the kinked demand curve exists because management tacitly believes that the competition will not be "undersold." On the other hand, a price hike by one firm allows competitors to capture its share of the market. Oligopolistic firms must make pricing decisions, and, therefore, they are *price makers,* rather than price takers. But as we will soon see in the kinked demand model, the high degree of interdependence among oligopolists restricts their pricing discretion.

In Exhibit 5, a kinked demand curve is drawn for Tucker Motor Company, which we assume competes with GM, Ford, and Chrysler in the automobile market. (I suggest you check out the movie titled *Tucker* at your video rental store.) The current price per car is $15,000, and the quantity demanded at this price is 3 million Tucker cars per year. Tucker's management assumes that if it raises its price even slightly above $15,000, the other automakers *will not follow* with higher prices. This price gap between the Tucker and other cars would drive many of Tucker's customers over to its rivals. The segment of the demand curve above $15,000 is therefore relatively flat. Stated differently, above the "kink" in the demand curve, demand is relatively elastic.

If Tucker raises the price to, say, $17,250 at point X, this price hike cuts Tucker's quantity demanded to 1.5 million cars per year. Since raising its price is ill-advised, management can consider a price reduction strategy. Suppose Tucker cuts the price of its cars to $12,250 at point Y. The model shows that Tucker gains few customers and the quantity demanded rises slightly to only 3.2 million cars per year. The reason for such a small sales boost is that GM, Ford, and Chrysler also cut their prices, so that each firm might keep its initial market share. However, the lower price does attract some new buyers who could not afford a car at the higher price. The segment of the demand curve below the kink is therefore relatively steep. Here demand is less elastic, meaning the quantity demanded is not very responsive to a price drop.

Given the kinked demand curve facing the oligopolist, management fears the worst and is afraid to raise or lower the price of its product. Under this model of oligopoly, the price established at the kink changes very infrequently. Price rigidity is eliminated only after large cost increases or decreases force a new kinked demand curve with a new higher or lower price at the kink.

Economists continue to debate the importance of the kinked demand model. Critics challenge the theory on theoretical and empirical grounds. On a theoretical level, there is no explanation for how the original price at

EXHIBIT 5

The Kinked Demand Curve

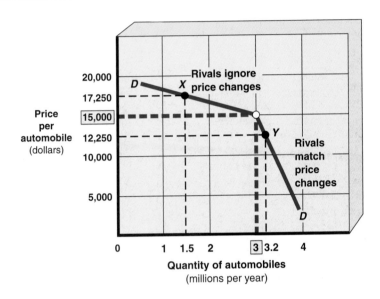

An oligopolist's demand curve may be kinked. In this graph, an auto-mobile producer believes it faces two demand curves. A price hike from $15,000 to $17,250 per auto causes a sizeable reduction in the quantity demanded from 3 million to 1.5 million autos (point X). Demand above the kink is elastic because rivals ignore the firm when it raises the price. Below the kink, the demand curve is less elastic. A price reduction from $15,000 to $12,250 per auto attracts very few new customers, and the quantity demanded increases only from 3 million to 3.2 million autos per year (point Y). Under the kinked demand curve theory, prices will be rigid.

the kink was determined. On empirical grounds, studies of certain oligopolistic industries fail to find price stickiness. On the other hand, widespread use of price lists in catalogs that remain fixed for a long time is consistent with kinked demand theory. In any case, the kinked demand theory does not provide a complete explanation of price and output decisions.

Price Leadership

Without formal agreement, firms can play a game of follow-the-leader that economists call **price leadership**. Price leadership is a pricing strategy in which a dominant firm sets the price for an industry and the other firms follow. Following this tactic, firms in an industry simply match the price of perhaps, but not necessarily, the biggest firm. For example, suppose GM initiates a price increase per car. Reacting to this price hike, other U.S.

Price leadership
A pricing strategy in which a dominant firm sets the price for an industry and the other firms follow.

INTERNATIONAL ECONOMICS

Major Cartels in Global Markets
Applicable Concept: cartel

Cartels flourished in Germany and other European countries in the first half of the 20th century. Many were international in membership. After World War II, European countries passed laws against such restrictive trade practices.

- *Organization of Petroleum Exporting Countries (OPEC).* OPEC was created by Iran, Iraq, Kuwait, Saudi Arabia, and Venezuela in Baghdad in 1960. Today, OPEC's membership consists of 12 countries that control about 80 percent of the world's oil reserves. Cartels are anticonsumer. OPEC's objective is to set oil production quotas for members and, in turn, influence global prices of

oil and gasoline. In the future, OPEC may become weaker if Russia and other countries in the Commonwealth of Independent States (CIS) compete with OPEC. The CIS possesses the world's largest oil reserves and may soon obtain Western technology necessary for efficient oil production.

- *International Telephone Cartel (CCITT).* The world's least known, and perhaps most effective, cartel is known by its French acronym, CCITT. This cartel is based in Switzerland and sets the minimum price you pay for an international telephone call. As a result, rates for international calls are much higher than competitive

long-distance telephone call rates in the United States. In fact, often 95 percent of the charge for an international call placed by AT&T, MCI, Sprint, and other U.S. telephone companies is remitted through the CCITT.

- *International Airline Cartel (IATA).* Most of the world's international airlines belong to the IATA. This cartel controls access to airports, fixes airline rates, and promotes mutual objectives for its members. The market power of the IATA may decline as more nations follow the example of the United States and reduce protection and regulation of airlines.

automakers quickly follow the leader's example and boost the price of their cars by an equal amount. Price leadership is not uncommon. In addition to GM, USX Corporation (steel), Alcoa (aluminum), DuPont (nylon), R. J. Reynolds (cigarettes), Goodyear Tire and Rubber (tires), and American Tobacco (cigarettes) are other examples of price leaders in U.S. industries.

The Cartel

The price leadership model assumes that firms do not collude to avoid price competition. Instead, firms avoid price wars by informally playing by the established pricing rules. Another way to avoid price wars is for oligopolists to agree to a peace treaty. Instead of allowing mutual interdependence to lead to rivalry, firms openly or in secret conspire with one another to form a monopoly called a **cartel**. A cartel is a group of firms formally agreeing to control the price and the output of a product. The goal of a cartel is to reap monopoly profits by replacing competition with coopera-

OPEC is one of the most successful cartels in history. See their site at http://www.opec.org.

Cartel
A group of firms formally agreeing to control the price and the output of a product.

CHECKPOINT   Which Model Fits the Cereal Aisle?

As you walk along the cereal aisle, notice the many different cereals on the shelf. For example, you will probably see General Mills Wheaties, Total, and Cheerios; Kellogg's Corn Flakes, Cracklin' Oat Bran, Frosted Flakes, and Rice Krispies; Quaker Cap'n Crunch and Quaker 100% Natural; and Post Super Golden Crisp, to name only a few. There are many different brands of the same product— cereal—on the shelves. Each brand is slightly different from the others. Is the breakfast cereal industry's market structure monopolistic competition or oligopoly?

tion. Cartels are illegal in the United States, but not in other nations. The best-known cartel is the Organization of Petroleum Exporting Countries (OPEC). The members of OPEC divide crude oil output among themselves according to quotas openly agreed upon at meetings of the OPEC oil ministries. Saudi Arabia is the largest producer and has the largest quota. The following is a brief summary of some of today's major global cartels.

Using Exhibit 6, we can demonstrate how a cartel works and why keeping members from cheating is a problem. Our analysis begins before oil-producing firms have formed a cartel. Assume each firm has the same cost curve shown in the exhibit. Price wars have driven each firm to charge $30 a barrel, which is equal to the minimum point on its *LRAC* curve. Because oil is a standardized product, as under perfect competition, each firm fears raising its price because it will lose all its customers. Thus, the typical firm is in long-run competitive equilibrium at a price of $30 per barrel ($MR_1$), producing 6 million barrels per day. In this condition, economic profits are zero, and the firms decide to organize a meeting of all oil producers to establish a cartel.

Now assume the cartel is formed and each firm agrees to reduce its output to 4 million barrels per day and charge $45 per barrel. If no firms cheat, each firm faces a higher horizontal demand curve, represented by MR_2. At the cartel price, each firm earns an economic profit of $40 million, rather than a normal profit. But what if one firm decides to cheat on the cartel agreement by stepping up its output and other firms stick to their quotas? Output corresponding to the point at which $MR_2 = MC$ is 8 million barrels per day. If a cheating firm expands output to this level, it can double its profit by earning an extra $40 million. Of course, if all firms cheat and the cartel breaks up, the price and output of each firm return to the initial levels, and economic profit again falls to zero.

EXHIBIT 6

Why a Cartel Member Has an Incentive to Cheat

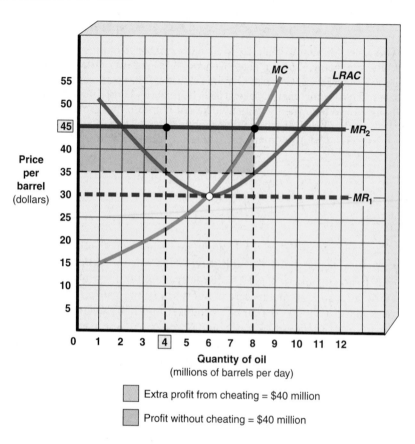

Extra profit from cheating = $40 million

Profit without cheating = $40 million

A representative oil producer operating in a perfectly competitive industry would be in long-run equilibrium at a price of $30 per barrel, producing 6 million barrels per day and making zero economic profit. A cartel can agree to raise the price of oil from $30 to $45 per barrel by restricting the firm to 4 million barrels per day. As a result of this quota, the cartel price is above $35 on the LRAC curve, and the firm earns a daily profit of $40 million. However, if the firm cheats on the cartel agreement, it will set the cartel price equal to the MC curve and earn a total profit of $80 million by adding an additional $40 million. If all firms cheated, the original long-run equilibrium would be re-established.

An Evaluation of Oligopoly

Oligopoly is much more difficult to evaluate compared to other market structures. None of the models just presented gives a definite answer to the question of efficiency under oligopoly. Depending on the assumptions made, an oligopolist can behave much like a perfectly competitive firm or more like a monopoly. Nevertheless, let's assume some likely changes that occur if a perfectly competitive industry is turned suddenly into an oligopoly selling a differentiated product.

First, the price charged for the product will be higher than under perfect competition. The smaller the number of firms there are in the oligopoly and the more difficult it is to enter the industry, the greater the oligopoly price will be in comparison to the perfectly competitive price.

Second, an oligopoly is likely to spend money on advertising, product differentiation, and other forms of nonprice competition. These expenditures can shift the demand curve to the right. As a result, both price and output may be higher under oligopoly than under perfect competition.

Third, in the long run, a perfectly competitive firm earns zero economic profit. The oligopolist, however, can earn a higher profit because it is more difficult for competitors to enter the industry.

Review of the Four Market Structures

Now that we have completed the discussion of perfect competition, monopoly, monopolistic competition, and oligopoly, you are prepared to compare these four market structures. Exhibit 7 summarizes the characteristics and gives examples of each market structure.

EXHIBIT 7   Comparison of Market Structures

Market Structure	Number of Sellers	Type of Product	Entry Condition	Examples
Perfect competition	Large	Homogeneous	Very easy	Agriculture*
Monopoly	One	Unique	Impossible	Public utilities
Monopolistic competition	Many	Differentiated	Easy	Retail trade
Oligopoly	Few	Homogeneous or differentiated	Difficult	Autos, steel, oil

*In the absence of government intervention.

An Economist Goes to the Final Four

Applicable Concepts: oligopoly and cartel

Many fascinating markets functioned during the Men's Final Four basketball tournament in April of 1992, and as an industrial organization economist, I observed them with great interest.

The competition began shortly after we got off the plane at the Minneapolis Airport. A group of high school students was giving away huge inflatable plastic hands with index fingers sticking up in the air. They were imprinted with the Pepsi-Cola slogan and logo and your choice of a Final Four team. And the group was giving away free cans of Pepsi. Uh huh! The latest battle in the Great Cola Wars was on, but this was just the beginning.

Giant inflatable "cans" of Coke and Pepsi appeared all over downtown Minneapolis—on the sidewalks, on top of gas stations—not to mention that entire sides of three story buildings were painted Coca-Cola red and white with the 64 NCAA basketball finalists and all the winners listed, bracket by bracket, just as they appeared in the newspaper. And on Sunday, following the first-round games, painters were three stories up on scaffolding, filling in the Coke sign's brackets for the final two teams, Duke and Michigan, in school colors no less. This was competition between showboating industry giants—a spectacular example of differentiated oligopoly. . . .

Then there were the hotels, which by joining a centralized booking service became a cartel. The first hotel that I booked had raised its normal price by 75 percent for the weekend. Others did the same. I later found a national chain motel that had not joined in the feeding frenzy. It charged a modest price, but it was well out into the suburbs. Still, by Saturday afternoon it was filled with Final Four Fans.

Fortunately, I did not have the same problem with the airline, rental car company or restaurants. Normal rates for transportation prevailed. National market oriented companies either do not want to bother with adjusting prices for local high demand special events or they do not wish to alienate their regular customers by taking advantage of the situation.

ANALYZE THE ISSUE

1. The author says that the Coke–Pepsi competition was an example of "differentiated oligopoly." What does he mean? In what ways were the soda giants differentiating their products?
2. Why didn't national companies adjust their prices in the face of increased Final Four demand?

Source: Michael Stoller, "An Economist Goes to the Final Four," *Margin* 8 (Spring 1993): 48–49.

KEY CONCEPTS

Imperfect competition	Nonprice competition	Mutual interdependence	Price leadership
Monopolistic competition	Oligopoly	Kinked demand curve	Cartel
Product differentiation			

SUMMARY

- **Imperfect competition** is the market structure between the extremes of perfect competition and monopoly. Monopolistic competition and oligopoly belong to the imperfect competition category.

- **Monopolistic competition** is a market structure characterized by (1) many small sellers, (2) a differentiated product, and (3) easy market entry and exit. Given these characteristics, firms in monopolistic competition have a negligible effect on the market price.

- **Product differentiation** is a key characteristic of monopolistic competition. It is the process of creating real or apparent differences between products.

- **Nonprice competition** includes advertising, packaging, product development, better quality, and better service. Under imperfect competition, firms may compete using nonprice competition, rather than price competition.

- ★ **Short-run equilibrium for a monopolistic competitor** can yield economic losses, zero economic profits, or economic profits. In the long run, monopolistic competitors make zero economic profits.

Short-run equilibrium for a monopolistic competitor

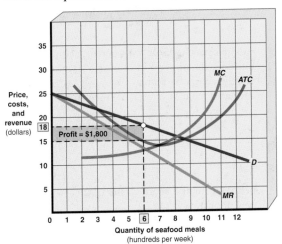

charges a higher price, restricts output, and does not produce where average costs are at a minimum.

Comparison of Monopolistic and Perfect Competition

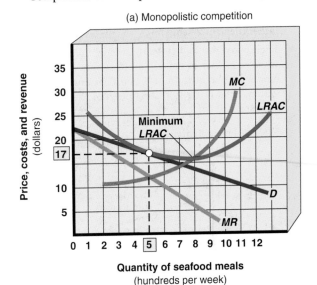

(a) Monopolistic competition

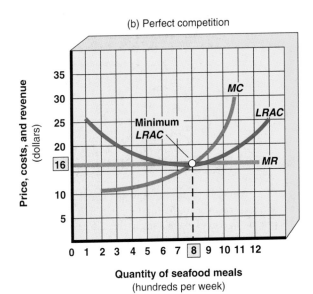

(b) Perfect competition

- ★ **Comparing monopolistic competition with perfect competition,** we find that the monopolistically competitive firm does not achieve allocative efficiency,

■ **Oligopoly** is a market structure characterized by (1) few sellers, (2) a homogeneous or a differentiated product, and (3) difficult market entry. Oligopolies are **mutually interdependent** because an action by one firm may cause a reaction on the part of other firms.

■ The **nonprice competition model** is a theory that might explain oligopolistic behavior. Under this theory, firms use advertising and product differentiation, rather than price reductions, to compete.

★ The **kinked demand curve** is a model that explains why prices may be rigid in an oligopoly. The kink is established because an oligopolist assumes that rivals will match a price decrease, but ignore a price increase.

Kinked demand curve

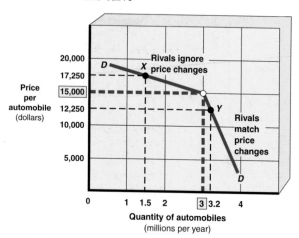

■ **Price leadership** is another theory of pricing behavior under oligopoly. When a dominant firm in an industry raises or lowers price, other firms follow suit.

★ A **cartel** is a formal agreement among firms to set prices and output quotas. The goal is to maximize profits, but firms have an incentive to cheat, which is a constant threat to a cartel.

Cartel

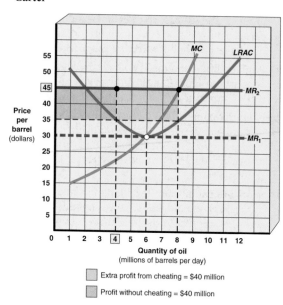

Extra profit from cheating = $40 million

Profit without cheating = $40 million

■ **Comparing oligopoly with perfect competition,** we find that the oligopolist allocates resources inefficiently, charges a higher price, and restricts output so that price may exceed average cost.

SUMMARY OF CONCLUSION STATEMENTS

■ The many-sellers condition is met when each firm is so small relative to the total market that each firm's pricing decisions have a negligible effect on the market price.

■ When a product is differentiated, buyers are not indifferent as to which seller's product they buy.

■ The demand curve for a monopolistically competitive firm is less elastic (steeper) than for a perfectly com-

petitive firm and more elastic (flatter) than for a monopolist.

■ The few-sellers condition is met when these few firms are so large relative to the total market that they can affect the market price.

■ Buyers in an oligopoly may or may not be indifferent as to which seller's product they buy.

STUDY QUESTIONS AND PROBLEMS

1. Compare the monopolistically competitive firm's demand curve to those of a perfect competitor and a monopolist.

2. Suppose the minimum point on the *LRAC* curve of a soft-drink firm's cola is $1 per liter. Under conditions of monopolistic competition, will the price of a liter bottle of cola in the long run be above $1, equal to $1, less than $1, or impossible to determine?

3. Exhibit 8 represents a monopolistically competitive firm in long-run equilibrium.

EXHIBIT 8

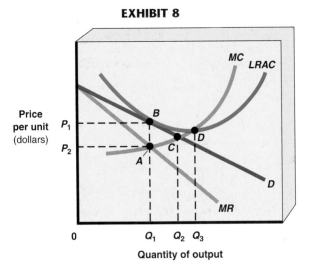

a. Which price represents the long-run equilibrium price?

b. Which quantity represents the long-run equilibrium output?

c. At which quantity is the *LRAC* curve at its minimum?

d. Is the long-run equilibrium price greater than, less than, or equal to the marginal cost of producing the equilibrium output?

4. Consider this statement: "Because price equals long-run average cost and profits are zero, a monopolistically competitive firm is efficient." Do you agree or disagree? Explain.

5. Assuming identical long-run cost curves, draw two graphs, and indicate the price and output that result in the long run under monopolistic competition and perfect competition. Evaluate the differences between these two market structures.

6. Draw a graph that shows how advertising affects a firm's *ATC* curve. Explain how advertising can lead to lower prices in a monopolistically competitive industry.

7. List four goods or services that you have purchased that were produced by an oligopoly. Why are these industries oligopolistic, rather than monopolistically competitive?

8. Why is mutual interdependence important under oligopoly, but not so important under perfect competition, monopoly, or monopolistic competition?

9. Suppose the jeans industry is an oligopoly in which each firm sells its own distinctive brand of jeans. Each firm believes its rivals will not follow its price increases, but will follow its price cuts. Explain the demand curve facing each firm. Given this demand curve, does this mean that firms in the jeans industry do or do not compete against one or another?

10. What might be a general distinction between oligopolists who advertise and those who do not?

11. Suppose IBM raised the price of its printers, but Hewlett-Packard (the largest seller) refused to follow. Two years later IBM cut its price, and Hewlett-Packard retaliated with an even deeper price cut, which IBM was forced to match. For the next five years, Hewlett-Packard raised its prices five times, and each time IBM followed suit within 24 hours. Does the pricing behavior of these computer industry firms follow the cartel model or the price leadership model? Why?

12. Evaluate the following statement: "A cartel will put an end to price wars, which is a barbaric form of competition that benefits no one."

ONLINE EXERCISES

Exercise 1

Visit Irin Reports (http://www.irin.com/colist.html), and follow these steps:

1. Review the annual reports of IBM Corporation and Apple Computers, Inc.

2. Explain how IBM and Apple have partial monopolies and yet they compete with each other.

3. Explain why IBM and Apple spend such a large amount of money on sales and marketing (see their income statements).

Exercise 2

Facial tissues, according to some analysts, are a product with low consumer loyalty. What is Kimberly-Clark (http://www.kimberly-clark.com/), maker of Kleenex, doing to increase product differentiation and brand loyalty?

Exercise 3

How does Chrysler (http://www.chrysler.com/) use the Internet to advertise its products? Is Chrysler different from General Motors (http://www.gm.com/) or Ford (http://www.ford.com/)? Are these companies operating within a monopolistically competitive or oligopolistic market environment?

Exercise 4

Why does Morton International produce many different types of table salt (http://www.morton.com/salt/prod/prflprod.htm)?

CHECKPOINT ANSWERS

Which Model Fits the Cereal Aisle?

The fact that there is a differentiated product does not necessarily mean that there are many firms competing along the cereal aisle. The different cereals listed in this example are produced by only four companies: General Mills, Kellogg's, Quaker, and Post. In fact, there are relatively few firms in the cereal industry, so even though they sell a differentiated product, the market structure cannot be monopolistic competition. If you said the cereal industry is an oligopoly, **YOU ARE CORRECT**.

PRACTICE QUIZ

For a visual explanation of the correct answers, visit the tutorial at http://tucker.swcollege.com.

1. An industry with many small sellers, a differentiated product, and easy entry would *best* be described as which of the following?
   a. Oligopoly
   b. Monopolistic competition
   c. Perfect competition
   d. Monopoly

2. Which of the following industries is the best example of monopolistic competition?
   a. Wheat
   b. Restaurant
   c. Automobile
   d. Water service

3. Which of the following is *not* a characteristic of monopolistic competition?
   a. A large number of small firms
   b. A differentiated product
   c. Easy market entry
   d. A homogeneous product

4. A monopolistically competitive firm will
   a. maximize profits by producing where $MR = MC$.
   b. probably not earn an economic profit in the long run.
   c. shut down if price is less than average variable cost.
   d. do all of the above.

5. The theory of monopolistic competition predicts that in long-run equilibrium a monopolistically competitive firm will
   a. produce the output level at which price equals long-run marginal cost.
   b. operate at minimum long-run average cost.
   c. overutilize its insufficient capacity.
   d. produce the output level at which price equals long-run average cost.

6. A monopolistically competitive firm is inefficient because the firm
   a. earns positive economic profit in the long run.
   b. is producing at an output where marginal cost equals price.
   c. is not maximizing its profit.
   d. produces an output where average total cost is not minimum.

7. A monopolistically competitive firm in the long run earns the same economic profit as
   a. a perfectly competitive firm.
   b. a monopolist.
   c. a cartel.
   d. none of the above.

8. One possible effect of advertising on a firm's long-run average cost curve is to
   a. raise the curve.
   b. lower the curve.
   c. shift the curve rightward.
   d. shift the curve leftward.

9. Monopolistic competition is an inefficient market structure because
   a. firms earn zero profit in the long run.
   b. marginal cost is less than price in the long run.
   c. there is a wider variety of products available compared to perfect competition.
   d. of all of the above.

10. The "Big Three" U.S. automobile industry is described as a (an)
    a. monopoly.
    b. perfect competition.
    c. monopolistic competition.
    d. oligopoly.

11. The cigarette industry in the United States is described as a (an)
    a. monopoly.
    b. perfect competition.
    c. monopolistic competition.
    d. oligopoly.

12. A characteristic of an oligopoly is
    a. mutual interdependence in pricing decisions.
    b. easy market entry.
    c. both a and b.
    d. neither a nor b.

13. The kinked demand theory attempts to explain why an oligopolistic firm
    a. has relatively large advertising expenditures.
    b. fails to invest in research and development (R and D).
    c. infrequently changes its price.
    d. engages in excessive brand proliferation.

14. According to the kinked demand theory, when one firm raises its price, other firms will
    a. also raise their prices.
    b. refuse to follow.
    c. increase their advertising expenditures.
    d. exit the industry.

15. Which of the following is evidence that OPEC is a cartel?
    a. Agreement on price and output quotas by oil ministries
    b. Ability to raise prices regardless of demand
    c. Mutual interdependence in pricing and output decisions
    d. Ability to completely control entry

CHAPTER ELEVEN

Labor Markets

In 1998, Oprah Winfrey, a talk show host, earned the impressive figure of $125 million, but Jerry Seinfeld, a comedian, did even better. He earned $225 million for starring in a very successful television series. The headlines might report that the Los Angeles Dodgers signed their star pitcher to a three-year contract for $8 million. Another headline may report a recent survey that found chief executive officers (CEOs) of large corporations were paid an average annual salary of $4 million. The president of the United States is paid $400,000 per year. The average college graduate earns about $40,000. The average high school graduate earns less than $25,000, while many others, including college students, toil for the minimum wage.

How are earnings determined? What accounts for the wide differences in earnings? This chapter provides answers by explaining different types of labor markets that determine workers' compensation and the quantity of workers firms hire. Understanding hiring decisions is indeed a key to understanding why some become rich and famous by playing baseball—a kid's game—while other workers might be exploited by firms with labor market power.

The chapter begins with development of a competitive labor market in which no single buyer or seller can influence the price (wage rate) of labor. The chapter concludes with a discussion of power. As in the product markets, labor market determinations are affected by market power. Power on the side of either unions or employers can alter wage and employment outcomes. For example, the chapter explains how unions affect wages and trends in union membership around the world.

In this chapter, you will learn to solve these economics puzzles:

■ What determines the wage rate an employer pays?

■ How do labor unions influence wages and employment?

■ Does the NCAA exploit college athletes?

The Labor Market Under Perfect Competition

In Chapters 8–10, you studied the price and quantity determinations of goods and services produced by firms operating under different market structures—perfect competition, monopoly, oligopoly, and monopolistic competition. As you have learned, market structure affects the price and the quantity of a good or service sold by firms to consumers. Similarly, as this chapter will demonstrate, the price (wage rate) paid to labor and the quantity of labor hired by firms are influenced by whether the labor market is competitive or not.

Recall from Chapter 8 that we assumed the hypothetical firm called Computech produces and sells electronic units for bank teller machines in a perfectly competitive market. Here we also assume Computech hires workers in a perfectly competitive labor market. In a perfectly competitive labor market, there are many sellers and buyers of labor services. Consequently, wages and salaries are determined by the intersection of the demand for labor and the supply of labor.

The Demand for Labor

How many workers should Computech hire? To answer this question, Computech must know how much workers contribute to its output. Column 1 of Exhibit 1 lists possible numbers of workers Computech might hire per day, and as discussed earlier in Chapter 7 on production costs, column 2 shows the total output per day. One worker would produce 5 units per day, 2 workers together would produce an output of 9 units per day, and so on. Note that columns 1 and 2 constitute a *production function* as represented earlier in Exhibit 2(a) in Chapter 7. Column 3 lists the additional output from hiring each worker. The first worker hired would add 5 units of output per day, the second would produce an additional 4 units (total product of 9 − 5 units produced), and so on. Recall from Chapter 7 that the additional output from hiring another unit of labor is defined as the *marginal product of labor* [see Exhibit 2(b) in Chapter 7]. Consistent with the *law of diminishing returns*, the marginal product falls as the firm hires more workers.[1]

---

[1] Recall from Chapter 7 that marginal product may increase with the addition of more labor at low rates of output due to specialization and division of labor. Then as output expands in the short run, the law of diminishing returns will cause marginal product to decrease.

EXHIBIT 1   Computech's Demand for Labor

Points	(1) Labor Input (workers per day)	(2) Total Output (units per day)	(3) Marginal Product (units per day)	(4) Product Price	(5) Marginal Revenue Product [(3) × (4)]
	0	0	—	$70	—
A	1	5	5	70	$350
B	2	9	4	70	280
C	3	12	3	70	210
D	4	14	2	70	140
E	5	15	1	70	70

Marginal revenue product (MRP)

The increase in total revenue to a firm resulting from hiring an additional unit of labor or other variable resource.

The next step in Computech's hiring decision is to convert marginal product into dollars by calculating the **marginal revenue product** (*MRP*). The marginal revenue product (*MRP*) is the increase in total revenue to a firm resulting from hiring an additional unit of labor or other variable resource. Stated simply, *MRP* is the dollar value of worker productivity. It is the extra revenue a firm earns from selling the output of an extra worker. Returning to Exhibit 1 in Chapter 8 on perfect competition, suppose the market equilibrium price for units is $70. Because Computech operates in a perfectly competitive market, the firm can sell any quantity of its product at the $70 market-determined price. Given this situation, the first unit of labor contributes a marginal revenue product of $350 per day to revenue ($70 per unit times the 5 units of output). Column 5 of Exhibit 1 lists the marginal revenue product of each additional worker hired.

Conclusion *A perfectly competitive firm's marginal revenue product is equal to the marginal product of its labor times the price of its product.*

Demand curve for labor

A curve showing the different quantities of labor employers are willing to hire at different wage rates in a given time period, ceteris paribus. It is equal to the marginal revenue product of labor.

Now assuming all other inputs are fixed, Computech can derive its **demand curve for labor,** which conforms to the law of demand explained in Chapter 3. The demand curve for labor is a curve showing the different quantities of labor employers are willing to hire at different wage rates. It is equal to the *MRP* of labor. The *MRP* numbers from Exhibit 1 are duplicated in Exhibit 2. As shown in the exhibit, the price of labor in terms of daily wages is measured on the vertical axis. The quantity of workers Computech will hire per day at each wage rate is measured on the horizontal axis. The demand curve for labor is downward sloping: As the wage rate falls, Computech will hire more workers per day. If the wage rate is above $350 (point *A*), Computech will hire no workers because the cost of a worker is more than the dollar value of any worker's contribution to total revenue (*MRP*). But what happens if Computech pays each worker $280

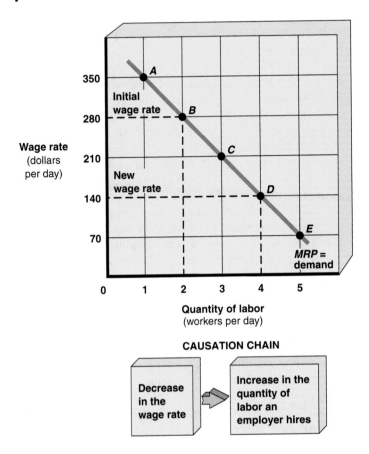

EXHIBIT 2

Computech's Demand Curve for Labor

CAUSATION CHAIN

Decrease in the wage rate ⇒ Increase in the quantity of labor an employer hires

Computech's downward-sloping demand curve for labor is derived from the marginal revenue product (MRP) of labor, which declines as additional workers are hired. The marginal revenue product is the change in total revenue that results from hiring one more worker (see Exhibit 1). At point B, Computech pays $280 per day and finds it profitable to pay this wage to 2 workers because each worker's MRP equals or exceeds the wage rate. If Computech pays a lower wage rate of $140 per day at point D, it is not profitable for the firm to hire the fifth worker because this worker's MRP of $70 is below the wage rate of $140 per day.

per day? At point *B*, Computech finds it profitable to hire 2 workers because the *MRP* of the first worker is greater than the wage rate (extra cost) and the second worker's *MRP* equals the wage rate. If the wage rate is $140 per day at point *D*, Computech will find it profitable to hire 4 workers. In this case, Computech will not hire the fifth worker. Why? The fifth worker contributes an *MRP* of $70 to total revenue (point *E*), but this amount is below the wage rate paid of $140. Consequently, Computech cannot maximize profits by hiring the fifth worker because it would be adding more to costs than to revenue.

Conclusion *A firm hires additional workers up to the point where the* MRP *equals the wage rate.*

Each firm in the market has a demand for labor based on its *MRP* data. Summing these individual demand curves for labor provides the market demand curve for labor in the electronic components industry. Another important point must be made. The demand for labor is called **derived demand**. The derived demand for labor and other factors of production depends on the consumer demand for the final goods and services the factors produce. If consumers are not willing to purchase products requiring electronic components, such as bank teller machines, there is no *MRP*, and firms will hire no workers to make electronic components for them. On the other hand, if customer demand for bank teller machines soars, the price of units rises, and the *MRP* of firms in the electronic components industry rises. The result is a rightward shift in the market demand curve for labor.

The Supply of Labor

The **supply curve of labor** is also consistent with the law of supply discussed in Chapter 3. The supply curve of labor is a curve showing the different quantities of labor workers are willing to offer employers at different wage rates. Summing the individual supply curves of labor for firms producing electronic units for bank teller machines provides the market supply curve of labor. As shown in Exhibit 3, as the wage rate rises, more workers are willing to supply their labor. At point *A*, 20,000 workers offer their services to the industry for $140 per day. At the higher wage rate of $280 per day (point *B*), the quantity of labor supplied is 40,000 workers. Higher wages attract workers from other industries that require similar skills, but have lower wage rates.

Ignoring differences in wage scales, why might the supply of less-skilled workers (carpenters) be greater than that of more-skilled workers (physicians)? The explanation for this difference is the **human capital** required to perform various occupations. Human capital is the accumulation of education, training, experience, and health that enables a worker to enter an occupation to be productive. Less human capital is required to be a carpenter than a physician. Therefore, many people are qualified, and the supply of carpenters is larger than the supply of physicians.

The Equilibrium Wage Rate

Wage rates are determined in perfectly competitive markets by the interaction of labor supply and demand. The equilibrium wage rate for the entire electronic components market, shown in Exhibit 4(a), is $210 per day. This wage rate clears the market because the quantity of 30,000 workers demanded equals the quantity of 30,000 workers who are willing to supply

Derived demand
The demand for labor and other factors of production that depend on the consumer demand for the final goods and services the factors produce.

Supply curve of labor
A curve showing the different quantities of labor workers are willing to offer employers at different wage rates in a given time period, ceteris paribus.

Human capital
The accumulation of education, training, experience, and health that enables a worker to enter an occupation and be productive.

The Market Supply Curve of Labor

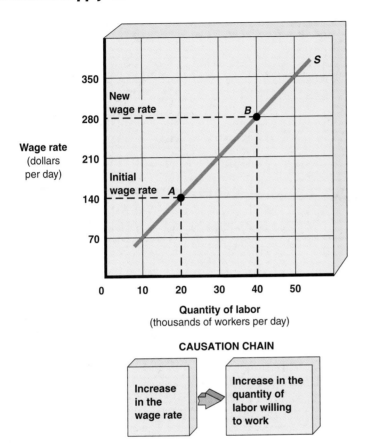

CAUSATION CHAIN

| Increase in the wage rate | ⇒ | Increase in the quantity of labor willing to work |

The upward-sloping supply curve of labor for the electronic components industry indicates that a direct relationship exists between the wage rate and the quantity of labor supplied. At point A, 20,000 workers are willing to work for $140 per day in this market. If the wage rate rises to $280 per day, 40,000 workers supply their services to the electronic parts labor market.

their labor services at that wage rate. In a competitive labor market, no single worker can set his or her wage above the equilibrium wage. Such a worker fears not being hired because there are so many workers who will work for $210 per day. Similarly, there are so many firms hiring labor that a single firm cannot influence the wage by paying workers more or less than the prevailing wage. Hence, a wage rate above $210 per day would create a surplus of workers seeking employment (unemployment) in the

What are the consequences of a minimum wage? Consider two different perspectives on the minimum wage. See Who Wins with a Minimum Wage? and President Clinton's Proposal to Increase the Minimum Wage at http://epn .org/epi/epminw.html *and* http: //www.sbsc.org:80/ct2-22-5.html, *respectively.*

EXHIBIT 4

A Competitive Labor Market Determines the Firm's Equilibrium Wage

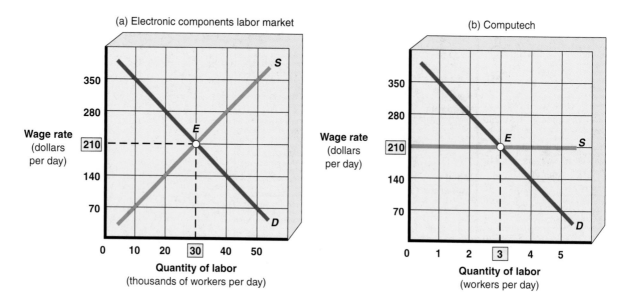

In part (a), the intersection of the supply of and the demand for labor curves determines the equilibrium wage rate of $210 per day in the electronic components industry. Part (b) illustrates that a single firm, such as Computech, is a "wage taker." The firm can hire all the workers it wants at this equilibrium wage, so its supply curve, S, is a horizontal line. Computech chooses to hire 3 workers, where the firm's demand curve for labor intersects its supply curve of labor.

electronic components market, and a wage rate below $210 per day would cause a shortage.

Although the supply curve of labor is upward-sloping for the electronic components market, this is not the case shown in Exhibit 4(b) for an individual firm, such as Computech. Because a competitive labor market assumes that each firm is too small to influence the wage rate, Computech is a "wage taker" and therefore pays the market-determined wage rate of $210 per day regardless of the quantity of labor it employs. For this reason, the labor supply to Computech is represented by a horizontal line at the equilibrium wage rate. Given this wage rate of $210 per day, Computech then hires labor up to the equilibrium point, E, where the wage rate equals the third worker's marginal revenue product.

Labor Unions

The perfectly competitive model does not apply to workers who belong to unions. Unions arose because workers recognized that acting together gave them more bargaining power than acting individually and being at the mercy of their employers. Some of the biggest unions are the Teamsters, United Auto Workers, National Education Association, and American Federation of Government Employees. A primary objective of unions is to improve working conditions and raise the wages of union members above the level that would exist in a competitive labor market. To raise wages, unions use three basic strategies: (1) increase the demand for labor, (2) decrease the supply of labor, and (3) exert power to force employers to pay a wage rate above the equilibrium wage rate.

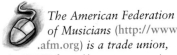

The American Federation of Musicians (http://www.afm.org) *is a trade union, the UAW* (http://www.uaw.org) *is an industrial union, the American Federation of Teachers* (http://www.aft.org) *is a public employee union, and the ABA* (http://www.abanet.org) *is an employee association.*

Unions Increase the Demand for Labor

Now suppose the workers form a union. One way to increase wages is to use a method called *featherbedding.* This means the union forces firms to hire more workers than are required or to impose work rules that reduce output per worker. Another approach is to boost domestic demand for labor by decreasing competition from other nations. This objective might be accomplished by the union lobbying Congress to protect the U.S. electronic parts industry against competition from Japan. Another approach might be to advertise and try to convince the public to "Look for the Union Label." Effective advertising would boost the demand for electronic products with union-made components and, in turn, the demand for union labor because it is *derived demand.* In addition, the union might lobby Congress and state legislatures to spend government funds to purchase only products using electronic components with the union label.

Exhibit 5 indicates the effect of union power used to increase the demand curve for labor. This exhibit is a reproduction of the labor market for electronic component workers from Exhibit 4(a). Begin at equilibrium point E_1, with the wage rate of $210 per day paid to each of 30,000 workers. Then the union causes the demand curve for labor to increase from D_1 to D_2. At the new equilibrium point, E_2, firms hire an additional 10,000 workers and pay each worker an extra $70 per day.

Made in the USA Foundation is a nonprofit organization of 60,000 members, including individuals, trade unions, and corporations. How does this organization try to increase the demand for union labor? See http://www.madeusa.org.

Unions Decrease the Supply of Labor

Exhibit 6 shows another way unions can use their power to increase the wage rate of their members by restricting the supply of labor. Now suppose the labor market is in equilibrium at point E_1, with 40,000 workers making electronic units and earning $210 per day. Then the union uses its power to shift the supply curve of labor leftward from S_1 to S_2 by, say, requiring a longer apprenticeship, charging higher fees, or using some other device designed to reduce union membership. For example, the union might lobby for legislation to reduce immigration or to guarantee shorter

EXHIBIT 5

A Union Causes an Increase in the Demand Curve for Labor

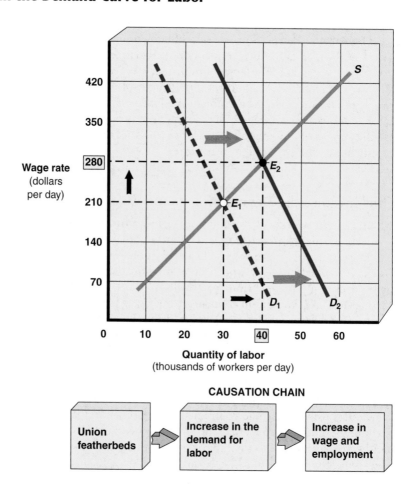

CAUSATION CHAIN

| Union featherbeds | ⇨ | Increase in the demand for labor | ⇨ | Increase in wage and employment |

A union shifts the demand curve for labor rightward from D_1 to D_2 by featherbedding or other devices. As a result, the equilibrium wage rate increases from $210 per day at point E_1 to $280 per day at point E_2, and employment rises from 30,000 to 40,000 workers.

working hours. As a result of these union actions, the equilibrium wage rate rises to $280 per day at point E_2, and employment is artificially reduced to 30,000 workers. It should be noted that self-serving practices of unions to limit the labor supply and raise wages can be disguised as standards of professionalism required by the American Medical Association and the American Bar Association, teacher certification requirements, Ph.D. requirements for university faculty, and so on.

EXHIBIT 6

A Union Causes a Decrease in the Supply Curve of Labor

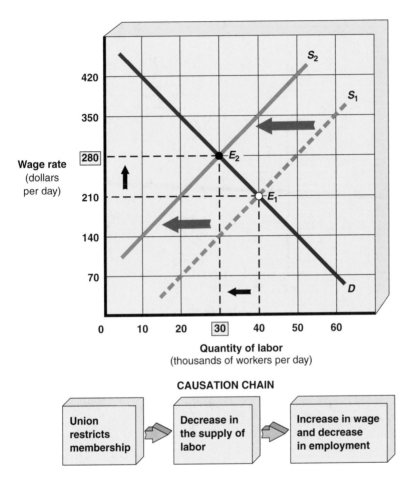

CAUSATION CHAIN

Union restricts membership	→	Decrease in the supply of labor	→	Increase in wage and decrease in employment

A union shifts the supply curve of labor leftward from S₁ to S₂ by restricting union membership or by using other techniques. As a result, the equilibrium wage rate rises from $210 per day at point E₁ to $280 per day at point E₂, and the number of workers hired falls from 40,000 to 30,000.

Unions Use Collective Bargaining to Boost Wages

A third way to raise the wage rate above the equilibrium level is to use **collective bargaining**. Collective bargaining is the process of negotiations between the union and management over wages and working conditions. By law, once a union has been certified as the representative of a majority of the workers, employers must deal with the union. If employers deny union demands, the union can strike and reduce profits until the firms agree to a higher wage rate.

Collective bargaining

The process of negotiations between the union and management over wages and working conditions.

EXHIBIT 7

Union Collective Bargaining Causes a Wage Rate Increase

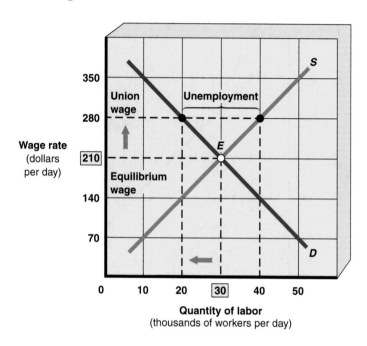

A *union exerts its power through collective bargaining. Instead of the competitive wage rate of $210 at point E, firms in the industry avoid a strike by agreeing in a labor contract to $280 per day. The effect is to artificially create a labor surplus (unemployment) of 20,000 workers at the negotiated wage.*

Visit UnionWeb and review A Short History of the Labor Movement, based on materials from the AFL–CIO. What obstacles did the labor movement overcome? How did the courts treat labor unions in the early days? See http://www .unionweb.org/history.htm *and* http://www.aflcio.org.

The result of collective bargaining is shown in Exhibit 7. Again, we return to the situation depicted for the electronic components market in Exhibit 4(a). At the equilibrium wage rate of $210 per day (point *E*), there is no surplus or shortage of workers. Then the industry is unionized, and a collective bargaining agreement takes effect in which firms agree to pay the union wage rate of $280 per day. At the higher wage rate, employment falls from 30,000 to 20,000 workers. However, the number of workers who wish to work for $280 per day is 40,000 workers. Consequently, there is a surplus of 20,000 unemployed workers in this industry. Because firms now hire fewer workers and pay higher wages, how might firms react? Employers might react by substituting capital for labor or by transferring operations overseas, where labor costs are lower than in the United States.

EXHIBIT 8   Factors Causing Changes in Labor Demand and Labor Supply

Changes in Labor Demand	Changes in Labor Supply
1. Unions	1. Unions
2. Prices of substitute inputs	2. Demographic trends
3. Technology	3. Expectations of future income
4. Demand for final products	4. Changes in immigration laws
5. Marginal product of labor	5. Education and training

Finally, there are several factors that can cause either the demand curve for labor or the supply curve of labor to shift. Exhibit 8 provides a list of these factors.

Union Membership Around the World

How important are unions as measured by the percentage of the labor force that belongs to a union? Let's start with the Great Depression, when millions of people were out of work and union membership was relatively low (see Exhibit 9). To boost employment and earnings, Franklin D. Roosevelt's National Industrial Recovery Act of 1933 (NIRA) established the right of employees to bargain collectively with their employers, but the act was declared unconstitutional by the Supreme Court in 1935. However, the 1935 National Labor Relations Act (NLRA), known as the Wagner Act, incorporated the labor provisions of the NIRA. The Wagner Act guaranteed workers the right to start unions and to engage in collective bargaining. The combined impact of this legislation and the production demands of World War II created a surge in union membership between 1935 and 1945.

Since World War II, union power has declined. Union membership has fallen from about 35 percent in 1945 to about 15 percent today. Since 1985, union membership has declined in such blue-collar industries as the automobile, steel, machinery, and electrical industries. On the other hand, union membership has gained in the public sector. For example, union membership has increased among public school teachers, state and local government employees, and postal workers.

Exhibit 10 shows the unionization rates in other countries. While in Sweden and Denmark nearly all workers belong to a union, union membership in the United States is far below that of other industrialized countries.

EXHIBIT 9

U.S. Union Membership, 1930–1997

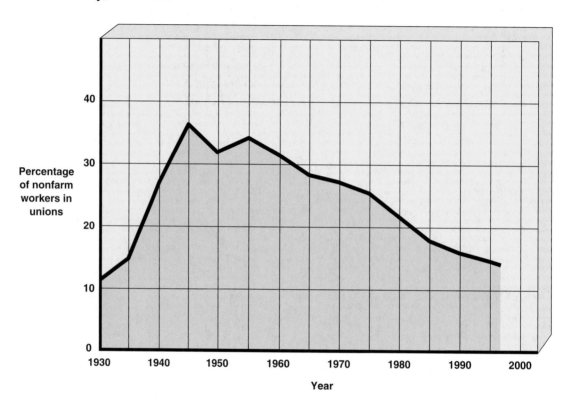

As a percentage of nonfarm workers, union membership in the United States grew most rapidly during the decade 1935–1945. Since the peak in 1945, union membership as a percentage of the labor force has fallen to about the level in 1935.

Source: The World Almanac and Book of Facts, 1999, First Search, All Databases.

Employer Power

So far, labor markets have been explained with employees possessing varying degrees of power to influence wage rates and employment, while employers were competitive with no market power. However, significant power can exist on the employer side of the labor market. The extreme case occurs in a **monopsony**. Monopsony is a labor market in which a single firm hires labor. For example, a single textile mill, mining company, or housing contractor might be the only buyer of labor in a particular market. The classical phrase for this situation is the "company town," where for miles around a small town everyone's livelihood depends on a single employer. The reason for the monopsony is the absence of other firms in the area that compete for labor.

Monopsony
A labor market in which a single firm hires labor.

EXHIBIT 10

Union Membership for Selected Countries, 1997

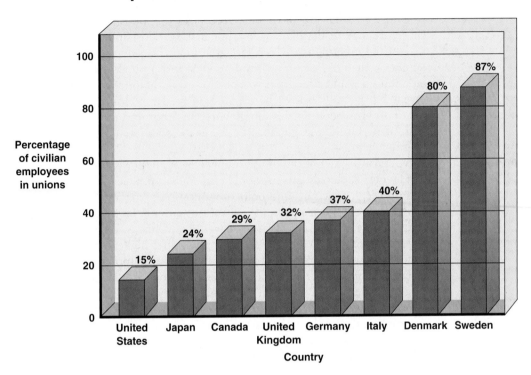

Union membership as a percentage of the civilian labor force in Sweden and Denmark is far above that of the United States. The unionization rates of other industrialized countries, such as Italy, the United Kingdom, Germany, Canada, and Japan, are also higher than the rate in the United States.

Source: U.S. Department of Labor, Bureau of International Labor Affairs, *Foreign Labor Trends 1996–1997,* published by country.

Marginal Factor Cost

This chapter began by assuming Computech operated in a competitive labor market in which no single employer in the electronic components market had any direct influence on the market wage rate. Recall from Exhibit 4 that Computech is a wage taker. More precisely, Computech hires the quantity of labor at the prevailing labor market equilibrium wage rate, which is determined by the point where the firm's downward-sloping *MRP* curve (demand curve for labor) intersects the horizontal supply curve of labor. The equilibrium wage rate is established by a competitive labor market beyond Computech's power to control.

Marginal factor cost (MFC)

The additional total cost resulting from a one-unit increase in the quantity of a factor.

Now we visit the small town of Plainsville and find General Griffin's, which is a monopsonist producing turkeys. As shown in Exhibit 11, the supply of labor curve facing the monopsonist is upward-sloping, rather than horizontal. The reason is that General Griffin's is the only firm hiring workers in Plainsville and it therefore faces the industry or entire supply curve of labor in the Plainsville labor market. This situation compares to that of the monopolist, which faces the industry demand curve for a particular product. As a result, the monopolist in a product market cannot sell an additional unit of a good without lowering the price, and the marginal revenue curve falls below the demand curve. For the monopsonist, a distinction exists between the supply curve of labor and the **marginal factor cost** (*MFC*) curve. Marginal factor cost is the additional total cost resulting from a one-unit increase in the quantity of a factor. Note that the *MFC* curve starts at the bottom of the supply curve of labor and then rises above it. Having made this observation, relax and take a deep breath; then we will proceed to the nuts and bolts of monopsonist theory.

If General Griffin's pays $1 per hour at point *A* on the upward-sloping supply curve of labor, only 1 worker will be willing to be hired. If the monopsonist wants to hire more labor, it must offer higher wages. If the firm raises its wage offer to $2 per hour for each worker (point B), the quantity of labor supplied increases to 2 workers per hour. In the exhibit, the total wage cost per hour in column 3 is computed by multiplying the wage rate per hour in column 1 times the number of workers per hour in column 2. At point *A*, the total wage cost per hour is $1, which equals the wage rate. At point *B*, the total wage cost per hour rises to $4, and *MFC* is greater than the wage rate of $2 per hour. The explanation is that all workers are assumed to perform the same job. Consequently, the first worker will demand to be paid the same wage rate as the second worker hired at the higher wage rate. Stated differently, General Griffin's must pay a higher wage to each additional worker as well as all previously hired workers. Comparing points *A* through *D* confirms that *MFC* is greater than the wage rate for a monopsonist, much like the monopolist's price, which is greater than the marginal revenue.

Conclusion *Because the monopsonist can hire additional workers only by raising the wage rate for all workers, the marginal factor cost exceeds the wage rate.*

Monopsonistic Equilibrium

How many workers will General Griffin's hire? To answer this question requires the demand curve for labor that traces labor's marginal revenue product (*MRP*), explained earlier in this chapter. Recall that *MRP* reflects the value or contribution of each additional worker because *MRP* is the increase in total revenue produced by hiring each additional worker. Also, as explained in Chapter 8, the profit-maximizing producer selects the level of output where marginal revenue equals marginal cost. Similarly, *the*

EXHIBIT 11

A Monopsonist Determines Its Wage Rate

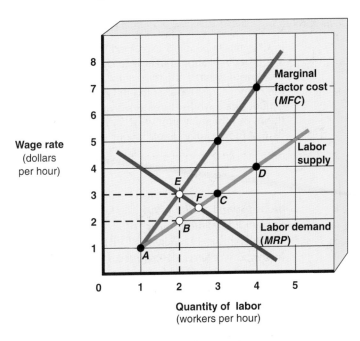

Points	(1) Wage rate (per hour)	(2) Labor input (workers per hour)	(3) Total wage cost (per hour) [(1) × (2)]	(4) Marginal factor cost (MFC) [Δ(3) ÷ Δ(2)]
	$0	0	$0	—
A	1	1	1	$1
B	2	2	4	3
C	3	3	9	5
D	4	4	16	7

The monopsonist, General Griffin's, faces the industry upward-sloping supply curve of labor in the small town of Plainsville. As the wage rate rises, all workers must be paid the same higher wage. As a result, the change in total wage cost (marginal factor cost in column 4) exceeds the wage paid to the last worker (column 1). The MFC curve therefore lies above the supply curve of labor.

The demand curve for labor is the marginal revenue product (MRP) or the worth to the monopsonist of each worker it hires. The intersection of the MFC and the MRP curves at point E determines that General Griffin's hires 2 workers per hour. Because this firm has a monopsony in the Plainsville labor market, it can pay $2 per hour at point B on the supply curve of labor, which is enough to attract 2 workers. However, the worker is exploited because the MRP at point E for the second worker is $3 per hour and the wage rate is only $2. In a competitive labor market, the equilibrium would be point F, paying a higher wage and employing more workers.

CHECKPOINT

Can the Minimum Wage Create Jobs?

In Chapter 4, Exhibit 5 explained that the effect of the minimum wage in a competitive labor market is to decrease the number of unskilled workers employed. Assume the minimum wage is $2.50, and consider the effect on the monopsonist represented in Exhibit 11. This means by law the monopsonist cannot hire a worker for a lower wage. Contrary to the case of perfect competition, can the minimum wage increase the number of persons working in the case of monopsony? Explain your answer using Exhibit 11.

For more about the NCAA, visit its Web site at http://www.ncaa.org.

monopsonist in the labor market hires the quantity of labor at which the marginal revenue product of labor equals its marginal factor cost.

In Exhibit 11, General Griffin's will follow the *MRP = MFC* rule by hiring 2 workers, determined by the intersection of the *MRP* and *MFC* curves at point *E*. But pay special attention to this point: The monopsonist has labor market power and does not have to pay $3 per hour, which equals the contribution of the second worker measured by his or her *MRP*. Instead of paying workers what their services are worth, the monopsonist follows the supply curve of labor, selects point *B*, and pays $2 per hour, rather than $3 per hour. Since $2 per hour is all the firm must pay to attract and hire 2 workers, the monopsonist can exploit labor by paying less than its marginal revenue product.

One alternative for labor facing a powerful employer is a powerful union and collective bargaining. Totally successful collective bargaining by a labor union could raise the wage rate from $2 per hour at point *B* to $3 per hour at point *E*. General Griffin's will resist the union's demands and

CHECKPOINT

If You Don't Like It, Mickey, Take Your Bat and Go Home

Mickey Mantle told of his salary negotiations in his autobiography *The Mick*. After winning baseball's Triple Crown in 1955, his salary increased from about $85,000 to $100,000. The next season he raised his batting average even higher, and the Yankee team owner offered him a pay cut. What is the most likely explanation for the owner's behavior—an increase in the supply of star baseball players, owner monopsony power, or the owner's desire that Mantle find another team for which to play?

Should College Athletes Be Paid?

Applicable Concept: monopsony

It was perfect football weather on a beautiful autumn Saturday at Minnesota State's stadium. There was a hush in the crowd of 80,000 as the clock showed 5 seconds left in the game and the scoreboard read Home 26 Visitor 30. The Screaming Eagles were playing the Fighting Irish, and the season was on the line. With time running out, the Eagles' All-American quarterback, Joe Wyoming, launched a desperation pass from his 45-yard line. The pass hit the extended fingers of a wide receiver who leaped over three defenders at the Irish 25-yard line and then ran into the end zone all alone. The home crowd roared with the joy of ecstasy after staring defeat in the face.

So the season had been in the hands of Joe Wyoming, who received a full scholarship, which cost the university more than $40,000 over four years. Because Joe led the Eagles to victory over Notre Dame, the team played in the Sugar Bowl, which paid Minnesota State $5 million for the appearance. In addition, next year's ticket sales, alumni contributions, and trademark licensing boosted revenues $10 million, while applications for admission to the university increased sharply.

Economist John Leonard argues that athletes are clearly underpaid in college sports because players cannot be paid salaries under National Collegiate Athletic Association (NCAA) rules. His study estimated that a star college football player who is named to an All-American team generates a marginal revenue product of $100,000 per year for the university. However, that athlete is paid only $5,000 per year.

In Chapter 10, a cartel was explained as firms that use a collusive agreement to act as a monopoly. NCAA regulations serve as a collusive agreement among colleges and universities to act as a monopsony and hire the services of college-bound athletes. Just like an output or sellers' cartel, such as the Organization of Petroleum Exporting Countries (OPEC), the NCAA must enforce the rules against cheaters.

Because this agreement holds players' wages far below their marginal revenue product, the gap creates an incentive for schools to offer "illegal" inducements of cars, money, clothes, and trips to attract good players. Such cheating benefits the college athletes whose wages are raised closer to their marginal revenue products. The school that is not caught benefits by recruiting better players, achieving athletic success, and receiving greater sports revenue. The other schools that follow the rules must depend on the NCAA to punish cheaters by taking away TV appearances, tournament play, bowl invitations, and scholarships.

ANALYZE THE ISSUE

Do you favor paying college athletes salaries determined by a competitive labor market, rather than an NCAA agreement? Explain.

offer a lower wage closer to point *B*. Thus, points *B* and *E* represent the boundaries of a potential final settlement. Such a negotiated final equilibrium wage rate depends on the tactics and resources of the negotiating parties.

Finally, recall from earlier in this chapter that in competitive labor markets additional workers are hired to the point where the wage rate is equal to *MRP*. At point *F*, the supply curve of labor intersects the *MRP* curve, and more workers would be hired for the $2.50 per hour paid to each worker.

Conclusion *A monopsonist hires fewer workers and pays a lower wage than a firm in a competitive labor market.*

KEY CONCEPTS

Marginal revenue product (*MRP*)

Demand curve for labor

Derived demand

Supply curve of labor

Human capital

Collective bargaining

Monopsony

Marginal factor cost (*MFC*)

SUMMARY

- **Marginal revenue product** (*MRP*) is determined by a worker's contribution to a firm's total revenue. Algebraically, the *MRP* equals the price of the product times the worker's marginal product (*MP*).

- ★ The **demand curve for labor** is the curve showing the quantities of labor a firm is willing to hire at different prices of labor. The marginal revenue product (*MRP*) of labor curve is the firm's demand curve for labor. Summing individual demand for labor curves gives the market demand curve for labor.

- **Derived demand** means that a firm demands labor because labor is productive. Changes in consumer demand for a product cause changes in demand for labor and for other resources used to make the product.

- ★ The **supply curve of labor** is the curve showing the quantities of workers willing to work at different prices of labor. The market supply curve of labor is derived by adding the individual supply curves of labor.

Demand curve for labor

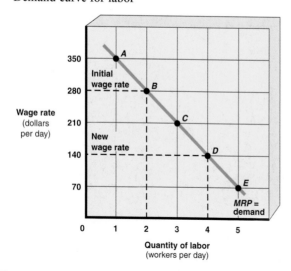

Supply curve of labor

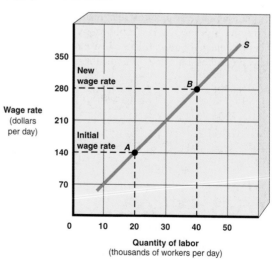

- **Human capital** is the accumulated investment people make in education, training, experience, and health in order to make themselves more productive. One explanation for earnings differences is differences in human capital.

- **Collective bargaining** is the process through which a union and management negotiate a labor contract.

★ **Monopsony** is a labor market in which a single firm hires labor. Because the monopsonist faces the industry supply curve of labor and each worker is paid the same wage, changes in total wage cost exceed the wage rate necessary to hire each additional worker. As a result, the **marginal factor cost** (*MFC*) of labor curve, which measures changes in total wage cost per worker, lies above the supply curve of labor. The monopsonist's wage rate and quantity of labor are determined where the *MFC* equals *MRP*. Since at this point the worker's *MRP* is greater than the wage paid, the monopsonist exploits the workers.

Monopsony

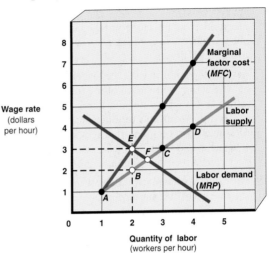

SUMMARY OF CONCLUSION STATEMENTS

- A perfectly competitive firm's marginal revenue product is equal to the marginal product of its labor times the price of its product.

- A firm hires additional workers up to the point where the *MRP* equals the wage rate.

- Because the monopsonist can hire additional workers only by raising the wage rate for all workers, the marginal factor cost exceeds the wage rate.

- A monopsonist hires fewer workers and pays a lower wage than a firm in a competitive labor market.

STUDY QUESTIONS AND PROBLEMS

1. Consider this statement: "Workers demand jobs, and employers supply jobs." Do you agree or disagree? Explain.

2. The Zippy Paper Company has no control over either the price of paper or the wage it pays its workers. The following table shows the relationship between the number of workers Zippy hires and total output:

Labor Input (workers per day)	Total Output (boxes of paper per day)
0	0
1	15
2	27
3	36
4	43
5	48
6	51

If the selling price is $10 per box, answer the following questions:
   a. What is the marginal revenue product (*MRP*) of each worker?
   b. How many workers will Zippy hire if the wage rate is $100 per day?
   c. How many workers will Zippy hire if the wage rate is $75 per day?
   d. Assume the wage rate is $75 per day and the price of a box of paper is $20. How many workers will Zippy hire?

3. Assume the Grand Slam Baseball Store sells $100 worth of baseball cards each day, with 1 employee operating the store. The owner decides to hire a second worker, and the 2 workers together sell $150 worth of baseball cards. What is the second worker's marginal revenue product (*MRP*)? If the price per card sold is $5, what is the second worker's marginal product (*MP*)?

4. What is the relationship between the marginal revenue product (*MRP*) and the demand curve for labor?

5. The market supply curve of labor is upward-sloping, but the supply curve of labor for a single firm is horizontal. Explain why.

6. Assume the labor market for loggers is perfectly competitive. How would each of the following events influence the wage rate paid those workers?
   a. Consumers boycott products made with wood.
   b. Loggers form a union that requires longer apprenticeships, charges high fees, and uses other devices designed to reduce union membership.

7. How does a human capital investment in education increase your lifetime earnings?

8. Suppose states pass laws requiring public school teachers to have a master's degree in order to retain their teaching certificates. What effect would this legislation have on the labor market for teachers?

9. Use the data in question 2, and assume the equilibrium wage rate is $90 per day, determined in a perfectly competitive labor market. Now explain the impact of a union-negotiated collective bargaining agreement that changes the wage rate to $100 per day.

10. Some economists argue that the American Medical Association and the American Bar Association create an effect on labor markets similar to that of a labor union. Do you agree?

11. The Jacksonville Jaguars is an expansion professional football team in the National Football League (NFL). NFL draft and employment rules create monopsony power for each member club. In 1995, the Jaguars were in the process of hiring players. Using the following hypothetical table of data, construct a graph to determine the number of quarterbacks the Jaguars hired and the salary paid to each quarterback. Assuming the labor market is competitive, what are the number of quarterbacks hired and the salary paid each?

(1) Salary (thousands of dollars)	(2) Number of Quarterbacks	(3) Total Cost of Quarterbacks (thousands of dollars)	(4) Marginal Factor Cost (*MFC*) (thousands of dollars)	(5) Marginal Revenue Product (*MRP*) (thousands of dollars)
$ 0	0	$ 0	—	—
100	1	100	$100	$700
200	2	400	300	600
300	3	900	500	500
400	4	1,600	700	400
500	5	2,500	900	300

ONLINE EXERCISES

Exercise 1

Visit Business Cycle Indicators Home Page (http://www .globalexposure.com), and select Wages/Labor. Then choose Index of average hourly compensation and Index of real average hourly compensation for the last 10 years. Compare these graphs.

Exercise 2

Visit GPO Gate, Catalog for Economic Report of the President (http://www.gpo.ucop.edu/catalog/erp99_appen _b.html). Select Table B-36, civilian employment and unemployment by sex and age, and follow these steps:

1. Compute the civilian population male and female employment ratio, and graph this data for the last 10 years.

2. Explain the trend in these data.

Exercise 3

Visit the Legal Information Institute (LII) at Cornell University, and examine the Labor-Management Reporting and Disclosure Act of 1959, or the Landrum-Griffin Act, as it is commonly known (http://www.law.cornell.edu /uscode/29.ch11.html). Why is this act considered the Bill of Rights for union members? What specific protections does it detail? What economic effect does this act have on the labor market?

Exercise 4

America's Labor Market Information System (ALMIS), a program sponsored by the Employment and Training Administration (ETA) at the U.S. Department of Labor, offers on-line labor market information (http://dwsa.state .ut.us/almis/). Review the national projections for the occupation of your choice. What are the projections for the occupation of your choice in the state in which you currently reside?

 CHECKPOINT ANSWERS

Can the Minimum Wage Create Jobs?

The minimum wage of $2.50 corresponds to point *F* in Exhibit 11. At this point, the labor supply and labor demand (MRP) curves intersect. Thus, the effect of the minimum wage is to force the monopsonist to operate at the equilibrium that would be established in a competitive labor market. If you said under monopsony the minimum wage could raise the wage rate and create additional employment, **YOU ARE CORRECT.**

If You Don't Like It, Mickey, Take Your Bat and Go Home

Baseball players had no free-agent rights in the 1950s. If Mantle did not like the salary offer, his only choice was to go back to his home in Oklahoma. Faced with that alternative, he accepted the salary cut. If you said each owner achieved monopsony power by prohibiting players from going to another team, **YOU ARE CORRECT.**

PRACTICE QUIZ

For a visual explanation of the correct answers, visit the tutorial at http://tucker.swcollege.com.

1. Marginal revenue product measures the increase in
   a. output resulting from one more unit of labor.
   b. total revenue resulting from one more unit of output.
   c. revenue per unit from one more unit of output.
   d. total revenue resulting from one more unit of labor.

2. Troll Corporation sells dolls for $10.00 each in a market that is perfectly competitive. Increasing the number of workers from 100 to 101 would cause output to rise from 500 to 510 dolls per day. Troll should hire the 101st worker only when the wage is
   a. $100 or less per day.
   b. more than $100 per day.
   c. $5.10 or less per day.
   d. none of the above.

3. Derived demand for labor depends on the
   a. cost of factors of production used in the product.
   b. market supply curve of labor.
   c. consumer demand for the final goods produced by labor.
   d. firm's total revenue less economic profit.

4. If demand for a product falls, the demand curve for labor used to produce the product will shift
   a. leftward.
   b. rightward.
   c. upward.
   d. downward.

5. The owner of a restaurant will hire waiters if the
   a. additional labor's pay is close to the minimum wage.
   b. marginal product is at the maximum.
   c. the additional work of the employees adds more to total revenue than to costs.
   d. waiters do not belong to a union.

6. In a perfectly competitive market, the demand curve for labor
   a. slopes upward.
   b. slopes downward because of diminishing marginal productivity.
   c. is perfectly elastic at the equilibrium wage rate.
   d. is described by all of the above.

7. A union can influence the equilibrium wage rate by
   a. featherbedding.
   b. requiring longer apprenticeships.
   c. favoring trade restrictions on foreign products.
   d. all of the above.
   e. none of the above.

8. In which of the following market structures is the firm *not* a price taker in the factor market?
   a. Oligopoly
   b. Monopsony
   c. Monopoly
   d. Perfect competition

9. The extra cost of obtaining each additional unit of a factor of production is called the marginal
   a. physical product.
   b. revenue product.
   c. factor cost.
   d. implicit cost.

10. A monopsonist's marginal factor cost curve lies above its supply curve because the firm must
    a. increase the price of its product to sell more.
    b. lower the price of its product to sell more.
    c. increase the wage rate to hire more labor.
    d. lower the wage rate to hire more labor.

11. In order to maximize profits, a monopsonist will hire the quantity of labor to the point where the marginal factor cost is equal to
    a. marginal physical product.
    b. marginal revenue product.
    c. total revenue product.
    d. any of the above.

12. BigBiz, a local monopolist, currently hires 50 workers and pays them $6 per hour. To attract an additional worker to its labor force, BigBiz would have to raise the wage rate to $6.25 per hour. What is BigBiz's marginal factor cost?
    a. $6.25 per hour.
    b. $12.50 per hour.
    c. $18.75 per hour.
    d. $20 per hour.

13. Suppose a firm can hire 100 workers at $8.00 per hour, but must pay $8.05 per hour to hire 101 workers. Marginal factor cost (*MFC*) for the 101st worker is approximately equal to
    a. $8.00.
    b. $8.05.
    c. $13.05.
    d. $13.00.

14. A monopsonist in equilibrium has a marginal revenue product of $10 per worker hour. Its equilibrium wage rate must be
    a. less than $10.
    b. equal to $10.
    c. greater than $10.
    d. equal to $5.

CHAPTER TWELVE

Income Distribution, Poverty, and Discrimination

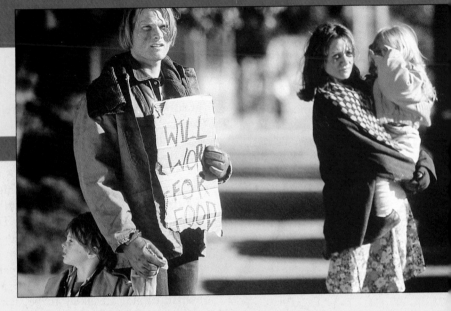

The previous chapter examined how variations in wages are determined in competitive and monopsonistic labor markets. These labor supply and demand models do not give the complete picture of labor markets. In this chapter, we turn our attention to the topics of distribution of income, poverty, and discrimination, which are important topics related to labor market wage decisions.

The chapter begins by exploring the controversial issue of how the total family income "pie" is cut into various size "slices" or shares for different groups of families. You will examine government data that indicate the trend over the years in the share of income for the richest fifth of the population and the poorest fifth. Here the hotly contested issue of whether the "rich got richer" at the expense of the poor is addressed. In addition, the inequality of income in the United States is compared to that of other countries.

Poverty is an unhappy consequence of an unequal income distribution. Eighteenth-century English poet and essayist Samuel Johnson stated "a decent provision for the poor is the true test of civilization." President Bill Clinton campaigned in 1992 on a pledge to "end welfare as we know it," and in 1996, the president signed a bipartisan landmark bill to reform welfare. Today, the consequences of this law are being felt throughout the nation. Another purpose of this chapter is to define poverty and ask what can be done about it.

The chapter concludes with the subject of discrimination, which is one possible explanation for unequal income distribution and poverty. Here you will apply the supply and demand model to explain why women earn less on average than men and blacks earn less than whites.

In this chapter, you will learn to solve these economics puzzles:

■ Could the rich become richer and other income groups also become better off?

■ How can a negative income tax solve the welfare controversy?

■ What is the effect on labor markets of laws that protect women from jobs deemed "too strenuous" or "too dangerous"?

The Distribution of Income

One function of labor markets is to determine the *distribution of income—* that is, how wages and salaries are divided among members of society. Recall from Chapter 2 that the For Whom question is one of three basic questions that any economic system must answer. Here we study the For Whom question in more detail.

Trends in Income Distribution

One way to analyze the distribution of income in the United States is illustrated in Exhibit 1. In column 1 of this exhibit, families are divided into six groups according to the percentage of the total annual money income they received. The remaining columns of the table give the percentages of the total money income for each of the six groups in 1929, 1947, 1970, 1980, 1990, and 1997. These data reveal changes in the distribution of income among families over time. For example, families with income in the top 5 percent in 1929 earned 10 percent more of the total income pie than they did in 1997. Otherwise, the distribution of income has not fluctuated greatly since 1947. However, there is the concern that since 1970 the percentage of income received by families in the lowest 20 percent has fallen, while the income percentages received by the families in the highest fifth and the highest 5 percent have risen.

The U.S. Bureau of the Census provides current and historical data on income distribution at http://www .census.gov/hhes/www/income .html.

As shown in Exhibit 1, there is an unequal distribution of income among families. Why didn't the highest 5 percent of the families receive 5 percent of the total income and each of the other five groups receive 20 percent of the total income? There are many reasons. For example, Exhibit 2 reveals that families headed by a college graduate fare better than those headed by an individual with only a high school degree. Recall from the previous chapter that human capital refers to education and skills that increase a worker's productivity. Workers with a greater investment in human capital are likely to be worth more to an employer. Data in this

EXHIBIT 1　The Division of the Total Annual Money Income Among Families, 1929–1997

Percentage of Families	1929	1947	1970	1980	1990	1997
Lowest fifth	3.5%	5.0%	5.5%	5.1%	4.6%	4.2%
Second-lowest fifth	9.0	11.9	12.2	11.5	10.8	9.9
Middle fifth	13.8	17.0	17.6	17.5	16.6	15.7
Second-highest fifth	19.3	23.1	23.8	24.3	23.8	23.0
Highest fifth	54.4	43.0	40.9	41.6	44.3	47.2
Highest 5%	30.0	17.5	15.6	15.3	17.4	20.7

Source: U.S. Bureau of the Census, http://www.census.gov/hhes/income/histinc/incfamdet.html, Table F-2.

EXHIBIT 2   Median Money Income of Families, 1997

Characteristic	Median Income*
All families	$44,568
Families headed by a male	32,960
Families headed by a female	21,023
Families with head aged 25–34 years	39,979
Families with head aged 65 years and over	30,660
Families with head non–high school graduate	25,465
Families with head high school graduate	40,040
Families with head attaining bachelor's degree	67,230

*Fifty percent of families earn less than the median income and 50 percent earn more.
Source: U.S. Bureau of the Census, http://www.census.gov/hhes/income/histinc/incfamdet.html, Tables F-7, F-11, and F-15.

table also indicate that the sex of the head of household influences family income. Families headed by a male generally earn more than those headed by a female.

Equality Versus Efficiency

Because the data presented in Exhibits 1 and 2 show that an unequal distribution of income exists in the United States, the normative question to be debated concerns the pros and cons of a more equal income distribution. Those who favor greater equality fear the link between the rich and political power. The wealthy may well use their money to influence national policies that benefit the rich. It is also argued that income inequality results in unequal opportunities for various groups. For example, children of the poor cannot obtain a college education, and, therefore, their underutilized productive capacity is a waste of human capital. The poor are also unable to afford health care, and this condition is a national concern.

Advocates of income inequality pose this question. Suppose you had your choice to live in egalitarian society *A*, where every person earns $30,000 a year, or society *B*, where 10 percent earn $20,000 and 90 percent earn $40,000. You would choose society *B* because the incentive to earn more and live better is worth the risk of earning less and living worse. After all, why is the average income higher in society *B*? The answer is that income inequality gives people an incentive to be productive. In contrast, people in society *A* lack such motivation because everyone earns the same income. Those who favor equality of income believe that critics ignore the nonmonetary incentives, such as pride in one's work and nation, that can motivate people.

A recent hotly debated topic concerning income inequality is whether the "rich got richer" during the 1980s. The data in Exhibit 1 reveal that the percentages of total income received by the highest 5 percent and the highest fifth did increase slightly, while the percentages received by each of the fifths below the highest decreased slightly.

> **Conclusion** *Measured by distribution of family money income, the richest families did become a little richer and the rest of the family groups a little poorer during the 1980s.*

It is important to note that simply observing changes in income distribution over time does not tell the whole story. Exhibit 3 traces real median family income, adjusted for rising prices, for the period 1980–1997. This measure indicates the trend of the average level of income received by all groups. Clearly, the trend for real median income during the 1980s was upward. This means the size of the income "pie" grew, and, therefore, the sizes of all the slices grew larger. However, consistent with the distribution data, the relative share of the pie for those with the biggest slice got slightly greater. Beginning in 1990, real median income fell steadily, and then it has risen since 1993.

The Lorenz Curve

Lorenz curve

A graph of the actual cumulative distribution of income compared to a perfectly equal cumulative distribution of income.

The distribution of income data presented in Exhibit 1 can be represented by the **Lorenz curve.** The Lorenz curve is a graph of the actual cumulative distribution of income compared to a perfectly equal cumulative distribution of income. This curve is a primary tool for measuring income distribution developed in 1905 by statistician M. O. Lorenz. Look at the hypothetical Lorenz curve in Exhibit 4. The vertical axis measures the *cumulative* percentage of family income, and the horizontal axis measures the *cumulative* percentage of families from poorest to richest. Starting at the lower left-hand corner on the graph, zero families earned zero percent of the cumulative percentage of money income. At the upper right-hand corner on the graph, 100 percent of the families earned 100 percent of the cumulative percentage of money income. The combination of other total family–total money income points between zero and 100 percent forms the Lorenz curve.

Reading along the horizontal axis, each fifth (20 percent) of the cumulative percentage of families corresponds to its cumulative share of income earned measured along the curve. At point *A*, the lowest 20 percent of families receive 10 percent of total or cumulative income. To read this, go from the 20 percent point on the horizontal line up to point *A* on the Lorenz curve. Then draw a horizontal line to the vertical axis, and read that it intersects this axis at 10 percent. Point *B* is interpreted as the lowest 40 percent of families earn 10 percent plus 15 percent, which equals a cumulative share of 25 percent. Similarly, point *C* is the cumulative share earned by the lowest 60 percent of families, which equals 40 percent. Finally, point *D* is a bit tricky to interpret. At this point, the lowest 80 percent of families receive about 62 percent of total income. And here is the twist. You must interpret that the richest 20 percent of families earn 38 percent of income (100 percent − 62 percent).

We now turn to the 45-degree line above the Lorenz curve that cuts the box in half. This line represents perfect equality: 20 percent of the families

EXHIBIT 3

Real Median Family Income, 1980–1997

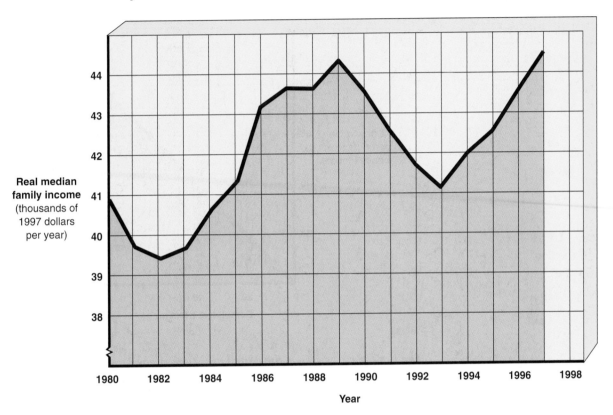

Real median income measures the income adjusted for inflation received by all families in the United States. Fifty percent of families earn less and 50 percent earn more than the median income. This measure fell and rose during the 1980s, but the trend was clearly upward during the 1980s. Between 1982 and 1989, the real median income increased by 13 percent. Beginning in 1990, real median income fell steadily, and then it has risen since 1993.

Source: *Economic Report of the President, 1999*, http://www.gpo.ucop.edu/catalog/erp99 .html, Table B-33.

receive 20 percent of total income, 40 percent of the families receive 40 percent of total income, and so on. The distance of the Lorenz curve from the perfect equality line is therefore a measure of unequal income distribution. The gap between points *C* and *E*, for example, indicates that 60 percent of families earn 20 percent less of total income than required for perfect equality. Similar measurements generate the shaded area between the Lorenz curve and the perfect equality line. Thus, the shaded area is a

EXHIBIT 4

A Hypothetical Lorenz Curve

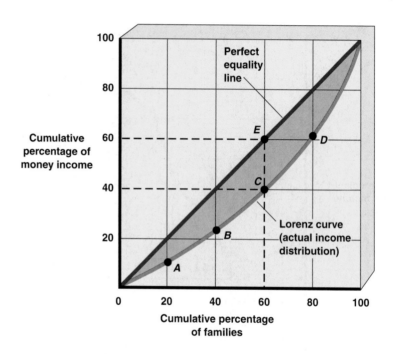

The Lorenz curve shows the cumulative percentage of money income earned from 0 to 100 percent by the cumulative percentage of families, also from 0 to 100 percent. If the income distribution followed the 45-degree perfect equality line, 20 percent of the families earn 20 percent of total money income, 40 percent receive 40 percent of total money income, and so on. The shaded area between the perfect equality line and the Lorenz curve measures the degree of inequality in the distribution of income. The more the Lorenz curve is bowed outward, the more unequal the distribution of income is.

measure of the degree of income inequality for our hypothetical data. A larger shaded area would mean greater income inequality, and the shape of the Lorenz curve would become more bowed outward. A smaller shaded area would represent a more equal income distribution, and the Lorenz curve would be a flatter curve.

It is very important to note that there are limitations associated with using money income statistics. Such data are not adjusted for government-provided food stamps, medical care, housing, or other goods and services. Money income also reflects income before taxes and does not measure unreported income or wealth. Still, used carefully, the Lorenz curve is a convenient tool for visualizing the degree of income inequality.

EXHIBIT 5

Lorenz Curves for Family Income Distribution, 1929 and 1997

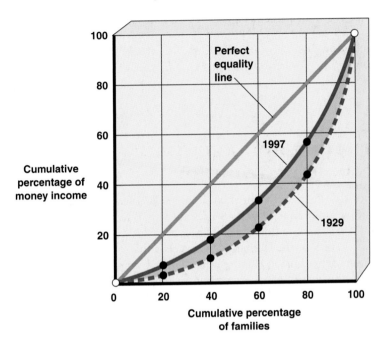

Percentage of families	1929		1997	
	Percentage share	Cumulative share	Percentage share	Cumulative share
Lowest fifth	3.5%	3.5%	4.2%	4.2%
Second-lowest fifth	9.0	12.5	9.9	14.1
Middle fifth	13.8	26.3	15.7	29.8
Second-highest fifth	19.3	45.6	23.0	52.8
Highest fifth	54.4	100.0	47.2	100.0

Since 1929, the Lorenz curve has shifted somewhat inward toward the perfect equality line. Thus, there has been a reduction in the inequality of distribution of family money income over these years.

Income Distribution Trend in the United States

In Exhibit 1, we looked at income distributions for selected years between 1929 and 1997. What can we conclude from these data using the Lorenz curve? Has the overall income distribution become more or less equal? The table in Exhibit 5 restates the income share data for 1929 and 1997 from Exhibit 1, and the cumulative percentage shares of families of quintiles are calculated from the percentage shares.

If you are a proponent of income equality, Exhibit 5 suggests that over-all money income distribution has changed little over the period. As shown in the exhibit, there is only a small shaded area between the 1929 and 1997 Lorenz curves. However, the share of income received by the top of families fell from 54 percent in 1929 to 47 percent in 1997.

Conclusion *The Lorenz curve has shifted only slightly inward and therefore closer to the perfect equality line between 1929 and 1997.*

International Comparisons of Income Distribution

How does the distribution of income in the United States compare with that of other countries? Exhibit 6 presents separate Lorenz curves for the United States, Russia, and Brazil. This exhibit indicates that the degree of income inequality in the United States exceeds that of Russia. On the other hand, income distribution is more equal in the United States than in Brazil. In general, the distribution of income in developed nations, such as the United States, Russia, Italy, and Sweden, is more equal than in developing nations, such as Brazil, Mexico, and China.

The U.S. Bureau of the Census provides current and historical data on, and information addressing, poverty at http://www.census.gov/hhes/www/poverty.html.

Poverty

Having discussed the broader question of measuring the degree of income distribution inequality, we now turn the spotlight on the fiercely debated issue of poverty. We are all disturbed by the thought of homelessness and hungry children. How can there be poverty in a nation of abundance, such as the United States? Can economists offer useful ideas to reform and improve our current welfare system? Most of the nation agrees that significant reforms to the welfare system must reduce poverty, cut welfare dependency, and save taxpayers money. The first step to understanding the problem is to ask this question: Who is poor?

Defining Poverty

What is poverty? Is it eating pork and beans when others are eating steak? Or is poverty a family having one car when others have two or more? Is the poverty standard only a matter of normative arguments? Indeed, the term *poverty* is a concept that is difficult to define. A person whose income is comparatively low in the United States may be viewed as well off in an undeveloped country. Or what we in the United States regard as poverty today might have seemed like a life of luxury 200 years ago.

EXHIBIT 6

Lorenz-Curves for Nations

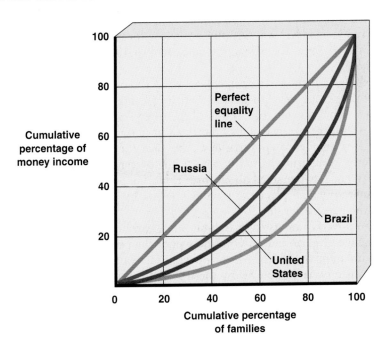

Comparing Lorenz curves for the United States, Russia, and Brazil reveals that income is distributed more equally in Russia than in the United States and Brazil. As illustrated by the Lorenz curve for Brazil, income inequality is usually greater in less-developed countries.

Source: The World Bank, World Development Report 1998, http://www.worldbank.org /data/databytopic.html, Table 2.8.

There are two views of poverty. One defines poverty in *absolute* terms, and the other defines poverty in *relative* terms. Absolute poverty can be defined as a dollar figure that represents some level of income per year required to purchase some minimum amount of goods and services essential to meeting a person's or a family's basic needs. In contrast, relative poverty might be defined as a level of income required to place a person or family in the lowest, say, 20 percent among all persons or families receiving incomes. An unequal distribution of income guarantees that some persons or families will occupy in relative terms the bottom rung of the income ladder. The U.S. government first established an official definition of the **poverty line** in 1964. The poverty line is the level of income below which a person or a family is considered as being poor. The poverty line is defined

Poverty line
The level of income below which a person or a family is considered as being poor.

in absolute terms: It is based on the cost of a minimal diet multiplied by three because low-income families spend about one-third of their income on food. In 1964, the poverty income level for a family of four was $3,000 ($1,000 for food × 3). Since 1969, the poverty line figure has been adjusted upward each year for inflation. In 1988, for example, the official poverty income level was $12,092 or below for a family of four. In 1997, a family of four needed an income of $16,400 to clear the poverty threshold.

Exhibit 7(a) shows the percentage of all persons in the U.S. population below the poverty level, beginning with 1959. The poverty rate for all persons was on a downward trend until the trend reversed in the early 1980s. Since 1980, the percentage has remained at about 14 percent. The exhibit also gives an idea of poverty levels by race for selected years. First, as shown by comparing parts (b) and (c), the percentage of blacks below the poverty line has remained about three times the percentage of whites since 1970. Second, the percentages in the 1990s by race have changed little from the percentages in 1975.

The poverty rate listed in Exhibit 8 has two major problems. First, this percentage gives no indication of how poor the people included are. A person with an income $1 below the poverty line counts, and so does a person whose income is $5,000 below the threshold. Second, the poverty rate is actually computed by comparing a family's census cash income from all sources to the poverty line. Cash income includes cash payments from Social Security, unemployment compensation, and Aid to Families with Dependent Children (AFDC). Cash income for the poor does not include noncash transfers, called **in-kind transfers**. In-kind transfers are government payments in the form of goods and services, rather than cash, including such government programs as food stamps, Medicaid, and housing. These antipoverty programs will be discussed in more detail in the next section.

In-kind transfers
Government payments in the form of goods and services, rather than cash, including such government programs as food stamps, Medicaid, and housing.

Who Are the Poor?

Exhibit 8 lists selected characteristics of families below the poverty level in 1997. Geographically, poor families are most likely to live in the South. An important characteristic of families living below the poverty line in the United States is family structure. The poverty rate was 32 percent for families headed by unmarried women compared to only 5 percent for married couples. In fact, there has been a sharp rise in families headed by unmarried women from 10 percent of all families in 1960 to 18 percent in 1997. Finally, poverty is greatly influenced by the lack of educational achievement of the head of household. As shown in the exhibit, 24 percent of the families with household heads that have not received a high school diploma are below the poverty line compared to only 2 percent for heads with at least a bachelor's degree.

EXHIBIT 7

Persons Below the Poverty Level as a Percentage of U.S. Population, 1959–1997

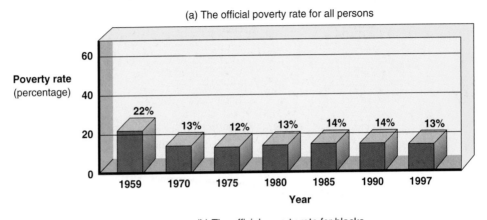

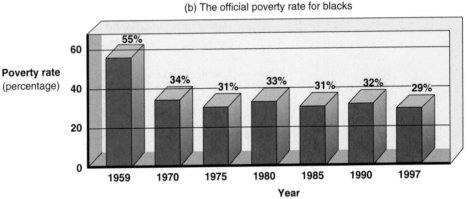

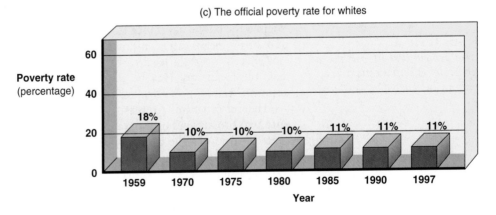

In part (a), the official poverty rate for all persons declined sharply between 1959 and the 1970s. After 1980, the poverty rate generally rose slightly. Comparison of parts (b) and (c) reveals that the poverty rate for blacks fell sharply between 1959 and 1970 and then has remained about three times the poverty rate of whites.

Source: U.S. Bureau of the Census, *Current Population Reports*, P60-201, http://www.census.gov/hhes /www/poverty.html, Table C-1.

EXHIBIT 8   Characteristics of U.S. Persons and Families Below the 1997 Poverty Level

Characteristic	Percentage Below the Poverty Line
Region	
South	15%
West	15
Midwest	10
Northeast	13
Type of Family	
Headed by married couple	5
Headed by male, no wife	13
Headed by female, no husband	32
Education of Household Head	
No high school diploma	24
High school diploma, no college	10
Bachelor's degree or more	2

Source: U.S. Bureau of the Census, *Current Population Reports,* P60-201, http://www.census.gov/hhes /www/poverty.html, Tables A, C3, and unpublished data.

Antipoverty Programs

The government has a number of programs specifically designed to aid the poor. The groups eligible for such assistance include disabled persons, elderly persons, and poor families with dependent children. People become eligible for public assistance if their income is below certain levels as measured by a **means test.** A means test is a requirement that a family's income not exceed a certain level to be eligible for public assistance. People who pass the means test may be *entitled* to government assistance. Thus, government welfare programs are often called *entitlement programs.*

Federal programs to assist the poor in the United States are classified into two broad types of programs: *cash* assistance and *in-kind transfers.* As stated previously, the current definition of the poverty threshold excludes in-kind transfers because these programs did not exist when the poverty rate measure was adopted over three decades ago.

Means test

A requirement that a family's income not exceed a certain level to be eligible for public assistance.

Cash Transfer Programs

The following are major government programs that alleviate poverty by providing eligible persons with cash payments needed to purchase food, shelter, clothing, and other basic needs.

Social Security (OASDHI). The technical name for our gigantic social insurance program is Old Age, Survivors, and Disability Health Insurance, or OASDHI. Under the Social Security Act passed in 1935, each worker must pay a payroll tax matched in equal amount by his or her employer. Look at your paycheck and you will find this deduction under FICA, which stands for Federal Insurance Contribution Act. Most of this money is used to pay current benefit recipients, and the remainder goes into the Social Security Trust Fund. Workers may retire at age 65 with full benefits or at 62 with reduced benefits. If a wage earner dies, Social Security provides payments to survivors, including spouse and children until about 18 years of age (age 21 if they are in school). In addition, payments are made to disabled workers.

Radical changes in policy are being debated. Since the creation of Social Security in 1935, money paid into the program has been invested exclusively in interest-bearing government securities, mainly long-term bonds. But the United States could obtain a higher return on investment and increase retirement savings for the baby-boom generation by channeling some of the money into the stock market, where stocks generally outperform bonds by a significant margin.

Although the Social Security Trust Fund now takes in more money in taxes and interest than it pays out in benefits, the program will not be able to pay all the benefits received by the baby-boom generation because, under the latest estimates, the trust fund will be depleted in 2030. Another reform idea is to create an investment account for each person covered by Social Security. The government would require workers to contribute a small amount each year beyond their current level of payroll taxes. These accounts would be held by the Social Security system, but individuals would be free to choose stock index funds, bond index funds, or some combination of these options. When a person retires, money accumulated in the account would be paid out in the form of an annuity, supplementing regular Social Security benefits.

The Social Security Administration manages SSI benefits, the Administration for Children and Families manages AFDC, and HUD sponsors low-income housing assistance. Visit their sites at http://www.ssa.gov, http://www.acf.dhhs.gov, *and* http://www.hud.gov, *respectively.*

Unemployment Compensation **Unemployment compensation** is a government insurance program that pays income for a short time period to unemployed workers. This unemployment insurance is financed by a payroll tax on employers, which varies by state and according to the size of the firm's payroll. This means employees do not have anything deducted from their paychecks for unemployment compensation. Although the federal government largely collects the taxes and funds this program, it is administered by the states. Any insured who becomes unemployed, and did not just quit his or her job, can become eligible for benefit payments after a short waiting period of usually one week.

Unemployment compensation

The government insurance program that pays income for a short time period to unemployed workers.

Aid to Families with Dependent Children (AFDC) AFDC is state administered, but partly financed with federal grants. This program provides aid to needy families with children who do not have the financial support of a parent, usually the father, because of divorce, desertion, disability, or death. To many people, AFDC embodies the "welfare mess." Critics argue

Pulling on the Strings of the Welfare Safety Net

Applicable Concept: welfare reform

The jury is still out on welfare reform. The following articles describe results of the new welfare scheme under the Personal Responsibility and Work Opportunity Act of 1996.

A *Washington Post* article reports welfare success in Los Angeles:

> Independent researchers have found the first solid evidence that welfare reform is beginning to work in the nation's largest cities, federal officials announced yesterday. While the welfare rolls have declined by nearly 4 million individuals since President Clinton signed dramatic overhaul legislation two years ago this Saturday, the biggest drops have occurred in rural states and suburban communities.
>
> In Los Angeles, the researchers found that 43 percent of poor families who were required to participate in the city's new welfare reform program got jobs, while only 32 percent of families randomly selected to remain in the traditional welfare program did. This represents an increase of one-third over the old welfare program. The typical welfare family subject to the reform initiatives earned $1,286 in the first six months of the program, while "control group" families earned $879, a difference of 46 percent. The study covered a period from 1996 to 1997.[1]

A *New York Times* article reports the impact on minorities:

> As the welfare rolls continue to plunge, white, black and Hispanic recipients are all leaving welfare at unprecedented rates. But the disproportionately large exodus of whites has altered the racial balance in a program long rife with racial conflict and stereotypes, according to figures that were compiled in an analysis of recent state data by The New York Times.
>
> The legacy of those stereotypes makes the discussion of race and welfare an unusually sensitive one. In the past, advocates and scholars have taken pains to note there were more white families on welfare than black. But that is no longer the case. Blacks now outnumber whites. The Hispanic share of the rolls is growing fastest. And black and Hispanic recipients combined outnumber whites by about 2 to 1. In addition, the remaining caseload is increasingly concentrated in large cities. Some analysts warn that the growing racial and urban imbalance could erode political support for welfare, especially when times turn tight. More immediately, the changing demographic suggest that states may need new strategies as they serve those left behind, like recipients who do not speak English. [2]

that AFDC provides an incentive for fathers to desert their families to receive payments.

In-Kind Transfers

The following are important government in-kind transfer programs that raise the standard of living for the poor.

Food Stamps The food stamp program began in 1964 as a federally financed program that is administered by state governments. The government issues coupons to the poor, who use them like money at the grocery store. The grocer cashes the stamps at a local bank, which redeems them at face value from the government. The cash value of stamps issued varies

Another *New York Times* article describes requests to charities:

Being off welfare is not the same as being out of poverty, according to some social service workers who say the decrease in welfare recipients has created a surge in people seeking shelter and food. They attributed the changes to sweeping welfare reform. "Now the sanctions are taking effect, and people really have no place to go," said Sasa Olessi Montano, executive director of the Young Women's Christian Association of Trenton.

Ms. Olessi Montano said the Y.W.C.A. had seen a "dramatic increase" in the number of families asking for shelter in the past few months, and the $30,000 yearly grant used to house them had already run out. The demand for food and clothing is outpacing the supply, she added. "It's bogus to say the welfare rolls are down and people are moving into jobs," Ms. Olessi Montano said. "That's not true. The need for services is growing by the minute." Treva Woung, program director for St. Rocco's Shelter in Newark, said she had seen a 50 percent increase in homeless single mothers who have been evicted from or denied state-subsidized housing. The shelter has beds for 60 women and children.[3]

The current approach to welfare reform is to cut the growth of welfare by turning control from the federal government to the states. Since state and local officials are closer to the people, welfare programs will improve. Analyze this article based on work disincentives, inefficiencies, and inequities.

[1] Judith Havemann, "Welfare Reform Success Cited in L.A.," *Washington Post*, August 20, 1998, p. A1.
[2] Jason Depule, "Shrinking Welfare Rolls Leave Record High Share of Minorities," *New York Times*, July 27, 1998, sec. A, p. 1.
[3] "As Welfare Rolls Drop, Requests to Charities Rise," *New York Times*, August 18, 1998, sec. B, p. 5.

with the eligible recipient's income and family size. The food stamp program has become a major part of the welfare system in the United States.

Medicaid   This is the largest in-kind transfer program. Medicaid provides medical services to eligible poor under 65 who pass a means test. AFDC families qualify for Medicaid in all states.

Housing Assistance   Federal and state governments have a number of different programs to provide affordable housing for poor people. The federal agency overseeing most of these programs is the Department of Housing and Urban Development (HUD). These programs include housing projects owned and operated by the government and subsidies to assist people who rent private housing. In both cases, recipients pay less than the market value for apartments and therefore receive an in-kind transfer.

Welfare Criticisms

The list of criticisms of welfare is indeed a long one. However, the majority of objections can be classified into the following three major criticisms:

- **Work Disincentives.** Because welfare provides income that is easier to obtain than by working, the poor are often induced to reduce their work effort. In fact, the more a recipient earns from a job, the fewer the benefits he or she receives. Moreover, the taxes to finance welfare payments have some disincentive effects on the work effort of taxpayers. Taxes reduce take-home pay and thus reduce the reward for work.

- **Inefficiencies.** Critics charge that the huge welfare bureaucracy in Washington, D.C., and throughout the nation results in more money in the pockets of bureaucrats than in the pockets of the poor. This major criticism is expressed by economics professor Thomas Sowell as follows:

  The amount necessary to lift every man, woman, and child in America above the poverty line has been calculated, and it is one-third of what is in fact spent on poverty programs. Clearly, much of the transfer ends up in the pockets of highly paid administrators, consultants, and staff as well as higher income recipients of benefits from programs advertised as antipoverty efforts.[1]

- **Inequities.** Today, many critics argue that poor persons with equal needs receive different benefits. For example, a needy family in California might receive welfare benefits twice as great as those received by the same needy family in South Carolina. The reason is that benefits under AFDC and Medicaid are essentially controlled by the states.

Reform Proposals

Given the criticisms of welfare prominent in the media and political speeches, how might the welfare system be revamped? Although there are numerous reform proposals, the various ideas can be classified into two broad approaches. First, the negative income tax system offers a major transformation of the entire patchwork of welfare programs. Second, workfare is a more likely alternative, involving a piecemeal approach, rather than a radical transformation.

Negative Income Tax

An idea first advanced by Stanford University's Milton Friedman (formerly of the University of Chicago) in the early 1960s to reduce work disincentives and welfare bureaucracy while providing for the poor is the **negative income tax**. The negative income tax (NIT) is a plan under which families below a certain break-even level of income would receive cash payments

What types of welfare reforms are necessary? For differing views, see the Urban Institute at http://www.urban.org/welfare/overview.htm, *the Electronic Policy Network at* http://epn.org/idea/welfare.html, *and The Heritage Foundation at* http://www.heritage.org:80//library/categories/healthwel/bg1063.html.

Negative income tax
A plan under which families below a certain break-even level of income would receive cash payments that decrease as their incomes increase.

---

[1]Thomas Sowell, *Markets and Minorities* (New York: Basic Books, Inc., 1981), p. 122.

that decrease as their incomes increase. A NIT system would combine all cash and in-kind transfer welfare programs into a single program administered by a single agency.

Exhibit 9 illustrates how a negative income tax might work. A low-income family of four receives a cash payment until it reaches a *break-even income* at $20,000 per year, where the family neither receives a payment nor pays income taxes. Above $20,000, the family pays income taxes. For example, a family with an income of $30,000 pays $5,000 in taxes, while a family with an income of $10,000 is paid an NIT subsidy of $5,000. A family with zero income is paid an NIT payment of $10,000. Thus, the government pays families an amount that varies inversely (negatively) with income.

Conclusion *The negative income tax is the reverse of a positive income tax system, in which people pay the government an amount that varies directly with their income.*

The basic idea behind the NIT system is simple: Families with incomes above the break-even income finance payments to families with incomes below the break-even income. Begin at zero income in the exhibit, and assume the income guarantee is set at the poverty income threshold of $10,000. Beyond the guaranteed minimum income of $10,000, government payments are reduced by, say, $.50 for each $1 earned. This rate, called the *phase-out rate*, determines the cash transfers to low-income families until the break-even income is reached.

The NIT system offers several potential advantages. First, the bureaucratic costs would be cut because an NIT program could be administered by a single agency. Second, poor people would not suffer the stigma of repeatedly standing in lines at the welfare office or using food stamps in the grocery store. Third, many economists argue that individuals are rational and know best how to spend their money. This means a cash subsidy is believed to be preferable to an in-kind transfer.

After 30 years of discussion and study, the negative income tax has not gained wide support other than among many economists. The NIT system is perceived as a political liability because voters perceive it as a "give-away" system for taxpayers' money. These critics believe in-kind welfare is preferable to cash assistance. When a recipient is given food stamps or a housing subsidy, he or she acquires food and housing, rather than, say, buying drugs and gambling. However, it is known that some food stamps are sold illegally for cash, which is used to buy drugs, alcohol, or whatever. Finally, a concern is that a generous guaranteed minimum income paid in cash might create a disincentive to work, rather than an incentive to work.

Workfare

The 1996 welfare reform bill titled the *Personal Responsibility and Work Opportunity Act* set a lifetime limit of five years of welfare benefits per family and gave the states block grants to run welfare programs. To overcome the disincentive to work produced by welfare programs, current

EXHIBIT 9

A Negative Income Tax Plan

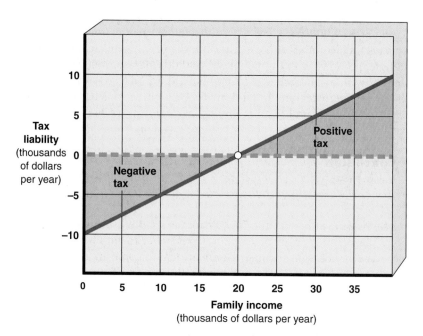

In this example, a family with no earned income receives a $10,000 payment from the government. From $0 to $20,000, payments are reduced by a phase-out rate of $.50 for each $1 of additional income. When income exceeds $20,000, payments fall to zero, and the family pays income taxes. Thus, a family with an income of $30,000 pays $5,000 in taxes.

welfare is aimed at increasing the work performed by welfare recipients and at increasing their participation in job-training programs. To keep their benefits, welfare recipients must perform some work activities within two years of receiving welfare or risk losing it. This idea is called *workfare*. Workfare programs require able-bodied adults to work for the local government or any available private-sector employer in order to be eligible for welfare benefits. The paramount question thus becomes how to create jobs for welfare recipients. A large public job plan would be costly and politically unpopular, especially among public employees who fear losing jobs. Another option is for the government to pay employers to hire welfare recipients. A variation on this idea is for the government to hire personnel firms that would earn a fee for each person placed in a job.

There are potential problems with subsidies for companies that hire welfare recipients. One problem is that subsidies can stigmatize welfare recipients and reduce their long-term employment prospects. Another potential problem is that subsidies could be a windfall payment to employers for hir-

CHECKPOINT   Does a Negative Income Tax Discourage Work?

Under a negative income system, people who work receive reduced payments from the government. Even worse, beyond the break-even income, workers must pay taxes. This means there is no basis in an NIT system to argue that the poor will have an incentive to work. Explain why you agree or disagree. (*Hint:* Construct a table using Exhibit 9, and consider after-tax income.)

ing people who would have been hired without the subsidies. Finally, there is a displacement problem because a subsidized welfare-recipient worker can take the job of an unsubsidized worker who has never received welfare benefits.

Discrimination

Poverty and discrimination in the workplace are related. Nonwhites and females earn less income when employer prejudice prevents them from receiving job opportunities. Discrimination also occurs when nonwhites and females do basically the same work as whites and males, but the nonwhites and females earn less. Exhibit 10 uses labor market theory to explain how discrimination can cause the equilibrium wage to be lower for nonwhites than for whites.

Exhibit 10(a) assumes that employers do not discriminate. This means employers hire workers regardless of race—that is, on the basis of their contribution to revenue (their *MRPs*). Hence, the interaction of the market demand curve, *D*, and the market supply curve, *S*, determines the equilibrium wage rate of $245 per day paid by nondiscriminating employers. The total number of black and white workers hired is 14,000 workers.

Now assume for the sake of argument that employers do practice job discrimination against black workers. The result, shown in Exhibit 10(b), is two different labor markets—one for whites and one for blacks. Because discrimination exists, the demand curve for labor for blacks is to the left of the demand curve for labor for whites, reflecting unjustified restricted employment practices. The supply curve of labor for blacks is also to the left of the supply curve of labor for whites because there are fewer blacks seeking employment than whites.

Given the differences in the labor market demand and the labor market supply curves, the equilibrium wage rate for whites of $280 is higher than the $210 paid to blacks. Comparison of these wage rates with the labor market equilibrium wage rate of $245 reveals that the effect of discrimination is to change the relative wages of white and black workers. Whites earn a higher wage rate than they would earn in a labor market that did

EXHIBIT 10

Labor Markets Without and With Racial Discrimination

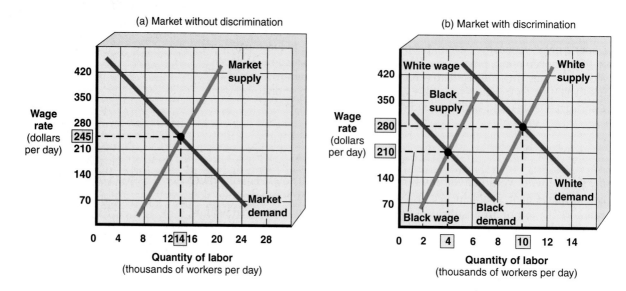

In part (a), there is no labor market discrimination against blacks. In this case, the equilibrium wage for all labor is $245 per day. Under discrimination in part (b), the labor demand and labor supply curves for white and black workers differ. As a result, the equilibrium wage rate for whites, $280, is higher than that for blacks, $210.

See the statement on comparable worth made by the MMA to the House Committee on Labor and Occupational Safety at http://www .mma-net.org/compworth.htm. *Links through the Internet search engines will provide pro and con opinions, and state laws, such as in IA and MN, can be accessed at* http://www.legis.state.ia.us /IACODE/1995/70A/18.html *and* http://www.doer.state.mn.us.

Comparable worth

The principle that employees who work for the same employer must be paid the same wages when their jobs, even if different, require similar levels of education, training, experience, and responsibility. It involves a nonmarket wage-setting process to evaluate and compensate jobs according to point scores assigned to different jobs.

not favor hiring them. Conversely, the black wage rate is decreased as a result of discrimination.

Comparable Worth

A controversial public policy aimed at eliminating labor market pay inequities is a concept called **comparable worth**. Comparable worth is the principle that employees who work for the same employer must be paid the same wages when their jobs, even if different, require similar levels of education, training, experience, and responsibility. Comparable worth is a nonmarket wage-setting remedy to the situation where jobs dominated by women pay less than jobs dominated by men. Because women's work is alleged to be undervalued, the solution is equal pay for jobs evaluated as having "comparable worth" according to point scores assigned to different jobs. In essence, comparable worth replaces labor-market-determined wages with bureaucratic judgments about the valuation of different jobs. For example, compensation paid to an elevator inspector and a nurse can be computed based on quantitative scores in a job-rating scheme. If the jobs' point totals are equal, the average elevator inspector and nurse must be paid equally by law.

Is a Librarian Worth the Same Wage as an Electrician?

Applicable Concept: comparable worth

In a recent *Forbes* ranking of the nation's top 100 chief executive officers by compensation, only one was a woman—Jill Barad of Mattel. On average, women earn about 75 percent as much as men in spite of laws against pay discrimination. Discrimination in wages and employment on the basis of sex was made illegal by two federal laws. In 1963, Congress passed the Equal Pay Act (EPA), which outlawed pay discrimination between men and women doing substantially the same job. This does not mean that unequal pay for the same work cannot exist, but if it does, the differential must be due to factors other than sex. These factors might include a seniority system, a merit system, or a system that measures earnings by quantity or quality of production.

Comparable worth laws have been passed in several states, Canada, Great Britain, and Australia. Proponents of comparable worth argue that the equal-pay-for-equal-work idea has failed. They observe that the pay is lower in female-dominated occupations and argue that female productivity and experience receive less reward in these jobs than do male productivity and experience in male-dominated jobs. In short, they maintain that women crowd into secretarial work, nursing, and retail sales because of discrimination against women. The increased supply of female labor in these crowded professions lowers the prevailing wage.

Comparable-worth advocates urge that the courts interpret such labor market inequalities as a violation of the sex-discrimination provisions of Title VII of the Civil Rights Act of 1964. This law addresses defined discriminatory practices more broadly than does the EPA. Title VII makes it unlawful to discriminate on the basis of race, sex, or national origin in classifying, assigning, or promoting employees; in extending or assigning facilities; in providing training, retraining, or apprenticeships; or in implementing any other terms, conditions, or privileges of employment.

If the courts accept comparable worth and expand the scope of Title VII, they will not consider whether employers intentionally pay less for "women's jobs," only whether there is compliance with an established rating scheme. The best-known case occurred in 1983, when the American Federation of State, County, and Municipal Employees won the first federal court case against the state of Washington. The defendant was found guilty of wage discrimination against women because the state had not followed its comparable-worth point system. To comply with Title VII, the court ordered Washington to upgrade nearly 15,000 female employees and award back pay estimated to cost $377 million. The case was appealed to higher courts, and the union ultimately lost the case.

Quantitative job evaluations are not new; however, their use is the cornerstone of the comparable-worth movement. In the Washington case, independent consultants gave a registered nurse more points than a computer systems analyst, and truck drivers received fewer points than clerks. In another case, job consultants studied the Minnesota job classification system and assigned point values to 762 state job classes. According to the point system, male-dominated jobs often paid more than female-dominated jobs even though the female jobs had greater "worth." The Minnesota Task Force on Pay Equity then recommended to the legislature that it raise the "underpaid" female job classes, not lower the "overpaid" male job classes.

Suppose the consultants use a job-scoring system and they determine that the wage rate for a secretary is $50 per hour, while the competitive labor market wage rate is $10 per hour. What is the effect of such a comparable-worth law?

CHECKPOINT

Should the Law Protect Females?

Do you want women serving in combat, mining coal, and building skyscrapers? Some states have enacted laws that protect women by keeping them out of jobs deemed "too strenuous" or "too dangerous." Would the likely effect of such laws be to decrease wages in male-dominated occupations, increase wages in female-intensive occupations, or decrease wages in female-intensive occupations?

KEY CONCEPTS

Lorenz curve
Poverty line

In-kind transfers
Means test

Unemployment
   compensation

Negative income tax
Comparable worth

SUMMARY

★ The **Lorenz curve** is a measure of inequality of income. Since 1947, the share of money income for each fifth of families ranked according to their income has been quite stable. Also, the degree of income inequality among families in the United States has changed little since 1929. During the 1980s, the richest families did become richer; however, the median income of all groups increased.

Lorenz curve

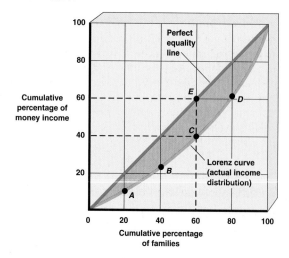

■ The **poverty line** is a level of cash income below which a family is classified as poor. The poverty income threshold is three times the cost of a minimal diet for a family. Today, about 12 percent of the U.S. population is officially classified as poor.

■ **In-kind transfers** are payments to the poor in the form of goods and services, rather than cash. Calculation of the poverty line counts cash income. On the other hand, in-kind transfers, such as food stamps, Medicaid, and housing, do not count as income for families classified as officially poor. Government cash transfers counted in the poverty line include payments from Social Security, unemployment compensation, and Aid to Families with Dependent Children.

■ **Welfare criticisms** include three major arguments: (1) Welfare reduces the incentive to work for the poor and taxpayers. (2) Welfare is inefficient because much of the money covers administrative costs, rather than providing benefits for the poor. (3) Because many antipoverty programs are controlled by the state, welfare benefits vary widely.

★ The **negative income tax** is a plan to set an income guarantee for all families. As a low-income family earns income, government payments (negative income tax) are phased out. After reaching a break-even income, families become taxpayers instead of being on the welfare rolls.

Negative income tax

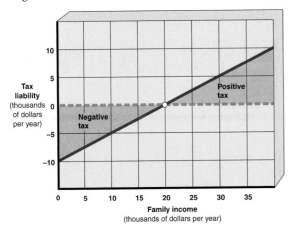

■ **Comparable worth** is the theory that workers in jobs determined to be of equal value by means of point totals should be paid equally. Instead of allowing labor markets to set wages, independent consultants award points to different jobs on the basis of such criteria as knowledge, experience, and working conditions.

SUMMARY OF CONCLUSION STATEMENTS

■ Measured by distribution of family money income, the richest families did become a little richer and the rest of the family groups a little poorer during the 1980s.

■ The Lorenz curve has shifted only slightly inward and therefore closer to the perfect equality line between 1929 and 1997.

■ The negative income tax is the reverse of a positive income tax system, in which people pay the government an amount that varies directly with their income.

STUDY QUESTIONS AND PROBLEMS

1. The following table contains data on the distribution of income in the countries of Alpha and Beta:

| | Alpha | | Beta | |
Percentage of Families	Percentage Share	Cumulative Share	Percentage Share	Cumulative Share
Lowest fifth	17.7%	_____	9.0%	_____
Second-lowest fifth	19.9	_____	14.2	_____
Middle fifth	20.4	_____	17.5	_____
Second-highest fifth	20.7	_____	21.9	_____
Highest fifth	21.3	_____	37.4	_____

a. Compute the cumulative distribution of income for each country.

b. Construct the Lorenz curve for each country.

c. For which country is the distribution of income more equal?

2. Suppose each family in the United States earned an equal money income. What would be the effect?

3. Explain the difference between poverty defined absolutely and poverty defined relatively. Which definition is the basis of the poverty line?

4. Calculate the official poverty threshold annual income for a family of four. Assume the minimally acceptable diet is estimated to be $5 per person per day and the minimum wage is $5 per hour. Will a head of a family of four earn the poverty threshold you have calculated?

5. What are in-kind transfers? Give examples. How are in-kind transfers considered in whether or not a family is below the poverty income threshold?

6. Would free health care reduce poverty, as measured by the government? Would free public housing, day care, and job training for the poor reduce the poverty rate? Explain.

7. What percentage of families in the United States was classified as poor in the 1990s? Which demographic groups have higher poverty rates?

8. List the major government cash assistance and in-kind transfer programs to assist the poor. Which of the programs are not exclusively for the poor?

9. What are the three major criticisms of welfare?

10. Assume the government implements a negative income tax plan with a guaranteed minimum income of $5,000 and a phase-out rate for payments of 50 percent. Provide the missing data in the following table:

A Negative Income Tax Plan

Family Income	Negative Tax	Total After-tax Income
$ 0	_____	_____
2,000	_____	_____
4,000	_____	_____
6,000	_____	_____
8,000	_____	_____
10,000	_____	_____

11. Critics of welfare argue that the role of government should be to break down legal barriers to employment, rather than using programs that directly provide cash or goods and services. For example, advocates of this approach would remove laws mandating minimum wages, comparable worth, union power, professional licensing, and other restrictive practices. Do you agree or disagree? Why?

ONLINE EXERCISES

Exercise 1

Visit Family Income Data Series (http://epn.org/epi/fids.html), and choose the Sources of Income Growth of Top Fifth. What conclusion is drawn concerning the relative importance of labor versus capital sources of income?

Exercise 2

Visit the U.S. Census Bureau (http://www.census.gov/ftp/pub/hhes/income/histinc/f02.html), and compare the income distribution in the United States over time. What can account for the change?

Exercise 3

Visit the U.S. Census Bureau (http://www.census.gov/ftp/pub/hhes/income/dewb94/index.html). Click on Moving Up and Down the Income Ladder. What are some of the causes of poverty?

Exercise 4

Visit the U.S. Census Bureau (http://www.census.gov/ftp/pub/hhes/www/incpov.html). What is the median household income for the most recent year reported? What is the poverty rate for that year? Find the poverty rate for the region including your hometown. How does it compare to the national average?

CHECKPOINT ANSWERS

Does a Negative Income Tax Discourage Work?

The following table is interpreted from Exhibit 9. Even though payments from the government decrease, total after-tax income increases from the combination of the income earned and the negative tax. After the break-even income of $20,000, total after-tax income continues to rise. If you said the NIT system assumes the poor are rational people who are motivated to earn more total after-tax income by working, **YOU ARE CORRECT.**

A Negative Income Tax Plan

Family Income	Negative Tax	Positive Tax	Total After-tax Income
$ 0	$10,000	$ 0	$10,000
5,000	7,000	0	12,000
10,000	5,000	0	15,000
15,000	2,500	0	17,500
20,000	0	0	20,000
25,000	0	−2,500	22,500
30,000	0	−5,000	25,000
35,000	0	−7,500	27,500

Should the Law Protect Females?

A law that limits women's access to certain occupations results in their crowding into the remaining occupations. The obstacles facing women in male-dominated occupations artificially restrict competition with men. If you said the increased labor supply in female-intensive occupations decreases their wages, while the decreased labor supply in male-intensive occupations increases wages for males, **YOU ARE CORRECT.**

PRACTICE QUIZ

For a visual explanation of the correct answers, visit the tutorial at http://tucker.swcollege.com.

1. In 1997, the wealthiest 5 percent of all U.S. families earned what percentage of total annual money income among families?
   a. More than 20 percent
   b. Less than 10 percent
   c. More than 25 percent
   d. More than 50 percent

2. A figure that measures the relationship between the cumulative percentage of money income on the vertical axis and the cumulative percentage of families on the horizontal axis is called the
   a. family-income curve.
   b. Washington curve.
   c. Lorenz curve.
   d. Gini curve.

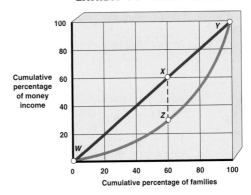

EXHIBIT 11   Lorenz curve

3. As shown in Exhibit 11, the perfect equality line is drawn between points
   a. W and Y along the curve.
   b. X and Z.
   c. W and Y along the straight line.
   d. W and X.

4. As shown in Exhibit 11, 20 percent of families earned a cumulative share of about ____ percent of income.
   a. 5
   b. 10
   c. 30
   d. 50

5. As shown in Exhibit 11, 40 percent of families earned a cumulative share of about ____ percent of income.
   a. 5
   b. 15
   c. 30
   d. 50

6. Since 1929, the overall income distribution in the United States has become
   a. much more unequal.
   b. much less unequal.
   c. slightly more unequal.
   d. slightly more equal.

7. Comparing the family income distributions of the United States, Russia, and Brazil, the conclusion is that income is distributed
   a. most equally in Brazil.
   b. most equally in the United States.
   c. about the same in all three countries.
   d. most equally in Russia.

8. In order to establish the poverty line that divides poor and nonpoor families, the government
   a. multiplies the cost of a minimal diet by three.
   b. multiplies the cost of a minimal diet by five.
   c. adds 50 percent to the cost of a minimal diet.
   d. adds 100 percent to the cost of a minimal diet.

9. The poverty line
   a. is defined as one-half average family income.
   b. includes in-kind transfers.
   c. includes Medicaid benefits.
   d. has been attacked for overstating poverty.

10. Which of the following is an in-kind subsidy?
    a. Social Security payments
    b. Unemployment compensation
    c. Food stamps
    d. Welfare payments

11. Which of the following is a cash assistance (not an in-kind transfer) program?
    a. Aid to Families with Dependent Children
    b. Medicare
    c. Medicaid
    d. Food stamps

12. The negative income tax (NIT) is a plan under which families
    a. above a level of income pay no tax.
    b. pay the same tax rate except for the poor.
    c. below a level of income pay no tax.
    d. below a level of income receive a cash payment.

13. Which of the following might decrease the supply curve of labor?
    a. Discrimination against blacks
    b. Discrimination against women
    c. Difficult licensing requirements
    d. All of the above

CHAPTER THIRTEEN

Antitrust and Regulation

> **P**eople of the same trade seldom meet together, even for merriment and diversion, but the conversation ends in a conspiracy against the public, or in some contrivance to raise prices.[1]
>
> —*Adam Smith*

As soon as Microsoft dominated the personal computer software industry, Bill Gates, its founder, was charged by the government with anticompetitive business practices. Meanwhile, the media compared the case to John D. Rockefeller's Standard Oil monopoly and the robber barons of the 1890s. In the past, antitrust laws have been successfully used against the nation's largest corporations. This threat of the high legal costs of defending against an antitrust suit serves as a powerful deterrent, preventing

monopolies from engaging in unfair actions intended to eliminate rivals. Here you will explore and form opinions on the Microsoft case, the Standard Oil case, and other major antitrust cases. In addition, this chapter compares antitrust laws in the United States to antitrust laws of other countries.

When antitrust policy is successful, consumers benefit from lower prices and more output. As you study antitrust policy in this chapter, you will learn that antitrust is somewhat of an art form, blended from economic theory and politics—perhaps more politics than economic theory. Interestingly, certain industries are exempt from

antitrust legislation: labor unions, professional baseball teams, public utilities, public transit companies, schools, hospitals, and suppliers of military equipment.

The second half of this chapter turns to government regulation, which affects virtually every business and consumer. Our food is regulated, toys are regulated, airline safety is regulated, and most industries must deal with some form of regulation. What are the reasons for regulation, and what are its consequences? The explanation begins with a brief survey of regulation in the United States. Although government regulation remains pervasive, a movement began in the late

---

[1] Adam Smith, *An Inquiry into the Nature and Causes of the Wealth of Nations* (1776; reprint, New York: Random House, The Modern Library, 1937), p. 128.

1970s to reduce regulation in industries such as transportation and telecommunications. In the last section, we discuss the rationale for three different types of regulation justified on the basis of market failure.

In this chapter, you will learn to solve these economics puzzles:

- Can universities and colleges improve education by engaging in price-fixing?
- Why doesn't the water company or electric company compete?
- Why is market failure an economic rationale for regulation?

Antitrust

Before the Civil War, industries were populated by small firms, and few economic problems were caused by monopoly. After the Civil War, during the rapid industrialization of the 1870s and 1880s, the railroads and telegraph linked diverse regions of the country and enabled firms to expand into national markets. In order to gain more control of expanding industries, many competing companies merged or formed a **trust**. A trust is a combination or cartel consisting of firms that place their assets in the custody of a board of trustees. The trust allows firms that have not actually merged to form a cartel or cohesive group of firms that control an industry in order to charge monopoly prices and profits. The long list of trusts formed during this period included the iron trust, sugar trust, copper trust, steel trust, coal trust, oil trust, tobacco trust, and even the paper-bag trust. The organizers of many of these trusts became widely known as *robber barons* because of their exploitation and bullying of anyone in their way.

During the last decades of the 19th century, many trusts used various tactics to avoid competition. Recall from Chapter 9 that Standard Oil acquired oil fields, railroads, pipelines, and ships and then denied access to rivals. Thus, competing firms had to merge with Standard Oil or go out of business. With the competition eliminated, John D. Rockefeller, the most well-known so-called robber baron, raised Standard Oil's prices and limited production, and consumers suffered along with Standard Oil's competitors.

Another anticompetitive strategy used by the industrial giants was **predatory pricing**. Predatory pricing is the practice of one or more firms temporarily reducing prices in order to eliminate competition and then raising prices. Often trusts would sell a product below cost until their weaker competitors were unable to withstand mounting losses and were forced from the industry. Perhaps even more alarming, some trusts resorted to political corruption. For example, the railroad and petroleum trusts employed corrupt legislators and judges to gain a competitive edge.

By the end of the 19th century, the threat of continuing economic and political abuses created a public opinion quite hostile to big business. Newspapers regularly printed news of the trusts' questionable business practices. The large number of politically influential farmers blamed the trusts for the high railroad charges that resulted in the unprofitability of farming. Consumers and labor unions also raised their voices against monopoly power. The influence of the trusts was discussed constantly in

Trust
A combination or cartel consisting of firms that place their assets in the custody of a board of trustees.

Predatory pricing
The practice of one or more firms temporarily reducing prices in order to eliminate competition and then raising prices.

the halls of Congress. In 1888, both major political parties added antimo-nopoly planks to their election platforms. Hatred and distrust of the cen-tralization of economic and political powers originated in the Jeffersonian tradition of the United States. Against this background of populist (pro-people) fear of big business and political power, Congress passed laws aimed at preventing firms from engaging in anticompetitive activities.

The following is a brief description of the major antitrust legislation that constitutes basic antitrust law.

The Sherman Act

The first antitrust law was the **Sherman Act**. The Sherman Act of 1890 is the federal antitrust law that prohibits monopolization and conspiracies to restrain trade. Today, this act remains the cornerstone of antitrust policy in the United States. It has two main provisions:

> *Section 1: Every contract, combination in the form of trust or other-wise, or conspiracy in restraint of trade or commerce among the sev-eral States, or with foreign nations, is hereby declared to be illegal. . . .*

> *Section 2: Every person who shall monopolize, or attempt to monop-olize, or combine or conspire with any other person or persons, to monopolize any part of the trade or commerce among the several States, or with foreign nations, shall be deemed guilty of a misde-meanor, and, on conviction thereof, shall be punished by a fine not exceeding five thousand dollars, or by imprisonment not exceeding one year, or by both said punishments, in the discretion of the court.[2]*

In response to the public outcry, Congress intended to craft this law with sweeping language against the trusts. But what does it really say? It is unclear exactly which business practices constitute a "restraint of trade" and therefore a violation of the law. As a result of the extremely vague lan-guage, there were numerous court battles, and the act was ineffective for years. For example, the federal government did not win its first notable cases against Standard Oil and American Tobacco until 1911.

The serious consequences of violations of the Sherman Act are reflected in the more recent case of Archer Daniels Midland Co. (ADM). In 1995, this agribusiness giant pleaded guilty to price-fixing involving lysine and citric acid. It paid a $100 million fine. In 1998, a federal jury convicted three past and present executives of conspiring with competitors to fix the prices of these products. They faced a maximum three-year prison sentence and at least a $350,000 fine.

The Clayton Act

As explained above, the Sherman Act was proving to be little more than a legislative mandate for the courts to spell out the meaning of antitrust laws. To define anticompetitive acts more precisely, Congress passed the **Clayton Act**. The Clayton Act of 1914 is an amendment that strengthened

Sherman Act
The federal antitrust law enacted in 1890 that prohibits monopo-lization and conspiracies to restrain trade.

For the complete text of the Sherman Act, the Clayton Act, and other antitrust legislation, visit the U.S. Department of Justice website at http://www.usdoj.gov/atr/foia /divisionmanual/ch2.htm.

Clayton Act
A 1914 amendment that strength-ens the Sherman Act by making it illegal for firms to engage in cer-tain anticompetitive business practices.

---

[2]In 1974, the act was amended so that violations would be treated as felonies.

the Sherman Act by making it illegal for firms to engage in certain anti-competitive business practices. Under this act, the following business practices are illegal, with the important controversial condition that the effect is to "substantially lessen competition or tend to create a monopoly":

1. *Price Discrimination.* A firm charges different customers different prices for the same product where the price differences are not related to cost differences. (Recall the discussion of this topic in the chapter on monopoly.)

2. *Exclusive Dealing.* A manufacturer requires a retailer to sign an agreement based on the condition that the retailer will not carry any rival products of the manufacturer.

3. *Tying Contracts.* The seller of one product requires the buyer to purchase some other product(s).

4. *Stock Acquisition of Competing Companies.* One firm buys the stock of a competing firm.

5. *Interlocking Directorates.* The directors of one company serve on the board of directors of another company in the same industry. Interlocking directorates are illegal whether or not the effect may be to "substantially lessen competition."

Although more specific than the Sherman Act, the Clayton Act is also vague. The key question is, Exactly when does a situation or action "substantially lessen competition"? To this day, the task of interpreting this ambiguous phrase remains with the courts, and the interpretation changes over time.

The Federal Trade Commission Act

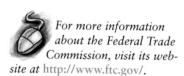

For more information about the Federal Trade Commission, visit its website at http://www.ftc.gov/.

Since the federal government faced a growing antitrust responsibility in the early 1900s, an agency was needed to investigate alleged anticompetitive practices and reach judgments. The **Federal Trade Commission Act** was enacted for this purpose. The Federal Trade Commission Act of 1914 is the federal act that established the Federal Trade Commission (FTC) to investigate unfair competitive practices of firms. This act contains perhaps the most general language of any antitrust act. It declares illegal "unfair methods of competition in commerce." The act established a five-member commission appointed by the president to determine the exact meaning of "unfair methods." Today, the FTC is concerned primarily with (1) enforcing consumer protection legislation, (2) prohibiting deceptive advertising, and (3) preventing collusion. When a complaint is filed with the FTC, the commission investigates. If there is a violation, the FTC can negotiate a settlement, issue a cease-and-desist order, or initiate a lawsuit.

The Robinson-Patman Act

The Clayton Act has been amended twice. Although price discrimination became an illegal practice under the Clayton Act, that section was not widely enforced at first. This situation changed with the passage of the **Robinson-Patman Act.** The Robinson-Patman Act of 1936 is an amendment to the Clayton Act that strengthens the Clayton Act against price discrimination. The Robinson-Patman Act is complex and controversial. Its basic purpose is to prevent large sellers from offering different prices to different buyers where the effect is to harm even a single small firm. In fact, the Robinson-Patman Act is often called the "Chain Store Act." The reason is that this act is an outgrowth of the competition between small independent sellers and chain stores that developed after World War I.

The Robinson-Patman Act encourages lawsuits by small independent firms because it broadens the list of illegal price discrimination practices. The Robinson-Patman Act, for example, makes it illegal for a firm to offer quantity discounts, free advertising, or promotional allowances to one buyer if the firm does not offer the same concessions to all buyers. Be careful to note that the legal prohibition on price discrimination in the Robinson-Patman Act is limited to situations where the effect is to "substantially lessen competition or tend to create a monopoly." The first You're the Economist offers the opportunity to debate issues concerning this act.

Additional information on the Robinson-Patman Act can be found at the following Internet address: http://www.lawmall.com/rpa/.

The Celler-Kefauver Act

Prior to 1950, the U.S. Supreme Court interpreted the Sherman Act as prohibiting mergers between competing firms by stock acquisition, but not prohibiting mergers by the sale of physical assets (plant, equipment, and so on). The **Celler-Kefauver Act** was the second amendment to the Clayton Act, and it was enacted to address this problem. The Celler-Kefauver Act of 1950 is an amendment to the Clayton Act that prohibits one firm from merging with a competitor by purchasing its physical assets if the effect is to substantially lessen competition. Consequently, this act is sometimes called the "Antimerger Act" because it closed the loophole in the Clayton Act and thereby prohibited anticompetitive mergers, which were the target of the original Clayton Act.

The five major antitrust laws are summarized in Exhibit 1.

Celler-Kefauver Act

A 1950 amendment to the Clayton Act that prohibits one firm from merging with a competitor by purchasing its physical assets if the effect is to substantially lessen competition.

EXHIBIT 1   Summary of Major Antitrust Laws

Law (Date Enacted)	Key Provisions
Sherman Act (1890)	Prohibits interstate price fixing and other conspiracies and combinations that restrain trade and attempts to monopolize.
Clayton Act (1914)	Bolsters and clarifies the Sherman Act by prohibiting specific business practices, including exclusive dealing, tying contracts, stock acquisition, and interlocking directorates.
Federal Trade Commission Act (1914)	Established an agency (the FTC) to help enforce antitrust laws by investigating unfair and deceptive business practices.
Robinson-Patman Act (1936)	Amends the Clayton Act by broadening the list of illegal price discrimination practices to include quantity discounts, free advertising, and promotional allowances offered to large buyers and not to small buyers. The Robinson-Patman Act is often called the "Chain Store Act."
Celler-Kefauver Act (1950)	Amends the Clayton Act by closing the loophole that permitted a firm to merge by acquisition of assets of a rival, rather than by acquisition of stocks, as outlawed in the original Clayton Act. The Celler-Kefauver Act is often called the "Antimerger Act."

Is Utah Pie's Slice of the Pie Too Small?

Applicable Concept: Robinson-Patman Act

In the 1950s the market for frozen dessert pies was small, but growing. The Salt Lake City market was supplied by distant plants in California that were owned by Carnation, Continental Baking, and Pet Milk. Until 1957, these three firms accounted for almost all the frozen fruit pies sold in the Salt Lake City market.

The Utah Pie Company had been baking dessert pies in Salt Lake City and selling them fresh for 30 years. This family-owned-and-operated business entered the frozen pie market in 1957. It was immediately successful and grabbed a huge share of the Salt Lake City market. During the relevant years, the market shares of the various competitors were as follows:

	1958	1959	1960	1961
Utah Pie	67	34	46	45
Pet	16	36	28	29
Carnation	10	9	12	9
Continental	1	3	2	8
All others	6	19	13	8

Utah Pie's strategy for penetrating the market was to set its prices below those of its competitors. Due to its immediate success, it built a new plant in 1958. Its local plants gave Utah Pie a locational advantage over its competitors. For most of the time in question, Utah Pie's prices were the lowest in the Salt Lake City market. The incumbent firms, of course, responded to Utah Pie's entry and lower prices by reducing their own prices. As a result, each of the larger firms sold frozen pies in Salt Lake City at prices lower than those charged for pies of like grade and quality in other geographic markets considerably closer to their California plants.

Utah Pie sued these three firms, claiming price discrimination. Ultimately, the case was reviewed by the Supreme Court [in 1967], which took a dim view of such pricing behavior: "Sellers may not sell like goods to different purchasers at different prices if the result may be to injure competition in either the sellers' or the buyers' market unless such discriminations are justified as permitted by the Act." Consequently, the Supreme Court found the defendants guilty of price discrimination. Inasmuch as no competitors had been forced from the market, it appears that price discrimination does not have to have an obvious predatory impact to be ruled illegal. All the Court saw in this case was a pattern of falling prices. It feared that such a pattern could result in a lessening of competition if one or more competitors fell out of the market.

ANALYZE THE ISSUE

Utah Pie sued its three outside competitors under the Robinson-Patman Act. Some have criticized this case because it is an example of the type of bizarre result that can be produced by antitrust policy. Do you agree? Explain.

Source: David L. Kaserman and John W. Mayo, *Government and Business: The Economics of Antitrust and Regulation* (Fort Worth: Dryden Press, 1995), p. 282.

Key Antitrust Cases

Antitrust policy can be compared to baseball or other sports. The House and Senate of U.S. Congress set the antitrust laws' "rules of the game," just like the American and National Leagues set the rules of baseball. For example, the rules of baseball say that a player hitting a homer must run from first to home base, rather than from third base to home base. Similarly, the Sherman Act forbids monopolization through predatory pricing by businesses. This brings us to the role of the umpire. After a game, a Little League player asked the first base umpire, "What do you call when the runner and the ball reach first base at exactly the same time?" The umpire replied, "There's no such thing as a tie. It's always the way I call it." That's how it is with court decisions on antitrust laws, and, just like with many of the umpire's calls, all the courts' decisions are not "crowd pleasers." With this point in mind, let's look at some important "calls" of the Supreme Court on antitrust cases.

An excellent source of antitrust information is found at the following Internet address: http://www.antitrust.org/.

The Standard Oil Case (1911)

The Theodore Roosevelt administration took action to break up Standard Oil under the Sherman Act. After 10 years of litigation, the Supreme Court ruled in 1911 that Standard Oil had achieved its monopoly position in the oil refining industry through illegal business practices. John D. Rockefeller's trust had used railroad rebates, discounts, espionage, control of supplies to rivals, and predatory pricing to gain a monopoly. The remedy was for the Standard Oil Trust to be broken into competing companies: Standard Oil of New York became Mobil, Standard Oil of California became Chevron, Standard Oil of Indiana became Amoco, and Standard Oil of New Jersey became Exxon.

The Standard Oil Trust case established a standard for antitrust rulings. The Supreme Court ruled that (a) Standard Oil was a monopoly with a 90 percent share of the refined-oil market and (b) Standard Oil achieved its monopoly through illegal business behavior intended to exclude rivals. The Court stated that point (b) was critical to its decision and not point (a). This doctrine became known as the **rule of reason**. The rule of reason is the antitrust doctrine that the existence of monopoly alone is not illegal unless the monopoly engages in illegal business practices. Stated differently, monopoly per se is not illegal. Thus, "big is not necessarily bad." Standard Oil and other dominant firms would be broken up not merely because of dominance, but also because of their abusive behavior.

Between 1911 and 1920, the rule of reason was also applied in breaking up the American Tobacco Trust and other trusts. In 1920, the Supreme Court also applied the rule of reason when it decided that U.S. Steel was not guilty under the Sherman Act. Although U.S. Steel controlled almost 75 percent of the domestic iron and steel industry, the Supreme Court ruled that it is not *size* that violates the law. Since there was no evidence of unfair pricing practices, U.S. Steel was a "good citizen" not in violation of the Sherman Act.

Rule of reason

The antitrust doctrine that the existence of monopoly alone is not illegal unless the monopoly engages in illegal business practices.

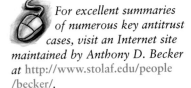 *For excellent summaries of numerous key antitrust cases, visit an Internet site maintained by Anthony D. Becker at* http://www.stolaf.edu/people/becker/.

The Alcoa Case (1945)

Thirty-four years after the Standard Oil case, the Supreme Court did a "flip flop" on the rule of reason. In 1940, the Aluminum Company of America (Alcoa) was the only producer of aluminum in the United States. Alcoa's monopoly was primarily the result of its patents and its ownership of a unique resource, bauxite. Moreover, Alcoa kept its prices low to avoid competition and prosecution, acting as a "good citizen" despite its size. The Court ruled Alcoa had violated the Sherman Act and declared:

> *Having proved that Alcoa had a monopoly of the domestic ingot market the government had gone far enough. . . . Congress did not condone "good trusts" and condemn "bad" ones; it forbade all.*[3]

Per se rule

The antitrust doctrine that the existence of monopoly alone is illegal, regardless of whether or not the monopoly engages in illegal business practices.

With the Alcoa decision, the courts turned from "big is not necessarily bad" to "big is bad." The rule of reason was transformed into the **per se rule**. The per se rule is the antitrust doctrine that the existence of monopoly alone is illegal regardless of whether or not the monopoly engages in illegal business practices. Instead of judgments based on the performance of a monopoly, antitrust policy in the United States was switched by Court interpretation to judgments based solely on the market structure. Interestingly, the Court's solution was not to break up Alcoa. Instead, the federal government subsidized its competitors. War plants were sold at bargain prices to Reynolds Aluminum and Kaiser Aluminum, and later more rivals entered the aluminum industry.

The IBM Case (1982)

In 1969, the U.S. Department of Justice brought antitrust action against IBM because of its dominance in the mainframe computer market. The government argued that IBM had a 72 percent share of the electronic digital computing industry. IBM argued that the relevant market was broader and included programmable calculators and other information-processing products. After 13 years of litigation, IBM had spent over $100 million on its defense and had constructed an entire building to store case documents. Finally, in 1982, the government dropped the case. One reason was that Digital Equipment, Apple Computer, and Japanese companies were competing with IBM. Another reason illustrates the mix of politics and antitrust policy. In 1982, Ronald Reagan was president, and he believed in a much less restrictive interpretation of antitrust laws. In any event, the IBM case represented a shift in the general sentiment among those enforcing the antitrust laws from the per se rule back to the rule of reason.

The AT&T Case (1982)

In 1978, the U.S. Department of Justice brought an antitrust suit against AT&T and the Bell System. The issue was complicated. At this time, AT&T was a *natural monopoly* regulated by the government. (Regulation

---

[3]United States v. Aluminum Co. of America, 148 F.2d 416 (2d Cir. 1945).

of a natural monopoly will be explained later in this chapter; see Exhibit 5.) The government allowed AT&T to have a monopoly in long-distance and local telephone service and in the production of telephones. The Federal Communications Commission (FCC) regulated long-distance rates, and state utility commissioners regulated local rates. What was the objective of giving one company the exclusive right to telephone services in the United States? In order to provide everyone with low-cost local services, the regulatory commissions set AT&T local charges low and AT&T long-distance rates high to cover the lower local rates.

In the 1970s, advances in technology changed the nature of the long-distance telephone industry. Telephone service was no longer a natural monopoly because fiber optics and satellites made cable connections obsolete. Competitors developed, and the government alleged these rivals were being charged unfairly high fees for access to AT&T's local telephone lines.

On the same day the IBM case ended in 1982, AT&T and the Department of Justice announced this case was settled. AT&T ("Ma Bell") divested itself of 22 local companies ("Baby Bells"), but retained its long-distance telephone service, its research facilities (Bell Laboratories), and its manufacturing facilities (Western Electric Company). As a result, local companies became regulated monopolies in their areas, and local phone rates rose sharply. In nationwide long-distance telephone service, AT&T's competition with MCI and Sprint lowered the price of long-distance telephone service. Moreover, individual customers were responsible for buying their own phones, rather than using only AT&T phones. The result has been a highly competitive market, offering a wide range of phone prices and a wide variety of phones.

The MIT Case (1992)

For years, the presidents of many of the nation's top universities—Cornell, Harvard, Yale, Columbia, Brown, Princeton, University of Pennsylvania, Dartmouth, and MIT—attended annual meetings to discuss tuition, faculty salaries, and financial aid packages. After such meetings, these schools often adjusted tuition charges, salary increases, and even fees for room and board. For example, one year Dartmouth planned to raise faculty salaries by 8.5 percent. The other schools wanted to hold the line at 6.5 percent, so Dartmouth was persuaded to cave in. At other meetings, the group's goal was to make sure each student who applied to more than one of the schools would be offered the same financial aid. At another meeting, Harvard and Yale accused Princeton of offering excessively generous scholarships to top students.

The U.S. Justice Department investigated and charged the eight Ivy League universities and MIT with an illegal conspiracy to fix prices. The eight Ivy League schools settled the case with a consent degree. This agreement required these schools to cease colluding on tuition, salaries, and financial aid in the future, and, in return, none of the schools admitted guilt for a price conspiracy. MIT refused to sign the consent order and pursued the case all the way to the Supreme Court. In 1992, the Court ruled

CHECKPOINT

Does Price-Fixing Improve Your Education?

Price-fixing agreements are among the monopolistic restraint-of-trade practices prohibited by Section 1 of the Sherman Act. The Supreme Court has concluded that no formal agreement is necessary for proof of conspiracy. Instead, conspiracy may be inferred from the acts of the accused even if the consequences might be considered socially desirable. The presidents of the universities charged with price-fixing defended their business practices with the argument that they openly met to fix prices in order to improve education. With the tuition and price of financial aid fixed, students and parents will choose their university on the basis of academic quality alone. Consider the discussion of pricing strategies for an oligopoly in Chapter 10. Can you give the presidents a better argument for their defense?

MIT had violated antitrust laws and concluded that students and parents have the right to compare prices when choosing a university.

The Microsoft Case (1995)

Microsoft Corporation dominates the computer software industry with nearly an 85 percent share of the personal computer operating system software market. In 1995, the U.S. Justice Department sued Microsoft to block the software company from buying Intuit Inc., which is the maker of Quicken personal-finance software. The suit, filed in the U.S. district court in San Francisco, stated that the $2 billion purchase essentially would give Microsoft a monopoly in the financial-software market, in which Quicken held a 70 percent market share. The deal would have been the largest in the history of the software industry.

The Justice Department stated that the acquisition would lead to higher prices and less innovation in personal-finance software and also would threaten the future of PC-based home banking. Instead of merger, Microsoft could use its Money program, a competitor of Quicken, to enter the market. However, this strategy would take much longer than buying Quicken because Money was not a very popular program. Microsoft agreed that if it were allowed to purchase Intuit, it would give Money to Utah-based Novell. The government said that was not enough of a concession; the proposal would not work because Novell would not be able to compete against Microsoft. Finally, Microsoft abandoned the proposed purchase of Intuit. As this text is written, the Justice Department is taking action against Microsoft for "tying" its Internet Explorer browser with its Windows95 operating software, which is the heart of 85 percent of the nation's personal computers.

Finally, the major antitrust cases are summarized in Exhibit 2.

EXHIBIT 2   Summary of Major Antitrust Cases

Case (Date)	Key Provision
Standard Oil (1911)	This case established the rule of reason, allowing a monopoly unless it engages in illegal practices.
Alcoa (1945)	This case overturned the rule of reason and established the per se rule, under which all monopolies are illegal.
IBM (1982)	The government dropped its case after 13 years and shifted antitrust policy back to the rule of reason.
AT&T (1982)	Technology made this government-regulated natural monopoly obsolete, and AT&T was found guilty of anticompetitive pricing.
MIT (1992)	Eight Ivy League schools agreed to stop colluding to fix prices, and MIT was found guilty of price-fixing while attending open meetings.
Microsoft (1995)	This recent case involved the merger of competing firms in the personal-finance software market.

Mergers and International Antitrust Policy

The decades of the 1980s and 1990s were characterized by a wave of mergers. Mergers are a concern to antitrust regulators because firms can avoid charges of price-fixing by merging into one firm. The antitrust policy toward merger depends on the type of merger and its likely effect on the relevant market.

Types of Mergers

A **horizontal merger** is a merger of firms that compete in the same market. The mergers of Coca-Cola and Pepsi-Cola, Ford Motor Company and General Motors, and Anheuser Bush and Coors are hypothetical examples of horizontal mergers. Horizontal mergers raise a "red flag" because they decrease competition in a market. For example, in 1986, the government blocked the proposed merger between Coca-Cola and Seven-Up.

A **vertical merger** is a merger of a firm with its suppliers. This type of merger is between companies at different stages of a production process. Hypothetical examples of vertical mergers would be General Motors merging with a major tire company and Ford Motor Company merging with a large number of car dealerships. The government often challenges vertical mergers. However, international competition has reduced antitrust scrutiny of vertical mergers. If this type of merger lowers costs by eliminating

Horizontal merger
A merger of firms that compete in the same market.

Vertical merger
A merger of a firm with its suppliers.

Conglomerate merger
A merger between firms in unrelated markets.

unnecessary supplier charges, U.S. firms will be more competitive in world markets.

A **conglomerate merger** is a merger between firms in unrelated markets. Suppose an insurance company buys a computer software company or a cigarette company merges with a hotel chain. Actual examples are Phillip Morris merging with Miller Brewing Company and General Motors merging with Electronic Data Systems Corporation. No antitrust action was taken to prevent these mergers because the products of the two firms were considered to be unrelated. Conglomerate mergers are generally allowed because they do not significantly decrease competition.

Antitrust Policies in Other Countries

Early antitrust laws were aimed at the domestic economy with little concern for international competitiveness. Because of the internationalization of competition in recent decades, some economists call for a relaxation of antitrust laws to allow firms to merge and compete more effectively in the world economy. Other economists disagree and argue that strong antitrust laws are necessary because small firms create most jobs and innovations.

One reason firms in other countries are so competitive with U.S. firms is that other countries' antitrust laws are weak in comparison to U.S. antitrust laws. For example, no other country breaks up companies for antitrust violations. There are two basic explanations. First, most other countries have less population than the United States. Because other countries have fewer potential customers, they view the international market as the target and design weak antitrust laws accordingly. Stated differently, other countries must sell their products internationally in order to achieve economies of scale and be competitive.

Second, other countries have weak antitrust laws based on their culture and history. In the United States, there is a strong belief in Adam Smith's individualistic competition among small firms. This "big is bad" ideology is the foundation of U.S. antitrust laws, but this belief is not prevalent in other countries. In other countries, "big is better," and in countries such as Japan and Germany, government and business work together to compete internationally. In contrast, there is a general mistrust of big government working directly with big businesses in the United States. Exhibit 3 provides brief descriptions of antitrust policies in various countries.

Regulation

The same distrust of big business that is the basis of antitrust laws also led to the evolution of regulation and federal regulatory agencies in the United States. The regulatory process in the United States has gone through several phases. In the first phase, from 1887 to the Great Depression, the railroads were the primary target. The Great Depression created a favorable environment in which regulation spread to the communications, financial, and other industries during the 1930s. After 1970, regulation increased steadily

EXHIBIT 3　Summary of Antitrust Policies Around the World

Country	Antitrust policy
Germany	■ Cartels are allowed and encouraged. The Federal Cartel Office is relatively small, and it has the authority to force price decreases if it determines a cartel has abused its power.
Britain	■ The British Monopoly Commission has the power to recommend structured changes, but it seldom does so. The commission, however, has reduced prices in some industries.
France	■ France has encouraged large-scale mergers. The Commission on Competition is very weak and often approves mergers.
European Economic Community (EEC)	■ The EEC's antitrust laws officially took precedence over member nations' laws in 1992. The EEC prohibits all agreements that have the effect of preventing, restraining, or distorting competition within the EEC.
Japan	■ Antitrust policies allow for cartel-like structures called *keiretsus*. A *keiretsu* links together companies, customers, suppliers, banks, and government agencies. Japan has a Fair Trade Commission that operates like the U.S. FTC. The Fair Trade Commission is weak and subordinated to Japan's pro-cartel Ministry of International Trade and Industry (MITI). We will discuss the MITI in more detail in the chapter on comparative economic systems.

in the areas of health, safety, and the environment until the 1980s, when a deregulation movement began and continues to have momentum in the 1990s.

Historical Origins of Regulation

The Early Years　The railroads came under regulation in the late 19th century as a result of their unfair pricing practices. At this time in history, railroads faced little competition from other carriers, so there was little to prevent railroads from overcharging. Railroads also practiced price discrimination against isolated rural customers by charging them higher rates for short hauls than they charged city customers for long hauls. To regulate rail prices, the Interstate Commerce Commission (ICC) was established in 1887. The ICC was also created to cut the costs of rail transportation by reducing duplicate trains, depots, and tracks.

The Great Depression Era　During the 1930s, regulation was extended to other industries. The Food and Drug Administration (FDA) was established in 1931 to oversee the safety of food and drugs. All surface transportation, including trucks, barges, and oil pipelines, came to be regulated by the ICC. The Civil Aeronautics Board (CAB) was created in 1938 to regulate air travel, and the Federal Communications Commission (FCC) was established in 1934 to regulate telephones, telegraphs, and broadcasting industries. In 1934, as a result of the stock market crash of 1929, the Securities and Exchange Commission (SEC) was created to combat fraud and malpractice in the securities industry.

The Health, Safety, and Environment Era The Occupational Safety and Health Administration (OSHA) was created in 1970 to reduce the incidence of injury and death in the workplace. This agency cites and fines employers who violate safety and health rules. In the same year, the Environmental Protection Agency (EPA) was established to set and enforce pollution standards. In 1972, the Consumer Product Safety Commission (CPSC) was established to protect the public against injury from unsafe products. The CPSC has the power to ban the sale of hazardous products.

The Deregulation Trend

Deregulation

The elimination or phasing out of government restrictions on economic activity.

In the 1970s, the higher production costs resulting from regulation generated widespread dissatisfaction with government regulation. The result was a movement toward **deregulation** in the late 1970s and the 1980s. Deregulation is the elimination or phasing out of government restrictions on economic activity. The major thrust of deregulation was in the transportation and telecommunications industries. The *Airline Deregulation Act of 1978* removed regulated airfares and restrictions against competition for air travel markets. The *Staggers Rail Act of 1980* deregulated the railroads, and the *Motor Carrier Act of 1982* deregulated bus transportation. The Civil Aeronautics Board (CAB), established in 1938 to regulate airline fares and air routes, was abolished in 1984. The You're the Economist at the end of the chapter examines the effects on the airline industry.

In telecommunications, the most important case was the deregulation and dismantling of AT&T. As explained above, technological innovations made competition in telecommunications possible and, as a result of an antitrust lawsuit, AT&T was broken up and forced to compete with MCI, Sprint, and other companies for long-distance service. In 1996, a telecommunications bill was passed that is making sweeping changes in U.S. telecommunications laws. The provisions of this bill deregulate cable rates, while allowing local and long-distance telephone companies and cable companies to compete. This bill also requires TV manufacturers to equip new sets with a computer chip to block shows labeled as offensive.

The trend in the 1990s was in the direction of further deregulation. Both the House of Representatives and the Senate approved budget bills that abolished around 200 federal agencies and programs. Although the specific impact on regulation is unclear at this time, these budget cuts could produce dramatic changes in government regulation.

The principal functions of the federal regulatory agencies presented above are summarized in Exhibit 4.

EXHIBIT 4   Federal Regulatory Agencies

Agency	Year Created	Function
Interstate Commerce Commission (ICC)	1887	Regulates interstate ground transportation, including the railroad, trucking, bus, and water carrier industries.
Food and Drug Administration (FDA)	1931	Protects the health of the nation against impure and unsafe foods, drugs, and cosmetics. Develops policy regarding labeling of all drugs.
Securities and Exchange Commission (SEC)	1934	Provides for complete financial disclosure and protects investors in stock and other securities against fraud.
Federal Communications Commission (FCC)	1934	Regulates television, radio, telephone, and telegraph services; satellite transmission; and cable TV.
Civil Aeronautics Board (CAB)	1938*	Regulated airline fares and routes.
Occupational Safety and Health Administration (OSHA)	1970	Enforces rules in cases involving safety and health violations in the workplace.
Environmental Protection Agency (EPA)	1970	Regulates pollution in the areas of air, water, waste, noise, radiation, and toxic substances.
Consumer Product Safety Commission (CPSC)	1972	Protects the public against unreasonable risks of injury from consumer products.

*Abolished in 1984.

Three Cases for Government Regulation

Government regulation involves political, social, and economic factors, and the general justification for regulation is to protect the public. In this section, three basic types of regulation are explained: (1) natural monopoly, (2) externalities, and (3) imperfect information. In each of these cases, the argument in favor of regulation is *market failure*. Recall from Chapter 4 that market failure is a situation in which the market operating on its own fails to lead to an efficient allocation of resources.

Natural Monopoly

The objective of antitrust policy is to create a level playing field for competing firms. Depending on the case, antitrust policy can result in breaking up a monopoly, preventing formulation of a monopoly, and/or punishing anticompetitive business practices of a monopoly. However, what happens when it is inefficient for more than one company to operate in a particular market? Stated another way, creation of a level playing field for competitors may not be in the best interest of economic efficiency. This situation exists in a *natural monopoly*. As explained earlier in Exhibit 1 in Chapter 9, a natural monopoly is an industry in which long-run average cost is minimized when only one firm serves the market. Recall that the services of such public utilities as local telephone, gas, electric, cable TV, and water companies are natural monopolies subject to government regulation. To avoid abuse of this type of monopoly, the prices or rates these public utilities can charge are determined by a federal, state, or local regulatory commission or board.

Exhibit 5 illustrates the demand curve, long-run marginal cost curve, and long-run average cost curve for a natural monopoly in the cable TV market—say, Vision Cable. Because of the advantages of larger firm size that create *economies of scale*, the long-run average cost (*LRAC*) curve is negatively sloped. Following the *average-marginal rule* explained in Chapter 7, the long-run marginal cost (*LRMC*) curve is below the falling *LRAC* curve. Given this condition, the firm's demand curve intersects the *LRAC* curve at a quantity of 80,000 subscribers and a cost of $15 per month equal to the price (point *B*). Suppose this output is divided equally between Vision Cable and another cable company. As discussed earlier in this chapter, the result of competition between cable television companies is that the cost per subscriber is much higher—and even higher if output is divided among more than two cable companies.

To take advantage of the lower cost, the policy prescription is to create a cable TV market served by only one producer—Vision Cable. The policy problem now is how to keep this unregulated natural monopoly from enjoying a substantial monopoly profit. Instead of providing services for 80,000 customers, Vision Cable will service only 40,000 customers by following the $MR = MC$ rule to maximize profits. The price that corresponds to this output is $25 per month at point *A*. Because the profit-maximizing price exceeds the *LRAC* curve, monopoly pricing creates too high a price and too small an output. Stated differently, the result is an inefficient cable TV market, in which there is an underallocation of resources to produce cable TV service.

For the cable TV market to be efficient, regulators must set a price ceiling at $10 per month, which is equal to long-run marginal cost at point *C* on the demand curve. This pricing strategy follows the competitive principle of **marginal cost pricing**. Marginal cost pricing is a system of pricing in which the price charged equals the marginal cost of the last unit produced. At a price of $10, Vision Cable suffers a loss because although the price covers long-run marginal cost, the price is not high enough to cover long-run average cost. This means the firm can survive in the long run only if the government subsidizes the loss.

What to do? Is there an option that does not require taxpayers' money? Yes! In practice, regulatory commissions have relaxed the objective of efficiency and have focused on establishing a "fair-return" price to be charged by the monopolist. In Exhibit 5, the commission would establish the fair-return price at $15 per month, where the demand curve intersects the *LRAC*

Marginal cost pricing
A system of pricing in which the price charged equals the marginal cost of the last unit produced.

EXHIBIT 5

A Regulated Monopoly

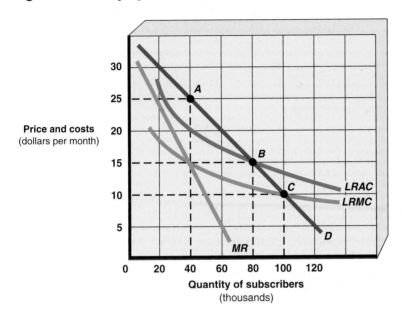

If an unregulated monopolist serves the cable TV market, it will set MR = LRMC, charge a price of $25 per month, and provide service to only 40,000 customers (point A). To improve the efficiency of the market by taking advantage of the lower costs of a natural monopoly, government regulators could set the price at $10, which equals long-run marginal cost (point C). This policy is efficient, but losses require public subsidies. The typical solution is to set a "fair-return" price of $15, which allows the monopolist to earn zero economic profit and serve 80,000 customers at point B. This condition does not fully correct the underallocation of resources caused by an unregulated natural monopoly.

curve at point B. Because the price ceiling equals long-run average cost, Vision Cable earns zero economic profit and serves 80,000 customers in the long run. However, remember from the chapter on production costs that, in economics, cost includes a normal profit, which is just enough to keep the firm in the cable industry.

Conclusion *Government regulators can achieve efficiency for a natural monopoly by setting a price ceiling equal to the intersection of the demand and the marginal cost curves, but this policy results in losses. An alternative is to set a price ceiling, called the fair-return price, that yields a normal profit, but is somewhat inefficient.*

Why Doesn't the Water Company Compete?

The local water company is considered to be a natural monopoly, and the government prohibits other firms from competing with the local water company. If a natural monopoly can produce water at a lower price than other firms, then why would the government protect the water company from competitors?

Externalities

The case of pollution was treated in detail in Exhibit 7(a) in Chapter 4. To refresh your memory, recall that the individual firm in a competitive market has no incentive to eliminate pollution voluntarily. Pollution is an *external cost* imposed on *third parties* who neither produce nor consume a good. Pollution causes polluting firms to overproduce, while causing firms that pay the cost of cleaning up the pollution to underproduce. Therefore, expenditure on pollution control would place firms at a competitive disadvantage with respect to firms that do not pay the cost of controlling pollution. If society wants less pollution, this type of market failure justifies government regulation from, say, the EPA. The exact nature of the regulation, however, may take a variety of forms, ranging from direct controls requiring specific pollution control equipment to taxation.

Without repeating the explanation given in Exhibit 7(b) in Chapter 4, note that the *external benefits* of a good, such as a vaccination, can lead to underproduction of the good. Again, regulation is necessary if society is to respond to externalities. In this case, the government solution can take various forms, including requiring consumption or providing special subsidies.

Imperfect Information

In some cases, consumers lack important information about a product, and they cannot make rational decisions. Without complete and reliable information, consumers may be unaware of the dangers of unsafe drugs, hazardous chemicals, and defective products. The source of imperfect information about products may simply be company errors. Much worse, companies may be able to boost sales by withholding valuable information about a problem with their products.

Let's consider a hypothetical case in which an unsafe Tucker Motors (TM) truck is sold. Suppose the safety defect is a gas tank that is located too close to the side of the truck. As a result, another vehicle can crash into the side of the TM truck and hit the gas tank. Such an accident can cause a deadly explosion. Assume further that Tucker Motors is aware of this safety problem, but the cost of recalling and fixing the trucks exceeds the estimated cost of lawsuits caused by the defective gas tanks. The market incentive is therefore for TM to withhold knowledge of this defect from uninformed consumers.

EXHIBIT 6

The Impact of Imperfect Information on the Market for TM Trucks

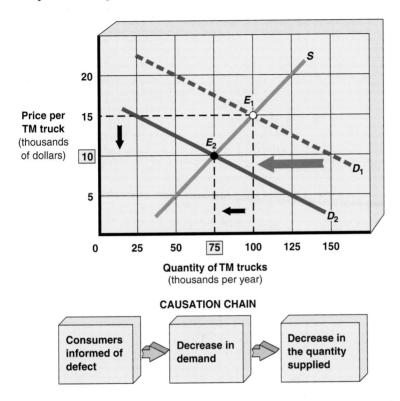

CAUSATION CHAIN

Consumers informed of defect → Decrease in demand → Decrease in the quantity supplied

An initial equilibrium is established at point E_1, with 100,000 TM trucks purchased each year for $15,000 per truck. This equilibrium is reached without consumers having knowledge of a safety defect. Once consumers are informed of the safety defect, the demand curve shifts leftward from D_1 to D_2. At the new equilibrium point of E_2, 75,000 TM trucks are purchased each year for $10,000 per truck. Thus, imperfect information has resulted in a waste of resources used to produce 25,000 TM trucks.

Exhibit 6 illustrates this case. With consumers unaware of the defect, the interaction of the supply and demand curves for TM trucks yields an equilibrium at E_1, with 100,000 trucks being sold per year at a price of $15,000 per truck. Next, suppose the Consumer Product Safety Commission (CPSC) exposes the problem, and the media report stories about wreck victims who have been severely burned and killed by the flames from the exploding gas tanks in TM trucks. Once the consuming public is aware of the defect, consumers' preferences for TM trucks change, and the demand curve decreases from D_1 to D_2. The result is a new equilibrium at E_2, with 75,000 TM trucks being sold per year at a price of $10,000 per

Does Airline Deregulation Mean Friendlier Skies?

Applicable Concept: regulation versus deregulation

The most publicized case of deregulation achievement is the airline industry. Under regulation by the Civil Aeronautics Board (CAB), airfare competition and the incentive to control costs were reduced or eliminated. The CAB set both fares and routes for carriers. Unable to compete with price, the carriers could compete only with costly nonprice competition, such as advertising. Once the CAB authorized a carrier to provide service between two cities, the frequency of service remained unregulated. When carriers purchased fleets of planes and provided too many flights for their protected routes, profits were squeezed because the percentage of seats filled with passengers (load factor) fell, and the average cost rose. Carriers would then attempt to boost profits by lobbying the CAB for higher fares. In addition to eliminating price competition between established carriers, the CAB restricted entrants into the industry. From 1938 until 1977, the CAB never awarded a major route to any new airline.

Successful deregulation of an industry would be expected to provide the following three results:

- The average price of the service falls.
- The volume and variety of services rise.
- New firms enter the industry, and other firms fail and exit the industry.

The Airline Deregulation Act of 1978 provided these results by changing the structure and business behavior of the airline industry. The CAB was eliminated under this act in 1984, and price competition produced the expected results of lower fares and greater quantity of service. Revenue per passenger mile of airline travel declined from 11.8 cents in 1978 to 9.9 cents in 1990 on an inflation-adjusted basis. The saving to consumers was $16 billion in 1986 alone.[1] Over this same period, air traffic increased from 227 billion to 458 billion passenger miles flown per year—a 102 percent increase. In 1995, the revenue per passenger mile was only 12.9 cents, and revenue passenger miles rose to 540 billion. After the barrier to entry was removed, the number of carriers increased sharply between 1978 and 1980 from 37 to 214. Since 1980, many carriers, such as the "few frills" People Express, exited the industry, and by 1996, the number of carriers dropped to 109.[2]

The airline deregulatory movement is not without criticism. One concern is that lots of airlines went "belly up," and these exits from the industry increased the percentage of all domestic air travel controlled by the industry's largest carriers. Today, American, United, and Delta account for about 60 percent of domestic air service. Moreover, under the pressure of competition, carriers searched for ways to cut costs, and they created the hub-and-spoke delivery system. This system allows carriers to gather passengers from the "spoke" routes using smaller, less efficient planes and fly them from the hub in fully occupied, bigger planes at lower cost. Many carriers have gained near monopoly power in "hub" airports. These dominant hub carriers can control access to terminal gates, takeoff time slots, and baggage service, and they can charge smaller lines high rates for using these airport rights.

Today, deregulation continues to exert downward pressure on fares. Low-fare tickets, cyberfares, and frequent flyer miles are popular, and fares are generally about one-third lower in real terms than before deregulation. Quality of service measured by complaints per 10,000 passengers is lower today than in the regulation era. Growing concentration is also a concern. Should the airlines remain deregulated or return to a government-enforced cartel? Defenders of deregulation argue that growth of market concentration and its abuses can be controlled by enforcing antitrust laws and allowing international competition.

ANALYZE THE ISSUE

Prior to deregulation, critics argued that airline safety would suffer. Instead, although the Federal Aviation Administration's budget was cut following deregulation, the accident rate involving fatalities has fallen. Give a rationale for why the critics' prediction did not come to pass.

[1]Ansel M. Sharp, Charles A. Register, and Richard H. Leftwich, *Economics of Social Issues* (Boston: Richard D. Irwin, 1994), pp. 174–175.
[2]*Statistical Abstract of the United States*, 1997, http://www.census.gov/prod/www/abs/cc97stab.html, Table 1046, p. 649 and Table 1055, p. 653.

truck. In other words, this case is an application of market supply and demand analysis as presented in Chapter 4.

Conclusion *Deficient information on unsafe products can cause consumers to overconsume a product.*

In the TM truck example, resources were used to produce 25,000 trucks that consumers would not purchase when given complete information. These resources were misallocated because they could have been used to produce other goods and services. The solution is for government to prevent companies from making false or deceptive claims by gathering and disseminating accurate information to consumers. This is the rationale for the safety testing of cars, EPA mileage ratings on cars, and warning labels on cigarettes. In extreme cases, a product may be deemed too unsafe, and it is outlawed from sale. Others disagree with this view and argue that the government should only provide information. Once consumers have sufficient information, they should be free to choose.

KEY CONCEPTS

Trust
Predatory pricing
Sherman Act of 1890
Clayton Act of 1914
Federal Trade Commission
    Act of 1914

Robinson-Patman Act of
    1936
Celler-Kefauver Act of
    1950
Rule of reason

Per se rule
Horizontal merger
Vertical merger
Conglomerate merger

Deregulation
Marginal cost pricing

SUMMARY

■ A **trust** is a cartel that places the assets of competing companies in the custody of a board of trustees. During the last decades of the 19th century, trusts engaged in anticompetitive strategies to eliminate competition and raise prices, such as *predatory pricing.*

■ The **Sherman Act of 1890** and the **Clayton Act of 1914** are the two most important antitrust laws. The Sherman Act marked the first attempt of the U.S. government to outlaw monopolizing behavior. Because this act was vague, the Clayton Act was passed to define anticompetitive behavior more precisely. The Clayton Act prohibited (1) price discrimination, (2) exclusive dealing, (3) tying contracts, (4) stock acquisition, and (5) interlocking directorates.

■ The **Federal Trade Commission Act of 1914** established the Federal Trade Commission (FTC) to investigate unfair competitive practices of firms.

■ The **Robinson-Patman Act of 1936** strengthened the Clayton Act by prohibiting certain forms of price discrimination. This law is called the "Chain Store Act" because it was aimed at large retail chain stores that were obtaining volume discounts.

■ The **Celler-Kefauver Act of 1950** strengthened the Clayton Act by declaring illegal the acquisition of the assets of one firm by another firm if the effect is to lessen competition.

■ The **rule of reason** and the **per se rule** are the two main philosophies the courts have used in interpreting antitrust law. Under the rule of reason, monopolists were not subject to prosecution unless they acted in an anticompetitive manner. The Supreme Court decision in the Alcoa case of 1945 replaced the rule of reason with the per se rule, which states that the mere existence of monopoly is illegal. Today, the trend is in favor of dominant firms because of international competition.

- A **horizontal merger** is a merger of two competing firms. A **vertical merger** is a merger of two firms where one produces an input used by the other firm. A **conglomerate merger** is a merger of two firms producing unrelated products.

- **Deregulation** is a movement that began in the 1980s to eliminate regulations primarily in the transportation and telecommunications industries. Today, the current trend is toward further deregulation resulting from federal budget cuts.

- ★ **Marginal cost pricing** is a competitive pricing strategy for a regulated natural monopoly. Using this approach, regulators set the monopolist's price equal to its marginal cost. Another method is for regulators to establish a fair-return price equal to long-run average cost and the monopolist earns zero economic profit. Regulation of a natural monopoly is justified on the basis

of market failure. Two other cases based on market failure include externalities and imperfect information.

Marginal cost pricing

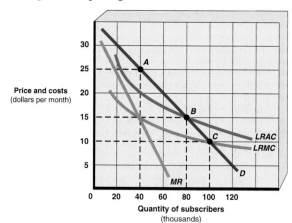

SUMMARY OF CONCLUSION STATEMENTS

- Government regulators can achieve efficiency for a natural monopoly by setting a price ceiling equal to the intersection of the demand and the marginal cost curves, but this policy results in losses. An alternative is to set a price ceiling, called the fair-return

price, that yields a normal profit, but is somewhat inefficient.

- Deficient information on unsafe products can cause consumers to overconsume a product.

STUDY QUESTIONS AND PROBLEMS

1. Describe the major provisions of the Sherman Act and the Clayton Act. Who is responsible for the enforcement of these laws?

2. Two business practices outlawed by the Clayton Act are tying contracts and interlocking directorates. Explain the difference in the conditions required for these two practices to be a violation of this antitrust law.

3. Distinguish between the Robinson-Patman Act of 1936 and the Celler-Kefauver Act of 1950.

4. Using cases presented in the text, explain the issue in the courts' interpretation of "monopoly versus monopolizing."

5. A controversy in many antitrust court cases involves the definition of the relevant market for a firm's product. How would you argue in the Alcoa case that the government's claim of the firm's high market share was in error?

6. In the MIT case, which students are harmed by the Ivy League schools' coordination of scholarship policy? Professional baseball is exempt from antitrust laws. Should colleges and universities also be exempt from antitrust laws?

7. Based on the antitrust laws, how would you expect the federal government to react to the following situations?
   a. A college bookstore deliberately reduces prices until its only rival is driven out of business. The bookstore then raises its prices.
   b. Real estate firms meet in an open meeting and agree to charge 6 percent commission on sales.
   c. Microsoft merges with WordPerfect by a stock acquisition.
   d. A small tax preparation company merges with a regional grocery store chain.

8. Based on the cases discussed in this text, is the following statement correct? "The antitrust laws in reality deal less with monopolies than with oligopolies."

9. Assume a regulatory agency is given authority over prices and entry conditions for a given industry. Also assume the agency decides to allow new entry, as the CAB actually did before deregulation, only when it is proven to be "necessary." Would this condition be expected to favor (a) existing regulated firms, (b) new entrants, or (c) consumers? Explain.

10. Exhibit 7 represents a natural monopolist.

EXHIBIT 7

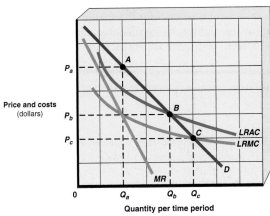

a. If the monopolist is not regulated, what price will it charge, and what quantity will it produce?

b. If the monopolist is required to use marginal cost pricing, what price will it charge, and what quantity will it produce? Why will the monopolist stay in business?

c. Assume regulators set a fair-return price at P_b. Why will the monopolist stay in business?

11. Assume a natural monopolist is required to use marginal cost pricing and a government subsidy covers the loss. What problems might be associated with a public subsidy?

12. Do you agree that "cost does not really matter" as a principle for safety regulation, or do you believe that the cost of a safety device must be justified on the basis of the value of human life removed from a hazard?

ONLINE EXERCISES

Exercise 1

Visit Antitrust Guidelines (http://www.usdoj.gov/atr/public/guidelines/guidelin.htm). Under International Operations, select Antitrust Enforcement Guidelines for International Operations. Explain how these guidelines may allow a monopoly.

Exercise 2

Visit GPO Gate, Catalog for Economic Report of the President (http://www.gpo.ucop.edu/catalog/erp97.html), and select Chapter 6, Refining the Role of Government in the U.S. Market Economy. Scroll down and browse The Telecommunications Act of 1996.

Exercise 3

Visit http://www.antitrust.org/news/mergers.html. Read about recent mergers. Summarize a particular case.

Exercise 4

Go to the Department of Justice website at http://www.usdoj.gov/01whatsnew/01_3.html. Choose the first DOJ Hot Topic, and write a brief report on the latest in antitrust enforcement.

CHECKPOINT ANSWERS

Does Price-Fixing Improve Your Education?

Accepting the schools' argument that they improve quality by price-fixing makes no more sense than allowing General Motors, Ford, Chrysler, and Japanese automakers to fix prices in order to improve quality. However, there is often a thin line between price-fixing and price leadership. Price leadership is not illegal as long as the price followers are not coerced. If you said price leadership is defendable and price fixing is not, **YOU ARE CORRECT.**

Why Doesn't the Water Company Compete?

Suppose new firms are allowed to compete with the water company, which is a natural monopolist. The concern is that the rivals will be outcompeted. New water companies must build plants, dig up the streets, and lay new water pipes and duplicate other resources in the same neighborhood. Because the competitors cannot produce water at a lower cost, they will leave the industry, and the resources used to compete with the natural monopolist will be wasted. If you said the government is not protecting the natural monopolist from competition so much as it is protecting against inefficient competitors wasting resources, **YOU ARE CORRECT.**

PRACTICE QUIZ

For a visual explanation of the correct answers, visit the tutorial at http://www.tucker.swcollege.com.

1. Which of the following is illegal under the Sherman Act?
   a. Attempts to monopolize
   b. Price-fixing
   c. Formation of cartels
   d. All of the above are illegal.

2. Officers of five large building-materials companies meet and agree that none of them will submit bids on government contracts lower than an agreed-upon level. This is an example of
   a. price-fixing.
   b. vertical restriction.
   c. a tying contract.
   d. an interlocking directorate.

3. A fabric shop cannot sell Singer sewing machines if it also sells other brands of sewing machines. This is an example of
   a. a resale price maintenance.
   b. territorial restrictions.
   c. a tying agreement.
   d. exclusive dealing.

4. Under the Clayton Act, horizontal mergers by stock acquisition were
   a. not considered.
   b. illegal if they could be shown to lessen competition.
   c. illegal under any circumstances.
   d. legal if they could be shown to lessen competition.

5. Under the Clayton Act, which of the following was illegal even if it was *not* shown to lessen competition substantially?
   a. Price discrimination
   b. Tying contracts
   c. Horizontal mergers by stock acquisition
   d. Interlocking directorates

6. The importance of the Federal Trade Commission Act of 1914 is that it
   a. set up an independent antitrust agency with the power to investigate complaints.
   b. strengthened the law against mergers.
   c. strengthened the law against price discrimination.
   d. did none of the above.

7. Which of the following is concerned primarily with price discrimination?
   a. The Sherman Act
   b. The Clayton Act
   c. The Robinson-Patman Act
   d. The Celler-Kefauver Act

8. Which of the following is concerned primarily with mergers?
   a. The Sherman Act
   b. The Clayton Act
   c. The Robinson-Patman Act
   d. The Celler-Kefauver Act

9. The Utah Pie case was brought under which of the following laws?
   a. The Sherman Act
   b. The Federal Trade Commission Act

c. The Robinson-Patman Act

d. The Celler-Kefauver Act

10. Although U.S. Steel controlled nearly 75 percent of the domestic iron and steel industry, in 1920 the Supreme Court ruled that the firm was *not* in violation of the Sherman Act because there was no evidence of abusive behavior. What antitrust doctrine was the court applying in this case?

    a. The rule of reason

    b. The per se rule

    c. The marginal cost pricing rule

    d. The natural monopoly rule

11. In which antitrust case did the Supreme Court begin to apply the per se rule to determine whether a firm was in violation of the Sherman Act?

    a. The Standard Oil case

    b. The Alcoa case

    c. The IBM case

    d. The MIT case

12. The Interstate Commerce Commission (ICC) was established in

    a. 1887.

    b. 1890.

    c. 1929.

    d. 1933.

13. Today, the Civil Aeronautics Board (CAB) regulates

    a. airline ticket prices.

    b. airline routes.

    c. airline safety.

    d. all of the above.

    e. none of the above; the CAB was abolished in 1984.

14. Which of the following provides the basis for regulation?

    a. Natural monopoly

    b. Externalities

    c. Imperfect information

    d. All of the above

15. Consider a regulated natural monopoly. If the regulatory commission wants to establish a fair-return price, then it should set a price ceiling where the demand curve crosses the monopoly's long-run

    a. marginal revenue curve.

    b. average revenue curve.

    c. marginal cost curve.

    d. average cost curve.

CHAPTER FOURTEEN

Environmental Economics

The private automobile is no doubt one of the most significant inventions of the last 100 years. America's love affair with the car reflects the unrivaled convenience of this mode of transport for traveling to work, commuting to school, picking up fast food, going to the drive-through window at the bank, or vacationing. When you use your car, you are making a private decision based on your benefits from driving compared to your costs, such as fuel, of making the trip. While your decision to drive is a private one, there are consequences that go far beyond the individual driver. The exhaust from cars causes air pollution, which impairs health as well as views, and may cause an international global warming problem. Within the next 50 years, global warming could cause melting of the polar ice caps, resulting in rising ocean levels and massive flooding of coastal areas throughout the world, as well as climate shifts that could render today's farms tomorrow's deserts.

The competitive market has been shown to be the best engine to generate economic efficiency. Yet unbridled use of the automobile threatens to choke our cities with congested roads, our nation with polluted air, and our world with rising global temperatures.

This chapter will address why competitive markets may fail to efficiently protect the environment. First, we will see that competitive markets produce more pollution than is efficient. Then we will see how we might correct the market failure. Finally, we will consider the pros and cons of government intervention to improve our environment.

In this chapter, you will learn to solve these economics puzzles:

■ Why do competitive markets produce too large a quantity and charge too low a price for products that pollute?

■ How can government legislation, taxes, and permits achieve environmental efficiency?

■ Can government intervention reduce environmental quality?

Competitive Markets and Environmental Efficiency

The competitive market has been shown in earlier chapters to achieve *economic efficiency*. This efficiency exists when the price to consumers, reflecting marginal benefit, equals marginal cost. Consumers, such as car buyers, consider purchase price and styling, along with performance features, such as acceleration, miles per gallon, and interior space, when comparing cars. Producers choose what type of car to make based on profit maximization. Assuming perfect competition, profit maximization occurs where price equals marginal cost. Admittedly, the auto industry does not exemplify perfect competition, but in this chapter, it is useful to accept that there is sufficient domestic and foreign competition to allow us to use the perfectly competitive model. We will not consider pollution in imperfectly competitive industries. Noncompetitive industries are not efficient, even in the absence of pollution.

Buyers and sellers consider only their personal or **private benefits and costs**. Private benefits and costs are benefits and costs to the decision-maker, ignoring benefits and costs to third parties. Third parties are people outside the market transaction who are affected by the product. As explained in Chapter 4, benefits and costs to third parties are known by a variety of names, including third-party effects, spillovers, and most commonly *external benefits and costs* or *externalities*. Recall that externalities are benefits or costs that are not considered by market buyers and sellers. Air pollution is an externality that affects third parties not driving automobiles.

Other externalities that degrade the environment include sulfur emissions from coal-burning electric power plants and the emission of chlorofluorocarbons (CFCs), associated with aerosol sprays and air conditioners. Sulfur emissions are widely thought to contribute to acid rain, resulting in tree deaths and fish kills. CFCs may be linked to a growing ozone hole, which increases the chance of skin cancer from the sun's ultraviolet rays.

Everyday occurrences include the secondhand effects of cigarette smoke on the health of nonsmokers, the use by farmers of pesticides that wash into soil and water with detrimental health effects, and even noise from your next-door neighbor who is having a loud party while you are trying to study for an economics exam. Externalities can be positive as well as negative. You benefit from your neighbor's well-kept yard.

When externalities are present, competitive markets are not likely to achieve economic efficiency. In competitive markets, price, which reflects private marginal benefit, equals private marginal cost. Efficiency for society requires consideration of both private and **social benefits and costs**. Social benefits are the sum of benefits to everyone in society, including both private benefits and external benefits. Social costs are the sum of costs to everyone in society, including both private costs and external costs. The condition for economic efficiency occurs when each unit of a good that is produced creates at least as much benefit to society as it does social cost. As a society, we do not want to produce any units of a good that creates more in additional social cost than it does in extra social benefit. In other words, we do not want our scarce resources used up on items that will not

Private benefits and costs
Benefits and costs to the decision-maker, ignoring benefits and costs to third parties. Third parties are people outside the market transaction who are affected by the product.

Social benefits and costs
The sum of benefits to everyone in society, including both private benefits and external benefits. Social costs are the sum of costs to everyone in society, including both private costs and external costs.

enhance our collective well-being. A succinct way of stating this condition for maximizing social welfare is to produce units of any good up to the point where

$$\text{marginal social benefit} = \text{marginal social cost}$$

Regulations require most automobiles to be equipped with catalytic converters to reduce auto emissions. Environmental regulations force market participants to include externalities in their decision-making. While regulations like the catalytic converter requirement reduce emissions, they are not necessarily the most efficient approach to achieving less pollution.

Fueled by current antigovernment fervor, alternative approaches emphasize setting a goal without mandating the technology to achieve the goal. For example, one approach allows businesses that wish to expand in areas with high levels of pollution an alternative to reducing factory pollution to meet air quality regulations. Instead of reducing their own emissions, they can pay another party to offset emissions to meet the regulation. It may be cheaper for the company to pay someone else to reduce emissions than to achieve an in-house reduction. Some states even have a program that allows expanding or new businesses to buy up 16-year-old "junkers" as a way of offsetting factory emissions. Old cars typically pollute more than new cars, and it may be cheaper to achieve an air quality standard by retiring old cars than by finding ways to reduce emissions from new factories.

Private and Social Costs

When Ford, General Motors, Chrysler, or any car producer chooses a production method, it is motivated by profit maximization. To maximize profit, the firm must choose the most efficient, least costly production method. Production costs include the costs of capital, labor, natural resources (such as land), and entrepreneurship. External costs to others, such as pollution, are not a part of production costs because the firm considers only its private costs. Social costs include private costs and external costs.

Competition and External Costs

Suppose there is a car company, such as GreenMachines, that considers social costs. It will choose a different production method with lower emissions. This cleaner production method must have a higher cost than the method used by other, more polluting firms, or else the other companies would already be using this method to minimize cost.

In a competitive market, consumers perceive all products as identical. They will pay no more for a GreenMachine than for other cars. In the short run, the cleaner car company will earn less than other firms, since its costs are higher. In the long run, GreenMachines will lose money and eventually go out of business. Only the lowest-cost firms will survive in the long run. Since price exactly equals private average (and marginal) cost in the long run, average cost for the environmentally conscious car company will lie above price, resulting in losses and eventual exit from the industry.

Exhibit 1(a) compares the typical and the "green" car companies in the short run. Exhibit 1(b) compares the two companies in the long run.

EXHIBIT 1

A Comparison of Costs for Typical and "Green" Firms

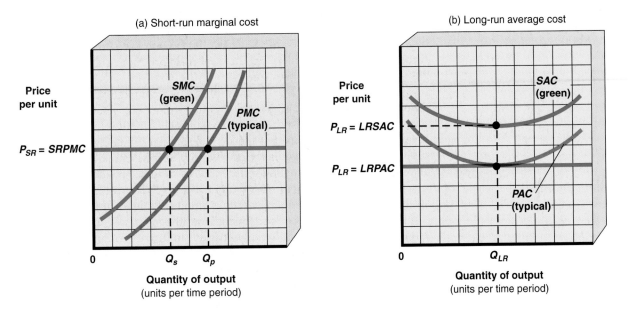

A "green" firm has higher costs in both the short run and the long run. The typical firm considers only private costs, as shown by PMC in part (a) and PAC in part (b). The "green" firm includes both private and external costs, shown by SMC in part (a) and SAC in part (b). These curves reflect social costs. In the short run, price in a competitive industry equals private marginal cost. The "green" firm produces a smaller quantity than the competitive firm. In the long run, price equals minimum long-run private average cost in a competitive industry. Minimum cost for the "green" firm is above price, so that the "green" firm loses money and eventually leaves the industry.

The typical car company chooses the lowest-cost method of production considering *private cost* only. Its costs are shown as *PMC* and *PAC*. The "green" company chooses the production method that has the lowest *social cost*, shown as *SMC* and *SAC*. In the short run, *SMC* lies above *PMC*, so that the "green" company produces less. In the long run, *SAC* lies above *PAC*, so that the "green" company loses money and eventually exits the industry.

Competitive Market Inefficiency When Externalities Exist

In competition, only firms that choose the lowest-cost method of production will survive. Firms that choose higher-cost methods will lose money and eventually exit the industry. There is no room for GreenMachines or any firm that does not minimize cost.

Rewarding firms that ignore externalities while punishing firms that recognize externalities is not socially efficient. Efficiency requires that price reflect marginal social benefit and equal marginal social cost. Competition results in a price that reflects marginal private benefit and equals marginal private cost. Efficiency requires that all relevant opportunity costs be included in marginal social cost, while competition forces firms to consider only private costs if they are to survive. If they are allowed to, competitive firms will ignore harmful by-products of their products, such as pollution, global warming, and congestion.

Exhibit 2 shows car market equilibrium in a competitive market of traditional firms compared to a market of environmentally sensitive "green" firms. Competitive industry supply, *PS*, sums the *private marginal costs* of "typical" individual firms that ignore externalities, while "green" industry supply, *SS*, sums the *social marginal costs* of GreenMachines, GreenMotors, and other firms that recognize external costs in their production decision.

When externalities are present, competition leads to a lower price and a larger quantity than the socially efficient point. By ignoring external costs, competitive firms produce "too much," and the market equilibrium price is "too low," compared to a socially efficient industry. Competition leads to too many cars bought and sold because neither the buyers nor the sellers take into account the external cost of cars. When there are external costs, the efficient point is at the intersection of the demand curve and the social supply curve, *SS*.

From society's point of view, the efficient outcome is an equilibrium of Q_s cars sold at price P_s. Associated with this outcome is a smaller quantity of pollution than at the competitive equilibrium. The quantity of pollution associated with quantity Q_s of cars is the efficient quantity of pollution.

If left to the competitive market, profit-maximizing producers would have no reason to reduce emissions. Emissions reductions, if they occurred at all, would be only an unintended by-product of technological change. For example, if manufacturers substitute a smaller engine so as to reduce car weight and increase miles per gallon, it is possible that the smaller engine would emit fewer pollutants. The emission reduction is a by-product of the market reward for a more fuel-efficient car, which consumers want and are willing to pay for. For emissions reduction to be worthwhile in its own right in a competitive market, it is necessary that consumers be willing to pay for a cleaner car.

Why won't consumers offer more for a cleaner car, just as they do for a more fuel-efficient car? First, consider choosing between two cars that are identical, except that one car gets 15 miles per gallon, while the other gets 30 miles per gallon. You will be willing to pay more for the second car because you will get to keep the full monetary benefit of reduced fuel purchases.

Now suppose you must choose between two identical cars, except that the "green" car emits only half as much pollution as the other car. You will not be willing to pay more for the "green" car because individually you will get only a negligible benefit. Benefits will extend to everyone, in the form of cleaner air and reduced global warming. Furthermore, if others

EXHIBIT 2

A Comparison of Equilibriums for Typical Competitive and "Green" Industries

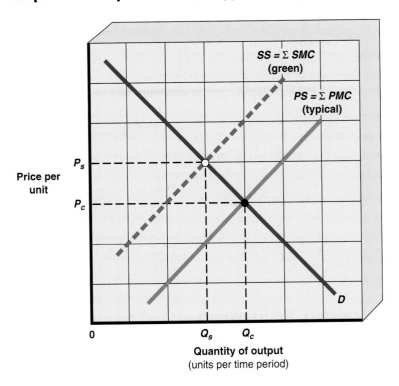

A typical competitive industry operates at price P_c, below the socially efficient price, P_s, that would be charged by "green" firms, which includes all social costs. The competitive industry produces too large a quantity, Q_c, compared to the socially efficient quantity, Q_s, and charges too low a price, P_c, compared to the socially efficient "green" industry price, P_s.

buy "green" cars, you will get the benefits whether or not you purchase a low-emissions vehicle. You are better off being a *free rider*. Recall from the definition of a public good in Chapter 4 that a free rider is someone who enjoys benefits without paying the cost. You will get the same benefit from cleaner air whether or not you buy the clean car. So you will choose to be a free rider and pay nothing for cleaner air, rather than paying extra to get a low-emissions vehicle and still breathing the same cleaner air.

The end result is that no one buys a low-emissions vehicle. Each individual chooses to free-ride, hoping to benefit from others who choose the "green" model. Once again, competitive markets are unlikely to be efficient.

Efficient Quantity of Pollution

The efficient production level for society is where marginal social benefit equals marginal social cost. The efficient amount of pollution is the amount generated at the socially efficient output level. It is of utmost importance to recognize that the efficient quantity of pollution is not zero. Zero pollution would require zero cars. Unless society places a sufficiently low value on cars, it is not likely to return to 19th-century transport modes so as to eliminate auto emissions. Even if society were willing, we might not prefer streets piled high with manure, as would be the case if we returned to the horse and carriage.

Other alternatives to consider are reduced-emission or emission-free cars, as well as other transport modes, including bus, rail, and bicycle. Bear in mind that each mode has associated private and external costs and benefits and that one cannot assert, for example, that an emission-free car is efficient. Solar cars powered by photovoltaic cells and hydrogen-powered cars are among virtually emission-free alternatives. The efficient car is not necessarily the one with the lowest emissions. Society values the reduced emissions, but also must consider the resources sacrificed to pay a premium for cleaner cars. Presently, the cost of solar and hydrogen cars is too high given society's willingness to pay for reduced emissions.

Achieving Environmental Efficiency

Competitive markets fail to produce the socially efficient quantity when there are externalities. Externalities are a cause of **market failure**. As explained in Chapter 4, market failure occurs when the private market fails to produce society's preferred outcome.

When there is market failure, we must consider alternatives to the market to achieve efficiency. Government has a potential role when there is market failure. Just as government can apply antitrust laws when an industry is not competitive, government can apply environmental laws when an industry ignores external costs. Not only are many cars required to have catalytic converters, but also many states require annual inspections to make sure the converters are working properly (and also to check that consumers have not removed the converters in order to improve gas mileage!).

In the environmental arena, as in other areas of government intervention, there is always the possibility of **government failure**. Government failure is present when the government fails to correct market failure. Government officials may fail to achieve an efficient outcome either by doing too little about pollution or by doing too much.

Government officials motivated to keep their jobs may be influenced by large campaign contributors as well as voter desires. A Michigan legislator is likely to be sympathetic to the concerns of the auto industry and will also be aware of the autoworker layoffs and unemployment that accompany reduced car production. The official may be less motivated by externalities that are borne by third parties who do not vote in Michigan. On the other hand, a New York legislator may support an overly strict standard. New York voters benefit from cleaner air and are less concerned about auto-industry job losses.

Visit the Global Network of Environment and Technology at http://www.gnet.org/ *to discover global information on environmental technologies.*

Market failure
A situation in which the price system creates a problem for society or fails to achieve society's goals.

Government failure
Government intervention that fails to correct market failure.

Much of the effort of environmental economists has gone toward improving the odds that government will help, rather than hinder, environmental goals. Economists generally favor **incentive-based regulations** over **command-and-control regulations**. Incentive-based regulations set an environmental goal, but are flexible in how buyers and sellers achieve the goal. Incentive-based regulations make it profitable for firms to reduce emissions. Command-and-control regulations set an environmental goal and dictate how the goal will be achieved. Firms unable to meet the goal pay penalties, but are not rewarded for exceeding the goal.

Economists favor incentive-based (IB) regulations over command-and-control (CAC) regulations on efficiency grounds. The advantage of IB compared to that of CAC is comparable to the advantages of a market system compared to those of a command system. Market systems are more efficient because they allow gains from comparative advantage. Businesses can pursue those activities where they have low opportunity costs. Similarly, allowing firms to choose how to achieve environmental goals will encourage firms that can improve at low cost to reduce emissions more than firms less able to achieve lower emissions.

Efficiency gains from IB regulations compared to those from CAC regulations are both short run and long run. In the short run, allowing firms to choose how they will achieve emission reduction is more efficient than prescribing a single approach because firms have differing opportunity costs in achieving lower emissions. In the long run, firms have an incentive to further reduce emissions by improving their technology. It is possible, although unlikely, that CAC will be as efficient as IB in the short run. Again, one can compare market and command systems. It is possible, though unlikely, that a command system will just happen to choose the lowest cost method of production. In the long run, however, command systems do not encourage innovative technology. There is no reward for improving, only a penalty for not meeting the standard. Let's consider how CAC and IB regulations reduce auto emissions.

Command-and-Control Regulations

In the 1970s, the U.S. government mandated the use of catalytic converters so as to reduce auto pollutants. The converter results in reduced hydrocarbon emissions associated with the burning of gasoline. While the catalytic converter undoubtedly reduces pollution, it suffers from several inefficiencies.

First, the requirement that cars have a catalytic converter is uniform throughout the country. The marginal car in a high-pollution region, such as Los Angeles, has a much higher external cost than the same car driven across the prairies of Kansas. Efficiency calls for stricter regulations in automobile-intensive regions, such as Los Angeles. Second, there may be other technologies that can achieve the same reduced emissions at a lower cost. Finally, automakers have little incentive to invest in better future technology, since regulations require the firm to meet, but not beat, the standard.

A more subtle inefficiency from environmental CAC regulations is that they may act as a barrier to entry to other firms, both domestic and international. The U.S. auto industry initially resisted environmental controls,

Incentive-based regulations
Governmental regulations that set an environmental goal, but are flexible in how buyers and sellers achieve the goal.

Command-and-control regulations
Governmental regulations that set an environmental goal and dictate how the goal will be achieved.

Visit the government's Environmental Protection Agency (EPA) at http://www.epa.gov/ *to discover more about its role in our economy.*

knowing that controls would drive up costs. Foreign manufacturers, such as the Japanese automakers, already met the proposed U.S. standards, but achieved their goal with a different technology. Catalytic converters put the Japanese at a temporary cost disadvantage. Japanese cars were required to have catalytic converters in spite of already meeting the air quality standard.

Incentive-Based Regulations

Effluent tax

A tax on the pollutant.

Effluent Taxes   The simplest type of incentive-based regulation is an **effluent tax**. An effluent tax is a tax on the pollutant. If car manufacturers face a tax that depends on emissions, they can no longer ignore externalities. They now consider the tax, based on emissions, along with private resource costs. Exhibit 3 shows how an effluent tax can achieve efficiency.

A less direct way of reducing pollutants is a gas tax. By increasing the price of gas to car owners, there is a smaller quantity demanded of gas and gas emissions. Over time, consumers faced with high gas prices seek more fuel-efficient cars, lowering emissions even more.

Taxes can achieve efficiency directly or indirectly and can be placed on buyers or sellers. While the tax approach may appear simple in theory, there are some important practical difficulties that limit the use of pollution taxes. First, how do we measure external cost? There is no market that buys and sells air pollution or global warming. So the tax is at best an approximation of external cost. Second, studies that have attempted to measure external cost find it to be quite large, requiring a substantial tax. It is widely thought that the price of a gallon of gas would have to increase by $1 to approximate external costs of auto emissions. Such a $1 tax, added to the approximately 40 cents in gas taxes that already go toward paying for roads, would be unpopular with voters and as a consequence unattractive to politicians.

Emissions-trading

Trading that allows firms to buy and sell the right to pollute.

Emissions-Trading   What if there were a market in which air pollution or global warming could be traded? As a result of the 1990 amendments to the Clean Air Act, there are markets for **emissions-trading**. Emissions-trading allows firms to buy and sell the right to pollute. The most active market so far is for sulfur emissions. Sulfur dioxide causes increased rain acidity. Acid rain can cause damage to lakes, trees, and even cars.

There are markets for air pollution rights. New factories that would add to pollution in an already polluted area may have to find *offsets* before they can relocate. An offset is a reduction in one pollution source that offsets a new pollution source. One offset described earlier is the program introduced in Maryland that allows new or expanding factories to buy up automobile "clunkers." Under this program, the factory offers to pay $500 to owners of cars that are at least 16 years old. The factory scraps the old clunkers, offsetting its new source of pollution. The clunker approach makes use of the fact that a small percentage of cars are responsible for a disproportionate share of pollution.

To set up trading for car emissions, the government could require auto manufacturers to buy permits for each unit of emissions. In the short run, firms would include the cost of permits along with private costs as a com-

EXHIBIT 3

Using an Effluent Tax to Achieve Environmental Efficiency

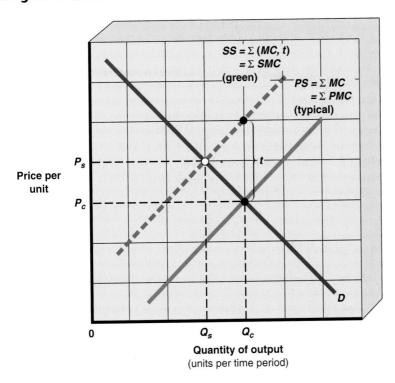

An effluent tax can achieve efficiency. The tax, t, equals marginal external cost, which is the difference between PMC and SMC. The firm now
has production costs including its private costs and the effluent tax, so it
makes product decisions as if it considered social marginal cost.

ponent of price. Price would increase most for the dirtiest vehicles. In the
long run, firms would have an incentive to build cleaner cars. Firms with
the cleanest fleet would need the fewest permits and might even profit by
selling permits to companies that cannot improve as quickly. Where Green-
Machines would go out of business in an unfettered competitive industry, it
would now be in position to succeed.

The real world helps us see problems that textbook theory does not
always reveal. Emissions-trading has the theoretical potential to achieve
environmental goals at the lowest cost, but, so far, real-world trading has
fallen short of efficiency. There are a number of obstacles to efficient trading, some minor and some major.

Taking the factory and clunker example, one minor problem is a **new-
source bias**. A new-source bias occurs when there is an incentive to keep
assets past the efficient point as a result of regulation. A firm faced with

New-source bias
*Bias that occurs when there is an
incentive to keep assets past the
efficient point as a result of regulation.*

the need to find offsets if it builds a new factory may stick with an older and dirtier factory, rather than paying for offsets. If there were no offset program, it might have been economical to retire the old factory in favor of a less-polluting new factory. But if the new factory cannot meet the air quality standard without offsets, the lowest-cost solution becomes extending the life of the old plant. There also may be a type of free-rider problem. Car owners about to junk their 15-year-old clunkers for $25 may keep them another year if a firm might be willing to pay $500. These minor problems are just growing pains of emissions-trading, and future emissions markets will find ways to reduce these undesirable outcomes.

The major problems will be harder to overcome. There may be small numbers of buyers or sellers, imperfect information on the value of a permit, concerns about permit value in the future, and so on. Firms will trade actively only if trading is a better alternative than other alternatives. Some firms may shut down or perhaps relocate in other countries where permits are not needed. But emissions-trading is probably here to stay. The government may initiate emissions-trading by distributing permits according to production or pollution over a designated period, or it may sell permits through an auction to the highest bidders. Buyers may be electric utilities, or they may be environmentalists. Environmentalists can achieve pollution reduction by outbidding utilities and then refusing to sell permits to utilities, forcing the utilities to reduce pollution.

Visit the Chicago Board of Trade EcoCenter at http://www.cbot.com /points_of_interest/ecocenter /ecocntr.html *to investigate market-based solutions to environmental concerns.*

The Chicago Board of Trade, or "Smog" Exchange, allows trading in pollution permits much like trading on the New York Stock Exchange. Companies are required to own a permit for each unit of emissions. Clean companies need fewer permits and offer to sell their extra permits on the exchange. Dirty companies need additional permits and are buyers on the exchange. They will buy only if the permit price is less than what it would cost them to reduce pollution by one more unit. Sellers of permits will charge at least what it costs them to reduce pollution by one more unit.

Exhibit 4 shows the price of sulfur dioxide allowances since trading began in late 1994 up to the present. Prices dropped steeply over the first year of trading, from almost $160 per permit to only $80. Permit prices have trended upward since then. One reason is that beginning in the year 2000 a second phase of the emissions trading program will begin. In the second phase, additional utilities that were not included in Phase I will now have to meet emissions requirements. So both Phase I and Phase II utilities are beginning to buy permits in anticipation of greater demand beginning in the year 2000.

There is concern that the benefits of emissions-trading will be diminished by lack of trading and opposition to the idea of creating a market to pollute. There is even a revival of interest in command-and-control regulation. If the government happens to pick the right approach and rewards cleaner technology, some economists favor CAC over the imperfect emissions-trading to date. For example, there are supporters of California's approach to reducing auto emissions. In 1998, 2 percent of cars sold in California must be emissions free. The command increases to 5 percent by 2001 and 10 percent by 2003. The mandate is likely to be met with electric vehicles (EVs).

EXHIBIT 4

Monthly Average Price of Sulfur Dioxide Allowances Under the Acid Rain Program

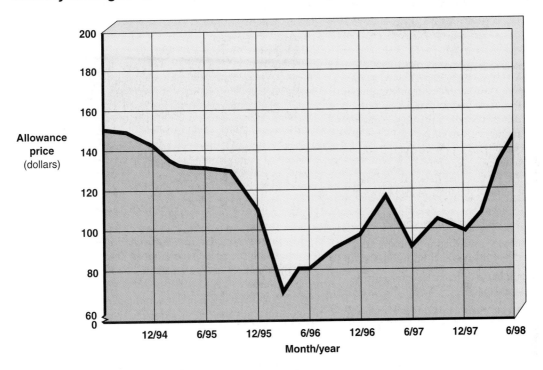

The Chicago Board of Trade allows trading in pollution permits much like trading on the New York Stock Exchange. This figure shows the sulfur dioxide allowance prices reported by brokerage firms and Fieldston Publications' market survey.

Source: Allowance Prices, http://ftp.epa.gov/docs/acidrain/ats/prices.html.

Critics of the California approach first point out that EVs are not emissions free if they require electricity from a power plant. Certainly, power plants also pollute, although there may be an advantage to transferring pollution away from the most densely populated areas. EVs powered by photovoltaic cells (PVCs) that use solar energy are closer to being emissions free, but there is still pollution in the PVC production process. Perhaps the greatest drawback to EVs is their poor performance to date. They suffer from poor acceleration, limited range, and limited ability to climb hills. Critics maintain that inferior products continue to be the legacy of CAC approaches.

As the following application demonstrates, the public is more comfortable with controls and rules than it is with prices and trading. There are a number of possible explanations for the public's view. First, people have difficulty accepting that any pollution is efficient. Nobody wants to think

Emissions: Let the Market Decide

Applicable Concepts: emissions-trading, command-and-control regulation

The evidence indicates that emissions trading—as opposed to command-and-control policies from environmental bureaucracies—has helped cut overall pollution at the lowest possible cost, say observers. According to the General Accounting Office, emissions trading will save utilities some $3.5 billion a year compared to command-and-control techniques.

The 1990 Clean Air Act created national trading rights in emissions of sulfur dioxide produced by coal-fired electric power plants.

The idea behind emissions trading is simple:

■ The government sets a maximum pollution standard for each utility plant which burns coal.

■ Each utility plant has a different cost for cutting sulfur dioxide emissions.

■ Plants which can cut their emissions fairly cheaply can trade their rights to pollute to other plants where clean-up would be more costly.

■ All new plants must buy their emission rights from existing plants—meaning that new plants cause no new net increase in sulfur dioxide emissions.

Three years ago, California's South Coast Air Quality Management District began allowing trading in nitrogen and sulfur oxides—two components of smog.

■ Since then, plants in the program have cut emissions by two-thirds below the target set by the agency.

■ The cost of cutting these emissions has been less than the national average, and job loss is just 4 percent of what it would have been under a command-and-control approach.

But environmentalists have challenged part of the program, and the agency has stopped all new emissions trading plans. Free-market advocates see that as a major step backward.

Proponents of emissions trading are urging the federal government to set up programs for particulate matter and ozone-causing emissions as well as greenhouse gases.

ANALYZE THE ISSUE

1. Why do some observers favor emissions-trading over a command-and-control approach?
2. In addition to sulfur dioxide, what other markets do proponents advocate for emissions-trading?
3. Why do you think some environmentalists oppose emissions-trading?

Source: Perspective, "Let the Market Decide," *Investor's Business Daily*, September 25, 1997.

about a higher risk of cancer due to a leak from a nuclear power plant. Economics teaches us that eliminating the risk of cancer due to a radioactive leak requires eliminating nuclear power. Are we willing to accept no electricity? If we want electric power, it will probably come from coal (causing acid rain from sulfur emissions) or oil (bringing the possibility of oil spills).

Another possible reason for the public's view is a distrust of experts. People were told by experts that nuclear power would be safe, hazardous wastes would not leak, and people near oil tanks would not have higher risks of cancer. When outcomes differ from what experts promise, the public favors safety over efficiency. No one wants to take a chance on illness or death if the experts are wrong again. And yet would you give up your car or favor a law that the speed limit be set at 20 miles per hour? These laws might increase safety, but they would certainly be inefficient.

Government and Environmental Efficiency

Market failure is likely for products with external costs. To achieve efficiency, buyers and sellers must consider external costs. Government has the power to establish laws, taxes, or permit systems so that market participants pay for external costs.

While government policy can potentially improve efficiency, there is no guarantee. The former Soviet Union, where government played a far more dominant role than in the United States, has environmental problems that dwarf those in the United States. In the former Soviet Union, air and water quality borders on ecocide, with high rates of illness due to environmental degradation. The Chernobyl disaster, in which a nuclear plant malfunctioned and released radioactivity, caused thousands of premature deaths.

In the United States, large numbers of U.S. Department of Defense sites are among the biggest environmental challenges. Hazardous wastes from the production of weapons are now leaking in burial sites including Oak Ridge, Tennessee, and Richland, Washington. The U.S. Forest Service frequently permits lumber companies to harvest trees from national forests at subsidized prices. Environmental officials have even gone to jail for illegally meeting with industries to weaken environmental regulations. And government has tended to ignore the cost to firms of complying with hundreds of thousands of pages of environmental legislation, a set of regulations more voluminous than the U.S. Tax Code. For all these reasons, as well as the widespread dissatisfaction with government in general, there is concern about the effectiveness of government policy in achieving environmental goals. Government officials may pursue self-interest, which could favor polluting industries over societal interests as a whole, especially if industry executives are major campaign contributors.

Ronald Coase, an economist at the University of Chicago and the winner of the 1991 Nobel Prize in economics, was among the first to caution against the assumption that government intervention in the environmental arena would improve on private-sector environmental performance. In his famous 1960 paper, "The Problem of Social Cost," he even questioned the fundamental assumption of market failure. According to the **Coase Theorem**, the private sector could achieve social efficiency with minimal government intervention. The role of the government should be limited to the legal establishment of property rights, with environmental disputes resolved in court. The Coase Theorem is the proposition that private market negotiations can achieve social efficiency regardless of the initial definition of property rights.

One example is a case of a train throwing off sparks, occasionally burning a farmer's crops. Exhibit 5 shows railroad profits increasing and farm profits decreasing as more trains run.

Coase Theorem

The proposition that private market negotiations can achieve social efficiency regardless of the initial definition of property rights.

EXHIBIT 5   Choosing the Efficient Amounts of Spark-Emitting Trains and Farm Crops

Number of Trains	Total Railroad Profit	Marginal Railroad Profit	Number of Crops	Total Farm Profit	Marginal Farm Profit
0	$ 0		10.5	$105	
		$20			$ −5
1	20		10	100	
		$20			−10
2	40		9	90	
		$20			−20
3	60		7	70	
		$20			−30
4	80		4	40	
		$20			−40
5	100		0	0	

Each train has an external cost. Emitted sparks can cause fires, which reduce the farmer's crops. If the railroad ignored external cost, it appears that the railroad would choose to run 5 trains so as to maximize profit, leaving the farmer with no crops. It also appears that in order to protect the farmer, there should be a law requiring the railroad to find a spark-free technology.

Suppose the courts establish a law that farmers have the right to spark-free trains. How could the railroad meet this tougher environmental standard? The railroad could change to a new, higher-cost technology. The cost must be higher, or the railroad would have chosen this environmentally friendly technology in the first place. If the cost is too high, the railroad might go out of business or relocate away from farms. Alternatively, it may be less expensive to offer the farmer money for any burned crops.

If the trains continue to throw off sparks, the first train will reduce the farmer's profits by $5 and will add $20 to the railroad's profits. The two parties will be able to negotiate a deal, with the farmer receiving a payment between $5 and $20 from the railroad. What about a second train? This train will add another $20 to railroad profits, but will reduce farm profits by $10. Again, the farmer will permit the railroad to run a second train as long as the railroad pays the farmer at least $10. If a third train runs, marginal social benefit will equal marginal social cost. Society will benefit from more train service, but will lose from fewer crops. The third train will be marginally worthwhile, but additional trains will not run. The fourth train will add $20 to railroad profits, but will reduce farm profit by $30. The railroad will lose money if it runs the fourth train. By clearly establishing the farmer's right to spark-free trains, the number of trains will be decreased from five to three trains.

Notice that the farmer will be better off if he allows sparks as long as the railroad compensates him for damage than if government requires a spark-free technology. The farmer earns $105 when there are no sparks. With sparks, the farmer will earn at least $105, receiving between $5 and $20 for permitting the first train, at least $10 (and possibly as much as $20) for permitting the second train, and another $20 for the third train.

With three trains, the farmer will still earn $70 from crops, for a total of at least $105.

This outcome is similar to the government solutions examined earlier. Efficiency leads to the efficient amount of pollution, which is typically not zero. No sparks may mean no trains. But Coase asks, Why assume that society is best served by assuming the railroad is the polluter and the farmer the victim? In the 1800s, sparking engines may have been the best available technology, and an occasional fire may have been a natural consequence.

So consider the outcome if trains are allowed to throw off sparks, so that property rights to produce sparks are given to the railroads in this next example. If the farmer does nothing, the railroad will run five trains, and the farmer will end up with no crops and no profit. The farmer will increase profit by $40 if only four trains run. Since the fifth train will add only $20 to railroad profit, the farmer can afford to pay as much as $40 (or as little as $20) to stop the fifth train. Similarly, the farmer will gain $30 by stopping the fourth train, more than enough to pay the railroad for foregoing $20 in profit. Once again, negotiations will stop at three trains, the efficient number.

This example demonstrates the Coase Theorem: As long as the courts clearly establish property rights, markets may achieve social efficiency *regardless of the initial assignment of property rights.* The great contribution of Coase was to focus attention on property rights, a focus that led to the emissions-trading approach. Emissions-trading allows firms to negotiate by buying and selling the right to pollute. But Coase wishes an even more limited role for government. The government should establish courts and then let markets negotiate.

Coase was instrumental in raising concern about government solutions. It might then seem a simple step to accept his claim that private markets would efficiently resolve environmental problems. In actuality, only a small number of environmental problems qualify for Coase Theorem solutions.

First, there are no **transactions costs** in the Coase Theorem. Transactions costs are the costs of negotiating and enforcing a contract. Turning to the courts is a costly process in terms of both time and money. And dealing with the source of the externality has its own costs. Have you ever tried to negotiate with a noisy neighbor at 2 A.M.? However, there are also transactions costs associated with government solutions. So Coasian negotiations may be preferable to government intervention even where there are substantial private transactions costs.

Second, there are no *income effects* in the Coase Theorem. As explained in the chapter on consumer choice theory, income effects are present when income changes affect purchasing patterns. Some parties may not be able to afford the efficient solution. A small farmer is unlikely to have enough money to pay for fewer trains, and you might not have enough money to convince your neighbor to turn down the volume.

Third, Coase assumes there are only two parties in the negotiation. Externalities are typically third-party problems, and there may be many third parties. Do all the farmers get together to negotiate with the railroad, and do all the neighbors get together to reduce noise from the party? With many parties, there is once again a **free-rider problem**. If noise levels

Transactions costs
The costs of negotiating and enforcing a contract.

Free-rider problem
The problem that if some individuals benefit, while others pay, few will be willing to pay for improvement of the environment or other public goods. As a result, these goods are underproduced.

INTERNATIONAL ECONOMICS

Beware of Global Warming Pact

Applicable Concepts: externalities, free-rider problem

For several years, the United States has been negotiating an international treaty on global warming. If you are still in the dark about what our nation's policy is you are not alone.

The draft United Nations' treaty will have a profound impact on all Americans. The draft treaty calls upon the U.S. and other "developed" countries to reduce carbon dioxide emissions to below 1990 levels. Essentially, if the United States assents to binding and target carbon dioxide emissions, we conform to an international scheme to manage our energy use.

Widespread opposition to the Clinton-Gore approach to global warming is growing, and the Senate recently passed a non-binding resolution that demonstrated the severity of concern for the administration's strategy.

The resolution, sponsored by Senator Robert Byrd, D–W.Va., and Senator Chuck Hagel, R–Neb., claims the United States should not be a signatory to any protocol or U.N. agreement that:

- Mandates new commitments to limit or reduce greenhouse gas emissions on developed countries unless developing countries are also part of the effort;

- Would result in serious harm to the U.S. economy.

The Byrd-Hagel resolution unanimously passed the Senate 95–0 in July [1997]. One of the major flaws of the global climate treaty is the fact that the United States would be bound by the stringency of the new treaty, while countries like China, Mexico, Brazil and India, so-called developing nations, would be exempt. To business and labor groups opposing the treaty, not only is this key element inequitable, but it's silly. Those businesses that could afford to would move overseas, taking many U.S. jobs with them.

Various private studies show that the economic impact of the proposed treaty would be harsh for American business, workers and consumers. The Clinton administration promised a full economic impact study by October of last year [1996], but has yet to produce one analysis of the proposal's impact on the economy. However, according to an Energy Department study, energy intensive industries would be substantially impacted if not devastated by the treaty.

Private studies parallel Energy Department findings. According to DRI/McGraw Hill, a $200-a-carbon tax, which is one option to bring carbon dioxide emissions below 1990 levels, would cost the U.S. economy $350 billion a year in reduced production of goods and services in human terms; 1.1 million workers could lose their jobs each year over a 15-year period.

Paying more for energy use translates to higher prices for consumer goods, higher costs for businesses and fewer jobs for American workers. In internal documents, the Environmental Protection Agency outlines a series of tax-increase options that could be instituted to meet U.S. obligations under the U.N. treaty. In addition to a carbon tax, a 50-cent gas tax is a real option to discourage energy use.

Clinton administration officials have stated that tax increases will not be a part of the final plan to conform with the treaty's requirements. According to economists and policy experts, the next and only alternative to taxes on all forms of energy is an energy rationing plan. Neither option sits well with the public.

ANALYZE THE ISSUE

1. Do free-rider problems make global agreements such as the United Nations treaty more difficult to achieve?
2. How do differing income levels between rich countries and poor countries complicate the United Nations treaty?

Source: Karen Kerrigan, "Beware Global Warming Pact," *South Florida Business Journal* 18 (September 26, 1997): 42.

CHECKPOINT   Is It Efficient to Buy Odor-Reducing Technology
                        If You Live Next to a Hog Farm?

You live next door to a hog farm. It is estimated that the smell from the hog
farm reduces the value of your home by $7,000. For $5,000, it is possible to
purchase technology that reduces the hog smell by half, so that your house
value decreases by only $3,500. Assuming the hog farm has the property right
to locate next door and that it is not required to reduce the hog smell, what
will you do? Will you do nothing or buy the new technology?

decrease, I get the benefit whether or not I contribute to the negotiations.
So why contribute? Stated as a concept, if some individuals benefit, while
others pay, the free-rider problem is that few will be willing to pay for
improvement of the environment or other public goods. As a result, these
goods are underproduced.

In sum, neither government nor the markets can be asserted as the best
solution. On balance, though, the effort to work toward improved government solutions seems worthwhile, given the outcome for the environment
of purely self-interested markets.

KEY CONCEPTS

Private benefits and costs   Incentive-based regulations   Effluent tax   Coase Theorem
Social benefits and costs   Command-and-control   Emissions-trading   Transactions costs
Market failure   regulations   New-source bias   Free-rider problem
Government failure

SUMMARY

- **Externalities** are benefits or costs that fall on third
  parties who are neither buyers nor sellers. Pollution
  is a negative externality or external cost that is a by-
  product of many industrial production processes.

- **Market failure** is present when the market produces
  a socially inefficient outcome. One instance is when
  there are externalities. All firms, including competitive
  firms, consider private costs, but disregard external
  costs, in making decisions.

- **Government failure** occurs when public-sector actions
  move us away from desired outcomes, such as efficiency. Government officials seeking campaign contri-

butions and votes may choose environmental measures that favor wealthy contributors over society's
best interests.

- **Command-and-control regulations** occur when the
  government dictates the approach to achieving an
  environmental goal. Command-and-control (CAC)
  regulations are generally inefficient on three grounds:
  They do not distinguish between high- and low-
  pollution areas, they do not allow firms to choose
  lower-cost technologies that could achieve the environmental standard, and they do not encourage
  improved technology to lower future emissions.

■ **Incentive-based regulations** build on markets to achieve environmental efficiency. Effluent taxes are taxes that reflect external costs. Emissions-trading allows firms to buy and sell the "right to pollute."

■ The **Coase Theorem** maintains that markets can be efficient in the presence of externalities with minimal government intervention. Even in the presence of externalities, markets may produce efficient outcomes so long as property rights are clearly established.

■ **Transactions costs, income effects,** and **free-rider problems** are obstacles to achieving environmental efficiency through markets. Transactions costs are the costs of negotiating an agreement, income effects are present when limited income prevents one party from being able to afford the efficient solution, and free-rider problems are present when participants are better off hiding than revealing their willingness to pay for an environmental improvement.

STUDY QUESTIONS AND PROBLEMS

1. Compare price and quantity in a competitive industry to those of a "green" industry for a product generating pollution.

2. Suppose a car sells for $20,000 in a market with no pollution restrictions. Will the car sell for more than $20,000, less than $20,000, or $20,000 when there are pollution restrictions? Explain.

3. You are considering whether to buy one house for $100,000 or another identical house located near high-voltage electric power lines for $90,000. Assume that it has been established that living near high-voltage lines increases the risk of cancer due to electromagnetic fields (EMFs). If you choose the $90,000 house, is the radiation from EMFs an externality? Explain.

4. It has been observed that large parties (eight or more) leave a lower average tip at a restaurant than smaller parties. Identify the effect, which also makes it more difficult to reach global environmental agreements, responsible for this phenomenon.

5. Suppose your instructor gives eight homework assignments during the semester. She indicates that anyone who does not turn in all eight assignments will automatically fail the course. Is this an example of a command-and-control or an incentive-based regulation? Explain any inefficiencies of your instructor's approach.

6. Environmentalists in Tennessee brought suit against the Champion Paper Company of North Carolina for polluting the Pigeon River, which flows from North Carolina into eastern Tennessee. Tennessee claimed that the coffee-colored water smelled bad and would not support fishing or swimming. Environmentalists requested that the river be restored to its pristine state, whereby water quality is restored to the level before the coming of industry. The Environmental Protection Agency heard the suit and applied an efficiency standard. Is pristine water an efficiency standard? Explain.

7. Draw a graph to demonstrate your answer to question 6.

8. California has mandated that 2 percent of its car fleet be emissions free within five years. This mandate has spurred electric vehicle research. Such vehicles could be powered by photovoltaic cells or by batteries that are recharged using an electric outlet. Would you agree that it is correct to conclude that electric vehicles that use electric outlets are emissions free? What about electric vehicles powered by photovoltaic cells?

9. Explain why consumers would not be willing to pay the full costs of a less-polluting car in the absence of government regulations.

10. Evaluate the following statement: "When products pollute, government solutions are more efficient than market solutions."

11. Provide an example of a market where you think the Coase Theorem applies. Explain why you think the market satisfies assumptions regarding transactions costs, income effects, and free riders.

12. In a study of ranching laws in the 1800s, an economic researcher found that as the laws restricted the ability of cattle to roam freely, agricultural output increased. Do this researcher's results support the Coase Theorem? Explain.

13. If we are to take action against global warming, we must reduce carbon emissions. Explain how to reduce carbon emissions using
    a. command-and-control regulation.
    b. an effluent tax.
    c. emissions-trading.

14. A global agreement known as the Montreal Protocol led to the phase-out of chlorofluorocarbons (CFCs), chemical compounds found in aerosol cans and refrigerants. CFCs may have contributed to the growing hole in the ozone. With a diminished ozone layer, there is an increased chance of skin cancer. Explain the effect of this agreement on the price of deodorants and air-conditioning. Also, is a ban on CFCs an efficient approach to the ozone hole problem?

ONLINE EXERCISES

Exercise 1

Browse Tropical Rainforest (http://www.euronet.nl/users /mbleeker/suriname/suri-eng.html#intro). This site provides a multimedia tour through the rainforest in South America.

Exercise 2

Visit GPO Catalog for the President (http://www.gpo .ucop.edu/catalog/erp97.html). Select Chapter 6, Refining the Role of Government in the U.S. Market Economy. Scroll down and browse the section titled Markets, Governments, and Complementarity.

Exercise 3

Visit NTIS Environment Home Page (http://www.ntis.gov /envirn/envirn.htm), and browse Environmental Topics.

Exercise 4

Visit the Environmental Protection Agency's website at http://www.epa.gov/epahome/press.htm. Click on the region you live in to see current press releases and media advisories. Choose one of these topics, and write a brief report.

CHECKPOINT ANSWERS

Is It Efficient to Buy Odor-Reducing Technology If You Live Next to a Hog Farm?

It is not efficient to purchase the new odor-reducing technology. It would cost $5,000, but would increase your house value by only $3,500. It is not efficient to cut the odor by half if the market will not compensate you sufficiently for reducing hog odors. If your only options are to do nothing and to buy the new technology and you said to do nothing, **YOU ARE CORRECT.** (A third option is to pay the hog farm to locate elsewhere. You would be willing to pay up to $7,000 to avoid the $7,000 lost due to the smell of the nearby farm.)

PRACTICE QUIZ

For a visual explanation of the correct answers, visit the tutorial at http://tucker.swcollege.com.

1. Recently, the city of New Orleans discovered chemical compounds in its drinking water that may cause cancer. Since New Orleans's drinking water comes from the Mississippi River, the source of these chemicals is the waste discharges of industrial plants upstream from New Orleans. This is an example of
   a. an external cost imposed on the citizens of New Orleans by the industrial plants upstream.
   b. a market failure where the market price of the output of these industrial plants does not fully reflect the social cost of producing these goods.
   c. an externality where the marginal social costs of producing these industrial goods differ from the marginal private costs.
   d. all of the above.

2. A government policy that charges steel firms a fee per ton of steel produced (an "effluent charge") where the fee is determined by the amount of pollutants discharged into the air or water will lead to
   a. a decrease in the market equilibrium quantity of steel produced.
   b. a decrease in the market equilibrium price of steel.
   c. an increase in the market equilibrium price of steel.
   d. the results in (a) and (b).
   e. the results in (a) and (c).

3. Social costs are
   a. the full resource costs of an economic activity.
   b. usually less than private costs.
   c. the costs of an economic activity borne by the producer.
   d. all of the above.

4. As a general rule, if pollution costs are external, firms will produce
   a. too much of a polluting good.
   b. too little of a polluting good.
   c. an optimal amount of a polluting good.
   d. an amount that cannot be determined without additional information.

5. Many economists would argue
   a. the optimal amount of pollution is greater than zero.
   b. all pollution should be eliminated.
   c. the market mechanism can handle pollution without any government intervention.
   d. central planning is the most efficient way to eliminate pollution.

6. Which of the following used marketable pollution permits as an incentive for reducing pollution?
   a. The 1970 Clean Air Act
   b. The Comprehensive Environmental Response, Compensation, and Liability Act of 1980
   c. The 1990 Clean Air Act amendments
   d. The Water Quality and Improvement Act of 1970

7. The disposable diaper industry is perfectly competitive. Which of the following is true?
   a. Since the industry is perfectly competitive, price and quantity are at the socially efficient levels.
   b. Competitive price is higher and competitive quantity lower than the socially efficient point.
   c. Competitive price is higher and competitive quantity higher than the socially efficient point.
   d. Competitive price is lower and competitive quantity higher than the socially efficient point.

8. An example of the command-and-control approach to environmental policy is
   a. placing a tax on high-sulfur coal to reduce its use and the corresponding sulfur emissions (which contribute to acid rain).
   b. requiring electric utilities to install scrubbers to reduce sulfur dioxide emissions (which contribute to acid rain).
   c. allowing coal producers to buy and sell permits to allow sulfur emissions.
   d. allowing individuals to sue coal producers if sulfur emissions exceed a government-set standard.

9. The profit-maximizing firm in Exhibit 6 creates water and air pollution as a consequence of producing its output of beef cattle. If pollution costs are borne by third parties, the firm will maximize economic profit by choosing to
   a. voluntarily incur costs to reduce its pollution.
   b. produce at output rate Q_3.
   c. produce at output rate Q_2.
   d. produce at output rate Q_4.

10. Use Exhibit 6 to complete the following: To maximize social welfare, the firm should produce at output rate
    a. Q_1.
    b. Q_2.
    c. Q_3.
    d. Q_4.

EXHIBIT 7
Impact of Flights on House Value

Number of Flights	Total Profits	Marginal Profits	Value of Wilbur's House
1	$10,000	$10,000	$100,000
2	18,000	8,000	95,000
3	24,000	6,000	90,000
4	28,000	4,000	85,000
5	30,000	2,000	80,000

11. As shown in Exhibit 7, if Orville has the property right to fly over Wilbur's house, but Wilbur is allowed to negotiate with Orville on the number of flights, what will be the number of flights?
    a. 2
    b. 3
    c. 4
    d. 5

12. As shown in Exhibit 7, if Wilbur has the property right to have no planes flying over his house, but Orville is allowed to negotiate with Wilbur, what will be the number of flights?
    a. 2
    b. 3
    c. 4
    d. 5

13. As shown in Exhibit 7, at the socially efficient number of flights, what will be the market value of Orville's house?
    a. $100,000.
    b. $95,000
    c. $90,000
    d. $85,000

EXHIBIT 6

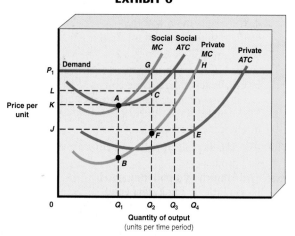

CHAPTER FIFTEEN

International Trade and Finance

Just imagine your life without world trade. For openers, you would not eat bananas from Honduras or chocolate from Nigerian cocoa beans. Nor would you sip French wine, Colombian coffee, or Indian tea. Also forget about driving a Japanese motorcycle or automobile. In addition, you could not buy Italian sweaters and most VCRs, televisions, fax machines, and personal computers because they are foreign made. Taking your vacation in Paris would also be ruled out if there were no world trade. And the list goes on and on, so the point is clear. World trade is important because it gives consumers more power by expanding their choices. Today, the speed of transportation and communication means producers must compete on a global basis for the favor of consumers.

The first part of this chapter explains why countries should specialize in producing certain goods and then trade them for imports. In his bid for the 1996 Republican nomination for president, Pat Buchanan's America First campaign sparked debate over foreign trade protectionism. Here you will study arguments for and against the United States protecting itself from "unfair" trade practices by other countries. In the second part of the chapter, you will learn how nations pay each other for world trade. Beginning in the summer of 1997, and continuing as this text is written in 1999, a financial crisis spread across East Asia, Japan, Russia, Brazil, and other nations. Economies sank into recession, and currencies collapsed. Here you will explore international bookkeeping and discover how supply and demand forces determine that, for instance, 1 dollar is worth 100 yen.

In this chapter, you will learn to solve these economics puzzles:

■ How does Babe Ruth's decision not to become a pitcher illustrate an important principle in international trade?

■ Is there a valid argument for trade protectionism?

■ Should the United States return to the gold standard?

Why Nations Need Trade

Exhibit 1 reveals which regions are our major trading partners. Leading U.S. exports are chemicals, machinery, airplanes, and computers. Major imports include cars, trucks, petroleum, electrical machinery and equipment, and clothing. Why does a nation even bother to trade with the rest of the world? Does it seem strange for the United States to import goods it could produce for itself? Indeed, why doesn't the United States become self-sufficient by growing all its own food (including bananas, sugar, and coffee), making all its own cars, and prohibiting sales of all foreign goods? This section explains why specialization and trade are a nation's keys to a higher standard of living.

The Production Possibilities Curve Revisited

Consider a world with only two countries—the United States and Japan. To keep the illustration simple, also assume *both* countries produce only two goods—grain and steel. Accordingly, we can construct in Exhibit 2 a *production possibilities curve* for each country. We will also set aside the *law of increasing opportunity costs*, explained in Chapter 2, and assume workers are equally suited to producing grain or steel. This assumption transforms the bowed-out shape of the production possibilities curve into a straight line.

Comparing parts (a) and (b) of Exhibit 2 shows that the United States can produce more grain than Japan. If the United States devotes all its resources to this purpose, 100 tons of grain are produced per day, represented by point *A* in Exhibit 2(a). The maximum grain production of Japan, on the other hand, is only 40 tons per day because Japan has less labor, land, and other factors of production than the United States. This capability is represented by point *D* in Exhibit 2(b).

Now consider the capacities of the two countries for production of steel. If all their respective resources are devoted to this output, the United States produces 50 tons per day (point *C*), and Japan produces only 40 tons per day (point *F*). Again, the greater potential maximum steel output of the United States reflects its greater resources. Both countries are also capable of producing other combinations of grain and steel along their respective production possibilities curves, such as point *B* for the United States and point *E* for Japan.

EXHIBIT 1

U.S. Trading Partners, 1998

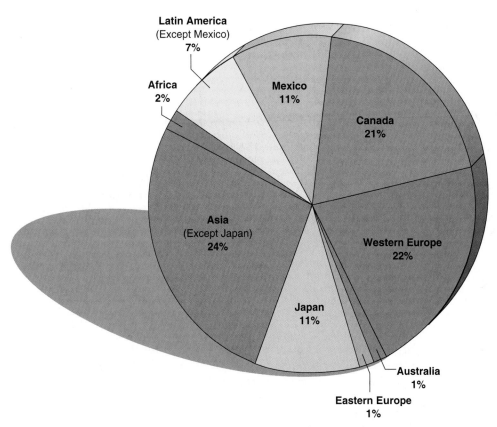

In 1998, Canada and Japan accounted for 32 percent of U.S. trade (merchandise exports and imports). Western Europe, Asia (except Japan), and Latin America (including Mexico) accounted for another 64 percent. Trade with Africa, Eastern Europe, and Australia was relatively small.

Source: Office of Trade and Economic Analysis, http://www.ita.doc.gov/industry/otea/usfth/tabcon.html, Tables 6 and 7.

Specialization Without Trade

Assuming no world trade, the production possibilities curve for each country also defines its *consumption possibilities*. Stated another way, we assume both countries are *self-sufficient* because without imports they must consume only the combination chosen along their production possibilities curve. Under the assumption of self-sufficiency, suppose the United States prefers to produce and consume 60 tons of grain and 20 tons of steel per

The World Trade Organization (WTO) (http://www.wto.org/) *provides data and analysis on international trade* (http://www.wto.org/wto/intltrad/internat.htm).

EXHIBIT 2

The Benefits of Trade

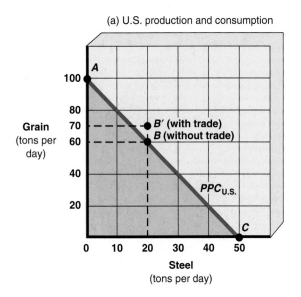

(a) U.S. production and consumption

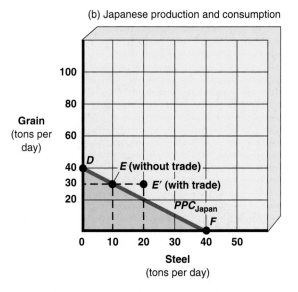

(b) Japanese production and consumption

As shown in part (a), assume the United States chooses point B on its production possibilities curve, PPC$_{U.S.}$. Without trade, the United States produces and consumes 60 tons of grain and 20 tons of steel. In part (b), assume Japan also operates along its production possibilities curve, PPC$_{Japan}$, at point E. Without trade, Japan produces and consumes 30 tons of grain and 10 tons of steel.

Now assume the United States specializes in producing grain at point A and imports 20 tons of Japanese steel in exchange for 30 tons of grain. Through specialization and trade, the United States moves to consumption possibility point B', outside its production possibilities curve. Japan also moves to a higher standard of living at consumption possibility point E', outside its production possibilities curve.

day (point *B*). Also assume Japan chooses to produce and consume 30 tons of grain and 10 tons of steel (point *E*). Exhibit 3 lists data corresponding to points *B* and *E* and shows that the total world output is 90 tons of grain and 30 tons of steel.

Now suppose the United States specializes by producing and consuming at point *A*, rather than point *B*. Suppose also Japan specializes by producing and consuming at point *F*, rather than point *E*. As shown in Exhibit 3, specialization in each country increases total world output per day by 10 tons of grain and 10 tons of steel. Because this extra world output has the potential for making both countries better off, why wouldn't the United States and Japan specialize and produce at points *A* and *F*, respectively?

EXHIBIT 3   Effect of Specialization on World Output

	Grain Production (tons per day)	Steel Production (tons per day)
Before specialization		
United States (at point *B*)	60	20
Japan (at point *E*)	30	10
Total world output	90	30
After specialization		
United States (at point *A*)	100	0
Japan (at point *F*)	0	40
Total world output	100	40

The reason is that although production at these points is clearly possible, neither country wants to consume these combinations of output. The United States prefers to consume less grain and more steel at point *B* compared to point *A*. Japan, on the other hand, prefers to consume more grain and less steel at point *E*, rather than point *F*.

Conclusion *When countries specialize, total world output increases, and, therefore, the potential for greater total world consumption also increases.*

Specialization with Trade

Now we return to Exhibit 2 and demonstrate how world trade benefits countries. Suppose the United States agrees to specialize in grain production at point *A* and to import 20 tons of Japanese steel in exchange for 30 tons of its grain output. Does the United States gain from trade? The answer is Yes. At point *A*, the United States produces 100 tons of grain per day. Subtracting the 30 tons of grain traded to Japan leaves the United States with 70 tons of its own grain production to consume. In return for grain, Japan unloads 20 tons of steel on U.S. shores. Hence, specialization and trade allow the United States to move from point *A* to point *B'*, which is a consumption possibility *outside* its production possibilities curve in Exhibit 2(a). At point *B'*, the United States consumes the same amount of steel and 10 more tons of grain compared to point *B* (without trade).

Japan also has an incentive to specialize by moving its production mix from point *E* to point *F*. With trade, Japan's consumption would be at point *E'*. At point *E'*, Japan has as much grain to consume as it had at point *E*, plus 10 more tons of steel. After trading 20 tons of the 40 tons of steel produced at point *F* for grain, Japan can still consume 20 tons of steel from its production, rather than only 10 tons of steel at point *E*. Thus, point E' is a consumption possibility that lies *outside* Japan's production possibilities curve.

Conclusion *International trade allows a country to consume a combination of goods that exceeds its production possibilities curve.*

Comparative and Absolute Advantage

Why did the United States decide to produce and export grain instead of steel? Why did Japan choose to produce steel, rather than grain? Here you study the economic principle that determines specialization and trade.

Comparative Advantage

Comparative advantage
The ability of a country to produce a good at a lower opportunity cost than another country.

The U.S. Department of Commerce, International Trade Administration (http://www.ita.doc.gov/), *provides foreign trade data by country and trade sector* (http://www.ita.doc.gov/industry/otea/usftu/usftu.html).

Engaging in world trade permits countries to escape the prison of their own production possibilities curves and produce bread, cars, or whatever goods they make best. The decision of the United States to specialize in and export grain and the decision of Japan to specialize in and export steel are based on **comparative advantage**. Comparative advantage is the ability of a country to produce a good at a lower opportunity cost than another country. Returning to our earlier example, we can calculate opportunity costs for the two countries and use comparative advantage to determine which countries should specialize in grain or steel. For the United States, the opportunity cost of producing 50 tons of steel is 100 tons of grain not produced, or 1 ton of steel costs 2 tons of grain. For Japan, the opportunity cost of producing 40 tons of steel is 40 tons of grain, or 1 ton of steel costs 1 ton of grain. Japan's steel is therefore cheaper in terms of grain foregone. This means Japan has a comparative advantage in steel production because less grain has to be given up to produce steel in Japan than in the United States. Stated differently, the opportunity cost of steel production is lower in Japan than in the United States.

The other side of the coin is to measure the cost of grain in terms of steel. For the United States, 1 ton of grain costs $\frac{1}{2}$ ton of steel. For Japan, 1 ton of grain costs 1 ton of steel. The United States has a comparative advantage in grain because its opportunity cost in terms of steel foregone is lower. Thus, the United States should specialize in grain because it is more efficient in grain production. Japan, on the other hand, is relatively more efficient at producing steel and should specialize in this product.

Conclusion *Comparative advantage refers to the relative opportunity costs between countries of producing the same goods. World output and consumption are maximized when each country specializes in producing and trading goods for which it has a comparative advantage.*

Absolute Advantage

So far, a country's production and international trade decisions depend on comparing what a country gives up to produce more of a good. It is important to note that comparative advantage is based on opportunity

CHECKPOINT　　　Do Nations with an Advantage Always Trade?

Comparing labor productivity, suppose the United States has an absolute advantage over Italy in the production of calculators and towels. In the United States, a worker can produce 4 calculators or 400 towels in 10 hours. In Italy, a worker can produce 1 calculator or 100 towels in the same time. Under these conditions, are specialization and trade advantageous?

costs regardless of the absolute costs of resources used in production. We have not considered how much labor, land, or capital either the United States or Japan uses to produce a ton of grain or steel. For example, Japan might have an **absolute advantage** in producing *both* grain and steel. Absolute advantage is the ability of a country to produce a good using fewer resources than another country. In our previous example, Japan might use fewer resources per ton to produce grain and steel than the United States. Maybe the Japanese work harder or have more skilled workers. In short, the Japanese may be more productive producers, but their absolute advantage does not matter in specialization and world trade decisions. If the United States has a comparative advantage in grain, it should specialize in grain even if Japan can produce grain and steel with fewer resources.

Perhaps a different example will clarify the difference between absolute advantage and comparative advantage. When Babe Ruth played for the New York Yankees, he was the best hitter and the best pitcher on the team. In other words, he had an *absolute advantage* in both hitting and throwing the baseball. For example, Babe Ruth could produce the same home runs as any other teammate with fewer times at bat. The problem was that if he pitched, he would bat fewer times because pitchers need rest after pitching. The coaches decided that the Babe had a *comparative advantage* in hitting. Other pitchers on the team could pitch almost as well as the Babe, but not one could touch his hitting. In terms of opportunity costs, the Yankees would lose fewer games if the Babe specialized in hitting.

Free Trade versus Protectionism

In theory, international trade should be based on comparative advantage and **free trade**. Free trade is the flow of goods between countries without restrictions or special taxes. In practice, despite the advice of economists, every nation protects its own domestic producers to some degree from foreign competition. Behind these barriers to trade are people whose jobs

Absolute advantage
The ability of a country to produce a good with fewer resources than another country.

The U.S. International Trade Commission (ITC) (http://www.usitc.gov/), *the Office of the U.S. Trade Representative* (http://www.ustr.gov/), *and the U.S. Department of State* (http://www.state.gov/www/issues /economic/trade_reports/) *issue reports on foreign trade barriers and unfair trade practices. The Bureau of Export Administration* (http://www.bxa.doc.gov/) *administers export control policies, issues export licenses, and prosecutes violators.*

Free trade
The flow of goods between countries without restrictions or special taxes.

Protectionism

The government's use of embargoes, tariffs, quotas, and other restrictions to protect domestic producers from foreign competition.

and incomes are threatened, so they clamor to the government for **protectionism**. Protectionism is the government's use of embargoes, tariffs, quotas, and other restrictions to protect domestic producers from foreign competition.

Embargo

Embargoes are the strongest limit on trade. An embargo is a law that bars trade with another country. For example, the United States and other nations in the world imposed an arms embargo on Iraq in response to Iraq's invasion of Kuwait in 1990. The United States also maintains embargoes against Cuba and Libya.

Tariff

Tariffs are the most popular and visible measures used to discourage trade. A tariff is a tax on an import. Tariffs are also called customs duties. The current U.S. tariff code specifies tariffs on nearly 70 percent of all U.S. imports. A tariff can be based on weight, volume, or number of units, or it can be *ad valorem* (figured as a percentage of the price). The average U.S. tariff is less than 5 percent, but individual tariffs vary widely. The purposes of tariffs are to reduce imports by raising import prices and to generate revenues for the U.S. Treasury.

During the worldwide depression of the 1930s, as one nation raised its tariffs to protect its industries, other nations retaliated by raising their tariffs. Under the Smoot-Hawley tariffs of the 1930s, the average tariff in the United States was an unbelievable 59 percent. In 1947, most of the world's industrialized nations mutually agreed to end the tariff wars by signing the *General Agreement on Tariffs and Trade (GATT)*. Since then, GATT nations have met periodically to negotiate lower tariff rates. GATT agreements have significantly reduced tariffs over the years among member nations. In the 1994 *Uruguay round*, Congress approved a vast new 116-nation GATT agreement that decreased tariffs by about one-third. The most divisive element of this agreement is the creation of the Geneva-based World Trade Organization (WTO), with the power to oversee GATT and enforce rulings in trade disputes. The concern is that the WTO might be far more likely to rule in favor of other countries in their trade disputes with the United States.

Quota

Another way to limit foreign competition is to impose a **quota**. A quota is a limit on the quantity of a good that may be imported in a given time period. For example, the United States may allow 10 million tons of sugar to be imported over a one-year period. Once this quantity is reached, no more sugar can be imported for the year. About 12 percent of U.S. imports are subject to import quotas. Examples include import quotas on sugar, dairy products, textiles, steel, and even ice cream. Quotas can limit imports from all foreign suppliers or from specific countries. Quotas, like all barriers to trade, invite nations to retaliate with more measures to restrict trade.

In addition to embargoes, tariffs, and quotas, some nations use more subtle measures to discourage trade. For example, some countries set up an overwhelming number of bureaucratic steps that must be taken in order to import a product.

Arguments for Protection

Free trade provides consumers with lower prices and larger quantities of goods from which to choose. Thus, removing import barriers might save each family a few hundred dollars a year. On the other hand, the problem is that imports could cost some workers their jobs and thousands of dollars per year from lost income. It is no wonder that, in spite of the greater total benefits to consumers, trade barriers exist. The reason is primarily because workers and owners from import-competing firms have more at stake than consumers, so they go to Washington and lobby for protection. The following are some of the most popular arguments for protection. These arguments have strong political or emotional appeal, but weak support from economists.

Infant Industry Argument

The infant industry argument, as the name suggests, is that a new domestic industry needs protection because it is not yet ready to compete with established foreign competitors. An infant industry is in a formative stage and must bear high start-up costs. These high costs result from the need to train an entire workforce, develop new technology, establish marketing channels, and reach economies of scale. With time to grow and protection, an infant industry can reduce costs and "catch up" with established foreign firms.

Economists ask where one draws the arbitrary line between an "infant" and a "grown-up" industry. It is also difficult to make a convincing case for protecting an infant industry in a developed country, such as the United States, where industries are well established. The infant industry argument, however, may have some validity for less-developed countries. Even for these countries, there is a danger. Once protection is granted, the new industry will not experience the competitive pressures necessary to encourage reasonably quick growth and participation in world trade. Also, once an industry is given protection, it is difficult to take it away.

National Security Argument

Another common argument is that defense-related industries must be protected with embargoes, tariffs, and quotas to ensure national security. By protecting critical defense industries, a nation will not be dependent on foreign countries for the essential defense-related goods it needs to defend itself in wartime. The national defense argument has been used to protect a long list of industries, including petrochemicals, munitions, steel, and rubber.

This argument gained validity during the War of 1812. England was the main trading partner of the United States, and then England became an enemy who blockaded our coast. Today, this argument makes less sense for the United States. The government stockpiles missiles, sophisticated electronics, petroleum, and most goods needed in wartime. These stockpiles prepare the Pentagon to fight a limited war, such as the 1991 Gulf War. In an all-out nuclear war, there would be little time to worry about strategic supplies.

Employment Argument

The employment argument suggests that restricting imports increases domestic jobs in protected industries. According to this protectionist argument, the sale of an imported good comes at the expense of its domestically produced counterpart. Lower domestic output therefore leads to higher domestic unemployment than would otherwise be the case.

It is true that protectionism can increase output and save jobs in some industries at home. Ignored, however, are the higher prices paid by consumers because protectionism reduces competition between domestic goods and imported goods. In addition, there are employment reduction effects to consider. For example, suppose a strict quota is imposed on steel imported into our nation. Reduced foreign competition allows U.S. steelmakers to charge higher steel prices. As a result, prices rise and sales fall for cars and other products using steel, causing production and employment to fall in these industries. Thus, the import quota on steel may save jobs in the steel industry, but more jobs are lost in the steel-consuming industries. In short, protectionism might cause a net reduction in the nation's total employment.

Cheap Foreign Labor Argument

Another popular claim is the cheap labor argument. It goes something like this: "How can we compete with such unfair competition? Labor costs $10.00 an hour in the United States, and firms in many developing countries pay only $1.00 an hour. Without protection, U.S. wages will be driven down, and our standard of living will fall."

A major flaw in this argument is that it neglects the reason for the difference in the wage rates between countries. A U.S. worker has more education, training, capital, and access to more advanced technology. Therefore, if U.S. workers produce more output per hour than workers in another country, U.S. workers will earn higher wages without a competitive disadvantage. Suppose textile workers in the United States are paid $10 per hour. If it takes 1 hour for a U.S. worker to produce a rug, the labor cost per rug is $10. Now suppose a worker in India earns $1 per hour, but requires 20 hours to produce a rug. In this case, the labor cost per rug is $20. Although the wage rate is 10 times higher in the United States, U.S. productivity is 20 times higher because a U.S. worker can produce 20 rugs in 20 hours, while the worker in India produces only 1 rug in the same amount of time.

INTERNATIONAL ECONOMICS

World Trade Slips on Banana Peel
Applicable Concept: protectionism

Growing bananas for European markets was a multibillion-dollar bright spot for Latin America's struggling economies. In fact, about half of this region's banana exports traditionally were sold to Europe. Then in 1993 the 15-nation European Union (EU) adopted a package of quotas and tariffs aimed at cutting Europe's banana imports from Latin America. The purpose of these restrictions was to give trade preference to 66 former banana-growing colonies of European nations in Africa, the Caribbean, and the Pacific. Ignored is the fact that Latin American growers grow higher-quality bananas at half the cost of EU-favored growers because of their low labor cost and flat tropical land near port cities.[1]

In September 1997, the World Trade Organization (WTO) ruled that the EU rules covering bananas unfairly discriminated against Latin American–grown bananas. The EU modified its banana rules, but the United States contended these

changes are merely cosmetic. In response, the Clinton administration announced punitive tariffs of 100 percent to be imposed in 1999 on millions of dollars of European imports, including items ranging from cashmere sweaters and Italian handbags to sheep's milk cheese, British biscuits, and German coffee-makers. Denmark and the Netherlands are exempt from the U.S. tariffs because they were the only nations voting against the EU banana rules.

An official of the EU immediately denounced the U.S. threat of sanctions and said a case would be filed before the WTO challenging the validity of these U.S. tariffs. On the other hand, the Clinton administration is pushing the case because American companies, including Chiquita Brands International Inc. and Dole Food Co., grow their bananas mostly in Latin America.

With America's trade deficit running at a record level, U.S. trade experts argue that the United States

had little choice but to act against the EU for failing to abide by the world trade group's ruling. "There are increasing voices in the United States questioning the wisdom of international trade and globalization," said Greg Masterl of the Economic Strategy Institute, a Washington think tank. "If the WTO proves that it can't arbitrate these disputes, then the case for the WTO is harder to prove."[2]

ANALYZE THE ISSUE

Make an argument in favor of the European import restrictions. Make an argument against this plan.

---

[1]James Brooke, "Forbidden Fruit in Europe: Latin Bananas Face Hurdles," *New York Times*, April 5, 1993, p. A1.
[2]The Associated Press, "U.S. Slaps Trade Sanction on Europe," *New York Times*, December 21, 1998, http://www.nytimes.com/aponline/w/AP-Banana-Trade-War.html.

Sometimes U.S. companies move their operations to foreign countries where labor is cheaper. Such moves are not always a success. The problem is that the savings from paying foreign workers a lower wage rate are offset by lower productivity. Other disadvantages of foreign operations include greater transportation costs to U.S. markets and political instability.

Free Trade Agreements

The trend in recent years has been for nations to negotiate a reduction in trade barriers. In 1993, Congress approved the *North American Free Trade Agreement (NAFTA)*, which linked the United States to its first- and third-largest trading partners, Canada and Mexico. Under NAFTA, which became

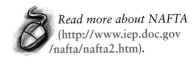

Read more about NAFTA (http://www.iep.doc.gov/nafta/nafta2.htm).

effective January 1, 1994, tariffs are being phased out over 15 years, and other impediments to trade will be eliminated among the three nations. For example, elimination of Mexican duties allows the United States to supply Mexico with more U.S. goods and to boost U.S. jobs. On the other hand, the NAFTA accord is expected to raise Mexico's wages and standard of living. As a result, the number of unauthorized Mexican immigrants to the United States should decline. The success of NAFTA remains controversial. At the conclusion of this chapter, we will use data to examine the impact of NAFTA.

The United States and other countries are considering other free trade agreements. In Europe, 15 nations have joined the *European Union (EU)*, which is dedicated to removing all trade barriers within Europe and thereby create a single European economy almost as large as the U.S. economy. In addition, a new currency, the *euro*, will replace marks, francs, lire, and other member currencies.[1]

The *Asian Pacific Economic Cooperation (APEC)* was formed in 1994 by the leaders of 18 Asian nations. This organization is based on a nonbinding agreement to reduce trade barriers between member nations.

Critics are concerned that regional free trade accords will make global agreements increasingly difficult to achieve. Some fear that trading blocs may erect new barriers, creating "Fortress North America," "Fortress Europe," and similar barriers to the worldwide reduction of trade barriers.

The Balance of Payments

Balance of payments

A bookkeeping record of all the international transactions between a country and other countries during a given period of time.

When trade occurs between the United States and other nations, many types of financial transactions are recorded in a summary called the **balance of payments.** The balance of payments is a bookkeeping record of all the international transactions between a country and other countries during a given period of time. This summary records the value of a nation's spending inflows and outflows made by individuals, firms, and governments. Exhibit 4 presents a simplified U.S. balance of payments for 1998.

Note the pluses and minuses in the table. A transaction that is a payment to the United States is entered as a positive amount. A payment by the United States to another country is entered with a minus sign. As our discussion unfolds, you will learn that the balance of payments provides much useful information.

Current Account

The first section of the balance of payments is the *current account*, which includes, as the name implies, trade in currently produced goods and services. The most widely reported and largest part of the current account is

---

[1]The EU consists of Austria, Belgium, Denmark, Finland, France, Germany, Greece, Ireland, Italy, Luxembourg, the Netherlands, Portugal, Spain, Sweden, and the United Kingdom.

EXHIBIT 4   U.S. Balance of Payments, 1998
(billions of dollars)

Type of Transaction	
Current account	
1. Merchandise exports	$+671
2. Merchandise imports	−919
Trade balance (lines 1–2)	−248
3. Service exports	+260
4. Service imports	−182
5. Investment income (net)	−22
6. Unilateral transfers (net)	−42
Current account balance (lines 1–6)	−234
Capital account	
7. U.S. capital inflow	+543
8. U.S. capital outflow	−305
Capital account balance (lines 7–8)	+238
9. Statistical discrepancy	−4
Net balance (lines 1–9)	0

Source: Survey of Current Business, http://www.bea.doc.gov/bea/dn1.htm, Table 1.

the **balance of trade.** The balance of trade is the value of a nation's merchandise imports subtracted from its merchandise exports. As shown in Exhibit 4, the United States had a *balance of trade deficit* of $248 billion in 1998. A trade deficit occurs when the value of a country's imports of goods (not services) exceeds the value of its exports of goods. When a nation has a trade deficit, it is called an *unfavorable balance of trade* because more is spent for imports than is earned from exports. Recall that net exports can have a positive (favorable) or negative (unfavorable) effect on GDP = $C + I + G + (X - M)$.

Exhibit 5 charts the annual balance of trade for the United States from 1975 through 1998. Observe that the United States experienced a *balance of trade surplus* in 1975. A trade surplus arises when the value of a country's merchandise exports is greater than the value of its merchandise imports. This is called a *favorable balance of trade* because the United States earned more from exports than it spent for imports. Since 1975, however, sizeable trade deficits have occurred. These trade deficits have attracted much attention because in part they reflect the popularity of foreign goods and the lack of competitiveness for goods "Made in U.S.A."

Balance of trade
The value of a nation's merchandise imports subtracted from its merchandise exports.

 *United States Foreign Trade Developments* (http://www.ita.doc.gov /industry/otea/usftu/usftu.html), *published by the International Trade Administration, includes a monthly analysis of U.S. trade balances.*

U.S. Balance of Trade, 1975–1998

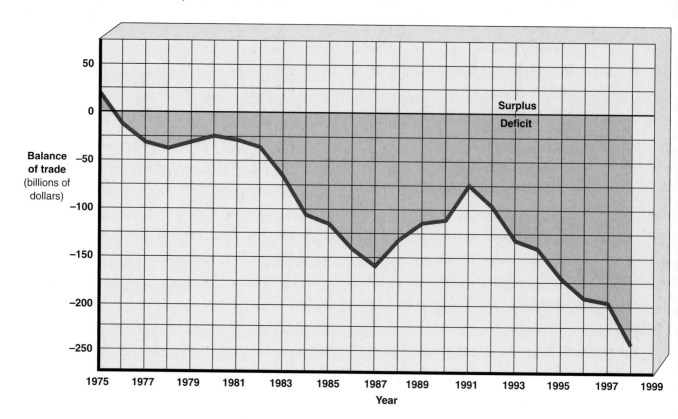

Since 1975, the United States has experienced trade deficits, in which the value of merchandise imports has exceeded the value of exports. These merchandise trade deficits attract much attention because in part they reflect the popularity of foreign goods in the United States. The Asian financial crisis contributed to the trade deficit in 1997 and 1998.

Source: Office of Trade and Economic Analysis, http://www.ita.doc.gov/industry/otea/usfth/tabcon.html, Table 1.

Because of the Asian financial crisis beginning in 1997, Asian consumers and businesses were unable to buy U.S. products, and U.S. exports fell. Moreover, Asian products were cheaper, and U.S. imports rose because of the declining value of the region's currencies compared to the dollar (discussed later in this chapter) and the price cuts from Asian businesses desperate for cash to pay their debts. This result contributed to the increase in the trade deficit in 1997 and 1998.

Lines 3–6 of the current account in Exhibit 4 list ways other than merchandise to move dollars back and forth between the United States and other countries. For example, a Japanese tourist who pays a hotel bill in Hawaii buys an export of services, which is a plus or credit to our current account (line 3). Similarly, an American visitor to foreign lands buys an import of services, which is a minus or debit to our services and therefore a minus to our current account (line 4). Income flowing back from U.S. investments abroad, such as plants, real estate, and securities, is a payment for use of the services of U.S. capital. Foreign countries also receive income flowing from the services of their capital owned in the United States. In 1998, line 5 of the table reports a net flow of −$22 billion to the United States.

Finally, we consider line 6, unilateral transfers. This category includes gifts made by our government, charitable organizations, or private individuals to other governments or private parties elsewhere in the world. For example, this item includes U.S. foreign aid to other nations. Similar unilateral transfers into the United States must be subtracted to determine the *net* unilateral transfers. Net unilateral transfers for the United States were −$42 billion in 1998.

Adding lines 1–6 gives the current account balance deficit of −$234 billion in 1998. This deficit means that foreigners were sending us more goods and services than we were sending them. Because the current account balance includes *both* goods and services, it is a broader measure than the trade balance. Since 1982, the trend in the current account balance has followed the swing into the red shown by the trade balance in Exhibit 5.

Capital Account

The second section of the balance of payments is the *capital account*, which records payment flows for financial capital, such as stocks, bonds, government securities, and real estate. For example, when Japanese investors buy U.S. Treasury bills, Rockefeller Center, or farmland in Hawaii, there is an inflow of dollars into the United States. As Exhibit 4 shows, foreigners made payments of $543 billion to our capital account (line 7). This exceeded the $305 billion outflow from the United States to purchase foreign-owned financial capital.

An important feature of the capital account is that the United States finances any deficit in its current account through this account. The capital account balance in 1998 was $238 billion. This surplus indicates that there was more foreign investment in U.S. assets than U.S. investment in foreign assets during this year.

Conclusion *A current account deficit is financed by a capital account surplus.*

The current account deficit should equal the capital account surplus, but line 9 in the table reveals that the balance of payments is not perfect. The capital account balance does not exactly offset the current account balance. Hence, a credit amount is simply recorded as a statistical discrepancy, and, therefore, the balance of payments always balances, or equals zero.

Should Everyone Keep a Balance of Payments?

Nations keep balances of payments and calculate accounts such as their merchandise trade deficit or surplus. If nations need these accounts, the 50 states should also maintain balances of payments to manage their economies. Or should they? What about cities?

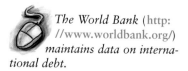

The World Bank (http://www.worldbank.org/) *maintains data on international debt.*

The International Debt of the United States

If each nation's balance of payments is always zero, what is all the talk about a U.S. balance of payments problem? The problem is with the *composition* of the balance of payments. Suppose the United States runs a $200 billion deficit in its current account. This means that the current account deficit must be financed by a net annual capital inflow in the capital account of $200 billion. That is, foreign lenders, such as banks and businesses, must purchase U.S. assets and grant loans to the United States that on balance equal $200 billion. For example, a Japanese bank could buy U.S. Treasury bonds. Recall from Exhibit 6 in the chapter on federal deficits and the national debt that this type of debt owed to lenders outside the United States is called *external debt*.

In 1984, the United States became a net debtor for the first time in about 70 years. This means that investments in the United States accumulated by foreigners—stocks, bonds, real estate, and so forth—exceeded the stock of foreign assets owned by the United States. In fact, during the decade of the 1980s, the United States moved from being the largest creditor nation in the world to being the largest debtor nation.

The concern over continuing trade deficits and the rising international debt that accompanies them is that the United States is artificially enjoying a higher standard of living. When the United States purchases more goods and services abroad than it exports, it might find itself "enjoying now and paying later." Suppose the Japanese and other foreigners decide not to make new U.S. investments and loans. In this case, the United States will be forced to eliminate its trade deficit by bringing exports and imports into balance. In fact, if other countries not only refuse to provide new capital inflows, but also decide to liquidate their investments, the United States would be forced to run a trade surplus. Stated differently, we would be forced to tighten our belts and accept a lower standard of living. A change in foreign willingness to purchase U.S. assets also affects the international value of the dollar—which is the topic to which we now turn.

Exchange Rates

Each transaction recorded in the balance of payments requires an exchange of one country's currency for that of another. Suppose you buy a Japanese car made in Japan—say, a Mazda. Mazda wants to be paid in yen and not dollars, so dollars must be traded for yen. On the other hand, suppose Pink Panther Airline Company in France purchases an airplane from McDonnell Douglas in the United States. Pink Panther has francs to pay the bill, but McDonnell Douglas wants dollars. Consequently, francs must be exchanged for dollars.

The critical question for Mazda, Pink Panther, McDonnell Douglas, and everyone involved in world trade is "What is the **exchange rate?**" The exchange rate is the number of units of one nation's currency that equals one unit of another nation's currency. For example, assume 1.81 dollars is exchangeable for 1 British pound. This means the exchange rate is 1.81 dollars = 1 pound. Alternatively, the exchange rate can be expressed as a reciprocal. Dividing 1 British pound by 1.81 dollars gives 0.552 pounds per dollar. Now suppose you are visiting England and want to buy a T-shirt with a price tag of 10 pounds. Knowing the exchange rate tells you the T-shirt costs $18.10 (10 pounds × $1.81/pound).

Conclusion *An exchange rate can be expressed as a reciprocal.*

We now turn to how an exchange rate is determined.

Supply and Demand for Foreign Exchange

The exchange rate for dollars, or any nation's currency, is determined by international forces of supply and demand. For example, consider the exchange rate of yen to dollars, shown in Exhibit 6. Like the price and the quantity of any good traded in markets, the quantity of dollars exchanged is measured on the horizontal axis, and the price per unit is measured on the vertical axis. In this case, the price per unit is the value of the U.S. dollar expressed as the number of yen per dollar.

The demand for dollars in the world currency market comes from Japanese individuals, corporations, and governments that want to buy U.S. exports. Because the Japanese buyers must pay for U.S. exports with dollars, they *demand* to exchange their yen for dollars. As expected, the demand curve for dollars or any foreign currency is downward-sloping. A decline in the number of yen per dollar means that one yen buys a larger portion of a dollar. This means U.S. goods and investment opportunities are less expensive to Japanese buyers because they must pay fewer yen for each dollar. Thus, as the yen price of dollars decreases, the quantity of dollars demanded by the Japanese to purchase Fords, stocks, land, and other U.S. products and investments increases. For example, suppose a CD recording of the hottest rock group has a $20 price tag. If the exchange rate is 200 yen to the dollar, a Japanese importer would pay 4,000 yen. If the price of dollars to Japanese buyers falls to 100 yen each, the same $20

The Pacific Exchange Rate Service (http://pacific.commerce.ubc.ca/xr/) provides a list of all the currencies of the world and the countries' exchange rate arrangements. Also, the Board of Governors of the Federal Reserve publishes current and historical exchange rates (http://www.bog.frb.fed.us/releases/H10/), and the Interactive Currency Table (http://www.xe.net/currency/table.htm), by Xenon Laboratories, provides exchange rate values and foreign exchange rate conversions.

Exchange rate
The number of units of one nation's currency that equals one unit of another nation's currency.

EXHIBIT 6

The Supply of and Demand for Dollars

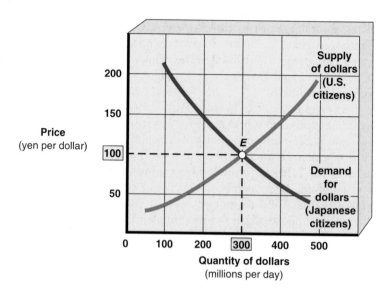

The number of Japanese yen per dollar in the foreign exchange market is determined by the demand for dollars by Japanese citizens and the supply of dollars by U.S. citizens. The equilibrium exchange rate is 100 yen per dollar, and the equilibrium quantity is $300 million per day.

CD will cost Japanese importers only 2,000 yen. This lower price causes Japanese buyers to increase their orders, which, in turn, increases the quantity of dollars demanded.

The supply curve of dollars is upward-sloping. This curve shows the amount of dollars offered for exchange at various yen prices per dollar in the world currency exchange market. Similar to the demand curve, the supply of dollars in this market flows from individuals, corporations, and governments in the United States that want to buy Mazdas, stocks, land, and other products and investments from Japan. Because U.S. citizens must pay for the Japanese goods and services in yen, they must exchange dollars for yen. An example will illustrate why the supply curve of dollars slopes upward. Suppose a Nikon camera sells for 100,000 yen in Tokyo and the exchange rate is 100 yen per dollar or .01 dollar per yen ($1/100 yen). This means the camera costs an American tourist $1,000. Now assume the exchange rate rises to 250 yen per dollar or .004 dollar per yen ($1/250 yen). The camera will now cost the American buyer only $400. Because the prices of the Nikon camera and other Japanese products fall when the number of yen per dollar rises, Americans respond by purchasing more Japanese imports, which, in turn, increases the quantity of dollars supplied.

The foreign exchange market in Exhibit 6 is in equilibrium at an exchange rate of 100 yen for $1. As you learned in Chapter 3, if the exchange rate is above equilibrium, there will be a surplus of dollars in the world currency market. Citizens of the United States are supplying more dollars than the Japanese demand, and the exchange rate falls. On the other hand, below equilibrium, there will be a shortage of dollars in the world currency market. In this case, the Japanese are demanding more dollars than Americans supply, and the exchange rate rises.

Shifts in Supply and Demand for Foreign Exchange

For most of the years between World War II and 1971, currency exchange rates were *fixed*. Exchange rates were based primarily on gold. For example, the German mark was fixed at about 25 cents. The dollar was worth $\frac{1}{35}$ of an ounce of gold, and 4 West German marks were worth $\frac{1}{35}$ of an ounce of gold. Therefore, 1 dollar equaled 4 marks, or 25 cents equaled 1 mark. In 1971, Western nations agreed to stop fixing their exchange rates and to allow their currencies to *float* according to the forces of supply and demand. Exhibit 7 illustrates that these rates can fluctuate widely. For example, in 1980, 1 dollar was worth about 230 Japanese yen. After gyrating up and down over the years, the exchange rate hit a postwar low of 94 yen per dollar in 1995.

Recall from Chapter 3 that the equilibrium price for products changes in response to shifts in the supply and demand curves. The same supply and demand analysis applies to equilibrium exchange rates for foreign currency. There are four important sources of shifts in the supply and demand curves for foreign exchange. Let's consider each in turn.

Tastes and Preferences   Exhibit 8(a) illustrates one important factor that causes the demand for foreign currencies to shift. Suppose the Japanese lose their "taste" for tobacco, U.S. government bonds, and other U.S. products and investment opportunities. This decline in the popularity of U.S. products in Japan decreases the demand for dollars at each possible exchange rate, and the demand curve shifts leftward from D_1 to D_2. This change causes the equilibrium exchange rate to fall from 150 yen to the dollar at E_1 to 100 yen to the dollar at E_2. Because the number of yen to the dollar declines, the dollar is said to *depreciate* or become *weaker*. **Depreciation** of currency is a fall in the price of one currency relative to another.

What happens to the exchange rate if the "Buy American" idea changes our tastes and the demand for Japanese imports decreases? In this case, U.S. citizens supply fewer dollars at any possible exchange rate, and the supply curve in Exhibit 8(b) shifts leftward from S_1 to S_2. As a result, the equilibrium exchange rate rises from 100 yen to the dollar at E_1 to 150 yen to the dollar at E_2. Because the number of yen per dollar rises, the dollar is said to *appreciate* or become *stronger*. **Appreciation** of currency is a rise in the price of one currency relative to another.

Depreciation of currency
A fall in the price of one currency relative to another.

Appreciation of currency
A rise in the price of one currency relative to another.

EXHIBIT 7

Changes in the Yen-per-Dollar Exchange Rate, 1980–1998

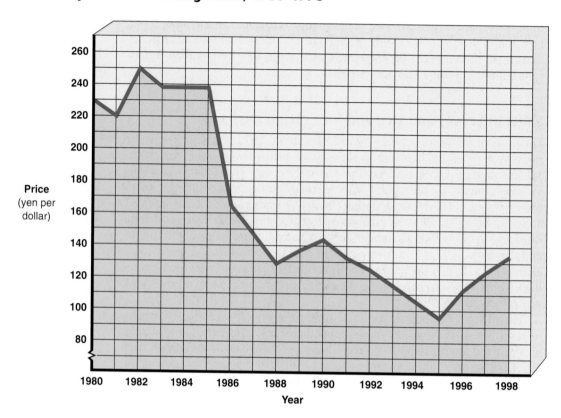

Today, most economies are on a system of flexible exchange rates. As demand and supply curves for currency change, exchange rates also change. In 1980, 1 dollar was worth about 230 Japanese yen. By 1995, the exchange rate had dropped to 94 yen per dollar.

Source: Economic Report of the President, 1999, http://www.gpo.ucop.edu/catalog/erp99 .html, Table B-106.

Relative Incomes   Assume income in the United States rises, while income in Germany remains unchanged. As a result, U.S. citizens buy more domestic products and more BMWs and other German imports. The results are a rightward shift in the supply curve for dollars and a decrease in the equilibrium exchange rate. Paradoxically, growth of U.S. income leads to the dollar depreciating or becoming weaker against the German mark.

Conclusion   The expansion in relative U.S. income causes a depreciation of the dollar.

Changes in the Supply and Demand Curves for Dollars

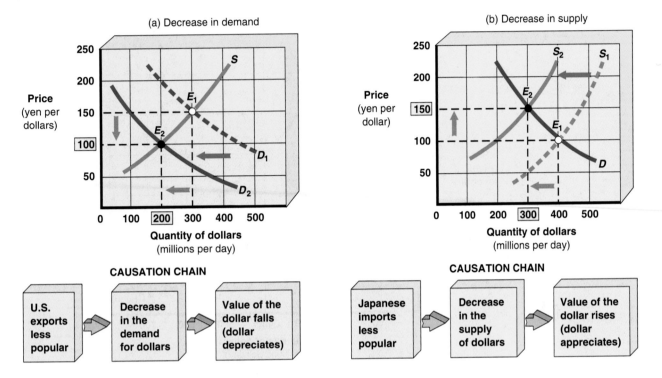

In part (a), U.S. exports become less popular in Japan. This change in tastes for U.S. products and investments decreases the demand for dollars, and the demand curve shifts leftward from D_1 to D_2. As a result, the equilibrium exchange rate falls from 150 yen to the dollar at E_1 to 100 yen to the dollar at E_2.

Part (b) assumes U.S. citizens are influenced by the "Buy American" idea. In this case, our demand for Japanese imports decreases, and U.S. citizens supply fewer dollars to the foreign currency market. The result is that the supply curve shifts leftward from S_1 to S_2 and the equilibrium exchange rate rises from 100 yen per dollar at E_1 to 150 yen per dollar at E_2.

Relative Price Levels Now we consider a more complex case, in which a change in a factor causes a change in both the supply and the demand curves for dollars. Assume the foreign exchange rate begins in equilibrium at 100 yen per dollar, as shown at point E_1 in Exhibit 9. Now assume the price level increases in Japan, but remains constant in the United States. The Japanese therefore want to buy more U.S. exports because they have become cheaper relative to Japanese products. This willingness of the

EXHIBIT 9

The Impact of Relative Price Level Changes on Exchange Rates

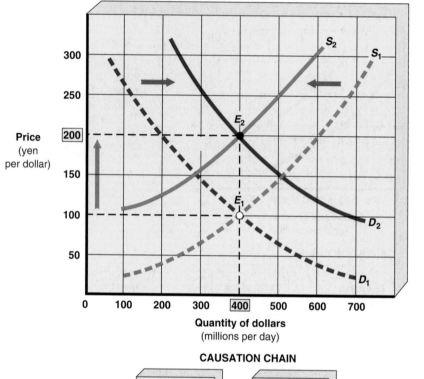

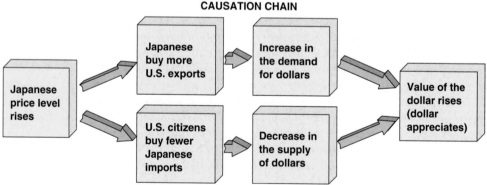

CAUSATION CHAIN

Begin at E_1, *with the exchange rate equal to 100 yen per dollar. Assume prices rise in Japan relative to those in the United States. As a result, the demand for dollars increases, and the supply of dollars decreases. The new equilibrium is at* E_2 *when the dollar appreciates (rises in value) to 200 yen per dollar.*

Japanese to buy U.S. goods and services shifts the demand curve for dollars rightward from D_1 to D_2. In addition, U.S. products are cheaper for U.S. citizens compared to Japanese imports. As a result, the willingness to import from Japan is reduced at each exchange rate, which means the supply curve of dollars decreases from S_1 to S_2. The result of the shifts in both the demand and the supply curves for dollars is to establish a new equilibrium at point E_2, and the exchange rate reaches 200 yen per dollar.

Conclusion *A rise in the Japanese relative price level causes the dollar to appreciate.*

Relative Real Interest Rates   Changes in relative real (inflation-adjusted) interest rates can have an important effect on the exchange rate. Suppose real interest rates in the United States rise, while those in France remain constant. To take advantage of more attractive yields, French investors buy an increased amount of bonds and other interest-bearing securities issued by private and government borrowers in the United States. This change increases the demand for dollars, which increases the equilibrium exchange rate of francs to the dollar, causing the dollar to appreciate (or the franc to depreciate).

There can also be an effect on the supply curve for dollars. When real interest rates rise in the United States, our citizens purchase fewer French securities. Hence, they offer fewer dollars at each and every exchange rate, and the supply curve for dollars shifts leftward. As a result, the equilibrium exchange rate increases, and the dollar appreciates from changes in both the demand for and the supply of dollars.

The Impact of Exchange Rate Fluctuations

Now it is time to stop a minute, take a breath, and draw some important conclusions. As you have just learned, exchange rates between most major currencies are flexible. Instead of being pegged to gold or another fixed standard, their value is determined by the laws of supply and demand. Consequently, shifts in supply and demand create a weaker or a stronger dollar. But it should be noted that exchange rates do not fluctuate with total freedom. Governments will often buy and sell currencies to prevent wide swings in exchange rates.

In summary, the strength or weakness of any nation's currency has a profound impact on its economy.

Conclusion *When the dollar is weak or depreciates, U.S. goods and services cost foreign consumers less, so they will buy more U.S. exports. At the same time, a weak dollar means foreign goods and services cost U.S. consumers more, so they will buy fewer imports.*

A weak dollar is therefore a "mixed blessing." A weak dollar ironically makes U.S. producers happy because they can sell their less expensive exports to foreign buyers. As export sales rise, jobs are created in the

INTERNATIONAL ECONOMICS

Return to the Gold Standard?

Applicable Concept: exchange rates

From the 1870s until the 1930s, most industrial countries were on the gold standard. The gold standard served as an international monetary system in which currencies were defined in terms of gold. Under the gold standard, a nation with a balance of payments deficit was required to ship gold to other nations to finance the deficit. Hence, a large excess of imports over exports meant a corresponding outflow of gold from a nation. As a result, that nation's money supply decreased, which, in turn, reduced the aggregate demand for goods and services. Lower domestic demand led to falling prices, lower production, and fewer jobs. A nation with a balance of payments surplus, on the other hand, would experience an inflow

of gold and the opposite effects. In this case, the nation's money supply increased, and its aggregate demand for goods and services rose. Higher aggregate spending, in turn, boosted employment and the price level. In short, the gold standard meant that governments could not control their money supplies and thereby conduct monetary policy.

The gold standard worked fairly well as a fixed exchange rate

system so long as nations did not face sudden or severe swings in flows from their stocks of gold. The Great Depression marked the beginning of the end of the gold standard. Nations faced with trade deficits and high unemployment began going off the gold standard, rather than contract their money supplies by following the rules of the gold standard.

Once the Allies felt certain they would win World War II, the finance ministers of Western nations met in 1944 at Bretton Woods, New Hampshire, to establish a new international monetary system. The new system was based on fixed exchange rates and an international central bank called the International Monetary Fund (IMF). The IMF made loans to countries faced with

United States. On the other hand, a weak dollar makes foreign producers unhappy because the prices of Japanese cars, French wine, and Italian shoes are higher. As U.S. imports fall, jobs in foreign countries are lost.

A strong dollar is also a "mixed blessing."

Conclusion *When the dollar is strong or appreciates, U.S. goods and services cost foreign consumers more, so they will buy fewer U.S. exports. At the same time, a strong dollar means foreign goods and services cost U.S. consumers less, so they will buy more foreign imports.*

A strong dollar therefore makes our major trading partners happy because the prices of Japanese cars, French wine, and Italian shoes are lower. A strong dollar, contrary to the implication of the term, makes U.S.

short-term balance of payments problems. Under this system, nations were expected to maintain fixed exchange rates within a narrow range. In the 1960s and early 1970s, the Bretton Woods system became strained as conditions changed. In the 1960s, inflation rates in the United States rose relative to those in other countries, causing U.S. exports to become more expensive and U.S. imports to become less expensive. This situation increased the supply of dollars abroad and caused an increasing surplus of dollars, thus putting downward pressure on the exchange rate. Monetary authorities in the United States worried that central banks would demand gold for their dollars, the U.S. gold stock would diminish sharply, and the declining money supply would adversely affect the economy.

Something had to give, and it did. In August 1971, President Richard Nixon announced that the United States would no longer honor its obligation to sell gold at $35 an ounce. By 1973, the gold standard was dead, and most of our trading partners were letting the forces of supply and demand determine exchange rates.

Today, there are those who advocate returning to the gold standard. These gold buffs do not trust the government to control the money supply without the discipline of a gold standard. They argue that if governments have the freedom to print money, political pressures will sooner or later cause them to increase the money supply too much and let inflation rage.

One argument against the gold standard is that no one can control the supply of gold. Big gold discoveries can cause inflation and have done so in the past. On the other hand, slow growth in mining gold can lead to slow economic growth and a loss of jobs. Governments therefore are unlikely to return to the gold standard because it would mean turning monetary policy over to uncontrollable swings in the stock of gold.

ANALYZE THE ISSUE

Return to Exhibit 6, and assume the equilibrium exchange is 150 yen per dollar and the equilibrium quantity is 300 million dollars. Redraw this figure, and place a horizontal line through the equilibrium exchange rate to represent a fixed exchange rate. Now use this figure to explain why a country would abandon the gold standard.

producers unhappy because their more expensive exports and related jobs decline. Conversely, a strong dollar makes foreign producers abroad happy because the prices of their goods and services are lower, causing U.S. imports to rise.

Finally, we return to the discussion earlier in this chapter of NAFTA in order to illustrate the impact of this free trade agreement and the effect of a strong dollar. Recall that in January 1994 NAFTA began a 15-year gradual phase-out of tariffs and other trade barriers. Exhibit 10 provides trade data for the United States and Mexico for the years surrounding the NAFTA agreement. As shown in the exhibit, both exports and imports of goods increased sharply. On the other hand, a small trade surplus of $2 billion in 1993 has turned into a huge trade deficit of $17 billion in 1998.

EXHIBIT 10   U.S. Trade Balances with Mexico, 1993–1998

Year	U.S. Exports to Mexico (billions)	U.S. Imports from Mexico (billions)	Exchange Rate: Pesos per Dollar	U.S. Trade Surplus (+) or Deficit (−) (billions)
1993	$42	$40	3.12	$ +2
1994	51	50	3.39	+1
1995	46	62	6.45	−16
1996	57	74	7.60	−16
1997	71	87	7.92	−17
1998	79	95	9.15	−16

Sources: Office of Trade and Economic Analysis, http://www.ita.doc.gov/industry/otea/usfth/tabcon.html, Tables 6, 7; and Federal Reserve, http://www.federalreserve.gov/releases/G5A/.

Before blaming this trade deficit entirely on NAFTA, you must note that the exchange rate rose from 3.12 pesos per dollar to 9.15. Prior to the peso's devaluation in 1995, Mexicans selling more goods to U.S. markets meant they earned more money to spend on goods from U.S. factories. However, the strong dollar put the price of U.S. goods out of reach for many Mexican consumers, so U.S. exports to Mexico dropped. At the same time, Mexican goods became less expensive for U.S. consumers, and U.S. imports from Mexico rose.

KEY CONCEPTS

Comparative advantage	Protectionism	Quota	Exchange rate
Absolute advantage	Embargo	Balance of payments	Depreciation of currency
Free trade	Tariff	Balance of trade	Appreciation of currency

SUMMARY

★ **Comparative advantage** is a principle that allows nations to gain from trade. Comparative advantage means that each nation *specializes* in a product for which its opportunity cost is lower in terms of the production of another product and then nations trade. When nations follow this principle, they gain. The reason is that world output increases and each nation ends up with a higher standard of living by consuming more goods and services than possible without specialization and trade.

Comparative advantage

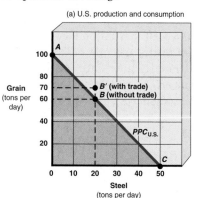

(a) U.S. production and consumption

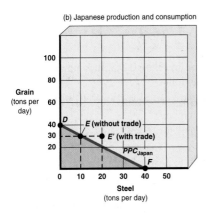

(b) Japanese production and consumption

- **Free trade** benefits a nation as a whole, but individuals may lose jobs and incomes from the competition from foreign goods and services.

- **Protectionism** is a government's use of embargoes, tariffs, quotas, and other methods to impose barriers intended to both reduce imports and protect particular domestic industries. **Embargoes** prohibit the import or export of particular goods. **Tariffs** discourage imports by making them more expensive. **Quotas** limit the quantity of imports or exports of certain goods. These trade barriers often result primarily from domestic groups that exert political pressure to gain from these barriers.

- The **balance of payments** is a summary bookkeeping record of all the international transactions a country makes during a year. It is divided into different accounts, including the *current account*, the *capital account*, and the *statistical discrepancy*. The current account summarizes all transactions in currently produced goods and services. The overall balance of payments is always zero after an adjustment for the statistical discrepancy.

★ The **balance of trade** measures only goods (not services) that a nation exports and imports. A balance of trade can be in deficit or in surplus. The balance of trade is the most widely reported and largest part of the current account. Since 1975, the United States has experienced balance of trade deficits.

Balance of trade

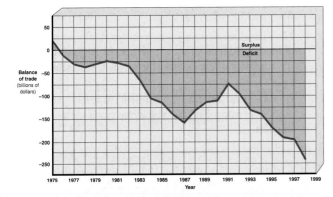

★ An **exchange rate** is the price of one nation's currency in terms of another nation's currency. Foreigners who wish to purchase U.S. goods, services, and financial assets demand dollars. The supply of dollars reflects the desire of U.S. citizens to purchase foreign goods, services, and financial assets. The intersection of the supply and demand curves for dollars determines the number of units of a foreign currency per dollar.

Exchange rate

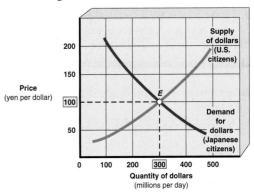

- **Shifts in supply and demand for foreign exchange** result from changes in such factors as tastes, relative price levels, relative real interest rates, and relative income levels.

- **Depreciation of currency** occurs when one currency becomes worth fewer units of another currency. If a currency depreciates, it becomes weaker. Depreciation of a nation's currency increases its exports and decreases its imports.

- **Appreciation of currency** occurs when one currency becomes worth more units of another currency. If a currency appreciates, it becomes stronger. Appreciation of a nation's currency decreases its exports and increases its imports.

SUMMARY OF CONCLUSION STATEMENTS

■ When countries specialize, the total world output increases, and, therefore, the potential for greater total world consumption also increases.

■ International trade allows a country to consume a combination of goods that exceeds its production possibilities curve.

■ Comparative advantage refers to the relative opportunity costs between countries of producing the same goods. World output and consumption are maximized when each country specializes in producing and trading goods for which it has a comparative advantage.

■ A current account deficit is financed by a capital account surplus.

■ An exchange rate can be expressed as a reciprocal.

■ The expansion in relative U.S. income causes a depreciation of the dollar.

■ A rise in the Japanese relative price level causes the dollar to appreciate.

■ When the dollar is weak or depreciates, U.S. goods and services cost foreign consumers less, so they will buy more U.S. exports. At the same time, a weak dollar means foreign goods and services cost U.S. consumers more, so they will buy fewer imports.

■ When the dollar is strong or appreciates, U.S. goods and services cost foreign consumers more, so they will buy fewer U.S. exports. At the same time, a strong dollar means foreign goods and services cost U.S. consumers less, so they will buy more foreign imports.

STUDY QUESTIONS AND PROBLEMS

1. The countries of Alpha and Beta produce diamonds and pearls. The production possibilities schedule below describes their potential output in tons per year.

Points on Production Possibilities Curve	Alpha		Beta	
	Diamonds	Pearls	Diamonds	Pearls
A	150	0	90	0
B	100	25	60	60
C	50	50	30	120
D	0	75	0	180

Using the data in the table, answer the following questions:

a. What is the opportunity cost of diamonds for each country?

b. What is the opportunity cost of pearls for each country?

c. In which good does Alpha have a comparative advantage?

d. In which good does Beta have a comparative advantage?

e. Suppose Alpha is producing and consuming at point *B* on its production possibilities curve and Beta is producing and consuming at point *C* on its production possibilities curve. Use a table such as Exhibit 3 to explain why both nations would benefit if they specialize.

f. Draw a graph, and use it to explain how Alpha and Beta benefit if they specialize and Alpha agrees to trade 50 tons of diamonds to Beta and Alpha receives 50 tons of pearls in exchange.

2. Bill can paint either two walls or one window frame in one hour. In the same time, Frank can paint either three walls or two window frames. To minimize the time spent painting, who should specialize in painting walls, and who should specialize in painting window frames?

3. Consider this statement: "The principles of specialization and trade according to comparative advantage among nations also apply to states in the United States." Do you agree or disagree? Explain.

4. Would there be any advantage to the U.S. government from using tariffs or quotas to restrict imports?

5. Suppose the United States passed a law that stated that we would refuse to purchase imports from any country that imposed any trade restrictions on our exports. Who would benefit and who would lose from such retaliation?

6. Now consider question 5 in terms of the impact on domestic producers that export goods. Does this policy adversely affect domestic producers that export goods?

7. Consider this statement: "Unrestricted foreign trade costs domestic jobs." Do you agree or disagree? Explain.

8. Do you support a constitutional amendment to prohibit the federal government from imposing any trade barriers, such as tariffs and quotas, except in case of war or national emergency? Why?

9. Discuss this statement: "Because each nation's balance of payments equals zero, it follows that there is actually no significance to a balance of payments deficit or surplus."

10. For each of the following situations, indicate the direction of the shift in the supply or the demand curve for dollars, the factor causing the change, and the resulting movement of the equilibrium exchange rate for the dollar in terms of foreign currency.
    a. GM, Ford, and Chrysler cars become more popular overseas.
    b. The United States experiences a recession, while other nations enjoy economic growth.
    c. Inflation rates accelerate in the United States, while inflation rates remain constant in other nations.
    d. Real interest rates in the United States rise, while real interest rates abroad remain constant.

e. The Japanese put quotas and high tariffs on all imports from the United States.
f. Tourism from the United States increases sharply because of a fare war among airlines.

11. The following table summarizes the supply and the demand for francs:

	U.S. Dollars per Franc				
	$.05	**$.10**	**$.15**	**$.20**	**$.25**
Quantity demanded (per day)	500	400	300	200	100
Quantity supplied (per day)	100	200	300	400	500

Using the above table:
a. Graph the supply and demand curves for francs.
b. Determine the equilibrium exchange rate.
c. Determine what the effect of a fixed exchange rate at $.10 per franc would be.

ONLINE EXERCISES

Exercise 1

Visit the Center for the Study of Western Hemispheric Trade (CSWHT) Tracking U.S. Trade Index (http://www.lanic.utexas.edu/cswht/tradeindex/). What change has occurred between the United States and its NAFTA trading partners since November 1995?

Exercise 2

Visit the Office of Trade and Economic Analysis (http://www.ita.doc.gov/tradestats/), and follow these steps:

1. Select U.S. Foreign Trade Highlights. Under U.S. Aggregate Foreign Trade Data, 1997 & Prior Years, choose Tables 9, 12, and 13. Which are the three top total U.S. trading partners? For the latest year reported, which country has the greatest trade surplus and trade deficit with the United States?

2. Click the Back button to return to the original site. Select U.S. Industry & Trade Outlook. Under Historical Tables, click on *tables*. Under Outlook Trends Table, choose Computers & Peripherals, and compare U.S. imports to exports of computers.

3. Click the Back button to return to the original site, and select State Export Data. Under Export Markets For Each State Ranked by 1997 Export Value, choose your state. What are the top three national export markets for your state? What has happened to your state's exports to these countries?

Exercise 3

Visit Economic Chart Dispenser (http://bos.business.uab.edu/charts/popular.shtm). Select Exchange Rate: Japanese Yen to one U.S. Dollar, and graph for 1990 to the present. What could have caused this change?

Exercise 4

Visit the Universal Currency Converter (http://www.xe.net/currency/). How much is the U.S. dollar currently worth in terms of the U.K. pound? What about the Japanese yen?

CHECKPOINT ANSWERS

Do Nations with an Advantage Always Trade?

In the United States, the opportunity cost of producing 1 calculator is 100 towels. In Italy, the opportunity cost of producing 1 calculator is 100 towels. If you said, because the opportunity cost is the same for each nation, specialization and trade would *not* boost total output and therefore Italy would not trade these products, **YOU ARE CORRECT.**

Should Everyone Keep a Balance of Payments?

The principal purpose of the balance of payments is to keep track of payments of national currencies. Because states and cities within the same nation use the same national currency, payments for goods and services traded between these parties do not represent a loss (outflow) or gain (inflow). If you said only nations need to use the balance of payments to account for flows of foreign currency across national boundaries, **YOU ARE CORRECT.**

PRACTICE QUIZ

For a visual explanation of the correct answers, visit the tutorial at http://tucker.swcollege.com.

1. With trade, the production possibilities for two nations lie
   a. outside their consumption possibilities.
   b. inside their consumption possibilities.
   c. at a point equal to the world production possibilities curve.
   d. none of the above.

2. Free trade theory suggests that when trade takes place,
   a. both nations will be worse off.
   b. one nation must gain at the other nation's expense.
   c. both nations will be better off.
   d. one nation will gain and the other nation will be neither better nor worse off.

3. Which of the following is *true* when two countries specialize according to their comparative advantage?
   a. It is possible to increase their total output of all goods.
   b. It is possible to increase their total output of some goods only if both countries are industrialized.
   c. One country is likely to gain from trade, while the other loses.
   d. None of the above is true.

4. According to the theory of comparative advantage, a country should produce and
   a. import goods in which it has an absolute advantage.
   b. export goods in which it has an absolute advantage.
   c. import goods in which it has a comparative advantage.
   d. export goods in which it has a comparative advantage.

EXHIBIT 11
Potatoes and Wheat Output (tons per hour)

Country	Potatoes	Wheat
United States	1	3
Ireland	1	2

5. In Exhibit 11, which country has the comparative advantage in the production of potatoes?
   a. The United States because it requires fewer resources to produce potatoes
   b. The United States because it has the lower opportunity cost of potatoes
   c. Ireland because it requires fewer resources to produce potatoes
   d. Ireland because it has the lower opportunity cost of potatoes

6. In Exhibit 11, the opportunity cost of wheat is
   a. ⅓ ton of potatoes in the United States and ½ ton of potatoes in Ireland.
   b. 2 tons of potatoes in the United States and 1½ tons of potatoes in Ireland.
   c. 8 tons of potatoes in the United States and 4 tons of potatoes in Ireland.
   d. ½ ton of potatoes in the United States and ⅔ ton of potatoes in Ireland.

7. In Exhibit 11, the opportunity cost of potatoes is
   a. ½ ton of wheat in the United States and ⅔ ton of wheat in Ireland.
   b. 2 tons of wheat in the United States and 1½ tons of wheat in Ireland.
   c. 16 tons of wheat in the United States and 6 tons of wheat in Ireland.
   d. 3 tons of wheat in the United States and 2 tons of wheat in Ireland.

8. If the countries in Exhibit 11 follow the principle of comparative advantage, the United States should
   a. buy all of its potatoes from Ireland.
   b. buy all of its wheat from Ireland.
   c. buy all of its potatoes and wheat from Ireland.
   d. produce both potatoes and wheat and not trade with Ireland.

9. A tariff increases
   a. the quantity of imports.
   b. the ability of foreign goods to compete with domestic goods.
   c. the prices of imports to domestic buyers.
   d. all of the above.

10. The infant industry argument for protectionism is based on which of the following views?
    a. Foreign buyers will absorb all of the output of domestic producers in a new industry.
    b. The growth of an industry that is new to a nation will be too rapid unless trade restrictions are imposed.
    c. Firms in a newly developing domestic industry will have difficulty growing if they face strong competition from established foreign firms.
    d. It is based on none of the above.

11. The figure that results when merchandise imports are subtracted from merchandise exports is
    a. the capital account balance.
    b. the balance of trade.
    c. the current account balance.
    d. always less than zero.

12. Which of the following international accounts records payments for exports and imports of goods, military transactions, foreign travel, investment income, and foreign gifts?
    a. The capital account
    b. The merchandise account
    c. The current account
    d. The official reserve account

13. Which of the following international accounts records the purchase and sale of financial assets and real estate between the United States and other nations?
    a. The balance of trade account
    b. The current account
    c. The capital account
    d. The balance of payments account

14. If a Japanese radio priced at 2,000 yen can be purchased for $10, the exchange rate is
    a. 200 yen per dollar.
    b. 20 yen per dollar.
    c. 20 dollars per yen.
    d. none of the above.

15. The United States
    a. was on a fixed exchange rate system prior to late 1971, but now is on a flexible exchange rate system.
    b. has been on a fixed exchange rate system since 1945.
    c. has been on a flexible exchange rate system since 1945.
    d. was on a flexible exchange rate system prior to late 1983, but now is on a fixed exchange rate system.

16. Suppose the exchange rate changes so that fewer Japanese yen are required to buy a dollar. We would conclude that
    a. the Japanese yen has depreciated in value.
    b. U.S. citizens will buy fewer Japanese imports.
    c. Japanese will demand fewer U.S. exports.
    d. none of the above will occur.

17. Which of the following would cause a decrease in the demand for French francs by those holding U.S. dollars?
    a. Inflation in France, but not in the United States
    b. Inflation in the United States, but not in France
    c. An increase in the real rate of interest on investments in France above the real rate of interest on investments in the United States
    d. None of the above

18. An increase in the equilibrium price of a nation's money could be caused by a (an)
    a. decrease in the supply of the money.
    b. decrease in the demand for the money.
    c. increase in the supply of the money.
    d. increase in the demand for the money.

19. If the dollar appreciates (becomes stronger), this causes
    a. the relative price of U.S. goods to increase for foreigners.
    b. the relative price of foreign goods to decrease for Americans.
    c. U.S. exports to fall and U.S. imports to rise.
    d. a balance of trade deficit for the United States.
    e. all of the above to occur.

20. Which of the following would cause the U.S. dollar to depreciate against the Japanese yen?
    a. Greater popularity of U.S. exports in Japan
    b. A higher price level in Japan
    c. Higher real interest rates in the United States
    d. Higher incomes in the United States

CHAPTER SIXTEEN

Comparative Economic Systems

> The inherent vice of capitalism is the unequal sharing of blessings. The inherent virtue of communism is the equal sharing of miseries.
>
> —*Winston Churchill*

The rapid emergence of the market system in Russia, China, and other communist countries continues to fascinate us. Newspapers and periodicals continue reporting the astonishing news that leaders in countries that used to be devoted followers of Marxism ideology now say they believe that capitalism, private property, and profit are ideas superior to the communist system. McDonald's joint venture in Moscow personifies this transformation toward a market system and the failure of communism. In 1996, President Boris Yeltsin swept to a strong victory and a second term as Russians rejected his communist opponent's call to roll back economic reforms. Today, Russia and other countries continue to experience economic crisis during their restructuring, but the commitment to free-market reforms remains. What caused this astonishing turn of events?

To understand how the pieces of the global economic puzzle fit together, this chapter begins with a discussion of the three basic types of economies. Then you will examine the pros and cons of the "isms" of capitalism, socialism, and communism. Here you will explore the worldwide clash between the ideas of Adam Smith and Karl Marx and study their current influence on economic systems. Finally, you will examine economic reforms in Cuba, Russia, and China. The chapter concludes with a look at the Japanese "malaise."

In this chapter, you will learn to solve these economics puzzles:

■ Why did drivers in the former Soviet Union remove the windshield wipers and side mirrors whenever they parked their cars?

■ What did Adam Smith mean when he said that an "invisible hand" promotes the public interest?

■ If the Soviets were foolish to run their economy on five-year plans, why do universities, businesses, and governments in a capitalistic economy plan?

Basic Types of Economic Systems

An **economic system** consists of the organizations and methods used to determine what goods and services are produced, how they are produced, and for whom they are produced. As explained earlier in Chapter 2, scarcity forces each economic system to decide what combination of goods to produce, how to produce such goods, and who gets the output once produced. The decision-making process involves interaction among many aspects of a nation's culture, such as its laws, form of government, ethics, religions, and customs. Economist Robert L. Heilbroner established a simple way to look at the basic methods that society can employ. Each economic system can be classified into one of three basic types: (1) *traditional*, (2) *command*, and (3) *market*.

The Traditional Economy

Why does England have a king or queen? Tradition answers the question. Historically, the **traditional economy** has been a common system for making economic decisions. The traditional economy is a system that answers the What, How, and For Whom questions the way they always have been answered. People in this type of society learn that copying the previous generation allows one to feel accepted. Anyone who changes ways of doing things asks for trouble from others. This is because people in such a society believe that what was good yesterday, and years ago, must still be a good idea today.

   Traditional systems operate in primitive tribes, the Ainu of Japan, the native people of Brazil's rain forest, and the Amish of Pennsylvania. In these societies, the way past generations decided what crops are planted, how they are harvested, and to whom they are distributed remains unchanged today. People perform their jobs in the manner established by their ancestors. The Amish are well known for rejecting tractors and using horsedrawn plows. Interestingly, the Amish reject Social Security because their society voluntarily redistributes wealth to members who are needy.

The Traditional Economy's Strengths and Weaknesses

The benefit of the traditional approach is that there is less friction among members because relatively little is disputed. Consequently, people in this system may cooperate more freely with one another. In today's industrial world, the Amish and other traditional economies appear very satisfied with their relatively uncomplicated systems. However, critics argue that the traditional system restricts individual initiative and therefore does not lead to the output of advanced goods and services, new technology, and economic growth.

The Command Economy

In a **command economy**, a dictator or group of central planners makes economic decisions for society. The command economy is a system that answers the What, How, and For Whom questions by central authority. The former Soviet Union in the past and Cuba today are nations with com-

Economic system
The organizations and methods used to determine what goods and services are produced, how they are produced, and for whom they are produced.

Traditional economy
A system that answers the What, How, and For Whom questions the way they always have been answered.

Command economy
A system that answers the What, How, and For Whom questions by central authority.

mand economies using national economic plans implemented through powerful government committees. Politically selected committees decide on everything, including the number, color, size, quality, and price of autos, brooms, sweaters, and tanks. The state owns the factors of production and dictates answers to the three basic economic questions. The authorities might decide to produce modern weapons instead of schools, or they might decide to devote resources to building huge monuments like the pyramids, built by the rulers of ancient Egypt to honor their dead kings and queens.

In the old Soviet economy, for example, the three basic economic questions were answered by a central planning agency called the *Gosplan*. The Gosplan set production quotas and prices for farms, factories, mines, housing construction, medical care, and other producing units. What should the cows be fed? If it is hay, how much land can be used to grow it? How much milk should the cows give? How many people will be dairy farmers? What wages should a dairy farmer earn? Should milk be given to everyone, to a few, or to any persons chosen by the leaders? The Gosplan tried to make all these choices. Today, in the Commonwealth of Independent States, the Gosplan is a relic of the discarded Soviet command system.

We can represent the command economy by the pyramid shown in Exhibit 1. At the top of the pyramid is a supremely powerful group of central planners, such as the old Soviet Gosplan. That agency established production targets and prices for goods and services. Then the Gosplan transmitted this information to a second layer of specialized state planning organizations. Among these specialized units, purchases of raw materials were made by one agency, fashion trends directed by another official organization, prices set by another body, employment and wages set by yet another government bureaucracy, and so on.

Production objectives were transmitted from the upper authority layers to the individual producing units, represented by the third layer of the pyramid in Exhibit 1. These producers supplied goods and services to the consumers, as commanded by the central authorities. The bottom portion of the pyramid illustrates the distribution, according to the master plan, of output for consuming units of individuals and households.

The Command Economy's Strengths and Weaknesses

Believe it or not, the command system can be defended. Proponents argue that economic change occurs much faster than in a traditional economy. This is one reason those dissatisfied with a traditional society might advocate establishment of a command system. The central authorities can ignore custom and order new ways of doing things. Another reason for adopting a command economy is the controversial belief that the government will provide economic security and equity. It is alleged that central authorities ensure that everyone is provided food, clothing, shelter, and medical care regardless of their ability to contribute to society.

The absolute power of central authorities to make right decisions is also the power to be absolutely wrong. Often the planners do not accurately set production goals, and either shortages or surpluses of goods and services are the result. For example, at one point the planners miscalculated and produced too few windshield wipers and side mirrors for Soviet cars. Faced

EXHIBIT 1

The Command Economy Pyramid

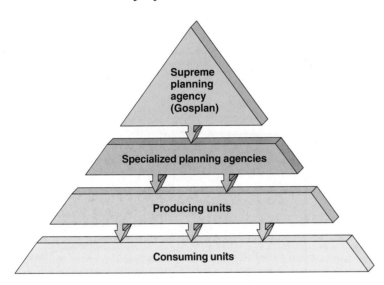

The principal feature of a command economy is the central planning board at the top, which transmits economic decisions down to the various producing and consuming units below. This process begins with an overall plan from a supreme planning board, such as the old Soviet Gosplan. The Gosplan established production targets and was the ultimate authority over a layer of specialized planning agencies, which authorized capital expansion, raw material purchases, prices, wages, and any other production decisions for individual producing units. Finally, the factories, farms, mines, and other producers distributed the specified output to consumers according to the approved master plan.

with shortages of these parts, Soviet drivers removed windshield wipers and side mirrors whenever they parked their cars to prevent theft. On the other hand, the Gosplan allocated some collective farms so much fertilizer that these farms could not use it all. To receive the same amount of fertilizer again the next year, farmers simply burned the excess fertilizer. As a result of such decision-making errors, people waited in long lines or stole goods. How does any decision-making group really know how many windshield wipers to produce each year and how much workers making them should earn?

Because profit is not the motive of producers in a command economy, quality and variety of goods also suffer. If the Gosplan ordered a state enterprise to produce 400,000 side mirrors for cars, for example, there was little incentive to make the extra effort required to create a quality product

EXHIBIT 2

Central Planners Fixing Prices

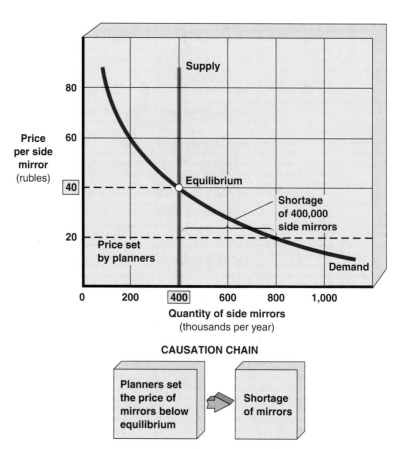

CAUSATION CHAIN

Planners set the price of mirrors below equilibrium ⟹ Shortage of mirrors

The central planners' goal is to keep prices low, so they set the price of a side mirror for a car at 20 rubles, which is below the market-determined equilibrium price of 40 rubles. At the set price, however, the quantity demanded is 800,000 side mirrors per year, and the quantity supplied is 400,000 per year. Thus, the shortage at the government-established price is 400,000 side mirrors per year. As a result, long lines form to buy side mirrors, and black markets appear.

in a variety of styles. The easiest way to meet the goal was to produce a low-quality product in one style regardless of consumer demand.

Exhibit 2 illustrates how the pricing policy of central planners causes shortages. The demand curve for side mirrors conforms to the law of demand. At lower prices in rubles, the quantity demanded increases. The supply curve is fixed at 400,000 side mirrors because it is set by the central planners and is therefore unresponsive to price variations.

Suppose one of the principal goals of the command economy is to keep the price low. To reach this goal, the central planners set the price of side mirrors at 20 rubles, which is below the equilibrium price of 40 rubles. At 20 rubles, more people can afford a side mirror compared to the equilibrium price that would be set by the marketplace. The consequence of this price set by the planners is a shortage. The quantity demanded at 20 rubles is 800,000 side mirrors, and the quantity supplied is only 400,000 mirrors. Thus, the model explains why side mirrors disappeared from stores long before many who were willing to buy them could do so.

The same graphical analysis applies to centrally planned rental prices for apartments. The central planners in the former Soviet Union set rents below the equilibrium rental prices for apartments. As the model predicts, low rents resulted in a shortage of housing. Meanwhile, the planners promised that improvements in housing would come in time. This pricing strategy is used today in China. Rent on a two-room apartment is about $100 a year, and a visit to the doctor costs less than 25 cents.

Conclusion *When central planners set prices below equilibrium for goods and services, they create shortages, which mean long lines, empty shelves, and black markets.*[1]

The Market Economy and the Ideas of Adam Smith

In a **market economy,** neither customs nor a single person or group of central planners answers the three basic economic questions facing society. The market economy is an economic system that answers the What, How, and For Whom questions using prices determined by the interaction of the forces of supply and demand. One of the first people to explain the power of a market economy was the Scottish economist Adam Smith. In the same year that the American colonies declared their political independence, Smith's *An Inquiry into the Nature and Causes of the Wealth of Nations* presented the blueprint for employing markets to improve economic performance. Professor Smith spent over 10 years observing the real world and writing about how nations could best improve their material well-being. He concluded that the answer was to use free markets because this mechanism provides the incentive for everyone to follow his or her *self-interest.*

Adam Smith is the *father of modern economics.* He intended to write a book that would influence popular opinion, and unlike many famous works, his book was an immediate success. The basic philosophy of his book is "the best government is the least government." This belief is known as *laissez faire,* a French expression meaning "allow to act." The consensus interpretation is that the role of the government is limited to providing national defense, providing education, maintaining infrastructure, enforcing contracts, and little else. This viewpoint includes the idea of free

Market economy
An economic system that answers the What, How, and For Whom questions using prices determined by the interaction of the forces of supply and demand.

For a short and well-written discussion of the life and works of Adam Smith, visit http://www.blupete .com/Literature/Biographies /Philosophy/Smith.htm.

---

[1]Recall from Exhibit 4 of Chapter 4 that a black market is an illegal market that emerges when a price ceiling is imposed in a free market.

trade among nations and rejects the idea that nations should impose trade barriers.

During Smith's lifetime, European nations such as England, France, and Spain intervened to control economic activities. In *The Wealth of Nations*, Smith argued that economic freedoms are "natural rights" necessary for the dignity of mankind. Smith believed that free competition among people who followed their self-interest would best benefit society because markets free of government interference produce the greatest output of goods and services possible. Smith was an advocate of free international trade and asked the question implied in the full title of his book: Why are some nations richer than others? He explained that the source of any nation's wealth is not really the amount of gold or silver it owns. This was an idea popular during Smith's time called *mercantilism*. Instead, he argued that it is the ability of people to produce products and trade in free markets that creates a nation's wealth.

The importance of a market is that it harnesses the power of self-interest to answer the What, How, and For Whom questions. Without central planning, markets coordinate the actions of millions of consumers and producers. Smith said that the market economy seemed to be controlled by an **invisible hand**. The invisible hand is a phrase that expresses the belief that the best interests of a society are served when individual consumers and producers compete to achieve their own private interests. Guided by an invisible hand, producers must compete with one another to win consumers' money. The *profit motive* in a competitive marketplace acts as a reward for efficient producers, while losses punish inefficient producers. Smith saw profit as the necessary driving force in an individualistic market system. The profit motive leads the butcher, the baker, and other producers to answer the What, How, and For Whom questions at the lowest prices. Consumers also compete with one another to purchase the best goods at the lowest price. Competition automatically regulates the economy and provides more goods and services than a system in which government attempts to accomplish the same task in the *public interest*. In Smith's own words:

> *Every individual necessarily labours to render the annual revenue of the society as great as he can. He generally, indeed, neither intends to promote the public interest, nor knows how much he is promoting it. By . . . directing that industry in such a manner as its produce may be of the greatest value, he intends only his own gain, and he is in this, as in many other cases, led by an* invisible hand *to promote an end which was no part of his intention. Nor is it always the worse for the society that it was no part of it. By pursuing his own interest he frequently promotes that of the society more effectually than when he really intends to promote it.*[2]

Invisible hand

A phrase that expresses the belief that the best interests of a society are served when individual consumers and producers compete to achieve their own private interests.

---

[2]Adam Smith, *An Inquiry into the Nature and Causes of the Wealth of Nations* (1776; reprint, New York: Random House, 1937), p. 423.

The Market Economy's Strengths and Weaknesses

In a market system, if consumers want Beanie Babies, they can buy them because sellers seek to profit from the sale of Beanie Babies. No single person or central planning board makes a formal decision to shift resources and tells firms how to produce what many might view as a frivolous product. Because no central body or set of customs interferes, the market system provides a wide variety of goods and services that buyers and sellers exchange at the lowest prices.

> **Conclusion** *A market economy answers the What to produce and How to produce questions very effectively.*

Those who attack the market economy point out the market failure problems of lack of competition, externalities, public goods, and income inequality, discussed in Chapter 4. For example, critics contend that competition among buyers and sellers results in people who are very wealthy and people who are very poor. In a market economy, output is divided in favor of people who earn higher income and own property. Some people will dine on caviar in a fine restaurant, while others will wander the street and beg for food and shelter. Supporters of the market system argue that this inequality of income must exist to give people incentives or rewards for the value of their contributions to others.

The Mixed Economy

In the real world, no nation is a pure traditional, command, or market economy. Even primitive tribes employ a few markets in their system. For example, members of a tribe may exchange shells for animal skins. In China, the government allows many private shops and farms to operate in free markets. While the United States is best described as a market economy, there is also a blend of the other two systems. The Amish operate a well-known traditional economy in our nation. The draft during wartime is an example of a command economy in which the government obtains involuntary labor. In addition, taxes "commanded" from taxpayers fund government programs, such as national defense and Social Security. If the economic systems of most nations do not perfectly fit one of the basic definitions, what term best describes their economies? A more appropriate description is that most countries employ a blend of the basic types of economic systems, broadly called a **mixed economy**. A mixed economy is a system that answers the What, How, and For Whom questions through a mixture of traditional, command, and market systems.

The traditional, command, and market economies can exist in a wide variety of political situations. For instance, the United States and Japan are politically "free" societies in which the market system flourishes. But China uses the market system in spite of its lack of political freedom. Moreover, some of the Western democracies engage in central economic planning. French officials representing government, business, and labor meet annually to discuss economic goals for industry for the next five-year period, but compliance is voluntary. In Japan, a government agency called the

Mixed economy
An economic system that answers the What, How, and For Whom questions through a mixture of traditional, command, and market systems.

INTERNATIONAL ECONOMICS

Choosing a System

Applicable Concept: basic types of economic systems

Because we in the United States live in a market-run society, we are apt to take for granted the puzzling nature of how a market economy works. But assume for a moment that we could act as economic advisers to a society that had not yet decided on its type of economic organization.

We could imagine the leaders of such a nation saying, "We have always experienced a highly tradition-bound way of life. Our men hunt and cultivate the fields and perform their tasks as they are brought up to do by the force of example and the instruction of their elders. Likewise, women are brought up with the knowledge of how to weave, cook and care for children. We know, too, something of what can be done by economic command. We are prepared, if necessary, to require by law that many of our people work on community projects for our national development. Tell us, is there any other way we can organize our society so that it will function successfully—or better yet, more successfully?" Suppose we answered, "Yes, there is another way. Organize your society along the lines of a market economy."

"Very well," say the leaders. "What do we then tell people to do? How do we assign them to their various tasks?"

"That's the very point," we would answer. "In a market economy, no one is assigned to any task. In fact, the main idea of a market society is that each person is allowed to decide for himself or herself what to do."

There is confusion among the leaders. "You mean there is no assignment of some people to mining and others to cattle raising? No manner of designating some for transportation and others for weaving? You leave this to people to decide for themselves? But what happens if they do not decide correctly? What happens if no one volunteers to go into the mines, or if no one offers to become a railway engineer?"

"You may rest assured," we tell the leaders, "none of that will happen. In a market society, all the jobs will be filled because it will be to people's advantage to fill them."

Our respondents accept this with uncertain expressions. "Now, look," one of them finally says, "let us suppose that we take your advice and allow our people to do as they please. Let's talk about something specific, like cloth production. Just how do we fix the right level of cloth output in the 'market society' of yours?"

"But you don't," we reply.

"We don't! Then how do we know there will be enough cloth produced?"

"There will be," we tell him. "The market will see to that."

"Then how do we know there won't be too much cloth produced?" he asks triumphantly.

"Ah, but the market will see to that too!"

"But what is this market that will do these wonderful things? Who runs it?"

"Oh, nobody runs the market," we answer. "It runs itself. In fact there isn't any such thing as '*the market*.' It's just a word we use to describe the way people behave."

"But I thought people behaved the way they wanted to!"

"And so they do," we say. "But never fear. They will want to behave the way you want them to behave."

"I am afraid," says the leader of the delegation, "that we are wasting our time. We thought you had in mind a serious proposal. What you suggest is inconceivable. Good day."

ANALYZE THE ISSUE

1. Professor Heilbroner explains that the market system differs from other systems. Describe how a traditional or a command system would make employment and production decisions compared to a market system.
2. Why might the leader find a market system inconceivable? Is it possible for economic activities not based on self-interest to take place in a market economy?

Source: Robert L. Heilbroner, *The Making of Economic Society*, 5th ed., pp. 12–13. © 1975 Reprinted by permission of Prentice-Hall, Inc., Upper Saddle River, N.J.

Ministry for International Trade and Industry (MITI) engages in long-term planning. One of the goals of the MITI is to encourage exports so Japan can earn the foreign currencies it needs to pay for oil and other resources.

The "Isms"

What type of economic system will society choose to answer the What, How, and For Whom questions? We could call most economies "mixed," but this would be too imprecise. In the real world, economic systems are labeled with various forms of the popular "isms"—capitalism, socialism, and communism.

Capitalism

Capitalism is an economic system characterized by private ownership of resources and markets. Capitalism is also called the *free enterprise system*. Regardless of its political system, a capitalistic economic system must possess two characteristics: (1) private ownership of resources and (2) decentralized decision-making using markets.

Private Ownership   Ownership of resources determines to a great degree who makes the What, How, and For Whom decisions. In a capitalist system, resources are primarily *privately* owned and controlled by individuals and firms, rather than having property rights *publicly* held by government on behalf of society. In the United States, most capital resources are privately owned, but the term *capitalism* is somewhat confusing because it stresses private ownership of factories, raw materials, farms, and other forms of *capital* even though public ownership of land exists as well.

Decentralized Decision-Making   This characteristic of capitalism allows buyers and sellers to exchange goods in markets without government involvement. A capitalist system operates on the principle of **consumer sovereignty**. Consumer sovereignty is the freedom of consumers to cast their dollar votes to buy, or not to buy, at prices determined in competitive markets. As a result, consumer spending determines what goods and services firms produce. In a capitalist system, most allocative decisions are coordinated by consumers and producers interacting through markets and making their own decisions guided by Adam Smith's invisible hand.

In the real world, there are many U.S. markets that are not perfectly open or free markets with the consumer as sovereign. For example, consumers cannot buy illegal drugs or body organs. In Chapter 4, you learned that the U.S. government sets the minimum prices (support prices) of wheat, milk, cheese, and other products. These markets are free only if the market price is above the support price. Similarly, the minimum wage law forces employers to pay a wage that must be above some dollar amount per hour regardless of market conditions.

Conclusion *No nation in the world fits precisely the two criteria for capitalism; however, the United States comes close.*

Capitalism
An economic system characterized by private ownership of resources and markets.

Consumer sovereignty
The freedom of consumers to cast their dollar votes to buy, or not to buy, at prices determined in competitive markets.

Capitalism's Strengths and Weaknesses

One of the major strengths of capitalism is its capacity to achieve *economic efficiency* because competition and the profit motive force production at the lowest cost. Another strength of pure capitalism is *economic freedom* because economic power is widely dispersed. Individual consumers, producers, and workers are free to make decisions based on their own self-interest. Economist Milton Friedman makes a related point: Private ownership limits the political power of government to deny goods, services, or jobs to their political adversaries.

Critics of capitalism cite several shortcomings. First, capitalism tends toward an unequal distribution of income. This inequality of income among citizens is the result of several factors. Private ownership of capital and the other factors of production can cause these factors to become concentrated in the hands of a few individuals or firms. Also, people are not all equal in their labor skills, and the marketplace rewards those with greater skills. These inequalities may be perpetuated because the rich can provide better education, legal aid, political platforms, and wealth to their heirs. Second, pure capitalism is criticized for its failure to protect the environment. The pursuit of profit and self-interest can take precedence over damage or pollution to the air, rivers, lakes, and streams. In Chapter 4, recall the graphical model used to illustrate the socially unacceptable impact on society of producers who pollute the environment.

Socialism

Socialism
An economic system characterized by government ownership of resources and centralized decision-making.

The idea of **socialism** has existed for thousands of years. Socialism is an economic system characterized by government ownership of resources and centralized decision-making. Socialism is also called *command socialism*. Under socialism, a command system owns and controls in the *public interest* the major industries, such as steel, electricity, and agriculture. However, some free markets can exist in farming, retail trade, and certain service areas. Just as no pure capitalist system exists in the real world, none of the socialist countries in the world today practices pure socialism. In fact, there are as many variants of socialism as there are countries called socialist.

Before discussing socialism further, you must realize that socialism is an economic system, and you must not confuse politics with economics. Great Britain, France, and Italy have representative democracies, but many of their major industries are or have been nationalized. In the United States, the federal government owns and operates the Tennessee Valley Authority, the National Aeronautics and Space Administration (NASA), and the U.S. Postal Service, while at the same time allowing private utilities and mail service firms to operate.

The Ideas of Karl Marx

Communism
A stateless, classless economic system in which all the factors of production are owned by the workers and people share in production according to their needs. This is the highest form of socialism toward which the revolution should strive.

In spite of the transition to capitalism in the former Soviet Union and Eastern Europe, socialism still prevails in China, Cuba, and many less-developed countries. The theory for socialism and **communism** can be traced to Karl Marx. Marx was a 19th-century German philosopher, revolutionary, and economist. Unlike other economists of the time who were followers of Adam Smith, Marx rejected the concept of a society operating through private interest and profit.

Karl Marx was born in Germany, the son of a lawyer. Marx was an outstanding student at Berlin University. In 1841, after receiving a doctorate in philosophy, he turned to journalism. In 1843, Marx married the daughter of a wealthy family and moved to Paris, but his political activities forced him to leave Paris for England. From the age of 31, he lived and wrote his books in London. In London, Marx lived an impoverished life while he and his lifelong friend Friedrich Engels wrote the *Communist Manifesto*, published in 1848. A massive work that followed, titled *Das Kapital*, was published in three volumes in 1867, 1884, and 1885.

These two works made Karl Marx the most influential economist in the history of socialism. In fact, he devoted his entire life to a revolt against capitalism. As Marx read *The Wealth of Nations*, he saw profits as unjust payments to owners of firms—the capitalists. Marx predicted that the market system would destroy itself because wealthy owners would go too far and exploit workers as unrelenting greed for profits would lead these wealthy owners to pay starvation wages. Moreover, the owners would force laborers to work in unsafe conditions, and many would not have a job at all.

Marx believed that private ownership and exploitation would produce a nation driven by a class struggle between a few "haves" and many "have-nots." As stated in the *Communist Manifesto*, "The history of all existing society is the history of class struggle. Freeman and slave, patrician and plebeian, lord and serf, guildmaster and journeyman, in a word, oppressor and oppressed."[3] Marx's vision was that the capitalists were the modern-day oppressors and the workers were the oppressed proletariat. Some day, Marx predicted, the workers would rise up in a spontaneous bloody revolution against a system benefiting only the owners of capital. Marx believed *communism* to be the ideal system, which would evolve in stages from capitalism through socialism. Communism is a stateless, classless economic system in which all the factors of production are owned by the workers and people share in production according to their needs. This is the highest form of socialism toward which the revolution should strive.

Under communism, no private property exists to encourage self-interest. There is no struggle between classes of people, and everyone cooperates. In fact, there is no reason to commit crime, and police, lawyers, and courts are unnecessary. Strangely, Marx surpassed Adam Smith in advocating a system with little central government. Marx believed that those who work hard, or who are more skilled, will be public spirited. Any "haves" will give voluntarily to "have-nots" until everyone has exactly the same material wellbeing. In Marx's own words, people would be motivated by the principle "from each according to his ability, to each according to his need." World peace would evolve as nation after nation accepted cooperation and rejected profits and competition. Under the idealized society of

Read the Communist Manifesto (http://www.marx.org/archive/1848-CM/).

---

[3]Karl Marx and Friedrich Engels, *The Communist Manifesto* (New York: International Press, 1848), p. 31.

communism, there would be no state. No central authority would be necessary to pursue the interest of the people.

Today, we call the economic systems of the former Soviet Union, Eastern Europe, China, Cuba, and other countries *communist*. However, the definition for *socialism* given in this chapter more accurately describes their real-world economic systems. Actually, no nation has achieved the ideal communist society described by Marx, nor has capitalism self-destructed as he predicted. Indeed, Marx would have been surprised to see the Communist revolution occur in Russia in 1917. At that time, Russia was an underdeveloped country, rather than an industrial country filled with greedy capitalists who exploited workers.

Characteristics of Socialism

Regardless of a society's political system, there are two basic characteristics that describe a socialistic economy: (1) public ownership and (2) centralized decision-making.

Public Ownership   Under socialism, the government owns most of the factors of production, including factories, farms, mines, and natural resources. Agriculture in the old Soviet Union illustrates how even this real-world socialist country deviated from total public ownership. In the former Soviet Union, there were three rather distinct forms of agriculture: state farms, collective farms, and private plots. In both the state-farm and the collective-farm sectors, central planning authorities determined prices and outputs. In contrast, the government allowed those holding small private plots on peasant farms to operate primarily in free markets that determined price and output levels. Reforms now allow farmers to buy land, tractors, trucks, and other resources from the state. If these reforms continue, they will dramatically end the collectivization of agriculture begun under Josef Stalin.

Centralized Decision-Making   Instead of the pursuit of *private interest*, the motivation of pure socialism is the *public interest* of the whole society. For instance, a factory manager cannot decide to raise or lower prices to obtain maximum profits for his or her factory. Regardless of inventory levels or the opportunity to raise prices, the planners will not permit this action. Instead of exploiting the ups and downs of the market, the goal of the socialist system is to make centralized decisions that protect workers and consumers from decentralized market decisions. Critics argue that the main objective of this centralization is to perpetuate the personal dictatorships of men such as Stalin in the old Soviet Union and Fidel Castro in Cuba.

Before the open market reforms, Soviet planners altered earnings to attract workers into certain occupations and achieve planned goals. For example, if space projects needed more engineers, then the state raised the earnings of engineers until the target number of people entered the engineering profession.

As shown earlier in Exhibit 2, central planners in the former Soviet Union also manipulated consumer prices. If consumers desired more cars

You make plans. You planned to go to college. You plan which career to follow. You plan to get married, and so on. Businesses plan. They plan to hire employees, expand their plants, increase profits, and so forth. Because individuals and businesses plan in a market economy, there is really no difference between our system and the command economy. Or is there?

than were available, the authorities increased the price of cars. If people wished to purchase less of an item than was available, then they lowered prices. The problem is that this decision process took time. And while the market awaited its orders from the Soviet planners, excess inventories of some items accumulated, and consumers stood in line for cheap products that never seemed to be available. There is an old Soviet saying, "If you see a line, get in it. Whatever it is, it's scarce, and you will not see it tomorrow."

The former Soviet factory system did not adhere completely to the command system. The government rewarded successful managers with bonuses that could be substantial. Better apartments, nice vacations, and medals were incentives for outstanding performance. Under economic reforms, plant managers now make decisions based on profitability instead of centralized controls.

Socialism's Strengths and Weaknesses

Proponents of the socialism model argue that this system is superior in achieving an equitable distribution of income. This is because government ownership of capital and other resources prevents a few individuals or groups from acquiring a disproportionate share of the nation's wealth. Also, supporters argue that rapid economic growth is achieved when planners have the power to direct more resources to producing capital goods and fewer resources to producing consumer goods (see Exhibit 4 of Chapter 2).

National goals may seem to be easily formulated and pursued under state directives, but there are problems. For example, proponents of such an economy can claim there is no unemployment because the government assigns all workers a job and allocates resources to complete their production goals. However, economic inefficiency results because the government often uses many workers to perform work requiring only one or two workers. Critics also point out that the absence of the profit motive for entrepreneurship or innovation suppresses economic growth.

Socialism is particularly vulnerable to the charge that it ignores the goal of economic freedom and instead creates a privileged class of government bureaucrats who assume the role of "capitalists." Central planners are the key translators of information about consumer preferences and production capabilities flowing to millions of economic units. This complex and cumbersome process is subject to errors and a lack of responsiveness to the wants of the majority of the population. Critics also question the argument that the distribution of income under socialism is more equitable than under capitalism. In the socialist system, perks for government officials, nepotism, and the illegal use of markets create disparities in income.

Comparing Economic Systems

In reality, all nations operate economic systems that blend capitalism and socialism. Exhibit 3 presents a continuum that attempts to place countries between the two extremes of pure socialism on the left and pure capitalism on the right. Economies characterized by a high degree of both private ownership and market allocation fit closest to pure capitalism. Hong Kong, Japan, the United States, and Canada fall at the capitalism end of the line. Conversely, economies characterized by much government ownership of resources and central planning are closest to pure socialism. Although the outcome of reforms is unclear in the former Soviet Union and China, at present these economies and Cuba fall close to the pure socialism end of the spectrum.

EXHIBIT 3

A Classification of Economic Systems

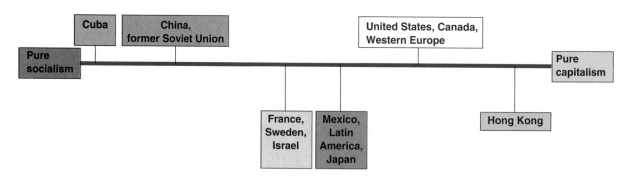

No nation has an economic system that is pure socialism or pure capitalism. All nations mix government ownership and reliance on markets. Cuba is closest to pure socialism, while Hong Kong comes closest to pure capitalism. Other real-world economies are placed between these two extremes on the basis of their use of government ownership versus markets.

Economies in Transition

By the early 1990s, the centrally planned economies in the old Soviet Union and Eastern Europe had collapsed. After more than 70 years in the Soviet Union and over 40 years in Eastern Europe and China, the failed communist economies made a startling switch to embrace capitalism. Faced with severe shortages of food, housing, cars, and other consumer goods, communism could no longer claim better living standards for its citizens. The following is a brief discussion of reforms aimed at introducing market power into the economic systems of Cuba, Russia, and China.

Cuba

Today, Cuba remains wedded to the communist system. However, the collapse of Soviet bloc aid coupled with the effects of the U.S. trade embargo have forced Castro, a die-hard Marxist, to reluctantly adopt limited free-market reforms. To earn foreign exchange, the dollar has been legalized, and the Cuban government has poured capital into tourism by building several new state-owned hotels and restoring historic sections of Havana. Also, Cuba has set up quasi-state enterprises that accept only hard currency. Since few Cubans have dollars or other hard currency, many are earning it by turning to illegal schemes, such as driving gypsy cabs, engaging in prostitution, or selling Cuba's famous cigars and coffee on the black market. Other Cubans have abandoned state jobs and opened small businesses under these new rules. However, these small-scale businesses cannot employ anyone beyond the family of the owner. Also, spare rooms in houses can be rented, and artisans can sell their work to tourists. In addition, the government allows farmers to sell produce left over after they have met the state's quota.

In spite of the private enterprise reforms, Cuba remains essentially a communist system. The vast majority of workers receive low state salaries in pesos and rations of staples. Profits from hotels and shops go directly into the Central Bank and help finance the Castro government. The state also discourages private enterprises by taxing them heavily on expected earnings, rather than on actual sales. In addition, there are highly restrictive regulations. For example, a restaurant in Havana is limited to 12 seats and cannot expand regardless of demand.

In 1999, President Clinton proposed a new U.S.-Cuba initiative. This five-point program called for an expansion of cash transfers, direct mail service, the sale of food to nongovernment entities, and expansion of cash transfers. These measures are intended to help the Cuban people without strengthening the Cuban government.

Russia

In August 1991, a failed coup ended Communist rule. The Communist Party and the KGB were shut down. To function efficiently, markets must offer incentives, and so workers, the public, and even foreign investors

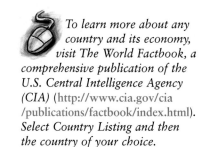

To learn more about any country and its economy, visit The World Factbook, a comprehensive publication of the U.S. Central Intelligence Agency (CIA) (http://www.cia.gov/cia /publications/factbook/index.html). *Select Country Listing and then the country of your choice.*

were permitted to buy state property. This meant individuals could own the factors of production and earn profits. Such market incentives are a dagger thrust into the heart of egalitarianism.

A key reform for Russia was to allow supply and demand to set higher prices for basic consumer goods. As shown earlier in Exhibit 2, when prices rise to their equilibrium level, the quantity supplied increases and the quantity demanded decreases without central planners. At the beginning of 1992, the Russian government removed direct government price controls on most market goods. As the model predicts, average prices leaped in 1992 by 2,600 percent, and a greater variety of goods started appearing on the shelves. Although workers had to pay more for basic consumer goods, they at least could find goods to buy.

Since 1992, Russia has created an independent central bank and implemented anti-inflationary monetary policies. As a result, the inflation rate fell to 14 percent in 1997. However, Russia continued to face financial crisis. In the late spring of 1998, its stock market crashed, payment on its foreign debt was suspended, and the ruble was devalued. Although Russia is far from a successful market economy, the nation is struggling to achieve an amazing economic transition.

The People's Republic of China

Unlike Russia, China has sought economic reform under the direction of its Communist Party. Fundamental economic reforms occurred in China after the death of Mao Tse Tung in 1976. Much of this reform was due to the leadership of Deng Xiaoping. Mao was devoted to the egalitarian ideal of communist ideology. Thoughts of self-interest were counterrevolutionary, and photographs of Marx, Lenin, and Mao hung on every street corner and in every office and factory. Deng shifted priorities by increasing production of consumer goods and wages of workers so they could buy more of these goods. International trade also expanded from less than 1 percent of U.S. merchandise trade in 1975 to 5 percent of U.S. merchandise trade in 1998.

To make China an industrial power by the year 2000, Chinese planners introduced a two-tier system for industry and agriculture in 1978. Each farm and state enterprise was given a contract to produce a quota. Any amount produced over the quota could be sold in an open market. Also, the Chinese government encouraged the formation of nonstate enterprises owned jointly by managers and their workforce and special economic zones open to foreign investment. In other words, a blend of capitalism and socialism would provide the incentives needed to increase output. As Deng Xiaoping explained, "It doesn't matter whether the cat is black or white as long as it catches mice." And this reform worked. It led to huge increases in farm and industrial output in the 1980s. In fact, some peasant farmers became some of the wealthiest people in China. After Deng's death in the mid-1990s, leadership of China passed to Jian Zemin, who continues the policy of free-market reforms.

The Japanese "Malaise"

The postwar transformation of the Japanese economy has been described as a remarkable success story. In 1950, Japan was starting to recover from the devastation of World War II. The real per capita GDP of Japan was one-eighth that of the United States. In the 1950s, "Made in Japan" meant cheap and poor-quality products. In the 1990s, "Made in Japan" means top-quality high-tech products, probably at the lowest price. By the 1990s, Japan's real per capita GDP exceeded that of the United States. This rapid economic growth happened in a country that has a land area smaller than California and a population half as large as that of the United States. Moreover, Japan lacks many natural resources, so almost all of its oil and other important minerals must be imported.

Many factors contributed to the success of Japan's capitalist economy. Let us consider some of the important features of the Japanese economy.

First, Japanese workers are very loyal to the firms that employ them. Part of the reason for this loyalty is the Confucian ethic, which requires loyalty for both employers and employees. Another part of the reason, although changing, is that almost all major Japanese corporations provide lifetime employment to age 55, when mandatory retirement occurs. A worker cannot be discharged except for criminal acts, excessive absenteeism, or other misconduct. This job security means employees have an incentive to strive for the long-run success of their firm. Another part of the reason for worker loyalty is labor-management cooperation. In Japan, unions often support wage reductions in order to avoid layoffs during periods of weak demand for their company's product. Other areas of labor-management cooperation include ways to improve product quality, work schedules, and company plans. For example, workers form *quality circles* to exchange suggestions for improving performance.

Second, taxes as a percentage of GDP are lower in Japan than other economies except the United States. As a result of low tax rates, there is a strong incentive to engage in entrepreneurship and make the Japanese economy grow rapidly. It should also be noted that there are many reasons for Japan's lower taxes. One reason often given is that Japan has been protected by the U.S. defense shield and therefore spends little on its military.

Third, the savings and investment rates of Japan are higher than those of other economies. The Japanese people save about 20 percent of their disposable income. One explanation for the high Japanese saving rate is a very limited social insurance system. Therefore, workers must save for their retirement. Also, Japan gives tax credits to encourage saving. Similarly, corporations channel the major share of their profits into investment.

Fourth, Japan has an industrial policy that combines government and businesses in joint ventures. The MITI, discussed earlier in this chapter, is an example of how the Japanese government actively follows policies to help certain industries to be profitable in international trade.

The average annual growth rate of real GDP for Japan during 1967–1976 was 7.0 percent compared with 4.2 percent during 1977–1992, 1.6 percent for 1993–1997, and −2.5 percent in 1998. Why the slowdown?

The Japanese Ministry of International Trade and Industry (http://www.miti .go.jp/index-e.html), *the Japan External Trade Organization* (http://www.jetro.go.jp/top/index .html), *and the Japan Economic Foundation* (http://www.jef.or.jp/) *provide news and information about Japanese trade and the Japanese economy.*

INTERNATIONAL ECONOMICS

China Seeks Free-Market Revolution
Applicable Concept: comparative economic systems

For more than 2,000 years, China had a "self-reliance" policy that caused China's economy to lag far behind advanced economies. In 1978, China adopted a new policy of economic reforms that are transforming one of the poorest economies in the world into one of the fastest-growing.

The rural economy is central to China's economic reform because about 70 percent of its population lives in rural areas. In the past, farmers worked collectively in people's communes. The government told the farmers what to produce and how much to produce. They could sell their products only to the state at a price fixed by the government, rather than in markets.

Under the reform system, households operate in a mixed world of state controls and free markets. A two-track pricing system still exists for some key goods and services, such as coal, petroleum, steel, and

transportation. On the other hand, the so-called household contract responsibility system assigns land owned by the state to farmers. An annual share of profits must be paid to the government, and the state does not cover losses. Farmers, however, have the authority to decide what to produce and the price at which to sell in open markets. As a result, everyone, farmers and consumers, is noticeably better off because everyone can find and afford more food.

As farming productivity rose sharply, fewer farmers were needed to work on the land, and this sur-

plus labor moved into emerging township and village nonstate enterprises. These enterprises are mostly in light industry and are owned collectively by townships or villages. As a result, the composition of rural output changed. When the reforms began, farming accounted for 70 percent of the total rural output and industry for 20 percent. Currently, industry's output share has jumped to more than 40 percent.[1]

The march toward reform is not trouble-free. An article in the *Boston Globe* provides additional insight into China's economic transformation:

> Unleashed from central controls, local officials are sinking government money into luxury developments instead of factories, into bureaucrats' pockets instead of farmers' hands. The get-rich-quick mentality has soaked up so much precious

Observers credit Japan's high growth rate in the past to its ability to utilize the technology developed by more advanced countries. Now the technology gap is closed, and Japanese manufacturing is as modern as, or more modern than, that of any other nation.

In the late 1990s, Japan experienced severe economic problems: A collapse in real estate and other asset prices created a massive debt problem for the Japanese financial system. Instead of dealing quickly with the bad loans, government and bank officials delayed establishing a system for bad-loan disposal. Cutbacks in lending by Japanese banks contributed to a credit crunch that contributed to recession in Japan and the rest of Asia. The Japanese crisis, its worst recession since World War II, and a slide in the yen triggered devaluations in other nations. United States exports to Japan fell, and fears about economic and political turmoil in Asia caused the Dow Jones industrial average to drop.

cash that hundreds of millions of farmers have been paid government-backed IOUs for their crops for two years running. Riots by farmers fed up with that system have been reported in 11 provinces.

Now Beijing is scrambling to rein in growth before the economy—and social unrest—spin out of control. But stuffing the genie back into the bottle might prove difficult. The flood of money has created a bubble, particularly in stocks and property, making some people in China very rich, very fast. The China Daily, China's official English-language newspaper, recently heralded the existence of 1 million millionaires. . . . These millionaires, many of whom just five years ago were still wearing Mao outfits and following the party's socialist dictates, now sport stylish Western-style suits with the label ostentatiously left on the cuff.[2]

Another article describes international trade problems.

The signs elbowing for attention on bustling Nanjing Road seem to scream in English. Coca-Cola! Kentucky Fried Chicken! Motorola pagers! In most sectors, competition has grown fierce and profit margins are narrowing. Deregulation of this state-controlled economy has been far slower than anticipated. The Asian economic slowdown and the collapse of some Asian currencies have made China relatively more expensive. And getting contracts honored in a nation still learning how to enforce its own laws remains difficult.

"It's taking too long and patience is running out," said Diane Long, former chairman of the American Chamber of Commerce in Shanghai. "China is not as cheap as it used to be, the government has been slow to grant licenses to industries,

and manufacturers remain plagued by distribution restrictions, which make it nearly impossible to service the products they sell."[3]

ANALYZE THE ISSUE

1. Why would China abandon the goal of income equality and shift from a centrally planned to a more market-oriented economy?
2. What groups are resisting the reforms?

[1]Liguang Wu, "Economic Reform in China: Retrospect," *Senior Economist*, November 1993, pp. 3–5.
[2]Maggie Farley, "China's Economic Boom Energizing Inflation," *Boston Globe*, August 13, 1993, p. 1A.
[3]Michael Zielenziger, "China's Road to Capitalism 'Malaise' Potholed, U.S. Firms Find," *Charlotte Observer*, June 21, 1998, p. 19A.

New legislation in Japan includes important measures to deal with financial sector problems. To support this effort, the government has made an unprecedently large sum of public funds available to recapitalize the banking system, amounting to about 12 percent of GDP.

KEY CONCEPTS

Economic system
Traditional economy
Command economy

Market economy
Invisible hand
Mixed economy

Capitalism
Consumer sovereignty

Socialism
Communism

SUMMARY

■ An **economic system** is the set of established procedures by which a society answers the What, How, and For Whom to produce questions.

★ Three basic types of economic systems are the traditional, command, and market systems. The **traditional system** is based on decisions made according to custom, and the **command system** answers the three economic questions through some powerful central authority. In contrast, the **market system** uses the impersonal mechanism of the interaction of buyers and sellers through markets to answer the What, How, and For Whom questions.

Command economy

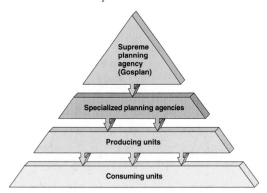

■ **Capitalism** is an economic system in which the factors of production are privately owned and economic choices are made by consumers and firms in markets. As prescribed by Adam Smith, there is an extremely limited role for government, and self-interest is the driving force, held in check, or regulated, by competition.

■ **Consumer sovereignty** is the determination by consumers of the types and quantities of products that are produced in an economy.

■ **Socialism** is an economic system in which the government owns the factors of production. The central authorities make the myriad of society's economic decisions according to a national plan. The collective good, or public interest, is the intended guiding force behind the central planners' decisions.

■ **Communism** is an economic system envisioned by Karl Marx to be an ideal society in which the workers own all the factors of production. Marx believed that workers who worked hard would be public spirited and would voluntarily redistribute income to those who are less productive. Such a communist nation described by Marx does not exist.

SUMMARY OF CONCLUSION STATEMENTS

■ When central planners set prices below equilibrium for goods and services, they create shortages, which mean long lines, empty shelves, and black markets.

■ A market economy answers the What to produce and How to produce questions very effectively.

■ No nation in the world fits precisely the two criteria for capitalism; however, the United States comes close.

STUDY QUESTIONS AND PROBLEMS

1. Give an example of how a nation's culture affects its economic system.

2. Explain the advantages and the disadvantages of any two of the three basic types of economic systems.

3. Suppose a national program of free housing for the elderly is paid for by a sizeable increase in income taxes. Explain a trade-off that might occur between economic security and efficiency.

4. "The schools are not in the business of pleasing parents and students, and they cannot be allowed to set their own agendas. Their agendas are set by politicians, administrators, and various constituencies that hold the keys to political power. The public system is built to see to it that the schools do what their government wants them to do—that they conform to the higher-order values their governors seek to impose."[4] Relate this statement to Exhibit 1.

---

[4]John Chubb and Terry More, *Politics, Markets, and the Nation's Public Schools* (Washington, D.C.: Brookings Institution, 1990), p. 38.

5. Suppose you are a farmer. Describe why you would be motivated to work in traditional, command, and market economies.

6. Karl Marx believed the market system was doomed. Why do you think he was right or wrong?

7. If all real-world economies are mixed economies, why is the U.S. economy described as capitalist, while the Chinese economy is described as socialist?

8. Suppose you are a factory manager. Describe how you might reach production goals under a system of pure capitalism and under a system of pure socialism.

 ## ONLINE EXERCISES

Exercise 1

Browse Capitalism: Frequently Asked Questions (http://www.ocf.berkeley.edu/~shadab/). Select topics of interest. For example, select How is democracy related to capitalism? or choose Is socialism ideal?

Exercise 2

Browse The Adam Smith Institute (http://www.adamsmith.org.) and Karl Marx (http://paul.spu.edu/~hawk/marxh.html).

Exercise 3

Visit Financial Times Home Page (http://www.usa.ft.com/), select First Time Visitors, and then select FREE

SUBSCRIPTION TO FT.com. Select HEADLINES, and then undertake a Search for "transition economies." Select an article that describes how transition economies are progressing.

Exercise 4

Visit the United Nations' Division for Economic Analysis and Projections (DEAP) (http://www.unece.org/deap/), part of the United Nations Economic Commission for Europe (UN/ECE). After reading the text of this home page, select Publications, and browse an article under Economic Survey of Europe or Economic Bulletin for Europe.

 ## CHECKPOINT ANSWERS

To Plan or Not to Plan—That Is the Question

When an individual or a business plans in a market economy, other individuals are free to make and follow their own plans. Suppose Hewlett-Packard decides to produce X number of laserjet printers and sell them at a certain price. The decision does not prohibit IBM from producing Y number of laserjet printers and selling them for less than Hewlett-Packard. If either firm makes a mistake,

only that firm suffers, and other industries are for the most part unaffected. Under a command system, a central economic plan would be made for all laserjet manufacturers. If the central planners order the wrong quantity or quality, there could be major harm to other industries and society. If you said there is a major difference between individual planning and central planning for all society, **YOU ARE CORRECT.**

PRACTICE QUIZ

For a visual explanation of the correct answers, visit the tutorial at http://tucker.swcollege.com.

1. The economic system in which all of the basic decisions are made through a centralized authority, such as government agency, is termed a
   a. market economy.
   b. capitalistic economy.
   c. command economy.
   d. traditional economy.

2. Command economies typically suffer from
   a. unemployment, but not underemployment.
   b. neither unemployment nor underemployment.
   c. both unemployment and underemployment.
   d. underemployment, but not unemployment.

3. Adam Smith stated that the only role of government in society should be to
   a. provide defense.
   b. enforce contracts.
   c. do absolutely nothing.
   d. do both (a) and (b).

4. When making economic decisions, Adam Smith urged society to
   a. follow the principle of self-interest.
   b. follow the principle of public interest.
   c. transfer wealth according to need.
   d. provide equal income for all citizens.

5. The doctrine of laissez faire
   a. advocates an economic system with extensive government intervention and little individual decision-making.
   b. was advocated by Adam Smith in his book *The Wealth of Nations*.
   c. was advocated by Karl Marx in his book *Das Kapital*.
   d. is described by none of the above.

6. In Adam Smith's competitive market economy, the question of what goods to produce is determined by the
   a. "invisible hand" of the price system.
   b. "invisible hand" of government.
   c. "visible hand" of public interest.
   d. "visible hand" of laws and regulations.

7. Adam Smith wrote that the
   a. economic problems of 18th-century England were caused by free markets.
   b. government should control the economy with an "invisible hand."
   c. pursuit of private self-interest promotes the public interest in a market economy.
   d. public or collective interest is not promoted by people pursuing their self-interest.

8. Adam Smith, in his book *The Wealth of Nations*, advocated
   a. socialism.
   b. an economy guided by an "invisible hand."
   c. government control of the "invisible hand."
   d. the adoption of mercantilism.

9. The economic system in which private individuals own the factors of production is
   a. a planned economy.
   b. capitalism.
   c. collectivism.
   d. socialism.

10. Which of the following is *not* a basic characteristic of capitalism?
    a. Economic decisions occur in markets.
    b. Factors of production are privately owned.
    c. Income is distributed on the basis of need.
    d. Businesses make their own product and price decisions.

11. According to Karl Marx, under capitalism,
    a. profits would be shared fairly.
    b. incomes would be distributed equally.
    c. workers would be exploited and revolt against owners of capital.
    d. workers would actually own the factors of production.

12. Karl Marx predicted which of the following?
    a. The market system would self-destruct.
    b. The "haves" would revolt against the "have-nots."
    c. The wealthy were entitled to profits as their reward for risk-taking.
    d. None of the above.

13. How many nations in the world today operate totally according to Karl Marx's theory of communism?
    a. None
    b. Several
    c. Only the United States
    d. Many

14. In Marx's ideal communist society, the state
    a. actively promotes income equality.
    b. follows the doctrine of laissez faire.
    c. owns resources and conducts planning.
    d. does not exist.

15. Karl Marx was a (an)
    a. 19th-century German philosopher.
    b. 18th-century Russian economist.
    c. 14th-century Polish banker.
    d. 19th-century Russian journalist.

CHAPTER SEVENTEEN

Growth and the Less-Developed Countries

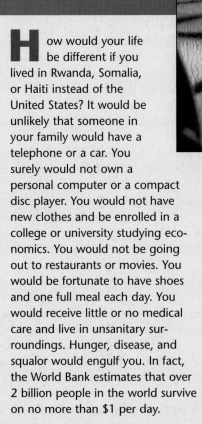

How would your life be different if you lived in Rwanda, Somalia, or Haiti instead of the United States? It would be unlikely that someone in your family would have a telephone or a car. You surely would not own a personal computer or a compact disc player. You would not have new clothes and be enrolled in a college or university studying economics. You would not be going out to restaurants or movies. You would be fortunate to have shoes and one full meal each day. You would receive little or no medical care and live in unsanitary surroundings. Hunger, disease, and squalor would engulf you. In fact, the World Bank estimates that over 2 billion people in the world survive on no more than $1 per day.

It is exceedingly difficult for Americans to grasp the fact that two-thirds of the world's population live close to the subsistence level.

This brings us to this chapter's important task of unraveling the secrets to economic growth and development. Why do some countries prosper, while others decline?

At different times in history, Egypt, China, Italy, and Greece were highly developed by the standards of their time. On the other hand, at one time the United States was a struggling, relatively poor country on the path to becoming a rich country. There were three stages: First, there was the agricultural stage. Then there was the manufacturing stage. Industries such as railroads, steel, and automobiles were driving forces toward economic growth. And, finally, there has been in recent years a shift toward service industries. This is the U.S. success story, but it is not the only road countries can follow to lift themselves from the misery of poverty.

In this chapter, you will learn to solve these economics puzzles:

■ Is there a difference between economic growth and economic development?

■ Why are some countries rich and others poor?

■ Is trade a better "engine of growth" than foreign aid and loans?

Comparing Developed and Less-Developed Countries

There is income disparity among family groups within the United States and other nations. In this section, the great inequality of income between the families of nations will be used to classify groups of rich versus poor nations.

Classifying Countries by GDP per Capita

There were more than 170 countries in the world in 1998. Exhibit 1 shows the World Bank's ranking of selected countries from high to low **GDP per capita**. GDP per capita is the value of final goods produced (GDP) divided by the total population. Although any system of defining rich versus poor countries is arbitrary, GDP per capita or average GDP is a fundamental measure of a country's economic well-being. At the top of the income ladder are 26 developed countries called the **industrially advanced countries**. Industrially advanced countries (IACs) are high-income nations that have market economies based on large stocks of technologically advanced capital and well-educated labor. The United States, Canada, Australia, New Zealand, Japan, and most of the countries of Western Europe are IACs. Excluded from the IACs are countries with high incomes, but with economies based on oil under the sand, resulting in a lack of widespread industrial development. The United Arab Emirates is an example of such a country excluded from the IAC list.

Countries of the world other than IACs are classified as underdeveloped or **less-developed countries**. Less-developed countries (LDCs) are nations without large stocks of technologically advanced capital and well-educated labor. LDCs are economies based on agriculture, such as most countries of Africa, Asia, and Latin America. Three-fourths of the world's population, consisting of about 150 countries, live in LDCs and share widespread poverty.

A closer examination of Exhibit 1 reveals that the differences in living standards between the IACs and LDCs are enormous. For example, the GDP per capita in the United States is $28,650 greater than the average income in Mozambique ($90). Stated differently, the 1998 average income in the United States is about 319 times larger than in Mozambique ($28,740/$90 = 319). What a difference! Imagine trying to live on only $90 for a year in the United States. You probably would not survive.

Exhibit 2 compares GDP per capita for IACs to LDCs by regions of the world for 1997. The average citizen in the IACs enjoyed an income of $24,847, which was 64 times that of the average citizen in South Asia ($24,847/$390 = 64). The exhibit also reveals that the greatest concentrations of world poverty are located in the rural areas of South Asia and Sub-Saharan Africa. The East Asia and Pacific regions have many countries characterized by bleak and pervasive poverty, but there are notable exceptions, nicknamed the "Four Tigers" of East Asia—Hong Kong, Singapore, South Korea, and Taiwan. These Pacific Rim countries are newly industrialized countries with living standards that approach or surpass some of those in the lower-tier IACs. We discuss these "tigers" at the end of this chapter.

The World Bank (http://www.worldbank.org/) *and the United Nations* (http://www.un.org/) *provide comprehensive information about different countries and their economies, including GDP per capita.*

GDP per capita
The value of final goods produced (GDP) divided by the total population.

Industrially advanced countries (IACs)
High-income nations that have market economies based on large stocks of technologically advanced capital and well-educated labor. The United States, Canada, Australia, New Zealand, Japan, and most of the countries of Western Europe are IACs.

Less-developed countries (LDCs)
Nations without large stocks of technologically advanced capital and well-educated labor. LDCs are economies based on agriculture such as most countries of Africa, Asia, and Latin America.

EXHIBIT 1 Annual GDP per Capita for Selected Countries, 1997

Country	GDP per Capita	Country	GDP per Capita
Industrially Advanced Countries (IACs)			
Luxembourg	$44,440	Hong Kong	$25,280
Switzerland	44,430	Finland	24,080
Japan	37,850	United Kingdom	20,710
Norway	36,090	Australia	20,540
Singapore	32,940	Italy	20,120
Denmark	32,500	Canada	19,290
United States	28,740	Ireland	18,280
Germany	28,260	New Zealand	16,480
Austria	27,980	Israel	15,900
Belgium	26,490	Spain	14,510
Sweden	26,220	Greece	12,010
France	26,050	South Korea	10,550
Netherlands	25,820	Portugal	10,450
Less-Developed Countries (LDCs)			
Chile	$5,020	Indonesia	$1,110
Brazil	4,720	Ukraine	1,040
Hungary	4,610	Georgia	840
Mexico	3,680	Zimbabwe	750
Poland	3,590	Jordan	570
South Africa	3,400	Pakistan	490
Turkey	3,130	Mongolia	390
Panama	3,080	Haiti	330
Thailand	2,800	Vietnam	320
Russia	2,740	Rwanda	210
Romania	1,420	Ethiopia	110
Morocco	1,250	Mozambique	90
Egypt	1,180		

Source: World Bank, http://www.worldbank.org/data/databytopic/keyrefs.htjl, Table 1.

Problems with GDP per Capita Comparisons

There are problems associated with using GDP per capita to compare rich versus poor countries. First, there is a measurement problem because each country tabulates GDP with differing degrees of accuracy. LDCs in general do not use sophisticated methods of gathering and processing GDP and population data. For example, in countries whose economies are based largely on agriculture, a family is more likely to produce goods and services outside the price system. In LDCs, families often grow their own food, make their own clothes, and build their own homes. Estimating the value of this output at market prices is a difficult task.

EXHIBIT 2

Average GDP per Capita for IACs and LDCs by Region, 1997

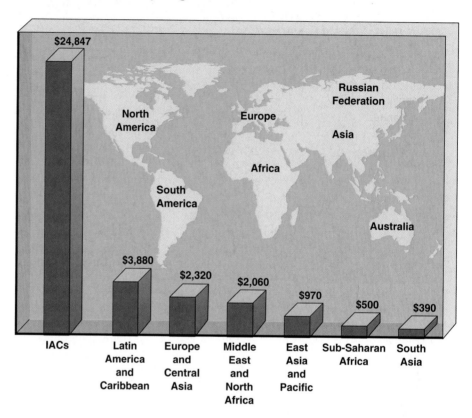

This exhibit represents average GDP per capita by regions of the world for 1997. The differences between the rich industrially advanced countries (IACs) and the poor less-developed countries (LDCs) in the various regions of the world are enormous. For example, the average citizen in the IACs had an income 70 times that of the average citizen in the LDCs of South Asia.

Source: World Bank, http://www.worldbank.org/data/databytopic/keyrefs.html, Table 1.

Conclusion *LDCs' GDP per capita is subject to greater measurement errors than data for IACs.*

Second, GDP per capita comparisons among countries can be misleading because they ignore the relative income distribution. Some countries have very high per capita incomes, yet most of the income goes to just a small percentage of wealthy families. The United Arab Emirates' GDP per capita is greater than that of several IACs. However, the United Arab Emirates earns its income from oil exports, and its income is actually distributed disproportionately to a relatively small number of wealthy families.

Conclusion *GDP per capita comparisons among nations can be misleading because GDP per capita does not measure income distribution.*

Third, GDP per capita comparisons among nations are subject to conversion problems. Making these data comparisons requires converting one nation's currency, say, Japan's yen, into a common currency, the U.S. dollar. Because, as explained in the chapter on international trade and finance, the value of a country's currency can rise or fall for many reasons, the true value of a nation's output can be distorted. For example, one government might maintain an artificially high exchange rate and another government might not during a given year.

Conclusion *A conversion problem may widen or narrow the GDP per capita gap between nations because the fluctuations in exchange rates do not reflect actual differences in the value of goods and services produced.*

Finally, there is a purchasing power parity problem. For example, in 1997, the GDP per capita of Japan ($37,850) exceeded that of the United States ($28,740). Based only on these data, one would conclude that the typical Japanese consumer is better off than the average American consumer. When one visits Japan, however, he or she quickly observes that the typical Japanese consumer is less well off than the average American. The reason is that despite Japan's higher average income, Japan has a higher average cost of living. For example, the price of a very modest home in Tokyo's suburbs is over $1 million.

The International Monetary Fund (IMF), discussed at the end of this chapter, has prepared revised estimates of GDP per capita using purchasing power comparisons, rather than exchange rates, to convert unadjusted GDP per capita data into U.S. dollars. Using this method, the LDCs often look better relative to the IACs.

Conclusion *Differences in purchasing power that affect living standards can alter the interpretation of international comparisons of GDP per capita.*

Quality-of-Life Measures of Development

GDP per capita measures market transactions, but this measure does not give a complete picture of differences in living standards among nations. Exhibit 3 presents other selected socioeconomic indicators of the quality of life. These are variables such as life expectancy at birth, literacy rate, child malnutrition rate, and per capita energy consumption.

Take a close look at the statistics in Exhibit 3. These data reflect the dimensions of poverty in many of the LDCs. For example, people born in the United States have a life expectancy that is 67 percent greater than in Mozambique. The literacy rate and dietary adequacy are also dramatically higher in Japan than Mozambique. Finally, per capita energy consumption measures the use of nonhuman energy to perform work. In IACs, most work is done by machines, and in LDCs, virtually all work is done

EXHIBIT 3   Quality-of-Life Indicators for Selected Countries

Country	(1) GDP per Capita, 1997	(2) Life Expectancy at Birth (years), 1997	(3) Literacy Rate, 1997[1]	(4) Malnutrition as % of Children under 5, 1990–96	(5) Per Capita Energy Consumption, 1995[2]
Japan	$37,850	81	99%	3%	3,964
United States	28,740	76	97	—	7,905
Bolivia	950	61	17	16	396
China	860	70	19	16	707
India	390	63	48	66	260
Bangladesh	270	57	62	68	67
Mozambique	90	45	60	47	38

[1]Percentage age 15 and over that can read and write.
[2]Kilograms of oil equivalent.

Source: World Bank, http://www.worldbank.org/data/wdi/wdi-worldview.html, **Tables 1.1 and 1.2; World Factbook,** http://www.odci.gov/cia
/publications/factbook/country.html.

by people. The average American uses 7,905 kilograms of (coal-equivalent) energy per year, while the average person in Mozambique uses only 38 kilograms.

How good an indicator of the quality of life is GDP per capita? Exhibit 3 reflects the principle that no measure is perfect. China, for example, has a GDP per capita less than Bolivia. Yet the life expectancy, literacy rate, child malnutrition rate, and per capita energy consumption either favor China or are equal to those indicated for Bolivia. In this case, using GDP per capita alone to compare standards of living is misleading. However, the data do confirm this conclusion: *In general, GDP per capita is highly correlated with alternative measures of quality of life.*

Read the World Bank's World Development Report (http://www .worldbank.org/).

Economic Growth and Development Around the World

Economic growth and development are major goals of IACs and LDCs. People all over the world strive for a higher quality of life for their generation and future generations. However, growth is closer to a life-or-death situation for many LDCs, such as Haiti, Rwanda, and Somalia.

Economic growth and economic development are somewhat different, but related, concepts. As shown in Exhibit 4, recall from Chapter 2 that economic growth is the ability of an economy to produce greater levels of output, represented by an outward shift of its production possibilities curve (*PPC*). Thus, economic growth is defined on a *quantitative* basis using the percentage change in GDP per capita. When a nation's GDP rises more rapidly than its population, GDP per capita rises, and the nation experiences

EXHIBIT 4

Economic Growth

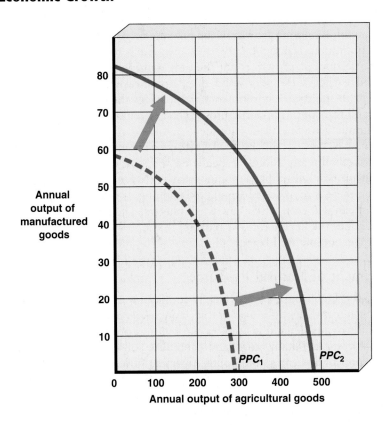

CAUSATION CHAIN

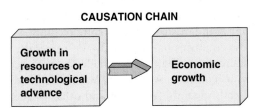

The economy begins with the capacity to produce combinations along production possibilities curve PPC$_1$. *Growth in the resource base or technological advance shifts the production possibilities curve outward from* PPC$_1$ *to* PPC$_2$. *Points along* PPC$_2$ *represent new production possibilities previously impossible. The distance that the curve shifts represents an increase in the nation's productive capacity.*

economic growth. Conversely, if GDP expands less than the population of a nation, GDP per capita falls, and the nation experiences negative economic growth.

Economic development is a broader concept that is more *qualitative* in nature. Economic development encompasses improvement in the quality of life, including economic growth in the production of goods and services. In short, continuous economic growth is necessary for economic development, but economic growth is not the only consideration. For example, as explained earlier, GDP per capita does not measure the distribution of income or the political environment that provides the legal, monetary, education, and transportation structures necessary for economic growth.

Economic growth and development involve a complex process that is determined by several interrelated factors. Like the performance of an NBA basketball team, success depends on the joint effort of team players, and one or two weak players can greatly reduce overall performance. However, there is no precise formula for winning. If your team has Michael Jordan, it can win even with a few weak players. The remainder of this section examines the key factors, or players, that operate together to produce a nation's economic well-being.

Endowment of Natural Resources

Most of the LDCs have comparatively limited bases of natural resources, including mineral deposits and arable land resources. In these countries, most of the available land is used for agricultural production, and clearing tropical forests to obtain more land can cause soil erosion. Also, tropical climates prevail in Central and South America, Africa, the Indian subcontinent, and Southeast Asia. The hot, humid climate in these regions is conducive to weed and insect infestations that plague agriculture.

Although a narrow base of resources does pose a barrier to economic growth and development, there is no single conclusion that can be drawn. For example, how have countries like Hong Kong, Japan, and Israel achieved high standards of living in spite of limited natural resource bases? Each of these countries has practically no minerals, no fertile land, and no domestic sources of energy. Nonetheless, these economies have become prosperous. In contrast, Argentina, Venezuela, and Brazil have abundant fertile land and minerals. Yet these and other countries have been growing slowly or not at all. Venezuela, for example, is one of the most oil-rich countries in the world. Ghana, Kenya, and Bolivia are also resource-rich countries that are poor, with little or no economic growth.

Conclusion *Natural resource endowment can promote economic growth, but a country can develop without a large natural resource base.*

Investment in Human Resources

A low level of human capital can also present a barrier to economic growth and development. Recall that human capital is the education, training, experience, and health that improves the knowledge and skills of workers to produce goods and services. In most of the LDCs, investment in human capital is much less than in the IACs. Look back at the third column in Exhibit 3. Consider how the literacy rate falls for the poorer countries. As the literacy rate falls, so does the ability to educate the labor force and create a basic foundation for economic growth. In fact, often the skills of labor in the poor countries are suited primarily to agriculture, rather than being appropriate for a wide range of industries and economic growth. Further complicating matters, there is a "brain drain" problem because the best educated and trained workers of poor countries pursue their education in wealthier countries. Column 2 of Exhibit 3 also gives a measure of health among countries with varying levels of GDP per capita. As the GDP per capita falls, the life expectancy at birth falls. Thus, richer countries have the advantage of a more educated and healthy workforce.

Conclusion *Investment in human capital generally results in increases in GDP per capita.*

Thus far, the discussion has been about the quality of labor. We must also talk about the quantity of labor because productivity is related to both the quality and the quantity of labor. Overpopulation is a problem for LDCs. In a nutshell, here is why: Other factors held constant, population (labor force) growth can increase a country's GDP. Yet rapid population growth can convert an expanding GDP into a GDP per capita that is stagnant, slow-growing, or negative. Stated another way, there is no gain if an increase in output is more than matched by an increase in the number of mouths that must be fed. Suppose the GDP of an LDC grows at, say, 3 percent per year. If there is no growth in population, GDP per capita also grows at 3 percent per year. But what if population also grows at 3 percent per year? The result is that GDP per capita remains unchanged. If the population growth is instead only 1 percent per year, GDP per capita rises 2 percent per year. Obstacles to population control are great and include strong religious and sociocultural arguments against birth control programs.

Conclusion *Rapid population growth combined with low human capital investment explains why many countries are LDCs.*

Exhibit 5 gives data that support the relationship between high population growth and low GDP per capita growth. The table classifies selected countries by GDP per capita growth rate and then lists the corresponding annual population growth rates between 1965 and 1996. Although these data do not include all countries in the world, several points can be made. First, the average growth rate of GDP per capita for IACs is about 3 percent per year. This output growth rate is achieved with a very slow average population growth rate of .7 percent. Second, the LDCs experience GDP per capita growth rates that are below the average rate for the IACs. In fact, in many of the poorest countries, the annual GDP per capita growth rate is negative. If this trend continues, these LDCs will never close their standard-of-living gap with the rest of the world. Third, the negative average output growth rate of -3.0 for the LDCs is combined with a relatively higher average annual population growth rate of 3.3 percent.

EXHIBIT 5   Annual Growth Rates for Selected Countries, 1965–1996

Country	(1) GDP per Capita Growth	(2) Population Growth
Industrially Advanced Countries (IACs)		
Hong Kong	5.6%	1.7%
Portugal	3.1	0.3
Ireland	2.7	0.7
Greece	2.5	0.6
United Kingdom	1.9	0.2
Less-Developed Countries (LDCs)		
Nicaragua	−4.2	2.9
Congo	−3.5	3.0
Iraq	−3.5	3.1
Madagascar	−0.2	2.6
Kuwait	−3.4	3.8
Saudi Arabia	−3.0	4.4
Libya	−2.9	3.6

Source: World Bank, http://www.worldbank.org/data/wdi/wdi-worldview.html, Table 1.4.

Conclusion *Nations that grow slowly or experience declines in GDP per capita will fail to catch up with the IACs' standard of living.*

Accumulation of Capital

It did not take long for Robinson Crusoe on a deserted island to invest in a net in order to catch more fish than he would catch with his hands. Similarly, farmers working with modern tractors can cultivate more acres than farmers working with horse-drawn plows. Recall from Chapter 1 that capital in economics means factories, tractors, trucks, roads, computers, irrigation systems, electricity-generation facilities, and other man-made goods used to produce goods and services.

LDCs suffer from a critical shortage of capital. The family in Somalia owns little in the way of tools except a wooden plow. To make matters worse, roads are terrible, there are few plants generating electricity, and telephone lines are scarce. As shown in Exhibit 6, recall from Chapter 2 that a high-investment country can shift its production possibilities outward, but investment in capital goods is not a "free lunch." When more resources are used to produce more factories and machines, there is an opportunity cost of fewer resources available for the production of current

EXHIBIT 6

Alpha's and Beta's Present and Future Production Possibilities Curves

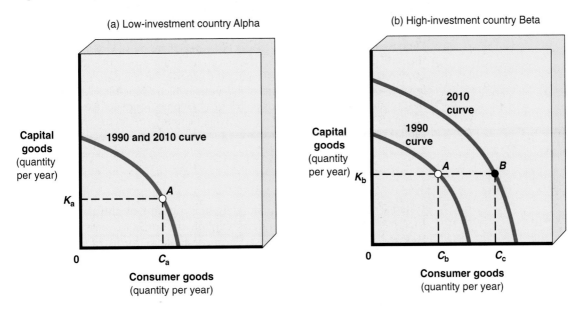

In part (a), each year Alpha produces only enough capital (K_a) to replace existing capital being worn out. Without greater capital and assuming other resources remain fixed, Alpha is unable to shift its production possibilities curve outward. In part (b), each year Beta produces K_b capital, which is more than the amount required to replenish its depreciated capital. In 2010, this expanded capital provides Beta with the extra production capacity to shift its production possibilities curve to the right. If Beta chooses point B on its curve, it has the production capacity to increase the amount of consumer goods from C_b to C_c without producing fewer capital goods.

consumer goods. This means that LDCs are often caught in a **vicious circle of poverty**. A vicious circle of poverty is the trap in which countries are poor and cannot afford to save. And low savings translate into low investment. Low investment results in low productivity, which, in turn, keeps incomes low. What savings that do exist among higher-income persons in poor LDCs are often invested in IACs. This phenomenon is often called "capital flight." These wealthy individuals are afraid to save in their own country because of the threat that their government may be overthrown and their savings could be lost.

The United States and other nations have attempted to provide LDCs with foreign aid so that they might grow. These countries desperately need more factories and **infrastructure**. Infrastructure is capital goods usually provided by the government, including highways, bridges, waste and water

Vicious circle of poverty
The trap in which countries are poor because they cannot afford to save and invest, but they cannot save and invest because they are poor.

Infrastructure
Capital goods usually provided by the government, including highways, bridges, waste and water systems, and airports.

Does Rapid Growth Mean a Country Is Catching Up?

Suppose country Alpha has a production possibilities curve closer to the origin than the curve for country Beta. Now assume Alpha experiences a 3 percent growth rate in GDP for 10 years and Beta experiences a 6 percent growth rate in GDP for 10 years. At the end of five years, which of the following is the best prediction of the standard of living? (1) Alpha's residents are better off. (2) Beta's residents are better off. (3) Which country's residents are better off cannot be determined.

systems, and airports. Unfortunately, the amount of capital given to the LDCs is relatively small, and, as explained above, workers in the LDCs lack the skills necessary to use the most modern forms of capital. More specifically, LDCs face a major obstacle to capital accumulation because of the lack of entrepreneurs to assume the risks of capital formulation.

Conclusion *There is a significant positive relationship between investment and economic growth and development.*

Technological Progress

As explained earlier in Chapter 2, holding natural resources, labor, and capital constant, advancing the body of knowledge applied to production shifts the production possibilities of a country. In fact, technological advancement has been at the heart of economic growth and development in recent history. During the last 250 years, brainpower has discovered new power-driven machines, advanced communication devices, new energy sources, and countless ways to produce more output with the same resources. How have innovative products improved your productivity? Consider—to name just a few products—the impact of CD-ROMs, fax machines, VCRs, personal computers, word-processing software, video cameras, and the Internet. In contrast, in many poor countries, waterwheels still bring water to the surface, cloth is woven on handlooms, and ox carts are the major means of transportation. This condition means large inputs of human effort are used relative to capital resources.

The United States and other IACs have provided the world with an abundant accumulation of technological knowledge that might be adopted by those LDCs without the resources to undertake the required cost of research and development. However, the results of this transfer process are mixed. Pacific Rim countries, such as Hong Kong, Singapore, Taiwan, South Korea, and Japan, have surely achieved rapid growth in part from the benefit of technological borrowing. Currently, Russia and other Eastern European nations are attempting to apply existing technological knowledge to boost their rates of growth.

The other side of the coin is that much available technology is not suited to LDCs. The old saying "You need to learn to walk before you can run" often applies to the LDCs. For example, the small farms of most LDCs are not suited for much of the agricultural technology developed for IACs' large farms. And how many factories in the LDCs are ready to use the most modern robotics in the production process? Stated differently, LDCs need appropriate technology, rather than necessarily the latest technology.

Conclusion *Many LDCs continue to experience low growth rates even though IACs provide advanced technologies for them to emulate.*

Political Environment

The discussion above leads to the generalization that in order for LDCs to achieve economic growth and development, they must wisely use natural resources, invest in human and physical capital, and adopt advanced technology. This list of policies is not complete. LDC governments must also create a political environment favorable to economic growth. All too often a large part of the problem in poor countries is the wasting of resources as a result of war and political instability. Political leaders must not be corrupt and/or incompetent. Instead of following policies that favor a small elite ruling class, LDC governments must adopt appropriate domestic and international economic policies, discussed under the following three headings of law and order, infrastructure, and international trade.

To learn more about any country and its economy, visit The World Factbook (http://www.odci.gov/cia /publications/factbook/index.html). *Select Country Listing and then any country of your choice.*

Law and Order A basic governmental function is to establish domestic law and order. This heading includes many areas, such as a stable legal system, stable money and prices, competitive markets, and private ownership of property. In particular, expropriation of private property rights among LDCs is a barrier to growth. Well-defined private property rights have fostered economic growth in the IACs because this institutional policy has encouraged an entrepreneurial class. Private ownership provides individuals with the incentive to save money and invest in businesses. A stable political environment that ensures private ownership of profits also provides an incentive for individuals in other countries to invest in developing poor countries.

Infrastructure Assuming an LDC government maintains law and order and the price system is used to allocate goods and services, it is vital that wise decisions be made concerning infrastructure. Indeed, many of the greatest problems of LDCs concern inadequate infrastructure. Without such public goods as roads, schools, bridges, and public health and sanitation services, poor countries are unable to generate the substantial external benefits that are an important ingredient in economic growth and development. From the viewpoint of individual firms, infrastructure must be provided by government because these public goods projects would be too costly for a firm to undertake.

Hong Kong: A Limping Pacific Rim Tiger

Applicable Concept: newly industrialized countries

As the map shows, the Pacific Rim countries are located along an arc extending from Japan and South Korea in the north to New Zealand in the south. The Four Tigers of East Asia are the newly industrialized countries of Hong Kong, Singapore, South Korea, and Taiwan. These "miracle economies" have often experienced higher economic growth rates, lower inflation rates, and lower unemployment rates than many of the other advanced countries. For example, the average growth rates from 1965 to 1996 range from 8.9 percent (South Korea) to 6.5 percent (Taiwan) compared to 2.4 percent for the United States and 4.5 percent for Japan. In addition to the Four Tigers, China, Malaysia, Indonesia, Thailand, and Vietnam have been high-growth economies. The Asian financial crisis beginning in 1997 resulted in economic turmoil and lower growth or recession for these countries. As noted on the map, Hong Kong's GDP growth rate "limped" to an estimated −4 percent in 1998.

Prior to the Asian financial crisis on the verge of the 21st century, Hong Kong was a great success story. When Adam Smith published his famous book, *The Wealth of Nations*, in 1776, Hong Kong was little more than a barren rock island almost void of natural resources except fish. Today, Hong Kong has

earned the reputation of a bustling free enterprise model in spite of the fact that six million people are crowded into only about 400 square miles. In fact, this is one of the highest population densities in the world.

Today, following the doctrine of Adam Smith, this economy is a paragon of laissez faire. Hong Kong has among the lowest individual and corporate income tax rates in the world and almost no legal restrictions on business. There is no capital gains tax, no interest tax, and no sales tax. Hong Kong has become the largest banking center in the Pacific region after Tokyo. International trade is also largely unrestricted, and Hong Kong depends to a large extent on trade through its magnificent harbor for its economic success. Its leading exports are electronics, clothing, textiles, toys and watches, domestic appliances, and plastics. Hong Kong's total exports per capita far exceed the average for either

the United States or Japan. Tariffs on imported goods are low, and Hong Kong is known as a safe-haven warehouse and trading center, with little or no interference from the government.

Hong Kong's people have proven that industrious people (entrepreneurs) working hard on a crowded island with minimum regulations and open trade can improve their living standard without natural resources. However, Hong Kong faces economic and political uncertainty. Under a 99-year lease signed in 1898, British rule transferred to the People's Republic of China in 1997. Will China allow Hong Kong to continue to follow Adam Smith's laissez-faire philosophy and return to high growth rates, or will Hong Kong change direction? It is anyone's guess.

ANALYZE THE ISSUE

One of the keys to Hong Kong's success is its free trade policy. Why is this so important for a developing country? What would be the effect of Hong Kong attempting to protect its domestic industries by raising tariffs and following other protectionist trade policies?

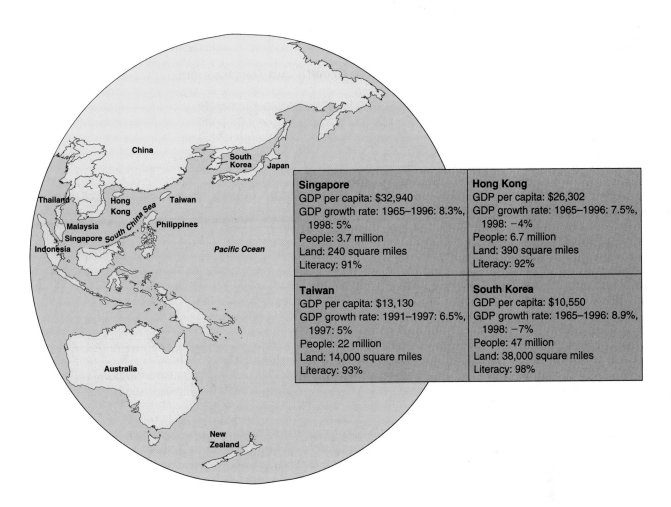

Singapore
GDP per capita: $32,940
GDP growth rate: 1965–1996: 8.3%, 1998: 5%
People: 3.7 million
Land: 240 square miles
Literacy: 91%

Hong Kong
GDP per capita: $26,302
GDP growth rate: 1965–1996: 7.5%, 1998: −4%
People: 6.7 million
Land: 390 square miles
Literacy: 92%

Taiwan
GDP per capita: $13,130
GDP growth rate: 1991–1997: 6.5%, 1997: 5%
People: 22 million
Land: 14,000 square miles
Literacy: 93%

South Korea
GDP per capita: $10,550
GDP growth rate: 1965–1996: 8.9%, 1998: −7%
People: 47 million
Land: 38,000 square miles
Literacy: 98%

International Trade   In general, LDCs can benefit from an expanding volume of trade. For example, this is the theory behind the North American Free Trade Agreement (NAFTA) and the General Agreement on Tariffs and Trade (GATT), discussed in the chapter on international trade and finance. As explained earlier in this chapter, policies such as tariffs and quotas restrain international trade and thereby economic growth and development. These trade policies are anti-growth because they restrict the ability of people in one country to trade with people in other countries. Similarly, a country that fixes the exchange rate of its own currency above the market-determined exchange rate makes that country's exports less attractive to foreigners. This means, in turn, that domestic citizens sell less of their goods to foreigners and earn less foreign currency with which to buy imports.

Read more about GATT (http://iisd1.iisd.ca/trade /wto/gatt.htm) *and NAFTA* (http://www.nafta.net/naftagre .htm).

Conclusion *Exchange rate controls artificially set by government above the market exchange rates reduce the volume of both exports and imports (international trade).*

EXHIBIT 7

Key Categories That Determine Economic Growth and Development

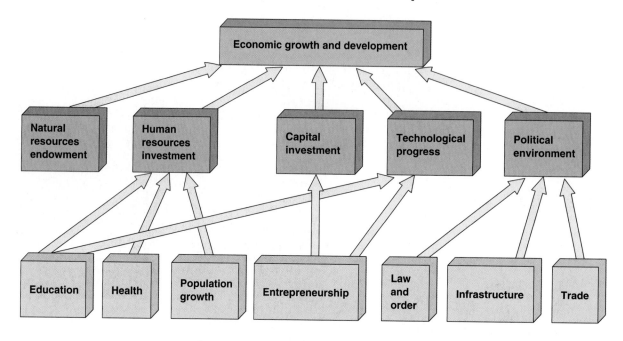

There are five basic categories that interact to determine the economic growth and development of countries: natural resources, human resources, capital, technological progress, and the political environment. The exhibit also indicates important factors that influence investment in human resources, capital, and the political environment. LDCs are faced with a formidable task. Since economic growth and development are multidimensional, LDCs must improve many factors in order to achieve economic progress.

Exhibit 7 summarizes the key factors explained above that determine the economic growth and development of countries. Analysis of this exhibit reveals that economic growth and development are the result of a multidimensional process. This means that it is difficult for countries to break the poverty barrier because they must follow various avenues and improve many factors in order to gain increased economic well-being. But it is important to remember that lack of one or more key factors, such as natural resources, does not necessarily keep an LDC in the trap of underdevelopment.

Conclusion *There is no single strategy for economic growth and development.*

The Helping Hand of Advanced Countries

How can poor countries escape the vicious circle of poverty? Low GDP per capita leads to low savings and investment, which lead, in turn, to low growth. Although there is no easy way for poor countries to become richer, the United States and other advanced countries can be an instrument of growth. The necessary savings can come from the LDCs' own domestic savings or from foreign external sources that include foreign private investment, foreign aid, and foreign loans.

Exhibit 8 illustrates how external funds can shift a country's production possibilities curve outward. Here you should review Exhibit 6. Suppose country Alpha is trapped in poverty and produces only enough capital (K_a) to replace the existing capital being worn out. Alpha's consumption level is at C_a, corresponding to point A on production possibilities curve PPC_1. Because C_a is at the subsistence level, Alpha cannot save and invest by substituting current consumption for capital and move upward along PPC_1. This inability to increase capital means Alpha cannot use internal sources of funds to increase its production possibilities curve in the future. There is a way out of the trap using external sources. Now assume Alpha receives an inflow of funds from abroad and buys capital goods that increase its rate of investment from K_a to K_b. At K_b, the rate of capital formation exceeds the value of capital depreciated, and Alpha's production possibilities curve shifts rightward to PPC_2. Economic growth made possible by external investment means Alpha can achieve economic growth without reducing its consumption level (C_a) at point B on PPC_2.

Foreign Private Investment

Many countries' development benefits from private-sector foreign investment from private investors. For example, Microsoft might finance construction of a plant in the Philippines to manufacture software, or Bank of America may make loans to the government of Haiti. These large multinational corporations and commercial banks supply scarce capital to the LDCs. A multinational corporation is a firm with headquarters in one country and one or more branch plants in other countries. Multinational firms often seek new investment opportunities in LDCs because these poor countries offer abundant supplies of low-wage labor and raw materials. But the political environment in the LDCs must be conducive to investment. Multinational corporations often become the largest employers, largest taxpayers, and largest exporters in the LDCs.

Foreign Aid

About 1 percent of the U.S. federal budget is spent on **foreign aid**. Foreign aid is the transfer of money or resources from one government to another for which no repayment is required. These transfers may be made as outright grants, technical assistance, or food supplies. Foreign aid flows from country to country through governments and voluntary agencies, such as

Foreign aid
The transfer of money or resources from one government to another for which no repayment is required.

EXHIBIT 8

The Effect of External Financing on an LDC's Production Possibilities Curve

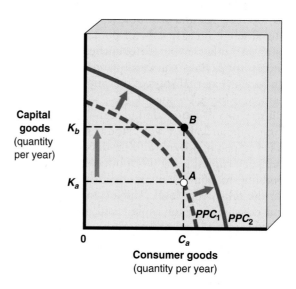

The poor country of Alpha is initially operating at point A on production possibilities curve PPC_1, with only enough capital (K_a) to replace depreciation. If C_a is the consumption level of subsistence, Alpha's economy cannot grow by reducing consumption. An inflow of external funds from abroad permits the LDC to increase its capital from K_a to K_b without reducing its consumption (C_a), and its production possibilities curve shifts outward to PPC_2.

Agency for International Development (AID)
The agency of the U.S. State Department that is in charge of U.S. aid to foreign countries.

Learn more about the Agency for International Development (http://www.info.usaid.gov/).

the Red Cross, CARE, and Church World Relief. The United States distributes most of its official development assistance through the **Agency for International Development,** established in 1961. The Agency for International Development (AID) is the agency of the U.S. State Department that is in charge of U.S. aid to foreign countries.

One reason that countries like the United States provide foreign aid to LDCs is the belief that it is a moral responsibility of richer countries to share wealth with poorer countries. A second reason is that it is in the best economic interest of the IACs to help the LDCs. When these countries become more prosperous, the IACs have more markets for their exports, and thereby all countries benefit from trade.

The LDCs often complain that foreign aid has too many economic and political strings attached. Loans are often offered on a "take it or leave it" basis, tied to policies other than basic trade policies, such as human rights, politics, or the military. Consequently, many LDCs argue for "trade, not aid." If the IACs would simply buy more goods from the LDCs, the LDCs could use their gains in export earnings to purchase more capital and other resources needed for growth. Many people in the United States feel that most foreign aid is a waste of money because it is misused by the recipient countries. This belief has caused Congress to grow increasingly reluctant to send taxpayers' money abroad except in the clearest cases of need or for reasons of national security.

Foreign Loans

A third source of external funds that can be used to finance domestic investment is loans from abroad. Governments, international organizations, and private banks all make loans to LDCs. Like foreign private investment and foreign aid, loans give LDCs the opportunity to shift their production possibilities curves outward. There are various types of loan sources for LDCs. Bilateral loans are made directly from one country to another. The principal agent for official U.S. bilateral loans is the U.S. Agency for International Development, introduced above.

One prominent multilateral lending agency is the **World Bank**. The 175-member World Bank is the lending agency affiliated with the United Nations that makes long-term low-interest loans and provides technical assistance to less-developed countries. Loans are made only after a planning period lasting a year or more. The World Bank was established in 1944 by major nations meeting in Bretton Woods, New Hampshire. Its first charge was to assist postwar reconstruction. Today, the World Bank is located in Washington, D.C., and its main purpose is to channel funds from rich countries to poor countries. The World Bank makes "last resort" loans to LDCs to finance basic infrastructure projects, such as dams, irrigation systems, and transportation facilities, for which private financing is not available. In addition, the World Bank helps LDCs get loans from private lenders by insuring the loans. Thus, the poor countries are able to complete projects and use the economic returns to pay off the lender with interest.

The World Bank is not the only multilateral lending agency making loans to LDCs. The World Bank's partner institution is the **International Monetary Fund**. The International Monetary Fund (IMF) is the lending agency that makes short-term conditional low-interest loans to developing countries. The IMF was also established at Bretton Woods in 1944. The purpose of the IMF is to help countries overcome short-run financial difficulties. Typically, the IMF makes conditional loans that require the debtor countries to implement fiscal and monetary policies that will alleviate balance-of-payments problems. The 182-member IMF is not a charitable institution. It operates like a credit union with funding quotas that earn interest on the loans. The United States is the IMF's largest shareholder, and thus has effective veto power over IMF decisions.

In recent years, the IMF has performed a major role in providing short-term loans to developing countries and to economies making the transition to capitalism. In the late 1990s, the IMF provided multibillion-dollar bailouts to Russia, Asia, Brazil, and other countries experiencing economic turmoil. Critics argue that as long as governments believe that the IMF will

World Bank
The lending agency that makes long-term low-interest loans and provides technical assistance to less-developed countries.

International Monetary Fund (IMF)
The lending agency that makes short-term conditional low-interest loans to developing countries.

Visit the International Monetary Fund (http://www.imf.org/).

CHECKPOINT

Is the Minimum Wage an Antipoverty Solution for Poor Countries?

Imagine you are an economic adviser to the president of a poor LDC. The president is seeking policies to promote economic growth and a higher standard of living for citizens of this country. You are asked whether adopting a minimum wage equal to the average of the IACs' average hourly wages would achieve these goals. Evaluate this policy.

bail them out, they will fail to correct their own problems. IMF supporters counter that if the IMF does not intervene, troubled economies will default on outstanding loans and cause a worldwide ripple effect. Critics respond that a flood of low-cost short-term loans from IMF encourages bad government policies and excessive risk-taking by banks. Consequently, the bailout in a crisis generates new financial crises and reduces world economic growth.

Finally, private banks also engage in lending to LDCs. Until the 1970s, LDCs borrowed primarily from the World Bank and foreign governments. In the 1970s, private banks began to lend to both governments and private firms in LDCs. During the 1980s, the news was full of stories that some U.S. banks had made so many risky loans to LDCs that default on these loans would lead to the failure of one major U.S. bank after another. As the story goes, "If you can't repay the bank for your car loan, you're in trouble. If a government can't repay the bank a billion dollars, the bank's in trouble."

In the late 1980s, the debt crisis was avoided by (1) writing off some of the loans, (2) lowering the interest rate of remaining loans, and (3) lending LDCs more money to pay interest on their debt. The U.S. government, other Western governments, and the IMF were active in these solutions. Was this a case of "throwing good money after bad" because many loans would never be repaid? The answer is No. Easing the debt burden salvaged some payments and was in the best interest of both rich and poor countries because a fresh start encouraged trade. Nevertheless, the huge outstanding debts of some of the LDCs (especially Mexico, Argentina, Chile, and Brazil) make another debt crisis a lingering possibility.

KEY CONCEPTS

GDP per capita
Industrially advanced
    countries (IACs)
Less developed countries
    (LDCs)

Vicious circle of poverty
Infrastructure
Foreign aid
Agency for International
    Development (AID)

World Bank
International Monetary
    Fund (IMF)

SUMMARY

- **GDP per capita** provides a general index of a country's standard of living. Countries with low GDP per capita and slow growth in GDP per capita are less able to satisfy basic needs for food, shelter, clothing, education, and health.

- **Industrially advanced countries (IACs)** are countries in which GDP per capita is high and output is produced by technologically advanced capital. Countries that earn high income without widespread industrial development, such as the oil-rich Arab countries, are not included in the IAC list.

- **Less-developed countries (LDCs)** are countries with low production per person. In these countries, output is produced without large amounts of technologically advanced capital and well-educated labor. The LDCs account for about three-fourths of the world's population.

- The **Four Tigers of the Pacific Rim** are Hong Kong, Singapore, South Korea, and Taiwan. These newly industrialized countries have achieved high growth rates and standards of living approaching those of many of the IACs.

- **GDP per capita comparisons** are subject to four problems: (1) The accuracy of LDC data is questionable, (2) GDP per capita ignores the degree of income distribution, (3) changes in exchange rates affect gaps between countries, and (4) there is no adjustment for the cost-of-living differences between countries.

- **Economic growth and economic development** are related, but somewhat different, concepts. Economic growth is measured quantitatively by GDP per capita, while economic development is a broader concept. In addition to GDP per capita, economic development includes quality-of-life measures, such as life expectancy at birth, adult literacy rate, and per capita energy consumption. Economic growth and development are the result of a complex process that is determined by five major factors: (1) natural resources, (2) human resources, (3) capital, (4) technological progress, and (5) the political environment. There is no single correct strategy for economic development, and a lack of strength in one or more of the five areas does not prevent growth.

- ★ The **vicious circle of poverty** is a trap in which the LDC is too poor to save and therefore it cannot invest and shift its production possibilities curve outward. As a result, the LDC remains poor. One way for a poor country to gain savings, invest, and grow is to use funds from external sources, such as foreign private investment, foreign aid, and foreign loans. Borrowing by many LDCs led to the debt crisis of the 1980s, which was resolved by writing off and restructuring the loans.

Vicious circle of poverty

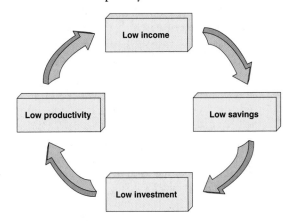

SUMMARY OF CONCLUSION STATEMENTS

- LDCs' GDP per capita is subject to greater measurement errors than data for IACs.

- GDP per capita comparisons among nations can be misleading because GDP per capita does not measure income distribution.

- A conversion problem may widen or narrow the GDP per capita gap between nations because the fluctuations in exchange rates do not reflect actual differences in the value of goods and services produced.

- Differences in purchasing power that affect living standards can alter the interpretation of international comparisons of GDP per capita.

- In general, GDP per capita is highly correlated with alternative measures of quality of life.

- Natural resource endowment can promote economic growth, but a country can develop without a large natural resource base.

- Investment in human capital generally results in increases in GDP per capita.

- Rapid population growth combined with low human capital investment explains why many countries are LDCs.

- Nations that grow slowly or experience declines in GDP per capita will fail to catch up with the IACs' standard of living.

- There is a significant positive relationship between investment and economic growth and development.

- Many LDCs continue to experience low growth rates even though IACs provide advanced technologies for them to emulate.

- Exchange rate controls artificially set by government above the market exchange rates reduce the volume of both exports and imports (international trade).

- There is no single strategy for economic growth and development.

STUDY QUESTIONS AND PROBLEMS

1. What is the difference between industrially advanced countries (IACs) and less-developed countries (LDCs)? List five IACs and five LDCs.

2. Explain why GDP per capita comparisons among nations are not a perfect measure of differences in economic well-being.

3. Assume you are given the following data for country Alpha and country Beta:

Country	GDP per Capita
Alpha	$15,000
Beta	25,000

   a. Based on the GDP per capita data given above, what country would you prefer to live in?

   b. Now assume you are given the following additional quality-of-life data. In which country would you prefer to reside?

Country	Life Expectancy at Birth	Daily per Capita Calorie Supply	Per Capita Energy Consumption*
Alpha	75	2,500	4,000
Beta	60	3,000	3,000

*Kilograms of oil equivalent.

4. What is the difference between economic development and economic growth? Give examples of how each of these concepts can be measured.

5. Do you agree with the argument that the rich nations are getting richer and the poor nations are getting poorer? Is this an oversimplification? Explain.

6. Explain why it is so difficult for poor LDCs to generate investment in capital in order to increase productivity and growth and therefore improve their standard of living.

7. Why is the quest for economic growth and development complicated?

8. Which of the following is associated with a high or low level of economic growth and development:

	High	Low
a. Overpopulation	_____	_____
b. Highly skilled labor	_____	_____
c. High savings rate	_____	_____
d. Political stability	_____	_____
e. Low capital accumulation	_____	_____
f. Advanced technology	_____	_____
g. Highly developed infrastructure	_____	_____
h. High proportion of agriculture	_____	_____
i. High degree of income inequality	_____	_____

9. Without external financing from foreign private investment, foreign aid, and foreign loans, poor countries are caught in the vicious circle of poverty. Explain. How does external financing help poor countries achieve economic growth and development?

10. What are some of the problems for LDCs of accepting foreign aid?

11. Why would an LDC argue for "trade, not aid"?

12. Explain the differences among the Agency for International Development (AID), the World Bank, and the International Monetary Fund (IMF).

ONLINE EXERCISES

Exercise 1

Visit Handbook of International Statistics (http://www.odci.gov/cia/publications/hies97/toc.htm), and follow these steps:

1. Select Economic Profile and Tables 2 and 4. Compare the economic profiles of OECD countries to those of newly industrializing economies.

2. Select Aggregate Trends and Table 10. Compare defense expenditures among nations.

3. Select Independent Republics of the Former Soviet Union and Table 26. Compare economic and social indicators among the republics of the former Soviet Union.

4. Select Foreign Trade and Aid and Table 117. Compare new industrializing economies' trade with the United States.

5. Select Environmental Topics and Table 132. Compare carbon dioxide emissions among nations.

Exercise 2

Visit the World Bank Group, and select the latest World Development Report (http://www.worldbank.org/).

Exercise 3

Visit the World Bank Group, and browse Regions and Countries (http://www.worldbank.org/html/extdr/regions.htm). Select a country, and read a brief.

Exercise 4

Visit the World Bank Group (http://www.worldbank.org/), and browse Development Topics.

Exercise 5

Visit the United Nations Social Indicators (http://www.un.org/Depts/unsd/social/main.htm), and select Income and Economic Activity. Compare per capita GDP among countries. Also compare male and female economic activity rates for different countries.

CHECKPOINT ANSWERS

Does Rapid Growth Mean a Country Is Catching Up?

GDP growth alone does not measure the standard of living. You must also consider population. Even though Beta experienced a greater GDP growth rate, its GDP per capita might be less than Alpha's because its population growth rate is greater. Of course, the reverse is also possible, but without population data, we cannot say. If you said which country's people are better off cannot be determined because the GDP must be divided by the population to measure the average standard of living, **YOU ARE CORRECT.**

Is the Minimum Wage an Antipoverty Solution for Poor Countries?

An important source of foreign investment for LDCs is multinational corporations that locate in these countries. LDCs compete with each other for the economic growth and development benefits that these multinational corporations can provide. For an LDC to win the competition, it must offer political stability, adequate infrastructure, a favorable business climate, and a cheap labor force. If you said you would not support the president's proposal to raise the minimum wage because it would place the LDC at a competitive disadvantage in the labor market, thereby reducing foreign private investment and growth, **YOU ARE CORRECT.**

PRACTICE QUIZ

For a visual explanation of the correct answers, visit the tutorial at http://tucker.swcollege.com.

1. An LDC is defined as a country
   a. without large stocks of advanced capital.
   b. without well-educated labor.
   c. with low GDP per capita.
   d. that is described by all of the above.

2. According to the definition given in the text, which of the following is *not* an LDC?
   a. India
   b. Egypt
   c. China
   d. Ireland

3. Which of the following is true when making GDP per capita comparisons among nations?
   a. The GDP per capita is subject to greater measurement errors for LDCs compared to IACs.
   b. The GDP per capita does not measure income distribution.
   c. The GDP is subject to fluctuations from changes in exchange rates.
   d. All of the above are true.

4. LDCs are characterized by
   a. high life expectancy.
   b. high adult literacy.
   c. high malnutrition.
   d. all of the above.
   e. none of the above.

5. According to the classification in the text, which of the following is an LDC?
   a. United Arab Emirates
   b. Israel
   c. Hong Kong
   d. Greece

6. When the government fixes the exchange rate above market exchange rates,
   a. international trade falls.
   b. the infrastructure improves.
   c. real GDP per capita rises.
   d. the vicious circle of poverty is broken.

7. Which of the following statements is *true*?
   a. An LDC is a country with a low GDP per capita, low levels of capital, and uneducated workers.
   b. The vicious circle of poverty exists because GDP must rise before people can save and invest.
   c. LDCs are characterized by rapid population growth and low levels of investment in human capital.
   d. All of the above are true.

8. An outward shift of the production possibilities curve represents
   a. economic growth.
   b. a decline in economic development.
   c. a decrease in human capital.
   d. a decrease in resources.

9. Which of the following problems do LDCs face?
   a. Low per capita income and high GDP growth rate.
   b. Low population growth and low per capita income.
   c. Rapid population growth and low human capital.
   d. Low per capita income and high saving rate.

10. Which of the following best defines the vicious circle of poverty?
    a. The GDP per capita must rise before people can save and invest.
    b. People cannot save while capital accumulates.
    c. Increased GDP per capita relates to lower population growth.
    d. Poverty, saving, and investment are related like a circle.

11. Which of the following is infrastructure?
    a. International Harvester tractor plant
    b. Waste and water system provided by government
    c. USAirways airplane
    d. Service of postal workers

12. Economic growth and development in LDCs are low because many of them lack
    a. capital investment.
    b. technological progress.
    c. a favorable political environment.
    d. all of the above.
    e. none of the above.

13. Which of the following makes short-term conditional low-interest loans to developing countries?
    a. The Agency for International Development (AID)
    b. The World Bank
    c. The International Monetary Fund (IMF)
    d. The New International Economic Order (NIEO)

14. Which of the following argues that IACs should help LDCs by imposing lower trade barriers on poor countries than on rich countries?
    a. The Agency for International Development (AID)
    b. The World Bank
    c. The International Monetary Fund (IMF)
    d. The New International Economic Order (NIEO)

Answers to Odd-Numbered Study Questions and Problems

Chapter 1

1. A poor nation, in which many lack food, clothing, and shelter, certainly experiences wants beyond the availability of goods and services to satisfy these unfulfilled wants. On the other hand, no wealthy nation has all the resources necessary to produce everything everyone in the nation wishes to have. Even if you had $1 million and were completely satisfied with your share of goods and services, other desires would be unfulfilled. There is never enough time to accomplish all the things that you can imagine would be worthwhile.

3. a. capital

5. a. microeconomic issue
   b. macroeconomic issue
   c. microeconomic issue
   d. macroeconomic issue

7. The real world is full of complexities that make it difficult to understand and predict the relationships between variables. For example, the relationship between changes in the price of gasoline and changes in consumption of gasoline requires abstraction from the reality that such variables as the fuel economy of cars and weather conditions often change at the same time as the price of gasoline.

9. The two events are associated, and the first event (cut in military spending) is the cause of the second event (higher unemployment in the defense industry). The point is that association does not necessarily mean causation, but it might.

11. d. statement of normative economics

Appendix to Chapter 1

1. a. The probability of living is *inversely* related to age. This model could be affected by improvements in diet, better health care, reductions in hazards to health in the workplace, or changes in the speed limit.

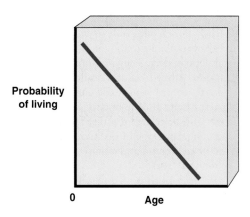

b. Annual income and years of formal education are *directly* related. This relationship might be influenced by changes in such human characteristics as intelligence, motivation, ability, and family background. An example of an institutional change that could affect this relationship over a number of years is the draft.

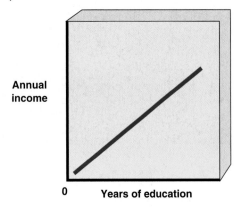

c. Inches of snow and sales of bathing suits are *inversely* related. The weather forecast and the price of travel to sunny vacation spots can affect this relationship.

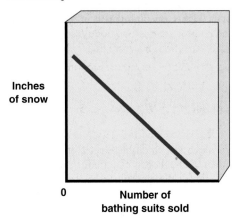

d. Most alumni and students will argue that the number of football games won is *directly* related to the athletic budget. They reason that winning football is great advertising and results in increased attendance, contributions, and enrollment that, in turn, increase the athletic budget. Success in football can also be related to other factors, such as school size, age and type of institution, number and income of alumni, and quality of the faculty and administrators.

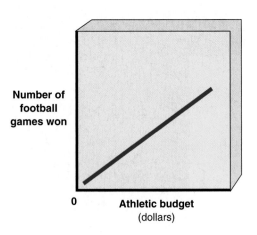

Chapter 2

1. Because the wants of individuals and society exceed the goods and services available to satisfy these desires, each must make choices. The consumption possibilities of an individual with a fixed income are limited, and the result is that additional consumption of one item necessarily precludes an expenditure on another next best choice. The foregone alternative is called the opportunity cost, and this concept also applies to societal decisions. If society allocates resources to the production of guns, then those same resources cannot be used at the same time to make butter.

3. Regardless of the price of a lunch, economic resources—land, labor, and capital—are used to produce the lunch. These scarce resources are no longer available to produce other goods and services.

5. Using marginal analysis, students weigh the benefits of attending college against the costs. There is an incentive to attend college when the benefits (improved job opportunities, income, intellectual improvement, social life, and so on) outweigh the opportunity costs.

7.

Flowerboxes	Opportunity Cost (Pies Foregone)
0	
1	4 (30 − 26)
2	5 (26 − 21)
3	6 (21 − 15)
4	7 (15 − 8)
5	8 (8 − 0)

9. Movements along the curve are efficient points and conform to the well-known "free lunch" statement. However, inefficient points are exceptions because it is possible to produce more of one output without producing less of another output.

11.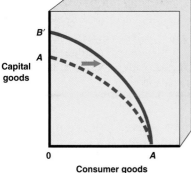

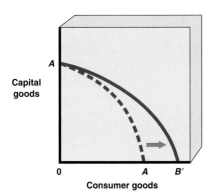

Chapter 3

1. If people buy a good or service because higher quality is associated with higher price, this is a violation of the ceteris paribus assumption. An increase in the quantity demanded results only from a decrease in price. Quality and other nonprice determinants of demand, such as tastes and preferences and the price of related goods, are held constant in the model.

3. a. Demand for cars decreases; oil and cars are *complements*.
   b. Demand for insulation increases; oil and home insulation are *substitutes*.
   c. Demand for coal increases; oil and coal are *substitutes*.
   d. Demand for tires decreases; oil and tires are *complements*.

5. One reason that the demand curve for word processing software shifted to the right might be that people desire new, higher-quality output features. The sup-

ply curve can shift to the right when new technology makes it possible to offer more software for sale at different prices.

7. a. Demand shifts to the right.
   b. Supply shifts to the left.
   c. Supply shifts to the right.
   d. Demand shifts to the right.
   e. Demand shifts to the right.
   f. Supply of corn shifts to the left.

9. a. The supply of compact disc players shifts rightward.
   b. The demand for compact disc players is unaffected.
   c. The equilibrium price falls, and the equilibrium quantity increases.
   d. The demand for compact discs increases because of the fall in the price of the disc players (a complementary good).

11. The number of seats (quantity supplied) remains constant, but the demand curve shifts because tastes and preferences change according to the importance of each game. Although demand changes, the price is a fixed amount, and to manage a shortage, colleges and universities use amount of contributions, number of years as a contributor, or some other rationing device.

Chapter 4

1.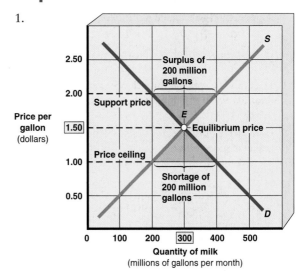

a. The equilibrium price is $1.50 per gallon, and the equilibrium quantity is 300 million gallons per month. The price system will restore the market's $1.50 per gallon price because either a surplus will drive prices down or a shortage will drive prices up.

b. The support price results in a persistent surplus of 200 million gallons of milk per month, which the government purchases with taxpayers' money. Consequently, taxpayers who do not drink milk are still paying for milk. The purpose of the support price is to bolster the incomes of milk farmers.

c. The ceiling price will result in a persistent shortage of 200 million gallons of milk per month, but 200 million gallons are purchased by consumers at the low price of $1.00 per gallon. The shortage places a burden on the government both to ration milk in order to be fair and to prevent black markets. The government's goal is to keep the price of milk below the equilibrium price of $1.50 per gallon, which would be set by a free market.

3. The labor market can be divided into two separate markets, one for skilled union workers and one for unskilled workers. If the minimum wage is above the equilibrium wage rate and is raised, the effect will be to increase the demand for, and the wage of, skilled union workers because the two groups are substitutes.

5. The equilibrium price rises.

7. The government can reduce emissions by (a) regulations that require smoke-abatement equipment or (b) pollution taxes that shift supply leftward.

9. Pure public goods are not produced in sufficient quantities by private markets because there is no feasible method to exclude free riders.

Chapter 5

1. Demand is elastic because the percentage change in quantity was greater than the percentage change in price.

3. If the price of used cars is raised 1 percent, the quantity demanded will fall 3 percent. If the price is raised 10 percent, the quantity demanded will fall 30 percent.

5.
$$E_d = \frac{\%\Delta Q}{\%\Delta P} = \frac{\dfrac{4{,}500 - 5{,}000}{5{,}000 + 4{,}500}}{\dfrac{3{,}500 - 3{,}000}{3{,}000 + 3{,}500}} = \frac{\dfrac{1}{19}}{\dfrac{1}{13}} = 0.68$$

The price elasticity of demand for the university is inelastic.

7. Demand for popcorn is perfectly inelastic, and total revenue will increase.

9. a. Sunkist oranges
   b. car
   c. foreign travel in the long run

11. Furniture sales fall by 30 percent and physician services by only 3 percent. Thus, the demand for physician services is much less responsive to a reduction in income than the demand for furniture.

13. The negative number tells you car tires are complements. If the price of cars rises by 10 percent, the quantity demanded of car tires falls by 20 percent.

15. The demand for a product becomes more inelastic, the greater the amount of a tax on this product is that sellers can pass on to consumers by raising the product's price.

Chapter 6

1. Utility is a subjective concept, and, therefore, this statement may or may not be true.

3. Marginal utility is 10 utils. When you attend the fourth party, total utility will increase, but marginal utility will be less than 10 utils.

5. In consumer equilibrium, the marginal utility ratio is 3/4, which is equal to the price ratio.

7. As people consume more of any product, eventually the satisfaction per unit decreases. Since the marginal utility from additional units falls, people will not buy a greater quantity unless the price falls.

9. The initial consumer equilibrium is as follows:

$$\frac{MU \text{ of steak meal}}{Price \text{ of steak meal}} = \frac{MU \text{ of hamburger meal}}{Price \text{ of hamburger meal}}$$

$$\frac{12 \text{ utils}}{\$10} = \frac{3 \text{ utils}}{\$5}$$

The marginal utility per dollar for each good equals 1.2. If the price of a hamburger meal falls to $2, this equality no longer holds. Now the marginal utility per dollar for a hamburger meal becomes higher at 1.5 (3 utils/$2). James can now increase his total utility by purchasing more hamburger meals per month. Given the law of diminishing returns, the marginal utility of hamburger meals falls until consumer equilibrium is restored.

Chapter 7

1. a. explicit cost
   b. explicit cost
   c. implicit cost
   d. implicit cost
   e. explicit cost
   f. implicit cost

3. a.

Labor	Marginal Product
1	8
2	10
3	12
4	13
5	12
6	10
7	8
8	6
9	3
10	−2

b.

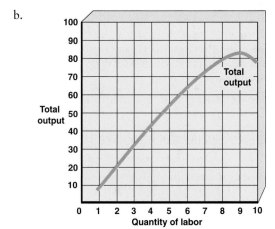

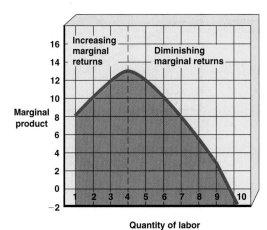

5. None. The position of a firm's short-run average total cost curve is not related to the demand curve.

7. The *ATC* and *AVC* curves converge as output expands because *ATC* = *AVC* + *AFC*. As output increases, *AFC* declines, so most of *ATC* is therefore *AVC*.

9. The average total cost–marginal cost rule states that when the marginal cost is below the average total cost, the addition to total cost is below the average total cost, and the average total cost falls. When the marginal cost is greater than the average total cost, the average total cost rises. In this case, the average total cost is at a minimum because it is equal to the marginal cost.

11. The marginal product for any number of workers is the slope of the total output curve. The marginal product is the derivative of the total output curve dTO/dQ, where *TO* is the total output and *Q* is the number of workers.

Chapter 8

1. A perfectly competitive firm will not advertise. Because all firms in the industry sell the same product, there is no reason for customers to be influenced by ads into buying one firm's product, rather than another firm's product.

3.

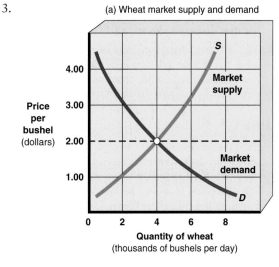

(a) Wheat market supply and demand

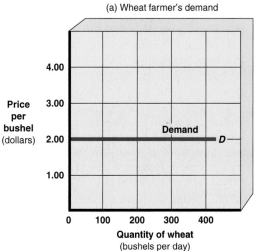

(a) Wheat farmer's demand

A single wheat farmer is a price taker facing a perfectly elastic demand curve because one seller in perfect competition has no control over its price. The reason is that each wheat farmer is one among many, sells a homogeneous product, and must compete with any new farmer entering the wheat market.

5. At a price of $150, the firm produces 4 units and earns an economic profit of $70 ($TR - TC = \$600 - \$530$). The firm breaks even at an output of 2 units.

7. This statement is incorrect. A firm can earn maximum profit (or minimum loss) when marginal revenue equals marginal cost. The confusion is between the "marginal" and the "total" concepts. Marginal cost is the change in total cost from one additional unit of output, and marginal revenue is the change in total revenue from one additional unit of output.

9. The statement is incorrect. The perfectly competitive firm must consider both its marginal revenue and its marginal cost. Instead of trying to sell all the quantity of output possible, the firm will sell the quantity where $MR = MC$ because beyond this level of output the firm earns less profit.

11. Advise the residential contractor to shut down because the market price exceeds the average variable cost and the firm cannot cover its operating costs.

Chapter 9

1. Each market is served by a single firm providing a unique product. There are no close substitutes for local telephone service, professional football in San Francisco, and first-class mail service. A government franchise imposes a legal barrier to potential competitors in the telephone and first-class mail services. An NFL franchise grants monopoly power to its members in most geographic areas.

3. The reason may be that the hospital has monopoly power because it is the only hospital in the area and patients have no choice. On the other hand, there may be many drugstores competing to sell drugs, and this keeps prices lower than those charged by the hospital.

5. In a natural monopoly, a single seller can produce electricity at a lower cost because the *LRAC* curve declines. One firm can therefore sell electricity at a cheaper price and drive its competitor out of business over time. Another possibility would be for two competing firms to merge and earn greater profit by lowering cost further.

7. In this special case, sales maximization and profit maximization are the same. The monopolist should

charge $2.50 per unit, produce 5 units of output, and earn $12.50 in profit. When the marginal cost curve is not equal to zero, the monopolist's $MR = MC$ output is less than 5 units of output, the price is higher than $2.50 per unit, and profit is below $12.50.

9. a. increase output
   b. decrease output

11. a. not price discrimination
    b. price discrimination
    c. not price discrimination if justified by a transportation cost difference
    d. price discrimination

Chapter 10

1. The monopolistically competitive firm's demand curve is less elastic (steeper) than a perfectly competitive firm's demand curve, but more elastic (flatter) than a monopolist's demand curve.

3. a. P_1
   b. Q_1
   c. Q_3
   d. greater than the marginal cost ($B > A$)

5.

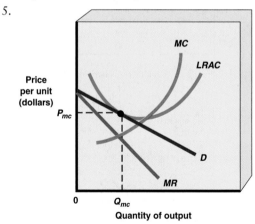

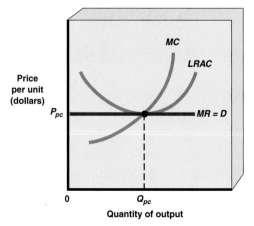

Because $P_{mc} > MC$, the monopolistically competitive firm fails to achieve allocative efficiency. The monopolistically competitive firm is also inefficient because it charges a higher price and produces less output than under perfect competition. The perfectly competitive firm sets P_{pc} equal to MC and produces a level of output corresponding to the minimum point on the $LRAC$ curve.

7. Answers might include automobiles, airline travel, personal computers, and cigarettes. An oligopoly is distinguished from monopolistic competition by being characterized as having few sellers, rather than many sellers; either a homogeneous or a differentiated product, rather than all differentiated products; and difficult entry, rather than easy entry.

9. Any maverick jeans firm that raises or lowers its price will earn less profits. Therefore, firms in the jeans industry face a kinked demand curve, and prices remain rigid. Although firms do not engage in price competition, they can engage in nonprice competition. Each firm can use advertising and style to market its brand-name product.

11. The pricing behavior follows the price leadership model. The price leader is Hewlett-Packard, which is the largest and most dominant firm in the computer printer industry. After a price war, IBM followed each of Hewlett-Packard's price hikes.

Chapter 11

1. This statement is incorrect. Workers supply their labor to employers. Demand refers to the quantity of labor employers hire at various wage rates based on the marginal revenue product of labor.

3. The MRP of the second worker is this person's contribution to total revenue, which is $50 ($150 − $100). Because $MRP = P \times MP$ and $MP = MRP/P$, the second worker's marginal product (MP) is 10 ($50/$5).

5. The firm in a perfectly competitive labor market is a price taker. Because a single firm buys the labor of a relatively small portion of workers in an industry, it can hire additional workers and not drive up the wage rate. For the industry, however, all firms must offer higher wages to attract workers from other industries.

7. Students investing in education are increasing their human capital. A student with greater human capital increases his or her marginal product. At a given product price, the MRP is higher, and firms find it profitable to hire the better educated worker and pay higher wages.

9. At a wage rate of $90 per day, Zippy Paper Company hires 3 workers because each worker's MRP exceeds or equals the wage rate. Setting the wage rate at $100 per day causes Zippy Paper Company to cut employment from 3 to 2 workers because the third worker's MRP is $10 below the union-caused wage rate of $100 per day.

11. As shown in the exhibit below, for a monopsony, the optimum quantity of labor is 3 quarterbacks, determined at point A, where the MFC curve intersects the MRP curve. However, the team can attract and hire 3 quarterbacks for an annual salary of $300,000 each at point B on the supply of labor curve, rather than paying a quarterback's contribution to the team's revenues (MRP), which is $500,000 per year at point A. In a competitive labor market, the Jacksonville Jaguars hire 4 quarterbacks and pay each $400,000 per year.

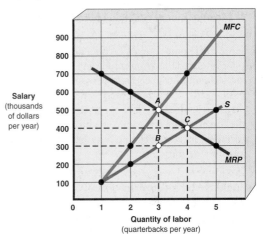

Chapter 12

1. a.

	Alpha		Beta	
Percentage of Families	**Percentage Share**	**Cumulative Share**	**Percentage Share**	**Cumulative Share**
Lowest fifth	17.7%	17.7%	9.0%	9.0%
Second-lowest fifth	19.9	37.6	14.2	23.2
Middle fifth	20.4	58.0	17.5	40.7
Second-highest fifth	20.7	78.7	21.9	62.6
Highest fifth	21.3	100.0	37.4	100.0

b.

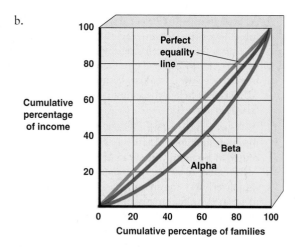

c. Because the Lorenz curve for Alpha is closest to the perfect equality line, Alpha's distribution of income is more equal compared to Beta.

3. Absolute poverty is defined as a dollar figure that represents some level of income per year required to purchase some minimum amount of goods and services essential to meeting a person's or a family's basic needs. Relative poverty is defined as a level of income required to place a person or family in, say, the lowest 20 percent among all persons or families receiving incomes. The poverty line is based on the absolute definition.

5. In-kind transfers are payments in the form of goods and services, rather than cash. Examples include such government programs as food stamps, Medicaid, and housing. Noncash income is not counted in a family's income to determine whether the family's income is below the poverty line.

7. The percentage of families in the United States classified as poor in the 1990s was about 14 percent. Poor families are more likely to live in the South. The age, race, and education of the head of the family are also important characteristics of poor families.

9. The three major criticisms are that welfare (1) reduces the work incentive, (2) is inefficient because the programs cost too much to administer, and (3) treats poor persons with the same needs unequally because the states pay different benefits.

11. This is an opinion question. To agree, you assume that markets are perfectly competitive and discrimination is therefore unprofitable. To disagree, you can argue that in reality labor markets will never be perfectly competitive and the government must therefore address the institutional causes of poverty.

Chapter 13

1. The Sherman Act outlaws price-fixing or anticompetitive practices designed to eliminate rivals. The Clayton Act clarifies the Sherman Act by outlawing specific business practices, including price discrimination, exclusive dealing, tying contracts, stock acquisition, and interlocking directorates. The U.S. Department of Justice and Federal Trade Commission (FTC) are responsible for enforcing these laws. Private firms can also bring suit against other firms under these laws.

3. Both the Robinson-Patman Act and the Celler-Kefauver Act were amendments to close loopholes in the Clayton Act. The Robinson-Patman Act expanded the list of illegal price discrimination practices to include quantity discounting, free advertising, and promotional allowances offered that "substantially lessen competition or tend to create a monopoly." The Celler-Kefauver Act closed the loophole in the Clayton Act whereby competing firms could merge by asset acquisition (not outlawed in the Clayton Act), rather than by acquiring stock (outlawed in the Clayton Act).

5. In fact, Alcoa argued that metals such as copper and steel are substitutes for aluminum. Therefore, the relevant industry to compute market share was the metals industry and not the aluminum industry. If the Court had chosen the U.S. metals industry as the relevant industry, Alcoa would not have a monopoly.

7. a. The federal government will charge the bookstore with predatory pricing in order to monopolize its college market for books, which is a violation of the Sherman Act.
   b. The federal government will charge the real estate firms with collusion to fix prices, which is a violation of the Sherman Act.
   c. The federal government will charge a violation of the Clayton Act because the combined market share of this horizontal merger would substantially lessen competition in the word processing market.
   d. The federal government will not charge a violation because this is a conglomerate merger between firms in unrelated industries.

9. The "necessary" condition would be expected to favor existing regulated firms by eliminating or greatly restricting competition and raising prices. The existing regulated firms are better organized politically than either new competitors or consumers. While consumers favor competition and lower prices, regulators would be expected to interpret "necessary" to mean that the service provided by existing firms is sufficient without new firms.

11. Although a public subsidy achieves efficiency, marginal-cost pricing is usually unpopular with vot-

ers, who must provide the monopolist with public funds. Moreover, a public subsidy gives the monopolist a disincentive to minimize costs.

Chapter 14

1. A competitive industry selling a pollution-generating product will charge a lower price and sell a larger quantity than would be the case for a "green" industry. The competitive industry has lower costs because it fails to include external costs. Lower costs allow a lower price. A lower price leads to a larger quantity demanded and sold.

3. If you choose the $90,000 house, the EMF radiation is *not* an externality. An externality is a third-party effect, whereby buyers and sellers of a product ignore the spillover effects of their transaction. In this case, the market reflects the risk of cancer, with the seller accepting a lower price and the buyer saving $10,000 to reflect the cancer risk.

   Houses have many characteristics that influence their price, including number of rooms, location, nearby schools, and environmental amenities. If you are willing to buy a house near a nuclear plant, or near EMF, you, the buyer, bear the consequences, not a third party.

5. An instructor who automatically flunks students who do not turn in all homework assignments is exhibiting command and control. She is dictating the production process for achieving knowledge. The inefficiencies are that students may turn in poorly done assignments or may copy assignments and that some students may understand the material without doing the homework or may have an alternative production method, such as the use of computer software, to achieve knowledge. The instructor's method is particularly inefficient if her assignments are busywork and do not really help the students to achieve knowledge.

7.

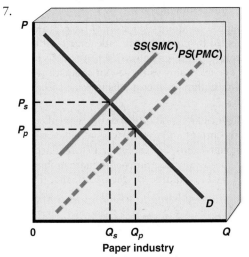

Paper industry

At Q_p, pollution from paper production leads to coffee-colored rivers. At socially efficient Q_s, there is less pollution, and rivers are less polluted. The rivers are unlikely to be pristine, which requires no production at all.

9. Consumers will share in the benefits of cleaner air if any individual buys a less polluting car. Since they enjoy the same benefit whether they pay extra or their neighbor pays extra for a cleaner car, they will let the neighbor buy the cleaner car. Of course, since their neighbor uses the same reasoning, no one ends up paying extra to buy a cleaner car.

11. Convincing examples should be sent to the author of the text. It is very difficult to find markets where the transactions costs of reaching an agreement are near zero. It is also difficult to find two-party situations, since most pollution spills over to many individuals. With many individuals involved, the free-rider problem arises, as a given individual wants to benefit from pollution agreements, but let others bear the cost. There can often be income effects, as fighting pollution may take a large amount of one's income. Candidates for markets where the Coase Theorem might apply include convincing your neighbor to leash her dog (you might help finance invisible fencing), enforcing laws concerning the fencing of cattle (see question 12 for a further discussion), and settling disputes when one builder interferes with the views of existing homes.

13. a. Command and control would dictate the use of an alternative technology with lower carbon emissions.
    b. An effluent tax would place a tax on carbon emissions so that firms could no longer ignore these costs. In turn, prices of carbon-emitting products would increase, and quantities would decrease.
    c. Permits would be issued giving the right to emit carbon. The number of permits would equal the socially efficient emissions level. Firms would be allowed to buy or sell these permits. Firms with higher marginal costs of emissions abatement would buy permits, while firms that could reduce emissions at a lower cost would profit from selling permits.

Chapter 15

1. a. In Alpha, the opportunity cost of producing 1 ton of diamonds is 1/2 ton of pearls. In Beta, the opportunity cost of producing 1 ton of diamonds is 2 tons of pearls.

b. In Alpha, the opportunity cost of producing 1 ton of pearls is 2 tons of diamonds. In Beta, the opportunity cost of producing 1 ton of pearls is 1/2 ton of diamonds.

c. Because Alpha can produce diamonds at a lower opportunity cost than Beta can, Alpha has a comparative advantage in the production of diamonds.

d. Because Beta can produce pearls at a lower opportunity cost than Alpha can, Beta has a comparative advantage in the production of pearls.

e.

	Diamonds (tons per year)	Pearls (tons per year)
Before specialization		
Alpha (at point *B*)	100	25
Beta (at point *C*)	30	120
Total output	130	145
After specialization		
Alpha (at point *A*)	150	0
Beta (at point *D*)	0	180
Total output	150	180

As shown in the above table, specialization in each country increases total world output per year by 20 tons of diamonds and 35 tons of pearls.

f.

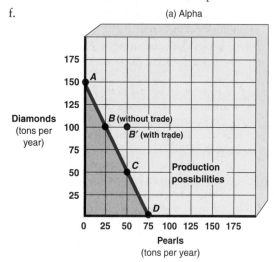

(a) Alpha

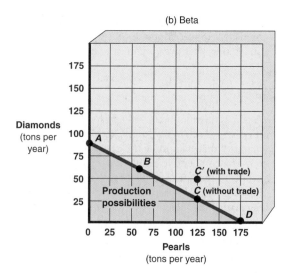

(b) Beta

Without trade, Alpha produces and consumes 100 tons of diamonds and 25 tons of pearls at point *B* on its production possibilities curve. Without trade, Beta produces and consumes 30 tons of diamonds and 120 tons of pearls (point *C*). Now assume Alpha specializes in producing diamonds at point *A* and imports 50 tons of pearls in exchange for 50 tons of diamonds. Through specialization and trade, Alpha moves its consumption possibility to point *B′*, outside its production possibilities curve.

3. The principle of specialization and trade according to comparative advantage applies to both nations and states in the United States. For example, Florida grows oranges, and Idaho grows potatoes. Trade between these states, just like trade among nations, increases the consumption possibilities.

5. United States industries (and their workers) that compete with restricted imports would benefit. Consumers would lose from the reduced supply of imported goods from which to choose and from higher prices for domestic products, resulting from lack of competition from imports.

7. Although some domestic jobs may be lost, new ones are created by international trade. Stated differently, the economy as a whole gains when nations specialize and trade according to the law of comparative advantage, but imports will cost jobs in some specific industries.

9. Although each nation's balance of payments equals zero, its current and capital account balances usually do not equal zero. For example, a current account deficit means a nation purchased more in imports than it sold in exports. On the other hand, this

nation's capital account must have a surplus to offset the current account deficit. This means that foreigners are buying more domestic capital (capital inflow) than domestic citizens are buying foreign capital (capital outflow). Thus, net ownership of domestic capital stock is in favor of foreigners.

11. a.

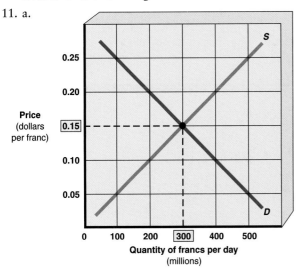

Quantity of francs per day
(millions)

b. $0.15 per franc
c. An excess quantity of 200 million francs would be demanded.

Chapter 16

1. Americans prefer large cars and canned soup. Europeans predominately buy small cars and dry soup. The role of women and minorities in the workplace is an excellent example of how culture relates to the labor factor of production.

3. Such a program would provide additional economic security for the elderly, but higher taxes could reduce the incentive to work, and economic efficiency might be reduced.

5. In a traditional agricultural system, a benefit would be that members of society would cooperate by helping to build barns, harvest, and so on. Under the command system, worrying about errors and crop failures would be minimized because the state makes the decisions and everyone in society has a basic income. In a market economy, a bumper crop would mean large profits and the capacity to improve one's standard of living.

7. Because most economies are mixed systems, this term is too broad to be very descriptive. The terms *capitalism* and *socialism* are more definitive concerning the role of private ownership, market allocations, and decentralized decision-making. Perestroika must confront the fact that embracing a market-oriented system means a transfer of power from the command bureaucracy to consumers. Markets are incompatible with the principle that socialist citizens are supposed to be concerned with the collective interest.

Chapter 17

1. The difference between IACs and LDCs is based on GDP per capita. This classification is somewhat arbitrary. A country with a high GDP per capita and narrow industrial development based on oil, such as the United Arab Emirates, is excluded from the IAC list. There are 21 countries listed in the text as IACs, including Switzerland, Japan, the United States, Singapore, and Hong Kong. The following countries are considered as LDCs: Argentina, Mexico, South Africa, Jordan, and Bangladesh.

3. a. Based only on GDP per capita, you would conclude that Alpha is a better place to live because this country produces a greater output of goods and services per person.
   b. Based on the additional evidence, you would change your mind and prefer to live in Beta because the quality of life data indicate a higher standard of living in this country.

5. As shown in Exhibit 5, the average growth rate of GDP per capita for an IAC was about 4 percent per year between 1965 and 1997. Over the same period of time, the GDP per capita for LDCs was generally below the average rate for the IACs. The argument is oversimplified because there is considerable diversity among the LDCs. For example, Nicaragua had an average growth rate of −4.2 percent, and Congo's average growth rate was −3.5 percent.

7. Economic growth and development are complicated because there is no single prescription that a country can follow. The text presents a multidimensional model with five basic categories: natural resources, human resources, capital, technological progress, and political environment. Because an LDC is weak in one or more of the key factors, such as natural resources, does not necessarily mean that the LDC cannot achieve economic success.

9. Because they are poor countries with low GDP per capita, they lack domestic savings to invest in capital, and lacking investment, they remain poor. The rich in these poor countries often put their savings abroad because of the fear of political instability. An inflow of external funds from abroad permits the LDC to increase its capital without reducing its consumption and to shift its production possibilities curve outward.

11. Poor countries are too poor to save enough to finance domestic capital formation. International trade is a way LDCs can generate savings from abroad. Exports provide the LDC with foreign exchange to pay for imports of capital stock that is necessary for economic growth and development.

Practice Quiz Answers

CHAPTER 1   Introducing the Economic Way of Thinking

1. c   2. d   3. c   4. c   5. a   6. a   7. a   8. a   9. a
10. c   11. a   12. b

APPENDIX TO CHAPTER 1   Applying Graphs to Economics

1. d   2. d   3. a   4. d   5. d   6. c   7. c   8. c

CHAPTER 2   Production Possibilities and Opportunity Cost

1. c   2. a   3. c   4. c   5. b   6. c   7. c   8. e   9. a
10. c   11. b

CHAPTER 3   Market Demand and Supply

1. e   2. a   3. b   4. b   5. a   6. b   7. c   8. b   9. c
10. b   11. c   12. c   13. d   14. d   15. c   16. d   17. d
18. c

CHAPTER 4   Markets in Action

1. a   2. a   3. c   4. d   5. d   6. d   7. c   8. b   9. a
10. b   11. c   12. a

CHAPTER 5   Price Elasticity of Demand and Supply

1. a   2. b   3. a   4. a   5. a   6. d   7. a   8. a   9. d
10. c   11. c   12. c

CHAPTER 6   Consumer Choice Theory

1. c   2. d   3. a   4. a   5. d   6. d   7. c   8. b   9. a
10. a   11. b

CHAPTER 7   Production Costs

1. d   2. b   3. c   4. c   5. d   6. d   7. c   8. d   9. d
10. c   11. c   12. b   13. c   14. b   15. d   16. c   17. d
18. e   19. c

CHAPTER 8   Perfect Competition

1. b. 2. b   3. b   4. b   5. c   6. d   7. b   8. d   9. b
10. b   11. a   12. d   13. b   14. d   15. d   16. a   17. d

CHAPTER 9   Monopoly

1. d   2. d   3. d   4. d   5. b   6. d   7. b   8. d   9. b
10. d   11. e

CHAPTER 10   Monopolistic Competition and Oligopoly

1. b   2. b   3. d   4. d   5. d   6. d   7. a   8. a   9. b
10. d   11. d   12. a   13. c   14. b   15. a

CHAPTER 11   Labor Markets

1. d   2. a   3. c   4. a   5. c   6. b   7. d   8. b   9. c
10. c   11. b   12. c   13. c   14. a

CHAPTER 12   Income Distribution, Poverty, and Discrimination

1. a.   2. c   3. a   4. a   5. b   6. d   7. d   8. a   9. d
10. c   11. a   12. d   13. d

CHAPTER 13   Antitrust and Regulation

1. d   2. a   3. a   4. b   5. d   6. a   7. c   8. d   9. c
10. a   11. b   12. a   13. e   14. d   15. d

CHAPTER 14   Environmental Economics

1. d   2. e   3. a   4. a   5. a   6. c   7. d   8. b   9. d
10. b   11. b   12. b   13. c

CHAPTER 15   International Trade and Finance

1. b   2. c   3. a   4. d   5. d   6. a   7. d   8. a   9. c
10. c   11. b   12. c   13. c   14. a   15. a   16. b   17. a
18. a   19. e   20. d

CHAPTER 16   Comparative Economic Systems

1. c   2. d   3. d   4. a   5. b   6. a   7. c   8. b   9. b
10. c   11. c   12. a   13. a   14. d   15. a

CHAPTER 17   Growth and the Less-Developed Countries

1. d   2. d   3. d   4. e   5. a   6. a   7. d   8. a   9. c
10. a   11. b   12. d   13. c   14. d

United States Gross Domestic Product and Related Statistics

United States Gross Domestic Product (in billions of dollars) and Related Statistics

	1929	1930	1931	1932	1933	1934	1935	1936	1937	1938
1. Gross domestic product	103.8	91.1	76.4	58.6	55.2	65.9	73.1	83.6	91.8	85.9
2. Personal consumption expenditures	77.5	70.2	60.7	48.7	45.9	51.4	55.9	62.2	66.8	64.2
3. Gross private domestic investment	16.7	10.6	5.9	1.1	1.7	3.7	6.7	8.7	12.2	7.1
4. Government consumption expenditures and gross investment	9.3	9.9	9.8	8.7	8.6	10.4	10.8	13.0	12.7	13.7
5. Net exports	0.4	0.3	0.0	0.0	0.1	0.3	-0.2	-0.2	0.0	0.9
6. Net domestic product	94.2	81.6	67.6	50.8	48.9	58.2	65.4	75.7	83.0	76.7
7. National income	86.3	75.3	60.1	43.7	41.2	50.1	57.8	65.7	73.9	67.3
8. Personal income	85.2	76.3	65.4	49.9	46.8	53.7	60.4	68.6	74.1	68.4
9. Disposable personal income	82.9	74.2	63.9	48.8	45.6	52.4	58.7	66.7	71.5	65.8
10. Real gross domestic product (in 1992 dollars)	790.9	719.7	674.0	584.3	577.3	641.1	698.4	790.0	831.5	801.2
11. Percent change in real GDP	—	-9.0	-6.4	-13.3	-1.2	9.5	6.3	13.1	4.3	-1.5
12. Real disposable income per capita (in 1992 dollars)	5,213.0	4,824.0	4,619.0	3,975.0	3,831.0	4,179.0	4,546.0	5,078.0	5,223.0	4,881.0
13. Consumer price index (1982–84 = 100)	17.1	16.7	15.2	13.7	13.0	13.4	13.7	13.9	14.4	14.1
14. Rate of inflation (percent)	0.0	-2.3	-9.0	-9.9	-5.1	3.1	2.2	1.5	3.6	-2.1
15. Civilian unemployment rate (percent)	3.2	8.7	15.9	23.6	24.9	21.7	20.1	16.9	14.3	19.0
16. Supply of money, M1 (in billions of dollars)	26.4	24.9	21.9	20.3	19.8	22.7	27.0	30.9	29.1	31.7
17. Percent change in M1	0.0	-5.7	-12.0	-7.3	-2.5	14.7	18.9	14.4	-5.8	8.9
18. Interest rate, 3-month T bills	—	0.5	1.4	0.9	0.5	0.3	0.1	0.1	0.5	0.1
19. Federal budget surplus or deficit (in billions of dollars)	0.7	0.7	-0.5	-2.6	-2.6	-3.6	-2.8	-4.4	-2.8	-1.2
20. Federal debt (in billions of dollars)	16.9	16.2	16.8	19.5	22.5	27.1	28.7	33.8	36.4	37.2

United States Gross Domestic Product (in billions of dollars) and Related Statistics (continued)

	1939	1940	1941	1942	1943	1944	1945	1946	1947	1948
1. Gross domestic product	91.9	101.2	126.7	161.6	198.3	219.7	223.2	222.6	244.6	269.7
2. Personal consumption expenditures	67.2	71.2	81.0	88.9	99.7	108.5	119.9	144.3	162.3	175.4
3. Gross private domestic investment	9.3	13.6	18.2	10.5	6.1	7.8	10.9	31.3	35.0	48.1
4. Government consumption expenditures and gross investment	14.6	15.0	26.5	62.7	94.9	105.6	93.3	39.9	36.6	40.8
5. Net exports	0.8	1.4	1.0	–0.3	–2.4	–2.2	–0.9	7.1	10.8	5.4
6. Net domestic product	82.8	91.7	115.7	148.1	181.9	200.3	202.1	198.8	218.3	241.4
7. National income	72.8	81.1	104.2	137.5	171.3	184.2	183.2	182.2	198.7	223.6
8. Personal income	72.8	78.3	96.0	122.3	151.8	165.7	171.3	179.0	191.8	210.7
9. Disposable personal income	70.6	76.0	92.9	117.7	134.3	147.0	150.8	160.7	170.7	190.1
10. Real gross domestic product (in 1992 dollars)	866.5	941.2	1,101.8	1,308.0	1,523.0	1,644.7	1,626.7	1,447.7	1,430.7	1,491.0
11. Percent change in real GDP	8.1	8.6	17.1	18.8	16.3	8.0	–1.1	–11.0	–1.2	4.2
12. Real disposable income per capita (in 1992 dollars)	5,250.0	5,548.0	6,339.0	7,065.0	7,282.0	7,452.0	7,267.0	7,150.0	6,759.0	6,994.0
13. Consumer price index (1982–84 = 100)	13.9	14.0	14.7	16.3	17.3	17.6	18.0	19.5	22.3	24.1
14. Rate of inflation (percent)	–1.4	0.7	5.0	10.9	6.1	1.7	2.3	8.3	14.4	8.1
15. Civilian unemployment rate (percent)	17.2	14.6	9.9	4.7	1.9	1.2	1.9	3.9	3.6	3.8
16. Supply of money, M1 (in billions of dollars)	36.0	41.9	48.2	62.6	79.9	90.7	102.4	107.6	112.2	110.7
17. Percent change in M1	11.9	16.4	15.0	29.9	27.6	13.5	12.9	5.1	4.3	–1.3
18. Interest rate, 3-month T bills	0.02	0.01	0.1	0.3	0.4	0.4	0.4	0.4	0.6	1.0
19. Federal budget surplus or deficit (in billions of dollars)	–2.8	–2.9	–4.9	–20.5	–54.6	–47.6	–47.6	–15.9	4.0	11.8
20. Federal debt (in billions of dollars)	48.2	50.7	57.5	79.2	142.6	204.1	260.1	271.0	257.1	252.0

United States Gross Domestic Product (in billions of dollars) and Related Statistics (continued)

	1949	1950	1951	1952	1953	1954	1955	1956	1957	1958
1. Gross domestic product	267.8	294.6	339.7	358.6	379.7	381.3	415.1	438.0	461.0	467.3
2. Personal consumption expenditures	178.9	192.7	208.7	219.7	233.5	240.7	259.1	271.9	266.7	296.3
3. Gross private domestic investment	36.7	54.2	60.3	54.0	56.3	53.8	69.0	72.2	70.6	64.5
4. Government consumption expenditures and gross investment	47.0	47.1	68.3	83.8	90.7	86.4	86.7	91.6	99.8	106.1
5. Net exports	5.2	0.7	2.4	1.0	-0.8	0.3	0.4	2.3	4.0	0.4
6. Net domestic product	238.6	264.7	306.5	322.3	341.2	340.8	372.4	390.9	410.2	414.8
7. National income	217.2	241.7	279.6	294.3	309.6	309.8	340.1	360.6	377.1	379.5
8. Personal income	207.8	229.7	258.6	276.0	292.9	295.7	317.3	340.5	359.6	370.3
9. Disposable personal income	189.8	209.6	230.2	242.5	258.0	263.9	282.7	301.8	318.3	329.4
10. Real gross domestic product (in 1992 dollars)	1,479.8	1,611.3	1,734.0	1,798.7	1,881.4	1,868.2	2,001.1	2,040.2	2,078.5	2,057.5
11. Percent change in real GDP	-0.8	8.9	7.6	3.7	4.6	-0.7	7.1	2.0	1.9	-1.0
12. Real disposable income per capita (in 1992 dollars)	6,915.0	7,415.0	7,501.0	7,613.0	7,861.0	7,822.0	8,202.0	8,432.0	8,481.0	8,421.0
13. Consumer price index (1982–84 = 100)	23.8	24.1	26.0	26.5	26.7	26.9	26.8	27.2	28.1	28.9
14. Rate of inflation (percent)	-1.2	1.3	7.9	1.9	0.8	0.7	-0.4	1.5	3.3	2.8
15. Civilian unemployment rate (percent)	5.9	5.3	3.3	3.0	2.9	5.5	4.4	4.1	4.3	6.8
16. Supply of money, M1 (in billions of dollars)	110.1	115.3	122.0	126.4	128.2	131.8	134.6	136.5	135.5	140.8
17. Percent change in M1	-0.5	4.7	5.8	3.6	1.4	2.8	2.1	1.4	-0.7	3.9
18. Interest rate, 3-month T bills	1.1	1.2	1.6	1.8	1.9	1.0	1.8	2.7	3.3	1.8
19. Federal budget surplus or deficit (in billions of dollars)	0.6	-3.1	6.1	-1.5	-6.5	-1.2	-3.0	3.9	3.4	-2.8
20. Federal debt (in billions of dollars)	252.6	256.9	255.3	259.1	266.0	270.8	274.4	272.7	272.3	279.7

United States Gross Domestic Product (in billions of dollars) and Related Statistics (continued)

	1959	1960	1961	1962	1963	1964	1965	1966	1967	1968
1. Gross domestic product	507.2	526.6	544.8	585.2	617.4	663.0	719.1	787.8	833.6	910.6
2. Personal consumption expenditures	318.1	332.2	342.6	363.4	383.0	411.4	444.3	481.9	509.5	559.8
3. Gross private domestic investment	78.8	78.8	77.9	87.9	93.4	101.7	118.8	130.4	128.0	139.9
4. Government consumption expenditures and gross investment	112.0	113.2	120.9	131.4	137.7	144.4	153.0	173.6	194.6	212.1
5. Net exports	-1.7	2.4	3.4	2.4	3.3	5.5	3.9	1.9	1.4	-1.3
6. Net domestic product	455.5	473.2	486.2	524.8	554.7	597.6	649.6	711.9	751.3	821.3
7. National income	413.9	429.8	444.8	479.0	506.3	544.1	592.0	648.9	685.5	747.3
8. Personal income	394.4	412.5	430.0	457.0	480.0	514.5	556.7	605.7	650.7	714.5
9. Disposable personal income	349.9	363.8	379.7	402.2	422.0	458.5	494.8	534.7	572.9	622.5
10. Real gross domestic product (in 1992 dollars)	2,210.2	2,222.9	2,314.3	2,454.8	2,559.4	2,708.4	2,881.1	3,069.2	3,147.2	3,293.9
11. Percent change in real GDP	7.4	2.4	2.3	6.1	4.3	5.8	6.4	6.5	2.5	4.7
12. Real disposable income per capita (in 1992 dollars)	8,660.0	8,681.0	8,814.0	9,098.0	9,294.0	9,825.0	10,311.0	10,735.0	11,081.0	11,468.0
13. Consumer price index (1982–84 = 100)	29.1	29.6	29.9	30.2	30.6	31.0	31.5	32.4	33.4	34.8
14. Rate of inflation (percent)	0.7	1.7	1.0	1.0	1.3	1.3	1.6	2.9	3.1	4.2
15. Civilian unemployment rate (percent)	5.5	5.5	6.7	5.5	5.7	5.2	4.5	3.8	3.8	3.6
16. Supply of money, M1 (in billions of dollars)	140.0	140.7	145.2	147.8	153.3	160.3	167.9	172.0	183.3	197.4
17. Percent change in M1	-1.2	0.5	3.2	1.8	3.7	4.6	4.7	2.5	6.6	7.7
18. Interest rate, 3-month T bills	3.4	2.9	2.4	2.8	3.2	3.6	3.9	4.9	4.3	5.3
19. Federal budget surplus or deficit (in billions of dollars)	-12.8	0.3	-3.3	-7.1	-4.8	-5.9	-1.4	-3.7	-8.6	-25.2
20. Federal debt (in billions of dollars)	287.5	290.5	292.6	302.9	310.3	316.1	322.3	328.5	340.4	368.7

United States Gross Domestic Product (in billions of dollars) and Related Statistics (continued)

	1969	1970	1971	1972	1973	1974	1975	1976	1977	1978
1. Gross domestic product	982.2	1,035.6	1,125.4	1,237.3	1,382.6	1,496.9	1,630.6	1,819.0	2,026.9	2,291.4
2. Personal consumption expenditures	604.7	648.1	702.5	770.7	851.6	931.2	1,029.1	1,148.8	1,277.1	1,428.8
3. Gross private domestic investment	155.0	150.2	176.0	205.6	242.9	245.6	225.4	286.6	356.6	403.8
4. Government consumption expenditures and gross investment	223.8	236.1	249.9	268.9	287.6	323.2	362.6	385.9	416.9	457.9
5. Net exports	−1.2	1.2	−0.3	−8.0	0.6	−3.1	13.6	−2.3	−23.7	−26.1
6. Net domestic product	884.8	930.1	1,011.0	1,111.2	1,247.3	1,340.9	1,443.8	1,617.2	1,796.4	2,031.6
7. National income	805.4	840.6	908.6	1,005.3	1,132.3	1,214.9	1,305.9	1,459.4	1,638.0	1,862.3
8. Personal income	779.3	837.1	900.2	988.8	1,107.5	1,215.9	1,319.0	1,459.4	1,616.1	1,862.9
9. Disposable personal income	669.4	728.1	791.2	856.8	967.0	1,056.8	1,162.6	1,277.1	1,406.1	1,585.8
10. Real gross domestic product (in 1992 dollars)	3,393.6	3,397.6	3,510.0	3,702.3	3,916.3	3,891.2	3,873.9	4,082.9	4,273.6	4,503.0
11. Percent change in real GDP	3.0	0.1	3.3	5.5	5.8	−0.6	−0.4	5.4	4.7	5.4
12. Real disposable income per capita (in 1992 dollars)	11,726.0	12,039.0	12,366.0	12,794.0	13,566.0	13,344.0	13,444.0	13,837.0	14,142.0	14,715.0
13. Consumer price index (1982–84 = 100)	36.7	38.8	40.5	41.8	44.4	49.3	53.8	56.9	60.6	65.2
14. Rate of inflation (percent)	5.5	5.7	4.4	3.2	6.2	11.0	9.1	5.8	6.5	7.6
15. Civilian unemployment rate (percent)	3.5	4.9	5.9	5.6	4.9	5.6	8.5	7.7	7.1	6.1
16. Supply of money, M1 (in billions of dollars)	203.9	214.4	228.3	249.2	262.8	274.2	287.4	306.3	331.1	358.4
17. Percent change in M1	3.3	5.1	6.5	9.2	5.5	4.3	4.8	6.6	8.1	8.2
18. Interest rate, 3-month T bills	6.7	6.5	4.4	4.1	7.0	7.9	5.8	5.0	5.3	7.2
19. Federal budget surplus or deficit (in billions of dollars)	3.2	−2.8	−23.0	−23.4	−14.9	−6.1	−53.2	−73.7	−53.7	−59.2
20. Federal debt (in billions of dollars)	365.8	380.9	408.2	435.9	466.3	483.9	541.9	629.0	706.4	776.6

United States Gross Domestic Product (in billions of dollars) and Related Statistics (continued)

	1979	1980	1981	1982	1983	1984	1985	1986	1987	1988
1. Gross domestic product	2,557.5	2,784.2	3,115.9	3,242.1	3,514.5	3,902.4	4,180.7	4,422.2	4,692.3	5,049.6
2. Personal consumption expenditures	1,593.5	1,706.4	1,941.3	2,076.8	2,283.4	2,492.3	2,740.8	2,892.7	3,094.5	3,349.7
3. Gross private domestic investment	480.9	465.9	556.2	501.1	547.1	715.6	715.1	722.5	747.2	773.9
4. Government consumption expenditures and gross investment	507.1	572.8	633.4	684.8	735.7	796.6	875.0	938.5	992.8	1,032.0
5. Net exports	−24.0	−14.9	−15.0	−20.5	−51.7	−102.0	−114.2	−131.5	−142.1	−106.1
6. Net domestic product	2,268.1	2,451.5	2,730.7	2,816.9	3,068.7	3,439.5	3,681.5	3,882.2	4,119.4	4,442.5
7. National income	2,078.5	2,244.5	2,501.4	2,600.8	2,793.3	3,164.4	3,383.4	3,550.3	3,813.0	4,145.3
8. Personal income	2,055.8	2,293.0	2,568.5	2,724.1	2,894.4	3,211.4	3,440.9	3,639.6	3,877.8	4,178.9
9. Disposable personal income	1,775.7	1,980.5	2,208.3	2,352.7	2,525.1	2,815.9	3,003.2	3,179.7	3,363.6	3,646.9
10. Real gross domestic product (in 1992 dollars)	4,630.6	4,615.0	4,720.7	4,620.3	4,803.7	5,140.1	5,340.1	5,487.7	5,649.5	5,865.2
11. Percent change in real GDP	2.8	−0.3	2.3	−2.1	4.0	7.0	3.6	3.1	2.9	3.8
12. Real disposable income per capita (in 1992 dollars)	14,951.0	14,867.0	15,064.0	15,034.0	15,293.0	16,286.0	16,604.0	16,939.0	17,109.0	17,650.0
13. Consumer price index (1982–84 = 100)	72.6	82.4	90.9	96.5	99.6	103.9	107.6	109.6	113.6	118.3
14. Rate of inflation (percent)	11.3	13.5	10.3	6.2	3.2	4.3	3.6	1.9	3.6	4.1
15. Civilian unemployment rate (percent)	5.8	7.1	7.6	9.7	9.6	7.5	7.2	7.0	6.2	5.5
16. Supply of money, M1 (in billions of dollars)	382.4	408.9	436.8	474.7	521.2	552.3	619.9	724.4	749.7	787.0
17. Percent change in M1	6.8	6.8	6.8	8.7	9.8	6.0	12.2	16.9	3.5	5.0
18. Interest rate, 3-month T bills	10.0	11.5	14.0	10.7	8.6	9.6	7.5	6.0	5.8	6.7
19. Federal budget surplus or deficit (in billions of dollars)	−40.7	−73.8	−79.0	−128.0	−207.8	−185.4	−212.3	−221.2	−149.8	−155.2
20. Federal debt (in billions of dollars)	829.5	909.1	994.8	1,137.3	1,371.7	1,564.7	1,817.5	2,120.6	2,346.1	2,601.3

United States Gross Domestic Product (in billions of dollars) and Related Statistics (continued)

	1989	1990	1991	1992	1993	1994	1995	1996	1997	1998
1. Gross domestic product	5,438.7	5,743.8	5,916.7	6,244.4	6,553.10	6,947.0	7,269.6	7,661.6	8,110.9	8,511.0
2. Personal consumption expenditures	3,594.8	3,839.3	3,975.1	4,219.8	4,459.2	4,717.9	4,953.9	5,215.7	5,493.7	5,807.9
3. Gross private domestic investment	829.2	799.7	736.2	790.4	876.2	1,007.9	1,043.2	1,131.9	1,256.0	1,367.1
4. Government consumption expenditures and gross investment	1,095.1	1,176.1	1,225.9	1,263.8	1,283.4	1,313.0	1,356.4	1,405.2	1,454.6	1,487.1
5. Net exports	−80.4	−71.3	−20.5	−29.5	−60.7	−90.9	−83.9	−91.2	−93.4	−151.2
6. Net domestic product	4,790.6	5,071.9	5,209.3	5,501.3	5,789.7	6,113.2	6,420.8	6,708.8	7,231.1	7,582.5
7. National income	4,397.3	4,652.1	4,761.6	4,990.4	5,266.8	5,590.7	5,923.7	6,256.0	6,646.5	6,994.7
8. Personal income	4,496.4	4,796.2	4,965.6	5,255.7	5,481.1	5,757.9	6,072.1	6,425.2	6,784.0	7,126.1
9. Disposable personal income	3,894.5	4,166.8	4,343.7	4,613.7	4,790.2	5,018.9	5,277.0	5,534.7	5,795.1	6,027.9
10. Real gross domestic product (in 1992 dollars)	6,062.0	6,136.3	6,079.4	6,244.4	6,386.6	6,610.7	6,761.7	6,994.8	7,269.8	7,551.9
11. Percent change in real GDP	3.4	1.2	−0.9	2.7	2.3	3.5	2.3	3.4	3.9	3.9
12. Real disposable income per capita (in 1992 dollars)	17,833.0	17,966.0	17,744.0	18,029.0	18,077.0	18,308.0	18,640.0	18,989.0	19,349.0	19,785.0
13. Consumer price index (1982–84 = 100)	124.0	130.7	136.2	140.3	144.5	148.2	152.4	156.9	160.5	163.0
14. Rate of inflation (percent)	4.8	5.4	4.2	3.0	3.0	2.6	2.8	3.0	2.3	1.6
15. Civilian unemployment rate (percent)	5.3	5.6	6.8	7.5	6.9	6.1	5.6	5.4	4.9	4.4
16. Supply of money, M1 (in billions of dollars)	794.2	825.8	897.3	1,024.0	1,129.9	1,150.7	1,128.7	1,082.8	1,076.0	1,092.3
17. Percent change in M1	0.9	4.0	8.6	14.2	10.2	1.8	−2.1	−4.3	−0.6	1.5
18. Interest rate, 3-month T bills	8.1	7.5	5.4	3.5	3.0	4.3	5.5	5.0	5.1	4.8
19. Federal budget surplus or deficit (in billions of dollars)	−152.5	−221.2	−269.4	−290.4	−255.0	−203.1	−163.9	−107.5	−21.9	69.2
20. Federal debt (in billions of dollars)	2,868.0	3,206.6	3,598.5	4,002.1	4,351.4	4,643.7	4,921.0	5,181.9	5,369.7	5,478.7

SOURCE: Survey of Current Business, Federal Reserve Bulletin, and *Economic Report of the President*.

Glossary

A

Absolute advantage The ability of a country to produce a good with fewer resources than another country. (Chapter 15)

Agency for International Development (AID) The agency of the U.S. State Department that is in charge of U.S. aid to foreign countries. (Chapter 17)

Appreciation of currency A rise in the price of one currency relative to another. (Chapter 15)

Arbitrage The practice of earning a profit by buying a good at a low price and reselling the good at a higher price. (Chapter 9)

Average fixed cost Total fixed cost divided by the quantity of output produced. (Chapter 7)

Average total cost Total cost divided by the quantity of output produced. (Chapter 7)

Average variable cost Total variable cost divided by the quantity of output produced. (Chapter 7)

B

Balance of payments A bookkeeping record of all the international transactions between a country and other countries during a given period of time. (Chapter 15)

Balance of trade The value of a nation's merchandise imports subtracted from its merchandise exports. (Chapter 15)

C

Capital The physical plants, machinery, and equipment used to produce other goods. Capital goods are man-made goods that do not directly satisfy human wants. (Chapter 1)

Capitalism An economic system characterized by private ownership of resources and markets. (Chapter 16)

Cartel A group of firms formally agreeing to control the price and the output of a product. (Chapter 10)

Celler-Kefauver Act A 1950 amendment to the Clayton Act that prohibits one firm from merging with a competitor by purchasing its physical assets if the effect is to substantially lessen competition. (Chapter 13)

Ceteris paribus A Latin phrase that means that while certain variables change, "all other things remain unchanged." (Chapter 1)

Change in demand An increase or decrease in the quantity demanded at each possible price. An increase in demand is a rightward shift in the entire demand curve. A decrease in demand is a leftward shift in the entire demand curve. (Chapter 3)

Change in quantity demanded A movement between points along a stationary demand curve, ceteris paribus. (Chapter 3)

Change in quantity supplied A movement between points along a stationary supply curve, ceteris paribus. (Chapter 3)

Change in supply An increase or decrease in the quantity supplied at each possible price. An increase in supply is a rightward shift in the entire supply curve. A decrease in supply is a leftward shift in the entire supply curve. (Chapter 3)

Clayton Act A 1914 amendment that strengthens the Sherman Act by making it illegal for firms to engage in certain anticompetitive business practices. (Chapter 13)

Coase Theorem The proposition that private market negotiations can achieve social efficiency regardless of the initial definition of property rights. (Chapter 14)

Collective bargaining The process of negotiations between the union and management over wages and working conditions. (Chapter 11)

Command economy A system that answers the What, How, and For Whom questions by central authority. (Chapter 16)

Command-and-control regulations Governmental regulations that set an environmental goal and dictate how the goal will be achieved. (Chapter 14)

Communism A stateless, classless economic system in which all the factors of production are owned by the workers and people share in production according to their needs. This is the highest form of socialism toward which the revolution should strive. (Chapter 16)

Comparable worth The principle that employees who work for the same employer must be paid the same wages when their jobs, even if different, require similar levels of education, training, experience, and responsibility. It involves a nonmarket wage-setting process to evaluate and compensate jobs according to point scores assigned to different jobs. (Chapter 12)

Comparative advantage The ability of a country to produce a good at a lower opportunity cost than another country. (Chapter 15)

Complementary good A good that is jointly consumed with another good. As a result, there is an inverse relationship between a price change for one good and the demand for its "go together" good. (Chapter 3)

Conglomerate merger A merger between firms in unrelated markets. (Chapter 13)

Constant returns to scale A situation in which the long-run average cost curve does not change as the firm increases output. (Chapter 7)

Constant-cost industry An industry in which the expansion of industry output by the entry of new firms has no effect on the firm's cost curves. (Chapter 8)

Consumer equilibrium A condition in which total utility cannot increase by spending more of a given budget on one good and spending less on another good. (Chapter 6)

Consumer sovereignty The freedom of consumers to cast their dollar votes to buy, or not to buy, at prices determined in competitive markets. (Chapter 16)

Cross-elasticity of demand The ratio of the percentage change in the quantity demanded of a good or service to a given percentage change in the price of another good or service. (Chapter 5)

D

Decreasing-cost industry An industry in which the expansion of industry output by the entry of new firms decreases the firm's cost curves. (Chapter 8)

Demand curve for labor A curve showing the different quantities of labor employers are willing to hire at different wage rates in a given time period, ceteris paribus. It is equal to the marginal revenue product of labor. (Chapter 11)

Depreciation of currency A fall in the price of one currency relative to another. (Chapter 15)

Deregulation The elimination or phasing out of government restrictions on economic activity. (Chapter 13)

Derived demand The demand for labor and other factors of production that depend on the consumer demand for the final goods and services the factors produce. (Chapter 11)

Diseconomies of scale A situation in which the long-run average cost curve rises as the firm increases output. (Chapter 7)

E

Economic profit Total revenue minus explicit and implicit costs. (Chapter 7)

Economic growth The ability of an economy to produce greater levels of output, represented by an outward shift of its production possibilities curve. (Chapter 2)

Economic system The organizations and methods used to determine what goods and services are produced, how they are produced, and for whom they are produced. (Chapter 16)

Economics The study of how society chooses to allocate its scarce resources to the production of goods and services in order to satisfy unlimited wants. (Chapter 1)

Economies of scale A situation in which the long-run average cost curve declines as the firm increases output. (Chapter 7)

Effluent tax A tax on the pollutant. (Chapter 14)

Elastic demand A condition in which the percentage change in quantity demanded is greater than the percentage change in price. (Chapter 5)

Embargo A law that bars trade with another country. (Chapter 15)

Emissions-trading Trading that allows firms to buy and sell the right to pollute. (Chapter 14)

Entrepreneurship The creative ability of individuals to seek profits by combining resources to produce innovative products. (Chapter 1)

Equilibrium A market condition that occurs at any price for which the quantity demanded and the quantity supplied are equal. (Chapter 3)

Exchange rate The number of units of one nation's currency that equals one unit of another nation's currency. (Chapter 15)

Explicit costs Payments to nonowners of a firm for their resources. (Chapter 7)

Externality A cost or benefit imposed on people other than the consumers and producers of a good or service. (Chapter 4)

F

Federal Trade Commission Act The federal act that in 1914 established the Federal Trade Commission (FTC) to investigate unfair competitive practices of firms. (Chapter 13)

Fixed input Any resource for which the quantity cannot change during the period of time under consideration. (Chapter 7)

Foreign aid The transfer of money or resources from one government to another for which no repayment is required. (Chapter 17)

Free trade The flow of goods between countries without restrictions or special taxes. (Chapter 15)

Free-rider problem The problem that if some individuals benefit, while others pay, few will be willing to pay for improvement of the environment or other public goods. As a result, these goods are underproduced. (Chapter 14)

G

GDP per capita The value of final goods produced (GDP) divided by the total population. (Chapter 17)

Government failure Government intervention that fails to correct market failure. (Chapter 14)

H

Horizontal merger A merger of firms that compete in the same market. (Chapter 13)

Human capital The accumulation of education, training, experience, and health that enables a worker to enter an occupation and be productive. (Chapter 11)

I

Imperfect competition A market structure between the extremes of perfect competition and monopoly. Monopolistic competition and oligopoly belong to the imperfect competition category. (Chapter 10)

Implicit costs The opportunity costs of using resources owned by the firm. (Chapter 7)

In-kind transfers Government payments in the form of goods and services, rather than cash, including such government programs as food stamps, Medicaid, and housing. (Chapter 12)

Incentive-based regulations Governmental regulations that set an environmental goal, but are flexible in how buyers and sellers achieve the goal. (Chapter 14)

Income effect The change in quantity demanded of a good or service caused by a change in real income (purchasing power). (Chapter 6)

Income elasticity of demand The ratio of the percentage change in the quantity demanded of a good or service to a given percentage change in income. (Chapter 5)

Increasing-cost industry An industry in which the expansion of industry output by the entry of new firms increases the firm's cost curves. (Chapter 8)

Industrially advanced countries (IACs) High-income nations that have market economies based on large stocks of technologically advanced capital and well-educated labor. The United States, Canada, Australia, New Zealand, Japan, and most of the countries of Western Europe are IACs. (Chapter 17)

Inelastic demand A condition in which the percentage change in quantity demanded is less than the percentage change in price. (Chapter 5)

Inferior good Any good for which there is an inverse relationship between changes in income and its demand curve. (Chapter 3)

Infrastructure Capital goods usually provided by the government, including highways, bridges, waste and water systems, and airports. (Chapter 17)

International Monetary Fund (IMF) The lending agency that makes short-term conditional low-interest loans to developing countries. (Chapter 17)

Investment The accumulation of capital, such as factories, machines, and inventories, that is used to produce goods and services. (Chapter 2)

Invisible hand A phrase that expresses the belief that the best interests of a society are served when individual consumers and producers compete to achieve their own private interests. (Chapter 16)

K

Kinked demand curve A demand curve facing an oligopolist that assumes rivals will match a price decrease, but ignore a price increase. (Chapter 10)

L

Labor The mental and physical capacity of workers to produce goods and services. (Chapter 1)

Land A shorthand expression for any natural resource provided by nature. (Chapter 1)

Law of demand The principle that there is an inverse relationship between the price of a good and the quantity buyers are willing to purchase in a defined time period, ceteris (Chapter 3)

Law of diminishing marginal utility The principle that the extra satisfaction of a good or service declines as people consume more in a given period. (Chapter 6)

Law of diminishing returns The principle that beyond some point the marginal product decreases as additional units of a variable factor are added to a fixed factor. (Chapter 7)

Law of increasing opportunity costs The principle that the opportunity cost increases as the production of one output expands. (Chapter 2)

Law of supply The principle that there is a direct relationship between the price of a good and the quantity sellers are willing to offer for sale in a defined time period, ceteris paribus. (Chapter 3)

Less-developed countries (LDCs) Nations without large stocks of technologically advanced capital and well-educated labor. LDCs are economies based on agriculture such as most countries of Africa, Asia, and Latin America. (Chapter 17)

Long run A period of time so long that all inputs are variable. (Chapter 7)

Long-run average cost curve The curve that traces the lowest cost per unit at which a firm can produce any level of output when the firm can build any desired plant size. (Chapter 7)

Lorenz curve A graph of the actual cumulative distribution of income compared to a perfectly equal cumulative distribution of income. (Chapter 12)

M

Macroeconomics The branch of economics that studies decision-making for the economy as a whole. (Chapter 1)

Marginal analysis An examination of the effects of additions to or subtractions from a current situation. (Chapter 2)

Marginal-average rule The rule that states when marginal cost is below average cost, average cost falls. When marginal cost is above average cost, average cost rises. When marginal cost equals average cost, average cost is at its minimum point. (Chapter 7)

Marginal cost The change in total cost when one additional unit of output is produced. (Chapter 7)

Marginal cost pricing A system of pricing in which the price charged equals the marginal cost of the last unit produced. (Chapter 13)

Marginal factor cost (MFC) The additional total cost resulting from a one-unit increase in the quantity of a factor. (Chapter 11)

Marginal product The change in total output produced by adding one unit of a variable input, with all other inputs used being held constant. (Chapter 7)

Marginal revenue The change in total revenue from the sale of one additonal unit of output. (Chapter 8)

Marginal revenue product (MRP) The increase in total revenue to a firm resulting from hiring an additional unit of labor or other variable resource. (Chapter 11)

Marginal utility The change in total utility from one additional unit of a good or service. (Chapter 6)

Market Any arrangement in which buyers and sellers interact to determine the price and quantity of goods and services exchanged. (Chapter 3)

Market economy An economic system that answers the What, How, and For Whom questions using prices determined by the interaction of the forces of supply and demand. (Chapter 16)

Market failure A situation in which the price system creates a problem for society or fails to achieve society's goals. (Chapters 4 and 14)

Market structure A classification system for the key traits of a market, including the number of firms, the similarity of the products they sell, and the ease of entry into and exit from the market. (Chapter 8)

Means test A requirement that a family's income not exceed a certain level to be eligible for public assistance. (Chapter 12)

Microeconomics The branch of economics that studies decision-making by a single individual, household, firm, industry, or level of government. (Chapter 1)

Mixed economy An economic system that answers the What, How, and For Whom questions through a mixture of traditional, command, and market systems. (Chapter 16)

Model A simplified description of reality used to understand and predict the relationship between variables. (Chapter 1)

Monopolistic competition A market structure characterized by (1) many small sellers, (2) a differentiated product, and (3) easy market entry and exit. (Chapter 10)

Monopoly A market structure characterized by (1) a single seller, (2) a unique product, and (3) impossible entry into the market. (Chapter 9)

Monopsony A labor market in which a single firm hires labor. (Chapter 11)

Mutual interdependence A condition in which an action by one firm may cause a reaction on the part of other firms. (Chapter 10)

N

Natural monopoly An industry in which the long-run average cost of production declines throughout the entire market. As a result, a single firm can supply the entire market demand at a lower cost than two or more smaller firms. (Chapter 9)

Negative income tax A plan under which families below a certain break-even level of income would receive cash payments that decrease as their incomes increase. (Chapter 12)

New-source bias Bias that occurs when there is an incentive to keep assets past the efficient point as a result of regulation. (Chapter 14)

Nonprice competition The situation in which a firm competes using advertising, packaging, product development, better quality, and better service, rather than lower prices. (Chapter 10)

Normal good Any good for which there is a direct relationship between changes in income and its demand curve. (Chapter 3)

Normal profit The minimum profit necessary to keep a firm in operation. A firm that earns normal profit earns total revenue equal to its total opportunity cost. (Chapter 7)

Normative economics An analysis based on value judgment. (Chapter 1)

O

Oligopoly A market structure characterized by (1) few sellers, (2) either a homogeneous or a differentiated product, and (3) difficult market entry. (Chapter 10)

Opportunity cost The best alternative sacrificed for a chosen alternative. (Chapter 2)

P

Per se rule The antitrust doctrine that the existence of monopoly alone is illegal, regardless of whether or not the monopoly engages in illegal business practices. (Chapter 13)

Perfect competition A market structure characterized by (1) a large number of small firms, (2) a homogeneous product, and (3) very easy entry into or exit from the market. Perfect competition is also referred to as pure competition. (Chapter 8)

Perfectly competitive firm's short-run supply curve The firm's marginal cost curve above the minimum point on its average variable cost curve. (Chapter 8)

Perfectly competitive industry's long-run supply curve The curve that shows the quantities supplied by the industry at different equilibrium prices after firms complete their entry and exit. (Chapter 8)

Perfectly competitive industry's short-run supply curve The supply curve derived from the horizontal summation of all firms' marginal cost curves in the industry above the minimum point of each firm's average variable cost curve. (Chapter 8)

Perfectly elastic demand A condition in which a small percentage change in price brings about an infinite percentage change in quantity demanded. (Chapter 5)

Perfectly inelastic demand A condition in which the quantity demanded does not change as the price changes. (Chapter 5)

Positive economics An analysis limited to statements that are verifiable. (Chapter 1)

Poverty line The level of income below which a person or a family is considered as being poor. (Chapter 12)

Predatory pricing The practice of one or more firms temporarily reducing prices in order to eliminate competition and then raising prices. (Chapter 13)

Price ceiling A legally established maximum price a seller can charge. (Chapter 4)

Price discrimination The practice of a seller charging different prices for the same product not justified by cost differences. (Chapter 9)

Price elasticity of demand The ratio of the percentage change in the quantity demanded of a product to a percentage change in its price. (Chapter 5)

Price elasticity of supply The ratio of the percentage change in the quantity supplied of a product to the percentage change in its price. (Chapter 5)

Price floor A legally established minimum price a seller can be paid. (Chapter 4)

Price leadership A pricing strategy in which a dominant firm sets the price for an industry and the other firms follow. (Chapter 10)

Price maker A firm that faces a downward-sloping demand curve and therefore it can choose among price and output combinations along the demand curve. (Chapter 9)

Price system A mechanism that uses the forces of supply and demand to create an equilibrium through rising and falling prices. (Chapter 3)

Price taker A seller that has no control over the price of the product it sells. (Chapter 8)

Private benefits and costs Benefits and costs to the decision-maker, ignoring benefits and costs to third parties. Third parties are people outside the market transaction who are affected by the product. (Chapter 14)

Product differentiation The process of creating real or apparent differences between goods and services. (Chapter 10)

Production function The relationship between the maximum amounts of output a firm can produce and various quantities of inputs. (Chapter 7)

Production possibilities curve A curve that shows the maximum combinations of two outputs that an economy can produce, given its available resources and technology. (Chapter 2)

Protectionism The government's use of embargoes, tariffs, quotas, and other restrictions to protect domestic producers from foreign competition. (Chapter 15)

Public good A good or service that, once produced, has two properties: (1) Users collectively consume benefits, and (2) there is no way to bar people who do not pay (free riders) from consuming the good or service. (Chapter 4)

Q

Quota A limit on the quantity of a good that may be imported in a given time period. (Chapter 15)

R

Resources The basic categories of inputs used to produce goods and services. Resources are also called factors of production. Economists divide resources into three categories: land, labor, and capital. (Chapter 1)

Robinson-Patman Act A 1936 amendment to the Clayton Act that strengthens the Clayton Act against price discrimination. (Chapter 13)

Rule of reason The antitrust doctrine that the existence of monopoly alone is not illegal unless the monopoly engages in illegal business practices. (Chapter 13)

S

Scarcity The condition in which human wants are forever greater than the available supply of time, goods, and resources. (Chapter 1)

Sherman Act The federal antitrust law enacted in 1890 that prohibits monopolization and conspiracies to restrain trade. (Chapter 13)

Short run A period of time so short that there is at least one fixed input. (Chapter 7)

Shortage A market condition existing at any price where the quantity supplied is less than the quantity demanded. (Chapter 3)

Social benefits and costs The sum of benefits to everyone in society, including both private benefits and external benefits. Social costs are the sum of costs to everyone in society, including both private costs and external costs. (Chapter 14)

Socialism An economic system characterized by government ownership of resources and centralized decision-making. (Chapter 16)

Substitute good A good that competes with another good for consumer purchases. As a result, there is a direct relationship between a price change for one good and the demand for its "competitor" good. (Chapter 3)

Substitution effect The change in quantity demanded of a good or service caused by the change in its price relative to substitutes. (Chapter 6)

Supply curve of labor A curve showing the different quantities of labor workers are willing to offer employers at different wage rates in a given time period, ceteris paribus. (Chapter 11)

Surplus A market condition existing at any price where the quantity supplied is greater than the quantity demanded. (Chapter 3)

T

Tariff A tax on an import. (Chapter 15)

Tax incidence The share of a tax ultimately paid by consumers and sellers. (Chapter 5)

Technology The body of knowledge applied to how goods are produced. (Chapter 2)

Total cost The sum of total fixed cost and total variable cost at each level of output. (Chapter 7)

Total fixed cost Costs that do not vary as output varies and that must be paid even if output is zero. These are payments that the firm must make in the short run, regardless of the level of output. (Chapter 7)

Total revenue The total number of dollars a firm earns from the sale of a good or service, which is equal to its price multiplied by the quantity demanded. (Chapter 5)

Total utility The amount of satisfaction received from all the units of a good or service consumed. (Chapter 6)

Total variable cost Costs that are zero when output is zero and vary as output varies. (Chapter 7)

Traditional economy A system that answers the What, How, and For Whom questions the way they always have been answered. (Chapter 16)

Transactions costs The costs of negotiating and enforcing a contract. (Chapter 14)

Trust A combination or cartel consisting of firms that place their assets in the custody of a board of trustees. (Chapter 13)

U

Unemployment compensation The government insurance program that pays income for a short time period to unemployed workers. (Chapter 12)

Unitary elastic demand A condition in which the percentage change in quantity demanded is equal to the percentage change in price. (Chapter 5)

Utility The satisfaction, or pleasure, that people receive from consuming a good or service. (Chapter 6)

V

Variable input Any resource for which the quantity can change during the period of time under consideration. (Chapter 7)

Vertical merger A merger of a firm with its suppliers. (Chapter 13)

Vicious circle of poverty The trap in which countries are poor because they cannot afford to save and invest, but they cannot save and invest because they are poor. (Chapter 17)

W

World Bank The lending agency that makes long-term low-interest loans and provides technical assistance to less-developed countries. (Chapter 17)

Index